THE
MICHELIN
GUIDE

GREAT BRITAIN | IRELAND

CONTENTS

Introduction

Restaurants & Hotels

Adrian Franklin/Stark

DEAR READER

We are delighted to present the 2020 edition of the Michelin guide to Great Britain and Ireland – a guide to the best places to eat and stay in England, Wales, Scotland, Northern Ireland and the Republic of Ireland.

● The guide caters for every type of visitor, from business traveller to families on holiday, and lists the best establishments across all categories of comfort and price – from cosy bistros and intimate townhouses to celebrated restaurants and luxurious hotels. So, whether you're visiting for work or pleasure, you'll find something that's right for you.

● All of the establishments in the guide have been selected by our team of famous Michelin inspectors, who are the eyes and ears of our readers. They always pay their own bills and their anonymity is key to ensuring that they receive the same treatment as any other guest. Each year, they search for new establishments to add to the guide – and only the best make it through. Once the annual selection has been made, the 'best of the best' are then recognised with awards: our famous One ❀, Two ❀❀ and Three ❀❀❀ Stars and our value-for-money Bib Gourmands ☺.

● Restaurants – our readers' favourite part – appear at the front of each locality, with the hotels following afterwards. Restaurants are ordered according to the quality of their food, with Michelin Stars placed at the top, followed by Bib Gourmands and then Michelin Plates ⦿.

● Being chosen by the Michelin Inspectors for inclusion in the guide is a guarantee of quality in itself and the Plate symbol points out restaurants where you will have a good meal.

The highlights of our 2020 guide

• In London, **Sketch (The Lecture Room & Library)** is promoted to Three Stars, while **La Dame de Pic** has been awarded Two Stars. In Ireland, **Aimsir**, known for its foraged and preserved produce, goes straight into the guide with Two Stars, while ever-chic **Greenhouse** in Dublin is promoted from One to Two Stars. In England, **The Dining Room** at Whatley Manor, with chef Niall Keating at the helm, also gains its second Star.

• London's new One Stars are **Da Terra**, where dishes inspired by Italy and Latin America are served by the chefs themselves; **Mãos** where up to 16 guests can enjoy Nuno Mendes' creations around a communal table; **Endo at the Rotunda**, a Japanese restaurant in the iconic former BBC HQ; and **Dysart Petersham**, which serves an ingredient-led menu in the charming surroundings of an early 1900s house.

- In other cities, Birmingham gains another Michelin Star thanks to **Opheem** and its sophisticated Indian food, while Manchester now has a Michelin Star thanks to the supremely stylish **Mana**.

- The Lake District has much to celebrate, with three new Michelin Stars: **Old Stamp House** is a sweet, intimate restaurant; **Allium at Askham Hall** makes great use of the produce just outside its door; and **Cottage in the Wood** is a hidden gem with a forward-thinking chef.

- For the second year running, there are several new Stars in the Republic of Ireland, including **Variety Jones** in Dublin, **Bastion** in Kinsale and The **Oak Room** in Adare. In Scotland, the two new Stars are **Condita** in Edinburgh and **Isle of Eriska**.

- This year's Bib Gourmands – awarded for good quality, good value cooking – are also widely dispersed, from **Provender** in Melrose, Scotland; **Land to Sea** in Dingle, Republic of Ireland; **Bancone** in London; and **The Sardine Factory** in Looe, Cornwall.

La Dame de Pic

Our mission always remains the same: to help you find the best restaurants and hotels on your travels. Please don't hesitate to contact us as we are always keen to hear your opinions on the establishments listed within these pages, as well as hearing about others that you feel could be of interest for future editions of the guide. We trust you will enjoy travelling with the 2020 edition of our Great Britain and Ireland guide.

2020...NEW AWARDS IN THIS YEAR'S GUIDE

STARS ✿...

✿✿✿

| London | Westminster (City of)/Mayfair | Sketch (The Lecture Room & Library) |

✿✿

London	City of London	La Dame de Pic
England	Malmesbury	The Dining Room
Republic of Ireland	Celbridge	Aimsir
	Dublin	Greenhouse

✿

London	Hackney/Shoreditch	Mãos
	Hammersmith & Fulham/ Shepherd's Bush	Endo at The Rotunda
	Richmond upon Thames/Richmond	Dysart Petersham
	Tower Hamlets/Bethnal Green	Da Terra
England	Ambleside	Old Stamp House
	Amersham	Artichoke
	Askham	Allium at Askham Hall
	Birmingham	Opheem
	Braithwaite	Cottage in the Wood
	Broadstairs	Stark
	Hetton	The Angel
	Lower Beeding	Interlude
	Manchester	Mana
	Nottingham	alchemilla
	Tenbury Wells	Pensons
	Whatcote	The Royal Oak
Scotland	Edinburgh	Condita
	Eriska (Isle of)	Isle of Eriska
Wales	Oxwich	Beach House
Northern Ireland	Belfast	The Muddlers Club

A complete list of Stars and Bib Gourmands 2020 are at the beginning of each region.

● **Republic of Ireland**

Adare	**The Oak Room**
Dublin	**Variety Jones**
Kinsale	**Bastion**

... AND BIB GOURMANDS

● **London**

Hackney/Shoreditch	**Two Lights**
Westminster (City of)/Soho	**Berenjak**
Westminster (City of)/Strand & Covent Garden	**Bancone**

● **England**

Bath	**Beckford Bottle Shop**
Brighton and Hove	**The Set**
Bristol	**BOX-E**
Colchester	**grain**
Ellastone	**Duncombe Arms**
Liverpool	**Pilgrim**
Looe	**Sardine Factory**
Newcastle upon Tyne	**Violets**
Oakham	**Hitchen's Barn**
Ramsgate	**Arya**
Wiveton	**Wiveton Bell**

● **Scotland**

Edinburgh	**Merienda**
Gullane	**Bonnie Badger**
Melrose	**Provender**

● **Northern Ireland**

Killinchy	**Balloo House**

● **Republic of Ireland**

Athlone	**Thyme**
Dingle	**Land to Sea**
Dublin, City Centre	**Uno Mas**
Dublin, Terenure	**Circa**

Starred establishments 2020

London — This location has at least one 3 star restaurant ✹✹✹

Dublin — This location has at least one 2 star restaurant ✹✹

Edinburgh — This location has at least one 1 star restaurant ✹

Stein

Eriska

Dalry

NORTHERN IRELAND
Belfast

Galway
Celbridge Dublin
Lisdoonvarna Blackrock
REPUBLIC OF IRELAND
Adare Kilkenny
Thomastown
Cork
Ballydehob Ardmore
Kinsale
Baltimore

Oxwich
Ilfracombe

Port Isaac
Padstow

GUERNSEY
JERSEY
St Helier ISLES OF SCILLY

SCOTLAND

Auchterarder
Peat Inn
Anstruther
Leith
Edinburgh

Newcastle-upon-Tyne

Braithwaite
Askham
Summerhouse
Grasmere
Bowness-on-
Ambleside
Windermere
Harome
Cartmel
Hetton
Oldstead
Langho
Fence
Leeds
South Dalton
Aughton
ENGLAND
Winteringham
Birkenhead
Manchester
Menai Bridge
Chester

Nottingham
Morston
Mountsorrel
Hunstanton
Machynlleth
Birmingham
Hambleton
Hampton in Arden
Tenbury Wells
Kenilworth
Cambridge
WALES
Stratford-
Whatcote
Great Milton
upon-Avon
Llanddewi
Cheltenham
Murcott
Burchett's Green
Little Dunmow
Skirrid
Oxford
Whitebrook
Malmesbury
Marlow
Amersham
Castle Combe
Shinfield
London
Penarth
Bristol
Newbury
Chew Magna
Colerne
Ascot
Egham
Seasalter
Bath
Broadstairs
East Chisenbury
Bray
Ripley
Dorking
Fordwich
Knowstone
Winchester
Bagshot
East Grinstead
Horsham
Lympstone
Lower Beeding
Torquay

11

Bib Gourmands 2020

● This location has at least one Bib Gourmand establishment

Helensburgh
Kilberry

NORTHERN
IRELAND
Aghalee ● Belfast ● Holywood
Moira ● Killinchy

Carrickmacross

Tuam
Galway
Athlone
REPUBLIC
OF IRELAND
Terenure ● Clontarf
Sallins ● Dublin

Doonbeg
Clonegall

Adare

Dingle
Killorglin
Duncannon

Timoleague

Ilfracombe

GUERNSEY

St Tudy
Padstow ●
JERSEY
Tavistock ●
Beaumont
Looe
Porthleven

12

SCOTLAND

Glasgow
Gullane
Edinburgh
Melrose

Ponteland
North Shields
Newcastle-
upon-Tyne
Skelton

Maltby

Thornton
York
Drighlington
Liverpool
Manchester
South Ferriby
Colwyn Bay
Sheffield
Chester
Nottingham
Ellastone
Wiveton
WALES
Oakham
Thorpe Market
ENGLAND
Stanton
Ludlow
Bury St. Edmunds
Welland
Howe Street
Aldeburgh
Ashendon
Hunsdon
Upper South Wraxall
Oxford
Colchester
Langford
Ripley
Abethin
Bristol
Gerrards Cross
London
Chelmsford
Bath
Upton
Ewell
Sherborne
New Alresford
Crundale
Ramsgate
Donhead-
West Hoathly
Tenterden
St-Andrew
Brighton and Hove
Seaview

THE MICHELIN GUIDE'S COMMITMENTS

EXPERIENCED IN QUALITY!

Whether they are in Japan, the USA, China or Europe, our inspectors apply the same criteria to judge the quality of each and every hotel and restaurant that they visit. The Michelin guide commands a worldwide reputation thanks to the commitments we make to our readers – and we reiterate these below:

Anonymous inspections

Our inspectors make regular and anonymous visits to hotels and restaurants to gauge the quality of products and services offered to an ordinary customer. They settle their own bill and may then introduce themselves and ask for more information about the establishment. Our readers' comments are also a valuable source of information, which we can follow up with a visit of our own.

Independence

To remain totally objective for our readers, the selection is made with complete independence. Entry into the guide is free. All decisions are discussed with the Editor and our highest awards are considered at a European level.

Our famous One ✿, Two ✿✿ and Three ✿✿✿ stars identify establishments serving the highest quality cuisine – taking into account the quality of ingredients, the mastery of techniques and flavours, the levels of creativity and, of course, consistency.

Selection and choice

The guide offers a selection of the best hotels and restaurants in every category of comfort and price. This is only possible because all the inspectors rigorously apply the same methods.

✿✿✿ THREE MICHELIN STARS
Exceptional cuisine, worth a special journey!
Our highest award is given for the superlative cooking of chefs at the peak of their profession. The ingredients are exemplary, the cooking is elevated to an art form and their dishes are often destined to become classics.

✿✿ TWO MICHELIN STARS
Excellent cooking, worth a detour!
The personality and talent of the chef and their team is evident in the expertly crafted dishes, which are refined, inspired and sometimes original.

✿ ONE MICHELIN STAR
High quality cooking, worth a stop!
Using top quality ingredients, dishes with distinct flavours are carefully prepared to a consistently high standard.

🙂 BIB GOURMAND
Good quality, good value cooking.
'Bibs' are awarded for simple yet skilful cooking for under £30 or €40.

ⅠО THE MICHELIN PLATE
Good cooking
Fresh ingredients, carefully prepared: simply a good meal.

Annual updates
All the practical information, classifications and awards are revised and updated every year to give the most reliable information possible.

Consistency
The criteria for the classifications are the same in every country covered by the MICHELIN guide.

The sole intention of Michelin is to make your travels safe and enjoyable.

 Follow our anonymous inspectors: @MichelinGuideUK

SEEK AND SELECT...
HOW TO USE THIS GUIDE

RESTAURANTS

Restaurants are listed by award.

Within each award category, they are ordered by comfort, from XxXxX to X.

Within each comfort category, they are then ordered alphabetically.

Awards:

✺✺✺ **Three Stars:** Exceptional cuisine, worth a special journey!

✺✺ **Two Stars:** Excellent cooking, worth a detour!

✺ **One Star:** High quality cooking, worth a stop!

⊘ **Bib Gourmand:** Good quality, good value cooking.

𝍐 **The Michelin Plate:** Good cooking.

Comfort:

Level of comfort, from XxXxX to X.

Red: our most delightful places.

HOTELS

Hotels are listed by comfort, from 🏨🏨🏨 to 🏠, followed by 🏚 for guesthouses.

Within each comfort category, they are then ordered alphabetically.

Red: our most delightful places.

Locating
the establishment

Location and coordinates on the town plan, with main sights.

Key words

Each entry comes with two keywords, making it quick and easy to identify the type of establishment and/or the food that it serves.

ENGLAND

BEAULIEU
✉ Brockenhurst ~ Hampshire ~ See Regio

✺ **Scott's**

FRENCH • CLASSIC XXX This elega
18C inn; head to the terrace for v
and efficient, and only top quality
dishes. Cooking has a classical ba
Specialities: Spiced scallops with
velouté. Roast duck breast, smoke
orange soufflé with Sichuan spice
Menu £30/50 (dinner only) –
Town plan: D1-a – *Palace Ln* ✉ SC
Closed December and January

⊘ **Sea Grill** 🆕

MEATS AND GRILLS • BISTRO XX
lage, this laid-back bar-restaurant
eggs are from their own chickens
Menu £28 – Carte £35/72
Specialities: Salted beef cheek, c
with vanilla ice cream.
Town plan: D1-c – *12 Robert St* ✉
www.seagrill.co.uk – *Closed Decem*

🏨 **Manor of Roses**

ROMANTIC • STYLISH With its ch
this charming 18C inn has a timele
marry antique furniture with mode
lised. The wicker-furnished conser
18 rooms – ⚕⚕£62/£125 – ⊒ £
Town plan: D1-a – *Palace Ln* ✉ SC

🏨 **Wentworth**

FRIENDLY • COSY Ivy-clad Victor
the bedrooms; some are traditic
bright and modern. 19C restaurant
28 rooms – ⚕⚕£61/106 – ⊒ £1
Town plan: D1-c – *35 Charles St* ✉
www.wentworth.com – *Closed Jan*

16

Other Special Features

🕸	Particularly interesting wine list
🍸	Notable cocktail list
≤	Great view
🦢	Peaceful establishment

Facilities & services

⇄	Restaurant with bedrooms
🏠	Hotel with a restaurant
🔲 &	Lift (elevator) • Wheelchair access
🆎	Air conditioning (in all or part of the establishment)
🎍	Outside dining available
🍽	Small plates
🕉	Restaurant offering vegetarian menus
🎭	Restaurant offering lower priced theatre menus
🧖	Wellness centre
🏋 ⅃₅	Sauna • Exercise room
🏊 🏊	Swimming pool: outdoor or indoor
🌿 🚫	Garden or park • Bookings not accepted
⛳	Golf course
🏛	Conference room
🍽	Private dining room
🅿 🚗	Car park • Garage
⊠	Credit cards not accepted
⊖	Nearest Underground station (London)
Ⓝ	New establishment in the guide

Prices

Prices are given in £ sterling, and in € euros for the Republic of Ireland.

Restaurants		Hotels	
Menu £13/28	Fixed price menu. Lowest/highest price.	🛉🛉 £100/120	Lowest/highest price for a double room.
Carte £20/35	À la carte menu. Lowest/highest price.	🖙🛉🛉 £100/120	Bed & breakfast rate.
		🖙 £5	Breakfast price where not included in rate.

17

Great Britain & Ireland

17
**Highland &
The Islands**

ATLANTIC

OCEAN

19
**Northern
Ireland**

Belfast

20
Republic of Ireland

*IRISH
SEA*

Dublin

21
Republic of Ireland

CorK

CELTIC

SEA

3

Alderney

Guernsey

Jersey

Channel Islands

Isles of Scilly

**Cornwall, Devon,
Isles of Scilly**
1

Plymouth

Central Scotland 16

Aberdeen

Dundee

Edinburgh

Glasgow

Borders, Edinburgh & Glasgow 15

Northumberland, Durham 14

Newcastle-upon-Tyne

Sunderland

Middlesbrough

Cumbria 12

Yorkshire 13

Blackpool

Leeds

Bradford

Kingston upon Hull

Cheshire, Lancashire 11

Liverpool

Manchester

Birkenhead

Sheffield

Stoke-on-Trent

Derbyshire, Leicestershire, Northamptonshire, Rutland, Lincolnshire, Nottinghamshire 9

Nottingham

Wales 18

Wolverhampton

Leicester

Norwich 8

Herefordshire, Worcestershire, Shropshire, Staffordshire, Warwickshire 10

Birmingham

Coventry

Norfolk, Suffolk, Cambridgeshire 8

Northampton

Ipswich

Oxfordshire, Buckinghamshire 6

Reading

Bedfordshire, Hertfordshire, Essex 7

Cardiff

Bristol

LONDON

Southend-on-Sea

Somerset, Dorset, Gloucestershire, Wiltshire 2

Southampton

Bournemouth

Portsmouth

Hampshire, Isle of Wight, Surrey, West Sussex 4

Brighton

East Sussex, Kent 5

NORTH SEA

FRANCE

GREAT BRITAIN

LONDON

London is one of the most cosmopolitan, dynamic, fashionable and cultured cities on earth, home not only to such iconic images as Big Ben, Tower Bridge and bear-skinned guards, but also Bengali markets, speedboat rides through the Docklands and stunning views of the city from the top of the very best of 21C architecture. From Roman settlement to banking centre to capital of a 19C empire, the city's pulse has never missed a beat; it's no surprise that a dazzling array of theatres, restaurants, museums, markets and art galleries populate its streets.

The city is one of the food capitals of the world, where you can eat everything from Turkish to Thai and Polish to Peruvian; diners here are an eclectic, well-travelled bunch who gladly welcome all-comers and every style of cuisine. Visit one of the many food markets like Borough or Brixton to witness the capital's wonderfully varied produce, or pop into a pop-up to get a taste of the latest trends. If it's traditional British you're after, try one of the many pubs in the capital; this was, after all, where the gastropub movement began.

- Michelin Road map n° 504
- Town plans pages: 160-205

NOT TO BE MISSED

STARRED RESTAURANTS

killertomato/iStock

BIB GOURMAND RESTAURANTS 🏵
Good quality, good value cooking

RESTAURANTS FROM A TO Z

Magone/iStock

RESTAURANTS BY CUISINE TYPE

Meats and Grills

Mediterranean Cuisine

Mexican

Middle Eastern

Modern British

Yauatcha

Modern Cuisine

Modern French

Moroccan

North African

Persian

Peruvian

Polish

Scandinavian

Seafood

South Indian

Spanish

coldsnowstorm/iStock

OUR TOP PICKS

RESTAURANTS WITH OUTSIDE DINING

coldsnowstorm/iStock

THE BEST PUBS 🍺

OUR SELECTION OF HOTELS

HOTELS FROM A TO Z

OUR MOST DELIGHTFUL HOTELS

CENTRAL LONDON - CAMDEN

Greater London

Top tips!

Thousands arrive in the city daily via King's Cross St Pancras; the Victorian masterpiece that is home to Eurostar and has more underground connections than any other London station. Those in the know head straight to **The Gilbert Scott** for traditional British cooking in the grand Gothic surrounds of the St. Pancras Renaissance Hotel. Neighbouring Camden Town, famed for its arty, alternative vibe, is one of the city's most popular areas to visit, with multiple markets and music venues, plus a plethora of pubs and clubs.

Further north is the gloriously green Primrose Hill; worth walking up for its panoramic views of the city. Take a stroll back down to long-standing local restaurant, **Odette's**, whose secret garden – open from May to September – is perfect for escaping the city noise.

BELSIZE PARK
Greater London

ⅰ○ Tandis   🏠 AC ⅰ☺

WORLD CUISINE · NEIGHBOURHOOD X Persian and Middle Eastern food whose appeal stretches way beyond the Iranian diaspora. The specialities are the substantial and invigorating khoresh stew and the succulent kababs; end with Persian sorbet with rosewater.

Carte £20/30

Town plan 11 P2-x – *73 Haverstock Hill* ✉ *NW3 4SL* ⊖ *Chalk Farm* –
✆ *020 7586 8079* – *www.tandisrestaurant.com*

BLOOMSBURY
Greater London

✿✿ Kitchen Table at Bubbledogs (James Knappett)   AC

MODERN CUISINE · CONTEMPORARY DÉCOR XX Ignore the throngs enjoying the curious combination of hotdogs with champagne and head for the curtain – behind it you'll find a horseshoe-shaped counter and a look of expectation on the faces of your fellow diners. Chef-owner James Knappett and his team prepare a surprise menu of around 14 dishes; the produce is some of the best you can find and the small dishes come with a clever creative edge, without being overly complicated.

With seating for just 19, the atmosphere is very convivial, especially if you're a fully paid-up member of the foodie community. The chefs interact with their customers over the counter and offer comprehensive explanations of each dish; they are helped out by James' wife Sandia, who is charm personified.

Specialities: Scallops with charcoal-infused cream, extra virgin olive oil and Exmoor caviar. Cornish glazed duck with damson purée, yoghurt, black garlic and turnips. Beetroot marmalade with sour cream ice cream and sweet woodruff granité.

Menu £150

Town plan 31 AN1-g – *70 Charlotte Street* ✉ *W1T 4QG* ⊖ *Goodge Street* –
✆ *020 7637 7770* – *www.kitchentablelondon.co.uk* – *Closed 1-14 January,
1-15 August, 22-29 December, Sunday, Monday, Tuesday, Wednesday - Saturday
lunch*

✿ Pied à Terre   ✿✿ AC ⅰ☺ ⇔

CREATIVE · ELEGANT XXX Over the last quarter of a century few London streets have seen more restaurants come and go than Charlotte Street, but one constant over that period has been David Moore's Pied à Terre. One of the reasons for its longevity has been its subtle reinventions: nothing ever too grandiose – just a little freshening up with some new art or clever lighting to keep the place looking relevant and vibrant. The room is undeniably intimate and the professional, thoughtful service goes a long way in ensuring the atmosphere remains serene and welcoming.

Of course, the restaurant's success is also due to the consistent standard of the cooking. The current chef continues to produce dishes based on classical French techniques but he also puts in a few nods to his own Greek background and this has given the cooking a bolder, more muscular edge than has been seen here for a while.

Specialities: Smoked quail with celeriac, truffle and hazelnuts. Honey-glazed lemon sole with asparagus, baby artichokes and morels. Chocolate crémeux with dulce de leche, passion fruit and fennel pollen.

Menu £43/145

Town plan 31 AN1-a – *34 Charlotte Street* ✉ *W1T 2NH* ⊖ *Goodge Street* –
✆ *020 7636 1178* – *www.pied-a-terre.co.uk* – *Closed 23 December-3 January,
Sunday, Saturday lunch*

✿ Hakkasan Hanway Place

CHINESE · EXOTIC DÉCOR XX Thanks to its sensual looks, air of exclusivity and glamorous atmosphere – characteristics now synonymous with the brand – the original Hakkasan wowed London when it first opened and, judging by the crowds, continues to do so today. The restaurant copes equally well with all types of customers, from large parties out to celebrate to couples on a date, and the well-organised and helpful staff are a fundamental part of that success.

Lunchtime dim sum here is a memorable, relaxed experience; at dinner try the Signature menus which represent better value than the à la carte. Thanks to the huge brigade in the kitchen, the Cantonese specialities are prepared with care and consistency; dishes are exquisitely presented and while there are moments of inventiveness, they never come at the expense of flavour.

Specialities: Smoked beef ribs with jasmine tea. Spicy prawn with lily bulb and almond. Jivara bomb.

Menu £38 (lunch) – Carte £35/135

Town plan 31 AP1-y – *8 Hanway Place* ⊠ *W1T 1HD* ⊖ *Tottenham Court Road* – *✆ 020 7927 7000 – www.hakkasan.com*

✿ The Ninth (Jun Tanaka)

AC

MEDITERRANEAN CUISINE · BRASSERIE X Jun Tanaka's career began in the early '90s and this – the ninth restaurant in which he has worked – is also the first he has owned. Although situated on foodie Charlotte Street, it's very much a neighbourhood spot, and both the lively downstairs with its counter for walk-ins and the more intimate first floor have a great feel to them.

The on-trend menu has sections including 'snacks', 'salads' and 'raw and cured', as well as 'meat' and 'fish'; staff suggest 3 starters, 2 mains and 2 vegetable dishes for two, although you're equally welcome to come in for a couple of plates and a glass of wine. Skilful cooking uses classical French techniques with a spotlight on the Mediterranean; dishes arrive at a good pace and certainly look the part – but the focus is firmly on flavour.

Specialities: Salted beef cheek with beetroot and horseradish. Chargrilled sea bream, lemon confit and miso. Pain perdu with vanilla ice cream.

Menu £28 (lunch) – Carte £39/59

Town plan 31 AN1-j – *22 Charlotte Street* ⊠ *W1T 2NB* ⊖ *Goodge Street* – *✆ 020 3019 0880 – www.theninthlondon.com – Closed 23 December-2 January, Sunday*

✿ Barbary

MEDITERRANEAN CUISINE · TAPAS BAR X A sultry, atmospheric restaurant from the team behind Palomar: a tiny place with 24 non-bookable seats squeezed around a horseshoe-shaped, zinc-topped counter. The menu of small sharing plates lists dishes from the former Barbary Coast. Service is keen, as are the prices.

Specialities: Ashkenazi chicken liver. Onglet shawarma. Baklawa.

Carte £21/38

Town plan 31 AQ2-k – *16 Neal's Yard* ⊠ *WC2H 9DP* ⊖ *Covent Garden* – *www.thebarbary.co.uk*

✿ Salt Yard

MEDITERRANEAN CUISINE · TAPAS BAR X A ground floor bar and buzzy basement restaurant specialising in good value plates of tasty Italian and Spanish dishes, ideal for sharing. Ingredients are top-notch; charcuterie is a speciality. Super wine list and sincere, enthusiastic staff.

Specialities: Jamón Ibérico, leek and Manchego. Chargrilled Ibérico Abanico with honey and spiced cannellini bean purée. Caramelised pear tart with sherry vinegar, pear salad, cream cheese and hazelnuts.

Carte £25/40

Town plan 31 AN1-d – *54 Goodge Street* ⊠ *W1T 4NA* ⊖ *Goodge Street* – *✆ 020 7637 0657 – www.saltyard.co.uk*

ⅡO Mere

MODERN CUISINE · DESIGN XX Monica Galetti's first collaboration with her husband, David, is an understatedly elegant basement restaurant flooded with natural light. Global, ingredient-led cooking features French influences with a nod to the South Pacific.

Menu £35 (lunch)/77 – Carte £55/75

Town plan 31 AN1-r – *74 Charlotte Street ✉ W1T 4QH ⊖ Goodge Street –*
℘ *020 7268 6565 – www.mere-restaurant.com – Closed Sunday*

ⅡO Noizé

MODERN FRENCH · NEIGHBOURHOOD XX A softly spoken Frenchman, an alumnus of Pied à Terre, took over the former Dabbous site and created a delightfully relaxed, modern bistro. The unfussy French food is served at fair prices; sauces are a great strength. The wine list, with plenty of depth and fair mark-ups, is another highlight.

Carte £35/50

Town plan 31 AN1-t – *39 Whitfield Street ✉ W1T 2SF ⊖ Goodge Street –*
℘ *020 7323 1310 – www.noize-restaurant.co.uk – Closed 25-27 August,*
21 December-2 January, Sunday, Monday, Saturday lunch

ⅡO Roka

JAPANESE · MINIMALIST XX The original Roka, where people come for the lively atmosphere as much as the cooking. The kitchen takes the flavours of Japanese food and adds its own contemporary touches; try specialities from the on-view Robata grill.

Carte £42/75

Town plan 31 AN1-k – *37 Charlotte Street ✉ W1T 1RR ⊖ Goodge Street –*
℘ *020 7636 5228 – www.rokarestaurant.com*

ⅡO Barrica

SPANISH · TAPAS BAR X You can always expect a fun and lively atmosphere at this authentic little tapas bar. The menu offers plenty of choice, with the more robust dishes being the standouts, like lamb neck with baby beetroot or ox cheeks with wild mushrooms.

Carte £19/30

Town plan 31 AN1-x – *62 Goodge Street ✉ W1T 4NE ⊖ Goodge Street –*
℘ *020 7436 9448 – www.barrica.co.uk – Closed 22 December-1 January, Sunday*

ⅡO Cigala

SPANISH · NEIGHBOURHOOD X Longstanding Spanish restaurant, with a lively and convivial atmosphere, friendly and helpful service and an appealing and extensive menu of classics. The dried hams are a must and it's well worth waiting the 30 minutes for a paella.

Menu £24 (lunch) – Carte £34/46

Town plan 32 AR1-a – *54 Lamb's Conduit Street ✉ WC1N 3LW ⊖ Russell Square –*
℘ *020 7405 1717 – www.cigala.co.uk – Closed 1 January, 24-26 December*

ⅡO Honey & Co

MIDDLE EASTERN · SIMPLE X The husband and wife team at this sweet little café were both Ottolenghi head chefs so expect cooking full of freshness and colour. Influences stretch beyond Israel to the wider Middle East. Open from 8am; packed at night.

Menu £32

Town plan 18 Q4-c – *25a Warren Street ✉ W1T 5LZ ⊖ Warren Street –*
℘ *020 7388 6175 – www.honeyandco.co.uk – Closed Sunday*

ⅡO Lore Of The Land ⓝ

EUROPEAN CONTEMPORARY · PUB X A pub with personality and charm, sitting in the shadow of the BT Tower. The cute upstairs dining room, decorated with paintings of food, offers a menu of carefully crafted sharing plates; Sunday roasts are a speciality. Beers from owner Guy Ritchie's Wiltshire brewery also feature.

Menu £20 (lunch) – Carte £30/44

Town plan 18 Q4-v – *4 Conway Street ✉ W1T 6BB ⊖ Great Portland Street –*
℘ *020 3927 4480 – www.gritchiepubs.com – Closed Sunday dinner, Monday*

Ⅴ○ Noble Rot

TRADITIONAL BRITISH · RUSTIC ※ A wine bar and restaurant from the people behind the wine magazine of the same name. Unfussy cooking comes with bold, gutsy flavours; expect fish from the Kent coast as well as classics like terrines, rillettes and home-cured meats.

Menu £16 (lunch)/20 – Carte £39/60

Town plan 32 AR1-r – *51 Lamb's Conduit Street* ✉ *WC1N 3NB* ⊖ *Russell Square* –
℘ *020 7242 8963* – *www.noblerot.co.uk* – *Closed Sunday*

⌂ Covent Garden

LUXURY · DESIGN Popular with those of a theatrical bent. Boldly designed, stylish bedrooms, with technology discreetly concealed. Boasts a very comfortable first floor oak-panelled drawing room with its own honesty bar. Easy-going menu in Brasserie Max.

58 rooms ⌸ – ♥♥ £450/650

Town plan 31 AP2-x – *10 Monmouth Street* ✉ *WC2H 9HB* ⊖ *Covent Garden* –
℘ *020 7806 1000* – *www.firmdalehotels.com*

CAMDEN TOWN
Greater London

Ⅴ○ York & Albany

MODERN CUISINE · INN ※※ This handsome 1820s John Nash coaching inn was rescued by Gordon Ramsay a decade ago after lying almost derelict. It's a moot point whether it's now an inn or more of a restaurant; the food is seasonal and sophisticated and the service is confident and bright. Stay over in one of the well-appointed bedrooms.

Menu £25 (lunch) – Carte £32/49

Town plan 12 Q3-s – *127-129 Parkway* ✉ *NW1 7PS* ⊖ *Camden Town* –
℘ *020 7592 1227* – *www.gordonramsayrestaurants.com/york-and-albany*

HATTON GARDEN
Greater London

Ⅴ○ Anglo

MODERN BRITISH · RUSTIC ※ As its name suggests, British produce is the mainstay of the menu at this pared-down, personally run restaurant, with 'home-grown' ingredients often served in creative ways. Cooking is well-executed with assured flavours.

Menu £25 (lunch), £45/65

Town plan 32 AS1-o – *30 St. Cross Street* ✉ *EC1N 8UH* ⊖ *Farringdon* –
℘ *020 7430 1503* – *www.anglorestaurant.com* – *Closed 22-30 December, Sunday, Monday*

HOLBORN
Greater London

Ⅴ○ Margot

ITALIAN · ELEGANT ※※※ Bucking the trend of casual eateries is this glamorous, elegant Italian, where a doorman greets you, staff sport tuxedos and the surroundings are sleek and stylish. The seasonal, regional Italian cooking has bags of flavour and a rustic edge.

Menu £26/29 – Carte £25/40

Town plan 31 AQ2-m – *45 Great Queen Street* ✉ *WC2 5AA* ⊖ *Holborn* –
℘ *020 3409 4777* – *www.margotrestaurant.com*

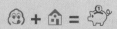

ENGLAND · LONDON

⅋○ Gezellig 　　　　88 AC ⅋⓪ ⇦

EUROPEAN CONTEMPORARY · **BRASSERIE** XX A warmly decorated brasserie with double-height ceilings and a mezzanine level, in the former Holborn Town Hall. Two of the three owners trained as sommeliers so wine is centre stage; the third is the chef, who produces modern European food that's big on flavour. A separate vegetarian menu is also offered.

Menu £22 (lunch) – Carte £31/53

Town plan 31 AQ2-e – *Holborn Hall, 193-197 High Holborn* ✉ *WC1V 7BD*
⊖ *Holborn* – ⌀ *020 3004 0004 – www.gezellig.co.uk – Closed Sunday*

🏨 Rosewood London 　　　　　　　🕏 🆂🅿🅰 🕼 Ⅼ♨ 🔄 🕭 AC 🏊 🚗

HISTORIC · **ELEGANT** A beautiful Edwardian building that was once the HQ of Pearl Assurance. The styling is very British and the bedrooms are uncluttered and smart. Cartoonist Gerald Scarfe's work adorns the walls of his eponymous bar. A classic brasserie with a menu of British favourites occupies the former banking hall.

306 rooms – 🛉🛉 £420/1150 – ⌷ £36 – 44 suites

Town plan 32 AR1-x – *252 High Holborn* ✉ *WC1V 7EN* ⊖ *Holborn* –
⌀ *020 7781 8888 – www.rosewoodhotels.com/london*

🏨 L'oscar 　　　　　　　　　　🕏 🔁 🕭 AC 🏊

HISTORIC BUILDING · **ELEGANT** No expense was spared in converting this Arts & Craft building and former HQ of the Baptist church. Silk, leather and marble have been used to create a seductive interior, with a peacock motif running through it. Baptist Grill is in the former chapel and serves a modern British menu.

39 rooms – 🛉🛉 £350/965 – ⌷ £30

Town plan 32 AR1-e – *2-6 Southampton Row* ✉ *WC1B 4AA* ⊖ *Holborn* –
⌀ *020 7405 5555 – www.loscar.com*

KING'S CROSS ST PANCRAS

Greater London

⅋○ Gilbert Scott 　　　　　　　　　🍸 🕭 AC ⇦

TRADITIONAL BRITISH · **BRASSERIE** XX Named after the architect of this Gothic masterpiece and run under the aegis of Marcus Wareing, this restaurant has the splendour of a Grand Salon but the buzz of a brasserie. The appealing menu showcases the best of British produce, whilst incorporating influences from further afield.

Menu £30/40 – Carte £31/73

Town plan 18 R4-d – *St Pancras Renaissance Hotel, Euston Road* ✉ *NW1 2AR*
⊖ *King's Cross St Pancras* – ⌀ *020 7278 3888 – www.thegilbertscott.com*

⅋○ Barrafina 🔘 　　　　　　　　⊗⅋ AC 🍽 ⇦

SPANISH · **TAPAS BAR** X This is the fourth and largest Barrafina, occupying a prime spot in the new Coal Drops Yard development. Expect their trademark counter seating and famous pan con tomate; the rest of the menu is inspired by the cuisine of Catalonia and features dishes that blend fish and meat (Mar Y Montana).

Carte £28/46

Town plan 12 R3-f – *27 Coal Drops Yard* ✉ *N1C 4AB* ⊖ *King's Cross St Pancras* –
www.barrafina.co.uk

⅋○ Coal Office 🔘 　　　　　　　　🏮 🕭 AC 🍽

MIDDLE EASTERN · **DESIGN** X A super-stylish collaboration between Israeli chef Assaf Granit and renowned designer Tom Dixon, with a long narrow interior, an open kitchen and striking pendant lights. The menu showcases Assaf's unique style of modern Israeli cuisine, with breads cooked to order in the wood-burning oven.

Carte £30/52

Town plan 12 R3-h – *2 Bagley Walk, Coal Drops Yard* ✉ *N1C 4PQ*
⊖ *King's Cross St Pancras* – ⌀ *020 3848 6085 – www.coaloffice.com*

¶○ **Hicce**

MODERN CUISINE · CONTEMPORARY DÉCOR X Pronounced ee-chay and meaning 'of the moment', this restaurant is incorporated into a high end clothing store and has the feel of a NYC loft party. Sip on a cocktail while you choose some of the daily changing small plates; must-tries include a starter sharing board and hot sticks cooked over coals.

Carte £ 22/37

Town plan 12 R3-v – *102 Stable Street, Coal Drops Yard* ✉ *N1C 4DQ*
⊖ *Kings Cross St Pancras –* ☎ *0203 869 8200 – www.hicce.co.uk*

PRIMROSE HILL

Greater London

¶○ **Michael Nadra Primrose Hill**

MODERN CUISINE · NEIGHBOURHOOD XX The menu resembles Michael Nadra's Chiswick operation, which means flavours from the Med but also the occasional Asian note. The bar offers over 20 martinis. The unusual vaulted room adds to the intimacy and service is very friendly.

Menu £ 26/56

Town plan 12 Q3-m – *42 Gloucester Avenue* ✉ *NW1 8JD* ⊖ *Camden Town –*
☎ *020 7722 2800 – www.restaurant-michaelnadra.co.uk/primrose –*
Closed Monday

¶○ **Odette's**

MODERN CUISINE · NEIGHBOURHOOD XX A long-standing local favourite with a warm and inviting interior and chatty yet organised service. The owner is passionate about his Welsh roots, and cooking is robust and elaborate, with braised dishes a highlight. Good value lunch and early evening menus; tasting and vegetarian menus also feature.

Menu £ 20 (lunch)/27 – Carte £ 36/52

Town plan 11 P3-b – *130 Regent's Park Road* ✉ *NW1 8XL* ⊖ *Chalk Farm –*
☎ *020 7586 8569 – www.odettesprimrosehill.com –*
Closed 24 December-6 January, Sunday dinner, Monday

SWISS COTTAGE

Greater London

¶○ **Bradley's**

MODERN CUISINE · NEIGHBOURHOOD XX A stalwart of the local dining scene and ideal for visitors to the nearby Hampstead Theatre. The thoughtfully compiled and competitively priced set menus of mostly classical cooking draw in plenty of regulars.

Menu £ 20 (lunch)/29 – Carte £ 33/44

Town plan 11 N2-e – *25 Winchester Road* ✉ *NW3 3NR* ⊖ *Swiss Cottage –*
☎ *020 7722 3457 – www.bradleysnw3.co.uk – Closed Sunday dinner*

WEST HAMPSTEAD

Greater London

¶○ **Hām**

MODERN CUISINE · NEIGHBOURHOOD X A bright, modern space that perfectly complements the style of cooking, which is light, seasonal and unfussy. The restaurant has a warm neighbourhood feel – its name means 'home' – and its brunches are also popular.

Menu £ 39 – Carte £ 20/41

Town plan 10 M2-h – *238 West End Lane* ✉ *NW6 1LG* ⊖ *West Hampstead –*
☎ *020 7813 0168 – www.hamwesthampstead.com – Closed Sunday dinner, Monday*

CENTRAL LONDON - CITY OF LONDON Greater London

Top tips!

The Romans developed this small area – this 'Square Mile' – around two thousand years ago and today it stands as the economic heartbeat of not only the capital, but the country as a whole; home to both the Stock Exchange and the Bank of England.

An army of bankers, lawyers and traders invade the area each morning, heading for corporate buildings including the iconic 'Gherkin' and the 'Cheesegrater', while tourists mill around St. Paul's Cathedral, which has stood at the highest point of the City of London since the 17th century. Whether they're schmoozing clients or grabbing a mouthful between meetings, all these people need somewhere to eat. Try **Kym's** in the Bloomberg Arcade for modern Chinese cooking in a buzzy atmosphere or Two Michelin-Starred **La Dame de Pic** at the impressive Beaux-Arts style Four Seasons Hotel, which will impress even the fussiest of customers.

Mauro_Repossini/iStock

Restaurants

❀❀ La Dame de Pic   ❀❀ 🕭 AC ⟷

MODERN FRENCH · DESIGN XX Anne-Sophie Pic's London outpost is a charmingly run brasserie deluxe situated in the impressive Beaux-Arts style Four Seasons Hotel; an airy, high-ceilinged room with lots of white, plenty of light and some attractive modern art.

Cooking is rooted in classic French techniques yet delivered in a light, modern manner and dishes are elegant, refined and original, with tremendous attention given to their finer details. The kitchen source excellent quality produce and the delicate combinations of these ingredients are exciting and intuitive, with no superfluous elements on the plate. The well-structured wine list highlights wines from the Rhône Valley – home of restaurant Maison Pic, the Valence institution owned by the Pic family.

Specialities: Scottish langoustine with shellfish butter, celeriac, apple and green anise emulsion. Dover Sole with smoked beetroot, rose and grapefruit. The white millefeuille.

Menu £42 (lunch) – Carte £75/114

Town plan 34 AY3-d – *Four Seasons H London at Ten Trinity Square, 10 Trinity Square* ✉ *EC3N 4AJ* ⊖ *Tower Hill* – ✆ *020 3297 3799* – *www.ladamedepiclondon.co.uk* – *Closed Sunday*

❀ City Social   ❀ 🍷 ⇐ 🕭 AC ⟷

MODERN CUISINE · ELEGANT XXX The buzz from the bar is the first thing you notice at Jason Atherton's handsome, well-run restaurant on the 24th floor of Tower 42. Dark and moody with a subtle art deco twist, it boasts impressive views of the City's ever-changing skyline – especially if you're sitting at one of the coveted window tables. Large parties should request one of the comfortable circular booths; those with bigger plans should ask for table 10, the proposal table.

Influences are largely European in their make-up. The kitchen has a deft touch but wisely acknowledges its customer base by making dishes quite robust in flavour and generous in size – this is elegant, refined but satisfying cooking. The wine list is also noteworthy, with a good mix of styles and prices.

Specialities: Yellowfin tuna tataki with cucumber salad, radish, avocado and ponzu dressing. Topside of Herdwick lamb with salsify, almond, olive tapenade and pomme soufflé. Hazelnut plaisir sucré with chocolate syrup and milk ice cream.

Carte £45/91

Town plan 33 AW2-s – *Tower 42, 25 Old Broad Street (24th Floor)* ✉ *EC2N 1HQ* ⊖ *Liverpool Street* – ✆ *020 7877 7703* – *www.citysociallondon.com* – *Closed Sunday, Saturday lunch*

❀ Club Gascon (Pascal Aussignac)   ❀ AC

FRENCH · ELEGANT XX Those living in Gascony enjoy a diet with the highest fat content in France yet they tend to live longer than their compatriots. This 'Gascon Paradox' is surely reason enough to explore further this most indulgent of cuisines. Longstanding chef-owner Pascal Aussignac is passionate about all things south western: get him started on the quality of the produce he uses and he'll talk the hind legs off an âne.

For Pascal's signature dishes, head to the 'Gascon' section of the menu; go for 'Season' for the ones celebrating the time of year; and 'Garden' for the vegetarian choices. Alternatively, the tasting menu is a good way to sample a variety of the robustly flavoured but refined dishes that will leave you feeling eminently satisfied.

Specialities: Barbecued foie gras with pine, mushroom and razor clams. Monkfish with pork crackling, crosnes and umami consommé. Gianduja with matcha sponge and passion fruit.

Menu £35 (lunch), £85/110 – Carte £46/86

Town plan 33 AU1-z – *57 West Smithfield* ✉ *EC1A 9DS* ⊖ *Barbican* – ✆ *020 7600 6144* – *www.clubgascon.com* – *Closed 1-8 January, Sunday, Saturday lunch*

ⅰ○ Bob Bob Cité ⓝ   🥂🍽 ⒶⒸ 🚹 ♻

FRENCH · BRASSERIE ✕✕ Sister to the iconic Soho original is this impressively ostentatious brasserie deluxe, set on the third level of the Cheesegrater building. Ensconce yourself in a booth, find the button and 'Press for Champagne'; the classic French dishes are hearty and full of flavour with some luxury touches.

Carte £45/83

Town plan 20 U5-u – *122 Leadenhall Street (Level 3)* ✉ *EC3V 4AB* ⊖ *Bank –*
✆ *020 3928 6600 – www.bobbobcite.com*

ⅰ○ Brigadiers   🍽 🏠🚹ⒶⒸ♻

INDIAN · EXOTIC DÉCOR ✕✕ The army mess clubs of India provide the theme for this large restaurant on the ground floor of the Bloomberg building. BBQ and street food from around India is the focus; with 'Feast' menus for larger parties. Beer and whisky are also a feature. The atmosphere is predictably loud and lively.

Menu £25 (lunch), £60/80 – Carte £22/55

Town plan 33 AV2-a – *1-5 Bloomberg Arcade* ✉ *EC4N 8AR* ⊖ *Mansion House –*
✆ *020 3319 8140 – www.brigadierslondon.com*

ⅰ○ Cigalon   ⒶⒸ ♻

FRENCH · ELEGANT ✕✕ Hidden away among the lawyers' offices on Chancery Lane, this bright, high-ceilinged former auction house pays homage to the food and wine of Provence and Corsica. Fresh, flavoursome French classics like salade niçoise, bouillabaisse and ratatouille remind you of sunny Mediterranean days.

Menu £27 (lunch)/38 – Carte £35/45

Town plan 32 AS2-x – *115 Chancery Lane* ✉ *WC2A 1PP* ⊖ *Chancery Lane –*
✆ *020 7242 8373 – www.cigalon.co.uk – Closed 21 December-6 January, Sunday, Saturday lunch*

ⅰ○ Fenchurch   🍽 ⪡🚹ⒶⒸ♻

MODERN CUISINE · DESIGN ✕✕ Arrive at the 'Walkie Talkie' early so you can first wander round the Sky Garden and take in the views. The smartly dressed restaurant is housed in a glass box within the atrium. Dishes are largely British and the accomplished cooking uses modern techniques.

Menu £39 (lunch), £60/85 – Carte £54/85

Town plan 34 AX3-a – *Sky Garden, 20 Fenchurch Street (Level 37)* ✉ *EC3M 3BY*
⊖ *Monument – ✆ 0333 772 0020 – www.skygarden.london*

ⅰ○ Kym's ⓝ   🏠 ⒶⒸ

CHINESE · DESIGN ✕✕ A smart, modern sister to A. Wong, with a friendly team and a buzzy atmosphere; it's named after the chef's grandmother and the original family restaurant. The emphasis is on roasting techniques from around China; choose the Three Treasure dish of crispy pork belly, soy chicken and Iberico pork char sui.

Carte £20/50

Town plan 33 AV3-g – *19 Bloomberg Arcade* ✉ *EC4N 8AR* ⊖ *Cannon Street –*
✆ *020 7220 7088 – www.kymsrestaurant.com – Closed 24 December-4 January, Sunday dinner*

ⅰ○ Vanilla Black   ⒶⒸ ⑲

VEGETARIAN · INTIMATE ✕✕ A vegetarian restaurant where real thought has gone into the creation of dishes, which deliver an array of interesting texture and flavour contrasts. Modern techniques are subtly incorporated and while there are some original combinations, they are well-judged.

Menu £29 (lunch)/42 – Carte £29/42

Town plan 32 AS2-e – *17-18 Tooks Court* ✉ *EC4A 1LB* ⊖ *Chancery Lane –*
✆ *020 7242 2622 – www.vanillablack.co.uk – Closed 24 December-3 January, Sunday*

ⅡO Yauatcha City

CHINESE · CONTEMPORARY DÉCOR XX A larger and more corporate version of the stylish Soho original with seating for 180, a couple of bars and a terrace at both ends. All the dim sum greatest hits are on the menu, from venison puffs to scallop shui mai – and desserts come from the patisserie downstairs.

Menu £ 38 (lunch), £ 48/75 – Carte £ 29/72

Town plan 34 AX1-w - *Broadgate Circle* ⊠ *EC2M 2QS* ⊖ *Liverpool Street* – *☏ 020 3817 9880 – www.yauatcha.com – Closed Sunday*

ⅡO Cabotte

FRENCH · WINE BAR X An appealing bistro de luxe with distressed décor and a rustic charm, offering accomplished French classics which are simple in style and rich in flavour. It is owned by two master sommeliers who share a passion for the wines of Burgundy, and its stunning wine list offers a top-notch selection.

Menu £ 45 – Carte £ 35/52

Town plan 33 AV2-c - *48 Gresham Street* ⊠ *EC2V 7AY* ⊖ *Bank* – *☏ 020 7600 1616 – www.cabotte.co.uk – Closed 21 December-2 January, Sunday, Saturday*

ⅡO José Pizarro

SPANISH · TAPAS BAR X The eponymous chef's third operation is a good fit here: it's well run, flexible and fairly priced – and that includes the wine list. The Spanish menu is nicely balanced, with the seafood dishes being the standouts.

Carte £ 17/56

Town plan 34 AX1-p - *36 Broadgate Circle* ⊠ *EC2M 1QS* ⊖ *Liverpool Street* – *☏ 020 7256 5333 – www.josepizarro.com – Closed Sunday*

Hotels

🏨 Four Seasons H. London at Ten Trinity Square

HISTORIC BUILDING · ELEGANT This extraordinary property, built in 1922, is the former headquarters of The Port of London Authority and boasts many original features including the impressive rotunda lounge with its domed ceiling and plaster reliefs. Classically furnished bedrooms; choose an Executive for more space and a contemporary look. Accomplished French cooking in La Dame de Pic. Asian dishes in Mei Ume.

100 rooms – ♥♥ £ 450/950 – ☲ £ 28 – 11 suites

Town plan 34 AY3-d - *10 Trinity Square* ⊠ *EC3N 4AJ* ⊖ *Tower Hill* – *☏ 020 3297 9200 – www.fourseasons.com/tentrinity*

✿✿ **La Dame de Pic** – See restaurant listing

🏨 Andaz London Liverpool Street

BUSINESS · DESIGN A contemporary and stylish interior hides behind the classic Victorian façade. Bright and spacious bedrooms boast state-of-the-art facilities. Various dining options include a brasserie with international influences, a compact Japanese restaurant and a traditional pub.

267 rooms – ♥♥ £ 169/499 – ☲ £ 28 – 14 suites

Town plan 34 AX2-t - *40 Liverpool Street* ⊠ *EC2M 7QN* ⊖ *Liverpool Street* – *☏ 020 7961 1234 – www.hyatt.com*

The Ned

HISTORIC BUILDING · CONTEMPORARY The former Midland bank headquarters, designed and built by Sir Edwin 'Ned' Lutyens in 1924; now a hotel and members club offering considerable luxury and style. Edwardian-style bedrooms feature rug-covered wooden floors and beautiful furniture. There are numerous restaurants housed in the vast hall; pay a visit to the former bank vaults – now a quirky bar.

250 rooms – **†** £190/550 – 4 suites

Town plan 33 AW2-n – *27 Poultry* ✉ *EC2R 8AJ* ⊖ *Bank* – *𝒸 020 3828 2000* – *www.thened.com*

Threadneedles

HISTORIC BUILDING · CONTEMPORARY A converted bank, dating from 1856, with a smart, boutique feel and a stunning stained-glass cupola in the lounge. Individually styled bedrooms feature Egyptian cotton sheets, iPod docks and thoughtful extras. Spacious Wheeler's with its marble, pillars and panelling specialises in grills and seafood.

74 rooms – **†** £149/599 – ⊡ £15

Town plan 33 AW2-y – *5 Threadneedle Street* ✉ *EC2R 8AY* ⊖ *Bank* – *𝒸 020 7657 8080* – *www.hotelthreadneedles.co.uk*

CENTRAL LONDON -
CITY OF WESTMINSTER Greater London

Top tips!

With Regent's Park to the north, and Hyde Park, Green Park and St James's Park further south, this area of the city is certainly greener than most. It's also home to the West End, which offers the largest and most diverse collection of restaurants, pubs, clubs and theatres in the country.

Sate your appetite before catching a show in Theatreland: Bib Gourmand award-holders **Kiln** and **Brasserie Zédel** offer great value; celebrated Indian restaurant **Veeraswamy** and buzzing **Barrafina** both hold Michelin Stars; while the iconic **Ivy** provides an opportunity for diners to spot stars of a different type.

For those staying over in the city, **Claridge's** is a glamorous art deco wonder in the heart of Mayfair, while **The Ritz**, in nearby St James's, provides similar levels of luxury, with its opulent Louis XVI décor and Michelin-Starred dining.

BAYSWATER AND MAIDA VALE

Greater London

🏵️ Hereford Road   🏠 ♿ AC

TRADITIONAL BRITISH · NEIGHBOURHOOD X A converted Victorian butcher's shop, now a relaxed and friendly neighbourhood restaurant. It specialises in tasty British dishes without frills, made using first-rate seasonal ingredients; offal is a highlight. Booths for six people are the prized seats.

Specialities: Potted crab. Devilled lamb's kidneys and mash. Sticky date pudding.

Menu £16 (lunch) – Carte £26/34

Town plan 27 AC2-s – *3 Hereford Road ⊠ W2 4AB ⊖ Bayswater –*
𝒞 020 7727 1144 – www.herefordroad.org – Closed 29-31 August,
22 December-5 January, Monday - Wednesday lunch

🏵️ Kateh   AC

MEDITERRANEAN CUISINE · NEIGHBOURHOOD X Booking is imperative if you want to join the locals who have already discovered what a little jewel they have in the form of this buzzy, busy Persian restaurant. Authentic stews, expert chargrilling and lovely pastries and teas.

Specialities: Japanese aubergine with minced veal and herbs. Quail stew with walnuts, pomegranate juice, coriander and parsley. Homemade baklava with milk ice cream.

Carte £23/35

Town plan 28 AE1-a – *5 Warwick Place ⊠ W9 2PX ⊖ Warwick Avenue –*
𝒞 020 7289 3393 – www.katehrestaurant.co.uk – Closed 1-3 January, Monday -
Friday lunch

🍴 Restaurant 104   AC

MODERN BRITISH · INTIMATE XX A cosy spot with only six tables; its set four course menu comes with a choice of mains and numerous extras. Classical combinations are finished with a modern style and dishes are delicate, easy to eat and full of flavour. This is confident cooking from a chef who has a real understanding of balance.

Menu £65

Town plan 27 AC1-h – *104a Chepstow Road ⊠ W2 5QS ⊖ Westbourne Park –*
𝒞 020 3417 4744 – www.104restaurant.com – Closed Sunday dinner, Monday,
Tuesday - Thursday lunch

🍴 Soutine   🍸 AC ⇄

FRENCH · BRASSERIE XX It may only have opened mid-2019 but consummate restaurateurs Corbin and King have created a warm, lively, Parisian-style bistro – albeit one with hints of Edwardiana – that feels like it's been here for years. The all-day menu offers a rollcall of French classics, from confit de canard to sole Véronique.

Carte £24/46

Town plan 11 P3-n – *60 St John's Wood High Street ⊠ NW8 7SH*
⊖ St John's Wood – 𝒞 020 3926 8448 – www.soutine.co.uk

🍴 Pomona's   🍸 🏠 ♿ AC 📋

WORLD CUISINE · NEIGHBOURHOOD X A large neighbourhood restaurant with a relaxed atmosphere. The all-day menu offers seasonal British dishes under the headings 'From the Earth/Land/Sea', while the sharing tasting menu is available with matching wine flights – and also comes in a vegetarian version. Start with cocktails in the bar or garden.

Carte £25/55

Town plan 27 AC2-a – *47 Hereford Road ⊠ W2 5AH ⊖ Bayswater –*
𝒞 020 7229 1503 – www.pomonas.co.uk

The Laslett

TOWNHOUSE · TRENDY Five grade II listed Victorian townhouses make up this well-kept hotel, which has a strong connection to its locality and the famed Notting Hill Carnival. Stylish, spacious bedrooms come with cool art, Penguin books and well-stocked fridges. Enjoy a restorative cocktail in the Russ Henderson bar.

51 rooms – 🛉 £199/650 – ☲ £16

Town plan 27 AC3-d – *8 Pembridge Gardens* ⊠ *W2 4DU* ⊖ *Notting Hill Gate* – ✆ *020 7792 6688* – *www.living-rooms.co.uk/hotel/the-laslett*

BELGRAVIA

Greater London

Marcus

MODERN CUISINE · ELEGANT XxxX The MasterChef maestro's eponymous flagship is set within one of the capital's most exquisite hotels: the Berkeley, in the heart of Belgravia. Wander through the glamorous Collins Room and you will be greeted by the cheerful team; the restaurant is eminently comfortable with touches of opulence, but the Chef's Table, with its view into the kitchen, provides the best seats in the house.

There's a steadfast Britishness to the menu, with produce arriving from all corners of the country, like Herdwick lamb, Orkney scallops, Dorset crab and Goosnargh duck. An array of menus include everything from light lunches to multi-course tasting menus, with a choice of two differently priced wine pairings – and plenty to please the vegetarians in your party.

Specialities: Scallops and beetroot cannelloni. Herdwick lamb with kale flowers and pesto. Coffee, mascarpone and bourbon.

Menu £45 (lunch), £90/135

Town plan 38 AK5-e – *Berkeley Hotel, Wilton Place* ⊠ *SW1X 7RL* ⊖ *Knightsbridge* – ✆ *020 7235 1200* – *www.marcusrestaurant.com* – *Closed Sunday*

Céleste

MODERN FRENCH · ELEGANT XxxX For those who regard a shared refectory table and a jam jar wine glass as simply anathema, there is Céleste, the sumptuously decorated and unapologetically formal restaurant on the ground floor of The Lanesborough hotel. With its crystal chandeliers, immaculately dressed tables, Wedgwood blue friezes and fluted columns, this is a room in which you feel truly cosseted, especially as it is one that's administered by a veritable army of staff.

Menus showcase seasonal British ingredients such as Cornish halibut and mackerel, Scottish langoustines and Yorkshire rhubarb in refined, classically based European dishes with intense flavours and modern touches. A wine list of impressive stature is the ideal accompaniment.

Specialities: Green asparagus blanched, Mimosa egg, Oscietra caviar and crème fraîche. Morels stuffed with chicken farce and mixed herb-smoked mashed potatoes. Chocolate pudding, roasted cereal, olive oil tuile and malted gelato.

Menu £39 (lunch) – Carte £72/100

Town plan 38 AK5-c – *The Lanesborough Hotel, Hyde Park Corner* ⊠ *SW1X 7TA* ⊖ *Hyde Park Corner* – ✆ *020 7259 5599* – *www.lanesborough.com*

Pétrus

FRENCH · LUXURY XxX The kitchen at Gordon Ramsay's sophisticated Belgravia restaurant clearly has a deep appreciation for classic French cuisine but isn't afraid of adding its own touches of originality and creativity. However, that doesn't mean there will be unexpected flavours or challenging combinations because it also has an inherent understanding of how to create satisfying and balanced dishes whose component parts all marry perfectly.

At the centre of the well-dressed dining room sits a striking circular wine store. Its contents are highly prized as the wine list includes, appropriately enough, Château Pétrus going back to 1928. Meanwhile, the service is undertaken by a courteous and highly professional team who make everyone feel as though they're having a special experience.

Specialities: Orkney scallop with kombu, bacon & egg sabayon. Fillet of Dexter beef with Roscoff onion, nasturtium and charcuterie sauce. 'Black Forest' kirsch mousse with Amarena and Morello cherry sorbet.

Menu £45 (lunch), £85/125

Town plan 38 AK5-v – 1 Kinnerton Street ⊠ SW1X 8EA ⊖ Knightsbridge – ℰ 020 7592 1609 – www.gordonramsayrestaurants.com/petrus

Amaya

INDIAN · DESIGN XxX Over 15 years since this ground-breaking restaurant first opened, it remains at the forefront of the Indian scene in London: oft-replicated but never bettered. Amaya loosely translates as 'without boundaries' and this is reflected in its open layout as well as its varied clientele, who range from families and friends to business types and couples.

Your senses are fired up by the shooting flames and enticing aromas emanating from the tawa, tandoor and sigri grills, and the resulting dishes are as wonderfully vibrant as you'd hope – from the salads prepared à la minute through to the addictive kebabs and the signature biryanis. Service is as bright and lively as the surroundings; another thing that keeps Amaya feeling so fresh.

Specialities: Black pepper chicken tikka. Tandoori wild prawns. Lime tart with limoncello jelly and spiced blueberry compote.

Menu £45 (lunch), £55/75 – Carte £40/79

Town plan 37 AJ5-k – Halkin Arcade, 19 Motcomb Street ⊠ SW1X 8JT ⊖ Knightsbridge – ℰ 020 7823 1166 – www.amaya.biz

Zafferano

ITALIAN · CLASSIC DÉCOR XxX The immaculately coiffured regulars continue to support this ever-expanding, long-standing and capably run Italian restaurant. They come for the reassuringly familiar, if rather steeply priced dishes from all parts of Italy.

Menu £33 (lunch) – Carte £36/85

Town plan 37 AJ5-f – 15 Lowndes Street ⊠ SW1X 9EY ⊖ Knightsbridge – ℰ 020 7235 5800 – www.zafferanorestaurant.com

Berkeley

GRAND LUXURY · ELEGANT A number of different designers have been used to update and modernise the bedrooms and the results are impressive. The Collins room remains a fine spot for afternoon tea with its Prêt-à-Portea theme and the Blue Bar enjoys a reputation as one of London's best. Great park views from the pool.

184 rooms – ♥♥ £570/1020 – ⊊ £38 – 28 suites

Town plan 38 AK5-e – Wilton Place ⊠ SW1X 7RL ⊖ Knightsbridge – ℰ 020 7235 6000 – www.the-berkeley.co.uk

Marcus – See restaurant listing

The Lanesborough

GRAND LUXURY · ELEGANT A multi-million pound refurbishment has restored this hotel's Regency splendour; its elegant Georgian-style bedrooms offering bespoke furniture, beautiful fabrics, tablet technologies and 24 hour butler service. Opulent Céleste serves rich French cooking under its domed glass roof.

93 rooms – ♥♥ £535/1245 – ⊊ £38 – 46 suites

Town plan 38 AK5-c – Hyde Park Corner ⊠ SW1X 7TA ⊖ Hyde Park Corner – ℰ 020 7259 5599 – www.lanesborough.com

Céleste – See restaurant listing

COMO The Halkin

LUXURY · ELEGANT Opened in 1991 as one of London's first boutique hotels and still looking pretty sharp today. Stylish bedrooms come with silk walls and marble bathrooms; those overlooking the garden at the back are quiet. Creative and colourful cuisine in Ametsa, from the team behind Spain's Arzak restaurant.

41 rooms – ♦♦ £385/760 – �) £25 – 6 suites

Town plan 38 AK5-b – *5 Halkin Street ⊠ SW1X 7DJ ⊖ Hyde Park Corner – ☏ 020 7333 1000 – www.comohotels.com/thehalkin*

The Wellesley

TOWNHOUSE · ART DÉCO Stylish, elegant townhouse inspired by the jazz age, with lovely art deco styling throughout. Impressive cigar lounge and bar with a super selection of whiskies and cognacs. Smart bedrooms have full butler service; those facing Hyde Park are the most prized. Modern Italian food in the discreet restaurant.

36 rooms – ♦♦ £405/565 – �) £26 – 14 suites

Town plan 38 AK5-w – *11 Knightsbridge ⊠ SW1X 7LY ⊖ Hyde Park Corner – ☏ 020 7235 3535 – www.thewellesley.co.uk*

Hari

BUSINESS · CONTEMPORARY An elegant and fashionable boutique-style hotel with a relaxed atmosphere and a hint of bohemia. Uncluttered, decently proportioned bedrooms come with oak flooring and lovely marble bathrooms. Cigar bar and terrace featuring a retractable roof. Italian dishes are served in the stylish restaurant.

85 rooms – ♦♦ £249/449 – �) £20 – 6 suites

Town plan 38 AK6-c – *20 Chesham Place ⊠ SW1X 8HQ ⊖ Knightsbridge – ☏ 020 7858 0100 – www.thehari.com*

HYDE PARK AND KNIGHTSBRIDGE

Greater London

✿✿ Dinner by Heston Blumenthal

TRADITIONAL BRITISH · CLASSIC DÉCOR XxX The fire that swept through the Mandarin Oriental hotel in 2018 mercifully left this restaurant largely untouched but, not a team to rest on their laurels, the chefs took the opportunity afforded by its closure to develop recipes and gain experience in other kitchens.

Heston Blumenthal's culinary quests led him to 'The Forme of Cury' – one of England's oldest recipe books – and it is from this and other historical works that dishes such as 'rice and flesh' and 'frumenty' (c. 1390) come – although the latter's 'grilled octopus with spelt, smoked sea broth and pickled dulse' wouldn't sound out of place in any 21C restaurant. Obsessed with consistency, the kitchen works with intelligence, efficiency and attention to detail to produce dishes that look deceptively simple but taste sublime.

Specialities: Mandarin, chicken liver parfait and grilled bread (c.1500). Spiced squab pigeon with onions, artichokes, ale and malt (c.1780). Tipsy cake with spit roast pineapple (c.1810).

Menu £45 (lunch) – Carte £90/105

Town plan 37 AJ5-x – *Mandarin Oriental Hyde Park Hotel, 66 Knightsbridge ⊠ SW1X 7LA ⊖ Knightsbridge – ☏ 020 7201 3833 – www.dinnerbyheston.com*

♦○ Bar Boulud

FRENCH · BRASSERIE XX Daniel Boulud's London outpost is fashionable, fun and frantic. His hometown is Lyon but he built his considerable reputation in New York, so charcuterie, sausages and burgers are the highlights.

Menu £26 (lunch) – Carte £37/60

Town plan 37 AJ5-x – *Mandarin Oriental Hyde Park Hotel, 66 Knightsbridge ⊠ SW1X 7LA ⊖ Knightsbridge – ☏ 020 7201 3899 – www.mandarinoriental.com*

ⅪO Zuma

JAPANESE · CONTEMPORARY DÉCOR XX Now a global brand but this was the original. The glamorous clientele come for the striking surroundings, bustling atmosphere and easy-to-share food. Go for the more modern dishes and those cooked on the robata grill.

Carte £40/141

Town plan 37 AH5-m – *5 Raphael Street* ⊠ *SW7 1DL* ⊖ *Knightsbridge* –
℘ *020 7584 1010 – www.zumarestaurant.com*

Mandarin Oriental Hyde Park

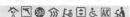

GRAND LUXURY · CONTEMPORARY This celebrated hotel, dating from 1889, is a London landmark. Recent refurbishments have focused on the spacious bedrooms, many of which have views of Hyde Park, as well as colours, fabrics and artwork inspired by its natural beauty. Enjoy afternoon tea in the charming Rosebery salon or relax in the luxurious spa with its 17m pool. Service remains as strong as ever.

181 rooms – ♛ £540/1475 – ☲ £80 – 32 suites

Town plan 37 AJ5-x – *66 Knightsbridge* ⊠ *SW1X 7LA* ⊖ *Knightsbridge* –
℘ *020 7235 2000 – www.mandarinoriental.com*

❀❀ **Dinner by Heston Blumenthal** · ⅪO **Bar Boulud** – See restaurant listing

Bulgari

LUXURY · ELEGANT Impeccably tailored hotel making stunning use of materials like silver, mahogany, silk and marble. Luxurious bedrooms with sensual curves, sumptuous bathrooms and a great spa – and there is substance behind the style. Sette is a stylish Italian restaurant from the people behind NYC's Scarpetta.

85 rooms – ♛ £640/850 – ☲ £34 – 23 suites

Town plan 37 AH5-k – *171 Knightsbridge* ⊠ *SW1 1DW* ⊖ *Knightsbridge* –
℘ *020 7151 1010 – www.bulgarihotels.com/london*

MAYFAIR
Greater London

❀❀❀ Alain Ducasse at The Dorchester

FRENCH · ELEGANT XXXX Coco Chanel once opined that "Luxury must be comfortable, otherwise it is not luxury," and at Alain Ducasse's elegant London outpost, the charming and professional team patiently understand that what is of utmost importance is making the diner feel at ease.

Although many of the much-loved Ducasse signatures are still in evidence, head chef Jean-Philippe Blondet has put his own stamp on the menu, so you'll find French classics like 'sauté gourmand' of lobster alongside more original dishes such as fermented cabbage with caviar and juniper berries. The kitchen sources the very best of British produce and dishes are visually striking with bold, generous flavours. Sauces are a highlight – and it's hard to resist the signature Rum Baba.

Specialities: Dorset crab with celeriac and caviar. Dry-aged beef with artichoke and bone marrow. 'Baba like in Monte-Carlo'.

Menu £70 (lunch), £105/185

Town plan 30 AK4-a – *Dorchester Hotel, Park Lane* ⊠ *W1K 1QA*
⊖ *Hyde Park Corner* – ℘ *020 7629 8866 – www.alainducasse-dorchester.com* –
Closed 1-13 January, 10-13 April, 2-25 August, Sunday, Monday, Saturday lunch

❀❀❀ Sketch (The Lecture Room & Library)

MODERN FRENCH · LUXURY XXXX There are few more joyously colourful and lavishly decorated restaurants in London than The Lecture Room & Library. As you're whisked past the braided rope and up the stairs to the first floor of Mourad Mazouz and Pierre Gagnaire's 18C palace of fun, you'll feel your expectations rise with every step. Once seated in your eminently comfortable armchair, a team of unfailingly attentive and professional staff are on hand to ensure that all those expectations are met.

The highly organised kitchen team do an extraordinary job in executing dishes bearing all the Pierre Gagnaire hallmarks: the main 'plate' comes surrounded by a number of complementary dishes and before long your table is covered with an assortment of vessels. Each element excels in terms of structure, composition, elegance and, above all, flavour. This is cooking that is original and immaculately rendered but also generous.

Specialities: 'Perfume of the Earth'. Fricassée of Cornish lobster tail with fresh turmeric root. Pierre Gagnaire's 'Grand Dessert'.

Carte £114/126

Town plan 30 AM2-h - 9 Conduit Street (1st Floor) ⊠ W1S 2XG ⊖ Oxford Circus - *𝒞 020 7659 4500 - www.sketch.london - Closed Sunday, Monday, Tuesday - Thursday lunch*

🕸🕸 Hélène Darroze at The Connaught   🕸 AC ⟷

MODERN CUISINE · LUXURY XxxX Its location within the iconic Connaught Hotel heightens expectations; take your seat in what must be one of the most elegant rooms in the capital and you will be handed a Solitaire board featuring 16 marbles. Each bears the name of a single ingredient; from these, you choose 5 or 7 – and the corresponding courses are delivered in any order you wish.

Cooking is largely informed by Darroze's homeland but she is not averse to using the occasional unexpected flavour. The visually appealing dishes are built around one high quality main ingredient and are bold, feminine and full of finesse. The wine list offers an impressive choice, and the service team also add to the experience with their professionalism, lack of pretension and personality.

Specialities: Tandoori scallop, carrot, citrus and coriander. Pigeon, foie gras, wild mushroom, turnip and Manuka honey. Signature Baba.

Menu £60 (lunch), £95/185

Town plan 30 AL3-e - Connaught Hotel, Carlos Place ⊠ W1K 2AL ⊖ Bond Street - *𝒞 020 3147 7200 - www.the-connaught.co.uk*

🕸🕸 Le Gavroche (Michel Roux Jnr)   🕸 AC ⟷

FRENCH · INTIMATE XxxX Anyone with any interest in Britain's post-war culinary history will be aware of this restaurant's significance, not just because of its celebration of French cuisine but also because of the well-known chefs who have passed through its kitchen over the years.

In an age of health-consciousness, there is something exhilarating about Michel Roux and head chef Rachel Humphrey's unapologetically extravagant French dishes – and the ingredients are of the highest order, whether that's the huge scallops or the succulent Goosnargh duck. Everyone has their favourite dish – be it soufflé Suissesse or omelette Rothschild – and the cheese board is one of London's best. You're guided through your meal by a charming team and the hum of satisfaction that pervades the room says it all.

Specialities: Soufflé Suissesse. Pigeon d'Anjou. Omelette Rothschild.

Menu £74 (lunch)/178 - Carte £70/180

Town plan 30 AK3-c - 43 Upper Brook Street ⊠ W1K 7QR ⊖ Marble Arch - *𝒞 020 7408 0881 - www.le-gavroche.co.uk - Closed Sunday, Monday, Saturday lunch*

🕸🕸 Greenhouse   🕸 AC ⟷

CREATIVE · ELEGANT XxX With its charming setting and understatedly elegant appearance, The Greenhouse is an oasis in the heart of the city. You enter via a tranquil garden – elements of which are brought inside through the use of natural materials, a pale green colour scheme and some pretty leaf-etched glass. Attentive, professional service puts you immediately at ease, with an experienced and wonderfully helpful sommelier on hand to guide you through the wine list; impressive in both its range and depth.

Cooking here is – and always has been – underpinned by top quality ingredients and a classical French base. Dishes are not only beautifully presented but also technically accomplished, with refined, perfectly judged contrasts of texture and flavour.

Specialities: Oeuf noir. Pigeon for two. Seasonal soufflé.

Menu £45 (lunch), £110/155

Town plan 30 AL3-m – *27a Hay's Mews* ⊠ *W1J 5NY* ⊖ *Hyde Park Corner –*
℘ 020 7499 3331 – www.greenhouserestaurant.co.uk –
Closed 22 December-3 January, Sunday, Monday, Saturday lunch

❀❀ Umu   ⅋ AC

JAPANESE • ELEGANT XxX The kaiseki menu is the best way to experience chef Yoshinori Ishii's cuisine – he trained at Kitcho in Kyoto; a bastion of tradition where the philosophy of kaiseki is preserved and celebrated. Due consideration is given to the provenance of the ingredients; the vegetables for the tempura are grown in Kent by a Japanese national, who imports the seeds from her home country, while fish comes courtesy of Cornish and Scottish fishermen to whom Yoshinori has taught the ikejime method of killing fish, in order to best preserve their quality.

The elegantly dressed and dimly lit restaurant offers a chic backdrop for the eye-catching and occasionally playful food; quiet corners providing intimacy, and the sushi counter, plenty of chatter and excitement.

Specialities: Tuna tartare with yam, myoga and Kaluga caviar. Grade 11 Wagyu beef hoba-yaki with Tokyo leek and miso nut sauce. Charamisu with matcha tea and Ginjo sake.

Menu £50 (lunch)/165 – Carte £100/200

Town plan 30 AL3-g – *14-16 Bruton Place* ⊠ *W1J 6LX* ⊖ *Bond Street –*
℘ 020 7499 8881 – www.umurestaurant.com – Closed 22 December-3 January, Sunday

❀ Alyn Williams at The Westbury   ⅋ � AC ⑩ ⇨

MODERN CUISINE • DESIGN XxxX Eponymous chef-owner Alyn Williams greets guests personally, running this elegant, rosewood panelled room within the Westbury Hotel with assured warmth and engaging confidence. His team, in their turn, are professional and attentive, with chefs joining front of house staff in delivering dishes to the smartly laid tables and interacting with guests.

The cooking displays an innate understanding of balance and dishes like Cornish gurnard bouillabaisse, fennel and red pepper or suckling pig with kohlrabi, wild garlic and boudin blanc are beautifully crafted, with precise, well-defined flavours. The various menus – à la carte, tasting, vegetarian tasting – offer excellent value for money and they'll happily let you mix and match between them.

Specialities: Native lobster with caviar and sauce Jacquéline. Suckling pig, apple, celeriac and boudin blanc. English strawberries, jelly, shiso and white chocolate.

Menu £35 (lunch)/90

Town plan 30 AM3-z – *Westbury Hotel, 37 Conduit Street* ⊠ *W1S 2YF*
⊖ *Bond Street – ℘ 020 7183 6426 – www.alynwilliams.com – Closed 1-17 January,
16 August-2 September, Sunday, Monday*

❀ The Square   ⅋ AC ⑩ ⇨

MODERN FRENCH • ELEGANT XxxX At the helm in the kitchen is Clément Leroy, a proud Frenchman equally keen to celebrate the UK's finest produce. Cornish mackerel and lobster, Lincolnshire eel, Scottish langoustines and Cumbrian beef all feature on his menu, albeit with the occasional imaginative or even playful twist – his Orkney scallops, for example, come with coffee and Marsala. The pastry section is headed up by Japanese-born Aya Tamura, who is Clément's wife; her desserts display the occasional Asian note and are equally intriguing and refined.

The room has a sleeker, more contemporary look these days and more is made of the artwork. Service remains as polished and attentive as ever and the wine list has enormous depth.

Specialities: Maldon oyster and bone marrow pot au feu. Crispy red mullet with black pepper jus. St. John's Wood honey, sweet potato and grapefruit.

Menu £37 (lunch), £95/110

Town plan 30 AM3-v – *6-10 Bruton Street* ⊠ *W1J 6PU* ⊖ *Green Park –*
℘ 020 7495 7100 – www.squarerestaurant.com – Closed 23-30 December, Sunday

Kai 🕸 AC 🕅 ⇔

CHINESE · INTIMATE XxX The owner and his long-standing chef Alex Chow are Malaysian and, while the cooking features dishes from several provinces in China, it is the southern region of Nanyang which is closest to their hearts. The addition of subtle Malaysian influences results in a light, fresh style of cooking.

The menu comprises 20% traditional dishes and 80% where a little innovation has been blended with some less familiar ingredients. However, the flavours remain true, balanced and refined and the dishes are vibrant and colourful. The lunch menu further proves this isn't your typical Chinese restaurant: instead of dim sum, they call their smaller versions of the dinner specialities 'Little plates of love-liness'. Vegetarians are well catered for and desserts are given a bigger billing than one usually sees.

Specialities: Seared scallop with spicy XO sauce, lotus root crisp and stir-fried vegetables. 18-hour slow-cooked pork belly with five spice and garlic. Durian & vanilla soufflé with salted caramel.

Carte £ 38/289

Town plan 30 AK3-n – *65 South Audley Street* ⊠ *W1K 2QU* ⊖ *Hyde Park Corner* – ✆ *020 7493 8988* – *www.kaimayfair.co.uk*

Murano (Angela Hartnett) 🕸 🕭 AC

ITALIAN · INTIMATE XxX Whether you're a newcomer or a regular, the welcome you'll receive at this understatedly elegant restaurant is an extremely warm one, no little thanks to owner Angela Hartnett. As passionate as ever, she spends much of her time here at her flagship, and with a brand new kitchen and a new head chef, the team at Murano are certainly firing on all cylinders.

The wonderfully appealing Italian menu has its roots in the north of the country and offers assured, accomplished dishes which exhibit a delicious vitality and freshness. Pasta is a highlight, vegetable dishes are well-represented and fish dishes show great purity and intensity. For dessert, choose the Amalfi lemon tart or the pistachio soufflé, both of which have become signatures.

Specialities: Pheasant agnolotti with rosemary jus and black truffle. Herdwick lamb, sweetbreads, peas, broad beans and goat's curd. Caramelised Amalfi lemon tart.

Menu £ 32 (lunch), £ 70/105

Town plan 30 AL4-b – *20 Queen Street* ⊠ *W1J 5PP* ⊖ *Green Park* – ✆ *020 7495 1127* – *www.muranolondon.com* – *Closed 24-28 December, Sunday*

Hide 🕸 🕭 🕭 AC 🕅 ⇔

MODERN BRITISH · DESIGN XX Hide is a collaboration between Hedonism Wines and chef Ollie Dabbous, and occupies some prime real estate opposite Green Park, which provides the inspiration for its decorative theme: the top floor is styled in light oak to represent the branches of the tree; the ground floor is slightly darker to signify the trunk; and the basement bar is darker still to represent the roots.

'Above' serves a tasting menu, which allows you to experience the full repertoire of this talented kitchen, and although 'Ground' is a slightly more casual, all-day affair, it shares the same vision: to bring out the natural flavours of the ingredients, in light and immaculately crafted dishes. The service team are charming and the wine list offers unparalleled depth.

Specialities: Nest egg. Wagyu with Oscietra caviar and rye in a warm oxtail broth. Sugared almond soufflé with preserved apricots and osmanthus ice cream.

Menu £ 38 (lunch)/115 – Carte £ 47/90

Town plan 30 AL4-d – *85 Piccadilly* ⊠ *W1J 7NB* ⊖ *Green Park* – ✆ *020 3146 8666* – *www.hide.co.uk*

Gymkhana 🕭 AC 🕮 🕅 ⇔

INDIAN · INTIMATE XX Inspired by Colonial India's gymkhana clubs, the interior is full of wonderful detail and plenty of wry touches, from the hunting trophies and ceiling fans to the glass wall lamps and Grandma Sethi's barometer. If you're on the ground floor ask for one of the booths but it's worth a little persistence to ensure you're seated downstairs, where the beaten brass topped tables, leather banquettes and the dimmest of lighting add to the intimate atmosphere.

There's an array of dishes inspired by the flavours of North India – don't procrastinate, just go straight for the 6 courser; included could be wild tiger prawns that show what a charcoal grill can do; kid goat methi keema with a pleasing richness and well-judged spicing; suckling pig vindaloo with complex flavours; or wild muntjac biryani, a triumph of flaky pastry.

Specialities: Kid goat methi keema, salli, pao. Wild muntjac biryani with pomegranate and mint raita. Saffron and pistachio kulfi falooda.

Menu £28 (lunch), £85/90 – Carte £35/62

Town plan 30 AM3-a – 42 Albemarle Street ⊠ W1S 4JH ⊖ Green Park –
✆ 020 3011 5900 – www.gymkhanalondon.com – Closed Sunday

✿ Hakkasan Mayfair   88 ⚘ & AC I⊙ ⇔

CHINESE • MINIMALIST XX This seductive subterranean spot beckons you in through its discreet entrance on Bruton Street, immediately transporting you to somewhere more exotic. If you're coming for lunchtime dim sum then sit on the ground floor, but if you're here for dinner ask for a table on the lower floor, which is markedly sexier thanks to its flattering lighting and energising atmosphere.

All the signature dishes which have made the reputation of this group can be found on the extensive menu; highlights include the roasted silver cod with champagne and honey, the delicious black truffle roasted duck and the wonderful spicy prawn with lily bulb and almond. Cooking is sophisticated, well-balanced and extremely tasty – and cocktails add to the fun.

Specialities: Crispy duck salad with pomelo, peanut and shallot. Stir-fried rib-eye of beef with black pepper. Exotic fruit selection with jasmine syrup.

Menu £32/38 – Carte £38/120

Town plan 30 AL3-a – 17 Bruton Street ⊠ W1J 6QB ⊖ Green Park –
✆ 020 7907 1888 – www.hakkasan.com

✿ Pollen Street Social (Jason Atherton)   88 ⚘ AC I⊙ ⇔

CREATIVE • ELEGANT XX Pollen Street Social is where it all started for Jason Atherton when he went solo and, even though he now has an impressive international portfolio of restaurants to his name, it's clear it remains his flagship operation. Top quality British produce lies at the heart of a menu which offers a hugely appealing selection of modern dishes; the cooking is clearly undertaken with great care and the confident kitchen brings out the best in those ingredients. There are moments of originality and innovation, even the occasional little playfulness, but never for its own sake.

The wine list has impressive breadth and is rooted in the classic regions – and the care and consideration customers receive from the sommeliers is another of the restaurant's strengths.

Specialities: Crab salad with apple, coriander and lemon purée, brown crab on toast. Suckling pig with celeriac and yeast, red & white wine poached pears and lardo roasted potatoes. Bronte pistachio soufflé, 70% chocolate, Madagascan vanilla ice cream.

Menu £37 (lunch) – Carte £65/85

Town plan 30 AM2-c – 8-10 Pollen Street ⊠ W1S 1NQ ⊖ Oxford Circus –
✆ 020 7290 7600 – www.pollenstreetsocial.com – Closed Sunday

✿ Veeraswamy   AC I⊙ ⊕⇔

INDIAN • DESIGN XX London's oldest surviving Indian restaurant may have opened in 1926 but it's always full of life – as soon as you get out of the lift, you become aware of the bustle and vitality. The traditionally attired doorman sets the tone for the restaurant, which is decorated in a subtle yet colourful style, thanks largely to the glass lanterns and chandeliers. It is also run with enormous charm by an enthusiastic team.

You can opt for royal recipes like Pista Ka Salan (chicken with pistachio and aniseed) or Patiala Shahi Raan (slow-cooked lamb shank) or for dishes from various regions of the country. The Hyderabadi lamb biryani has been on the menu since opening day but, like all the dishes, boasts a fresh, invigorating taste thanks to the judicious spicing.

Specialities: Tandoori green prawns. Lamb rogan josh. Rose kulfi.

Menu £45/65 – Carte £37/75

Town plan 31 AN3-t – Victory House, 99 Regent Street (Entrance on Swallow St) ⊠ W1B 4RS ⊖ Piccadilly Circus – ✆ 020 7734 1401 – www.veeraswamy.com

Sabor (Nieves Barragán)

SPANISH · TAPAS BAR Heddon Street may not quite resemble a side street in Seville but it can sometimes lead to serendipitous discoveries. Sabor is the brainchild of chef Nieves Barragán, and she has created something authentic and truly joyful with co-owner José Etura, who has assembled a charming service team.

There are three distinct areas: on the ground floor is the bar and opposite, a counter serving tapas from all over Spain. Upstairs is El Asador, the only area for which bookings are taken; here you sit at communal tables enjoying specialities from Galicia and Castile. There are two must-haves: succulent Segovian suckling pig – quartered, halved or whole – and roasted in the specially built oven, and the melt-in-the-mouth octopus cooked in vast copper pans. You'll be licking your lips for hours.

Specialities: Payoyo croquetas with black olive and sun-dried tomato. Wood oven-roasted suckling pig. Rhubarb and mascarpone tartaleta.

Carte £ 35/60

Town plan 30 AM3-p – 35-37 Heddon Street ⊠ W1B 4BR ⊖ Oxford Circus – ℰ 020 3319 8130 – www.saborrestaurants.co.uk – Closed 23 December-2 January, Sunday dinner

Park Chinois

CHINESE · EXOTIC DÉCOR Old fashioned glamour, strikingly rich surroundings and live music combine to great effect at this sumptuously decorated restaurant. The menu traverses the length of China, with dim sum at lunchtimes and afternoon tea at weekends.

Menu £ 30 (lunch) – Carte £ 40/105

Town plan 30 AM3-f – 17 Berkeley Street ⊠ W1J 8EA ⊖ Green Park – ℰ 020 3327 8888 – www.parkchinois.com

Scott's

SEAFOOD · ELEGANT Scott's is proof that a restaurant can have a long, proud history and still be fashionable, glamorous and relevant. It has a terrific clubby atmosphere and if you're in a two then the counter is a great spot. The choice of prime quality fish and shellfish is impressive.

Carte £ 36/89

Town plan 30 AK3-h – 20 Mount Street ⊠ W1K 2HE ⊖ Bond Street – ℰ 020 7495 7309 – www.scotts-restaurant.com

Benares

INDIAN · CHIC Set in a commanding location in the heart of Berkeley Square; enjoy Indian street food and cocktails in the lounge, or dine from the à la carte or tasting menus in the lively restaurant. British ingredients like Scottish salmon and New Forest vension feature, as do techniques like pickling and preserving.

Menu £ 29 (lunch), £ 50/98 – Carte £ 70/95

Town plan 30 AL3-q – 12a Berkeley Square House, Berkeley Square ⊠ W1J 6BS ⊖ Green Park – ℰ 020 7629 8886 – www.benaresrestaurant.com – Closed Sunday lunch

Ella Canta

MEXICAN · DESIGN Martha Ortiz is one of Mexico's most celebrated chefs and she also has a London outpost here at the InterContinental. The cooking draws on themes of history, philosophy and fantasy to create dishes that are colourful, creative and original. Great drinks list and charming staff.

Menu £ 25 (lunch) – Carte £ 34/63

Town plan 30 AL4-k – InterContinental London Park Lane Hotel, 1 Hamilton Pl, Park Lane ⊠ W1J 7QY ⊖ Hyde Park Corner – ℰ 020 7318 8715 – www.ellacanta.com – Closed Sunday dinner, Monday lunch

ⅠⅠ○ Galvin at Windows

MODERN CUISINE · FRIENDLY XᵪX The cleverly laid out room makes the most of the spectacular views across London from the 28th floor of the Hilton Hotel. There's a classical French base to the menu but the Korean chef also incorporates influences from his homeland. Service is relaxed and friendly.

Menu £37 (lunch), £82/119

Town plan 30 AL4-e – *London Hilton Hotel, 22 Park Lane (28th floor)* ✉ *W1K 1BE* ⊖ *Hyde Park Corner* – ℰ *020 7208 4021* – *www.galvinatwindows.com* – *Closed Sunday dinner*

ⅠⅠ○ Lucky Cat by Gordon Ramsay Ⓝ

ASIAN · CHIC XᵪX Gordon Ramsay's foray into Asian culture is a moody, masculine space in the former Maze, with a striking bar, a banging soundtrack and a cool, fun feel. Accomplished Japanese and Chinese dishes blend British ingredients and are designed for sharing; the bonito fried duck leg bao is a must-try.

Menu £36 (lunch), £70/125 – Carte £35/75

Town plan 30 AK2-t – *10 Grosvenor Square* ✉ *W1K 6JP* ⊖ *Marble Arch* – ℰ *020 7107 0000* – *www.gordonramsayrestaurants.com*

ⅠⅠ○ Momo

MOROCCAN · EXOTIC DÉCOR XX An authentic Moroccan atmosphere comes courtesy of the antiques, berber rugs, gold seating and moucharabieh wooden screens – you'll feel you're eating near the souk. Go for the classic dishes: briouats, pigeon pastilla, mechoui, and tagines with mountains of fluffy couscous.

Menu £25 (lunch), £45/80 – Carte £25/100

Town plan 30 AM3-n – *25 Heddon Street* ✉ *W1B 4BH* ⊖ *Oxford Circus* – ℰ *020 7434 4040* – *www.momoresto.com*

ⅠⅠ○ Sketch (The Gallery)

MODERN CUISINE · CHIC XX The striking 'Gallery' has a smart look from India Mahdavi and artwork from David Shrigley. At dinner the room transmogrifies from art gallery to fashionable restaurant, with a menu that mixes the classic, the modern and the esoteric.

Menu £59 (lunch) – Carte £38/109

Town plan 30 AM2-h – *9 Conduit Street* ✉ *W1S 2XG* ⊖ *Oxford Circus* – ℰ *020 7659 4500* – *www.sketch.london*

ⅠⅠ○ Black Roe

WORLD CUISINE · BISTRO XX A dark and moody spot offering appealing, flavoursome dishes with Pacific Rim influences: choose from the likes of sashimi, gyoza and ramen, as well as more substantial dishes cooked on a Kiawe wood grill. Add in a buzzy atmosphere and decent cocktails and you have all the elements for a fun night out.

Menu £60/75 – Carte £25/72

Town plan 30 AM2-b – *4 Mill Street* ✉ *W1S 2AX* ⊖ *Oxford Circus* – ℰ *020 3794 8448* – *www.blackroe.com* – *Closed Sunday*

⅋○ Bombay Bustle   🗚 🍴 🍹

INDIAN · ELEGANT ✗✗ Tiffin tin carriers on Mumbai's railways inspired Jamavar's second London restaurant. A charming train theme runs through it; the ground floor is the livelier; downstairs is more 'first class'. Before a curry, biryani or dish from the tandoor order some tasting plates, made from family recipes.

Menu £28 (lunch), £55/65 – Carte £31/49

Town plan 30 AM2-k – *29 Maddox Street* ✉ *W1S 2PA* ⊖ *Oxford Circus –*
☎ 020 7290 4470 – www.bombaybustle.com

⅋○ Emilia 🆕   🚬 ⅋ 🗚

ITALIAN · MINIMALIST ✗✗ From the same stable as Portland comes this bright, hassle-free restaurant adjoining Bonhams auction house. The cooking is influenced by the region of Emilia-Romagna – hence the name; the pasta dishes are standouts. The ground floor wine bar serves an abridged version of the same menu.

Carte £31/70

Town plan 30 AL2-u – *7 Haunch of Venison Yard (Off Brook Street)* ✉ *W1K 5ES*
⊖ *Bond Street* – *☎ 020 7468 5868 – www.emiliarestaurant.co.uk –*
Closed 23 December-2 January, Sunday

⅋○ Goodman Mayfair   🗚

MEATS AND GRILLS · BRASSERIE ✗✗ A worthy attempt at recreating a New York steakhouse; all leather and wood and macho swagger. Beef is dry- or wet-aged in-house and comes with a choice of four sauces; rib-eye is the speciality.

Menu £25 (lunch) – Carte £31/107

Town plan 30 AM2-e – *26 Maddox Street* ✉ *W1S 1QH* ⊖ *Oxford Circus –*
☎ 020 7499 3776 – www.goodmanrestaurants.com –
Closed Sunday

⅋○ Heddon Street Kitchen   🍸 🚬 ⅋ 🗚 🗢 🗢

MODERN CUISINE · BRASSERIE ✗✗ Gordon Ramsay's follow up to Bread Street is spread over two floors and is about all-day dining: breakfast covers all tastes, there's weekend brunch, and an à la carte offering an appealing range of European dishes executed with palpable care.

Carte £35/68

Town plan 30 AM3-y – *3-9 Heddon Street* ✉ *W1B 4BE* ⊖ *Oxford Circus –*
☎ 020 7592 1212 – www.gordonramsayrestaurants.com

⅋○ Indian Accent   🗚

INDIAN · ELEGANT ✗✗ The third branch, after New Delhi and NYC, is set over two levels, with a bright, fresh look. The kitchen takes classic dishes from all regions of India and blends them with European and Asian notes and techniques. The resulting dishes are colourful, sophisticated and full of flavour.

Menu £80/85 – Carte £41/56

Town plan 30 AM3-c – *16 Albemarle Street* ✉ *W1S 4HW* ⊖ *Green Park –*
☎ 020 7629 9802 – www.indianaccent.com

⅋○ Jamavar   🍸 🗚 🍹 🗢 🗢

INDIAN · EXOTIC DÉCOR ✗✗ Leela Palaces & Resorts are behind this smartly dressed Indian restaurant. The menus, including vegetarian, look to all parts of India, with a bias towards the north. The 'small plates' section includes Malabar prawns, and kid goat shami kebab; from the tandoor the stone bass tikka is a must; and the biryanis are also good.

Menu £24 (lunch), £60/80 – Carte £34/56

Town plan 30 AL3-v – *8 Mount Street* ✉ *W1K 3NF* ⊖ *Bond Street –*
☎ 020 7499 1800 – www.jamavarrestaurants.com

ⅱ○ Jean-Georges at The Connaught

MODERN CUISINE · INTIMATE ✕✕ Low-slung bespoke marble-topped tables and comfy sofas make this room at the front of The Connaught hotel somewhere between a salon and a restaurant. It has something for all tastes, from Asian-inspired dishes to fish and chips. The truffle-infused pizza is a best seller.

Carte £57/88

Town plan 30 AL3-e – *Connaught Hotel, Carlos Place* ✉ *W1K 2AL* ⊖ *Bond Street* – ✆ *020 7107 8861* – *www.the-connaught.co.uk*

ⅱ○ Kanishka ❶

INDIAN · INTIMATE ✕✕ The focus is on north east India at this boldly decorated restaurant from chef Atul Kochhar. Chillies play a prominent role in the cooking; the chicken tikka pie is a speciality; and side dishes like Angoori hing aloo are well worth ordering. The ground floor is more fun than the basement level.

Menu £29/69 – Carte £37/52

Town plan 30 AM2-v – *17-19 Maddox Street* ✉ *W1S 2QH* ⊖ *Oxford Circus* – ✆ *020 3978 0978* – *www.kanishkarestaurant.com* – *Closed Sunday lunch*

ⅱ○ No 5 Social ❶

MODERN BRITISH · ELEGANT ✕✕ What was formerly Little Social now sports a smart, stylish look, with on-trend copper, dark wood, and duck egg blue upholstery ensuring it fits in perfectly with its Mayfair surroundings. The seasonal menu name-checks British regions and suppliers, and dishes are modern and creative with plenty of flavour.

Menu £25 – Carte £42/60

Town plan 30 AM2-r – *5 Pollen Street* ✉ *W1S 1NE* ⊖ *Oxford Circus* – ✆ *020 7870 3730* – *www.no5social.com* – *Closed Sunday*

ⅱ○ Nobu

JAPANESE · TRENDY ✕✕ Nobu restaurants are now all over the world but this was Europe's first and opened in 1997. It retains a certain exclusivity and is buzzy and fun. The menu is an innovative blend of Japanese cuisine with South American influences.

Carte £30/95

Town plan 30 AL4-c – *COMO Metropolitan Hotel, 19 Old Park Lane* ✉ *W1Y 4LB* ⊖ *Hyde Park Corner* – ✆ *020 7447 4747* – *www.noburestaurants.com*

ⅱ○ Nobu Berkeley St

JAPANESE · TRENDY ✕✕ This branch of the glamorous chain is more of a party animal than its elder sibling at The COMO Metropolitan. Start with cocktails then head upstairs for Japanese food with South American influences; try dishes from the wood-fired oven.

Carte £30/95

Town plan 30 AM3-b – *15 Berkeley Street* ✉ *W1J 8DY* ⊖ *Green Park* – ✆ *020 7290 9222* – *www.noburestaurants.com*

ⅱ○ Sakagura

JAPANESE · EXOTIC DÉCOR ✕✕ A contemporary styled Japanese restaurant part owned by the Japan Centre and Gekkeikan, a sake manufacturer. Along with an impressive drinks list is an extensive menu covering a variety of styles; highlights include the skewers cooked on the robata charcoal grill.

Carte £27/65

Town plan 30 AM3-s – *8 Heddon Street* ✉ *W1B 4BS* ⊖ *Oxford Circus* – ✆ *020 3405 7230* – *www.sakaguralondon.com*

ⅱ○ Sexy Fish

ASIAN · DESIGN ✕✕ Everyone will have an opinion about the name but what's indisputable is that this is a very good looking restaurant, with works by Frank Gehry and Damien Hirst, and a stunning ceiling by Michael Roberts. The fish comes with various Asian influences but don't ignore the meat dishes like the beef rib skewers.

Menu £36 (lunch) – Carte £35/60

Town plan 30 AM3-w – *4-6 Berkeley Square* ✉ *W1J 6BR* ⊖ *Green Park* – ✆ *020 3764 2000* – *www.sexyfish.com*

StreetXO

CREATIVE · TRENDY XX The menu at Madrid chef David Muñoz's London outpost is inspired by European, Asian and even South American cuisines. Dishes are characterised by explosions of colour and a riot of different flavours, techniques and textures. The quasi-industrial feel of the basement room adds to the moody, noisy atmosphere.

Menu £30 (lunch)/40 – Carte £45/68

Town plan 30 AM3-t – *15 Old Burlington Street* ⊠ *W1S 2JL* ⊖ *Oxford Circus –*
℘ 020 3096 7555 – www.streetxo.com –
Closed Monday lunch

Tamarind

INDIAN · CONTEMPORARY DÉCOR XX Tamarind now has a light and airy first floor space, as well as its basement where you can watch the chefs working at the tandoor counter. Cooking is lighter than before, with a delicate balance of herbs and spices. Sharing plates are the highlight; choose between a curry and a biryani for your main course.

Menu £30/69 – Carte £30/65

Town plan 30 AL4-h – *20 Queen Street* ⊠ *W1J 5PR* ⊖ *Green Park –*
℘ 020 7629 3561 – www.tamarindrestaurant.com

Theo Randall

ITALIAN · CLASSIC DÉCOR XX There's an attractive honesty about Theo Randall's Italian food, which is made using the very best of ingredients. The somewhat corporate nature of the hotel in which it is located can sometimes seem a little at odds with the rustic style of food but the room is bright, relaxed and well run.

Menu £29 (lunch) – Carte £35/63

Town plan 30 AL4-k – *InterContinental London Park Lane Hotel, 1 Hamilton Pl, Park Lane* ⊠ *W1J 7QY* ⊖ *Hyde Park Corner –*
℘ 020 7318 8747 – www.theorandall.com

Tokimeitē

JAPANESE · CHIC XX Yoshihiro Murata, one of Japan's most celebrated chefs, teamed up with the Zen-Noh group to open this good looking, intimate restaurant on two floors. Their aim is to promote Wagyu beef in Europe, so it's understandably the star of the show.

Menu £30 (lunch)/50 – Carte £38/159

Town plan 30 AM3-k – *23 Conduit Street* ⊠ *W1S 2XS* ⊖ *Oxford Circus –*
℘ 020 3826 4411 – www.tokimeite.com –
Closed Sunday

Le Boudin Blanc

FRENCH · RUSTIC X Appealing, lively French bistro in Shepherd Market, spread over two floors. Satisfying French classics and country cooking are the draws, along with authentic Gallic service. Good value lunch menu.

Menu £19 (lunch) – Carte £30/66

Town plan 30 AL4-q – *5 Trebeck Street* ⊠ *W1J 7LT* ⊖ *Green Park –*
℘ 0207 499 3292 – www.boudinblanc.co.uk

Kitty Fisher's

MODERN CUISINE · BISTRO X Warm, intimate and unpretentious restaurant – the star of the show is the wood grill which gives the dishes added depth. Named after an 18C courtesan, presumably in honour of the profession for which Shepherd Market was once known.

Carte £38/68

Town plan 30 AL4-s – *10 Shepherd Market* ⊠ *W1J 7QF* ⊖ *Green Park –*
℘ 020 3302 1661 – www.kittyfishers.com –
Closed Sunday

Claridge's

GRAND LUXURY · CLASSIC Claridge's has a long, illustrious history dating back to 1812 and this iconic and very British hotel has been a favourite of the royal family over generations. The hotel is known for its wide corridors and its sumptuous bedrooms – but its most striking feature is its ornate art deco styling.

197 rooms ☑ – ♥♥ £540/1200 – 62 suites

Town plan 30 AL2-c – *Brook Street* ✉ *W1K 4HR* ⊖ *Bond Street* –
✆ *020 7629 8860 – www.claridges.co.uk*

Connaught

GRAND LUXURY · CLASSIC One of London's most famous hotels, the Connaught offers effortless serenity and exclusivity and an elegant British feel. All the luxurious bedrooms come with large marble bathrooms and butler service; some overlook a small oriental garden, others look down onto mews houses. Refined French cooking in Hélène Darroze; something for everyone in all-day Jean-Georges.

121 rooms – ♥♥ £420/990 – ☑ £38 – 25 suites

Town plan 30 AL3-e – *Carlos Place* ✉ *W1K 2AL* ⊖ *Bond Street* –
✆ *020 7499 7070 – www.the-connaught.co.uk*

❀❀ **Hélène Darroze at The Connaught** · ⏱○ **Jean-Georges at The Connaught** –
See restaurant listing

Dorchester

GRAND LUXURY · CLASSIC One of the capital's iconic properties offering every possible facility and exemplary levels of service. The striking marbled and pillared promenade provides an elegant backdrop for afternoon tea. Bedrooms are eminently comfortable; some overlook Hyde Park. The Grill is for all things British; Alain Ducasse waves Le Tricolore; China Tang celebrates the cuisine of the Orient.

250 rooms ☑ – ♥♥ £595/925 – 51 suites

Town plan 30 AK4-a – *Park Lane* ✉ *W1K 1QA* ⊖ *Hyde Park Corner* –
✆ *020 7629 8888 – www.dorchestercollection.com*

❀❀❀ **Alain Ducasse at The Dorchester** – See restaurant listing

Four Seasons

GRAND LUXURY · CONTEMPORARY It raised the bar for luxury hotels: a striking red and black lobby sets the scene, while the spacious, sumptuous and serenely coloured bedrooms have a rich, contemporary look and boast every conceivable comfort. Italian influenced menu in Amaranto, with its outdoor terrace. Great views from the stunning rooftop spa.

192 rooms – ♥♥ £450/1550 – ☑ £32 – 42 suites

Town plan 30 AL4-v – *Hamilton Place, Park Lane* ✉ *W1J 7DR*
⊖ *Hyde Park Corner* – ✆ *020 7499 0888 – www.fourseasons.com/london*

The Beaumont

LUXURY · ART DÉCO A stunningly styled art deco hotel which was once a garage for Selfridges but now exudes understated luxury. It is themed around the sheer glamour of travel and the attention to detail is exemplary, from the undeniably masculine bedrooms to the lively, cool cocktail bar and busy brasserie.

73 rooms – ♥♥ £460/650 – ☑ £23 – 10 suites

Town plan 30 AK2-x – *Brown Hart Gardens* ✉ *W1K 6TF* ⊖ *Bond Street* –
✆ *020 7499 1001 – www.thebeaumont.com*

45 Park Lane

LUXURY · CONTEMPORARY It was the original site of the Playboy Club and used to be a car showroom, before being reborn as The Dorchester's sister hotel. The bedrooms, all with views over Hyde Park, are wonderfully sensual and the marble bathrooms are beautiful.

46 rooms – ♥♥ £895/1300 – ☑ £36 – 11 suites

Town plan 30 AK4-r – *45 Park Lane* ✉ *W1K 1PN* ⊖ *Hyde Park Corner* –
✆ *020 7493 4545 – www.45parklane.com*

Brown's

LUXURY · CLASSIC Opened in 1837 by James Brown, Lord Byron's butler. This urbane and very British hotel with an illustrious past offers a swish bar with Terence Donovan prints, bedrooms in neutral hues and a classic English sitting room for afternoon tea.

115 rooms – ♙ £480/1000 – ☲ £36 – 33 suites

Town plan 30 AM3-d - *33 Albemarle Street* ⊠ *W1S 4BP* ⊖ *Green Park* –
℘ *020 7493 6020 – www.roccofortehotels.com*

Westbury

BUSINESS · CONTEMPORARY With its smart, comfortable, individually designed bedrooms, its terrific art deco inspired suites and its elegant, iconic Polo bar, this hotel is as stylish now as it was when it first opened in the 1950s. All the exclusive brands are right outside the front door.

225 rooms – ♙ £279/779 – ☲ £26 – 13 suites

Town plan 30 AM3-z - *37 Conduit Street* ⊠ *W1S 2YF* ⊖ *Bond Street* –
℘ *020 7629 7755 – www.westburymayfair.com*

❀ **Alyn Williams at The Westbury** – See restaurant listing

Flemings

TOWNHOUSE · CONTEMPORARY A luxurious boutique hotel made up of a series of conjoined Georgian townhouses. Bedrooms are very pleasantly decorated and the keen team provide charming and attentive service. Stylish drawing room for afternoon tea; seasonal British dishes served in the wood-panelled basement restaurant.

129 rooms – ♙ £265/500 – ☲ £29 – 10 suites

Town plan 30 AL4-m - *7-12 Half Moon Street* ⊠ *W1J 7BH* ⊖ *Green Park* –
℘ *020 7499 0000 – www.flemings-mayfair.co.uk*

REGENT'S PARK AND MARYLEBONE

Greater London

❀ Locanda Locatelli (Giorgio Locatelli)

ITALIAN · CHIC XX A few minutes in the company of Giorgio Locatelli, whether face to face or through the medium of television, reveals a man who is passionate about Italian food and it is that very passion that has kept Locanda Locatelli at the top for so long. The restaurant may be into its second decade but still looks as dapper as ever and remains in the premier league of London's most fashionable addresses.

The other reason for its enduring popularity is the great food and the consistency that the kitchen maintains. The hugely appealing menu covers many of the regions of Italy and provides plenty of choice for everyone including coeliacs, as the terrific pasta dishes available include gluten-free options. Unfussy presentation and superlative ingredients allow natural flavours to shine through.

Specialities: Pappardelle with broad beans and rocket. Rabbit with Parma ham, polenta and chargrilled radicchio. Ricotta mousse with pistachio sponge, candied fruit and pistachio ice cream.

Carte £50/100

Town plan 29 AJ2-r - *8 Seymour Street* ⊠ *W1H 7JZ* ⊖ *Marble Arch* –
℘ *020 7935 9088 – www.locandalocatelli.com*

❀ Portland

MODERN CUISINE · INTIMATE XX The cooking at Portland respects the principles of sourcing and seasonality; in fact the menu is often reprinted after lunch as ingredients are used up and replaced by different ones. The kitchen believes in doing as little as possible to the raw produce to allow their natural flavours to come through. The bread, flavoured with treacle and porter, is stunning. Plates are never fussy or over crowded but neither will one leave here unsated.

The open kitchen is a dominant feature so the chefs are on show, but wine here is as big a feature as the food. The pared-down look of the room is just the right side of austere, helped by some original art on the walls, and the service team are knowledgeable and happy to make recommendations.

Specialities: Isle of Mull scallops with pickled Yorkshire rhubarb and roasted salsify. Cotswold venison with juniper and hay-baked purple carrots. Baked apple terrine with hazelnut ice cream and lemon thyme soft-serve.

Menu £30 (lunch)/69 – Carte £49/60

Town plan 30 AM1-p – *113 Great Portland Street* ⊠ *W1W 6QQ*
⊖ *Great Portland Street* – ☏ *020 7436 3261* – *www.portlandrestaurant.co.uk* – *Closed 22 December-3 January, Sunday, Monday - Tuesday lunch*

✲ Roganic   🄰🄲 🏵

MODERN BRITISH • MINIMALIST ✗✗ Keen followers of London's restaurant landscape will remember Roganic as a two year pop-up back in 2011. In 2018, it returned to London with several members of the original team on board; not a copy of Simon Rogan's Lake District restaurant, but bringing elements of it to the capital – and with some of the dishes designed to reflect the London location.

Cooking is confidently executed and full of flavour; many ingredients come from their farm in Cartmel and the cuisine style – which uses plenty of techniques, including pickling and curing – is such that diners will inevitably feel closer to nature than they usually do when eating out in the capital. Service is engaging and personable, with chefs delivering many of the dishes to the tables themselves.

Specialities: Chicken with cod's roe and carrot. Monkfish with brassicas. Rhubarb with buttermilk and Earl Grey.

Menu £35 (lunch), £65/85

Town plan 30 AK1-d – *5-7 Blandford Street* ⊠ *W1U 3DB* ⊖ *Bond Street* –
☏ *020 3370 6260* – *www.roganic.uk* – *Closed 1-6 January, Sunday, Monday*

✲ Texture (Agnar Sverrisson)   🕸 🄰🄲 🏵 ♿

CREATIVE • DESIGN ✗✗ Iceland is chef-owner Agnar Sverrisson's country of birth so it is no surprise to find lamb, cod (whose crisp skin is served with drinks), langoustine and skyr, the dairy product that nourished the Vikings; the bread, and the olive oils are very good too. There's considerable technical skill and depth to the cooking but dishes still appear light and refreshing and, since the use of cream and butter is largely restricted to the desserts, you even feel they're doing you good.

The Champagne Bar at the front has become a destination in itself and is separated from the restaurant by a large cabinet so you never feel too detached from it. The high ceilings add a little grandeur to the room and the service is very pleasant, with staff all willing and ready with a smile.

Specialities: Scallops with coconut, soup, kaffir lime leaves and lemongrass. Cod with avocado, brandade, tomatoes and chorizo. Icelandic skyr with ice cream, Gariguette strawberries and rye breadcrumbs.

Menu £29 (lunch), £89/99 – Carte £70/116

Town plan 30 AK2-p – *34 Portman Street* ⊠ *W1H 7BY* ⊖ *Marble Arch* –
☏ *020 7224 0028* – *www.texture-restaurant.co.uk* – *Closed 5-13 April, 9-24 August, 23 December-6 January, Sunday, Monday, Tuesday - Wednesday lunch*

✲ Trishna (Karam Sethi)   🄰🄲 🏵 ♿

INDIAN • NEIGHBOURHOOD ✗ The coast of southwest India provides the kitchen with most of its influences and the interesting menu is full of vibrant, exciting dishes, ranging from the playful – try their own mini version of 'fish and chips' as a starter – to the original: the succulent guinea fowl comes with lentils, fennel seed and star anise. However, the undoubted star of the show is a version of the dish made famous by the original Trishna in Mumbai: brown crab, in this case from Dorset, comes with lots of butter and a little kick of wild garlic; it is so wondrously rich you'll be licking your lips for days afterwards.

The various tasting menus often provide the most rounded experience but all the dishes are as fresh tasting and beautifully spiced as they are colourful. Much thought has also gone into matching wines with specific dishes.

Specialities: Aloo tokri chaat. Dorset brown crab with coconut oil, pepper, garlic and curry leaf. Mango and saffron kheer.

Menu £25 (lunch), £60/70 – Carte £34/58

Town plan 30 AK1-r – *15-17 Blandford Street* ⊠ *W1U 3DG* ⊖ *Baker Street* – ℰ *020 7935 5624 – www.trishnalondon.com*

ⅈ○ Orrery   🛱 𝖠𝖢 ⇔

MODERN CUISINE · NEIGHBOURHOOD XxX The most recent redecoration left this comfortable restaurant, located in what were converted stables from the 19C, looking lighter and more contemporary; the bar and terrace are also smarter. Expect quite elaborate, modern European cooking, strong on presentation and with the occasional twist.

Menu £27 (lunch), £59/89 – Carte £27/89

Town plan 18 Q4-a – *55 Marylebone High Street* ⊠ *W1U 5RB* ⊖ *Regent's Park* – ℰ *020 7616 8000 – www.orrery-restaurant.co.uk*

ⅈ○ Arros QD Ⓝ   𝖠𝖢

MEDITERRANEAN CUISINE · CONTEMPORARY DÉCOR XX From celebrated Spanish chef Quique Dacosta comes this huge, strikingly decorated restaurant celebrating rice, and in particular the Valencian dish paella. Ask for a table on the ground floor so you can watch the action in the open kitchen and see the flames from the wood-fired stoves.

Menu £28 (lunch)/85 – Carte £42/76

Town plan 31 AN2-y – *64 Eastcastle Street* ⊠ *W1W 8NQ* ⊖ *Oxford Circus* – ℰ *020 3883 3525 – www.arrosqd.com* – *Closed Sunday dinner*

ⅈ○ Chiltern Firehouse   🛱 𝖠𝖢 ⇔

WORLD CUISINE · TRENDY XX How appropriate – one of the hottest tickets in town is a converted fire station. The room positively bursts with energy but what makes this celebrity hangout unusual is that the food is rather good. Nuno Mendes' menu is full of vibrant North and South American dishes that are big on flavour.

Carte £37/63

Town plan 30 AK1-a – *Chiltern Firehouse Hotel, 1 Chiltern Street* ⊠ *W1U 7PA* ⊖ *Baker Street* – ℰ *020 7073 7676 – www.chilternfirehouse.com*

ⅈ○ Fischer's   𝖠𝖢

AUSTRIAN · BRASSERIE XX An Austrian café and konditorei that summons the spirit of old Vienna; from the owners of The Wolseley et al. It's open all day and breakfast is a highlight – the viennoiserie are great. The schnitzels are also good; upgrade to a Holstein.

Carte £19/55

Town plan 30 AK1-b – *50 Marylebone High Street* ⊠ *W1U 5HN* ⊖ *Baker Street* – ℰ *020 7466 5501 – www.fischers.co.uk*

ⅈ○ Lurra   🛱 𝖠𝖢 𝄃𝄃

BASQUE · DESIGN XX Its name means 'land' in Basque and reflects their use of the freshest produce, cooked over a charcoal grill. Choose tasty nibbles or sharing plates like 14 year old Galician beef, whole grilled turbot or slow-cooked shoulder of lamb.

Carte £20/65

Town plan 29 AJ2-c – *9 Seymour Place* ⊠ *W1H 5BA* ⊖ *Marble Arch* – ℰ *020 7724 4545 – www.lurra.co.uk* – *Closed Sunday dinner, Monday lunch*

⫶○ Meraki

GREEK · BRASSERIE 🎤🎤 A lively Greek restaurant from the same owners as Roka and Zuma; its name a fitting reference to the passion put into one's work. Contemporary versions of classic Greek dishes; much of the produce is imported from Greece, including the wines.

Menu £20 (lunch) – Carte £25/60

Town plan 30 AM1-m – *80-82 Great Titchfield Street* ⊠ *W1W 7QT*
⊖ *Goodge Street* – ☏ *020 7305 7686* – *www.meraki-restaurant.com* –
Closed Sunday dinner

⫶○ Les 110 de Taillevent

FRENCH · ELEGANT 🎤🎤 Ornate high ceilings and deep green banquettes create an elegant look for this French brasserie deluxe, which is more food orientated than the Paris original. It also offers 110 wines by the glass: 4 different pairings for each dish, in 4 different price brackets.

Menu £28 (lunch)/32 – Carte £48/65

Town plan 30 AL2-f – *16 Cavendish Square* ⊠ *W1G 9DD* ⊖ *Oxford Circus* –
☏ *020 3141 6016* – *www.les-110-taillevent-london.com* –
Closed 17-23 August, Sunday

⫶○ Ooty

SOUTH INDIAN · BRASSERIE 🎤🎤 Named after a hill station in Tamil Nadu, Ooty is a roomy, stylish restaurant whose creative kitchen adds contemporary touches to the southern Indian specialities. Service is attentive and sweet-natured. Ooty Station is a more casual all-day space and Ooty Club is the handsome bar downstairs.

Menu £25 (lunch) – Carte £25/66

Town plan 30 AK1-h – *66 Baker Street* ⊠ *W1U 7DJ* ⊖ *Baker Street* –
☏ *020 3727 5014* – *www.ooty.co.uk* – *Closed Sunday*

⫶○ Roux at The Landau

FRENCH · ELEGANT 🎤🎤 There's been a change to a more informal style for this restaurant run under the aegis of the Roux organisation – it's now more akin to a modern bistro in looks and atmosphere and is all the better for it. The cooking is classical French and informed by the seasons; shellfish is a highlight.

Menu £35/90 – Carte £39/80

Town plan 30 AM1-n – *Langham Hotel, 1c Portland Place, Regent Street* ⊠ *W1B 1JA* ⊖ *Oxford Circus* – ☏ *020 7965 0165* – *www.rouxatthelandau.com* –
Closed Sunday, Monday

⫶○ Rovi

WORLD CUISINE · BRASSERIE 🎤🎤 Yotam Ottolenghi's bright and colourful brasserie uses lots of fermenting and chargrilling. Dishes are designed for sharing, influences come from far and wide and vegetables are given equal billing as meat and fish.

Carte £25/75

Town plan 31 AN1-u – *59 Wells Street* ⊠ *W1A 3AE* ⊖ *Oxford Circus* –
☏ *020 3963 8270* – *www.ottolenghi.co.uk/rovi* –
Closed Sunday dinner

⫶○ Royal China Club

CHINESE · ORIENTAL 🎤🎤 Service is fast-paced and to the point, which is understandable considering how busy this restaurant always is. The large menu offers something for everyone and the lunchtime dim sum is very good; at dinner try their more unusual Cantonese dishes.

Carte £35/80

Town plan 30 AK1-c – *40-42 Baker Street* ⊠ *W1U 7AJ* ⊖ *Baker Street* –
☏ *020 7486 3898* – *www.royalchinagroup.co.uk* –
Closed 25-27 December

ⓘ◯ Xier ⓝ   AC ⓘ⊘

INNOVATIVE · DESIGN XX A 10 course set menu, along with a vegetarian alternative, is offered upstairs in the formal surroundings of Xier. Here the cooking is ambitious, original and informed by the Italian chef's international travels. XR on the ground floor is a more casual alternative and serves European dishes.

Menu £90

Town plan 30 AK1-g – *13-14 Thayer Street* ⊠ *W1U 3JR* ⊖ *Bond Street* –
℘ *020 7486 3222* – *www.xierlondon.com* – *Closed Sunday, Monday, Tuesday - Saturday lunch*

ⓘ◯ Bonnie Gull   🛖 AC

SEAFOOD · SIMPLE X Sweet Bonnie Gull calls itself a 'seafood shack' – a reference perhaps to its modest beginnings as a pop-up. Start with something from the raw bar then go for classics like Cullen skink, Devon cock crab or fish and chips. There's another branch in Soho.

Carte £32/50

Town plan 30 AM1-b – *21a Foley Street* ⊠ *W1W 6DS* ⊖ *Goodge Street* –
℘ *020 7436 0921* – *www.bonniegull.com*

ⓘ◯ Carousel ⓝ   AC

MODERN CUISINE · RUSTIC X A unique, fun and well-run dining operation in which international and up-and-coming chefs showcase their talents. The chef changes every fortnight; each one cooking dishes for a set menu which is then eaten at two large communal tables. Advance bookings only for the one sitting per evening.

Menu £45

Town plan 30 AK1-v – *71 Blandford Street* ⊠ *W1U 8AB* ⊖ *Baker Street* –
℘ *020 7487 5564* – *www.carousel-london.com* – *Closed Sunday, Monday - Friday lunch, Saturday*

ⓘ◯ Clipstone   🛖 AC 🍷

MODERN CUISINE · COSY X Sister to Portland, just around the corner, is this wonderful neighbourhood spot. Ingredients are good quality and cooking is an object lesson in flavour and originality. Add a cleverly conceived wine list, some cocktails and a relaxed, buzzy atmosphere and you've a recipe for all-round contentment.

Menu £26 (lunch), £39/48 – Carte £26/48

Town plan 30 AM1-d – *5 Clipstone Street* ⊠ *W1W 6BB* ⊖ *Great Portland Street* –
℘ *020 7637 0871* – *www.clipstonerestaurant.co.uk* – *Closed Sunday*

ⓘ◯ Dinings

JAPANESE · COSY X It's hard not to be charmed by this sweet little Japanese place, with its ground floor counter and basement tables. Its strengths lie with the more creative, contemporary dishes; sharing is recommended but prices can be steep.

Carte £21/80

Town plan 29 AH1-c – *22 Harcourt Street* ⊠ *NW1 4HH* ⊖ *Edgware Road* –
℘ *020 7723 0666* – *www.dinings.co.uk/harcourt* – *Closed Sunday - Saturday lunch*

ⓘ◯ Donostia   🍷

BASQUE · TAPAS BAR X The two young owners were inspired to open this pintxos and tapas bar by the food of San Sebastián. Sit at the counter for Basque classics like cod with pil-pil sauce, chorizo from the native Kintoa pig and slow-cooked pig's cheeks.

Menu £20 (lunch) – Carte £20/45

Town plan 29 AJ2-s – *10 Seymour Place* ⊠ *W1H 7ND* ⊖ *Marble Arch* –
℘ *020 3620 1845* – *www.donostia.co.uk* – *Closed Sunday - Monday lunch*

LONDON · ENGLAND

⅏○ Jikoni

INDIAN · ELEGANT ⅩⅩ Indian tablecloths and colourful cushions create a homely feel at this idiosyncratic restaurant. Born in Kenya of Indian parents and brought up in London, chef Ravinder Bhogal takes culinary inspiration from these sources and more.

Carte £ 28/45

Town plan 30 AK1-n – *19-21 Blandford Street* ⊠ *W1U 3DH* ⊖ *Baker Street –* ℰ *020 7034 1988 – www.jikonilondon.com – Closed Sunday dinner, Monday*

⅏○ Lima

PERUVIAN · NEIGHBOURHOOD Ⅹ Lima is one of those restaurants that just makes you feel good about life – and that's even without the pisco sours. The Peruvian food at this informal, fun place is the ideal antidote to times of austerity: it's full of punchy, invigorating flavours and fantastically vivid colours.

Carte £ 26/56

Town plan 31 AN1-h – *31 Rathbone Place* ⊠ *W1T 1JH* ⊖ *Goodge Street –* ℰ *020 3002 2640 – www.limalondongroup.com*

⅏○ Opso

GREEK · NEIGHBOURHOOD Ⅹ A modern Greek restaurant which has proved a good fit for the neighbourhood – and not just because it's around the corner from the Hellenic Centre. It serves small sharing plates that mix the modern with the traditional.

Carte £ 35/51

Town plan 30 AK1-s – *10 Paddington Street* ⊠ *W1U 5QL* ⊖ *Baker Street –* ℰ *020 7487 5088 – www.opso.co.uk – Closed 23 December-5 January*

⅏○ Picture Fitzrovia

MODERN BRITISH · SIMPLE Ⅹ An understated, simply designed neighbourhood restaurant; sit at the bar with a cocktail or under the skylight in the main room. Choose from the concise seasonal à la carte or go for the six course tasting menu (of which a vegetarian version is also available.) Good value Wednesday Wine Club.

Menu £ 35 (lunch)/45 – Carte £ 33/42

Town plan 30 AM1-t – *110 Great Portland Street* ⊠ *W1W 6PQ* ⊖ *Oxford Circus –* ℰ *020 7637 7892 – www.picturerestaurant.co.uk – Closed Sunday*

⅏○ Picture Marylebone

MODERN BRITISH · DESIGN Ⅹ The younger and smaller sister to Picture Fitzrovia, situated five minutes away, and owned by the same experienced trio. The à la carte and six course tasting menus (one vegetarian) offer carefully crafted dishes which are full of colour and flavour – and there's a great value set lunch menu too.

Menu £ 18 (lunch)/45 – Carte £ 33/40

Town plan 30 AL1-m – *19 New Cavendish Street* ⊠ *W1G 9TZ* ⊖ *Bond Street –* ℰ *020 7935 0058 – www.picturerestaurant.co.uk – Closed Sunday, Monday*

⅏○ Riding House Café

MODERN CUISINE · RUSTIC Ⅹ It's less a café, more a large, quirkily designed, all-day New York style brasserie and cocktail bar. The small plates have more zing than the main courses. The 'unbookable' side of the restaurant is the more fun part.

Carte £ 17/42

Town plan 30 AM1-k – *43-51 Great Titchfield Street* ⊠ *W1W 7PQ* ⊖ *Oxford Circus –* ℰ *020 7927 0840 – www.ridinghousecafe.co.uk*

⅏○ The Wigmore

TRADITIONAL BRITISH · PUB Ⅹ The impressively high ceiling can only mean one thing – this was once a bank. Booths, high tables, a sizeable bar and bold emerald green tones lend a clubby feel to this addendum to The Langham. Classic, hearty British dishes are given an update.

Carte £ 22/46

Town plan 30 AM1-e – *Langham Hotel, 15 Langham Place, Upper Regent Street* ⊠ *W1B 1JA* ⊖ *Oxford Circus –* ℰ *020 7965 0198 – www.the-wigmore.co.uk – Closed Sunday*

🍴 Zoilo   🍸 & AC 🔄

ARGENTINIAN · FRIENDLY 🍴 Sharing is the order of the day here so grab a seat at the counter and discover Argentina's regional specialities. Typical dishes include baked Provolone cheese, crab on toast, and grilled lamb sweetbreads. It all comes with an appealing all-Argentinian wine list.

Carte £30/60

Town plan 30 AK2-z – *9 Duke Street* ✉ *W1U 3EG* ⊖ *Bond Street* –
℘ *020 7486 9699* – *www.zoilo.co.uk* –
Closed Sunday, Monday lunch

🏨 Langham   ✿ ☝ 🕸 🕸 ₤ 🖳 & AC 🏄

LUXURY · ELEGANT Was one of Europe's first purpose-built grand hotels when it opened in 1865. Now back to its best, with its famous Palm Court for afternoon tea, its stylish Artesian bar and bedrooms that are not without personality and elegance.

380 rooms – ♥♥ £475/825 – ⊑ £35 – 31 suites

Town plan 30 AM1-n – *1c Portland Place, Regent Street* ✉ *W1B 1JA*
⊖ *Oxford Circus* – ℘ *020 7636 1000* – *www.langhamhotels.com/london*
🍴 **Roux at The Landau** • 🍴 **The Wigmore** – See restaurant listing

🏨 Charlotte Street   ✿ ⊑ & AC 🏄

LUXURY · CONTEMPORARY Stylish interior designed with a charming, understated English feel. Impeccably kept and individually decorated bedrooms. Popular in-house screening room. Colourful restaurant whose terrace spills onto Charlotte Street; grilled meats a highlight.

52 rooms – ♥♥ £480/552 – ⊑ £18 – 5 suites

Town plan 31 AN1-e – *15 Charlotte Street* ✉ *W1T 1RJ* ⊖ *Goodge Street* –
℘ *020 7806 2000* – *www.charlottestreethotel.co.uk*

🏨 Chiltern Firehouse   ✿ ⊑ & AC

TOWNHOUSE · CONTEMPORARY From Chateau Marmont in LA to The Mercer in New York, André Balazs' hotels are effortlessly cool. For his London entrance, he sympathetically restored and extended a Gothic Victorian fire station. The style comes with an easy elegance; it's an oasis of calm and hardly feels like a hotel at all.

26 rooms ⊑ – ♥♥ £600/900 – 12 suites

Town plan 30 AK1-a – *1 Chiltern Street* ✉ *W1U 7PA* ⊖ *Baker Street* –
℘ *020 7073 7676* – *www.chilternfirehouse.com*

🍴 **Chiltern Firehouse** – See restaurant listing

🏨 Mandrake   ✿ ⊑ & AC

LUXURY · DESIGN In a city with so many different hotels, The Mandrake still manages to stand out. It's filled with art and sculpture, has a great bar called Waeska and you can gaze up at the living walls or chill in the greenhouse in Jurema. No two bedrooms are the same but all are striking and luxurious.

33 rooms ⊑ – ♥♥ £330/1500

Town plan 31 AN1-r – *20-21 Newman Street* ✉ *W1T 1PG*
⊖ *Tottenham Court Road* – ℘ *020 3146 7770* – *www.themandrake.com*

🏨 The London Edition   ✿ ₤ ⊑ & AC 🏄

BUSINESS · DESIGN Formerly Berners, a classic Edwardian hotel, strikingly reborn through a partnership between Ian Schrager and Marriott – the former's influence most apparent in the stylish lobby and bar. Ask for a bedroom with a balcony.

173 rooms – ♥♥ £350/895 – ⊑ £30 – 6 suites

Town plan 31 AN2-b – *10 Berners Street* ✉ *W1T 3NP* ⊖ *Tottenham Court Road* –
℘ *020 7781 0000* – *www.editionhotels.com/london*

Sanderson

LUXURY · MINIMALIST Formerly home of Sanderson Textiles, this hotel was designed by Philippe Starck and his influence is still evident, especially in the large lobby. The Purple Bar is dark and moody; the stylish Long Bar has an equally popular terrace. Bedrooms are bright, light, pared-back and crisply decorated.

150 rooms – ₦ £219/459 – ☲ £20

Town plan 31 AN1-c – *50 Berners Street* ✉ *W1T 3NG* ⊖ *Oxford Circus* –
✆ *020 7300 1400 – www.sandersonlondon.com*

Zetter Townhouse Marylebone

TOWNHOUSE · ELEGANT Once home to Edward Lear, now a stylish Georgian townhouse full of character. It's crammed with furniture, has a rich red colour scheme and open fires. The comfortable bedrooms are equally quirky and very English in character; the best has a roll-top bath on its rooftop terrace.

24 rooms – ₦ £258/750

Town plan 29 AJ2-b – *28-30 Seymour Street* ✉ *W1H 7JB* ⊖ *Marble Arch* –
✆ *020 7324 4544 – www.thezettertownhouse.com*

Dorset Square

TOWNHOUSE · CONTEMPORARY Having reacquired this Regency townhouse, Firmdale refurbished it fully before reopening it in 2012. It has a contemporary yet intimate feel and visiting MCC members will appreciate the cricketing theme, which even extends to the cocktails in their sweet little basement brasserie.

38 rooms ☲ – ₦ £246/558

Town plan 17 P4-s – *39-40 Dorset Square* ✉ *NW1 6QN* ⊖ *Marylebone* –
✆ *020 7723 7874 – www.firmdalehotels.com*

SOHO
Greater London

✿ Barrafina

SPANISH · TAPAS BAR 𝄪 The menu at Barrafina is reassuringly familiar and supplemented by an appealing little blackboard menu of the day's best produce – from which it's well worth ordering a few dishes like crisp anchovies or octopus with capers. The dishes all burst with flavour, leave a lasting impression and are easy to share, although you'll find yourself ordering more when you look around and see what your neighbours are having.

Expect to queue if you're not here just before opening time – but a seat at the L-shaped counter in the bright and animated room will be well worth the wait. As well as hiring delightful staff, another thing that owners, the Hart Brothers, get right is that once you've got your seats you won't be hurried out of them too quickly.

Specialities: Gamba roja al ajillo. Solomillo de Rubia Gallega. Crema Catalana.

Carte £20/40

Town plan 31 AP2-v – *26-27 Dean Street* ✉ *W1D 3LL* ⊖ *Tottenham Court Road* –
✆ *020 7440 1456 – www.barrafina.co.uk*

✿ Social Eating House

MODERN CUISINE · BRASSERIE 𝄪 The coolest joint in Jason Atherton's stable comes with distressed walls, moody lighting and a laid-back vibe – it also has a terrific speakeasy-style bar upstairs. The serving team may look as though they've just been chopping wood outside but they know the menu backwards and contribute enormously to the overall fun of the place.

The 'Sampler' menu is an easy way of experiencing the full breadth of the kitchen's talents, although the à la carte also shows the modern cooking style to full effect. Influences are international, with effective combinations of flavours being punchy and well-judged. Food miles from the largely British suppliers are shown on the reverse of the menu. Cumbrian steaks are a speciality and are 40, 45 or 60 day aged and expertly cooked on the Josper grill. The well-chosen wine list includes some eclectic choices by the glass.

Specialities: Scallop ceviche with avocado, artichoke, sunflower seeds and horseradish. Corn-fed duck with pickled turnip, puntarelle, salsa verde and lentils. Dark chocolate délice with cocoa nib yoghurt and tarragon ice cream.

Menu £ 28 – Carte £ 48/68

Town plan 31 AN2-t – *58 Poland Street* ⊠ *W1F 7NR* ⊖ *Oxford Circus –*
✆ *020 7993 3251 – www.socialeatinghouse.com – Closed Sunday*

Brasserie Zédel

FRENCH · BRASSERIE XX A grand French brasserie, which is all about inclusivity and accessibility, in a bustling subterranean space restored to its original art deco glory. Expect a roll-call of classic French dishes and some competitive prices.

Specialities: Salade d'endives au Roquefort. Steak haché, sauce au poivre et frites. Île flottante.

Menu £14/20 – Carte £17/45

Town plan 31 AN3-q – *20 Sherwood Street* ⊠ *W1F 7ED* ⊖ *Piccadilly Circus –*
✆ *020 7734 4888 – www.brasseriezedel.com*

Bao

TAIWANESE · SIMPLE X There are some things in life worth queueing for – and that includes the delicious eponymous buns here at this simple, great value Taiwanese operation. The classic bao and the confit pork bao are standouts, along with 'small eats' like trotter nuggets. There's also another Bao in Windmill St.

Specialities: Classic bao. Taiwanese fried chicken. Fried Horlicks ice cream.

Carte £15/30

Town plan 31 AN2-f – *53 Lexington Street* ⊠ *W1F 9AS* ⊖ *Tottenham Court Road –*
✆ *020 3011 1632 – www.baolondon.com – Closed Sunday dinner*

Berenjak 🄽

PERSIAN · VINTAGE X Based on the hole-in-the-wall 'kabab' houses of Tehran, with exposed brick and painted plasterwork; the best place to sit is at the open kitchen counter opposite the tandoor, mangal barbecue and vertical rotisserie. Cooking is fresh and tasty; try the coal-cooked aubergine and the goat shoulder kabab.

Specialities: Coal-cooked aubergine with whey, walnuts and dried mint. Minced lamb shoulder kabab with onions and black pepper. Baklava ice cream sandwich.

Menu £ 30 – Carte £ 22/26

Town plan 31 AP2-b – *27 Romilly Street* ⊠ *W1D 5AL* ⊖ *Leicester Square –*
✆ *020 3319 8120 – www.berenjaklondon.com – Closed Sunday*

Hoppers

SOUTH INDIAN · SIMPLE X Street food inspired by the flavours of Tamil Nadu and Sri Lanka features at this fun little spot from the Sethi family (Trishna, Gymkhana). Hoppers are bowl-shaped pancakes made from fermented rice and coconut – ideal with a creamy kari. The 'short eats' are great too, as are the prices, so expect a queue.

Specialities: Lamb kothu. Black pork kari. Love cake ice cream sandwich.

Menu £ 20 (lunch) – Carte £15/30

Town plan 31 AP2-z – *49 Frith Street* ⊠ *W1D 4SG* ⊖ *Tottenham Court Road –*
✆ *020 3011 1021 – www.hopperslondon.com – Closed Sunday*

Kiln

THAI · SIMPLE Sit at the far counter to watch chefs prepare fiery Thai food in clay pots, woks and grills. The well-priced menu includes influences from Laos, Myanmar and Yunnan – all prepared using largely British produce. The counter is for walk-ins only but parties of four can book a table downstairs.

Specialities: Aged lamb and cumin skewer. Wok-fried mackerel with garlic. Burmese beef neck and wild ginger curry.

Carte £10/25

Town plan 31 AN3-k – *58 Brewer Street* ⊠ *W1F 9TL* ⊖ *Piccadilly Circus –*
www.kilnsoho.com

Kricket

INDIAN · SIMPLE A trendy pop-up turned permanent with branches also in White City and Brixton; not many Indian restaurants have a counter, an open kitchen, sharing plates and cocktails. Well-priced dishes under the headings of 'Meat', 'Fish' and 'Veg' are made with home-grown ingredients. Bookings are only taken for groups of 4 or more at dinner.

Specialities: Keralan fried chicken, curry leaf mayonnaise and pickled mooli. Butternut squash, makhani sauce, fresh paneer, hazelnut crumble and puffed wild rice. Mishti doi, rhubarb mint.

Carte £20/35

Town plan 31 AN3-t – *12 Denman Street* ⊠ *W1D 7HH* ⊖ *Piccadilly Circus –*
℘ 020 7734 5612 – www.kricket.co.uk – Closed Sunday

Palomar

MIDDLE EASTERN · TRENDY A hip slice of modern-day Jerusalem in the heart of theatreland, with a zinc kitchen counter running back to an intimate wood-panelled dining room. Like the atmosphere, the contemporary Middle Eastern cooking is fresh and vibrant.

Specialities: Kubaneh with tomato and tahini. Shakshukit beef and lamb with pine nuts. Malabi with hibiscus syrup and Iranian pistachios.

Carte £20/32

Town plan 31 AP3-s – *34 Rupert Street* ⊠ *W1D 6DN* ⊖ *Piccadilly Circus –*
℘ 020 7439 8777 – www.thepalomar.co.uk

Gauthier - Soho

FRENCH · INTIMATE Detached from the rowdier elements of Soho is this charming Georgian townhouse, with dining spread over three floors. Alex Gauthier offers assorted menus of his classically based cooking, with vegetarians particularly well looked after.

Carte £35/60

Town plan 31 AP2-k – *21 Romilly Street* ⊠ *W1D 5AF* ⊖ *Leicester Square –*
℘ 020 7494 3111 – www.gauthiersoho.co.uk – Closed Sunday, Monday

Bob Bob Ricard

TRADITIONAL BRITISH · VINTAGE Small but perfectly formed, BBR actually sees itself as a glamorous grand salon; ask for a booth. The menu is all-encompassing – from pies and burgers to oysters and caviar. Prices are altered depending on how busy they are, with up to a 25% reduction at off-peak times.

Carte £38/86

Town plan 31 AN2-s – *1 Upper James Street* ⊠ *W1F 9DF* ⊖ *Oxford Circus –*
℘ 020 3145 1000 – www.bobbobricard.com

100 Wardour St

MODERN CUISINE · CONTEMPORARY DÉCOR For a night out with a group of friends, this D&D place is worth considering. At night, head downstairs for cocktails, live music (well, this was once The Marquee Club) and a modern, Med-influenced menu with the odd Asian touch. During the day, the ground floor offers an all-day menu.

Menu £42 – Carte £31/58

Town plan 31 AN2-v – *100 Wardour Street* ⊠ *W1F 0TN*
⊖ *Tottenham Court Road – ℘ 020 7314 4000 – www.100wardourst.com*

ⅰ○ Tamarind Kitchen   AC

INDIAN · **EXOTIC DÉCOR** XX A more relaxed sister to Tamarind in Mayfair, this Indian restaurant comes with endearingly earnest service and a lively buzz. There's a nominal Northern emphasis to the fairly priced menu, with Awadhi kababs a speciality, but there are also plenty of curries and fish dishes.

Menu £18 (lunch), £24/40 – Carte £20/36

Town plan 31 AN2-m – *167-169 Wardour Street* ✉ *W1F 8WR*
⊖ *Tottenham Court Road* – ℰ *020 7287 4243 – www.tamarindkitchen.co.uk –*
Closed Monday lunch

ⅰ○ Temper   🕸 ఈ AC

BARBECUE · **CONTEMPORARY DÉCOR** XX A fun, basement restaurant all about barbecue and meats. The beasts are cooked whole, some are also smoked in-house and there's a distinct South African flavour to the salsas that accompany them. Kick off with some tacos – they make around 1,200 of them every day.

Carte £20/40

Town plan 31 AN2-r – *25 Broadwick Street* ✉ *W1F 0DF* ⊖ *Oxford Circus –*
ℰ *020 3879 3834 – www.temperrestaurant.com – Closed Monday lunch*

ⅰ○ Vasco and Piero's Pavilion   AC ⇔

ITALIAN · **FRIENDLY** XX Regulars and tourists have been flocking to this institution for over 40 years; its longevity is down to a twice daily changing menu of Umbrian-influenced dishes rather than the matter-of-fact service or simple decoration.

Carte £28/40

Town plan 31 AN2-q – *15 Poland Street* ✉ *W1F 8QE* ⊖ *Oxford Circus –*
ℰ *020 7437 8774 – www.vascosfood.com – Closed Sunday, Saturday lunch*

ⅰ○ Yauatcha Soho   🍸 ఈ AC 🍴 🕦

CHINESE · **DESIGN** XX The bright ground floor features well-spaced tables and cabinets full of pastries and chocolates – but ask to sit in the more atmospheric basement, with its celestial ceiling lights, tropical fish tanks and glimpses into the kitchen. The menu provides plenty of choice and over-ordering is easy to do.

Carte £29/72

Town plan 31 AN2-k – *15 Broadwick Street* ✉ *W1F 0DL*
⊖ *Tottenham Court Road* – ℰ *020 7494 8888 – www.yauatcha.com*

ⅰ○ yeni ⓝ   ఈ AC

TURKISH · **CONTEMPORARY DÉCOR** XX Anatolian-inspired cooking from experienced chef-owner Civan Er, who made his name at acclaimed sister restaurant Yeni Lokanta in his home city of Istanbul. Daily changing menu of vibrant, gutsy, flavoursome dishes; techniques are rooted in tradition, with dishes cooked over oak in the Josper oven.

Carte £28/57

Town plan 31 AN2-g – *55 Beak Street* ✉ *W1F 9SH* ⊖ *Piccadilly Circus –*
ℰ *020 3475 1903 – www.yeni.london – Closed Sunday*

ⅰ○ Nopi   🍸 AC 🍴 🕦

MEDITERRANEAN CUISINE · **DESIGN** X The bright, clean look of Yotam Ottolenghi's charmingly run all-day restaurant matches the fresh, invigorating food. The sharing plates take in the Mediterranean, the Middle East and Asia and the veggie dishes stand out.

Carte £31/49

Town plan 31 AN3-g – *21-22 Warwick Street* ✉ *W1B 5NE* ⊖ *Piccadilly Circus –*
ℰ *020 7494 9584 – www.ottolenghi.co.uk – Closed Sunday dinner*

ⅰ○ Barshu   AC ⇔

CHINESE · **EXOTIC DÉCOR** X The fiery and authentic flavours of China's Sichuan province are the draw here; help is at hand as the menu has pictures. It's well run and decorated with carved wood and lanterns; downstairs is better for groups.

Carte £20/58

Town plan 31 AP2-g – *28 Frith Street* ✉ *W1D 5LF* ⊖ *Leicester Square –*
ℰ *020 7287 8822 – www.barshurestaurant.co.uk*

🍴○ **Beijing Dumpling**

CHINESE · NEIGHBOURHOOD 𝕏 This relaxed little place serves freshly prepared dumplings of both Beijing and Shanghai styles. Although the range is not as comprehensive as the name suggests, they do stand out, especially varieties of the famed Xiao Long Bao.

Menu £25 – Carte £14/38

Town plan 31 AP3-e – *23 Lisle Street* ✉ *WC2H 7BA* ⊖ *Leicester Square –*
📞 *020 7287 6888 – www.beijingdumpling.co.uk*

🍴○ **Blanchette**

FRENCH · SIMPLE 𝕏 Run by three frères, Blanchette takes French bistro food and gives it the 'small plates' treatment. It's named after their mother – the ox cheek Bourguignon is her recipe. Tiles and exposed brick add to the rustic look.

Menu £39/45 – Carte £28/50

Town plan 31 AN2-c – *9 D'Arblay Street* ✉ *W1F 8DR* ⊖ *Oxford Circus –*
📞 *020 7439 8100 – www.blanchettelondon.co.uk*

🍴○ **Bocca di Lupo**

ITALIAN · TAPAS BAR 𝕏 Atmosphere, food and service are all best when sitting at the marble counter, watching the chefs at work. Specialities from across Italy come in large or small sizes and are full of flavour and vitality. Try also their gelato shop opposite.

Carte £25/55

Town plan 31 AN3-e – *12 Archer Street* ✉ *W1D 7BB* ⊖ *Piccadilly Circus –*
📞 *020 7734 2223 – www.boccadilupo.com*

🍴○ **Casita Andina**

PERUVIAN · RUSTIC 𝕏 Respect is paid to the home-style cooking of the Andes at this warmly run and welcoming Peruvian picantería. Dishes are gluten-free and as colourful as the surroundings of this 200 year old house.

Menu £12 – Carte £16/20

Town plan 31 AN3-n – *31 Great Windmill Street* ✉ *W1D 7LP* ⊖ *Piccadilly Circus –*
📞 *020 3327 9464 – www.andinalondon.com/casita – Closed Monday - Tuesday lunch*

🍴○ **Cây Tre**

VIETNAMESE · MINIMALIST 𝕏 Bustling Vietnamese restaurant offering specialities from all parts of the country. Dishes are generously sized and appealingly priced; their various versions of pho are always popular. Come in a group to compete with the noise.

Menu £13 (lunch)/25 – Carte £14/27

Town plan 31 AP2-m – *42-43 Dean Street* ✉ *W1D 4PZ* ⊖ *Tottenham Court Road –*
📞 *020 7317 9118 – www.caytrerestaurant.co.uk*

🍴○ **Ceviche Soho**

PERUVIAN · FRIENDLY 𝕏 This is where it all started for this small group that helped London discover Peruvian food. It's as loud and cramped as it is fun and friendly. Start with a pisco-based cocktail then order classics like tiradito alongside dishes from the grill such as ox heart anticuchos.

Menu £10/12 – Carte £12/25

Town plan 31 AP2-w – *17 Frith Street* ✉ *W1D 4RG* ⊖ *Tottenham Court Road –*
📞 *020 7292 2040 – www.cevicherestaurants.com*

🍴○ **Copita**

SPANISH · TAPAS BAR 𝕏 This tapas bar – a sister to Barrica – is packed most nights; perch on one of the high stools or stay standing and get stuck into the daily menu of small, colourful dishes. Staff add to the lively atmosphere and everything on the thoughtfully compiled Spanish wine list is available by the glass or copita.

Carte £18/40

Town plan 31 AN2-h – *27 D'Arblay Street* ✉ *W1F 8EP* ⊖ *Oxford Circus –*
📞 *020 7287 7797 – www.copita.co.uk – Closed Sunday*

85

⁙○ Darjeeling Express   🗚C

INDIAN · **BRASSERIE** ⅍ With Royal Mughlai ancestry and a great love of food gained from cooking traditional family recipes, the owner couldn't be better qualified. Her open kitchen is run by a team of housewives; the influences are mostly Bengali but there are also dishes from Kolkata to Hyderabad. Lively and great fun.

Carte £24/29

Town plan 31 AN2-x – *Kingly Court, Carnaby Street (Top Floor)* ⊠ *W1B 5PW* ⊖ *Oxford Circus* – ℰ *020 7287 2828* – *www.darjeeling-express.com* – *Closed Sunday*

⁙○ Dehesa   🏠 🗚C 🍴 ⇔

MEDITERRANEAN CUISINE · **TAPAS BAR** ⅍ Repeats the success of its sister restaurant, Salt Yard, by offering flavoursome and appealingly priced Spanish and Italian tapas. Busy, friendly atmosphere in appealing corner location. Good drinks list too.

Menu £15 (lunch) – Carte £20/35

Town plan 30 AM2-i – *25 Ganton Street* ⊠ *W1F 9BP* ⊖ *Oxford Circus* – ℰ *020 7494 4170* – *www.dehesa.co.uk*

⁙○ Duck & Rice   🗚C

CHINESE · **INTIMATE** ⅍ Something a little different – a converted pub with a Chinese kitchen – originally set up by Alan Yau. Beer and snacks are the thing on the ground floor; upstairs, with its booths and fireplaces, is for Chinese favourites and comforting classics.

Carte £21/49

Town plan 31 AN2-w – *90 Berwick Street* ⊠ *W1F 0QB* ⊖ *Tottenham Court Road* – ℰ *020 3327 7888* – *www.theduckandrice.com*

⁙○ Ember Yard   🗚C 🍴 ⇔

MEDITERRANEAN CUISINE · **TAPAS BAR** ⅍ Those familiar with the Salt Yard Group will recognise the Spanish and Italian themed menus – but their 4th fun outlet comes with a focus on cooking over charcoal or wood. There's even a seductive smokiness to some of the cocktails.

Menu £20 (lunch), £30/45 – Carte £29/48

Town plan 31 AN2-e – *60 Berwick Street* ⊠ *W1F 8SU* ⊖ *Oxford Circus* – ℰ *020 7439 8057* – *www.emberyard.co.uk*

⁙○ Evelyn's Table   🗚C 🍴

MODERN CUISINE · **SIMPLE** ⅍ A former beer cellar of a restored 18C inn – much is made of the whole cramped, underground, speakeasy thing. Watching the chefs behind the counter is all part of the appeal; their modern European dishes are designed for sharing, with fish from Cornwall a highlight.

Carte £39/56

Town plan 31 AP3-u – *The Blue Posts, 28 Rupert Street* ⊠ *W1D 6DJ* ⊖ *Piccadilly Circus* – ℰ *07921 336010* – *www.theblueposts.co.uk* – *Closed Monday - Tuesday lunch*

⁙○ French House ⓝ

TRADITIONAL BRITISH · **PUB** ⅍ This historic Soho watering hole, once a favourite haunt of writers and artists such as Dylan Thomas, Brendan Behan and Francis Bacon, has only seven tables in its oxblood and wood-panelled upstairs restaurant. It's run in a bohemian style and offers honest British cooking with integrity and flavour.

Carte £25/50

Town plan 31 AP2-n – *49 Dean Street* ⊠ *W1D 5BG* ⊖ *Leicester Square* – ℰ *020 7437 2477* – *www.frenchhousesoho.com* – *Closed Sunday, Monday dinner, Friday dinner, Saturday*

🍽️○ Jinjuu

ASIAN • DESIGN 🍴 American-born celebrity chef Judy Joo's restaurant is a celebration of her Korean heritage. The vibrant dishes, whether Bibimbap bowls or Ssam platters, burst with flavour and are as enjoyable as the fun surroundings. There's another branch in Mayfair.

Menu £14 (lunch), £40/60 – Carte £17/60

Town plan 31 AN2-d – *15 Kingly Street* ⊠ *W1B 5PS* ⊖ *Oxford Circus* –
☏ *020 8181 8887* – *www.jinjuu.com*

🍽️○ Jugemu

JAPANESE • SIMPLE 🍴 Like all the best izakaya, this one is tucked away down a side street and easy to miss. It has three small tables and a 9-seater counter from where you can watch the chef-owner at work. Popular with a homesick Japanese clientele, it keeps things traditional; the sashimi is excellent.

Carte £15/50

Town plan 31 AN2-a – *3 Winnett Street* ⊠ *W1D 6JY* ⊖ *Piccadilly Circus* –
☏ *020 7734 0518* – *Closed Sunday, Saturday lunch*

🍽️○ Koya Soho

JAPANESE • SIMPLE 🍴 A simple, sweet place serving authentic Udon noodles and small plates; they open early for breakfast. Counter seating means everyone has a view of the chefs; bookings aren't taken and there is often a queue, but the short wait is worth it.

Carte £14/32

Town plan 31 AP2-z – *50 Frith Street* ⊠ *W1D 4SQ* ⊖ *Tottenham Court Road* –
☏ *020 7494 9075* – *www.koya.co.uk*

🍽️○ Mele e Pere

ITALIAN • FRIENDLY 🍴 There's a small dining room on the ground floor but all the fun happens downstairs, where you'll find a large vermouth bar with vintage posters and plenty of seating in the buzzy vaulted room. The rustic Italian dishes hit the spot and the pre-theatre menu is great value.

Menu £19 (lunch), £18/20 – Carte £29/48

Town plan 31 AN3-h – *46 Brewer Street* ⊠ *W1F 9TF* ⊖ *Piccadilly Circus* –
☏ *020 7096 2096* – *www.meleepere.co.uk*

🍽️○ Pastaio

ITALIAN • OSTERIA 🍴 Get ready to queue and even share a table – but at these prices who cares? This buzzy spot, a stone's throw from Carnaby Street, is all about pasta. It's made in-house daily by the all Italian team, with short and long semolina pasta extruded through bronze dies. The tiramisu is great too.

Carte £24/28

Town plan 31 AN2-p – *19 Ganton Street* ⊠ *W1F 9BN* ⊖ *Oxford Circus* –
☏ *020 3019 8680* – *www.pastaio.london*

🍽️○ Rambla

SPANISH • TAPAS BAR 🍴 The owner's childhood in Barcelona is celebrated here with an interesting range of Catalan-inspired dishes, which are punchy in flavour and designed to be shared. It's a simple, unpretentious place dominated by an open kitchen; the best seats are at the counter.

Carte £22/39

Town plan 31 AP2-q – *64 Dean Street* ⊠ *W1D 4QQ* ⊖ *Tottenham Court Road* –
☏ *020 7734 8428* – *www.ramblalondon.com*

🍽️○ XU

TAIWANESE • CHIC 🍴 They've squeezed a lot into the two floors to create the feel of 1930s Taipei, including an emerald lacquered tea kiosk and mahjong tables. Don't miss the numbing beef tendon and classics like Shou Pa chicken. Tofu is made in-house and Chi Shiang rice is flown in from Taiwan.

Carte £24/45

Town plan 31 AP3-s – *30 Rupert Street* ⊠ *W1D 6DL* ⊖ *Piccadilly Circus* –
☏ *020 3319 8147* – *www.xulondon.com*

Café Royal

GRAND LUXURY · HISTORIC One of the most famous names of the London so-cial scene for the last 150 years is now a luxury hotel. The bedrooms are beautiful, elegant and discreet and the wining and dining options many and varied. Take afternoon tea in the gloriously rococo Oscar Wilde lounge, once home to the iconic Grill Room.

160 rooms – **††** £470/1000 – ☷ £36 – 16 suites

Town plan 31 AN3-r – *68 Regent Street* ✉ *W1B 4DY* ⊖ *Piccadilly Circus* –
✆ *020 7406 3333* – *www.hotelcaferoyal.com*

Ham Yard

LUXURY · ELEGANT This stylish hotel from the Firmdale group is set around a courtyard – a haven of tranquillity in the West End. Each of the rooms is different but all are supremely comfortable. There's also a great roof terrace, a theatre, a fully stocked library and bar... and even a bowling alley.

91 rooms – **††** £380/770 – ☷ £27 – 7 suites

Town plan 31 AN3-p – *1 Ham Yard* ✉ *W1D 7DT* ⊖ *Piccadilly Circus* –
✆ *020 3642 2000* – *www.hamyardhotel.com*

Soho

LUXURY · PERSONALISED Stylish and fashionable hotel that mirrors the vi-brancy of the neighbourhood. Boasts two screening rooms, a comfortable draw-ing room and up-to-the-minute bedrooms; some vivid, others more muted but all with hi-tech extras.

96 rooms ☷ – **††** £402/636 – 6 suites

Town plan 31 AN2-n – *4 Richmond Mews* ✉ *W1D 3DH* ⊖ *Tottenham Court Road* –
✆ *020 7559 3000* – *www.firmdalehotels.com*

Dean Street Townhouse

TOWNHOUSE · CONTEMPORARY In the heart of Soho and where bedrooms range from tiny to bigger; the latter have roll-top baths in the room. All are well designed and come with a good range of extras. Cosy ground floor lounge.

39 rooms – **††** £180/510 – ☷ £15

Town plan 31 AP2-t – *69-71 Dean Street* ✉ *W1D 3SE* ⊖ *Piccadily Circus* –
✆ *020 7434 1775* – *www.deanstreettownhouse.com*

Hazlitt's

TOWNHOUSE · HISTORIC Dating from 1718, the former house of essayist and critic William Hazlitt still welcomes many a writer today in its role as a charming townhouse hotel. It has plenty of character and is warmly run. No restaurant so breakfast in bed really is the only option – and who is going to object to that?

30 rooms – **††** £260/320 – ☷ £12

Town plan 31 AP2-u – *6 Frith Street* ✉ *W1D 3JA* ⊖ *Tottenham Court Road* –
✆ *020 7434 1771* – *www.hazlittshotel.com*

ST JAMES'S

Greater London

Ritz Restaurant

MODERN BRITISH · LUXURY XXXX Executive Chef John Williams MBE and his traditionally structured kitchen have taken classic dishes, including some Escoffier recipes, and by using enormous skill and adding touches of modernity and finesse have lifted these dishes to new heights, while still respecting their spirit and heri-tage. Unsurprisingly, the ingredients used are from the far end of the ledger marked 'extravagant' and, alongside a 'Menu Surprise' and the à la carte, come dishes for two on the 'Arts de le Table' menu that could include Beef Wellington and Gateaux St Honoré finished off at the table.

There is no restaurant in London grander than The Ritz. The lavish Louis XVI decoration makes this the place for the most special of special occasions – so it should come as no surprise that they insist on a jacket and tie.

Specialities: Norfolk crab with apple, avocado and caviar. Tournedos of beef with salsify, lovage and smoked bone marrow. Crêpes Suzette.

Menu £59 (lunch), £67/125 – Carte £70/140

Town plan 30 AM4-c – *Ritz Hotel, 150 Piccadilly* ✉ *W1J 9BR*
⊖ *Green Park* –
✆ *020 7300 2370* –
www.theritzlondon.com

⊗ Seven Park Place   AC ⇌

MODERN CUISINE · COSY ✗✗✗ 2019 saw William Drabble celebrate 10 years in charge of the kitchen here at St James's Hotel and Club and it's a rare night he's not at the stove. He trained and worked in some significant kitchens before joining the hotel and his style of food is unapologetically classic, both in the flavour combinations of his dishes and also in the techniques he uses to create them.

Sauces are a particular strength but at the heart of his philosophy is the sourcing of great British ingredients, like Rhug Estate chicken, Scottish seafood and Lune Valley lamb. Keeping things simple allows the seasonal ingredients to speak for themselves; try his signature poached tail of native lobster with cauliflower purée and lobster butter sauce.

Specialities: Poached native lobster tail with cauliflower purée and lobster butter sauce. Assiette of Lune Valley lamb with calçot onions and thyme jus. Coffee soaked savarin, gianduja mousse, mascarpone and hazelnuts.

Menu £28 (lunch), £65/95

Town plan 30 AM4-k – *St James's Hotel and Club, 7-8 Park Place* ✉ *SW1A 1LS*
⊖ *Green Park* – ✆ *020 7316 1615* –
www.stjameshotelandclub.com –
Closed Sunday, Monday

⊗ Aquavit   🍷 🏠 & AC 🐾 ⇌

SCANDINAVIAN · BRASSERIE ✗✗ A younger, more down-to-earth sister to the original in NYC – well-suited to its surroundings in St James's Market – Aquavit London features a design inspired by Gothenburg City Hall and comes with a central bar, plenty of marble, wood, leather and light – and the warm, informal kind of atmosphere enjoyed at all the best brasseries.

The cooking delivers as much panache as the Scandinavian styling, with classic Nordic dishes like beef Rydberg or meatballs with lingonberries featuring excellent ingredients, clear natural flavours, and a subtle modern touch. Be sure to include a selection of sharing plates from the smörgåsbord – perhaps some shrimp Skagen or in-house marinated matje herring; and don't miss the Norwegian omelette for dessert.

Specialities: Smoked eel with baby gem, tomato and lovage. Beef Rydberg. Norwegian omelette with sea buckthorn and vanilla.

Menu £27 (lunch), £22/30 – Carte £32/66

Town plan 31 AN3-d – *St. James's Market, 1 Carlton Street* ✉ *SW1Y 4QQ*
⊖ *Piccadilly Circus* – ✆ *020 7024 9848* –
www.aquavitrestaurants.com –
Closed 23-27 December, Sunday dinner

⊗ Ikoyi (Jeremy Chan)   & AC 🐾

CREATIVE · SIMPLE ✗ The somewhat colourless development that is St James's Market is the unlikely setting for one of the capital's more innovative restaurants. It's named after the prosperous neighbourhood in Lagos, Nigeria which gives a clue as to its USP: the two owners, friends since childhood, have put together a kitchen that uses home-grown ingredients enlivened with flavours from West Africa.

There is nothing gimmicky here – it's all about using ingredients that may be un-familiar while still ensuring that the main constituent of the dish, be it monkfish or duck, remains the star of the show. Kick off with Moin Moin with prawns or the buttermilk-soaked plantain with a Scotch Bonnet dip – they will certainly get your taste-buds in the mood. Jollof rice is a must and here it comes with crab – when the lid is lifted you'll find the smoky aromas intoxicating.

Specialities: Plantain & smoked Scotch Bonnet with red mullet velouté, white as-paragus and banga. Aged Beef & Carrot Maafe. Wild rice and fonio.

Menu £35/100

Town plan 31 AN3-b – *1 St. James's Market* ⊠ *SW1Y 4AH* ⊖ *Piccadilly Circus* – ☏ *020 3583 4660* – *www.ikoyilondon.com* – *Closed 24 December-4 January, Sunday*

⫶○ Chutney Mary

INDIAN • DESIGN XXX A long-standing and popular Indian restaurant, which is more relaxed and fashionable than its St James's address might suggest. The ap-pealing menu offers lots of choice and the well-judged, flavourful dishes have been subtly updated, whilst still respecting the foundations of Indian cooking.

Menu £46/56 – Carte £50/78

Town plan 30 AM4-c – *73 St James's Street* ⊠ *SW1A 1PH* ⊖ *Green Park* – ☏ *020 7629 6688* – *www.chutneymary.com*

⫶○ Imperial Treasure ❶ &⃞ AC ⟨Y⟩ ⟨⟩

CHINESE • ELEGANT XXX The first London outpost of this group is housed in an imposing former bank, which provides a luxurious backdrop for the traditional, mostly Cantonese cooking. White leather, onyx walls and wood partitions pro-vide some intimacy amongst the opulence. The signature Peking duck is worth the expense.

Menu £38 (lunch), £68/128 – Carte £48/130

Town plan 31 AP3-t – *9 Waterloo Place* ⊠ *SW1Y 4BE* ⊖ *Piccadilly Circus* – ☏ *020 3011 1328* – *www.imperialtreasure.com/uk*

⫶○ The Wolseley AC ⟨Y⟩ ⟨⟩

MODERN CUISINE • ELEGANT XXX This feels like a grand and glamorous Euro-pean coffee house, with its pillars and high vaulted ceiling. Appealing menus offer everything from caviar to a hotdog. It's open from early until late and boasts a large celebrity following.

Carte £25/55

Town plan 30 AM3-q – *160 Piccadilly* ⊠ *W1J 9EB* ⊖ *Green Park* – ☏ *020 7499 6996* – *www.thewolseley.com*

⫶○ 45 Jermyn St ⟨⟩ AC ⟨⟩

TRADITIONAL BRITISH • BRASSERIE XX Style and comfort go hand in hand at this bright, contemporary brasserie. The menu is a mix of European and British classics; the beef Wellington and lobster spaghetti are finished off at your table. Sodas, coupes and floats pay tribute to its past as Fortnum's Fountain restaurant.

Menu £27/39 – Carte £30/77

Town plan 31 AN3-f – *45 Jermyn Street* ⊠ *SW1 6DN* ⊖ *Piccadilly Circus* – ☏ *020 7205 4545* – *www.45jermynst.com*

⫶○ Franco's 🕸 ⟨⟩ AC ⟨⟩ ⟨⟩

ITALIAN • TRADITIONAL XX Have an aperitivo in the clubby bar before sitting down to eat at one of London's oldest yet rejuvenated Italian restaurants. The kitchen focuses on the classics and they live up to expectations; the regulars, of whom there are many, all have their favourites.

Menu £32 – Carte £36/64

Town plan 30 AM3-u – *61 Jermyn Street* ⊠ *SW1Y 6LX* ⊖ *Green Park* – ☏ *020 7499 2211* – *www.francoslondon.com* – *Closed Sunday*

ⅼ◯ Cafe Murano

ITALIAN · FRIENDLY ✗✗ Angela Hartnett and her chef have created an appealing and flexible menu of delicious North Italian delicacies – the lunch menu is very good value. It's certainly no ordinary café and its popularity means pre-booking is essential.

Menu £19/23 – Carte £29/44

Town plan 30 AM4-m – *33 St. James's Street* ✉ *SW1A 1HD* ⊖ *Green Park* – ✆ *020 3371 5559 – www.cafemurano.co.uk* – *Closed 24-26 December, Sunday dinner*

ⅼ◯ Farzi Café

INDIAN · CONTEMPORARY DÉCOR ✗✗ A great spot for a meal before heading next door to the Theatre Royal, this glitzy, buzzy two-floored restaurant serves modern, reinterpreted versions of classic Indian dishes, with some interesting global touches. Spicing is clean, distinct and multi-layered – and Zodiac-themed cocktails add to the fun.

Carte £26/58

Town plan 31 AP3-w – *8 Haymarket* ✉ *SW1Y 4BP* ⊖ *Piccadilly Circus* – ✆ *020 3981 0090 – www.farzilondon.com*

ⅼ◯ Ginza Onodera

JAPANESE · ELEGANT ✗✗ Re-fitted and re-launched in 2017 on the site of what was Matsuri for over 20 years. A staircase leads down to the smart restaurant and the three counters: sushi, teppanyaki and the robata grill. The emphasis is on traditional Japanese cuisine and top-end ingredients.

Menu £23 (lunch) – Carte £29/70

Town plan 31 AN3-w – *15 Bury Street* ✉ *SW1Y 6AL* ⊖ *Green Park* – ✆ *020 7839 1101 – www.onodera-group.com*

ⅼ◯ Portrait

MODERN CUISINE · CONTEMPORARY DÉCOR ✗✗ Set on the top floor of the National Portrait Gallery with views of local landmarks. Carefully prepared modern European food; dishes are sometimes created in celebration of current exhibitions. Good value pre-theatre and weekend set menus.

Menu £33 – Carte £37/87

Town plan 31 AP3-n – *National Portrait Gallery, St Martin's Place (3rd Floor)* ✉ *WC2H 0HE* ⊖ *Charing Cross* – ✆ *020 7312 2490* – *www.npg.org.uk/portraitrestaurant* – *Closed Sunday - Wednesday dinner*

ⅼ◯ Quaglino's

MODERN CUISINE · DESIGN ✗✗ This colourful, glamorous restaurant manages to be cavernous and cosy at the same time, with live music and a late night bar adding a certain sultriness to proceedings. The kitchen specialises in contemporary brasserie-style food.

Menu £23/33 – Carte £37/64

Town plan 30 AM4-j – *16 Bury Street* ✉ *SW1Y 6AJ* ⊖ *Green Park* – ✆ *020 7930 6767 – www.quaglinos-restaurant.co.uk*

ⅼ◯ Sake No Hana

JAPANESE · MINIMALIST ✗✗ A modern Japanese restaurant within a Grade II listed '60s edifice – and proof that you can occasionally find good food at the end of an escalator. As with the great cocktails, the menu is best enjoyed when shared with a group.

Carte £33/133

Town plan 30 AM4-n – *23 St. James's Street* ✉ *SW1A 1HA* ⊖ *Green Park* – ✆ *020 7925 8988 – www.sakenohana.com* – *Closed Sunday*

ⅱ○ Wild Honey St James ⓝ   🅰🅲

MODERN BRITISH · CONTEMPORARY DÉCOR XX Elegant without being overly formal, this grand brasserie is set in the impressive surrounds of the Sofitel London St James – in what was previously the hall of this Grade II listed former bank. Anthony Demetre's accomplished modern European dishes are the perfect match for the surroundings.

Menu £27 – Carte £45/57

Town plan 31 AP3-g – *Sofitel London St James Hotel, 8 Pall Mall* ⊠ *SW1Y 5NG* ⊖ *Piccadilly Circus* – ☏ *020 7968 2900* – *www.wildhoneystjames.co.uk*

ⅱ○ Scully   🅰🅲 🎮

WORLD CUISINE · FRIENDLY X The eponymous chef-owner's travels and family heritage inform his style of food. The small plates feature an array of international influences and the bold, diverse flavours give them an appealing vitality. The kitchen makes good use of the shelves of pickles and spices.

Carte £45/60

Town plan 31 AN3-r – *4 St. James's Market* ⊠ *SW1Y 4AH* ⊖ *Piccadilly Circus* – ☏ *020 3911 6840* – *www.scullyrestaurant.com* – *Closed Sunday dinner*

🏨 Ritz   🏖 ƙる ⬆ 🅰🅲 🕍

GRAND LUXURY · CLASSIC Opened in 1906 as a fine example of Louis XVI architecture and decoration, The Ritz is one of London's most celebrated hotels. The Palm Court is famed for its afternoon tea and the Rivoli Bar is beautiful. Lavishly appointed bedrooms are constantly being refreshed and refurbished while respecting the hotel's heritage; many overlook the park.

136 rooms – ♥♥ £425/930 – ⴲ £42 – 25 suites

Town plan 30 AM4-c – *150 Piccadilly* ⊠ *W1J 9BR* ⊖ *Green Park* – ☏ *020 7493 8181* – *www.theritzlondon.com*

⁂ **Ritz Restaurant** – See restaurant listing

🏨 Haymarket   🏖 🖼 ƙる ⬆ & 🅰🅲 🕍

LUXURY · PERSONALISED Housed in a John Nash Regency building, this hotel not only boasts a great location but is stylishly decorated with works of art and sculpture. Large, comfortable bedrooms come in soothing colours and there's an impressive basement pool. Brumus restaurant a good choice for pre-theatre dining.

50 rooms ⴲ – ♥♥ £312/516 – 3 suites

Town plan 31 AP3-x – *1 Suffolk Place* ⊠ *SW1Y 4HX* ⊖ *Piccadilly Circus* – ☏ *020 7470 4000* – *www.haymarkethotel.com*

🏨 Sofitel London St James   🏖 🛎 ƙる ⬆ & 🅰🅲 🕍

LUXURY · ELEGANT This well-located hotel – a Grade II listed former bank – blends chic French styling with its British heritage. Enjoy afternoon tea in the lounge, which takes its inspiration from an English rose garden, or head to informal all-day restaurant, Wild Honey, for modern European dishes in the original banking hall.

183 rooms – ♥♥ £375/795 – ⴲ £26 – 16 suites

Town plan 31 AP3-a – *6 Waterloo Place* ⊠ *SW1Y 4AN* ⊖ *Piccadilly Circus* – ☏ *020 7747 2200* – *www.sofitelstjames.com*

ⅱ○ **Wild Honey St James** – See restaurant listing

🏨 Stafford   🏖 🐾 ƙる ⬆ 🅰🅲 🕍

LUXURY · ELEGANT A charming 'country house in the city' which mixes the old and the new, with bedrooms divided between the main house, a converted 18C stables and a more modern mews. The Game Bird restaurant offers traditional British food with salmon and game the highlights. The legendary American Bar is certainly worth a visit.

107 rooms – ♥♥ £350/780 – ⴲ £26 – 15 suites

Town plan 30 AM4-u – *16-18 St James's Place* ⊠ *SW1A 1NJ* ⊖ *Green Park* – ☏ *020 7493 0111* – *www.thestaffordlondon.com*

St James's Hotel and Club

BUSINESS · CONTEMPORARY 1890s house, formerly a private club, in a wonderfully central yet quiet location. Modern, boutique-style interior with over 300 European works of art from the '20s to the '50s. Fine finish to the compact but well-equipped bedrooms.

60 rooms – †† £250/400 – ☐ £22 – 10 suites

Town plan 30 AM4-k – *7-8 Park Place* ⊠ *SW1A 1LS* ⊖ *Green Park –*
☏ *020 7316 1600 – www.stjameshotelandclub.com*

❀ **Seven Park Place** – See restaurant listing

STRAND AND COVENT GARDEN
Greater London

Bancone 🟢

MODERN CUISINE · CONTEMPORARY DÉCOR X It's all about freshly made pasta at great prices – and all in the centre of town; the highlight is 'silk handkerchiefs' with walnut butter. Start by sharing some focaccia or panelle with smoked duck. As the name means 'counter' this is where most want to sit, although there are tables available.

Specialities: Charred hispi cabbage with chilli and garlic. Bucatini with cod cheeks, black olives and sun-dried tomato. Poached Comice pears, yoghurt foam & honeycomb.

Carte £20/30

Town plan 31 AQ3-y – *39 William IV Street* ⊠ *WC2N 4DD* ⊖ *Charing Cross –*
☏ *020 7240 8786 – www.bancone.co.uk*

Cinnamon Bazaar

INDIAN · EXOTIC DÉCOR X Vivek Singh's Covent Garden restaurant provides relaxed, all-day contemporary Indian dining in a bright, colourful space which evokes a marketplace. Menus are influenced by the trade routes of the subcontinent, with twists that encompass Afghanistan, the Punjab and the Middle East.

Specialities: Kerala shrimp cocktail. Rogan josh shepherd's pie. Saffron poached pear.

Menu £17 (lunch), £21/24 – Carte £20/38

Town plan 31 AQ3-b – *28 Maiden Lane* ⊠ *WC2E 7JS* ⊖ *Leicester Square –*
☏ *020 7395 1400 – www.cinnamon-bazaar.com*

Delaunay

MODERN CUISINE · ELEGANT XXX The Delaunay was inspired by the grand cafés of Europe but, despite sharing the same buzz and celebrity clientele as its sibling The Wolseley, is not just a mere replica. The all-day menu is more mittel-European, with great schnitzels and wieners.

Menu £28/75 – Carte £28/75

Town plan 32 AR2-x – *55 Aldwych* ⊠ *WC2B 4BB* ⊖ *Temple –* ☏ *020 7499 8558 –*
www.thedelaunay.com

The Ivy

TRADITIONAL BRITISH · ELEGANT XXX This slickly run stalwart of the London Theatre dining scene offers comforting classics alongside Asian-inspired dishes. For a last minute table, try the beautiful oval bar with its no-bookings policy and watch the world – and perhaps a few celebrities – go by. Service is both personable and professional.

Menu £25/29 – Carte £32/95

Town plan 31 AP2-p – *1-5 West Street* ⊠ *WC2H 9NQ* ⊖ *Leicester Square –*
☏ *020 7836 4751 – www.the-ivy.co.uk*

Rules

TRADITIONAL BRITISH · TRADITIONAL XX London's oldest restaurant boasts a fine collection of antique cartoons, drawings and paintings. Tradition continues in the menu, specialising in game from its own estate.

Carte £39/71

Town plan 31 AQ3-n – *35 Maiden Lane* ⊠ *WC2E 7LB* ⊖ *Leicester Square –*
☏ *020 7836 5314 – www.rules.co.uk*

ⅈ◯ Spring   点 AC 🍸 ⇆

ITALIAN · ELEGANT ✗✗ Spring occupies the 'new wing' of Somerset House that for many years was inhabited by the Inland Revenue. It's a bright, feminine space under the aegis of chef Skye Gyngell. Her cooking is Italian-influenced and ingredient-led.

Menu £ 32 (lunch) – Carte £ 51/71

Town plan 32 AR3-c – *New Wing, Somerset House (Entrance on Lancaster Place)* ✉ WC2R 1LA ⊖ Temple – ℰ 020 3011 0115 – www.springrestaurant.co.uk – Closed Sunday

ⅈ◯ Balthazar   🍸 点 AC 🍸 ⇆

FRENCH · BRASSERIE ✗✗ Those who know the original Balthazar in Manhattan's SoHo district will find the London version of this classic brasserie uncannily familiar in looks, vibe and food. The Franglais menu keeps it simple and the cocktails are great.

Menu £ 20/23 – Carte £ 31/70

Town plan 31 AQ2-t – *4-6 Russell Street* ✉ WC2B 5HZ ⊖ Covent Garden – ℰ 020 3301 1155 – www.balthazarlondon.com

ⅈ◯ Clos Maggiore   🕸 AC 🍸

FRENCH · CLASSIC DÉCOR ✗✗ One of London's most romantic restaurants – but be sure to ask for the enchanting conservatory with its retractable roof. The sophisticated French cooking is joined by a wine list of great depth. Good value and very popular pre/post theatre menus.

Menu £ 30 (lunch) – Carte £ 44/64

Town plan 31 AQ3-a – *33 King Street* ✉ WC2E 8JD ⊖ Leicester Square – ℰ 020 7379 9696 – www.closmaggiore.com

ⅈ◯ Eneko Basque Kitchen & Bar   点 AC 🍸

BASQUE · DESIGN ✗✗ Set in the One Aldwych Hotel, this stylish, ultra-modern restaurant features curved semi-private booths and a bar which seems to float above like a spaceship. Menus offer a refined reinterpretation of classic Basque dishes.

Menu £ 22/27 – Carte £ 24/97

Town plan 32 AR3-r – *One Aldwych Hotel, 1 Aldwych* ✉ WC2B 4BZ ⊖ Temple – ℰ 020 7300 0300 – www.eneko.london – Closed Sunday, Monday

ⅈ◯ Frog by Adam Handling   🍸 AC ⅈ⊘ 🍸 ⇆

MODERN CUISINE · BRASSERIE ✗✗ The chef put his name in the title to signify that this is the flagship of his bourgeoning group. His dishes, which change regularly, are attractive creations and quite detailed in their composition. The well-run room is not without some understated elegance.

Menu £ 65/96 – Carte £ 54/76

Town plan 31 AQ3-z – *34-35 Southampton Street* ✉ WC2E 7HG ⊖ Charing Cross – ℰ 020 7199 8370 – www.frogbyadamhandling.com

ⅈ◯ J.Sheekey   点 AC

SEAFOOD · CHIC ✗✗ Festooned with photographs of actors and linked to the theatrical world since opening in 1890. Wood panels and alcove tables add famed intimacy. Accomplished seafood cooking.

Menu £ 25/30 – Carte £ 34/118

Town plan 31 AP3-v – *28-32 St. Martin's Court* ✉ WC2N 4AL ⊖ Leicester Square – ℰ 020 7240 2565 – www.j-sheekey.co.uk

ⅈ◯ Petersham   🏞 点 AC ⅈ⊘

MEDITERRANEAN CUISINE · ELEGANT ✗✗ Along with a deli, shop and florist is this elegant restaurant with contemporary art, Murano glass and an abundance of fresh flowers. The Italian-based menu uses produce from their Richmond nursery and Devon farm. The lovely terrace is shared with La Goccia, their more informal spot for sharing plates.

Menu £ 30/34 – Carte £ 43/70

Town plan 31 AQ3-p – *2 Floral Court* ✉ WC2E 9FB ⊖ Covent Garden – ℰ 020 7305 7676 – www.petershamnurseries.com

⁑○ Tredwells

MODERN BRITISH · BRASSERIE XX Chef-owner Chantelle Nicholson's contemporary cooking makes good use of British ingredients and also displays the occasional Asian twist. It's set over three floors, with a subtle art deco feel. A good choice for a Sunday roast.

Menu £29/41 – Carte £30/55

Town plan 31 AP2-s – *4a Upper St Martin's Lane* ✉ *WC2H 9EF*
⊖ *Leicester Square* – ✆ *020 3764 0840* – *www.tredwells.com*

⁑○ Cora Pearl ⓝ

MODERN BRITISH · ELEGANT X Sister to Kitty Fisher's, and similarly named after an infamous courtesan, this elegant restaurant is set in a characterful townhouse and has a rich, cosy bistro feel, as well as attentive 'old school' service. The concise menu focuses on seasonal British produce in fresh, unfussy boldly flavoured dishes.

Carte £27/55

Town plan 31 AQ3-r – *30 Henrietta Street* ✉ *WC2F 8NA* ⊖ *Covent Garden* –
✆ *020 7324 7722* – *www.corapearl.co.uk* – *Closed Sunday dinner*

⁑○ J.Sheekey Atlantic Bar

SEAFOOD · INTIMATE X An addendum to J. Sheekey restaurant. Sit at the bar to watch the chefs prepare the same quality seafood as next door but at slightly lower prices; fish pie and fruits de mer are the popular choices. Open all day.

Menu £30 (lunch) – Carte £32/54

Town plan 31 AP3-v – *33-34 St. Martin's Court* ✉ *WC2 4AL* ⊖ *Leicester Square* –
✆ *020 7240 2565* – *www.jsheekeyatlanticbar.co.uk*

⁑○ Barrafina

SPANISH · TAPAS BAR X The second Barrafina is not just brighter than the Soho original – it's bigger too, so you can wait inside with a drink for counter seats to become available. Try more unusual tapas like ortiguillas, frit Mallorquin or the succulent meats.

Carte £27/52

Town plan 31 AQ3-x – *10 Adelaide Street* ✉ *WC2N 4HZ* ⊖ *Charing Cross* –
✆ *020 7440 1456* – *www.barrafina.co.uk*

⁑○ Barrafina

SPANISH · TAPAS BAR X The third of the Barrafinas is tucked away at the far end of Covent Garden; arrive early or prepare to queue. Fresh, vibrantly flavoured fish and shellfish dishes are a real highlight; tortillas y huevos also feature.

Carte £27/52

Town plan 31 AQ2-a – *43 Drury Lane* ✉ *WC2B 5AJ* ⊖ *Covent Garden* –
✆ *020 7440 1456* – *www.barrafina.co.uk*

⁑○ Din Tai Fung ⓝ

TAIWANESE · SIMPLE X A fun, canteen style dim sum restaurant with a bustling atmosphere and a no-bookings system; the first London branch of this successful Taiwanese export, famed for their Xiao long bao. You order off a pre-printed form and dishes come fast; watch the chefs at work through the glass wall of the kitchen.

Carte £25/40

Town plan 31 AQ3-g – *5-6 Henrietta Street* ✉ *WC2E 8PS* ⊖ *Covent Garden* –
✆ *020 3034 3888* – *www.dintaifung-uk.com*

⁑○ Dishoom

INDIAN · RUSTIC X Expect long queues at this group's original branch. It's based on a Bombay café, of the sort opened by Iranian immigrants in the early 20C. Try vada pau (Bombay's version of the chip butty), a curry or grilled meats; and finish with kulfi on a stick. It's lively, a touch chaotic but great fun.

Carte £20/28

Town plan 31 AP2-j – *12 Upper St Martin's Lane* ✉ *WC2H 9FB*
⊖ *Leicester Square* – ✆ *020 7420 9320* – *www.dishoom.com*

Ⅰ○ Frenchie   🍷 ⅙ AC 🔋

MODERN CUISINE · BISTRO ✗ A well-run modern-day bistro – younger sister to the Paris original, which shares the name given to chef-owner Greg Marchand when he was head chef at Fifteen. The adventurous, ambitious cooking is informed by his extensive travels.

Menu £29 (lunch), £52/65 – Carte £52/65

Town plan 31 AQ3-c – *16 Henrietta Street* ✉ *WC2E 8QH* ⊖ *Covent Garden* –
☎ *020 7836 4422* – *www.frenchiecoventgarden.com*

Ⅰ○ Little Kolkata Ⓝ

INDIAN · SIMPLE ✗ What started as two friends holding pop-up supper clubs has led to this simply styled but delightfully friendly restaurant. Cooking comes from the East of India, particularly Calcutta, with many of the recipes handed down through the generations; dishes are fresh and vibrant with punchy, refreshing flavours.

Carte £20/35

Town plan 31 AQ2-v – *51-53 Shelton Street* ✉ *WC2H 9JU* ⊖ *Covent Garden* –
☎ *020 7240 7084* – *www.littlekolkata.co.uk* – *Closed Sunday dinner*

Ⅰ○ Oystermen

SEAFOOD · RUSTIC ✗ Covent Garden isn't an area usually associated with independent restaurants but this bustling and modestly decorated little spot is thriving. From its tiny open kitchen come oysters, crabs and expertly cooked fish.

Carte £29/49

Town plan 31 AQ3-r – *31-32 Henrietta Street* ✉ *WC2E 8NA* ⊖ *Covent Garden* –
☎ *020 7240 4417* – *www.oystermen.co.uk*

Ⅰ○ RedFarm Ⓝ   🍷 ⅙ AC 🥢 🔋 ⇄

ASIAN · CHIC ✗ The original resides in New York and its buzzy London counterpart shares its rustic, Asia-meets-America vibe. Three floors of fun come with a cocktail bar, communal tables and chatty service; modern Chinese dishes include super crispy shrimp-stuffed chicken and the made-for-Instagram Pac-Man dumplings.

Menu £23 – Carte £30/56

Town plan 31 AQ2-3-h – *9 Russell Street* ✉ *WC2B 5HZ* ⊖ *Covent Garden* –
☎ *020 3883 9093* – *www.redfarmldn.com*

🏨 Savoy   ☆ 🗔 🛗 ⅙ AC 🏋 🚗

GRAND LUXURY · ART DÉCO One of the grande dames of London's hotel scene. Luxurious bedrooms come in Edwardian or Art Deco styles; many have magnificent views over the Thames and the stunning suites pay homage to past guests. Enjoy tea in the Thames Foyer; sip a cocktail in the iconic American Bar or elegant Beaufort bar. Dine in the famous Savoy Grill or enjoy seafood and steaks in Kaspar's.

267 rooms ⌤ – 👫 £550/1400 – 45 suites

Town plan 31 AQ3-s – *Strand* ✉ *WC2R 0EU* ⊖ *Charing Cross* – ☎ *020 7836 4343* –
www.thesavoylondon.com

🏨 One Aldwych   ☆ 🗔 🏊 🛗 ⅙ AC 🏋 🅿

GRAND LUXURY · CONTEMPORARY A stylish hotel featuring over 400 pieces of contemporary artwork. Bedrooms are understated in style with fine linen and fresh fruit and flowers delivered daily. Charlie and the Chocolate Factory themed afternoon tea. Gluten and dairy-free British dishes in Indigo; Basque cooking in Eneko.

103 rooms – 👫 £380/685 – ⌤ £32 – 13 suites

Town plan 32 AR3-r – *1 Aldwych* ✉ *WC2B 4RH* ⊖ *Temple* – ☎ *020 7300 1000* –
www.onealdwych.com

Ⅰ○ **Eneko Basque Kitchen & Bar** – See restaurant listing

St Martins Lane

LUXURY · DESIGN The unmistakable hand of Philippe Starck is evident at this most contemporary of hotels. Unique and stylish, from the starkly modern lobby to the state-of-the-art bedrooms, which come in a blizzard of white.

204 rooms – **†∮** £219/399 – ⌣ £20 – 2 suites

Town plan 31 AP3-e – *45 St Martin's Lane* ⊠ *WC2N 4HX* ⊖ *Charing Cross* – ℰ *020 7300 5500* – *www.stmartinslane.com*

Henrietta ⌗▢⌕⌹

BOUTIQUE HOTEL · DESIGN Cosy boutique townhouse in the heart of Covent Garden; stylish, contemporary bedrooms offer good facilities including Bluetooth speakers and Nespresso machines. Ask for one of the quieter rooms at the back; 18, with its balcony and city views, is best. Cocktail bar and restaurant serving original modern dishes.

18 rooms – **†∮** £250/400 – ⌣ £21 – 1 suite

Town plan 31 AQ3-f – *14-15 Henrietta Street* ⊠ *WC2E 8QH* ⊖ *Covent Garden* – ℰ *020 3794 5313* – *www.henriettahotel.com*

VICTORIA

Greater London

⌘ **Dining Room at The Goring**

TRADITIONAL BRITISH · ELEGANT XxX The Goring is a model of British style and understatement and its ground floor dining room the epitome of grace and decorum. It appeals to those who 'like things done properly' and is one of the few places in London for which everyone appears to dress up – indeed, many are investees who've come straight from the Palace. Even those who decry tradition will be charmed by the atmosphere and the earnestness of the well-choreographed service team.

The hotel has long enjoyed a reputation for serving classic British food but the kitchen makes judicious use of modern techniques and superb ingredients to produce dishes – whether old favourites like Eggs Drumkilbo or something more contemporary such as slow-cooked halibut with nasturtiums – that display an impressive understanding of balance, flavour and texture.

Specialities: Eggs Drumkilbo. Glazed lobster omelette. Warm Eccles cake with Beauvale cheese and apple vinegar.

Menu £52 (lunch)/64

Town plan 38 AL6-a – *Goring Hotel, 15 Beeston Place* ⊠ *SW1W 0JW* ⊖ *Victoria* – ℰ *020 7769 4475* – *www.thegoring.com* – *Closed Saturday lunch*

⌘ **Quilon**

INDIAN · DESIGN XxX Head chef Sriram Aylur and his experienced team – many of whom have worked together for over fifteen years – focus here on the cuisine of the southwest coast of India, a highlight of which is naturally its sublime seafood. Being free from ghee means that dishes are wonderfully healthy, with an appealing purity and lightness.

Ingredients are first-rate and cooking confident and assured; dishes may look simple but offer a terrific balance of flavours, with superb sauces and well-judged spicing. Popadums, pickles and chutneys kick things off with a rarely seen freshness and vibrancy. After that, the tasting menus – of which there are vegetarian, non-vegetarian and seafood versions – are the best way to experience the full repertoire of the kitchen.

Specialities: Fish peera. Lemon sole cafreal. Tropical fruits with sweet chilli syrup.

Menu £31 (lunch), £70/85 – Carte £40/61

Town plan 39 AN5-a – *St James' Court Hotel, 41 Buckingham Gate* ⊠ *SW1E 6AF* ⊖ *St James's Park* – ℰ *020 7821 1899* – *www.quilon.co.uk*

✿ A. Wong (Andrew Wong)

CHINESE · NEIGHBOURHOOD ❌ Flavours, traditions and techniques from all across China are celebrated here by Andrew Wong and his kitchen team. Inspired by his travels through the provinces, he presents his own interpretations of classic Chinese dishes using modern techniques and a creative eye but without ever compromising their integrity and authenticity.

Umami-rich dishes come packed with flavour, whether that's dishes to share like 'Xian city lamb burger' and 'crispy aromatic Peking duck London 1963' or the varied and competitively priced lunchtime dim sum. If you want the full gastronomic experience, come in the evening for the 13 course Taste of China menu which offers a 3-hour culinary voyage around China. Ask for a seat at the kitchen counter if you want to know how it's all done.

Specialities: Shanghai steamed dumplings with ginger infused vinegar. Shaanxi pulled lamb 'burger' with Xinjiang pomegranate salad. 'Postcard from Yunnan' with banana, chocolate and white truffle.

Menu £95 – Carte £24/54

Town plan 38 AM7-w – *70 Wilton Road* ✉ *SW1V 1DE* ⊖ *Victoria* –
☎ *020 7828 8931* – *www.awong.co.uk* – *Closed 22 December-6 January, Sunday, Monday lunch*

🍽 The Cinnamon Club

INDIAN · HISTORIC ❌❌ Locals and tourists, business people and politicians – this smart Indian restaurant housed in the listed former Westminster Library attracts them all. The fairly elaborate dishes arrive fully garnished and the spicing is quite subtle.

Menu £31 (lunch) – Carte £38/66

Town plan 39 AP6-c – *30-32 Great Smith Street* ✉ *SW1P 3BU*
⊖ *St James's Park* – ☎ *020 7222 2555* – *www.cinnamonclub.com*

🍽 Roux at Parliament Square

MODERN CUISINE · ELEGANT ❌❌ Light floods through the Georgian windows of this comfortable restaurant within the offices of the Royal Institute of Chartered Surveyors. Carefully crafted, elaborate and sophisticated cuisine, with some interesting flavour combinations.

Menu £42 (lunch), £59/89 – Carte £42/59

Town plan 39 AP5-x – *Royal Institution of Chartered Surveyors, 11 Great George Street, Parliament Square* ✉ *SW1P 3AD* ⊖ *Westminster* – ☎ *020 7334 3737* – *www.rouxatparliamentsquare.co.uk* – *Closed 1-5 January, 21-30 December, Sunday, Saturday*

🍽 Rex Whistler

MODERN CUISINE · CLASSIC DÉCOR ❌❌ A hidden gem, tucked away on the lower ground floor of Tate Britain; its most striking element is Whistler's restored mural, 'The Expedition in Pursuit of Rare Meats', which envelops the room. The menu is stoutly British and the remarkably well-priced wine list has an unrivalled 'half bottle' selection.

Menu £35 (lunch)/57

Town plan 39 AP7-w – *Tate Britain, Millbank* ✉ *SW1P 4RG* ⊖ *Pimlico* –
☎ *020 7887 8825* – *www.tate.org.uk/visit/tate-britain/rex-whistler-restaurant* –
Closed Sunday - Saturday dinner

🍽 Siren Ⓝ

SEAFOOD · ELEGANT ❌❌ Nathan Outlaw's latest venture – the first new restaurant at the Goring Hotel in 109 years – is inspired by the Goring family's ties with Cornwall, and showcases the very best of Cornish seafood, with a focus on wonderfully fresh fish, delivered daily. The elegant, orangery-style dining room overlooks the gardens.

Carte £50/102

Town plan 38 AL6-a – *Goring Hotel, 15 Beeston Place* ✉ *SW1W 0JW* ⊖ *Victoria* –
☎ *020 7396 9000* – *www.thegoring.com*

Aster

MODERN CUISINE · CONTEMPORARY DÉCOR XX The flagship eatery of the Nova SW1 development combines two spaces: a stylish, airy first floor restaurant and a more casual café/bar on the ground floor beneath. The modern European brasserie menu offers something for everyone, from oysters and caviar to chicken schnitzel and beef stroganoff.

Menu £30 – Carte £28/56

Town plan 38 AM6-a – *150 Victoria Street* ⊠ *SW1E 5LB* ⊖ *Victoria –*
℘ *020 3875 5555 – www.aster-restaurant.com – Closed Sunday dinner*

Enoteca Turi

ITALIAN · NEIGHBOURHOOD XX In 2016 Putney's loss was Pimlico's gain when, after 25 years, Giuseppe and Pamela Turi had to find a new home for their Italian restaurant. They brought their warm hospitality and superb wine list with them, and the chef has introduced a broader range of influences from across the country.

Menu £30 (lunch) – Carte £40/68

Town plan 38 AK7-s – *87 Pimlico Road* ⊠ *SW1W 8PU* ⊖ *Sloane Square –*
℘ *020 7730 3663 – www.enotecaturi.com – Closed Sunday*

Kerridge's Bar & Grill

MODERN BRITISH · BRASSERIE XX The menu bears all the hallmarks of chef Tom Kerridge by focusing on British dishes and the best of British ingredients; some old classics are also brought back to life and good use is made of the rotisserie. When it comes to glamour and grandeur, the huge room offers plenty of bang for your buck.

Menu £30 – Carte £45/68

Town plan 31 AQ4-x – *The Corinthia Hotel, Whitehall Place (Entrance 10 Northumberland Avenue)* ⊠ *SW1A 2BD* ⊖ *Embankment – ℘ 020 7321 3244 – www.kerridgesbarandgrill.co.uk*

Osteria Dell' Angolo

ITALIAN · NEIGHBOURHOOD XX At lunch, this Italian opposite the Home Office is full of bustle and men in suits; at dinner it's a little more relaxed. Staff are personable and the menu is reassuringly familiar; homemade pasta and seafood dishes are good.

Menu £23 (lunch) – Carte £25/85

Town plan 39 AP6-n – *47 Marsham Street* ⊠ *SW1P 3DR* ⊖ *St James's Park –*
℘ *020 3268 1077 – www.osteriadellangolo.co.uk – Closed Sunday, Saturday lunch*

Lorne

MODERN CUISINE · SIMPLE X A small, simply furnished restaurant down a busy side street. The experienced chef understands that less is more and the modern menu is an enticing list of unfussy, well-balanced British and European dishes. Diverse wine list.

Menu £27 (lunch) – Carte £37/50

Town plan 38 AM7-e – *76 Wilton Road* ⊠ *SW1V 1DE* ⊖ *Victoria –*
℘ *020 3327 0210 – www.lornerestaurant.co.uk – Closed 23 December-2 January, Sunday dinner, Monday lunch*

Olivomare

SEAFOOD · DESIGN X A busy, well-run Italian championing the cuisine of Sardinia; the monthly changing menu offers appealingly simple dishes created with high quality produce; much of which is also available in their deli next door. It's dimly lit, with a stark white interior and also boasts a striking feature wall.

Carte £35/49

Town plan 38 AL6-b – *10 Lower Belgrave Street* ⊠ *SW1W 0LJ* ⊖ *Victoria –*
℘ *020 7730 9022 – www.olivorestaurants.com*

⁐ The Orange

MODERN CUISINE · PUB The old Orange Brewery is as charming a pub as its stucco-fronted façade suggests. Try the fun bar or book a table in the more sedate upstairs room. Seasonal menus offer modern British dishes, with spelt or wheat-based pizzas a speciality. The upstairs bedrooms are stylish and comfortable.

Menu £25/43 – Carte £31/43

Town plan 38 AK7-k – *37 Pimlico Road* ⊠ *SW1W 8NE* ⊖ *Sloane Square* – ℰ *020 7881 9844 – www.theorange.co.uk*

The Other Naughty Piglet

MODERN CUISINE · SIMPLE A light, spacious restaurant with friendly staff and a relaxed atmosphere, set on the first floor of The Other Palace theatre. Eclectic modern small plates are designed for sharing and accompanied by an interesting list of natural wines.

Menu £18 (lunch), £27/30 – Carte £26/44

Town plan 38 AM5-t – *The Other Palace, 12 Palace Street* ⊠ *SW1E 5JA* ⊖ *Victoria* – ℰ *020 7592 0322 – www.theothernaughtypiglet.co.uk* – *Closed 22 December-2 January, Sunday, Monday lunch*

Corinthia

GRAND LUXURY · ELEGANT The restored Victorian splendour of this grand, luxurious hotel cannot fail to impress. Tasteful and immaculately finished bedrooms are some of the largest in town; suites come with butlers. The stunning spa is over four floors. Dine on creative dishes in elegant Northall or updated British classics in Kerridge's Bar & Grill.

283 rooms ⊒ – ♥♥ £480/1260 – 27 suites

Town plan 31 AQ4-x – *Whitehall Place* ⊠ *SW1A 2BD* ⊖ *Embankment* – ℰ *020 7930 8181 – www.corinthia.com*

⁐ **Kerridge's Bar & Grill** – See restaurant listing

Goring

LUXURY · ELEGANT Under the stewardship of the founder's great grandson, this landmark hotel has been restored and renovated while maintaining its traditional atmosphere and pervading sense of Britishness. Expect first class service and immaculate, very comfortable bedrooms, many of which overlook the garden.

69 rooms – ♥♥ £315/1100 – ⊒ £32 – 5 suites

Town plan 38 AL6-a – *15 Beeston Place* ⊠ *SW1W 0JW* ⊖ *Victoria* – ℰ *020 7396 9000 – www.thegoring.com*

❀ **Dining Room at The Goring** · ⁐ **Siren** – See restaurant listing

CENTRAL LONDON - ISLINGTON

Greater London

Top tips!

This borough epitomizes the idea of London as a city of joined up villages, and in recent years has become something of a foodie mecca.

In the south, trendy Clerkenwell is home to the original **St. John** restaurant, pioneer of nose-to-tail eating and long-term holder of a Michelin Star. It's also where you'll find Exmouth Market, with its cornucopia of artisan stalls and street food, surrounded by restaurants, bars and cafés; try Moorish cuisine from the wood-fired oven in **Moro** or tapas in next door **Morito**.

Upper Street – which runs right through the heart of Islington – is another foodie hotspot, offering everything from Mexican and Brazilian to Vietnamese and Thai. If you're after cooking with influences a little closer to home, head to busy bistro **Oldroyd** for easy-to-eat European small plates.

ARCHWAY
Greater London

🍴○ St John's Tavern

MODERN CUISINE · PUB · A Junction Road landmark with friendly service and a great selection of artisan beers. Tapas is served in the front bar; head to the vast, hugely appealing rear dining room for well-crafted British and Mediterranean dishes.

Menu £22 (lunch), £25/35 – Carte £22/35

Town plan 12 Q1-s – *91 Junction Road* ⊠ *N19 5QU* ⊖ *Archway* – *𝒸 020 7272 1587* – *www.stjohnstavern.com*

CANONBURY
Greater London

🕾 Primeur

MODERN CUISINE · SIMPLE · A relaxed neighbourhood restaurant whose concertina doors fold back to reveal a quirky interior with counter seating around the edges and a huge communal table. Plates are small and designed for sharing; understated but packed with flavour – simplicity is key, allowing the ingredients to really shine.

Specialities: Asparagus with sauce gribiche. Cavatelli with aubergine, pine nuts and ricotta. Baked rhubarb custard.

Carte £22/35

Town plan 13 T2-p – *116 Petherton Road* ⊠ *N5 2RT* ⊖ *Canonbury* – *𝒸 020 7226 5271* – *www.primeurn5.co.uk* – *Closed Sunday dinner, Monday, Tuesday - Thursday lunch*

🕾 Trullo

ITALIAN · NEIGHBOURHOOD · A neighbourhood gem split over two floors; its open kitchen serving an ingredient-led daily menu. Harmonious, tried-and-tested combinations create rustic, full-flavoured Italian dishes, including meats and fish cooked on the charcoal grill and delicious fresh pasta, hand-rolled before each service.

Specialities: Pappardelle beef shin ragu. Scallops with borlotti beans, rosemary and caper dressing. Amalfi lemon tart.

Carte £24/41

Town plan 13 S2-t – *300-302 St Paul's Road* ⊠ *N1 2LH* ⊖ *Highbury & Islington* – *𝒸 020 7226 2733* – *www.trullorestaurant.com* – *Closed 23 December-3 January*

CLERKENWELL
Greater London

✿✿ St John

TRADITIONAL BRITISH · SIMPLE · There's no standing on ceremony here at St John; indeed, very little ceremony at all, and that makes eating here such a joyful experience. There's little distraction from the surroundings either, which come in a shade of detention centre white.

This is the place to try new flavours, whether that's cuttlefish or ox tongue. Game is a favourite and the only gravy will be the blood of the bird – this is natural, 'proper' food. Seasonality is at its core – the menu is rewritten for each service – and nothing sums up the philosophy more than the potatoes and greens: they are always on the menu but the varieties and types change regularly. The waiters spend time in the kitchen so they know what they're talking about and are worth listening to. There are dishes for two as well as magnums of wine for real trenchermen. Do order the warm madeleines for the journey home.

Specialities: Brown shrimps with white cabbage. Lamb sweetbreads with peas and mint. Eccles cake with Lancashire cheese.

Carte £36/50

Town plan 33 AU1-k – *26 St. John Street* ⊠ *EC1M 4AY* ⊖ *Farringdon* – *𝒸 020 7251 0848* – *www.stjohnrestaurant.com* – *Closed Sunday dinner, Saturday lunch*

ⅰ○ Luca

🛋 ᚛ AⅭ

ITALIAN · DESIGN XX Owned by the people behind The Clove Club, but less a little sister, more a distant cousin. There's a cheery atmosphere, a bar for small plates and a frequently changing menu of Italian dishes made with quality British ingredients.

Menu £26 (lunch)/68 – Carte £40/62

Town plan 33 AU1-c – *88 St John Street* ⊠ *EC1M 4EH* ⊖ *Farringdon –*
℘ 020 3859 3000 – www.luca.restaurant – Closed 22 December-6 January, Sunday

ⅰ○ Comptoir Gascon

AⅭ

FRENCH · BISTRO X A buzzy restaurant; sister to Club Gascon. Rustic specialities from the SW of France include wine, bread, cheese and plenty of duck, with cassoulet and duck rillettes perennial favourites and the duck burger popular at lunch. There's also produce on display to take home.

Carte £23/44

Town plan 32 AT1-a – *61-63 Charterhouse Street* ⊠ *EC1M 6HJ* ⊖ *Farringdon –*
℘ 020 7608 0851 – www.comptoirgascon.com – Closed 25 December-1 January,
Sunday, Monday, Saturday lunch

ⅰ○ Palatino

᚛ AⅭ

ITALIAN · DESIGN X Stevie Parle's airy, canteen-like, all-day restaurant has an open kitchen, yellow booths and an industrial feel. The seasonal Italian menu has a strong emphasis on Rome, with dishes like rigatoni with veal pajata.

Menu £16/20 – Carte £16/41

Town plan 19 T4-p – *71 Central Street* ⊠ *EC1V 8AB* ⊖ *Old Street –*
℘ 020 3481 5300 – www.palatino.london – Closed 23 December-3 January, Sunday

🏠 The Rookery

AⅭ

TOWNHOUSE · PERSONALISED A row of charmingly restored 18C houses which remain true to their roots courtesy of wood panelling, flagstone flooring, open fires and antique furnishings. Highly individual bedrooms have feature beds and Victorian bathrooms.

33 rooms – 👫 £240/280 – 🖵 £12 – 3 suites

Town plan 33 AU1-p – *12 Peters Lane, Cowcross Street* ⊠ *EC1M 6DS*
⊖ *Farringdon – ℘ 020 7336 0931 – www.rookeryhotel.com*

FINSBURY

Greater London

✿ Angler

🕸 🍷 🛋 ᚛ AⅭ

SEAFOOD · DESIGN XX As the restaurant's name suggests, fish is the mainstay of the menu – the majority of it from Cornwall and Scotland – and the kitchen has the confidence to know that when it's this good, it needs little in the way of adornment. That's not to say there isn't a certain vibrancy to the cooking, and the satisfying dishes display plenty of colour, balance and poise.

The restaurant itself may be on the top floor of the South Place hotel but feels very much like a separate, stand-alone establishment with its own personality. The first thing you notice is the ornate mirrored ceiling and the brightness of the room. It also feels very intimate and comes with its own terrace where, on a warm evening, you'll see the cocktails go flying out.

Specialities: Tartare of Cornish mackerel with oyster cream, green apple and shiso. Newlyn cod with new season's garlic, morels, and Scottish langoustines. P. B.C-peanut, banana, chocolate.

Menu £36 (lunch) – Carte £65/75

Town plan 33 AW1-v – *South Place Hotel, 3 South Place* ⊠ *EC2M 2AF*
⊖ *Moorgate – ℘ 020 3215 1260 – www.anglerrestaurant.com –*
Closed 25 December-3 January, Sunday, Saturday lunch

Morito

SPANISH • **TAPAS BAR** X From the owners of next door Moro comes this authentic and appealingly down to earth little tapas bar. Seven or eight dishes between two should suffice but over-ordering is easy and won't break the bank.

Specialities: Grilled asparagus with seasoned yoghurt and chilli butter. Octopus with cherry tomatoes, dill, red onion and crispy capers. Chocolate mousse, roasted almonds and olive oil.

Carte £18/33

Town plan 19 S4-b - *32 Exmouth Market ✉ EC1R 4QE ⊖ Farringdon -*
✆ 020 7278 7007 - www.morito.co.uk - Closed 24 December-2 January

The Drunken Butler

FRENCH • **REGIONAL** XX The chef-owner's quiet enthusiasm pervades every aspect of this small but bright restaurant. The cooking is classical French at heart but also informed by his travels and Persian heritage; dishes provide plenty of colour, texture and flavour.

Menu £30 (lunch), £49/69 - Carte £30/69

Town plan 19 S4-k - *20 Rosebery Avenue ✉ EC1R 4SX ⊖ Farringdon -*
✆ 020 7101 4020 - www.thedrunkenbutler.com - Closed 1-9 January, 10-19 August, Monday, Tuesday

Quality Chop House

TRADITIONAL BRITISH • **COSY** X In the hands of owners who respect its history, this 'progressive working class caterer' does a fine job of championing gutsy British grub; game is best but steaks from the butcher next door are also worth ordering. The terrific little wine list has lots of gems. The Grade II listed room, with its trademark booths, has been an eating house since 1869.

Menu £26 (lunch), £40/60 - Carte £38/65

Town plan 19 S4-h - *88-94 Farringdon Road ✉ EC1R 3EA ⊖ Farringdon -*
✆ 020 7278 1452 - www.thequalitychophouse.com -
Closed 23 December-1 January, Sunday dinner

Moro

MEDITERRANEAN CUISINE • **FRIENDLY** X It's the stuff of dreams - pack up your worldly goods, drive through Spain, Portugal, Morocco and the Sahara, and then back in London, open a restaurant and share your love of Moorish cuisine. The wood-fired oven and chargrill fill the air with wonderful aromas and food is vibrant and colourful.

Carte £33/45

Town plan 19 S4-m - *34-36 Exmouth Market ✉ EC1R 4QE ⊖ Farringdon -*
✆ 020 7833 8336 - www.moro.co.uk - Closed 24 December-2 January

South Place

BUSINESS • DESIGN Restaurant group D&D's first venture into the hotel business is a stylish affair; unsurprising as its interior was designed by Conran & Partners. Bedrooms are a treat for those with an eye for aesthetics and no detail has been forgotten. The ground floor hosts 3 South Place, a bustling bar and grill.

80 rooms - †† £240/460 - ☕ £15 - 1 suite

Town plan 33 AW1-v - *3 South Place ✉ EC2M 2AF ⊖ Moorgate -*
✆ 020 3503 0000 - www.southplacehotel.com

✿ **Angler** - See restaurant listing

Zetter

TOWNHOUSE • CONTEMPORARY A stylish, well-kept and professionally run hotel with two distinct sides to it. The main part of the hotel is within a converted Victorian warehouse and features understated bedrooms with a cool retro edge. The more idiosyncratic Zetter Townhouse across the square is elegant and traditional in style.

59 rooms ☕ - †† £138/510

Town plan 19 S4-s - *St John's Square, 86-88 Clerkenwell Road ✉ EC1M 5RJ*
⊖ Farringdon - ✆ 020 7324 4444 - www.thezetter.com

HIGHBURY
Greater London

⊛ Farang

THAI · FRIENDLY 〤 Seb and Dan had a series of pop-ups for their Thai street food before moving into this permanent home. Dishes have an authentic heart and use a mix of Thai and British produce. The small menu is supplemented by a number of specials, while the 'Feasting' menus are great for larger groups.

Specialities: Kale, soy, chilli and garlic bites with burnt chilli dipping sauce. Curried egg noodles with smoked chicken, pickled mustard and chilli jam. Pandan & banana ice cream with coconut cream, butterscotch and cashews.

Carte £ 25/34

Town plan 13 T1-b – *72 Highbury Park* ⊠ *N5 2XE* ⊖ *Arsenal* –
☎ *020 7226 1609* – *www.faranglondon.co.uk* –
Closed 23-29 December, Sunday, Monday, Tuesday - Friday lunch

HOLLOWAY
Greater London

⊛ Westerns Laundry

MODERN BRITISH · BISTRO 〤 Sister to Primeur and with the same industrial feel; set on the ground floor of a former laundry, with a pleasant front terrace. Sit at the kitchen counter or at one of the communal tables. The fish-focused menu is accompanied by natural wines and the confidently executed dishes are full of flavour.

Specialities: Salt cod croquettes. Pollock with leeks and lobster butter. Rum & raisin cake with Chantilly cream.

Carte £ 22/42

Town plan 13 S2-w – *34 Drayton Park* ⊠ *N5 1PB* ⊖ *Holloway Road* –
☎ *020 7700 3700* – *www.westernslaundry.com* –
Closed Sunday dinner, Monday, Tuesday - Thursday lunch

ISLINGTON
Greater London

⊛ Plaquemine Lock

CREOLE · PUB 〤 A unique and very colourful pub named after a small city in Louisiana and with a menu centred around Creole and Cajun traditions. Dishes like gumbo with okra, blackened chicken, and crawfish with corn and potatoes are carefully cooked and packed with flavour. Big Easy style cocktails add to the fun.

Specialities: Green tomato and blackened avocado, fire-roasted salsa and pickled celery salad. Creole jambalaya with chicken, shrimp and house made andouille sausage. Pecan pie with cane sugar ice cream.

Carte £ 25/32

Town plan 13 S3-e – *139 Graham Street* ⊠ *N1 8LB* ⊖ *Angel* – ☎ *020 7688 1488* –
www.plaqlock.com

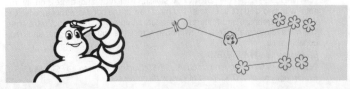

ﾘ○ Galley 🍷 AC 📋

SEAFOOD · BRASSERIE XX A smart, colourful seafood restaurant with a brasserie feel; there's a bar at the front and a few prized booths, but the best seats in the house are at the kitchen counter. The hot or cold seafood platters are great to share.

Menu £25/40 – Carte £27/44

Town plan 13 S3-a – *105-106 Upper Street* ✉ *N1 1QN* ⊖ *Highbury & Islington –*
✆ *020 7684 2538 – www.galleylondon.co.uk*

ﾘ○ Drapers Arms 🏠 🍴

TRADITIONAL BRITISH · PUB X An imposing neighbourhood pub with warming fires, shabby-chic styling, a relaxed, unpretentious feel, a bevy of eager-to-please staff and a courtyard garden. They offer gutsy and satisfying seasonal British dishes, a great selection of regional ales and a well-thought-out wine list.

Carte £25/38

Town plan 13 S3-x – *44 Barnsbury Street* ✉ *N1 1ER* ⊖ *Highbury & Islington. –*
✆ *020 7619 0348 – www.thedrapersarms.com*

ﾘ○ Oldroyd 📋

MODERN BRITISH · INTIMATE X The eponymous Oldroyd is Tom, who left his role with the Polpo group to open this busy little bistro. It's all about small plates – ingredients are largely British, influences are from within Europe and dishes are very easy to eat.

Menu £16 (lunch) – Carte £25/35

Town plan 13 S3-w – *344 Upper Street* ✉ *N1 0PD* ⊖ *Angel –* ✆ *020 8617 9010 –*
www.oldroydlondon.com

ﾘ○ Pig and Butcher 🏠 AC 📋 🍴

TRADITIONAL BRITISH · PUB X Dating from the mid-19C, when cattle drovers taking livestock to Smithfield Market would stop for a swift one, and now fully restored. There's a strong British element to the daily menu; meat is butchered and smoked in-house.

Carte £31/49

Town plan 13 S3-b – *80 Liverpool Road* ✉ *N1 0QD* ⊖ *Angel –* ✆ *020 7226 8304 –*
www.thepigandbutcher.co.uk – Closed Monday - Thursday lunch

ﾘ○ Top Cuvée ⓝ 📋

MEDITERRANEAN CUISINE · NEIGHBOURHOOD X An unpretentious and personally run neighbourhood bistro; sit at the bar counter to watch the friendly team at work. The concise menu offers fresh, carefully cooked small plates with Mediterranean influences and a rustic edge. A great drinks list reflects time spent by the owner working in bars.

Menu £20 (lunch) – Carte £23/32

Town plan 13 T1-n – *177B Blackstock Road* ✉ *N5 2LL* ⊖ *Arsenal –*
✆ *020 3294 1665 – www.topcuvee.com – Closed Monday, Tuesday, Wednesday -*
Friday lunch

ﾘ○ 12:51 ⓝ AC 📋 🍸

MODERN CUISINE · NEIGHBOURHOOD X A chatty young team serve you at this narrow and cluttered two-floored bistro, which is decorated with record sleeves and local artists' work. The menu of interesting, well-priced sharing plates is split into 'snacks', 'plates' and 'desserts', which are influenced by the chef's Scottish-Caribbean heritage.

Menu £15 (lunch) – Carte £26/40

Town plan 13 S3-n – *107 Upper Street* ✉ *N1 1QN* ⊖ *Angel –* ✆ *07934 202269 –*
www.1251.co.uk – Closed 23-30 December

CENTRAL LONDON - KENSINGTON AND CHELSEA Greater London

Top tips!

The smallest borough in London is also one of the richest; it's smart residential streets and elegant garden squares somewhat fitting for a borough conferred with royal status. It's home to Kensington Palace, where Queen Victoria resided from birth until her accession – and the imperious Royal Albert Hall, later built by the widowed queen in memory of her husband.

The area's well-heeled residents mean that the demand for upmarket restaurants is high – and the district has certainly attracted some big-name chefs. **Gordon Ramsay**'s Three-Starred flagship sits on Royal Hospital Road, whilst one of his protégées has gained Two Stars of her own at **CORE by Clare Smyth** in nearby Notting Hill.

Those 'eating in' should head to Portobello Road Market for a great selection of seasonal fruit and vegetables (alongside antiques and fashion) – or for luxury ingredients, take a trip to Harrods Food Hall.

xeipe/iStock

CHELSEA
Greater London

✿✿✿ Gordon Ramsay   ⅋ AC ⅃⊚

FRENCH · ELEGANT XxX He may be one of the most famous chefs on the planet but Gordon Ramsay remains fiercely committed to maintaining the highest of standards at his flagship restaurant. The charming Jean-Claude, who has run the restaurant since day one, oversees a team who get the service just right: yes, it's polished and professional, but it also has personality.

The menu features plenty of dishes which might be called 'classic Ramsay' like the lobster ravioli, navarin of lamb and lemonade parfait, but there are newer dishes too, such as roast sweetbread with Jerusalem artichokes, courtesy of head chef, Matt Abé. Cooking is elegant, balanced and full of flavour; executed not only with great confidence, but also with an extraordinary lightness of touch.

Specialities: Ravioli of lobster, langoustine and salmon with sorrel. Herdwick lamb with courgette, romesco, black olive and marjoram. Raspberry soufflé with almond ice cream.

Menu £70 (lunch), £120/185

Town plan 37 AJ8-c – *68-69 Royal Hospital Road* ✉ *SW3 4HP* ⊖ *Sloane Square –*
✆ *020 7352 4441 – www.gordonramsayrestaurants.com – Closed Sunday, Monday*

✿✿ Claude Bosi at Bibendum   ⅋ AC

FRENCH · ELEGANT XxX Bibendum sits on the first floor of the historic art deco building which was built as Michelin's London HQ in 1911 and its handsome interior cannot fail to impress. The iconic stained glass windows allow light to flood in – a fact best appreciated at lunch when the Michelin Man can be seen in all his glory; in fact, his presence is everywhere, from the butter dish to the salt and pepper pots.

Claude Bosi's cooking shows a man proud of his French heritage and confident of his abilities. His dishes are poised and well-balanced with bold, assured flavours. Choose the à la carte menu for classics like Brittany rabbit with langoustine and artichoke barigoule or turbot à la Grenobloise – and don't miss the soufflé for dessert, particularly if it's chocolate.

Specialities: Duck jelly with smoked sturgeon and special selection caviar. Brittany rabbit with langoustine and artichoke barigoule. Black Forest soufflé with Griottine ice cream.

Menu £65 (lunch), £120/185 – Carte £71/107

Town plan 37 AH7-s – *Michelin House, 81 Fulham Road* ✉ *SW3 6RD*
⊖ *South Kensington – ✆ 020 7581 5817 – www.bibendum.co.uk –*
Closed 1-7 January, 6-14 April, 30 August-8 September, Monday, Tuesday,
Wednesday lunch

✿ **Five Fields** (Taylor Bonnyman)   ⅋ ⅋ AC ⊹

MODERN CUISINE · NEIGHBOURHOOD XxX Over the years this charming Chelsea restaurant has built up a loyal local following. It is a formally run yet intimate place, with a discreet atmosphere and a warm, comfortable feel. The room is luxuriously decorated in crisp creams and the smart, suited staff are professional and engaging.

The chef-owner – blessed with the great name of Taylor Bonnyman – has worked in some illustrious kitchens around the world. His dishes are skilfully conceived, quite elaborate constructions; attractively presented and packed with flavour. Produce is top-notch and includes the occasional Asian ingredient; many of the herbs and vegetables come from the restaurant's own kitchen garden in East Sussex. Alongside the classics, the extensive wine list also offers some more esoteric bottles from Eastern Europe and the Middle East.

Specialities: Foie gras with pickled shimeji mushrooms, rainbow carrots and beetroot. Venison with salsify, sour cream and rye. Pineapple baba with Chantilly cream and Somerset brandy.

Menu £65 (lunch), £80/95

Town plan 37 AJ7-s – *8-9 Blacklands Terrace* ✉ *SW3 2SP* ⊖ *Sloane Square –*
✆ *020 7838 1082 – www.fivefieldsrestaurant.com – Closed 1-12 January,*
10-23 August, 21-27 December, Sunday, Monday, Tuesday - Wednesday lunch

Elystan Street (Philip Howard)

MODERN BRITISH · ELEGANT XX Elystan Street is a neighbourhood restaurant, but the neighbourhood it happens to be in is Chelsea, so as well as unfussy cooking and friendly service, you can expect elegance and style in spades. It's a collaboration between Philip Howard and Rebecca Mascarenhas, and with its huge windows and well-judged lighting, is an equally charming spot for a light lunch or an intimate dinner.

Cooking is pared-back and relaxed, yet there's a vigour and an energy to it which suggests that it comes from the heart. Dishes have a classical base but there's a lightness of touch, as well as a focus on vegetables, pasta and salads. Many dishes have Mediterranean influences and flavours are well-defined and eminently satisfying. Desserts are a highlight.

Specialities: Cashew nut hummus with roast vegetables, curry dressing, nut milk and lime. Fillet of Cornish cod with garlic leaf & nettle pesto, creamed potatoes and buttered morels. Lemon tart with yoghurt.

Menu £30 (lunch) – Carte £46/84

Town plan 37 AH7-e – *43 Elystan Street* ⊠ *SW3 3NT* ⊖ *South Kensington* – ℰ *020 7628 5005* – *www.elystanstreet.com*

Colbert

FRENCH · BRASSERIE XX With its posters, chessboard tiles and red leather seats, Colbert bears more than a passing resemblance to a Parisian pavement café. It's an all-day, every day operation with French classics from croque monsieur to steak Diane.

Carte £26/65

Town plan 38 AK7-t – *50-52 Sloane Square* ⊠ *SW1W 8AX* ⊖ *Sloane Square* – ℰ *020 7730 2804* – *www.colbertchelsea.com*

No. Fifty Cheyne

MODERN BRITISH · ELEGANT XX High-end comfort food is the order of the day at this colourfully painted former pub close to the Thames. Dining takes place in an elegant, high-ceilinged room festooned with flowers, art and chandeliers; head upstairs for cocktails in the plush deep red cocktail bar or the country house style drawing room.

Menu £35 (lunch) – Carte £42/68

Town plan 23 P7-m – *50 Cheyne Walk* ⊠ *SW3 5LR* ⊖ *South Kensington* – ℰ *020 7376 8787* – *www.fiftycheyne.com* – *Closed Monday lunch*

Adam Handling Chelsea

MODERN BRITISH · ELEGANT XX The eponymous chef's latest opening is in the beautifully restored Cadogan Hotel; to the front there's an elegant cocktail bar; further back, two high-ceilinged dining rooms with ornate plasterwork and a subtle contemporary style. Modern menus showcase the freshest of ingredients in creative British dishes.

Menu £50 – Carte £20/70

Town plan 37 AJ6-n – *Belmond Cadogan Hotel, 75 Sloane Street* ⊠ *SW1X 9SG* ⊖ *Knightsbridge* – ℰ *020 8089 7070* – *www.adamhandling.co.uk*

il trillo

ITALIAN · FRIENDLY XX The Bertuccelli family have been making wine and running a restaurant in the Tuscan Hills for over 30 years. Two of the brothers now run this smart local which showcases the produce and wine from their region. Delightful courtyard.

Menu £34/38 – Carte £32/70

Town plan 36 AE8-s – *4 Hollywood Road* ⊠ *SW10 9HY* ⊖ *Earl's Court* – ℰ *020 3602 1759* – *www.iltrillo.net* – *Closed Monday, Tuesday - Friday lunch*

Kahani

INDIAN · ELEGANT XX Service is charming at this smart, easy-going basement restaurant. It's name means 'Story' in Urdu; the story in question being that of chef-owner Peter Joseph, whose influences include his Indian heritage, the concept of sharing food picked up on his travels in Spain and the best of British produce.

Menu £25/70 – Carte £26/70

Town plan 37 AJ6-g – *1 Wilbraham Place* ⊠ *SW1X 9AE* ⊖ *Sloane Square* – ℰ *020 7730 7634* – *www.kahanidining.com* – *Closed Monday lunch*

ⅰ○ Kutir ⓝ

INDIAN · EXOTIC DÉCOR XX A pretty end-of-terrace townhouse in an elegant Chelsea street; there's a lively buzz throughout the various smart yet cosy rooms – if you're on a date, ask to sit upstairs. Assorted menus – including a vegetarian tasting menu – offer refined and original cooking from different Indian regions.

Menu £20/65 – Carte £32/45

Town plan 37 AJ7-h – *10 Lincoln Street* ⊠ *SW3 2TS* ⊖ *Sloane Square –*
℘ *020 7581 1144 – www.kutir.co.uk – Closed Monday*

ⅰ○ Medlar

MODERN CUISINE · NEIGHBOURHOOD XX A charming, comfortable and very popular restaurant with a real neighbourhood feel, from two alumni of Chez Bruce. The service is engaging and unobtrusive; the kitchen uses good ingredients in dishes that deliver distinct flavours in classic combinations.

Menu £25 (lunch), £32/53

Town plan 23 N7-x – *438 King's Road* ⊠ *SW10 0LJ* ⊖ *South Kensington –*
℘ *020 7349 1900 – www.medlarrestaurant.co.uk*

ⅰ○ Bandol

FRENCH · DESIGN X Stylishly dressed restaurant with a 100 year old olive tree evoking memories of sunny days spent on the French Riviera. Sharing plates take centre stage on the Provençal and Niçoise inspired menu; seafood is a highlight.

Menu £20 (lunch) – Carte £30/57

Town plan 36 AE8-b – *6 Hollywood Road* ⊠ *SW10 9HY* ⊖ *Earl's Court –*
℘ *020 7351 1322 – www.barbandol.co.uk*

ⅰ○ Rabbit

MODERN BRITISH · RUSTIC X The Gladwin brothers followed the success of The Shed with another similarly rustic and warmly run restaurant. Share satisfying, robustly flavoured plates; game is a real highlight, particularly the rabbit dishes.

Menu £17 (lunch), £25/42 – Carte £20/50

Town plan 37 AH7-r – *172 King's Road* ⊠ *SW3 4UP* ⊖ *Sloane Square –*
℘ *020 3750 0172 – www.rabbit-restaurant.com – Closed 23 December-2 January, Sunday dinner, Monday lunch*

ⅰ○ The Sea, The Sea ⓝ

SEAFOOD · TRENDY X A modern fishmonger's by day and a chic champagne and seafood bar in the evening; set in a charming semi-pedestrianised mews off Sloane Square. Cold lunchtime platters make way for more interesting sharing plates; must-tries include the crab with seaweed waffle, and the lobster rice sandu.

Carte £29/60

Town plan 37 AJ7-v – *174 Pavilion Road* ⊠ *SW1X 0AW* ⊖ *Sloane Square –*
℘ *020 7824 8090 – www.theseathesea.net – Closed Sunday, Monday*

🏠 Belmond Cadogan ⓝ

GRAND TOWNHOUSE · DESIGN An intimate hotel dating from 1895; a top-to-toe 2019 refurbishment was sympathetically undertaken, meaning that none of the building's immense charm and character was lost. Bedrooms are sumptuous and service, superbly efficient. Enjoy afternoon tea in the delightful lounge or creative British dishes in the elegant restaurant.

54 rooms – 👫 £550/950 – 8 suites

Town plan 37 AJ6-n – *75 Sloane Street* ⊠ *SW1X 9SG* ⊖ *Knightsbridge –*
℘ *020 7048 7141 – www.belmond.com*

ⅰ○ **Adam Handling Chelsea** – See restaurant listing

The Capital

LUXURY · CLASSIC A fine, thoroughly British hotel, known for its discreet atmosphere and its conscientious and attentive service. Comfortable, immaculately kept bedrooms are understated in style. Enjoy afternoon tea in the intimate Sitting Room and seasonal British dishes in the stylish Restaurant.

50 rooms – ♥♥ £349/420 – ☒ £20 – 1 suite

Town plan 37 AJ5-a – *22-24 Basil Street* ✉ *SW3 1AT*
⊖ *Knightsbridge* – ☎ *020 7589 5171* –
www.capitalhotel.co.uk

Egerton House

TOWNHOUSE · CLASSIC Compact but comfortable townhouse in a very good location, well-maintained throughout and owned by the Red Carnation group. High levels of personal service make the hotel stand out.

28 rooms – ♥♥ £315/630 – ☒ £29

Town plan 37 AH6-e – *17-19 Egerton Terrace* ✉ *SW3 2BX*
⊖ *South Kensington* – ☎ *020 7589 2412* –
www.egertonhousehotel.com

Franklin

TOWNHOUSE · ELEGANT A discreet, elegant and charmingly run boutique hotel within a lovingly restored, red-brick Victorian townhouse. The quietest rooms are those that overlook the lovely communal garden at the back. Modern Italian menu.

35 rooms – ♥♥ £250/400 – ☒ £25 – 9 suites

Town plan 37 AH6-h – *24 Egerton Gardens* ✉ *SW3 2DB*
⊖ *South Kensington* – ☎ *020 7584 5533* –
www.starhotelscollezione.com

Knightsbridge

LUXURY · PERSONALISED Charming and attractively furnished townhouse in a Victorian terrace, with a very stylish, discreet feel. Every bedroom is immaculately appointed and has a style all of its own; fine detailing throughout.

44 rooms ☒ – ♥♥ £318/400

Town plan 37 AH6-s – *10 Beaufort Gardens* ✉ *SW3 1PT*
⊖ *Knightsbridge* – ☎ *020 7584 6300* –
www.knightsbridgehotel.com

The Levin

TOWNHOUSE · CLASSIC Little sister to The Capital next door, The Levin has an impressive façade and a contemporary interior. Comfortable bedrooms have a subtle art deco style and marvellous champagne mini bars; the best room is the open-plan top floor suite. Enjoy a light breakfast in the lobby.

12 rooms – ♥♥ £300/450 – ☒ £13

Town plan 37 AJ5-c – *28 Basil Street* ✉ *SW3 1AS*
⊖ *Knightsbridge* – ☎ *020 7589 6286* –
www.thelevinhotel.co.uk

No.11 Cadogan Gardens

TOWNHOUSE · PERSONALISED A classic townhouse hotel; fashioned out of four red-brick houses and exuberantly dressed, with bold colours and furnishings. Theatrically decorated bedrooms vary in size from cosy to spacious. Modern British classics are served in the basement restaurant, Hans' Bar & Grill.

56 rooms – ♥♥ £250/395 – ☒ £24 – 7 suites

Town plan 37 AJ7-x – *11 Cadogan Gardens* ✉ *SW3 2RJ*
⊖ *Sloane Square* – ☎ *020 7730 7000* –
www.11cadogangardens.com

KENSINGTON
Greater London

✿ Kitchen W8

MODERN CUISINE · NEIGHBOURHOOD ⅩⅩ Kitchen W8 is a joint venture between experienced restaurateurs Rebecca Mascarenhas and Philip Howard and their influence is clear to see. It's the sort of restaurant every neighbourhood should have because it succeeds on so many levels. Whether you're here for a special occasion or a quick bite for lunch, the staff will get the tone of the service just right and the food will be meticulously prepared yet easy to eat.

Head Chef Mark Kempson puts as much care into the great value lunch and early evening menu as he does the main à la carte. His confident cooking delivers great flavours and subtle degrees of originality so that the dishes have personality and depth. The restaurant may not be quite as informal as the name suggests but it is certainly free of pomp or pomposity.

Specialities: Grilled Cornish mackerel, smoked eel, sweet mustard and leek. Roast rump of veal, young garlic, white asparagus, Jersey Royals and morels. Yoghurt parfait, with lemon curd, warm vanilla beignets and basil.

Menu £25 (lunch), £30/75 – Carte £36/52

Town plan 35 AC5-a – 11-13 Abingdon Road ✉ W8 6AH
⊖ High Street Kensington – ✆ 020 7937 0120 – www.kitchenw8.com

ⅠⅠ○ Launceston Place

MODERN CUISINE · NEIGHBOURHOOD ⅩⅩ A favourite of many thanks to its palpable sense of neighbourhood, pretty façade and its nooks and crannies which make it ideal for trysts or tête-à-têtes. The menu is fashionably terse and the cooking is quite elaborate, with dishes big on originality and artfully presented.

Menu £25 (lunch), £55/65 – Carte £42/70

Town plan 36 AE5-a – 1a Launceston Place ✉ W8 5RL ⊖ Gloucester Road –
✆ 020 7937 6912 – www.launcestonplace-restaurant.co.uk – Closed Monday, Tuesday lunch

ⅠⅠ○ Akira ⓝ

JAPANESE · ELEGANT ⅩⅩ Japan House promotes all things Japanese so it's appropriate that upstairs there's a stylish restaurant celebrating the country's cuisine. The open kitchen is the focal point of the room, which offers both counter and table seating. The best things on the menu are dishes from the robata charcoal grill.

Menu £40 (lunch), £60/72 – Carte £38/50

Town plan 36 AD5-h – Japan House, 101-111 Kensington High Street ✉ W8 5SA
⊖ High Street Kensington – ✆ 020 3971 4646 – www.japanhouseakira.london –
Closed Sunday dinner

ⅠⅠ○ Clarke's

MODERN CUISINE · NEIGHBOURHOOD ⅩⅩ Its unhurried atmosphere, enthusiastic service and dedication to its regulars are just a few reasons why Sally Clarke's eponymous restaurant has instilled such unwavering loyalty for over 30 years. Her kitchen has a light touch and understands the less-is-more principle.

Menu £34 (lunch)/39 – Carte £42/100

Town plan 27 AC4-c – 124 Kensington Church Street ✉ W8 4BH
⊖ Notting Hill Gate – ✆ 020 7221 9225 – www.sallyclarke.com –
Closed 24-30 August, 24-31 December

ⅠⅠ○ Zaika

INDIAN · CONTEMPORARY DÉCOR ⅩⅩ The cooking focuses on the North of India and the influences of Mughal and Nawabi, so expect rich and fragrantly spiced dishes. The softly-lit room makes good use of its former life as a bank, with its wood-panelling and ornate ceiling.

Menu £21/55 – Carte £20/40

Town plan 36 AD5-r – 1 Kensington High Street ✉ W8 5NP
⊖ High Street Kensington – ✆ 020 7795 6533 – www.zaikaofkensington.com –
Closed Monday lunch

Mazi

GREEK · FRIENDLY X It's all about sharing at this simple, bright Greek restaurant where traditional recipes are given a modern twist to create vibrant, colourful and fresh tasting dishes. The garden terrace at the back is a charming spot in summer.

Menu £20 (lunch) – Carte £30/75

Town plan 27 AC3-a – *12-14 Hillgate Street* ✉ *W8 7SR* ⊖ *Notting Hill Gate* – ✆ *020 7229 3794* – *www.mazi.co.uk* – *Closed Monday lunch*

The Shed

MODERN BRITISH · RUSTIC X It's more than just a shed but does have a higgledy-piggledy charm and a healthy dose of the outdoors. One brother cooks, one manages and the third runs the farm which supplies the produce for the earthy, satisfying dishes.

Menu £25/42 – Carte £23/34

Town plan 27 AC3-s – *122 Palace Gardens Terrace* ✉ *W8 4RT* ⊖ *Notting Hill Gate* – ✆ *020 7229 4024* – *www.theshed-restaurant.com* – *Closed Sunday, Monday lunch*

The Milestone

LUXURY · PERSONALISED Elegant and enthusiastically run hotel with decorative Victorian façade and a very British feel. Charming oak-panelled sitting room is popular for afternoon tea; snug bar in former stables. Meticulously decorated bedrooms offer period detail. Ambitious cooking in discreet Cheneston's restaurant.

62 rooms ⌑ – ♦♦ £405/935 – 6 suites

Town plan 36 AE5-u – *1-2 Kensington Court* ✉ *W8 5DL* ⊖ *High Street Kensington* – ✆ *020 7917 1000* – *www.milestonehotel.com*

NORTH KENSINGTON
Greater London

CORE by Clare Smyth (Clare Smyth)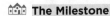

MODERN BRITISH · CONTEMPORARY DÉCOR XxxX The moment you step inside Clare Smyth's Notting Hill restaurant you know you're in for an unforgettable experience. It has a reassuringly welcoming atmosphere that puts all diners at ease and that's largely down to her warm and engaging service team. Secondly, it's decorated in a bright, yet understated way that makes for a truly comforting feel.

Purity and elegance are the hallmarks of Clare's cooking. There are no elements of 'look at me' bravado – just beautifully balanced dishes that reflect her heritage, professional experience and personality. A typical dish to illustrate just how skilled this kitchen is must surely be the Charlotte potato with dulse beurre blanc and roe, a nod to her Northern Irish upbringing; here a seemingly simple ingredient is elevated to something extraordinary and shows the real depth of the cooking.

Specialities: 'Potato and roe' - dulse beurre blanc, herring and trout roe. 'Lamb carrot' - braised lamb, sheep's milk yoghurt. Lemonade parfait with honey and yoghurt.

Menu £70 (lunch), £95/145

Town plan 27 AB2-e – *92 Kensington Park Road* ✉ *W11 2PN* ⊖ *Notting Hill Gate* – ✆ *020 3937 5086* – *www.corebyclaresmyth.com* – *Closed Sunday, Monday, Tuesday - Wednesday lunch*

Ledbury (Brett Graham)

MODERN CUISINE · NEIGHBOURHOOD XxX Look around the smart but unshowy Ledbury and you may catch sight of a chef or two having dinner - that's because Aussie Brett Graham is considered a "chef's chef" and it's easy to see why. His cooking is informed by the seasonal ingredients available and his deep-rooted knowledge of husbandry and his close relationships with his suppliers are revealed throughout his menu.

Dishes demonstrate how adept the kitchen is at harnessing the true flavours of ingredients, often with complementing layers – it takes great skill to make something with such depth look so simple. Game is a highlight – particularly the Sika deer which is raised on the owner's estate in Oxfordshire. The service is personable and free from affectation; the wine list is strong across all regions; and the atmosphere, hospitable and grown up.

Specialities: White beetroot baked in clay with Exmoor caviar and smoked eel. Muntjac with smoked bone marrow, red leaves and vegetables. Brown sugar tart with stem ginger ice cream.

Menu £80 (lunch), £125/150

Town plan 27 AB2-c – *127 Ledbury Road* ⊠ *W11 2AQ*
⊖ *Notting Hill Gate* – ℰ *020 7792 9090* –
www.theledbury.com –
Closed Monday - Tuesday lunch

ⅈO Caractère 🆕

EUROPEAN CONTEMPORARY · **NEIGHBOURHOOD** XX Emily Roux, scion of the Roux dynasty, and her husband, chef Diego Ferrari, have turned this former pub into a warm, convivial neighbourhood restaurant. The menu reflects their French and Italian backgrounds. Be sure to order celeriac 'cacio e pepe' – a delicious and clever reworking of the Roman classic.

Menu £39 (lunch)/78 – Carte £44/60

Town plan 27 AB1-u – *209 Westbourne Park Road* ⊠ *W11 1EA*
⊖ *Westbourne Park* – ℰ *020 8181 3850* –
www.caractererestaurant.com –
Closed Monday, Tuesday

ⅈO Flat Three 🔳 ⅈⓋ

CREATIVE · **DESIGN** XX The open kitchen is the main feature of this roomy, basement restaurant. The flavours of Korea and Japan feature heavily in the elaborately constructed, original and creative dishes which deliver plenty of flavour. Service can be rather formal.

Menu £33 (lunch), £39/59

Town plan 27 AA4-k – *120-122 Holland Park Avenue* ⊠ *W11 4UA*
⊖ *Holland Park* – ℰ *020 7792 8987* –
www.flatthree.london –
Closed Sunday, Monday, Wednesday - Thursday lunch

ⅈO Granger & Co. Notting Hill 🔳 ⅈ 🔳

WORLD CUISINE · **FRIENDLY** X Bill Granger's first London restaurant is a great fit for this neighbourhood – and its airy, relaxed style a perfect match to his cooking. Food is fun and comes with a riot of flavours; alongside plenty of tasty breakfast dishes are signatures like chicken schnitzel or sticky chilli belly pork.

Carte £23/38

Town plan 27 AC2-x – *175 Westbourne Grove* ⊠ *W11 2SB*
⊖ *Bayswater* – ℰ *020 7229 9111* –
www.grangerandco.com

ⅈO 108 Garage 🔳

MODERN BRITISH · **NEIGHBOURHOOD** X This former garage has a utilitarian look that's all bare brick, exposed ducting and polished concrete. A 6 course menu is offered, with a choice of main course and dessert, and the vibrant, modern dishes feature plenty of contrasts and originality. Sit at the counter if you want to chat with the chefs.

Menu £35 (lunch)/65 – Carte £39/50

Town plan 27 AA1-e – *108 Golborne Road* ⊠ *W10 5PS*
⊖ *Westbourne Park* – ℰ *020 8969 3769* –
www.108garage.com –
Closed 23 August-2 September, 23 December-5 January, Sunday, Monday, Tuesday - Thursday lunch

LONDON · ENGLAND

🍴○ **Orasay**   A/C 🛋 ♿

MODERN BRITISH · FRIENDLY 🗡 A relaxed, contemporary bistro named after the Scottish island where chef-owner Jackson Boxer holidayed as a child. Small plates of modern British food rely on excellent seasonal ingredients, which are expertly cooked to produce clean, natural flavours. Subtle Mediterranean and Asian influences feature.

Menu £20 (lunch) – Carte £32/52

Town plan 27 AA2-g – *31 Kensington Park Road* ⊠ *W11 2EU* ⊖ *Ladbroke Grove –* ℰ *020 7043 1400 – www.orasay.london – Closed Sunday dinner, Monday, Tuesday lunch*

🍴○ **Six Portland Road**   A/C

FRENCH · NEIGHBOURHOOD 🗡 An intimate and personally run neighbourhood restaurant owned by Oli Barker, previously of Terroirs. The menu changes frequently and has a strong French accent; dishes are reassuringly recognisable, skilfully constructed and very tasty.

Menu £20 (lunch), £45/65 – Carte £20/65

Town plan 27 AA4-n – *6 Portland Road* ⊠ *W11 4LA* ⊖ *Holland Park –* ℰ *020 7229 3130 – www.sixportlandroad.com – Closed 15-29 August, 24 December-4 January, Sunday, Saturday lunch*

🍴○ **Zayane**   A/C

MOROCCAN · NEIGHBOURHOOD 🗡 An intimate neighbourhood restaurant owned by Casablanca-born Meryem Mortell and evoking the sights and scents of North Africa. Carefully conceived dishes have authentic Moroccan flavours but are cooked with modern techniques.

Carte £21/35

Town plan 27 AA1-z – *91 Golborne Road* ⊠ *W10 5NL* ⊖ *Westbourne Park –* ℰ *020 8960 1137 – www.zayanerestaurant.com – Closed Sunday dinner, Monday*

🏠 **The Portobello**   ↕

TOWNHOUSE · CLASSIC An attractive Victorian townhouse in a Kensington terrace. Its small, comfortable lounge has an honesty bar. Bedrooms are individually furnished in an English style with antique furniture; some have four-poster beds. Ask for a 'Signature' room overlooking a private garden at the back.

21 rooms 🖵 – 👫 £195/455

Town plan 27 AB2-n – *22 Stanley Gardens* ⊠ *W11 2NG* ⊖ *Notting Hill Gate –* ℰ *020 7727 2777 – www.portobellohotel.com*

SOUTH KENSINGTON

Greater London

🍴○ **Bombay Brasserie**   A/C 🍴 🕈

INDIAN · EXOTIC DÉCOR 🗡🗡🗡 A well-run, well-established and comfortable Indian restaurant, featuring a very smart bar and conservatory. Creative dishes sit alongside more traditional choices on the various menus and vegetarians are well-catered for.

Menu £27 (lunch), £51/127 – Carte £39/60

Town plan 36 AE6-y – *Courtfield Road* ⊠ *SW7 4QH* ⊖ *Gloucester Road –* ℰ *020 7370 4040 – www.bombayb.co.uk – Closed Monday lunch*

🍴○ **Cambio de Tercio**   🐕 A/C 🍴 ♿

SPANISH · COSY 🗡🗡 A long-standing, ever-improving Spanish restaurant. Start with small dishes like the excellent El Bulli inspired omelette, then have the popular Pluma Iberica. There are super sherries and a wine list to prove there is life beyond Rioja.

Menu £24 (lunch) – Carte £45/60

Town plan 36 AE7-a – *163 Old Brompton Road* ⊠ *SW5 0LJ* ⊖ *Gloucester Road –* ℰ *020 7244 8970 – www.cambiodetercio.co.uk – Closed 23 December-2 January*

⑩ Ognisko

POLISH · ELEGANT XX Ognisko Polskie – The Polish Hearth Club – was founded in 1940 in this magnificent townhouse; its elegant restaurant serves traditional dishes from across Eastern Europe and the cooking is without pretence and truly from the heart.

Menu £18/22 – Carte £29/37

Town plan 37 AG5-r – *55 Prince's Gate, Exhibition Road* ✉ *SW7 2PN*
⊖ *South Kensington* – ✆ *020 7589 0101* – *www.ogniskorestaurant.co.uk*

⑩ Yashin Ocean House

JAPANESE · CHIC XX The USP of this chic Japanese restaurant is 'head to tail' eating, although, as there's nothing for carnivores, 'fin to scale' would be more precise. Stick with specialities like the whole dry-aged sea bream for the full umami hit.

Carte £25/100

Town plan 36 AF7-y – *117-119 Old Brompton Road* ✉ *SW7 3RN*
⊖ *Gloucester Road* – ✆ *020 7373 3990* – *www.yashinocean.com*

⑩ Capote y Toros

SPANISH · TAPAS BAR X Expect to queue at this compact and vividly coloured spot which celebrates sherry, tapas, ham... and bullfighting. Sherry is the star; those as yet unmoved by this most underappreciated of wines will be dazzled by the variety.

Carte £30/60

Town plan 36 AE7-v – *157 Old Brompton Road* ✉ *SW5 0LJ* ⊖ *Gloucester Road* –
✆ *020 7373 0567* – *www.cambiodetercio.co.uk* – *Closed 22 December-2 January, Sunday, Monday, Tuesday - Saturday lunch*

⑩ Go-Viet

VIETNAMESE · CONTEMPORARY DÉCOR X A Vietnamese restaurant from experienced chef Jeff Tan. Lunch concentrates on classics like pho and bun, while dinner provides a more sophisticated experience, offering interesting flavourful dishes with a distinct modern edge.

Carte £22/51

Town plan 36 AF7-v – *53 Old Brompton Road* ✉ *SW7 3JS* ⊖ *South Kensington* –
✆ *020 7589 6432* – *www.vietnamfood.co.uk*

⑩ Margaux

MEDITERRANEAN CUISINE · NEIGHBOURHOOD X An earnestly run modern bistro with an ersatz industrial look. The classically trained kitchen looks to France and Italy for its primary influences and dishes are flavoursome and satisfying. The accompanying wine list has been thoughtfully compiled.

Menu £15 (lunch), £40/55 – Carte £27/56

Town plan 36 AE7-m – *152 Old Brompton Road* ✉ *SW5 0BE* ⊖ *Gloucester Road* –
✆ *020 7373 5753* – *www.barmargaux.co.uk*

🏠 Blakes

LUXURY · DESIGN Behind the Victorian façade is one of London's first 'boutique' hotels. Dramatic, bold and eclectic décor, with oriental influences and antiques from around the world. International dishes in the spacious ground floor restaurant.

45 rooms ⊞ – 👬 £275/470 – 7 suites

Town plan 36 AF7-n – *33 Rowland Gardens* ✉ *SW7 3PF* ⊖ *Gloucester Road* –
✆ *020 7370 6701* – *www.blakeshotels.com*

🏠 The Pelham

LUXURY · ELEGANT Great location if you're in town for museum visiting. It's a mix of English country house and city townhouse, with a panelled sitting room and library with honesty bar. Sweet and intimate basement restaurant with Mediterranean menu.

52 rooms – 👬 £240/370 – ⊞ £15 – 2 suites

Town plan 37 AG6-z – *15 Cromwell Place* ✉ *SW7 2LA* ⊖ *South Kensington* –
✆ *020 7589 8288* – *www.pelhamhotel.co.uk*

Number Sixteen

TOWNHOUSE · ELEGANT Elegant 19C townhouses in a smart neighbourhood; well-run by charming, helpful staff. Tastefully furnished lounges feature attractive modern art. First floor bedrooms benefit from large windows and balconies; basement rooms are the quietest and two have their own terrace. Airy Orangery restaurant for afternoon tea and light meals overlooking the pretty garden.

41 rooms – †† £300/486 – ⬜ £18

Town plan 36 AF7-d – *16 Sumner Place* ⬚ *SW7 3EG*
⊖ *South Kensington* – ☏ *020 7589 5232* –
www.firmdalehotels.com

The Gore

TOWNHOUSE · PERSONALISED Idiosyncratic, hip Victorian house close to the Royal Albert Hall, whose charming lobby is covered with pictures and prints. Individually styled bedrooms have plenty of character and fun bathrooms. Bright and casual bistro.

50 rooms ⬜ – †† £170/350

Town plan 36 AF5-n – *190 Queen's Gate* ⬚ *SW7 5EX*
⊖ *Gloucester Road* – ☏ *020 7584 6601* –
www.gorehotel.com

CENTRAL LONDON - SOUTHWARK

Greater London

Top tips!

A must-see if you're in Southwark, Borough Market dates back to the 12th century and specialises in food from around the world, with organic and farm produce, fresh fruit and vegetables, and street food to takeaway. Restaurants within the market include Bib Gourmand award-holder **Padella**, a lively Italian bistro dedicated to pasta; **Roast**, which is known for its British food and its promotion of UK producers; and **Elliot's**, which serves earthy, satisfying dishes accompanied by natural wines. If you're after a special occasion place to stay, you can't beat **Shangri-La** in The Shard, which provides panoramic city views through its floor-to-ceiling windows. Travel further south to Peckham and you'll find lively **Levan**, which is loved by locals, and husband-and-wife run Bib Gourmand holder **Kudu**.

Bermondsey

✿ Story (Tom Sellers)   ⓖ AC

MODERN CUISINE · CONTEMPORARY DÉCOR XxX Story's rather strange location on an island in the middle of the road turns out to be a blessing as, once ensconced inside this intimate restaurant, you feel pleasantly detached from the outside world. The picture window allows light to flood in, but the focus here is on chef Tom Sellers and his team at work in the glass kitchen.

Tom is a chef who puts great store on presentation and creativity and his 10 course surprise menu contains playful elements, like the imaginative savoury Oreo, 'Storeo', and the bread and 'dripping' where your candle melts to provide the dip for your sourdough. Alongside these come perfectly balanced dishes like 'venison, cauliflower and yeast', which show respect for the classics whilst also elevating them to new levels.

Specialities: Bread and 'dripping'. Venison, cauliflower and yeast. Almond and dill.
Menu £100 (lunch)/145

Town plan 42 AY5-u – *199 Tooley Street* ✉ *SE1 2JX*
⊖ *London Bridge* – ☎ *020 7183 2117* –
www.restaurantstory.co.uk – *Closed 22 December-3 January, Sunday, Monday lunch*

ⓐ José   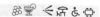

SPANISH · MINIMALIST X Standing up while eating tapas feels so right, especially at this snug, lively bar that packs 'em in like boquerones. The vibrant dishes are intensely flavoured – five per person should suffice; go for the daily fish dishes from the blackboard. There's a great list of sherries too.

Specialities: Croquetas. Pluma Ibérica 5J. Crema Catalana.

Carte £23/30

Town plan 42 AX5-v – *104 Bermondsey Street* ✉ *SE1 3UB*
⊖ *London Bridge* – ☎ *020 7403 4902* – *www.josepizarro.com*

�○ Le Pont de la Tour

FRENCH · ELEGANT XxX Few restaurants can beat the setting, especially when you're on the terrace with its breathtaking views of Tower Bridge. For its 25th birthday it got a top-to-toe refurbishment, resulting in a warmer looking room in which to enjoy the French-influenced cooking.

Menu £30 – Carte £35/75

Town plan 34 AY4-e – *36d Shad Thames, Butlers Wharf* ✉ *SE1 2YE*
⊖ *London Bridge* – ☎ *020 7403 8403* – *www.lepontdelatour.co.uk*

�○ Butlers Wharf Chop House

TRADITIONAL BRITISH · BRASSERIE XX Grab a table on the terrace in summer and dine in the shadow of Tower Bridge. Rustic feel to the interior; noisy and fun. The menu focuses on traditional English ingredients and dishes; grilled meats a speciality.

Menu £29 (lunch) – Carte £34/58

Town plan 34 AY4-n – *36e Shad Thames, Butlers Wharf* ✉ *SE1 2YE*
⊖ *London Bridge* – ☎ *020 7403 3403* – *www.chophouse-restaurant.co.uk*

⅟○ Coal Shed

MEATS AND GRILLS · DESIGN XX Coal Shed was established in Brighton before opening here in this modern development by Tower Bridge. It's set over two floors and specialises in steaks but there's also plenty of seafood on offer. Desserts are good too; try the various 'sweets'.

Menu £15/24 – Carte £30/44

Town plan 34 AX4-s – *Unit 3.1, One Tower Bridge, 4 Crown Square*
✉ *SE1 2SE* ⊖ *London Bridge* – ☎ *020 3384 7272* –
www.coalshed-restaurantlondon.co.uk

⫶○ Duddell's

CHINESE · HISTORIC XX A former church, dating from 1703, seems an unlikely setting for a Cantonese restaurant but this striking conversion is the London branch of the Hong Kong original. Lunchtime dim sum is a highlight but be sure to order the Peking duck which comes with 8 condiments in two servings.

Menu £25 (lunch) – Carte £36/69

Town plan 33 AW4-c – 9A St. Thomas Street ⊠ SE1 9RY ⊖ London Bridge –
𝒞 020 3957 9932 – www.duddells.co/london

⫶○ Casse Croûte

FRENCH · BISTRO X Squeeze into this tiny bistro and you'll find yourself trans-ported to rural France. A blackboard menu offers three choices for each course but new dishes are added as others run out. The cooking is rustic, authentic and heartening.

Carte £31/37

Town plan 42 AX5-t – 109 Bermondsey Street ⊠ SE1 3XB ⊖ London Bridge –
𝒞 020 7407 2140 – www.cassecroute.co.uk – Closed Sunday dinner

⫶○ Flour & Grape

ITALIAN · SIMPLE X The clue's in the name – pasta and wine. A choice of 7 or 8 antipasti are followed by the same number of homemade pasta dishes, with a dessert menu largely centred around gelato. Add in a well-chosen wine list with some pretty low mark-ups and it's no wonder this place is busy.

Carte £15/28

Town plan 42 AX6-e – 214 Bermondsey Street ⊠ SE1 3TQ ⊖ London Bridge –
𝒞 020 7407 4682 – www.flourandgrape.com – Closed Monday lunch

⫶○ Garrison

MEDITERRANEAN CUISINE · PUB X Known for its charming vintage look, booths and sweet-natured service, The Garrison boasts a warm, relaxed vibe. Open from breakfast until dinner, when a Mediterranean-led menu pulls in the crowds.

Carte £26/40

Town plan 42 AX5-z – 99-101 Bermondsey Street ⊠ SE1 3XB ⊖ London Bridge. –
𝒞 020 7089 9355 – www.thegarrison.co.uk

⫶○ Gunpowder at Tower Bridge 🆕

INDIAN · CONTEMPORARY DÉCOR X In contrast to the first Gunpowder, this branch sits within a modern development, is spread over two floors and takes bookings; ask for one of the booths. The well-priced dishes allow for uninhibited ordering; crispy pork ribs, spiced venison doughnuts and soft-shell crab are must-haves.

Menu £25 – Carte £16/40

Town plan 34 AY4-v – One Tower Bridge, 4 Duchess Street ⊠ SE1 2SE
⊖ London Bridge – 𝒞 020 3598 7946 – www.gunpowderlondon.com –
Closed Sunday dinner

⫶○ Pique-Nique

FRENCH · BISTRO X Set in a converted 1920s park shelter is this fun French restau-rant with a focus on rotisserie-cooked Bresse chicken. Concise menu of French classics; go for the 6 course 'Menu autour du poulet de Bresse' which uses every part of the bird.

Carte £24/44

Town plan 42 AX5-n – Tanner St Park ⊠ SE1 3TD ⊖ London Bridge –
𝒞 020 7403 9549 – www.pique-nique.co.uk – Closed Sunday dinner

⫶○ Pizarro

MEDITERRANEAN CUISINE · NEIGHBOURHOOD X José Pizarro has a refresh-ingly simple way of naming his establishments: after José, his tapas bar, came Pi-zarro, a larger restaurant a few doors down. Go for the small plates, like prawns with piquillo peppers and jamón.

Carte £28/50

Town plan 42 AX6-r – 194 Bermondsey Street ⊠ SE1 3TQ ⊖ London Bridge –
𝒞 020 7378 9455 – www.josepizarro.com

ⅈⓄ Santo Remedio

MEXICAN · COLOURFUL X The cooking inspiration comes from the owner's time spent in Mexico City, the Yucatan and Oaxaca. Ingredients are a mix of imported – like grasshoppers to liven up the guacamole – and home-grown like Hertfordshire pork. Spread over two floors, the rooms are as colourful as the food.

Menu £15 (lunch) – Carte £24/32

Town plan 34 AX4-r – *152 Tooley Street* ⊠ *SE1 2TU* ⊖ *London Bridge* –
☏ *020 7403 3021* – *www.santoremedio.co.uk*

ⅈⓄ Tom Simmons

MODERN CUISINE · SIMPLE X The eponymous chef went from being a contestant on 'MasterChef: The Professionals' to having his name above the door of his own restaurant here in this modern development near Tower Bridge. His Welsh heritage comes through on the modern menu, with its use of Welsh lamb and beef.

Menu £21 (lunch), £23/29 – Carte £18/56

Town plan 34 AY4-c – *2 Still Walk* ⊠ *SE1 2RA* ⊖ *London Bridge* –
☏ *020 3848 2100* – *www.tom-simmons.co.uk* – *Closed 1-8 January, Sunday, Monday*

🏨 Shangri-La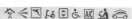

LUXURY · ELEGANT When your hotel occupies floors 34-52 of The Shard, you know it's going to have the wow factor. The pool is London's highest and north-facing bedrooms have the best views. An East-meets-West theme includes the restaurant's menu and afternoon tea when you have a choice of traditional English or Asian.

202 rooms – †† £535/865 – � £36 – 17 suites

Town plan 33 AW4-s – *The Shard, 31 St Thomas Street* ⊠ *SE1 9QU*
⊖ *London Bridge* – ☏ *020 7234 8000* – *www.shangri-la.com/london*

🏨 Bankside Ⓝ

BOUTIQUE HOTEL · CONTEMPORARY A purpose-built hotel but one with personality, thanks to the impressive collection of artwork scattered around; there's even an Artist in Residence. Bedrooms are bright and stylish and there's a laid-back all-day brasserie on the ground floor.

161 rooms ⊠ – †† £342/599

Town plan 32 AT3-c – *2 Blackfriars Road, Upper Ground* ⊠ *SE1 9JU*
⊖ *Southwark* – ☏ *020 3943 2220* – *www.artyardbarandkitchen.com*

Peckham

🏵 Kudu

MODERN CUISINE · NEIGHBOURHOOD X Run by a young husband and wife team who have attracted a fun and young local clientele. Patrick's South African roots are evident in dishes like the mussel potjie and the 'braai' lamb neck; the brioche-style bread with bacon butter is memorable. Amy and her service team are delightful.

Specialities: Octopus potjie with red pepper and garlic. Confit duck, maitake, celeriac and spring greens. Malted chocolate ganache with sesame ice cream.

Menu £20 (lunch) – Carte £30/45

Town plan 26 V8-k – *119 Queen's Road* ⊠ *SE15 2EZ*
⊖ *Queens Road Peckham (Rail).* – ☏ *020 3950 0226* – *www.kudu-restaurant.com*
– *Closed Monday, Tuesday, Wednesday - Thursday lunch*

ⅈⓄ Artusi

ITALIAN · NEIGHBOURHOOD X An enthusiastically run Italian restaurant which shows Peckham is on the rise. The kitchen displays clear respect for the seasonal ingredients, dishes are kept honest and the prices are more than fair.

Carte £21/30

Town plan 26 U9-a – *161 Bellenden Road* ⊠ *SE15 4DH* ⊖ *Peckham Rye* –
☏ *020 3302 8200* – *www.artusi.co.uk*

⁌◯ Levan ⓝ   🅰🄲 🍴

EUROPEAN CONTEMPORARY · NEIGHBOURHOOD ✗ Lively and friendly local restaurant named after DJ Larry Levan so the music's good too. Sharing plates of mostly European influence feature, accompanied by natural wines from small producers. Be sure to start with the comté fries.

Carte £24/37

Town plan 26 U8-r – *12-16 Blenheim Grove* ✉ *SE15 4QL* ↔ *Peckham Rye –*
📞 *020 7732 2256 – www.levanlondon.co.uk – Closed 22 December-2 January, Sunday dinner, Monday*

SOUTHWARK
Greater London

⊛ Padella   ⌀🍴 🅰🄲

ITALIAN · BISTRO ✗ This lively little sister to Trullo offers a short, seasonal menu where hand-rolled pasta is the star of the show. Sauces and fillings are inspired by the owners' trips to Italy and prices are extremely pleasing to the pocket. Sit at the ground floor counter overlooking the open kitchen.

Specialities: Wiltshire burrata with olive oil. Tagliarini with courgette, brown shrimp and chilli. Rhubarb and almond tart.

Carte £12/22

Town plan 33 AW4-d – *6 Southwark Street, Borough Market* ✉ *SE1 1TQ*
↔ *London Bridge – www.padella.co*

⁌◯ Roast   🍸 ♿ 🅰🄲 🛇

MODERN BRITISH · FRIENDLY ✗✗ Known for its British food and for promoting UK producers – not surprising considering the restaurant's in the heart of Borough Market. They take quite a lot of large tables but the bright room is big enough to cope.

Carte £35/66

Town plan 33 AV4-e – *The Floral Hall, Borough Market* ✉ *SE1 1TL*
↔ *London Bridge –* 📞 *020 3006 6111 – www.roast-restaurant.com – Closed Sunday dinner*

⁌◯ Union Street Café   🍸 ♿ 🅰🄲 🛇

ITALIAN · DESIGN ✗✗ Occupying a former warehouse, this Gordon Ramsay restaurant has been busy since day one and comes with a New York feel, a faux industrial look and a basement bar. The Italian menu keeps things simple and stays true to the classics.

Menu £19/23 – Carte £30/50

Town plan 33 AU4-u – *47-51 Great Suffolk Street* ✉ *SE1 0BS* ↔ *London Bridge –*
📞 *020 7592 7977 – www.gordonramsayrestaurants.com – Closed Sunday dinner*

⁌◯ Anchor & Hope   ⌀🍴 🏠

MODERN BRITISH · PUB ✗ As popular as ever thanks to its congenial feel and lived-in looks but mostly because of the appealingly seasonal menu and the gutsy, bold cooking that delivers on flavour. No reservations so be prepared to wait at the bar.

Menu £18 (lunch) – Carte £23/44

Town plan 32 AT4-n – *36 The Cut* ✉ *SE1 8LP* ↔ *Southwark. –* 📞 *020 7928 9898 – www.anchorandhopepub.co.uk – Closed 24 December-2 January, Sunday dinner, Monday lunch*

⁌◯ Bala Baya   ♿ 🅰🄲 🍴

MIDDLE EASTERN · DESIGN ✗ A friendly, lively restaurant which celebrates the Middle Eastern heritage of its passionate owner. Dishes are fresh, vibrant and designed for sharing and the bright, modern interior is inspired by the Bauhaus architecture of Tel Aviv.

Menu £25 (lunch), £33/53 – Carte £31/60

Town plan 33 AU4-a – *Arch 25, Old Union Yard Arches, 229 Union Street* ✉ *SE1 0LR* ↔ *Southwark –* 📞 *020 8001 7015 – www.balabaya.co.uk – Closed Sunday dinner*

⬭◯ **El Pastór** ⊘🗱 AC 🍴

MEXICAN • BISTRO X A lively, informal restaurant under the railway arches at London Bridge; inspired by the taquerias of Mexico City. Flavours are beautifully fresh, fragrant and spicy; don't miss the Taco Al Pastór after which the restaurant is named.

Carte £14/32

Town plan 33 AV4-r – *7a Stoney St, Borough Market* ✉ *SE1 9AA*
⊖ *London Bridge* – ℰ *020 7440 1461* –
www.tacoselpastor.co.uk – Closed Sunday dinner

⬭◯ **Elliot's**

MODERN CUISINE • RUSTIC X A lively, unpretentious restaurant which sources its ingredients from Borough Market, in which it stands. The appealing menu is concise and the cooking is earthy, pleasingly uncomplicated and very satisfying. Four plates per person will suffice; try the Isle of Mull cheese puffs. Natural wines are a focus.

Carte £22/60

Town plan 33 AV4-h – *12 Stoney Street, Borough Market* ✉ *SE1 9AD*
⊖ *London Bridge* – ℰ *020 7403 7436* –
www.elliotscafe.com – Closed Sunday

⬭◯ **Lobos** AC 🍴

SPANISH • TAPAS BAR X A dimly lit, decidedly compact tapas bar under the railway arches – sit upstairs to enjoy the theatre of the open kitchen. Go for one of the speciality meat dishes like the leg of slow-roasted milk-fed Castilian lamb.

Carte £20/48

Town plan 33 AW4-a – *14 Borough High Street* ✉ *SE1 9QG*
⊖ *London Bridge* – ℰ *020 7407 5361* –
www.lobostapas.co.uk

⬭◯ **Native** ⓝ AC ⟷

INNOVATIVE • RUSTIC X Wild food and foraging underpin this restaurant occupying an ersatz industrial space close to Borough Market; Ivan runs the kitchen and Imogen the service. It also boasts strong eco credentials and seeks to reduce waste; start with the 'snacks' made from what that would otherwise be discarded.

Carte £31/50

Town plan 33 AV4-v – *32 Southwark Street* ✉ *SE1 1TU*
⊖ *London Bridge* – ℰ *07507 861570* –
www.eatnative.co.uk – Closed 23 December-4 January, Sunday, Monday

⬭◯ **Oxo Tower Brasserie** 🍷 ≤ 🛖 AC

MODERN CUISINE • DESIGN X Set on the eighth floor of the iconic converted factory and providing stunning views of the Thames and beyond. The open-plan kitchen produces modern, colourful and easy-to-eat dishes with influences from the Med. Great views too from the bar.

Menu £30 (lunch) – Carte £27/49

Town plan 32 AS3-a – *Oxo Tower Wharf, Barge House Street (8th Floor)* ✉ *SE1 9PH* ⊖ *Southwark* – ℰ *020 7803 3888* –
www.oxotower.co.uk

⬭◯ **Tapas Brindisa** ⊘🗱 🛖 🍴ⓥ

SPANISH • TAPAS BAR X A blueprint for many of the tapas bars that subsequently sprung up over London. It has an infectious energy and the well-priced, robust dishes include Galician-style octopus and black rice with squid; try the hand-carved Ibérico hams.

Carte £14/38

Town plan 33 AV4-k – *18-20 Southwark Street, Borough Market* ✉ *SE1 1TJ*
⊖ *London Bridge* – ℰ *020 7357 8880* –
www.brindisatapaskitchens.com

🍴 Tate Modern (Restaurant)　　　　　🅰️ 🔲 🔲

MODERN BRITISH · DESIGN 🍴 Allow time to get to this bright, open restaurant on the 9th floor of Tate Modern's Blavatnik Building as the lifts are often crowded. The modern menus champion seasonal British ingredients in flavoursome, uncomplicated dishes and the wine list is varied and well-priced.

Menu £29/35

Town plan 33 AU3-s – *Blavatnik Building (9th floor), Tate Modern, Bankside* ✉ *SE1 9TG* ⊖ *Southwark* – ☏ *020 7401 5108* – *www.tate.org.uk* – *Closed Sunday - Thursday dinner*

🏨 Sea Containers London　　🔲 🔲 🔲 🔲 🔲 🔲 🔲 🔲 🔲

BUSINESS · DESIGN The former Sea Containers house now has slick, stylish look evoking the golden age of the transatlantic liner. Rooms come with a bright splash of colour; Suites have balconies and Superiors, a river view. Globally influenced small plates in the smart restaurant, with meat and fish from the grill & clay oven.

359 rooms – 🛏 £348/1111 – 🍽 £16 – 5 suites

Town plan 32 AT3-x – *20 Upper Ground* ✉ *SE1 9PD* ⊖ *Southwark* – ☏ *020 3747 1000* – *www.seacontainerslondon.com*

coldsnowstorm/iStock

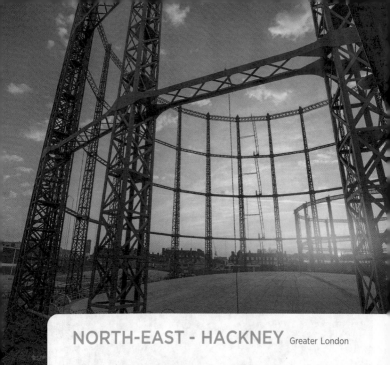

NORTH-EAST - HACKNEY Greater London

Top tips!

The regeneration of Hackney continues apace and this hipster hub is home to some of the city's most cutting edge restaurants. Check out **Nest** in Hackney, which focuses on one meat at a time; feast on fantastically fresh fish at **Cornerstone** in Hackney Wick, and enjoy southern French food eaten communally at **Sardine** in Hoxton.

If you're here on a Saturday, make time for a visit to Hackney's Broadway Market, just north of Regent's Canal: a Victorian street market selling all manner of fresh produce, with artisan food stalls and plenty of organic, gluten free, vegetarian and vegan options.

Further south, Shoreditch is Michelin Star central with **Brat**, **Clove Club**, **Leroy** and **Lyle's** all holders of this exclusive award – and putting paid to the outdated notion that Stars are all about linen napkins, starched tablecloths and amuse bouches.

Chris Bishop/iStock

DALSTON
Greater London

ⅼ◯ Angelina

ITALIAN · INTIMATE ✗ A fun and intimate neighbourhood spot owned by two friends and offering an unusual mix of Japanese and Italian cuisines; sit at the marble counter to watch the chefs at work in the open kitchen. Good value set menu; highlights include the seasonal nibbles and the tempura snacks.

Menu £38/43

Town plan 14 U2-c – *56 Dalston Lane* ⊠ *N16 8BH*
⊖ *Dalston Junction* – ℰ *020 7241 1851* – *www.angelina.london* – *Closed Monday, Tuesday, Wednesday* – *Thursday lunch*

ⅼ◯ Jidori

JAPANESE · BISTRO ✗ A sweet, unadorned yakitori-style restaurant serving succulent skewers of chicken, cooked on a charcoal-fired Kama-Asa Shoten grill imported from Japan. Charming staff and a good selection of cocktails, sake and craft beers.

Carte £17/28

Town plan 14 U2-y – *89 Kingsland High Street* ⊠ *E2 8BP*
⊖ *Dalston Kingsland* – ℰ *020 7686 5634* – *www.jidori.co.uk* – *Closed Sunday*

HACKNEY
Greater London

ⅼ◯ Casa Fofō

MODERN CUISINE · NEIGHBOURHOOD ✗ A cosy, relaxed neighbourhood restaurant with a spacious rear terrace and a homely, rustic feel. The seven course menu changes daily according to the best produce available and the well-balanced modern dishes feature daring flavour combinations. Wine pairings focus on organic and unfiltered wines.

Menu £39

Town plan 14 V2-v – *158 Sandringham Road* ⊠ *E8 2HS*
⊖ *Hackney Downs* – ℰ *020 3021 0747* – *www.casafofolondon.co.uk* –
Closed 23 December-3 March, Monday, Tuesday, Wednesday - Friday lunch

ⅼ◯ Laughing Heart

MODERN CUISINE · WINE BAR ✗ A wine bar for our age and as joyful as the name suggests. It comes with a great vibe, lovely service and a flexible menu of cleverly paired seasonal ingredients with occasional Asian flavours. Natural wines are the focus of the wine list and the small wine shop downstairs.

Menu £39 – Carte £27/43

Town plan 14 U3-f – *277 Hackney Road* ⊠ *E2 8NA*
⊖ *Hoxton* – ℰ *020 7686 9535* – *www.thelaughingheartlondon.com* –
Closed Sunday, Monday - Saturday lunch

ⅼ◯ Nest

MODERN BRITISH · NEIGHBOURHOOD ✗ A snug, modestly decorated and very warmly run restaurant created by three friends. The set menu focuses on seasonal British produce; their commendable "use all" ethos means they focus on one meat every 6 weeks – it could be Belted Galloway or Goosnargh duck – which they use in different ways.

Menu £38/44

Town plan 14 V2-s – *177 Morning Lane* ⊠ *E9 6LH*
⊖ *Homerton* – ℰ *020 8986 0065* – *www.nestfood.co.uk* –
Closed 22 December-7 January, Sunday, Monday, Tuesday, Wednesday - Saturday lunch

Silver Lining ⓝ ⒶⒸ 🍸

MODERN BRITISH · BISTRO ✗ Start with drinks at their next door cocktail bar, 'Every Cloud', before moving on to this dark, intimate restaurant with its relaxed, welcoming feel. The seasonal small plates are fresh and full of flavour; this is skilful cooking from an experienced chef who understands that less is more.

Carte £21/39

Town plan 14 V2-m – 13 Morning Lane ⊠ E9 6ND ⊖ Hackney Central –
☏ 020 8510 1782 – www.silverlininge9.com – Closed Sunday, Monday, Tuesday - Friday lunch

HACKNEY WICK

Greater London

Cornerstone ♿ ⒶⒸ 🍸

SEAFOOD · NEIGHBOURHOOD ✗ Superbly presented fish dishes – which change according to seasons and catches – are the highlight here, which is hardly surprising as the owner-chef previously worked for Nathan Outlaw. The pared-back room is dominated by a large open kitchen. Save room for the Cornish burnt cream.

Carte £35/54

Town plan 3 F3-c – 3 Prince Edward Road ⊠ E9 5LX ⊖ Hackney Wick (Rail) –
☏ 020 8986 3922 – www.cornerstonehackney.com –
Closed 22 December-6 January, Sunday, Monday, Tuesday lunch

Gotto Trattoria 🍽

ITALIAN · BRASSERIE ✗ The sister to Soho's Mele e Pere is a modern trattoria in a canal-side setting. The imported Italian ingredients are treated with respect and some of the recipes – such as the ever-present lasagne – are family secrets. Many of the cocktails use their homemade vermouth.

Carte £18/26

Town plan 3 F3-t – 27 East Bay Lane ⊠ E15 2GW ⊖ Hackney Wick (Rail) –
☏ 020 3424 5035 – www.gotto.co.uk

HOXTON

Greater London

☺ Petit Pois 🍸 🍽

MODERN BRITISH · NEIGHBOURHOOD ✗ Some restaurants just have a certain honesty about them. The small, even cramped, dining room is full of life and the service team take it in their stride. The flavoursome cooking is all about allowing the main ingredient to shine. The chocolate mousse is scooped at the table.

Specialities: Foie gras parfait, cornichons and herb toast. Steak frites, béarnaise sauce. Chocolate mousse.

Menu £14 (lunch) – Carte £26/35

Town plan 20 U4-a – 9 Hoxton Square ⊠ N1 6NU ⊖ Old Street – *☏ 020 7613 3689*
– www.petitpoisbistro.com – Closed 24-27 December

The Frog Hoxton 🍽 ♿ ⒶⒸ 🍸🍴 🕓

MODERN CUISINE · NEIGHBOURHOOD ✗ An unpretentious place with a concrete floor, graffiti-style murals, an open kitchen and a small café-cum-bar featuring over 200 beers. Creative, modern, boldly flavoured dishes incorporate influences from all over the world; service is super friendly, with some dishes delivered by the chefs themselves.

Carte £36/48

Town plan 20 U4-x – 45-47 Hoxton Square ⊠ N1 6PD ⊖ Old Street –
☏ 020 3813 9832 – www.thefroghoxton.com – Closed Sunday, Monday

⫶○ **Sardine**   AC 🎐

FRENCH · COSY ⫶ A trendy, compact restaurant with a communal table at the heart of proceedings. The food comes from Southern France, and dishes are rustic, unfussy and very tasty; try the lamb à la ficelle, cooked over an open fire.

Menu £16/20 – Carte £27/36

Town plan 19 T4-r – *Parasol Art Gallery, 15 Micawber Street* ✉ *N1 7TB*
⊖ *Old Street* – ☏ *020 7490 0144 – www.sardine.london*

LONDON FIELDS
Greater London

⫶○ **Hill & Szrok**   ⊘⫶ 🏠

MEATS AND GRILLS · NEIGHBOURHOOD ⫶ Butcher's shop by day; restaurant by night, with a central marble-topped table, counters around the edge and a friendly, lively feel. Daily blackboard menu of top quality meats, including steaks aged for a minimum of 60 days. No bookings.

Carte £19/32

Town plan 14 V3-z – *60 Broadway Market* ✉ *E8 4QJ*
⊖ *Bethnal Green* – ☏ *020 7254 8805 –*
www.hillandszrok.co.uk – Closed Monday - Saturday lunch

⫶○ **Pidgin**   🍸

MODERN BRITISH · NEIGHBOURHOOD ⫶ A cosy, single room restaurant with understated décor and a buzzy neighbourhood vibe, tucked away on a residential Hackney street. Creative modern British dishes deliver an array of different textures and flavours. The no-choice menu changes weekly, as do the interesting wine pairings.

Menu £49

Town plan 14 V2-d – *52 Wilton Way* ✉ *E8 1BG*
⊖ *Hackney Central* – ☏ *020 7254 8311 –*
www.pidginlondon.com – Closed 23 December-3 January, Monday, Tuesday - Friday lunch

NEWINGTON GREEN
Greater London

⫶○ **Cérès**

MEDITERRANEAN CUISINE · NEIGHBOURHOOD ⫶ An intimate, personally run neighbourhood restaurant with understated décor, chatty service and a relaxed feel. The chef-owner is of French-Italian heritage and the frequently changing Mediterranean menu offers fresh, tasty, colourful dishes cooked with passion and care; desserts are a highlight.

Carte £25/40

Town plan 13 T2-c – *74 Green Lanes* ✉ *N16 9EJ*
⊖ *Canonbury* – ☏ *020 7689 0922 –*
www.cereslondon.co.uk – Closed Sunday, Monday, Tuesday - Saturday lunch

⫶○ **Jolene**   AC

MEDITERRANEAN CUISINE · RUSTIC ⫶ A bakery first and foremost, serving wonderful pastries, biscuits and cakes, as well as delicious bread and pasta from flour they mill themselves. All-day dining means that homemade croissants and sourdough morph into simple lunches and more adventurous dinners. The sausage rolls are to die for!

Carte £17/40

Town plan 13 T2-u – *21 Newington Green* ✉ *N16 9PU*
⊖ *Canonbury* – ☏ *0203 887 2309 –*
www.jolenen16.com – Closed Monday

LONDON · ENGLAND

SHOREDITCH
Greater London

The Clove Club (Isaac McHale)

MODERN CUISINE · CLASSIC DÉCOR XX The first of Isaac McHale's restaurants is set in the ornate and rather glamorous former Shoreditch Town Hall. Chefs perform centre stage in the smart, blue-tiled kitchen – sit here rather than in the adjacent bar so you don't miss out on the buzz.

Set menus – for which you must prepay online – are the order of the day, and these are tweaked constantly, since this is a kitchen fanatical about sourcing only top-notch seasonal British produce. Dishes are understated in appearance but offer maximum flavour; there is originality, verve and flair but combinations are always expertly judged and complementary. Seafood dishes are a highlight; don't miss the deliciously juicy raw Orkney scallop, served with hazelnut, clementine and Périgord truffle.

Specialities: Tartare of hay-smoked trout with potato and sansho pepper. Slow-roast Lincolnshire chicken with walnut emulsion. Loquat sorbet & mousse with amaranth and popcorn.

Menu £65 (lunch), £95/145

Town plan 20 U4-c – Shoreditch Town Hall, 380 Old Street ⊠ EC1V 9LT
⊖ Old Street – ℰ 020 7729 6496 – www.thecloveclub.com –
Closed 23 December-7 January, Sunday, Monday lunch

Brat (Tomos Parry)

TRADITIONAL BRITISH · NEIGHBOURHOOD X Brat takes inspiration from the cooking styles found in the Basque country, and in particular the town of Getaria. Cooking over fire is paramount, and the stove, grill and hand-built oven provide the focal point of the room.

The restaurant's name is the Old English word for turbot and this is the house speciality: grilled whole in a handmade basket over lump wood charcoal with a sauce made from the released collagen and gelatine. There are plenty of other dishes to enjoy first; some of which are inspired by chef Tomos Parry's Welsh roots, such as the pork and laverbread salami, or baby peas with Carmarthen ham.

Here, it's all about wonderful ingredients and natural flavours – and there is something very joyful about that. You don't just eat at Brat – you tuck in.

Specialities: Soused red mullet. Grilled whole turbot. Burnt cheesecake with rhubarb.

Carte £25/65

Town plan 20 U4-r – 4 Redchurch Street (1st Floor) ⊠ E1 6JL
⊖ Shoreditch High Street – www.bratrestaurant.com – Closed Sunday dinner

Leroy (Sam Kamienko)

MODERN BRITISH · NEIGHBOURHOOD X How can you not fall for a place where the first thing you see is a couple of shelves of vinyl? Putting all their experience to bear, the owners have created a restaurant with a relaxed, easy vibe and great food.

Increased turnover means the quality of the ingredients they can use is better than ever; as Sam the chef says, "We can now buy brill or turbot instead of mackerel and calf's sweetbreads instead of liver". The core ingredient shines through in every dish – whether that's razor clams with garlic and parsley, boudin noir with watercress or the delicious skewers of honeyed quail. There's no clear division between starters and main courses – just order a few dishes to share and marvel at how much skill must go into making something unshowy.

Specialities: Cured grey mullet with tomato and lovage. John Dory with spring vegetables and ham broth. Chocolate ganache and boozy prunes.

Menu £22 (lunch) – Carte £37/46

Town plan 20 U4-d – 18 Phipp Street ⊠ EC2A 4NU ⊖ Old Street –
ℰ 020 7739 4443 – www.leroyshoreditch.com – Closed 22 December-2 January,
Sunday, Monday lunch

ENGLAND · LONDON

✿ Lyle's (James Lowe)   A/C

MODERN BRITISH · SIMPLE X Lipton, the tea people, once owned the building and the pared-down, ersatz industrial look of the restaurant is bang on trend. For added animation, help is at hand from the open kitchen, while warmth and personality come courtesy of the delightful service team, who share the passion of the kitchen, offer great advice and really know their menu.

The dishes may appear to be as unadorned as the room but don't be fooled – they are technically accomplished, thoughtfully composed and deliver far more depth and sophistication than their terse menu descriptions suggest. The superb seasonal British ingredients provide flavours that are clean and unadulterated and a joy to experience. Dinner sees a set menu but at lunch you can choose an array of dishes at prices that are more than fair.

Specialities: Peas & Ticklemore. Dexter flank, bitter leaves and anchovy. Espresso meringue and caramel.

Menu £59 – Carte £35/45

Town plan 20 U4-g – *Tea Building, 56 Shoreditch High Street* ⊠ *E1 6JJ*
⊖ *Shoreditch High Street* – ℰ *020 3011 5911* –
www.lyleslondon.com – *Closed 23 December-6 January, Sunday*

✿ Popolo   ⊘🍴 A/C 🍽

MEDITERRANEAN CUISINE · DESIGN X Skimmed concrete floors and exposed brick walls give this restaurant a utilitarian feel; sit at the counter and chat to the chefs as they work. Italian, Spanish and North African influences feature on the menu of small plates. Pasta is a highlight and classic, simply cooked dishes allow the ingredients to shine.

Specialities: Deep-fried olives, labneh and dukkah. Pork cheek agnolotti with porcini butter. Burnt honey panna cotta with pistachio advieh.

Carte £24/35

Town plan 20 U4-b – *26 Rivington Street* ⊠ *EC2A 3DU*
⊖ *Old Street* – ℰ *020 7729 4299* –
www.popoloshoreditch.com – *Closed Sunday, Monday - Saturday lunch*

✿ Two Lights ❶   A/C 🍽

MODERN CUISINE · FRIENDLY X This fun, trendy, simply furnished Shoreditch spot is named after Two Lights State Park in Maine, where the head chef – a Clove Club alumnus – is originally from. The pleasingly unstructured menu offers playful and creative modern American dishes which are well-priced and will leave you feeling satisfied.

Specialities: Oven-roasted artichoke with sunflower seed miso. Ray wing with Jersey Royals and dill pickle butter. Vanilla custard tart with bourbon caramel.

Menu £20 (lunch) – Carte £26/42

Town plan 20 U4-s – *28 Kingsland Road* ⊠ *E2 8DA* ⊖ *Old Street* –
ℰ *020 3976 0076* – *www.twolights.restaurant* – *Closed 22 December-6 January, Monday, Tuesday lunch*

ⅼ○ Merchants Tavern   & A/C ⇔

TRADITIONAL BRITISH · BRASSERIE XX The 'pub' part – a Victorian warehouse – gives way to a large restaurant with the booths being the prized seats. The cooking is founded on the sublime pleasures of seasonal British cooking, in reassuringly familiar combinations.

Menu £25 (lunch) – Carte £25/40

Town plan 20 U4-t – *36 Charlotte Road* ⊠ *EC2A 3PG*
⊖ *Old Street* – ℰ *020 7060 5335* –
www.merchantstavern.co.uk – *Closed Sunday dinner*

✿✿✿, ✿✿, ✿, ☺ & ⅼ○

⊕ Andina

PERUVIAN · SIMPLE X Andina may be smaller and slightly more chaotic that its sister Ceviche, but this friendly picantería with live music is equally popular. The Peruvian specialities include great salads and skewers, and ceviche that packs a punch.

Carte £12/25

Town plan 20 U4-w – *1 Redchurch Street* ✉ *E2 7DJ*
⊖ *Shoreditch High Street* – ✆ *020 7920 6499* –
www.andinarestaurants.com

⊕ Princess of Shoreditch

TRADITIONAL BRITISH · PUB X There has been a pub on this corner site since 1742 but it is doubtful many of the previous incarnations were as busy or as pleasant as the Princess is today. The best dishes are those with a rustic edge, such as goose rillettes or chicken pie.

Carte £28/45

Town plan 19 T4-a – *76-78 Paul Street* ✉ *EC2A 4NE*
⊖ *Old Street* – ✆ *020 7729 9270* –
www.theprincessofshoreditch.com

⊕ St Leonards

MODERN BRITISH · BISTRO X Urban industrial meets stylish Scandic at this relaxed open-plan restaurant, where seasonal vegetables and meats are chargrilled to perfection and served straight from the hearth; think whole roast duck with mint and olives. Shellfish also feature – as do some cracking snacks and cocktails.

Menu £22 (lunch) – Carte £28/50

Town plan 19 T4-n – *70 Leonard Street* ✉ *EC2A 4QX*
⊖ *Old Street* – ✆ *020 7739 1291* –
www.stleonards.london – *Closed 22 December-2 January, Sunday, Monday*

🏨 Ace Hotel

BUSINESS · MINIMALIST What better location for this achingly trendy hotel than hipster-central itself – Shoreditch. Locals are welcomed in, the lobby has a DJ, urban-chic rooms have day-beds if you want friends over and the minibars offer everything from Curly Wurlys to champagne. British favourites in the stylish brasserie.

258 rooms – 🛏 £180/420 – ⌧ £15 – 3 suites

Town plan 20 U4-p – *100 Shoreditch High Street* ✉ *E1 6JQ*
⊖ *Shoreditch High Street* – ✆ *020 7613 9800* –
www.acehotel.com

🏨 The Curtain

BUSINESS · TRENDY A trendy, fun hotel which used to be a warehouse used for raves. The stylish, comfortable bedrooms feature original art and steam showers. Enjoy afternoon tea in the Green Room, soul food in Red Rooster or brasserie dishes in rooftop Lido. Live music in members club, LP.

120 rooms ⌧ – 🛏 £275/450 – 5 suites

Town plan 20 U4-e – *45 Curtain Road* ✉ *EC2A 3PT*
⊖ *Old Street* – ✆ *020 3146 4545* –
www.thecurtain.com

🏨 Nobu H. Shoreditch

BUSINESS · DESIGN The UK's first Nobu hotel is an impressive modern building with a super-stylish interior, hidden away in the streets of Shoreditch. Comfortable bedrooms have a subtle industrial feel and offer state-of-the-art TVs. The 35th branch of the renowned Nobu restaurant serves its modern Japanese cuisine in the basement.

150 rooms – 🛏 £190/300 – ⌧ £18 – 4 suites

Town plan 19 T4-h – *10-50 Willow Street* ✉ *EC2A 4BH*
⊖ *Old Street* – ✆ *020 7683 1200* –
www.nobuhotelshoreditch.com

🏠 Boundary ☆ ⊟ ♿

LUXURY · DESIGN A converted warehouse boasting individually styled bed-rooms, studios and duplex loft suites which are cool, stylish and bursting with personality. Rooftop has a relaxed Mediterranean flavour; Albion is an all-day café with something for everyone.

17 rooms – 👫 £145/650 – 🍽 £20 – 5 suites

Town plan 20 U4-b – *2-4 Boundary Street* ✉ *E2 7DD* ⊖ *Shoreditch High Street* – ☎ *020 7729 1051* – *www.boundary.london*

SOUTH HACKNEY

Greater London

ⅰ○ Empress 🏠

TRADITIONAL BRITISH · PUB 🗶 An 1850s neighbourhood pub with a short, simple and pleasingly seasonal menu of traditional British dishes with the occasional Mediterranean influence. Service is friendly and you can bring your own bottle on Tuesday nights.

Carte £16/45

Town plan 3 F3-d – *130 Lauriston Road, Victoria Park* ✉ *E9 7LH* ⊖ *Homerton.* – ☎ *020 8533 5123* – *www.empresse9.co.uk* – *Closed Monday lunch*

NORTH-EAST Greater London

Top tips!

The North-East is arguably the most exciting area of London; home to a wide range of different cultures and communities, as well as the business centre of Canary Wharf – and popular with the city's creatives. It was the site of the 2012 Olympic Games and continues to be an area of urban regeneration, with plenty of new housing and business start-ups as well as art galleries, restaurants, cafés and clubs galore.

Head to Old Spitalfields Market for vintage and vinyl, plus everything from doughnuts or dumplings to 'dirty' food and delis. Boldly flavoured Burmese specialities are served at **Lahpet** – or eat at the buzzing **Blixen** with its appealing European menu and basement bar.

If only a Michelin Star will do, try the surprise menu at **Da Terra** in Bethnal Green, where you'll find hints of Latin America and Italy in the original and truly memorable dishes.

Electric Egg/Shutterstock.com

REDBRIDGE
Greater London

South Woodford

�Ⅰ○ **Grand Trunk Road**

INDIAN · CONTEMPORARY DÉCOR ✗✗ Named after one of Asia's oldest and longest routes, which provided inspiration for the menu. Dishes are well-balanced and original with a modern touch; breads come from a charcoal-fired tandoor and vegetable dishes are a highlight.

Menu £20 (lunch), £39/49 – Carte £32/70

Town plan 4 G2-w – *219 High Road* ✉ *E18 2PB* ⊖ *South Woodford –*
☏ 020 8505 1965 – www.gtrrestaurant.co.uk – Closed Monday

Wanstead

⊙ **Provender**

FRENCH · BISTRO ✗ A welcoming and busy neighbourhood bistro, courtesy of experienced restaurateur Max Renzland. The fairly priced French cooking is pleasingly rustic and satisfying; the classic dishes are the ones to go for. Look out for the good value menus during the week.

Specialities: Soupe à l'oignon. Lapin à la moutarde. Tarte Tatin.

Menu £17 (lunch) – Carte £25/45

Town plan 4 G2-x – *17 High Street* ✉ *E11 2AA* ⊖ *Snaresbrook –* ☏ *020 8530 3050*
– www.provenderlondon.co.uk

TOWER HAMLETS
Greater London

Bethnal Green

✿ **Da Terra** ⓝ

MODERN CUISINE · CONTEMPORARY DÉCOR ✗✗ The surprise menu here comprises 8 or 10 original, refined and truly captivating courses. To reflect the chef's heritage and his extensive culinary peregrinations, there are hints of Latin America and Italy in the influences. The harmony of flavours is exemplary and a great deal of thought clearly goes into the contrast of textures. The chefs bring the dishes to the table themselves and explain their make-up – the zeal they all have for their craft is palpable.

The discreetly dressed restaurant sits within the restored Victorian splendour of the Town Hall hotel – start with a cocktail in the bar across the hall. As you enter the restaurant you're greeted by the sight of orderly activity in the open kitchen – be sure to sit in this part of the room if you want to keep watching.

Specialities: Scallop with fennel and apple. Beef with artichoke and chard. Topinambur with white chocolate.

Menu £73/90

Town plan 20 V4-x – *Town Hall Hotel, 8 Patriot Square* ✉ *E2 9NF*
⊖ *Bethnal Green –* ☏ *020 7062 2052 – www.daterra.co.uk – Closed 2-18 August,*
23 December-7 January, Sunday, Monday, Tuesday, Wednesday - Friday lunch

✿ **Mãos** ⓝ (Nuno Mendes)

INNOVATIVE · CONTEMPORARY DÉCOR ✗✗ A "kitchen, table and wine room" is how chef Nuno Mendes describes his restaurant on the first floor of the Blue Mountain School – a collaborative space for fashion, design, art and food. It certainly offers a genuinely immersive experience and a night out like no other.

Before settling down to eat together at the 16-seater table, guests are served drinks and snacks by the open kitchen and encouraged to engage with their fellow diners as well as the chefs. It's then on to the wine room to make your choices for the evening ahead.

The surprise menu of around 16 courses offers a masterclass in originality, balance and depth. Combinations are bold but never challenging, each ingredient has a purpose and the craftsmanship is hugely impressive, resulting in flavours that will be long remembered.

Specialities: Mushroom and kombu chawanmushi. Grilled hogget, prawn miso and hispi cabbage. Celeriac with white truffle.

Menu £150

Town plan 20 U4-k – 41 Redchurch Street ⊠ E2 7DJ ⊖ Shoreditch High Street – ℰ 020 7739 9733 – www.bluemountain.school – Closed Sunday, Monday, Tuesday, Wednesday - Friday lunch

Brawn
⊗⊗ AC

TRADITIONAL BRITISH · NEIGHBOURHOOD X The kind of place everyone needs in their neighbourhood: passionately run with a relaxed, upbeat vibe and serving good value, reliably tasty food alongside some interesting wines. The menu evolves with the seasons and dishes are hearty and boldly flavoured. Sit in the back room to enjoy the buzz from the kitchen.

Specialities: Raw scallop, turnip, apple and lovage. Ricotta, borage and walnut agnolotti. Buttermilk panna cotta, loquat and pistachio.

Carte £29/44

Town plan 20 U4-z – 49 Columbia Road ⊠ E2 7RG ⊖ Bethnal Green – ℰ 020 7729 5692 – www.brawn.co – Closed 23 December-3 January, Sunday, Monday lunch

Smokestak
🍷 🏠 AC

MEATS AND GRILLS · RUSTIC X A buzzing barbecue restaurant with an open kitchen and an industrial feel. Highlights include the brisket and ribs: these are brined, oak-smoked, coated with a sweet and sour BBQ sauce and chargrilled – the results being unctuous and incredibly satisfying. The charming staff are happy to guide you.

Specialities: Crispy ox cheek with anchovy mayo. Beef brisket, mustard barbecue sauce. Sticky toffee pudding, clotted cream ice cream.

Carte £18/30

Town plan 20 U4-f – 35 Sclater Street ⊠ E1 6LB ⊖ Shoreditch High Street – ℰ 020 3873 1733 – www.smokestak.co.uk

Blanchette
AC 📋

FRENCH · BISTRO X Sister to the Soho original with the same lively buzz, funky music and tasty French dishes, but here the menu heads further south, with a few North African influences too. 3 or 4 plates per person should suffice.

Menu £20 (lunch) – Carte £23/36

Town plan 20 U4-h – 204 Brick Lane ⊠ E1 6SA ⊖ Shoreditch High Street – ℰ 020 7729 7939 – www.blanchettelondon.co.uk – Closed Monday - Thursday lunch

Lahpet
🍷 AC ⓥ

BURMESE · BISTRO X This pop-up-turned-permanent is a buzzing spot run by two friends, both of Burmese heritage; sit at the counter and order some cocktails to start. Authentic Burmese cooking comes with bold, unique flavours. Dishes arrive as and when they are ready; 3 or 4 dishes per person are about right.

Carte £20/40

Town plan 20 U4-y – 58 Bethnal Green Road ⊠ E1 6JW ⊖ Shoreditch High Street – ℰ 020 3883 5629 – www.lahpet.co.uk – Closed 23-28 December, Monday - Thursday lunch

Marksman
🏠 AC

TRADITIONAL BRITISH · PUB X With its quirky, brown-tiled façade, this pub has long been a local landmark; the wood-panelled bar retains the feel of a traditional boozer, while the first floor dining room is more modern. Simply cooked, seasonal British dishes are wonderfully fresh, well-balanced and full of flavour.

Menu £26 (lunch) – Carte £28/39

Town plan 20 U4-m – 254 Hackney Road ⊠ E2 7SJ ⊖ Hoxton. – ℰ 020 7739 7393 – www.marksmanpublichouse.com – Closed 25-31 December, Monday - Friday lunch

⍩○ Sager + Wilde ⍩ 🏠

MEDITERRANEAN CUISINE · RUSTIC ⅄ Friendly neighbourhood restaurant – a former wine bar – set underneath a railway arch. Tasty, well-priced, creative dishes have a Mediterranean heart and an eye-catching modern style, with some interesting combinations.

Carte £24/40

Town plan 20 V4-s – 250 Paradise Row ✉ E2 9LE
⊖ Bethnal Green – ℰ 020 7613 0478 –
www.sagerandwilde.com –
Closed 24-26 December, Monday lunch

🏛 Town Hall 🏠 🖼 ⌶♨ ⬆ ⅃ AC 🎿

LUXURY · DESIGN Grand Edwardian and Art Deco former council offices converted into a stylish, trendy hotel, whilst retaining many original features. Striking, individually decorated bedrooms come with retro furnishings and frequently changing art.

97 rooms ⌸ – 🛉 £150/180 – 57 suites

Town plan 20 V4-x – Patriot Square ✉ E2 9NF
⊖ Bethnal Green – ℰ 020 7871 0460 –
www.townhallhotel.com
❀ **Da Terra** – See restaurant listing

Spitalfields

❀ Galvin La Chapelle (Jeff Galvin) 🏠 ⅃ AC 🕭 ⟷

FRENCH · ELEGANT ⅄⅄⅄ Built in 1890 as a girls' school, this splendid Grade II listed structure with its vaulted ceiling, arched windows and marble pillars was an inspired choice for a venue. It lends itself effortlessly to its role as a glamorous restaurant: a magnificent open space with a mezzanine for private dining, and plenty of tables, whether in booths, in the wings or right in the middle of the action. The atmosphere is bustling yet relaxed and unstuffy.

Cooking is assured and precise, with a classical French foundation and a sophisticated modern edge. There are no unnecessary fripperies – just three courses of reassuringly familiar combinations with the emphasis on bold, harmonious flavours and, whilst dishes may sound complicated, they are anything but. Musttries include the tagine of Bresse pigeon and the tarte Tatin.

Specialities: Lasagne of Dorset crab with beurre Nantais and pea shoots. Tagine of Bresse pigeon, couscous, confit lemon and harissa sauce. Tarte Tatin with Normandy crème fraîche.

Menu £38 – Carte £55/77

Town plan 34 AX1-v – 35 Spital Square ✉ E1 6DY
⊖ Liverpool Street – ℰ 020 7299 0400 –
www.galvinrestaurants.com –
Closed 1-2 January, 24-27 December

❀ Blixen 🍸 ⅃ AC ⟷

MEDITERRANEAN CUISINE · CHIC ⅄ A charmingly run and good-looking restaurant with lots of natural light; set in a former bank. The appealing European menu offers keenly priced modern dishes. Service is enthusiastic, the atmosphere's buzzing and you'll want to return for cocktails in the basement bar or a weekend brunch.

Specialities: Chicken parfait with ginger and walnut, port jelly, pickles and toast. Roast snapper fillet with chorizo gyoza, cauliflower, purple kale and red wine jus. Rhubarb and almond tart with cardamom ice cream.

Carte £24/40

Town plan 34 AY1-w – 65a Brushfield Street ✉ E1 6AA
⊖ Liverpool Street – ℰ 020 7101 0093 –
www.blixen.co.uk – Closed Sunday dinner

Gunpowder ⤨ ❏ ♿ 🍽

INDIAN · SIMPLE 🍽 A loud, buzzy restaurant with just ten tightly packed tables, serving vibrant small plates from across the Indian regions. The name is a reference to the chef's daily-made spice mix and his menu takes its influence from old family recipes. Standout dishes include deep-fried crab and crispy pork ribs.

Specialities: Spicy venison and vermicelli doughnut with fennel and chilli chutney. Maa's Kashmiri lamb chops. Old Monk rum pudding.

Carte £15/29

Town plan 34 AY1-g – *11 White's Row* ✉ *E1 7NF*
⊖ *Liverpool Street* – ☎ *020 7426 0542* – *www.gunpowderlondon.com* –
Closed Sunday

St John Bread and Wine 🔡 🍽

TRADITIONAL BRITISH · BISTRO 🍽 An appealing restaurant with a stripped back style. The highly seasonal menu offers starter-sized dishes perfect for sharing and the cooking is British, uncomplicated and very satisfying. Breakfast includes a wonderful rare breed bacon sandwich.

Specialities: Beetroot, red cabbage and crème fraîche. Deep-fried skate cheeks and tartare sauce. Eccles cake and Lancashire cheese.

Carte £24/42

Town plan 34 AY1-a – *94-96 Commercial Street* ✉ *E1 6LZ*
⊖ *Liverpool Street* – ☎ *020 7251 0848* – *www.stjohnrestaurant.com*

🍽○ Hawksmoor 🔡

MEATS AND GRILLS · FRIENDLY 🍽 A buzzy, relaxed restaurant with friendly staff. It's not really about the starters or the puds here – the star is the great British beef, hung for 35 days, which comes from Longhorn cattle in the heart of the Yorkshire Moors.

Menu £29 – Carte £26/29

Town plan 34 AY1-s – *157a Commercial Street* ✉ *E1 6BJ*
⊖ *Shoreditch High Street* – ☎ *020 7234 9940* – *www.thehawksmoor.com*

🍽○ Som Saa 🍹 ♿ 🔡

THAI · RUSTIC 🍽 Som Saa's success took it from pop-up to permanent restaurant, with a lively atmosphere and a rustic, industrial look. Menus showcase the diversity of Thai cuisine. 4 or 5 dishes between two are recommended – and do try a cocktail or two!

Menu £25 (lunch)/35 – Carte £20/45

Town plan 34 AY1-t – *43a Commerical Street* ✉ *E1 6BD*
⊖ *Aldgate East* – ☎ *020 7324 7790* – *www.somsaa.com* – *Closed Sunday, Monday lunch*

🏠 Batty Langley's 📱 ♿ 🔡

TOWNHOUSE · ELEGANT It looks and feels like a Georgian house, thanks to the antique furniture and attention to detail, yet even the façade was rebuilt. The luxurious rooms come with flowing drapes, reproduction fireplaces and lovely bathrooms. An oasis of composed elegance.

29 rooms – 🚹 £260/320 – ⊡ £12 – 5 suites

Town plan 34 AY1-y – *12 Folgate Street* ✉ *E1 6BX* ⊖ *Liverpool Street* –
☎ *020 7377 4390* – *www.battylangleys.com*

Whitechapel

Cafe Spice Namaste 🔡 🍽Ⓥ

INDIAN · NEIGHBOURHOOD 🍽🍽 Fresh, vibrant and fairly priced Indian cuisine from Cyrus Todiwala, served in a colourfully decorated room that was once a magistrate's court. Engaging service from an experienced team.

Specialities: Beetroot and coconut samosa. Goan pork vindaloo. Cardamom, ginger and saffron crème brûlée.

Carte £25/43

Town plan 34 AZ3-z – *16 Prescot Street* ✉ *E1 8AZ* ⊖ *Tower Hill* –
☎ *020 7488 9242* – *www.cafespice.co.uk* – *Closed Sunday, Saturday lunch*

141

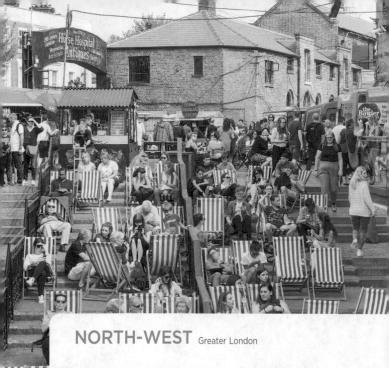

NORTH-WEST Greater London

Top tips!

To the west is Hammersmith, which developed gradually from the early 18th century, when the embankment upstream from the bridge became home to rows of houses with flower-decked balconies and enviable views of the river.

This part of the Thames is the centre of the annual boat race course, a cut-throat rowing race between Oxford and Cambridge Universities – and is also home to the iconic **River Café**, founded in 1987 by Ruth Rogers and the late Rose Gray – and where it all began for TV chef Jamie Oliver. The restaurant has held a Michelin Star since 1997 and its menu bursts with authentic Italian flavours.

Not far away in leafy Fulham you will find the **Harwood Arms**, another holder of a Michelin Star – this time in the typically British surroundings of a down-to-earth pub.

BRENT
Greater London

Church End

⁑○ Shayona

INDIAN · FAMILY ⊠ Opposite the striking Swaminarayan Temple is this simple, sattvic restaurant: it's vegetarian and 'pure' so avoids onion or garlic. Expect curries from the north, dosas from the south and Mumbai street food. No alcohol so try a lassi.

Menu £12 (lunch) – Carte £12/24

Town plan 2 C3-a – *54-62 Meadow Garth* ⊠ *NW10 8HD* ⊖ *Stonebridge Park* – ℰ *020 8965 3365* – *www.shayonarestaurants.com* – *Closed 27-28 October*

Kensal Green

⁑○ Parlour 🍸 🏠

MODERN BRITISH · PUB ⊠ A fun, warmly run and slightly quirky neighbourhood hangout. The menu is a wonderfully unabashed mix of tradition, originality and reinvention, and dishes are fresh and full of flavour. Don't miss the cow pie which even Dan, however Desperate, would struggle to finish.

Menu £18/36 – Carte £35/45

Town plan 16 L4-r – *5 Regent Street* ⊠ *NW10 5LG* ⊖ *Kensal Green* – ℰ *020 8969 2184* – *www.parlourkensal.com* – *Closed 22 December-2 January, Monday*

EALING
Greater London

Acton Green

⁑○ Le Vacherin AC

FRENCH · BRASSERIE ⊠⊠ Authentic feel to this comfortable brasserie, with its brown leather banquette seating, mirrors and belle époque prints. French classics from snails to duck confit; beef is a speciality.

Menu £22 (lunch), £29/30 – Carte £28/54

Town plan 6 C4-f – *76-77 South Parade* ⊠ *W4 5LF* ⊖ *Chiswick Park* – ℰ *020 8742 2121* – *www.levacherin.com* – *Closed Monday lunch*

⁑○ Duke of Sussex 🏠

MEDITERRANEAN CUISINE · PUB ⊠ Bustling Victorian pub, whose striking dining room was once a variety theatre complete with proscenium arch. Stick to the Spanish dishes; stews and cured meats are the specialities.

Carte £19/54

Town plan 6 C4-f – *75 South Parade* ⊠ *W4 5LF* ⊖ *Chiswick Park.* – ℰ *020 8742 8801* – *www.thedukeofsussex.co.uk*

Ealing

⁑○ Charlotte's W5 🍸 🏠 ⅙ AC 📖

MODERN CUISINE · NEIGHBOURHOOD ⊠ It's all about flexibility at this converted stable block – you can come for a drink, a snack or a full meal. Every dish is available in a choice of three sizes and every bottle of wine is offered by the glass or carafe. The charming service team add to the buzz.

Menu £15 (lunch)/30 – Carte £29/42

Town plan 1 B3-c – *Dickens Yard, Longfield Avenue* ⊠ *W5 2UQ* ⊖ *Ealing Broadway* – ℰ *020 3771 8722* – *www.W5.charlottes.co.uk*

⍐ **Kiraku**

JAPANESE · FRIENDLY ⅹ The name of this cute little Japanese restaurant means 'relax and enjoy' - easy with such charming service. The extensive menu includes zensai, skewers, noodles, rice dishes and assorted sushi; ask if you want them in a particular order.

Carte £14/35

Town plan 2 C3-v – *8 Station Parade, Uxbridge Road* ✉ *W5 3LD*
⊖ *Ealing Common* – ℰ *020 8992 2848* –
www.kiraku.co.uk – *Closed 25 December-1 January, Monday, Tuesday - Thursday lunch*

South Ealing

⍐ **Ealing Park Tavern** 🛖

MODERN BRITISH · PUB ⅹ An impressive Arts and Crafts property, dating from 1886 and brought up to date thanks to a splendid refurbishment from the Martin Brothers. Cooking is robust yet with a refined edge. The pub also boasts its own brewery at the back.

Carte £22/30

Town plan 6 C4-e – *222 South Ealing Road* ✉ *W5 4RL*
⊖ *South Ealing* – ℰ *020 8758 1879* –
www.ealingparktavern.com

HAMMERSMITH AND FULHAM

Greater London

Fulham

⭐ **Harwood Arms** 🕸 🗚

MODERN BRITISH · PUB ⅹ The menu here is British to its core and game season is certainly not to be missed as the owners' shoots produce plenty of bounty for the kitchen – but that kitchen is so skilled and so resolutely governed by the country's seasonal produce that it's worth calling in at this Fulham pub any time of year.

'Delicious' is usually the word most being uttered by your fellow diners as dishes are all about delivering wonderfully satisfying flavours. The Harwood also never forgets it's a pub – it may all be laid up for dining but it's rare not to see someone at the bar enjoying a pint and a Scotch egg – and you get to enjoy the sort of dishes you always hope to find in such a place: cheese and onion pie, whole lemon sole, venison faggots and chocolate malt cake.

Specialities: Crab tartlet. Deer Wellington. Marmalade ice cream sandwich.

Menu £33 (lunch)/50

Town plan 22 M7-a – *Walham Grove* ✉ *SW6 1QP*
⊖ *Fulham Broadway.* - ℰ *020 7386 1847* –
www.harwoodarms.com – *Closed Monday lunch*

⍐ **Harlequin** 🆕

MODERN CUISINE · SIMPLE ⅹ A sweet neighbourhood spot with an open kitchen and a relaxed feel; the chef is from South Africa and this is subtly reflected in the cooking. The good value set menu changes monthly and the kitchen use superbly fresh, seasonal ingredients to create carefully crafted, boldly flavoured dishes.

Menu £45

Town plan 22 M8-h – *194 Wandsworth Bridge Road* ✉ *SW6 2UF*
⊖ *Parsons Green* – ℰ *020 7736 7169* –
www.harlequinrestaurant.co.uk – *Closed 22 December-14 January, Sunday, Monday, Tuesday, Wednesday - Friday lunch*

PETROSSIAN

FONDÉ À PARIS EN 1920

Caviar. Smoked Fish. Fish Roe.

London Office
Tel : 0044 (0)7 562 799 020 / sales@petrossian.co.uk

⁑○ Koji   ⚗️🍷 A/C 🍴

JAPANESE · WINE BAR 🍴 A fun, contemporary wine bar serving Japanese food. The menu mixes the modern and the classic, with tempura and dishes from the robata grill particularly popular; food is full of flavour and the kitchen clearly know their craft.

Carte £36/75

Town plan 22 M8-e – *58 New King's Road* ⊠ *SW6 4LS* ⊖ *Parsons Green –*
𝒞 020 7731 2520 – www.koji.restaurant – Closed Monday, Tuesday - Friday lunch

⁑○ Manuka Kitchen   A/C 🍴

MODERN CUISINE · RUSTIC 🍴 The two young owners run their simple little restaurant with great enthusiasm and their prices are keen. Like the magical Manuka honey, the chef is from New Zealand; his menu is varied and his food is wholesome and full of flavour.

Menu £27 (lunch) – Carte £27/36

Town plan 22 M8-k – *510 Fulham Road* ⊠ *SW6 5NJ* ⊖ *Fulham Broadway –*
𝒞 020 7736 7588 – www.manukakitchen.com – Closed 24-26 December, Sunday dinner, Monday

⁑○ Tendido Cuatro   A/C 🍴

SPANISH · NEIGHBOURHOOD 🍴 Along with tapas, the speciality is paella. Designed for a hungry two, they vary from seafood to quail and chorizo; vegetarian to cuttlefish ink. Vivid colours used with abandon deck out the busy room.

Carte £25/50

Town plan 22 M8-x – *108-110 New Kings Road* ⊠ *SW6 4LY* ⊖ *Parsons Green –*
𝒞 020 7371 5147 – www.cambiodetercio.co.uk – Closed 23 December-2 January, Sunday dinner, Monday

Hammersmith

🕃 River Café (Ruth Rogers)   ⚗️ 🍴 ♿ 🕃

ITALIAN · MEDITERRANEAN 🍴🍴 Over thirty years since the River Café opened, the ethos here is still very much the same, with superlative ingredients at the centre of everything they do. The team seem like one big happy family and servers welcome you with genuine enthusiasm.

The menu is written anew for each service and bursts with authentic Italian flavours; there's a vigour and honesty to the cooking and dishes are made with top-class produce and come in hearty portions. Pasta is a must-have, as is the perennial Chocolate Nemesis; one bite of the latter and you'll understand why it never comes off the menu. This iconic restaurant's location on the banks of the Thames is as much part of the experience as the cooking – ask for a seat on the riverside terrace, or failing that, sit by the window.

Specialities: Chargrilled squid with fresh chilli and rocket. Wood-roasted turbot on the bone. Chocolate Nemesis.

Carte £68/95

Town plan 21 K7-c – *Thames Wharf, Rainville Road* ⊠ *W6 9HA* ⊖ *Barons Court –*
𝒞 020 7386 4200 – www.rivercafe.co.uk – Closed Sunday dinner

🕃 L' Amorosa   A/C

ITALIAN · NEIGHBOURHOOD 🍴🍴 Former Zafferano head chef Andy Needham has created a warm and sunny Italian restaurant – one that we'd all like to have in our high street. The quality of the produce shines through and homemade pasta dishes are a highlight.

Specialities: Burrata ravioli with lobster, chilli, garlic and olive oil. Ossobuco with saffron risotto and Amalfi lemon gremolata. Summer berries, natural yoghurt sorbet and Genovese basil sugar.

Carte £27/35

Town plan 21 K7-s – *278 King Street* ⊠ *W6 0SP* ⊖ *Ravenscourt Park –*
𝒞 020 8563 0300 – www.lamorosa.co.uk – Closed Sunday dinner, Monday, Tuesday - Saturday lunch

ⅰ○ Indian Zing   🏠 AC 🕐

INDIAN · NEIGHBOURHOOD XX Chef-owner Manoj Vasaikar seeks inspiration from across India. His cooking balances the traditional with the more contemporary and delivers many layers of flavour – the lamb dishes and breads are particularly good. The restaurant is always busy yet service remains courteous and unhurried.

Menu £19 (lunch) – Carte £23/39

Town plan 21 K7-a – 236 King Street ⊠ W6 0RF ⊖ Ravencourt Park –
☎ 020 8748 5959 – www.indian-zing.co.uk

ⅰ○ Anglesea Arms   🏠

MODERN BRITISH · PUB X One of the daddies of the gastropub movement. The seasonal menu gives the impression it's written by a Brit who occasionally holidays on the Med – along with robust dishes are some that display a pleasing lightness of touch.

Carte £24/36

Town plan 15 K6-e – 35 Wingate Road ⊠ W6 0UR ⊖ Ravenscourt Park –
☎ 020 8749 1291 – www.angleseaarmspub.co.uk – Closed 24-26 December

ⅰ○ Azou   AC

NORTH AFRICAN · NEIGHBOURHOOD X Silks, lanterns and rugs add to the atmosphere of this personally run, North African restaurant. Most come for the very filling tajines, served with triple steamed couscous. Many of the dishes are designed for sharing.

Carte £23/45

Town plan 21 J7-u – 375 King Street ⊠ W6 9NJ ⊖ Stamford Brook –
☎ 020 8563 7266 – www.azou.co.uk – Closed Sunday - Saturday lunch

Shepherd's Bush

🏵 Endo at The Rotunda   ⩽ AC

JAPANESE · DESIGN XXX The former BBC TV Centre on Wood Lane may be an unlikely setting for a Japanese restaurant but Yokohama-born Endo Kazutoshi has created a stylish and good-looking space on the top floor; the highlight of which is a beautiful counter fashioned from 200-year-old hinoki wood.

He was trained in Edomae techniques but has considerable international experience, so the nigiri is interspersed with dishes of a more modern composition. Ingredients are either imported from Japan, such as rice from Yamagata, or are the best the UK has to offer, like scallops from Orkney; he also uses fish caught by Japanese fishermen in Cornwall. The preparations are impressive and the flavours subtle and well-judged. Endo guides diners through the experience himself and explains each element of the omakase in an engaging and charming way.

Specialities: Yamadanishiki "kunkou" salmon nigiri. Miyazaki wagyu beef with Rokko miso. Rice soufflé.

Menu £60 (lunch), £150/180 – Carte £47/98

Town plan 15 K5-v – The Helios, 101 Wood Lane (8th Floor) ⊠ W12 7FR
⊖ Wood Lane – ☎ 020 3972 9000 – www.endoatrotunda.com – Closed Monday, Tuesday

ⅰ○ Shikumen   � & AC

CHINESE · INTIMATE XX Impressive homemade dim sum at lunch and excellent Peking duck are the standouts at this unexpectedly sleek Cantonese restaurant in an otherwise undistinguished part of Shepherd's Bush.

Carte £22/63

Town plan 15 K6-s – 58 Shepherd's Bush Green ⊠ W12 8QE ⊖ Shepherd's Bush –
☎ 020 8749 9978 – www.shikumen.co.uk

⅏○ Kricket

INDIAN · CONTEMPORARY DÉCOR X The third and largest of the Kricket clan is in the Television Centre development; the open kitchen with its long counter is its main feature and a good place to sit. Modern Indian small plates use traditional flavours in original combinations; must-tries are the breads, lamb raan and suckling pig shoulder vindaloo.

Carte £16/32

Town plan 15 K5-k – *2 Television Centre, 101 Wood Lane* ⊠ *W12 7FR*
⊖ *White City* – ℰ *020 3958 2867* – *www.kricket.co.uk* – *Closed Sunday dinner*

HARINGEY

Greater London

Crouch End

⅏○ Bistro Aix

FRENCH · BISTRO X Dressers, cabinets and contemporary artwork lend an authentic Gallic edge to this bustling bistro, a favourite with many of the locals. Traditionally prepared French classics are the highlights of an extensive menu.

Menu £20/25 – Carte £29/50

Town plan 3 E2-v – *54 Topsfield Parade, Tottenham Lane* ⊠ *N8 8PT*
⊖ *Crouch Hill* – ℰ *020 8340 6346* – *www.bistroaix.co.uk* – *Closed Monday - Friday lunch*

⅏○ Through the Woods

MODERN BRITISH · SIMPLE X There's no sign – just a logo; it's all about understatement and simplicity at this cute little spot. Dinner is served to everyone at 8pm so arrive on time. One owner sings and serves; the other cooks natural tasting, largely plant-based dishes using mostly organic produce, for the weekly changing menu.

Menu £45

Town plan 3 E2-r – *212 Middle Lane* ⊠ *N8 7LA* – *www.throughthewoods.london* – *Closed 1-8 January, Sunday-Wednesday, Thursday-Saturday lunch*

SOUTH-EAST Greater London

Top tips!

A jewel in the South-East's crown is Greenwich, home to the National Maritime Museum, the Meridian Line, the Royal Observatory and the beautifully restored 19th century ship, the Cutty Sark.

Head to the Greenwich Peninsula for fun and food; here you'll find the O2 Arena and the Emirates Air Line cable car as well as plenty of shops, cafés and restaurants. **Craft London** is a striking space featuring a coffee shop, cocktail bar and restaurant in one, while **Peninsula** offers great views across the river to go with its creative cooking.

Another vibrant area is the tree-lined South Bank, which buzzes with visitors enjoying al fresco coffee and outdoor performances of music and theatre, and is home to must-visit attraction, the London Eye. Head further south to Clapham for dinner at Michelin-Starred **Trinity** – or to Bib Gourmand awarded **Upstairs at Trinity** for a more relaxed meal from the same chef.

P. Prince/Loop Images /age fotostock

BROMLEY
Greater London

Farnborough

⫯○ Chapter One $\otimes \, \overline{\underline{\forall}} \quad \widehat{\pi} \, \& \, \underline{AC} \, i\!\heartsuit \, \Leftrightarrow \, \boxed{P}$

MODERN CUISINE · CLASSIC DÉCOR XxX This long-standing restaurant has many regulars; its wide-ranging menus offering keenly priced, carefully prepared modern European dishes. Cooking is light and delicate, mixing classic and modern flavours. The property dates from the 1930s and there are subtle references to this period in the elegant décor.

Menu £25 (lunch)/43

Town plan 8 G6-c - *Farnborough Common, Locksbottom* ⊠ *BR6 8NF* –
✆ *01689 854848* –
www.chapteronerestaurant.co.uk

GREENWICH
Greater London

⫯○ Peninsula $\leqslant \, \& \, \underline{AC} \, i\!\heartsuit \, \Im \, \Leftrightarrow \, \textstyle\textcircled{\small\Longleftrightarrow}$

MODERN CUISINE · ELEGANT XxX Don't be put off by its being in a somewhat corporate hotel – the floor-to-ceiling windows ensure great views across the river. The menu is also creative and ambitious, with the occasional Nordic touch; the dishes are skilfully executed and attractively presented.

Menu £35/75

Town plan 7 F4-p – *InterContinental London - The O2 Hotel (2nd floor),*
1 Waterview Drive, Greenwich Peninsula ⊠ *SE10 0TW*
⊖ *North Greenwich* – ✆ *020 8463 6913* –
www.iclondon-theo2.com – *Closed Sunday, Monday, Tuesday - Saturday lunch*

⫯○ Craft London $\overline{\underline{\forall}} \quad \& \, \underline{AC}$

MODERN BRITISH · DESIGN X Chef Stevie Parle has created a striking space beside the O2 that includes a coffee shop, a cocktail bar, and a restaurant championing seasonal British produce. They do their own curing and smoking, and roast their own coffee.

Carte £32/60

Town plan 7 F4-f – *Peninsula Square* ⊠ *SE10 0SQ*
⊖ *North Greenwich* – ✆ *020 8465 5910* –
www.craft-london.co.uk – *Closed 22 December-2 January, Sunday dinner, Monday, Tuesday, Wednesday lunch*

LAMBETH
Greater London

Brixton

⫯○ Kricket ⓝ $\boxed{\Xi} \, i\!\heartsuit$

INDIAN · RUSTIC X Originally a Brixton pop-up, Kricket has returned to a permanent site under two railway arches in the heart of the busy borough; don't be alarmed at the sound of the trains rumbling by overhead. Tasty, well-priced dishes take their influences from all over India, with deft spicing, pleasing textures and plenty of choice for vegetarians.

Carte £15/30

Town plan 25 S9-C – *41-43 Atlantic Road* ⊠ *SW9 8JL*
⊖ *Brixton* – ✆ *020 3826 4090* –
www.kricket.co.uk – *Closed Sunday dinner, Monday, Tuesday - Thursday lunch*

ⅈ○ Nanban [A/C]

JAPANESE · SIMPLE ⅹ A ramen-bar-cum-izakaya, tucked away at the back of Brixton Market and owned by former MasterChef winner, Tim Anderson. Food is fresh and full of flavour; the spicy, super-crispy chicken karaage will have you coming back for more.

Carte £ 21/35

Town plan 25 S9-n – *426 Coldharbour Lane* ✉ *SW9 8LF* ⊖ *Brixton –*
✆ *020 7346 0098 – www.nanban.co.uk – Closed Monday - Friday lunch*

ⅈ○ Naughty Piglets

MODERN BRITISH · NEIGHBOURHOOD ⅹ A friendly neighbourhood bistro with a basement wine bar, set away from the bustle of central Brixton; sit at the counter or one of the raised tables for the best atmosphere. Daily changing blackboard menus offer seasonal British small plates with global touches, and dishes are fresh, tasty and well-priced.

Carte £ 23/35

Town plan 7 E4-r – *28 Brixton Water Lane* ✉ *SW2 1PE* ⊖ *Brixton –*
✆ *020 7274 7796 – www.naughtypiglets.co.uk – Closed 22 December-2 January, Sunday, Monday - Thursday lunch*

Clapham Common

❀ Trinity (Adam Byatt)   ✿ 🎐 [A/C]

MODERN CUISINE · CHIC ⅹⅹ The joy of genuine neighbourhood restaurants is that customers tend to be treated less like numbers and chefs listen more to their opinions. This is certainly true at chef-owner Adam Byatt's Clapham restaurant, which has built its considerable reputation on giving locals exactly what they want.

The skilled kitchen wisely avoids reinventing the wheel. Dishes boast classic combinations and are refreshingly free from unnecessary decorative flourishes so that the focus remains firmly on the primary ingredient, whether that's roast cod served with a squid ink linguine or Bresse pigeon with rainbow chard. Don't miss the crispy pig's trotter with sauce Gribiche – and it's well worth pre-ordering the tarte Tatin with prune and Armagnac ice cream for two.

Specialities: Crispy pig's trotters with sauce gribiche and crackling. Wild turbot 'bonne femme' with morels and creamed ratte potatoes. Tarte Tatin with prune and Armagnac ice cream.

Menu £ 40 (lunch), £ 60/70

Town plan 24 Q9-a – *4 The Polygon* ✉ *SW4 0JG* ⊖ *Clapham Common –*
✆ *020 7622 1199 – www.trinityrestaurant.co.uk*

☺ Sorella   🍽 ♿ [A/C] 🍷 ⅈ○

ITALIAN · BISTRO ⅹ The cooking found in Italy's Amalfi region inspired this 'sister' to The Dairy. Expect a great buzz, fair prices and enthusiastic service. 4-5 sharing plates per couple should do it; be sure to include some pasta. Dishes may look simple but the kitchen infuses them with bags of flavour.

Specialities: Pappardelle with pork and 'nduja ragu. Veal fillet with cacio e pepe cocoa beans. Pump Street chocolate mousse.

Carte £ 25/39

Town plan 24 Q9-b – *148 Clapham Manor Street* ✉ *SW4 6BX*
⊖ *Clapham Common – ✆ 020 7720 4662 – www.sorellarestaurant.co.uk –*
Closed 21-29 December, Sunday dinner, Monday, Tuesday lunch

🏵 Upstairs (at Trinity)

MODERN BRITISH · CONTEMPORARY DÉCOR X The open-plan kitchen is the focus of this more relaxed room upstairs from Trinity. It's all about sharing the visually appealing, flavoursome and reasonably priced plates, which bring a hint of the Mediterranean with them.

Specialities: Barbecued purple sprouting broccoli with hazelnuts and bagna càuda. Cassoulet of octopus with white beans, crispy bread and fine herbs. Chocolate cremosa with salted caramel ice cream.

Carte £25/37

Town plan 24 Q9-a – *4 The Polygon* ✉ SW4 0JG
⊖ *Clapham Common* – ☎ *020 3745 7227* –
www.trinity-upstairs.co.uk – *Closed Sunday dinner, Monday, Tuesday lunch*

🏮 Bistro Union

MODERN BRITISH · NEIGHBOURHOOD X The little sister to Trinity is a classic neighbourhood restaurant with a rustic look, mirrored walls and friendly, relaxed atmosphere. Dishes have British, French and Italian influences and the menu is appealingly flexible, whether you're here for weekend brunch, a light lunch or a full dinner.

Carte £25/40

Town plan 7 E4-s – *40 Abbeville Road* ✉ SW4 9NG
⊖ *Clapham South* – ☎ *020 7042 6400* –
www.bistrounion.co.uk

🏮 Dairy

MODERN BRITISH · RUSTIC X The rustic, easy-to-eat food, which comes as small sharing plates, is driven by seasonality – some of the produce comes from their own farm. The higgledy-piggledy, homemade look of this fun, lively neighbourhood restaurant adds to its charm.

Menu £28 (lunch)/48 – Carte £32/47

Town plan 24 Q9-d – *15 The Pavement* ✉ SW4 0HY
⊖ *Clapham Common* – ☎ *020 7622 4165* –
www.the-dairy.co.uk – *Closed Sunday dinner, Monday*

Herne Hill

🏮 Llewelyn's

TRADITIONAL BRITISH · NEIGHBOURHOOD X A neighbourhood restaurant in a village-like location. Cooking is British with Mediterranean influences and dishes to share are a feature. Expect quality ingredients in hearty portions, with no unnecessary elaboration.

Carte £20/32

Town plan 7 E4-n – *293-295 Railton Road* ✉ SE24 0JP
⊖ *Herne Hill* – ☎ *020 7733 6676* –
www.llewelyns-restaurant.co.uk – *Closed 22 December-3 January, Sunday dinner, Monday*

Kennington

🏮 Kennington Tandoori

INDIAN · NEIGHBOURHOOD XX Kowsar Hoque runs this contemporary Indian restaurant with great pride and his eagerness and professionalism filters through to his staff. The food is prepared with equal care – try the seasonal specialities and the excellent breads.

Carte £20/34

Town plan 40 AS8-a – *313 Kennington Road* ✉ SE11 4QE
⊖ *Kennington* – ☎ *020 7735 9247* –
www.kenningtontandoori.com – *Closed Monday - Friday lunch*

Stockwell

⑪○ **Canton Arms**   🚫🍴 ⌂

TRADITIONAL BRITISH · **PUB** 🌂 An appreciative crowd of all ages come for the earthy, robust and seasonal British dishes which suit the relaxed environment of this pub so well. Staff are attentive and knowledgeable.

Carte £ 24/37

Town plan 24 R8-a – *177 South Lambeth Road* ⊠ *SW8 1XP* ⊖ *Stockwell.* – *⌀ 020 7582 8710* – *www.cantonarms.com* – *Closed 23 December-2 January, Sunday dinner, Monday lunch*

LEWISHAM

Greater London

Forest Hill

⑪○ **Babur**

INDIAN · **NEIGHBOURHOOD** 🌂🌂 Good looks and innovative cooking make this passionately run and long-established Indian restaurant stand out. Influences from the south and north west feature most and seafood is a highlight - look out for the 'Treasures of the Sea' menu.

Carte £ 35/45

Town plan 7 F4-s – *119 Brockley Rise* ⊠ *SE23 1JP* ⊖ *Honor Oak Park* – *⌀ 020 8291 2400* – *www.babur.info*

Lewisham

⑪○ **Sparrow**

MODERN BRITISH · **FRIENDLY** 🌂 A bright and buzzing neighbourhood spot whose name symbolises the culinary diversity of its globally influenced menus, as well as one of the owner's Sri Lankan heritage. Weekend brunches also offer an eclectic choice of dishes.

Carte £ 25/35

Town plan 7 F4-w – *2 Rennell Street* ⊠ *SE13 7HD* ⊖ *Lewisham* – *⌀ 020 8318 6941* – *www.sparrowlondon.co.uk* – *Closed 21 December-6 January, Sunday dinner, Monday, Tuesday lunch*

DATES & WALNUTS
100% wholemeal

£3.95

Vegan & sugar free.

PAIN DE CAMPAGNE
600g

TRADITIONAL FRENCH COUNTRY
BREAD, MIX OF RYE & WHITE

£2.95

Vegan, free from nuts & sugar

SOUTH-WEST Greater London

Top tips!

Some of the city's most charming locations can be found in the South-West, including riverside Chiswick, the Royal Botanic Gardens at Kew and villagey Richmond, with its vast Royal Park where deer roam. Stroll along the river and across meadows towards Petersham, before rewarding yourself with lunch at **Petersham Nurseries Café** or Michelin-Starred **Dysart Petersham**.

In addition to its vast common and its thriving village perched on a hilltop, Wimbledon takes great pride in its acclaimed tennis championship, which draws international stars every summer. Fittingly delicious eats are all around: try **Black Radish** for modern British food, inspired by the Parisian bistronomy movement; neighbourhood favourite **Light House** for wholesome Mediteranean dishes; or **White Onion** for classical French cooking in a relaxed bistro deluxe.

simonbradfield/iStock

HOUNSLOW
Greater London

Chiswick

⁣ La Trompette

MODERN BRITISH · NEIGHBOURHOOD ✗✗ It's easy to see why this neighbourhood restaurant has a loyal following: it has a grounded head chef who ensures the food is consistent, a well-chosen wine list and service that is as discreet as it is free of undue pomp. It is also a restaurant that seems happy in Chiswick and never gives the impression it would prefer to be in Mayfair; the locals repay the compliment by creating a warm, relaxed atmosphere.

The menu changes twice a day and there's little difference between the style of dishes served at lunch and dinner. The set price menu is balanced and appealing and, while the influences are varied, its heart is French with occasional nods to the Mediterranean. The dishes themselves are free of unnecessary adornment, so the focus remains on the top quality ingredients.

Specialities: Roast veal sweetbread with chestnut mushrooms and ricotta & spring green agnolotti. Grilled turbot with wild garlic spätzle, new season morels and peas. Rhubarb crumble soufflé with vanilla ice cream.

Menu £40 (lunch), £58/75

Town plan 21 J7-y – *3-7 Devonshire Road* ✉ *W4 2EU* ⊖ *Turnham Green –*
☎ 020 8747 1836 – www.latrompette.co.uk

⁣ Charlotte's W4

MODERN CUISINE · NEIGHBOURHOOD ✗✗ Sister to Charlotte's W5 in Ealing is this bright and unpretentious neighbourhood bistro, which is run by an enthusiastic young team and offers a menu of flavoursome, well-prepared dishes with European influences and a modern edge. The lunch and early evening menus offer good value for money.

Menu £17 (lunch), £30/35

Town plan 21 J7-a – *6 Turnham Green Terrace* ✉ *W4 1QP* ⊖ *Turnham Green –*
☎ 020 8742 3590 – www.charlottes.co.uk

⁣ Michael Nadra

MODERN CUISINE · NEIGHBOURHOOD ✗✗ Half way down a residential side street is this intimate little place where the closely set tables add to the bonhomie. Dishes are modern, colourful and quite elaborate in their make-up; it's worth going for the sensibly priced set menu and the chosen wines.

Menu £26/46 – Carte £38/46

Town plan 21 J7-z – *6-8 Elliott Road* ✉ *W4 1PE* ⊖ *Turnham Green –*
☎ 020 8742 0766 – www.restaurant-michaelnadra.co.uk – Closed 24-28 December, Monday

KINGSTON UPON THAMES
Greater London

Surbiton

⁣ The French Table

MEDITERRANEAN CUISINE · NEIGHBOURHOOD ✗✗ Husband and wife run this lively local: he cooks and she runs the show, assisted by her team of friendly staff. Expect zesty and satisfying French-Mediterranean cooking, as well as great bread, as they also run the bakery next door.

Menu £29 (lunch)/45

Town plan 6 C5-a – *85 Maple Road* ✉ *KT6 4AW* – *☎ 020 8399 2365 –*
www.thefrenchtable.co.uk – Closed 1-6 January, 21 August-7 September, Sunday, Monday

Wimbledon

🍴 **Black Radish**   A/C

MODERN BRITISH · DESIGN 🍴 A proudly and passionately run neighbourhood restaurant with a simple yet stylish Scandic-inspired look. The chef takes his inspiration from the modern Parisian bistronomy movement and his dishes show understanding and respect for each ingredient, offering harmonious flavours with a subtle twist.

Menu £44/49 – Carte £35/45

Town plan 6 D5-c – *28 The Ridgway* ✉ *SW19 4QW* ⊖ *Wimbledon –*
☏ 020 8617 3960 – www.blackradishsw19.com – Closed 1-11 August, Sunday, Monday, Tuesday - Friday lunch

🍴 **Light House**   ♿ A/C

MEDITERRANEAN CUISINE · NEIGHBOURHOOD 🍴 A neighbourhood favourite offering Mediterranean cooking in smart, comfortable surroundings. The food is wholesome and confident, with plenty of bold flavours; Italian dishes and puddings are the highlights and staff are calm and cheery.

Menu £25 – Carte £28/40

Town plan 6 D5-u – *75-77 Ridgway* ✉ *SW19 4ST* ⊖ *Wimbledon –*
☏ 020 8944 6338 – www.lighthousewimbledon.com – Closed Sunday dinner

🍴 **Takahashi**   A/C

JAPANESE · FRIENDLY 🍴 The eponymous chef-owner of this sweet spot is a Nobu alumnus and his wife runs the service with a personal touch. Mediterranean ingredients bring a creative edge to the pure, delicately flavoured dishes. Sushi and sashimi are a highlight.

Menu £36 (lunch), £38/120 – Carte £30/95

Town plan 6 D5-s – *228 Merton Road* ✉ *SW19 1EQ* ⊖ *South Wimbledon –*
☏ 020 8540 3041 – www.takahashi-restaurant.co.uk – Closed Monday, Tuesday, Wednesday - Friday lunch

🍴 **The White Onion**   ♿ A/C 🔄

MODERN CUISINE · BISTRO 🍴 A relaxed bistro deluxe with a handsome marble-topped bar and an attentive young team. Flavoursome classic French cooking has clever modern touches. Great value set lunch and a terrific selection of wine by the glass and carafe.

Menu £24 (lunch) – Carte £32/53

Town plan 6 D5-w – *67 High Street* ✉ *SW19 5EE* ⊖ *Wimbledon –*
☏ 020 8947 8278 – www.thewhiteonion.co.uk – Closed 27 July-13 August, 25 December-14 January, Sunday dinner, Monday, Tuesday - Thursday lunch

RICHMOND-UPON-THAMES

Greater London

Barnes

🍴 **Rick Stein**   🍷 ← 🏠

SEAFOOD · ELEGANT 🍴🍴 In a stunning spot beside the Thames; its glass extension offering the best views. Dishes from the celebrity chef's travels inform the menu, so expect Indonesian seafood curry alongside old favourites like cod and chips with mushy peas.

Menu £26 (lunch) – Carte £28/95

Town plan 21 J8-r – *Tideway Yard, 125 Mortlake High Street* ✉ *SW14 8SN –*
☏ 020 8878 9462 – www.rickstein.com

East Sheen

⅋○ **Victoria**   ⇔ ⌂ **P**

MODERN BRITISH · PUB ⅍ A proper local, with a lived-in feel, especially in the bars; if you're here to eat head for the conservatory, which overlooks a terrace. The appealing menu offers a good range of dishes and comes with a distinct Mediterranean slant, with Middle Eastern influences never far away.

Carte £25/41

Town plan 6 C4-h – *10 West Temple Sheen* ⊠ *SW14 7RT*
⊖ *Mortlake (Rail). –* ℘ *020 8876 4238 –*
www.victoriasheen.co.uk

Kew

⁕ **The Glasshouse**   ⅋⅋ **A/C**

MODERN CUISINE · ROMANTIC ⅍⅍ 2019 saw the 20th birthday of this very model of a modern neighbourhood restaurant. The quirkily-shaped room comes with textured walls and some vibrant artwork and, as the name implies, it's a bright spot, with floor-to-ceiling windows at the front. Tables may be rather formally laid but the service is undertaken by a team who are sociable and engaging and the atmosphere, thanks largely to the high number of locals who call this place their own, is never less than animated.

The kitchen concentrates on recognisable combinations and flavours that complement one another – ox cheek with mushrooms, rabbit with broad beans, hake with potted shrimps – and a strong sense of seasonality. A wonderful panna cotta with strawberries is the perfect example of what this place is all about.

Specialities: Scottish salmon sashimi with pickled rhubarb, ginger and crème fraîche. Sea bream with king prawn samosa, black rice, chilli, coriander and garlic. Warm chocolate croustade with milk ice cream and roasted nuts.

Menu £40 (lunch)/58

Town plan 6 C4-z – *14 Station Parade* ⊠ *TW9 3PZ*
⊖ *Kew Gardens –* ℘ *020 8940 6777 –*
www.glasshouserestaurant.co.uk – Closed Sunday dinner, Monday

Richmond

⁕ **Dysart Petersham**   ⌂ ⅋ ⅋⅋ ⇔ **P**

MODERN CUISINE · INTIMATE ⅍⅍ Built in the early 1900s as part of the Arts and Crafts movement, The Dysart is named after the family who once lived in Ham House. It's run as a restaurant rather than a pub, with service that is confident yet relaxed, and the warm, homely space blends its period features with more contemporary design elements. Tables are well-spaced but still leave room for an antique grand piano – this comes into its own at their regular music recitals.

Cooking has evolved in recent years and the Dysart now offers a classic, ingredient-led menu which features well-crafted dishes with bold flavours. You won't find any unnecessary gimmicks here; just good quality ingredients cooked with care and understanding. Fish is handled with particular aplomb and desserts are creative and satisfying.

Specialities: Charred mullet with radish, ginger and champagne. Longhorn beef with kombu braised Swiss chard, Belle de Fontenay potatoes and red wine jus. Valrhona chocolate & praline bar with cherries and raspberry sorbet.

Menu £30 – Carte £41/63

Town plan 6 C4-d – *135 Petersham Road* ⊠ *TW10 7AA –*
℘ *020 8940 8005 –*
www.thedysartpetersham.co.uk – Closed Sunday dinner, Monday, Tuesday, Wednesday

🍴○ Petersham Nurseries Café

MODERN CUISINE · RUSTIC X On a summer's day there can be few more delightful spots for lunch, whether that's on the terrace or in the greenhouse. The kitchen uses the freshest seasonal produce in unfussy, flavoursome dishes that have a subtle Italian accent.

Carte £40/65

Town plan 6 C4-k – *Church Lane (off Petersham Rd)* ✉ *TW10 7AG* –
☎ 020 8940 5230 – www.petershamnurseries.com –
Closed Sunday dinner, Monday, Tuesday - Saturday dinner

WANDSWORTH

Greater London

Battersea

🍴○ Hatched

MODERN BRITISH · NEIGHBOURHOOD X The large open kitchen is the focus of this relaxed and simply styled room. The ethos is about using quality ingredients, prepared with skill, and with the addition of some international flavours which reflect the chef-owner's travels. Gnocchi is a standout.

Carte £35/48

Town plan 23 N9-d – *189 St John's Hill* ✉ *SW11 1TH*
⊖ *Clapham Junction – ☎ 020 7738 0735 –*
www.hatchedsw11.com –
Closed Sunday dinner, Monday, Tuesday - Thursday lunch

🍴○ Nutbourne

MODERN BRITISH · NEIGHBOURHOOD X The 3rd restaurant from the Gladwin brothers; named after the family farm and vineyards in West Sussex. British produce drives the eclectic daily menu, with meats cooked on the open fire; dishes are hearty, wholesome and full of flavour.

Menu £42 – Carte £27/50

Town plan 23 P8-n – *Unit 29, Ransomes Dock, 35-37 Parkgate Road* ✉ *SW11 4NP* – *☎ 020 7350 0555 –*
www.nutbourne-restaurant.com –
Closed Monday

🍴○ Sinabro

MODERN CUISINE · NEIGHBOURHOOD X The main room feels almost kitchen-like, courtesy of a wall of stainless steel; sit at the wooden counter – made by the chef-owner's father. Confidently prepared dishes rely largely on classic French flavours but are modern in style.

Carte £35/49

Town plan 23 P9-r – *28 Battersea Rise* ✉ *SW11 1EE*
⊖ *Clapham Junction – ☎ 020 3302 3120 –*
www.sinabro.co.uk –
Closed 10-24 August, Sunday, Monday, Tuesday - Thursday lunch

🍴○ Soif

FRENCH · NEIGHBOURHOOD X A busy bistro-cum-wine-shop with a great atmosphere. The satisfying French food takes regular excursions across the border into Italy and the thoughtfully compiled wine list includes plenty of natural wines from artisan winemakers.

Carte £26/45

Town plan 23 P9-c – *27 Battersea Rise* ✉ *SW11 1HG*
⊖ *Clapham Junction – ☎ 020 7223 1112 –*
www.soif.co – Closed Monday - Wednesday lunch

Nine Elms

🍽 **Darby's**

MODERN BRITISH · **BRASSERIE** XX A stylish neighbourhood brasserie from Robin Gill – of The Dairy and Sorella fame – and named after his late father, an accomplished Irish-born jazz musician. The ingredient-led menu offers modern versions of the classics: expect oysters, homemade bread and charcuterie, and prime cuts of meat and fish.

Carte £35/52

Town plan 24 R7-f – *3 Viaduct Gardens* ✉ *SW11 7AY* ⊖ *Vauxhall* – ℰ *020 7537 3111* – *www.darbys-london.com* – *Closed Sunday - Monday dinner*

Wandsworth

❀ **Chez Bruce** (Bruce Poole)

FRENCH · **BRASSERIE** XX There are few restaurants that engender such loyalty from their regulars as Chez Bruce. Maybe that's because they get to enjoy top quality cooking without having to schlep up to the West End; or perhaps it's because they like to be surrounded by the same familiar faces every time they come here. Add in sprightly service and fair prices and you realise that the longevity of this restaurant is no accident.

The cooking of chef Matt Christmas, who has worked with owner Bruce Poole for over a decade, is all about flavour and balance; the plates are never overcrowded and ingredients are not required to fight for supremacy. The base is largely classical French but with a pronounced Mediterranean influence – this is a kitchen where things are done the traditional way.

Specialities: Fishcake with creamed Cornish mussels, quail eggs and samphire. Anjou pigeon with spiced pastilla, roast foie gras, bitter leaf stir-fry and pears. Apple croustade with vanilla ice cream and butterscotch sauce.

Menu £40 (lunch)/57

Town plan 6 D5-e – *2 Bellevue Road* ✉ *SW17 7EG* ⊖ *Tooting Bec* – ℰ *020 8672 0114* – *www.chezbruce.co.uk*

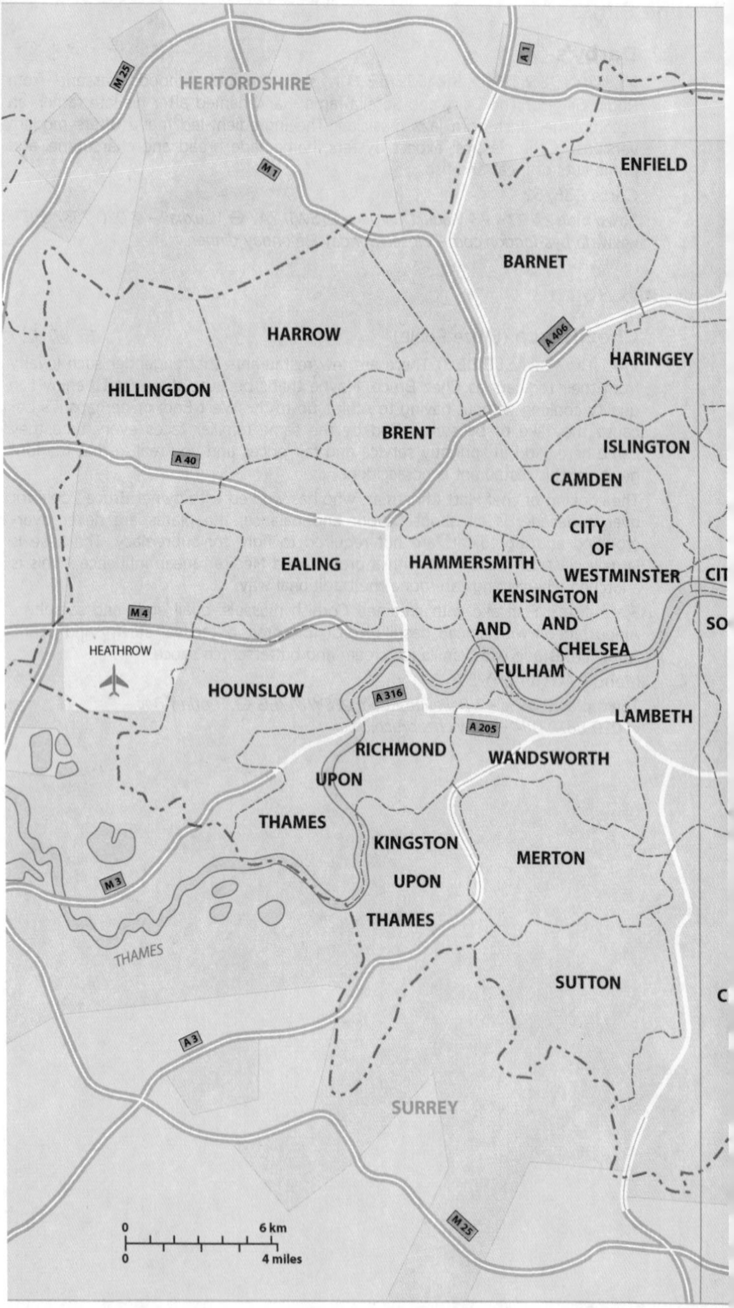
HERTORDSHIRE
M 25
M 1
A 1
ENFIELD
BARNET
HARROW
A 406
HARINGEY
HILLINGDON
BRENT
ISLINGTON
A 40
CAMDEN
CITY
OF
WESTMINSTER
EALING
HAMMERSMITH
KENSINGTON
AND
AND
CHELSEA
FULHAM
M 4
HEATHROW
HOUNSLOW
A 316
A 205
LAMBETH
RICHMOND
UPON
THAMES
WANDSWORTH
KINGSTON
UPON
THAMES
MERTON
M 3
THAMES
SUTTON
A 3
SURREY
M 25
0
6 km
0
4 miles

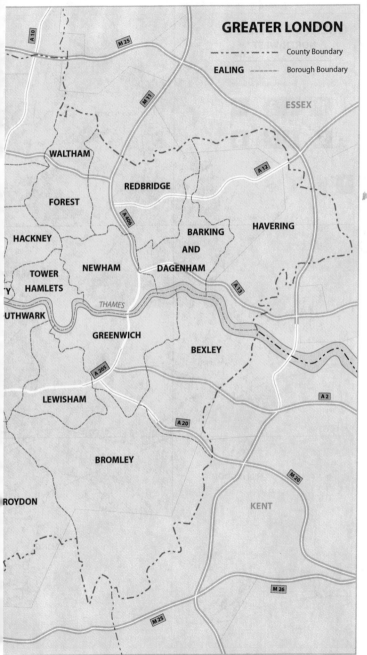

GREATER LONDON

EALING ----- Borough Boundary
-··-··-··- County Boundary

LONDON ENGALND

ESSEX

WALTHAM

REDBRIDGE

FOREST

HAVERING

HACKNEY

BARKING

AND

DAGENHAM

NEWHAM

TOWER
HAMLETS

Y

UTHWARK

THAMES

GREENWICH

BEXLEY

LEWISHAM

A 20

A 2

BROMLEY

M 20

ROYDON

KENT

M 26

M 25

161

GREATER LONDON
NORTH-WEST

0 — 3 km
0 — 2 miles

Greater London Boundary

| 1 | 2 | 3 | 4 |
| 5 | 6 | 7 | 8 |

1

Watford North

ALDENHAM COUNTRY PARK

Watford Junction Park

WATFORD

Bushey

Moor Park

BISHOP'S WOOD

Batchworth

Carpenders Park

Old Redding

Northwood

Hatch End

Uxbridge Rd

HARROW

Northwood Hills

PINNER PARK

Headstone Lane

Potter St

Pinner

Harrow and Wealdstone

North Harrow

Eastcote Rd

Harrow-on-the-Hill

West Ruislip

Eastcote Rd

Eastcote

Rayners Lane

West Harrow

HARROW PARK

Ruislip Manor

Ruislip

Ickenham

Ruislip Gardens

South Harrow

Sudbury Hill Harrow

Sudbury Hill

Hillingdon

South Ruislip

Western Av.

Northolt

HILLINGDON

Kingshill Av.

Ruislip Church Rd

Ruislip Rd

South Greenford

Perivale

Greenford

Western

EALING

Castle Bar Park

Drayton Green

West Ealing

Falling Lane

Uxbridge Rd the Broadway

Hanwell

West Drayton Station

Southall

Uxbridge Rd

Hayes and Harlington

Western Rd

Northfields

162

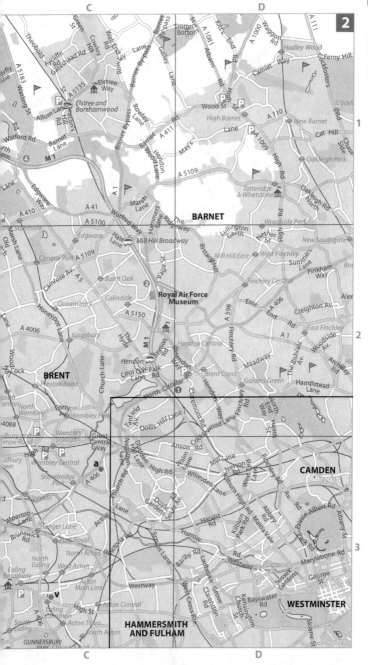

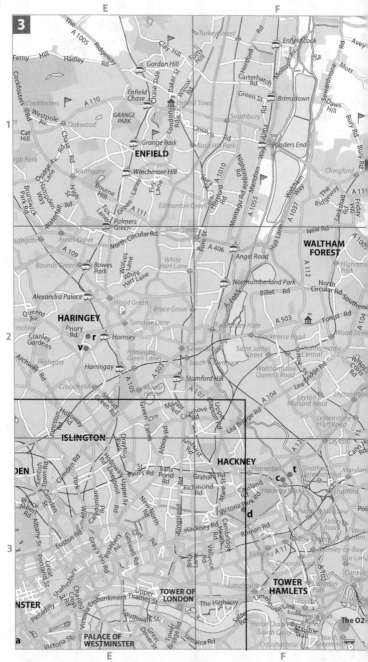

GREATER LONDON
NORTH-EAST

0   3 km
0   2 miles

Greater London Boundary

1   **2**   **3**   **4**
5   **6**   **7**   **8**

1

4

Honey Lane
Woodridden Hill
Coppice Row
Theydon Bois
Pynest Green Lane
Nursery Rd
Golding's Hill
Abridge Rd
St. Church Rd
Earl's Pth
GREAT MONK WOOD
London Rd
Hoe
A121
A1168
BUCKHURST HILL
Debden
A113
Gravel A1112
HAINAULT FOREST COUNTRY PARK
Bournebridge Lane
Oak Hill Rd
Epping New Rd
A1069
High Rd
Loughton
Oakwood Hill
M11
Chigwell
Pudding Lane
Manor
Rd
North Rd
Whitehall Rd
Palmerston Rd
Buckhurst
Vicarage
Romford Rd
Orange Tree Hill
Monkham's Lane
Roding Valley
A113
Chigwell Lane
Grange Hill
Grange Hill
Rd
Collier Row Rd
Chase Cross Rd
Havering
Woodford
A123
Manor
Hainault
A1112
Broadmead Rd
Chigwell Rd
Fairlop Forest
Rd
REDBRIDGE
HAVERING
W
A1400
Clayhall Av.
Tomswood Hill
Painters Rd
Billet Rd
Whalebone Lane North
West A125
Eastern Av. East
South Woodford
A113
Redbridge
Cranbrook Rd
Horns Rd
Barkingside
Eastern Av.
Chadwell Heath Lane
Eastern Av.
Mawney Rd
ROM
Wanstead
A12
Gants Hill
Newbury Park
Barley Lane
High
A118
London Rd
Crow Lane
Valley Way
Blake Hall Rd
A406
Cranbrook Rd
North
Seven Kings Rd
Goodmayes
Chadwell Heath
A124
Rd
Aldersbrook
Ilford
Ley High
A1083
Bennett's Castle Lane
Valence Av.
Woolley Lane
A1112
WANSTEAD FLATS PARK
Manor Park
A123
Loxford Lane
Wanstead
Green Lane
BARKING AND DAGENHAM
Dagenham East
Forest Gate
Woodgrange Park
A124
Becontree
Dagenham Heathway
Rainham Rd
A118
Plashet Rd
Plashet Grove
East Ham
Upton
Lodge
Av.
A1240
B178 A1112
Upton Park
River
A123
Way
Ripple Rd
New
Dagenham Dock
Cherry Tree Rd
NEWHAM
A117
Alfred's Way
Bastable Av.
Choats
Rd
Choats Manor Way
Prince Regent Lane
A13
Newham Way
Beckton
Royal Docks Rd
River
Rd
A2016 Way
Tollgate Rd
Custom House
Prince Regent
Royal Albert
Beckton Park
Gallions Reach
THAMES
Renwick
Cross
A2016
West Silvertown
Cyprus
LONDON CITY AIRPORT
Bentham
A2041
Pontoon Dock
London City Airport
King George V
A2016 Way

165

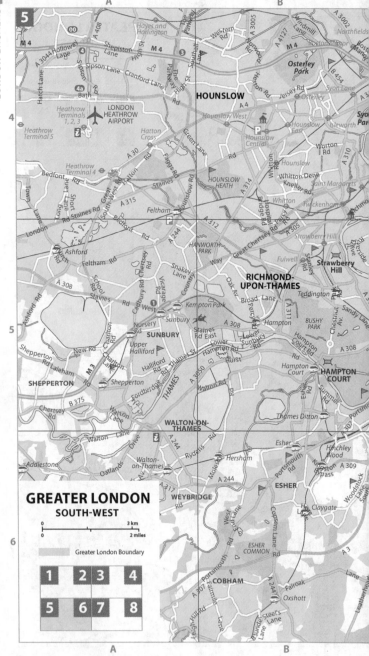

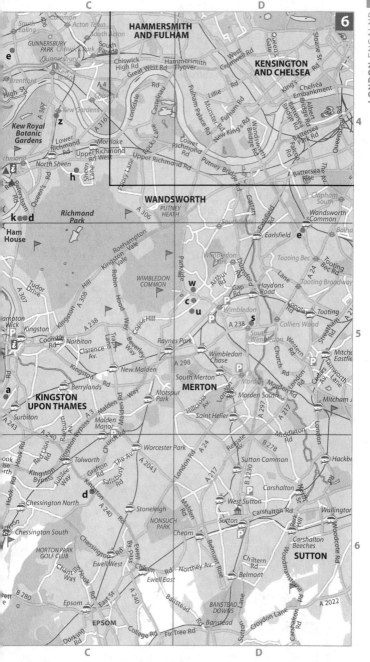

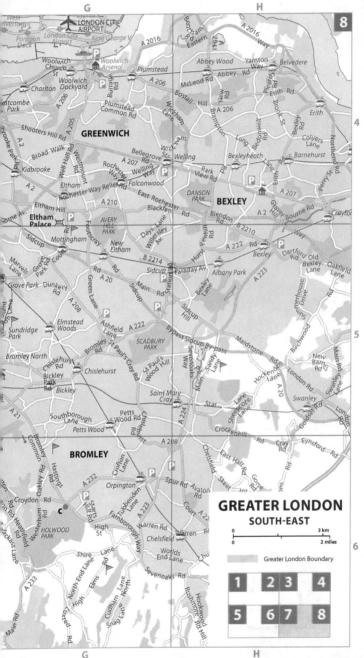

GREATER LONDON
SOUTH-EAST

| 0 | | | | 3 km |
| 0 | | | 2 miles | |

Greater London Boundary

1	2	3	4
5	6	7	8

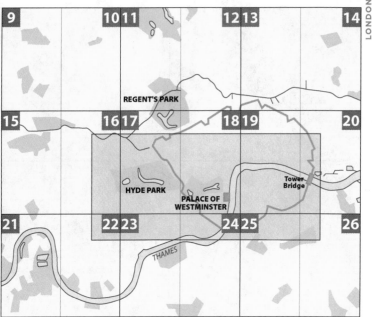

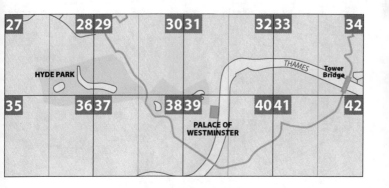

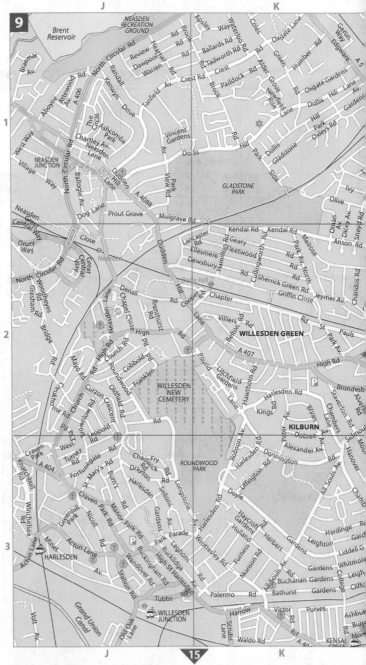

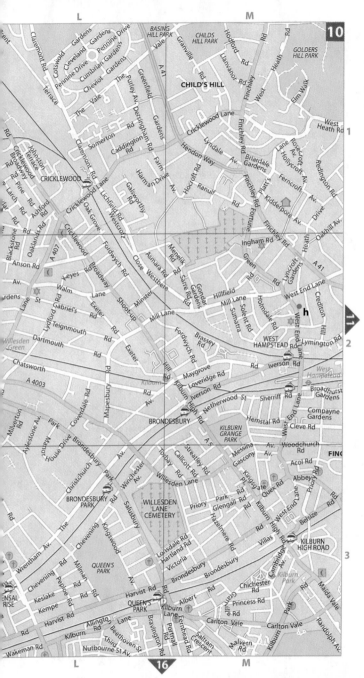

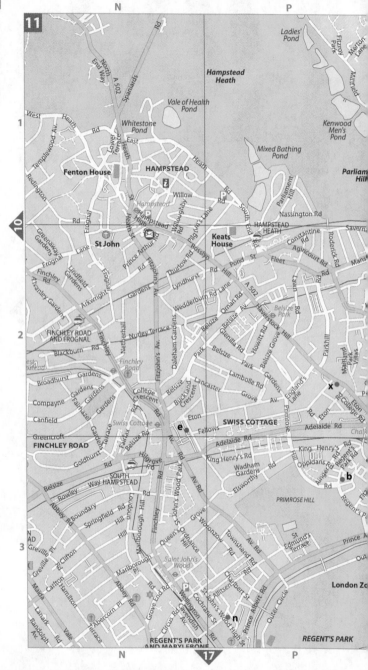

Ladies' Pond

Fitzroy Park

Merton Lane

Mitfield

Hampstead Heath

North End Way

Spaniards Rd

A 502

Vale of Health Pond

Kenwood Men's Pond

1

West Heath

Whitestone Pond

Heath

Templewood Av.

Lower Terrace

East Heath Rd

Mixed Bathing Pond

Parliam Hill

Redington Rd

Fenton House

HAMPSTEAD

Heath

Greenaway Gardens

St

Hampstead High St

Willow

Lower Terrace

10

Rd

Hampstead High St

Willoughby Rd

Pilgrim's Lane

South End Rd

Parliament Hill

Nassington Rd

Savern

Lindfield Gardens

Frognal

St John

Lane

Prince Arthur Rd

Thurlow Rd

Rosslyn Hill

Keats House

HAMPSTEAD HEATH

Pond St

Constantine Rd

Agincourt Rd

Roderick Rd

Finchley Gardens

Arkwright Rd

Frognal Gardens

Fitzjohns Av.

Lyndhurst Rd

Hill

A 502

Fleet

Lawn Rd

Mans

Ranstey Gardens

FINCHLEY ROAD AND FROGNAL

Netherhall

Nutley Terrace

Gardens

Wedderburn Rd

Lane

Ornan Rd

Haverstock Hill

Belsize Park

2

Blackburn Rd

Finchley Rd

Daleham Gardens

Belsize

Av.

Howitt Rd

Glenilla Rd

Belsize Grove

Parkhill

Park Villas

esh stead

Broadhurst Gardens

Gardens

Finchley Road

Belsize

Park

Belsize

Park

Gardens

Lambolle Rd

England's

Lane

Compayne Gardens

Fairhazel Gardens

Gardens

College Crescent

Belsize

Buckland Crescent

Lancaster

Grove

Av.

x

Eton College

Pe

Canfield

Swiss Cottage

Eton

Primrose Rd

Eton

Adelaide Rd

Chal

Greencroft

FINCHLEY ROAD

Fairfax Rd

Belsize Rd

e

Fellows

SWISS COTTAGE

Rd

Rd

Goldhurst

Rd

Hilgrove Rd

Adelaide Rd

King Henry's

Rd

King Henry's Rd

Regent's Park Rd

Belsize

Rowley

SOUTH HAMPSTEAD

Way

Rd

King Henry's Rd

Wadham Gardens

Oppidans Rd

Ainger

Rd

b

Regent's P

Abbey Rd

Boundary Rd

Springfield Rd

Loudoun Hill

Elsworthy

Rd

PRIMROSE HILL

Regent's P

3

N AD

Greville Pl.

Clifton Hill

Hamilton

Marlborough Hill

Queen's Grove

Ordnance Hill

Wotonzow Rd

Townshend Rd

St Edmund's Terrace

Prince A

Out

Carlton

Marshx

Abbey Rd

Marlborough Pl.

Saint John's Wood

Grove End Rd

Wellington Rd

Allitsen Rd

Cochrane St

St John's Wood High St

Prince Albert Rd

Outer Circle

London Zo

Lanark Rd

Randolph Av.

Vale

Abercorn Pl.

Circus Rd

Cavendish

n

Prince Albert Rd

REGENT'S PARK

12

Q R

Highgate

Oakeshott Av.
Makepeace Av.
Langbourne Av.

Hillwich
Swains Lane

Highgate Lane

Highgate Hill
Archway Rd

Magdala Av.
Anatola Rd
Bredgar Rd
Hargrave Park
Bickerton Rd

Archway

Hargrave Rd
Holloway Rd
Elthorne Rd
St. John's Villas
Fairbridge

St. John's Way
Hatchard Rd
Cornwallis Rd
Bavaria Rd
Mitford Rd
Sussex

Hornsey
Hanley Rd
Colbyn
Thorpedale
Way Crescent

UPPER
HOLLOWAY

WHITTINGTON
PARK

A 1
Kingsdown
Alexander Rd
Tollington
Way
Windsor Rd
Manor Gardens

1

DARTMOUTH
PARK

St. Alban's
Crofdown
Woodsome Rd
Laurier Rd
York Rd

Highgate Rd
Dartmouth Park Rd
Chetwynde Rd
Spencer Rise

Junction Rd

Station Rd

Foxham Rd
Tytherton Rd

Mercers Rd

Tufnell Park Rd

St. George's Av.

Tufnell Park Rd
Tabley
Corbyn
Dalmeny Rd

Holloway Rd

Pakhurst Rd

Camden
Penn Rd
Hillmarton Rd
Sturmer

GOSPEL
OAK

Gordon House Rd

ble St.

Lady Somerset Rd

Burghley
Fortess
Countess Rd
Montpelier Grove
Anson
Bickuock
Leighton Grove
Carleton Rd

Hilldrop Rd
Crescent
Camden
Brecknock Rd
Hungerford Rd

Beatson Rd
Hartham Rd

Tufnell Park

KENTISH
TOWN

Leighton Rd
Islip St

Torriano Av.

Camden Mews

North

Caledonian Road

CALEDONIAN
PARK

Caledonian Rd

A 52U3

2

Grafton
Crescent
Weeding Rd
Regis Rd
Holmes Rd

Leighton
Caversham Rd
Galsford St
Patshull Rd
Lawford Rd
Bartholomew Rd
Rochester Rd
Rochester Pl.
Royal St

Bartholomew

Camden Rd

A 503

Camden Park Rd

Murray Mews
St. Augustine's Rd

Brewery

York Way
Blundell St

Market

Rd

KENTISH TOWN
WEST

Prince of Wales
Harmood
Castlehaven Rd

Ferdinand St
Chalk Farm Rd
Hartland Rd
Hawley Rd
Kentish

College

Agar

Grove

Tileyard Rd

Brandury Way

m

Jamestown Rd
Kentish Town Rd
Bayham St
Georgiana St
Pratt St

CAMDEN
ROAD

Barker Drive

Freight Lane
York Way

Copenhagen St
Bingfield St

Camley St
Carnouside Drive

3

CAMDEN
TOWN

Parkway
Albert St
Camden High St
Bayham St
Plender St
College Pl.

Delancey St

s

Gloucester
Gate

St Katharine's
Church

Cumberland
Terrace

TERRACES

Park

Albany St
Mornington Crescent
Eversholt St

Camden
Crowndale Rd
Charrington St
Chalton St
Pancras Rd

Way

Handyside St

f
v h

London Canal
Museum

Goods Way

King's
Cross

Wharfdale Rd

Caledonian Rd
Catshot
Pentonville Rd

REGENT'S
PARK

East

Barnby St
Wellington St

St Pancras

d

York Way

Q 18 R

175

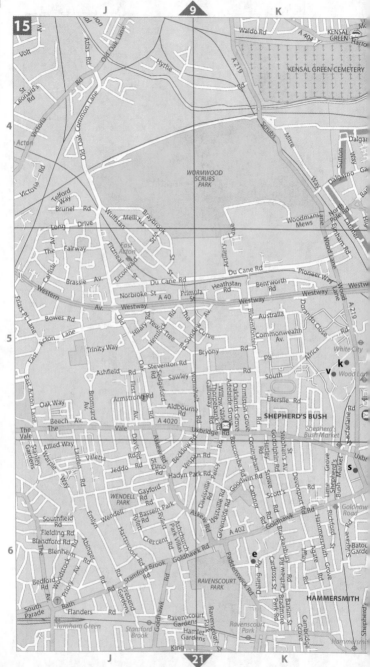

J　　　　　　　　　　K

Waldo Rd　　A 404　　KENSAL
GREEN　　Harro　　Mc

KENSAL GREEN CEMETERY

Volt.

St
Leonard's
Rd

Atlas Rd

Old Oak Common Lane

Hythe

A 219

Rd

Scrubs

Mitre

Dalgar

4

Acton

Victoria　Rd

Victoria

Telford
Way

Brunel　Rd

Wulfstan

Mellitus

Braybrook

WORMWOOD
SCRUBS
PARK

North
Pole

Way

Dalgarno Ga

Bas

Dalgarno

Long　Drive

Fairway

The

Carlisle

Brassie　Av.

Friars Pl Lane

Fitzneal

East
Acton
Way

Elcom　St

St

St

Du Cane Rd

Norbroke St
A 40

Heathstan
Rd

Primula

Pioneer Way

Wood

Westw

Woodmansi
Mews

Artillery

Lane

Elpham Rd

Lane

Lane

Bentworth
Rd

Westway

Westway

A 219

Westw

Western

Av.

Bowes Rd

East　Acton　Lane

Westway

Old

Hilary
Rd

Yew
Tree

Hemlock Tree

Rd

The
Curve

Subway

Bloemfontein

Australia
Rd

Commonwealth
Av.

Dorando Close

Rd

Africa

White City

5

Trinity Way

Ashfield　Rd

Oak

Steventon Rd

Sedgeford

Sawley

Bryony

South

Rd

Rd

Ph

k

v

Wood Lan

Oak Way

First

Bromyard

Armstrong Rd

Wormholt

Galloway

Willow Vale

Thorpebank

Oaklands Grove
Adelaide Grove

Ormiston Grove

Ellerslie　Rd

SHEPHERD'S BUSH

Shepherd's
Bush Market

Macfarlane

Beech　Av.

The
Vale

The
Vale

Davis St

Aldbourne
Rd

A 4020

Alkew Rd

Uxbridge　Rd

Boscombe Rd

Coningham

Stephen's Av.

Goldhurst Rd

Hetley

Stowe

Rd

Rd

Grove

Shepherd's Bush Market

Uxbr

Allied Way

Stanley
Gardens

Marple
Way

Lidden Rd

Valetta

Jeddo

Rd

St
Elmo

Beckllow

Vespan Rd

Hadyn Park Rd

Goodwin Rd

Scott's

Devonport

Rd

Rd

s

Southfield
Rd

Fielding Rd

Blandford Rd

The
Blenheim

Emlyn

Wendell

Gayford
Rd

Bassein Park

Ryfold

Ryfold

Crescent

Davisville Rd

Westville Rd

Greenside Rd

Askew　Rd

Goldhawk Rd

Coningham

Brackenbury

Goldhawk　Rd

A 402

Hammersmith Grove

Banim St

Cardross St

Bradmore

Park Rd

Richford

Goldhaw
Road

Batou
Garde

Agate Rd

Tig

6

Bedford
Rd

Woodstock

Bath

South
Parade

Flanders

Priory

Abinger

Stamford Brook

Prebend
Gardens

Goldhawk　Rd

Paddenswick Rd

e

Dalling

Rd

RAVENSCOURT
PARK

HAMMERSMITH

Turnham Green

Stamford
Brook

Raven scourt
Gardens

Ravenscourt
Rd

Ravens court St

Hamlet
Gardens

King

Ravenscourt
Park

Cambridge
Grove

Hammersm

Shepher

REGENT'S PARK AND MARYLEBONE

REGENT'S PARK

Maida Vale

Lanark Rd

Ashworth Rd

Elgin Av.

Hamilton

Maida Vale

Randolph Av.

Lauderdale Rd

Sutherland Av.

Warrington Crescent

Randolph Crescent

Clifton

Maida Vale

Vale

Warwick Av.

Warwick Avenue

Delamere Terrace

Blomfield

Maida

canal

TER AND A VALE

Harrow Rd

Westway

Gloucester Terrace

Porchester Terrace

Eastbourne

Inverness Terrace

Queensway

Porchester Terrace

Queensborough Terrace

Inverness Terrace

Leinster Gardens

Leinster Terrace

Craven Hill

Bayswater Rd

Lancaster Gate

Kensington Gardens

Orangery

Round Pond

Kensington Palace

Palace Av.

De Vere Gardens

Queen's Gate Terrace

Elvaston Pl.

Cornwall Gardens

Gloucester Rd

Palace Gate

Kensington Rd

Queen's Gate

Serpentine Gallery

Albert Memorial

Royal Albert Hall

Exhibition Rd

SCIENCE MUSEUM

Natural History Museum

Cromwell Rd

Gloucester Road

Harrington Rd

John's Wood Rd

Lodge Rd

Lisson Grove

Regent's Canal

Park Rd

Hanover Terrace

Baker

Outer Circle

TERRACES

Hanover Terrace

The Holme

Boating Lake

QUEEN MARY GARDENS

Sussex Place

Regent's College

Nottingham Terrace

Cornwall Terrace

Madame Tussaud

Circle Rd

Ivor Pl.

Rossmore Rd

Lilestone

Salisbury

Frampton

Penfold

Orchardson St

Edgware Rd

John Aird Court

Westway

North Wharf Rd

South Wharf Rd

Marylebone Flyover

Chapel St

Edgware Road

Church St

Broadley

Bell

Lisson Grove

Conway St

MARYLEBONE

Ivor Pl.

Baker Street

S •

York St

Crawford

Montagu

Dorset St

Paddington

Blandford

REGENT'S PARK AND MARYLEBONE

WALLACE COLLECTION

Gloucester Terrace

Bishop's Bridge Rd

Praed St

St Michael's St

Sussex Gardens

Bathurst

Hyde Park Gardens

Bayswater Rd

Sussex Mews

Chilworth

Craven Rd

London St

Edgware Rd

Connaught St

Upper Berkeley St

Hyde Park St

Upper Berkeley St

Portma

Marble Arch

Oxford St

North Row

Green St

Upper Brook St

Upper Grosven

Park

Lane

Park

Hyde Park

Carriage Drive

North Carriage Drive

The Long Water

Carriage

The Serpentine

Serpentine Rd

Serpentine Rd

West

HYDE PARK AND KNIGHTSBRIDGE

Hyde Pa Corne

South Carriage Drive

South Carriage Drive

Kensington Rd

Knightsbridge

Knightsbridge

Wilton Crescent

Harriet Walk

Sloane St

BELGRAVIA

VICTORIA AND ALBERT MUSEUM

Brompton Rd

Beauchamp Pl.

Hans Rd

Pont St

Cadogan

Lyall St

Eaton Mews

Thurloe Pl.

Brompton Rd

Walton

South Kensington

Pelham St

Thurloe Pl.

Harrington Rd

CHELSEA

Cabon Mews

Cadogan Lane

Pavillion Rd

Sloane St

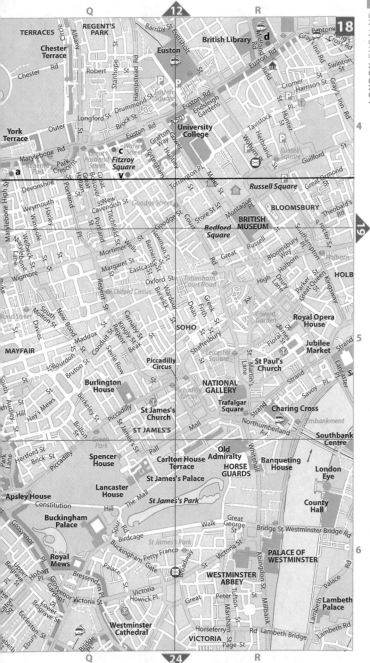

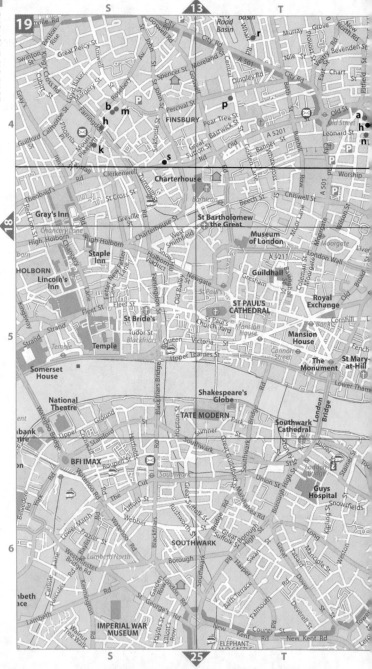

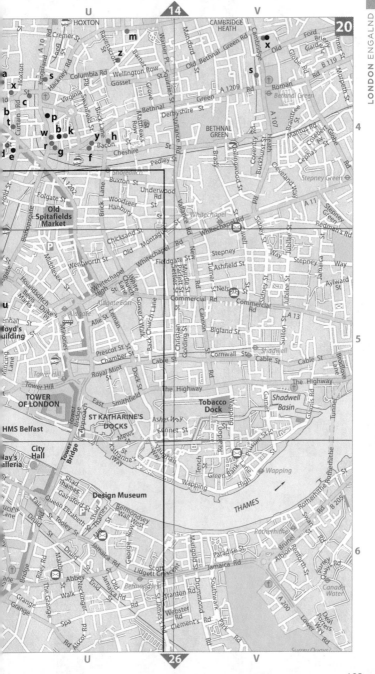

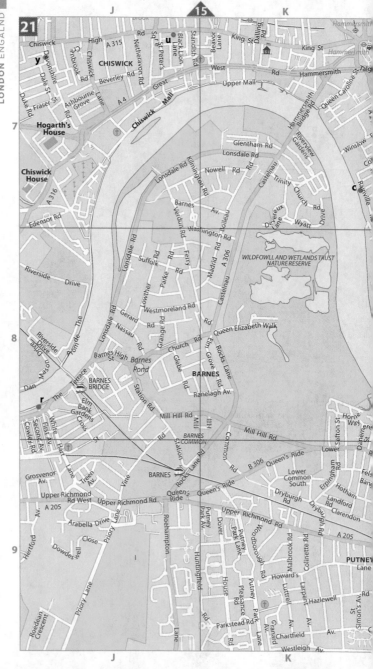

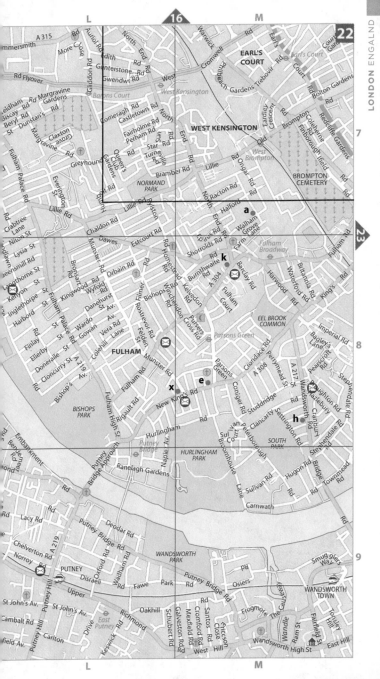

23

17

P

N

CHELSEA

Harrington Rd

Kensington

Pelham St

SOUTH KENSINGTON

Michelin House

Sloane

Draycott Av.

Cadogan St

Cadogan Gdns

Sloane Square

Sloane St

Holbein Pl.

Lower Sloane St

Draycott Pl.

Harrington Gardens

Wetherby Gardens

Gloucester Rd

P

Old Brompton Rd

Cranley Gardens

Onslow Gardens

Sydney St

Dovehouse St

Sumner Pl.

St

Sloane

King's Rd

Royal Av.

Pimlico

Cresswell Gardens

The Boltons

Tregunter Rd

Redcliffe Gardens

Gilston Rd

Cresswell Gardens

Evelyn Gardens

Drayton Gardens

Manresa Rd

Old Church St

Chelsea Manor St

Oakley St

Flood St

Smith St

St Luke

Royal Hospital

National Army Museum

7

Finborough Rd

Ifield Rd

Fulham Rd

Beaufort St

Elm Park Rd

Fulham Park Rd

Redcliffe Gardens

Church St

King's Rd

Cheyne Walk

The St

Cheyne

Embankment

Queen's House

x

m

Gunter Grove

Edith Grove

King's Rd

Hortensia Rd

Tadema Rd

Cheyne Walk

Chelsea

Albert

Bridge

22

P

Fulham Rd

Lots Rd

Burnaby St

Cremorne Rd

Battersea

Church Rd

Hester Rd

Parkgate Rd

Worfield St

n

Carriage Drive North

Carriage Drive Nor

Carriage Drive West

Battersea Park Lake

Carriage Drive

Imperial Rd

Bagley's Lane

Stephendale Rd

IMPERIAL WHARF

Gwynne Rd

Vicarage Crescent

Battersea High St

B 305

Bridge Lane

Surrey Lane

Petworth St

Prince of Wales Drive

Prince

of

Wales

Brynmaor Rd

Warriner Gardens

Batte

8

Lombard Rd

Bridges Court Rd

York Rd

York Rd

Falcon Rd

Shuttleworth Rd

Abercrombie St

BATTERSEA

A 3205

Burns Rd

Reform St

Dagnall St

Sheepcote Lane

Culvert Rd

Rowditch Lane

Eversleigh Rd

Tyneham Rd

Townmead

William Morris Way

YORK GARDENS

Ingrave St

Este Rd

A 3220

Ashbury Rd

Kingsley St

Morrison St

Sabine Rd

Elsley Rd

Gideon Rd

Shelgate Rd

Wynter St

Maysoule Rd

Daphne St

Thomas Baines Rd

Grant Rd

Falcon Lane

A 3036

Lavender

Sisters Av.

Mysore Rd

Thirsk Rd

Elspeth Rd

Stormont Rd

Forthbridge Rd

Eland Rd

Gowrie Rd

St John's Hill

Bridgend

York Rd

Nantes Close

St John's Hill

Spencer Rd

Strathblaine Rd

Bolingbroke Grove

Comyn Rd

A 3

Beauchamp Rd

Carmsa Crescent

Eccles Rd

Webb's Rd

r

c

Clapham Common

9

RTH

Alma Rd

Fulton Rd

Dempster Rd

Trinity Rd

St John's Hill Grove

Harbut Rd

Marcilly Rd

d

North Side Wandsworth Common

SPENCER PARK

Chivalry Rd

Northcote Rd

Mallinson Rd

Bennerley Rd

Salcott Rd

Wakehurst Rd

Belleville Rd

Clapham Common West Side

Grandison Rd

Cairns Rd

The

Av.

N

P

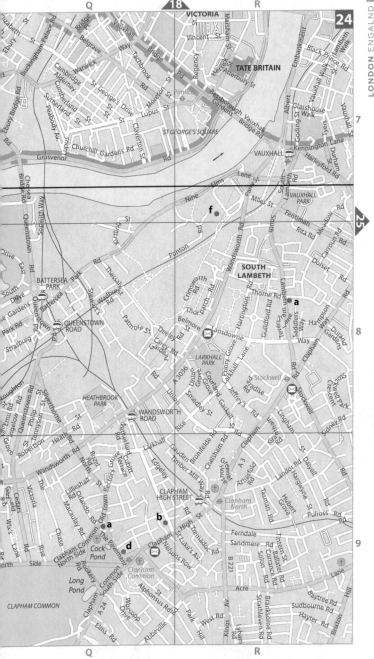

MUSEUM

19

ELEPHANT AND CASTLE

New Kent Rd

WALWORTH

KENNINGTON

THE OVAL
Kennington Oval
Oval

KENNINGTON PARK

CAMBERWELL

Camberwell Green

CAMBERWELL

MOSTYN GARDENS

MYATTS FIELD

Camberwell Station Rd

DENMARK HILL

LOUGHBOROUGH JUNCTION

RUSKIN PARK

BRIXTON

n C

A 2217

A 23

A 202

A 215

A 216

20

Surrey Quays

SOUTH BERMONDSEY

7

8

QUEENS ROAD
PECKHAM

EAST DULWICH

PECKHAM
RYE

NUNHEAD

NUNHEAD
CEMETERY

9

PECKHAM
RYE PARK

U

V

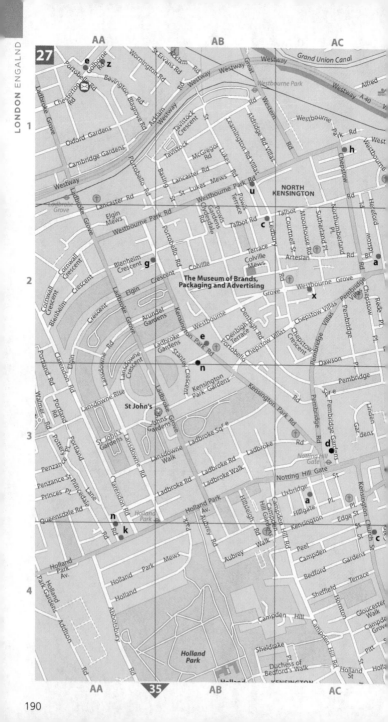

AG AH AJ

29

Church St · Edgware St · Penfold Pl · Lisson St · Bell St · Cosway St
Marylebone Rd · Bickenhall St
Westway · Harrow · Edgware Road · Marylebone · Flyover · Harcourt St · Homer St · York St · Knox St · Upper Montagu St · Gloucester Pl · York St · Crawford St · Dorset St
North Wharf · Harbet Rd
North Wharf Rd · Praed St · Chapel St · Old Marylebone Rd · Crawford St
Shouldham St · Seymour Pl · Montagu Pl · Gloucester Pl · Montagu St
REGENT'S PARK AND MARYLEBONE
South Wharf Rd · Winsland St · St Michael's St · Sussex Gardens · Norfolk Pl · Molyneux St · *Bryanston Square* · *Montagu Square*
Praed St · Star St · Norfolk Pl · Norfolk Crescent · Edgware Rd · Harrowby St · Nutford Pl · George St · Seymour St · Bryanston Mews West · Great Cumberland Pl · Montagu St · Gloucester
London St · Sussex Gardens · Sussex Gardens · Southwick St · Radnor Pl · Park West Pl · Edgware Rd · Upper Berkeley St
2
Bathurst Mews · Sussex Gardens · Radnor Mews · *GLOUCESTER SQUARE* · Hyde Park St · Connaught St · Kendal St · George's Fields · Seymour St · Edgware Rd · Seymour St · Bryanston St · *Marble Arch*
Strathearn Pl · *SUSSEX SQUARE* · Hyde Park Gardens Mews · Clarendon Pl · Albion St · Connaught Pl · Oxford St
Westbourne St · Stanhope Terrace · Brook St · *HYDE PARK GARDENS* · Hyde Park St · Bayswater Rd · Oxford St
Bayswater Rd · North Carriage Drive · Park Lane
North Carriage Drive **The Ring**

Fountain Garden
West Carriage Drive
3
Hyde Park

Park Lane

The Long Water
Serpentine Sackler Gallery
West Carriage Drive
Serpentine Rd · Serpentine Rd
The Serpentine
4
Serpentine Gallery
Princess Diana Memorial Fountain

HYDE PARK AND KNIGHTSBRIDGE
South

AG **37** AH AJ

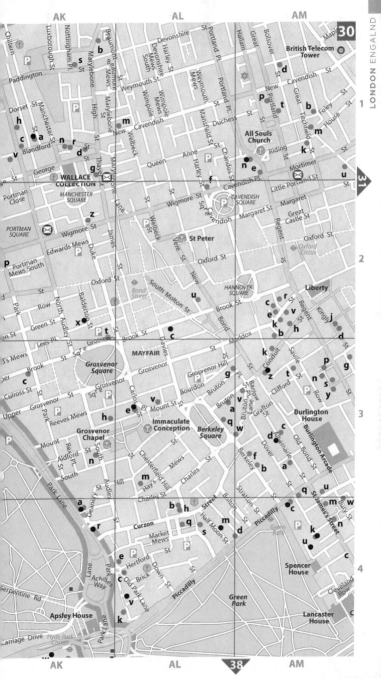

AN AP AQ

30

Russell Square
BLOOMSBURY
BRITISH MUSEUM
Bloomsbury Square Gardens
St George
Bedford Square
Goodge Street
Tottenham Court Road
Soho Square
St Giles-in-the-Fields
High Holborn
Oxford St
Eastcastle
SOHO
St Anne's
Covent Garden
Royal Opera House
Covent Garden Market
London Transport Museum
Jubilee Market
St Paul's Church
Golden Square
Leicester Square
London Coliseum
Piccadilly Circus
Piccadilly
St James's Church
ST JAMES'S
National Portrait Gallery
NATIONAL GALLERY
Theatre Royal
St Martin in the Fields
Trafalgar Square
Charing Cross
Victoria Embankment Gardens
St James's Square
Institute of Contemporary Art
Old Admiralty
Waterloo Place
Carlton House Terrace
Queen's Chapel
HORSE GUARDS
Banqueting House
St James's Palace
Clarence House
St James's Park
Horse Guards Parade
Nº 10 Downing Street
Richmond Terrace
THAMES

AN 39 AP AQ

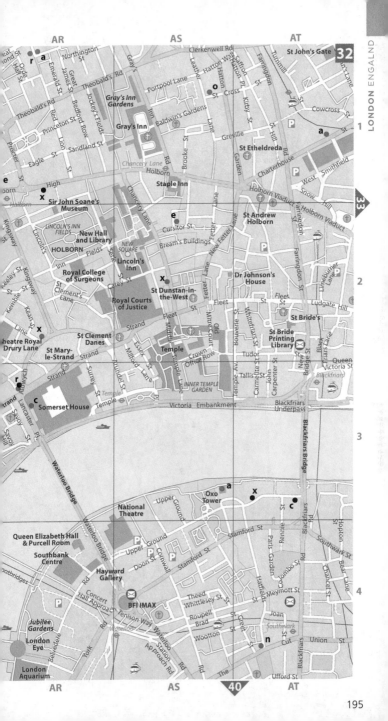

AU AV AW

c
Charterhouse
Fann St
Golden Lane
Chiswell St
Bunhill Row
BUNHILL FIELDS
Christ
Wilson
P

k
Charterhouse St
Lindsey St
Beech St
Silk St
Milton
Lane
Ropemaker St
Finsbury St
A 501
Lackington St
Wilson
Barbican
Art Center
P
Barbican
Lane
Aldersgate
New
Union St
Moor
Moorgate
v
South Pl
Eldon
FINSBURY
CIRCUS

West
Smithfield
z
St Bartholomew
the Great
Long Lane
West
Smithfield
Hosier
Lane
Little Britain
Montague St
Museum
of London
Fore St
London Wall
A 1211
London Wall
London

Newgate St
Glittspur
Little
Britain
Angel
St
St Paul's
Noble St
Gresham St
Basinghall Av.
Guildhall
Basinghall St
Coleman St
Moorgate
Throgmorton
St Margaret
Lothbury
AN-
Winchester
Gre

2
P
Amen
Court
Ludgate Hill
ST PAUL'S
CATHEDRAL
St Paul's Church Yard
Carter Lane
Foster Lane
Gutter Lane
Wood St
St Vedast
Cheapside
St Mary-le-Bow
New Change
Bread St
King St
Ironmonger Lane
c
Old Jewry
Poultry
St Mary
Aldermary
Bow Lane
Queen St
Victoria
a
Bucklersbury
g
n
Bank of England
Mansion
House
Bank
St Stephen
Royal Exchange
St Michael's
Lombard St
Gracechurch St
s
y
Lothbury
Old

Queen Victoria St
Baynard
Castle
Upper Thames St
High Timber St
Queen St
Mansion House
Cloak Lane
College St
Upper Thames St
Cousin Lane
Cannon Street
Monument
The
Monument
Pudding Lane
Lower
Eas

3
Millennium Bridge
Southwark Bridge
P
London Bridge

Shakespeare's
Globe
Hopton St
Holland St
s TATE MODERN
Sumner St
Park St
Bear
Gardens
Rose Theatre
St
i
Park St
Stoney St
Southwark
Cathedral
a
Tooley St
Duke St Hill
Joiner
THAME
THAMES

Hopton St
Bear Lane
Great Guildford St
Southwark St
Great Suffolk St
Lavington St
Thrale St
Southwark St
h
r
e
v
Borough
Market
k
d
c
London
Bridge
Thomas St
Tooley St
Weston
The

4
Suffolk St
Union St
Great Suffolk St
Union St
Redcross Way
Redcross Way
Borough High St
Guys
Hospital
s
Great Maze Pond
Stainer St

Copperfield St
Loman St
Ayres St
Union St
Newcomen St

AU
41
AV
AW

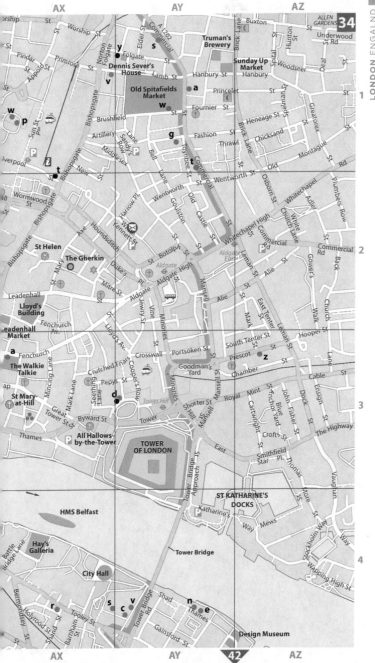

AA | AB | AC

27

Holland Park

Holland House

Duchess of Bedford's Walk

KENSINGTON

Campden St

Holland St

Hornton

Holla

Mews

18 Stafford Terrace

Phillimore

Addison Rd

Addison Villas

Holland

Abbotsbury Rd

Abbotsbury Close

Addison Crescent

Oakwood Lane

Oakwood Court

Ilchester

Melbury

Stafford Terrace

Phillimore Gardens

Argyll Rd

Allen

Sheffield Terrace

Kensington

Russell Rd

Holland Rd

Addison

Leighton House

Strangways Terrace

Holland Park Rd

Melbury Rd

Melbury Court

Abingdon

a

Earls

Napier Rd

Abbots Terrace

St Mary Kensington High St

Earls Terrace

Abingdon Villas

Olympia Way

Russell Rd

Kensington High St

Kensington High St

Warwick

EDWARDES SQUARE

Earls Walk Court

Earl's Walk

Hammersmith Rd

Bishop King's Rd

North End Rd

Avonmore Rd

Warwick Rd

Warwick Rd

Pembroke Gardens Close

Pembroke Gardens

Pembroke Rd

Pembroke Pl

Stratford Rd

Lexham Mews

Lexham Gardens

Avonmore

Lisgar Terrace

Matheson Rd

Pembroke Rd

Gardens

Logan Pl

Cornwall Crescent

Earls Court Rd

Cromwe

Redf

Vernon End Rd

Fitzjames Av.

Fitzjames Av.

Stanwick Rd

P

Pembroke Rd

West Cromwell Rd

Templeton Pl

Cromwell Rd

Edith Rd

Gunterstone Rd

North End Rd

Mornington Av.

Warwick Rd

EARL'S COURT

NEVERN SQUARE

Earl's Cour

Glazbury Rd

Gwendwr Rd

Gwendwr

West Cromwell Rd

Bramber

Longridge Rd

Trebovir Rd

Rd

Talgarth Rd

West Kensington ⊖

Gardens

Penywern

Baron's Court

Barton Rd

Vereker Rd

North End Rd

Challoner Rd

Beaumont Av.

Dieppe Close

Beaumont Crescent

Mund St

Fairley Rd

Warwick Rd

Comeragh Rd

Castletown Rd

Charleville Rd

Gledstanes Rd

Fairholme Rd

Perham Rd

St Andrew's Rd

Sun Rd

North End Rd

Archel Rd

Ivatt Pl

Argyll Pl

Empress Approach

WEST KENSINGTON

Marchbank Rd

West Brompton

Old Brompton Rd

Greyhound Rd

Queen's Club Gardens

Normand Rd

Turneville Rd

Archel Rd

Archel Rd

Chesson Rd

Chesson Rd

Thaxton Rd

Lillie Rd

Ongar Rd

Seagrave Rd

P

Musard Rd

Star Rd

Bramber Rd

North End Rd

Lillie Rd

Sedlescombe Rd

Tamworth Rd

Stafford

NORMAND PARK

Clem Attlee Court ✉

Racton Rd

Anselm Rd

Halford

Rd

Lillie

AA | AB | AC

198

Kensington Church St
St Mary Abbots
Old Court Pl
Kensington High St
Palace Ave.
Kensington

Albert Memorial

h
Roof Garden
Kensington Square
High Street Kensington

r u

De Vere Gardens
Victoria Rd
Palace Gate
Kensington Rd
Kensington Gore

Queen's Gate

Royal Albert Hall

n

Prince
Consort
Rd

St Alban's Grove

Kensington Gate
Hyde Park Gate

a

Canning Pl.
Queen's Gate Mews
Queen's Gate Terrace

Cottesmore Gardens
Stanford Rd
Victoria Rd
Gloucester Rd

Eldon Rd
Kynance Mews
Cornwall Gardens

Petersham Pl.
Elvaston
Petersham Mews
Elvaston Mews
Queen's Gate Pl.

Ayrton Rd

Imperial College Rd

SCIENCE MUSEUM

St Margarets Lane
St Mary's Pl
Lexham Gardens
Pennant Mews

McLeod's Mews
Grenville Pl.
Southwell Gardens
QUEEN'S GATE GARDENS
Atherstone Mews
Queen's Gate Pl. Mews

Museum Lane

Natural History Museum

Cromwell Rd

Cromwell Rd Cromwell Rd Cromwell Rd

Ashburn Gardens
Gloucester Road
Ashburn Pl
Stanhope Mews West

Queen's Gate Mews East
Stanhope Mews
Queensberry Pl.

Harrington Rd

Cromwell Rd Cromwell

y

Stanhope Gardens

P

Courtfield Gardens
Courtfield Rd

Harrington Gardens
Gloucester Rd

SOUTH KENSINGTON

Rd's Court Gardens
Bakston Gardens
Hesper Mews
Bramham Gardens

Courtfield Gardens
Colbeck Mews
Harrington Gardens
Wetherby Gardens
Bina Gardens
Brechin Pl

v d

Onslow Mews East
Old Brompton Rd

7

Hogarth
Earl's Court Rd

m

Onslow Gardens
Neville St
Old
Church St

Bolton Gardens
Bolton Gardens
Old Brompton Rd The

a v
Drayton

y

Cranley Mews
Roland Gardens
Roland Way

Cresswell
The Boltons

n

Elm Pl.
Evelyn Gardens

Coleherne Gardens
Redcliffe Gardens
Coleherne Mews
Redcliffe Mews
Ifield

Little Boltons
Priory Walk
Gilston Rd
Harley Gardens
Thistle Grove
Grove Gardens
Fulham Rd

Elm Park Gardens
Elm Park Lane
Beaufort St
Elm Park Rd

8

BROMPTON CEMETERY

Coleherne Rd
Finborough Rd
Wesgate Terrace
Redcliffe St
Redcliffe Gardens
Finborough Rd

Seymour Walk
Hollywood Walk
Redcliffe Rd
Tregunter Rd
Fawcett St

b
s

Fulham Rd
Callow St
Limeston
Nightingale Pl.
Park Walk
Elm
Chelsea Park Gardens

King's Rd
Beaufort St
The Vale

37

29

36

AG AH AJ

HYDE PARK AND KNIGHTSBRIDGE

West Carr Drive

South Carriage Drive

South Carriage Drive

South

Prince's Gate

Kensington Rd

Knightsbridge

x

Exhibition Rd

Montrose Court

Exhibition Rd

Prince's Gate

Ennismore Gardens

Cathedral Church of the Dormition and All Saints

Trevor Pl.

k

Knightsbridge

Knightsbridge St

William Mews

5

Ennismore Gardens

Ennismore Mews

Ennismore Gardens Mews

Montpelier Square

Montpelier Pl.

Lancelot Pl.

m

a

c

Pavilion Rd

Lowndes Square

Sloane St

r

Princes Gardens

Exhibition

Princes Gardens

Montpelier Walk

Rutland

Cheval Pl.

Brompton Rd

Hans Rd

Beaufort Gardens

Hans Crescent

P

Hans Pl.

Pavilion Rd

k

f

Cadogan

Hyde Park Chapel

Holy Trinity

Brompton Rd

Yeoman's Row

s

Beauchamp Pl.

Walton Pl.

Hans

P

n

Sloane St

Brompton Oratory

Egerton Gardens

e

h

VICTORIA AND ALBERT MUSEUM

St Columba

Pont St

Pavilion Rd

6

Cromwell Gardens

Thurloe Pl.

Ovington St

LENNOX GARDENS

Clabon

Sloane St

Exhibition Rd

Thurloe Sq

Thurloe Pl

Alexander Pl.

Egerton Gardens

South Terrace

Brompton Rd

Walton St

Hasker St

Milner St

CHELSEA

Halsey St

Moore

Cadogan Square

Sloane St

g

Old Brompton

South Kensington

Pelham

St

Ixworth Pl.

Denyer St

Rawlings St

Cadogan

St

Moore St

Mews

x

v

Holy Trinity

Melton Court

Pelham Crescent

s

Sloane Ave.

Draycott

Rosemoor St

Cadogan

Draycott Terrace

Symons St

Sloan Squa

Sumner Pl.

Fulham Rd

Michelin House

Lucan Pl.

P

Petyward

Sloane Ave.

Ave.

Draycott

Bray Pl.

s

King's Rd

Lower

7

Sydney Mews

Pond Pl.

Bury Walk

Ixworth

P

Whitehead's Grove

Elystan Pl.

h

Cheltenham Terrace

Saatchi Gallery

Turks Row

Fulham Rd

Sydney St

Cale St

Markham St

Royal Ave.

Walpole St

Franklin's Row

South Parade

Dovehouse

Godfrey St

Jubilee Pl.

Burnsall St

King's Rd

St Leonard's Terrace

e

St Luke's

St Luke's St

Astell St

r

Smith St

Burton's Court

Hospital

Chelsea Square

Britten St

Chelsea Manor St

Radnor

Shawfield St

Smith Terrace

TEDWORTH SQUARE

8

Church St

Manresa

Sydney St

King's Rd

Flood St

Chelsea Manor St

Redesdale St

Redburn St

Christchurch St

Caversham St

Tite St

Royal Hospital Rd

West Rd

National Army Museum

c

Mulberry Walk

CARLYLE SQUARE

Mallord St

Glebe Pl.

Bramerton St

Oakley St

Margaretta Terrace

Flood Walk

Oakley Gardens

Flood St

Chelsea Manor

Swan Walk

Chelsea Physic Garden

Embankment Gardens

King's Rd

Old Church St

Upper Cheyne Row

Cheyne Walk

Queen's House

Royal Hospital Rd

Chelsea Embankment

Embankment Gardens

AG AH AJ

age Drive

Hyde Park Carnel

w **c**

e

Wilton Row

Wilton Crescent

Grosvenor Crescent

Halkin St

b

Montrose Pl

Grosvenor St

Chester St

Wilton Mews

Wilton Pl

Constitution Hill

Wellington Arch

Constitution Hill

The Mall

BUCKINGHAM PALACE GARDENS

Buckingham Palace

Birdcage Walk

Buckingham Gate

Catherine Pl

Wilfred St

Castle Lane

5

Wilton Crescent

BELGRAVIA

v

Halkin St

Belgrave Square

Belgrave Sqre

Lowndes Pl

Upper Belgrave St

Eaton Pl

Eaton Mews

Belgrave Pl

Eccleston Mews

Hobart Pl

Grosvenor Gardens

a

Buckingham Palace Rd

Allington St

Bressenden Pl

a

Victoria

St

Palace

t

Royal Mews

Catherine Pl

c

Chesham Pl

Lyall St

Chesham St

Eaton Pl

Eaton Mews North

Eaton Mews South

Eaton St

Chester Sqr

Eccleston Mews S

Lower Belgrave St

b

Ebury St

Eccleston St

Victoria

Carlisle

St

Westminster Cathedral

6

nt St

Elizabeth St

Eaton Gate

South Eaton Pl

Ebury St

Eccleston Mews

Eccleston St

Eccleston Bridge

Belgrave Rd

P

Bulleid Way

Bridge Pl

Gillingham St

Guildhouse St

Longmoore St

w **e**

Wilton Rd

Vauxhall Bridge Rd

Francis St

Willow Pl

P

Cliveden Pl

Eaton Terrace

t

Royal Court Theatre

Sloane Square

Holbein Pl

Bourne St

Chester Terrace

Graham Terrace

Ebury St

Semley Pl

Ebury St

South Eaton Pl

P

Belgrave Rd

Hugh St

Belgrave St

ECCLESTON SQUARE

St George's Drive

Warwick Way

Denbigh St

Churton St

Denbigh Pl

Charlwood St

WARWICK SQUARE

Denbigh St

7

Pimlico Rd

k

Bloomfield Terrace

Ranelagh Grove

s

Buckingham Palace Rd

Warwick Way

Bridge Rd

Cambridge St

Warwick Way

Alderney St

Winchester St

Sutherland St

P

George's

Cambridge St

Gloucester St

Denbigh St

Denbigh Pl

George's

Claverton St

Royal Hospital

Chelsea

Bridge

Ebury Bridge Rd

RANELAGH GARDENS

Chelsea Bridge Rd

Cumberland St

Westmoreland Terrace

Turpentine Lane

Peabody Av

YS siding

Chichester

Lupus St

Glasgow Terrace

Churchill Gardens

Churchill Gardens

8

Chelsea Embankment

Grosvenor Rd

Grosvenor Rd

39

AN   31   AP   AQ

The Mall
Park
N° 10 Downing Street
Richmond Terrace
St James's Park Lake
King Charles St
Whitehall
Parliament St
Victoria Embankment
Birdcage Walk
Great George St
Bridge St
Westminster Bridge
Old Queen St
x
Queen Anne's Gate
St Margaret's Church
St Margaret St
Birdcage Walk
France
Tothill St
Victoria St
Dean Farrar St
Great Smith St
Dean's Yard
WESTMINSTER ABBEY
PALACE OF WESTMINSTER
Abingdon St
Petty
Buckingham Gate
a
Palmer St
St James's Park
Broadway
Caxton St
Abbey Orchard St
St Ann's St
Great Smith St
Great College St
Victoria St
Howick Pl.
Old Pye St
Artillery Row
Strutton Ground
Great Peter St
Tufton St
c
Great Peter St
Victoria Tower Gardens
Chadwick St
Monck St
St John
Millbank
Thirleby Rd
Emery Hill St
Greencoat Pl
Horseferry Rd
Medway St
Marsham St
n
Romney St
ster ral
Rochester Row
Maunsel St
VICTORIA
Horseferry Rd
Thorney St
Lambeth Bridge
Stillington St
Willow Pl.
Vauxhall Bridge Rd
Vincent Square
Page St
Regency St
Vincent St
Marsham St
John Islip St
Millbank
Lambeth
Tachbrook St
Charlwood St
Bridge
Douglas St
Chapter St
Montaigne Close
Erasmus St
Herrick St
TATE BRITAIN
w
Blackw
Salam
Belgrave Rd
Moreton Pl.
Moreton St
Causton St
John Islip St
Ponsonby Pl.
Millbank
Randall
Tinworth St
Denbigh St
Lupus St
Pimlico
Vauxhall Bridge Rd
Bessborough Gardens
Vauxhall Bridge Rd
Glasshouse
Claverton St
Chichester St
ST GEORGE'S SQUARE
Aylesford St
Bessborough Pl
Bridgefoot
Albert Embankment
SPRING GARDEN
Godding
Kennington
Grosvenor Rd
THAMES
VAUXHALL
Wandsworth Rd
Bondway
South Lambeth Rd
Harleyf
Grosvenor
Nine Elms Lane
Parry St
Langley Lane

AN   AP   AQ

Eye
London Aquarium
County Hall
Florence Nightingale Museum

LAMBETH PALACE GARDENS
Lambeth Palace
The Garden Museum

GERALDINE MARY HARMSWORTH PARK
IMPERIAL WAR MUSEUM

KENNINGTON
THE OVAL
KENNINGTON PARK

5
41
6
7
8

SOUTH
King James's
Borough Rd
Gladstone St

Waterloo Rd
Cornwall Rd
The Cut
Mitre Rd
Ufford St
Chaplin Close
Valentine Pl
Surrey Row
Pocock St
Rushworth St
Webber St
Baron's Pl
Webber Row
Lancaster St
Blackfriars Rd
Dodson St
Gerridge St
Morley St
Bayliss Rd
Frazier St
Murphy St
Greenham Close
Denham
Lambeth North
Carlisle Lane
Lower Marsh
Spur Rd
Station Approach Rd
Addington St
York Rd
Westminster Bridge Rd
Upper Marsh
Church St
End
Royal St
Centaur St
Hercules Rd
Cosser St
Kennington Rd
St George's Rd
King Edward Walk
Lambeth Rd
St George's Rd
Lambeth Rd
London Rd
Garden Row
Gaywood St
Colnbrook St
Palace Rd
Salamanca St
China Walk
Newport St
Juxon St
Walnut Tree Walk
Fitzalan St
Lollard St
Brook Drive
Austral St
Brook Drive
Hayles St
Elliott's Row
Oswin St
Churchyard Row
Dante Rd
Renfrew Rd
Dugard Way
Newington Butts
Walcot Sqre
St Mary's Gardens
Monkton St
Gilbert Rd
Wincott St
Reedworth St
Kennington Rd
Denny St
Chester Way
Opal St
Kennington Park Rd
Penton Pl
Alberta St
Kennington Lane
Old Paradise St
Whitgift St
Newport St
Lambeth Walk
Jonathan St
Tyers St
Sancroft St
Orsett St
Wickham St
Black Prince Rd
Courtenay St
Cardigan St
Cleaver St
Kennington Green
Kennington
Braganza St
Morgan St
St Oswald's Pl
Tyers Terrace
Loughborough St
Newburn St
Vauxhall St
Kennington Lane
Fairham St
Royal
Durham St
Montford Pl
KENNINGTON
Milverton St
Methley St
Ravensdon St
Stannary St
Kennington Park Pl
Sharsted St
Faunce St
Harmsworth St
Doddington Grove
Westcott Rd
Chapter Rd
Fleming Rd
Ebbisham Drive
Clayton St
Bowling Green
Oval

a

41

33

AU AV AW

Copperfield
Loman St
Surrey Row
Pocock
Rushworth
Suffolk
Glasshill St
Webber St
Sawyer St
Marshalsea Rd
Redcross Way
Ayres St
Borough High St
Newcomen
Mermaid Court
Weston St
Snowsfields
Kipling St
Crosby Row
Long Lane
Le

Bittern
Bridge
Great Suffolk St
Lant St
Borough
St George's
the Martyr
Tabard St
Great Dover St
Pilgrimage St
Tennis St
Staple St
Mantple
Weston St
Wild

SOUTHWARK

Borough
Keil St
Keyworth St
St Oswld
London Rd
Southwark Bridge Rd
Gaunt St
Tiverton St
Swain St
Harper Rd
Terrace
Bath
Rockingham St
TRINITY CHURCH
SQUARE
MERRICK
SQUARE
Trinity St
Spurgeon St
Deverell St
Tabard St
Great Dover St
Bittle
Close
Potle
Pardoner St
Law

40

St George's Rd
Ontin
Newington
Causeway
New
Kent
Meadow
Row
Falmouth
County St
Harper Rd
County St
New Kent Rd
Deverell St
Bartholomew St
Great Dover St

ELEPHANT
AND CASTLE
Elephant
and Castle
Churchyard Row
Newington
Butts
New Kent Rd
New Kent Rd
Searles
Munton Rd
Rodney Pl
John
Maurice Close
WALWORTH
St
Darwin
Mason

Hampton St
Steedman St
Robert
Dashwood Way
Walworth Rd
Deacon Way
Heygate
Brandon St
Rodney
Chatham
Rd
Catesby St
Tatum
Elsted St
Tisdall Pl
Dean's
Buildings
Dawes St
Crampton St
Iliffe St
Iliffe Yard
Amelia St
Wansey
Larcom
Charleston St
Wadding St
Stead
Orb
Brandon
Browning
King and Queen's St
Morecambe St
East St
East St
Sedan

Penton Pl
Manor Pl
Penton Pl
Penrose St
Walworth Rd
East St
Bronti Close
Portland St
Sandford Row
Trafalgar
St
Wooler St
Aylesbury Rd
Rd

PASLEY PARK
Chapter
Carter
Penrose St
Penrose Grove
Date St
Liverpool Grove
Inville
St
Beaconsfield
Larmore
Lorrimore Rd
Deco St
Fielding
Gateway
Merrow St
Queen's Row
Lytham St
Phelp St
Westmoreland Rd
Portland St
Hopwood Rd
Villa St
Alban Rd

AU AV AW

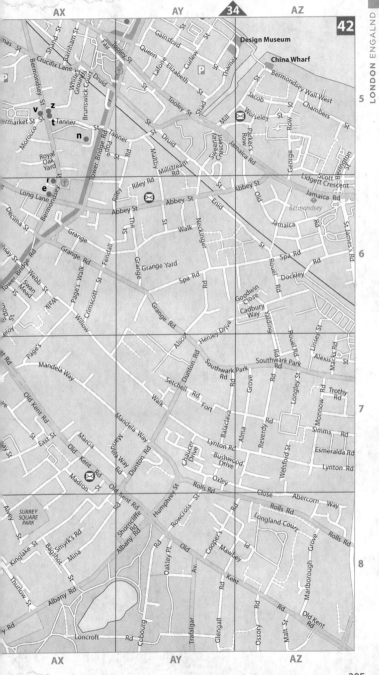

AX   AY   AZ

...mas St
Crucifix Lane
Bermondsey
Whites Grounds
Brunswick Court
St Druid
Gainsford St
Queen
Lafone
Elizabeth
Curlew St
Thames St
Design Museum
China Wharf
Bermondsey Wall West
Jacob St
Chambers
Wolseley St
Parker's Row
Scott
Bevington
Row
George Row
St

v z
t
Tanner
n
Morocco
Tanner St
Druid St
Maltby St
Sweeney Crescent
Jamaica Rd
Mill St
Shad
Tooley St
St

Royal Oak Yard
Tower Bridge Rd
St

r
e
Long Lane
Bermondsey
Decima St
Grange
Riley Rd
Riley Rd
Abbey St
Millstream Rd
The St
Abbey St
Enid
Neckinger
Walk
Abbey St
Old
Jamaica Rd
Lidgett Crescent
Jamaica Rd
Bermondsey
Jamaica
St James's St

Grange Rd
Fendall St
Grange St
Grange Yard
Spa Rd
Spa Rd
Rouel Rd
Dockley
Spa Rd

Webb St
Swan Mead
Page's Walk
Crimscott St
Willow
Grange Rd
Alscot
Henley Drive
Goodwin Close
Cadbury Way
Falding
Rouel Rd
Linsey St
Macks Rd
Alexis St

Page's
Mandela Way
Dunton Rd
Southwark Park Rd
Southwark Park Rd
Grove
Longley St
Monnow Rd
Trothy Rd

Setchell Rd
Walk
Fort
Balaclava Rd
Alma
Reverdy
Welsford St
Simms Rd
Esmeralda Rd
Lynton Rd

Old Kent Rd
Marcia
East St
Old Kent Rd
Mandela Way
Dunton Rd
Chaucer Drive
Lynton Rd
Bushwood Drive
Oxley
Rolls Rd
Close
Abercorn Way

Madron
SURREY SQUARE PARK
Shorncliffe Rd
Albany Rd
Humphrey St
Rowcross St
Old
Cooper's
Mawbey
Rolls Rd
Longland Court
Rolls Rd
Grove
Marlborough Grove

Kinglake St
Bagshot
Smyrk's Rd
Mina
Alvey St
Oakley Pl
Kent
Av.
Id
Old Kent Rd

Thurlow St
Albany Rd
Loncroft Rd
Cobourg Rd
Trafalgar Rd
Glengall Rd
Malt St
Ossory Rd
Old Kent Rd

5

6

7

8

AX   AY   AZ

ENGLAND

A vision of England sweeps across historic buildings and rolling landscapes, but from the rugged splendour of Cornwall's cliffs to pounding Northumbrian shores, this image seeks parity with a newer picture of Albion: refined cities whose industrial past has been reshaped by a shiny, interactive reality. The country's bones and bumps are a reassuring constant: the windswept moors of the south west and the craggy peaks of the Pennines, the summery orchards of the Kentish Weald, the constancy of East Anglian skies and the mirrored calm of Cumbria's lakes.

Renewed interest in all things regional means restaurants are increasingly looking to serve dishes rooted in their locality. Think Melton Mowbray pie in Leicestershire or Lancashire hotpot in the north west – and what better place to eat cheese than where it was made? Seafood is an important part of the English diet: try shrimps from Morecambe Bay, oysters from Whitstable, crab from Cromer and fish from Brixham. Sunday pub roasts are another quintessential part of English life – and a trip to the South West wouldn't be complete without a cream tea.

• Michelin Road maps
  n° 502, 503, 504 and 713

1 Cornwall, Devon, Isles of Scilly

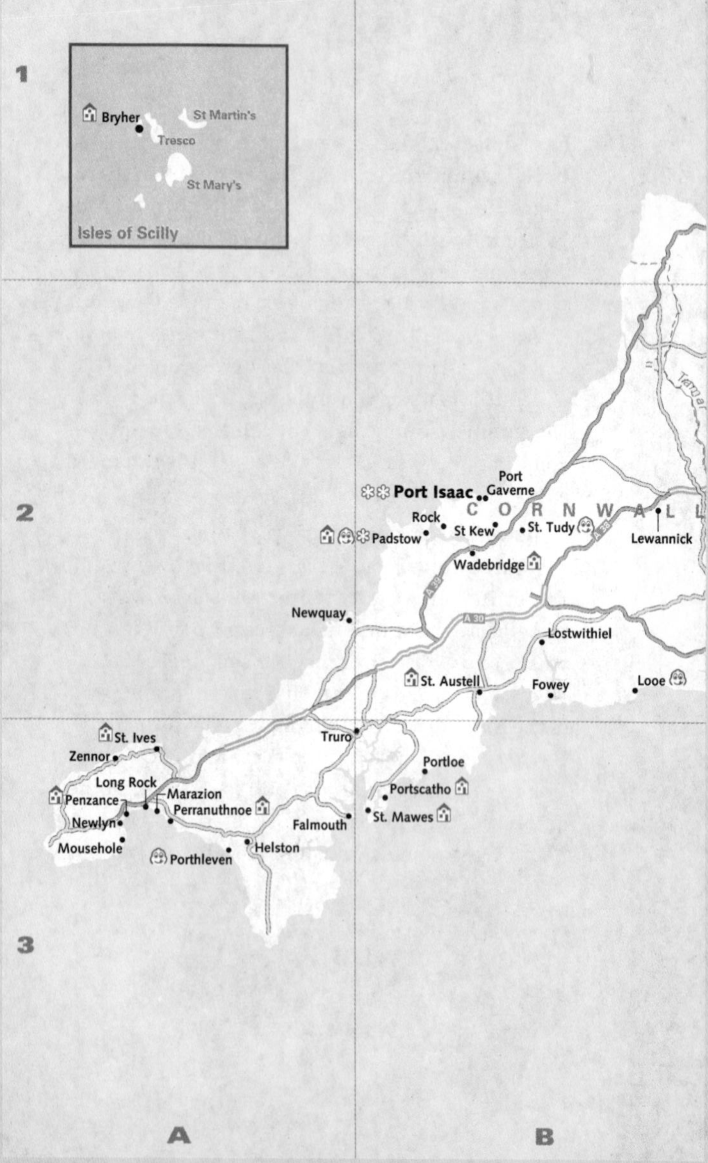

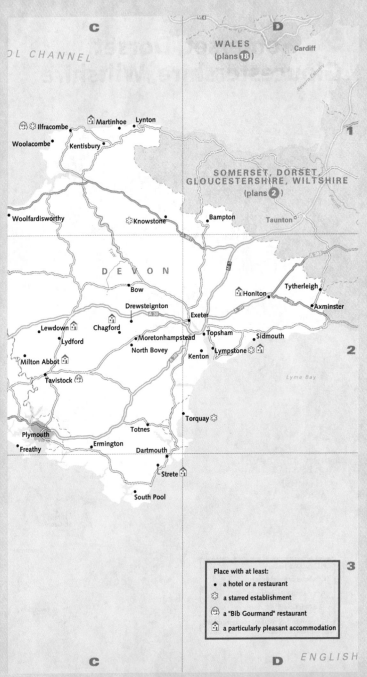

2

Somerset, Dorset, Gloucestershire, Wiltshire

A B

1

WALES
(plans 18)

o Merthyr
Tydfil

Swansea o

Newport o

Cardiff

Wrington •

2

S O M E R S E T

Dulverton •

CORNWALL, DEVON,
ISLES OF SCILLY
(plans 1)

Taunton •   Long Sutton •

Fivehead •

Yeovil •

Hinton
St. George •

Beaminster
•

3

Place with at least:
• a hotel or a restaurant
✿ a starred establishment
😊 a "Bib Gourmand" restaurant
🏠 a particularly pleasant accommodation

Bridport •

West Bexington •

Lyme Bay

A B

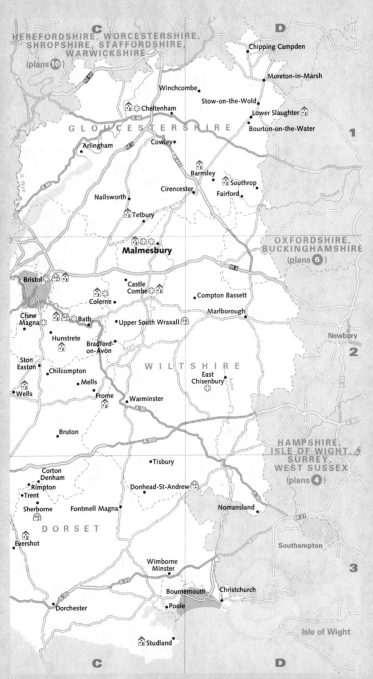

Chipping Campden

Moreton-in-Marsh

Winchcombe

Cheltenham

Stow-on-the-Wold

Lower Slaughter

Bourton-on-the-Water

G L O U C E S T E R S H I R E

Arlingham

Cowley

R. Wye

Barnsley

Thames

Cirencester

Southrop

Nailsworth

Fairford

Tetbury

Malmesbury

Bristol

Castle Combe

Colerne

Compton Bassett

Marlborough

Chew Magna

Bath

Upper South Wraxall

Newbury

Hunstrete

Bradford-on-Avon

Avon

Ston Easton

W I L T S H I R E

Chilcompton

Mells

East Chisenbury

Wells

Frome

Warminster

Avon

Bruton

Tisbury

Corton Denham

Rimpton

Donhead-St-Andrew

Trent

Nomansland

Sherborne

Fontmell Magna

D O R S E T

Southampton

Evershot

Wimborne Minster

Bournemouth

Christchurch

Dorchester

Poole

Isle of Wight

Studland

211

Channel Islands 3

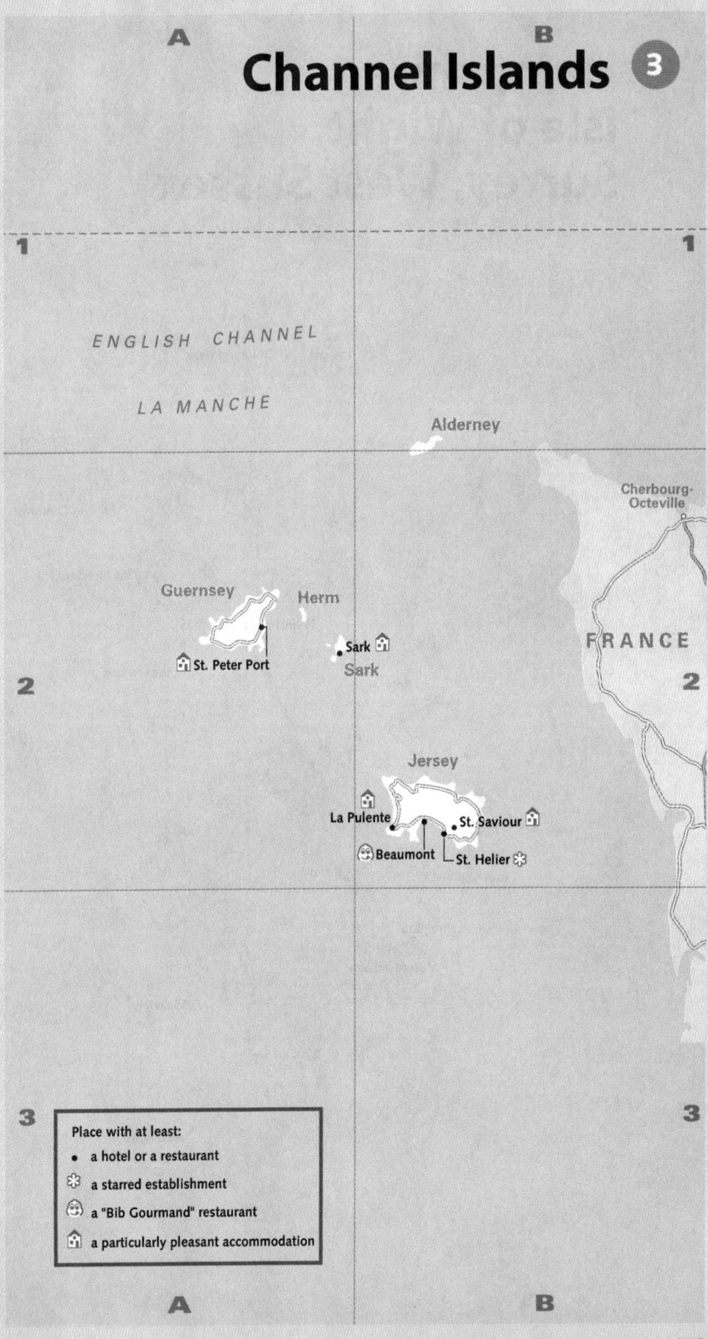

ENGLISH CHANNEL

LA MANCHE

Alderney

Cherbourg-
Octeville

Guernsey   Herm

Sark 🏠
St. Peter Port   Sark

F R A N C E

Jersey

La Pulente
St. Saviour 🏠
Beaumont   St. Helier ✱

Place with at least:

- •   a hotel or a restaurant
- ✱   a starred establishment
- 😀   a "Bib Gourmand" restaurant
- 🏠   a particularly pleasant accommodation

213

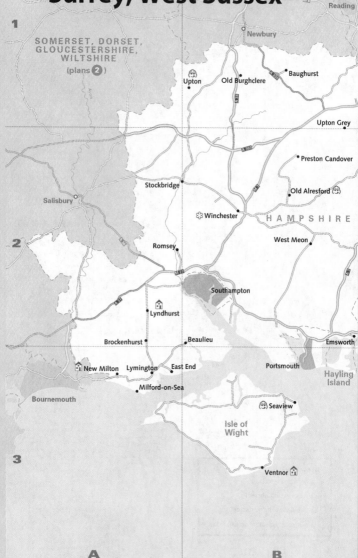

Reading

SOMERSET, DORSET,
GLOUCESTERSHIRE,
WILTSHIRE
(plans ②)

Newbury

Upton   Old Burghclere   Baughurst

Upton Grey

Preston Candover

Stockbridge   Old Alresford

Salisbury   Winchester   HAMPSHIRE

West Meon

Romsey

Southampton

Lyndhurst

Brockenhurst   Beaulieu   Emsworth

New Milton   Lymington   East End   Portsmouth   Hayling Island

Milford-on-Sea

Bournemouth   Seaview

Isle of Wight

Ventnor

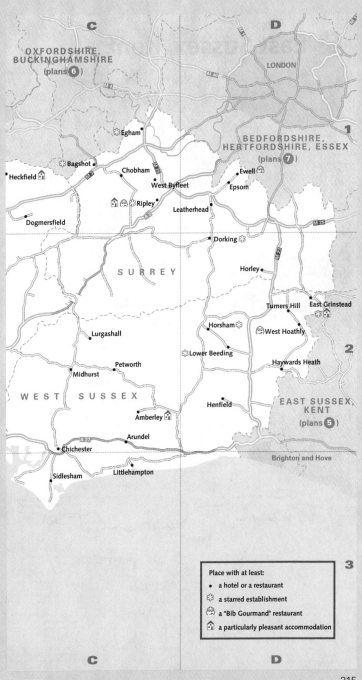

5 East Sussex, Kent

A
B
BEDFORDSHIRE
HERTFORDSHIRE, ESSEX
(plans 7)
LONDON
A 127
A 13
R. THAMES
1
Wilmington
A 2
M 26
M 20
West Malling
M 25
HAMPSHIRE,
ISLE OF WIGHT,
SURREY, WEST SUSSEX
(plans 4)
A 21
KENT
Bidborough
Royal
Tunbridge Wells
Matfield
Crawley
2
Kilndown
Ticehurst
EAST SUSSEX
Hastings and
St. Leonards
A 259
Bexhill
Brighton and Hove
A 27
Alfriston
Eastbourne
3
A
B

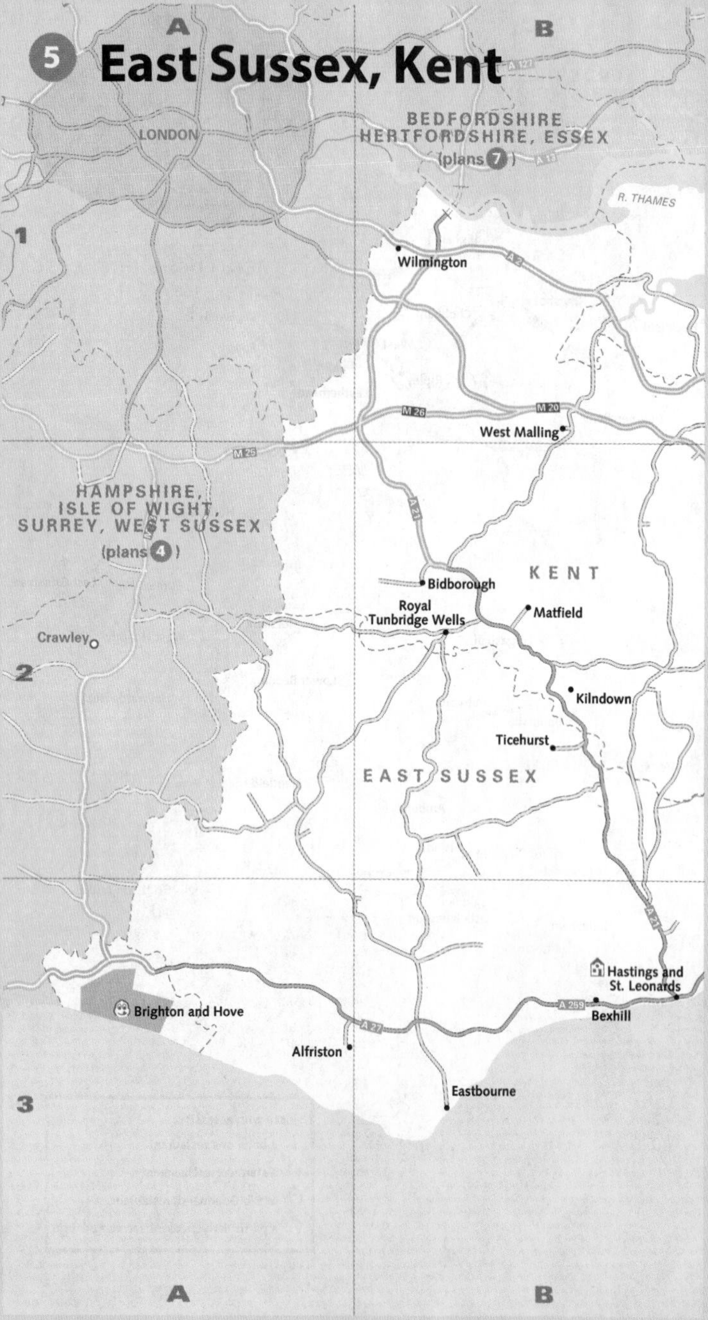

HEREFORDSHIRE,
WORCESTERSHIRE,
SHROPSHIRE,
STAFFORDSHIRE,
WARWICKSHIRE
(plans 10)

SOMERSET, DORSET,
GLOUCESTERSHIRE,
WILTSHIRE
(plans 2)

Great Tew

Hethe

Chipping Norton

Churchill

Kingham

Wootton

Woodstock

Hampton Poyle

Murcott

Burford

Minster Lovell

South Leigh

Oxford

OXFORDSHIRE

Filkins

Langford

Clanfield

Northmoor

Thames

Kelmscott

Fyfield

Stadhampton

Berrick Salome

East Hendred

Letcombe Regis

Swindon

Goring

Yattendon

Place with at least:

- • a hotel or a restaurant
- ✸ a starred establishment
- 🍴 a "Bib Gourmand" restaurant
- 🏠 a particularly pleasant accommodation

Newbury

HAMPSHIRE,
ISLE OF WIGHT,
SURREY, WEST SUSSEX
(plans 4)

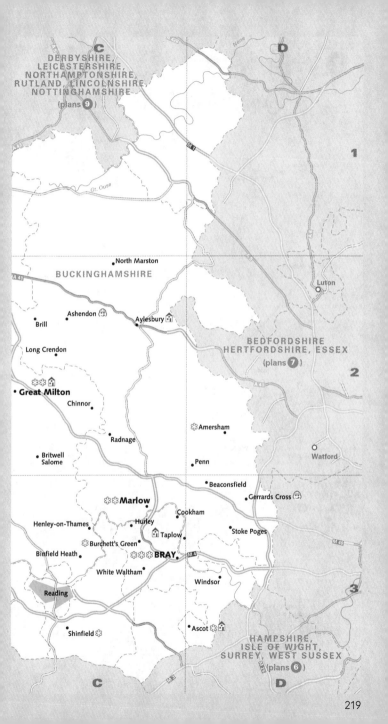

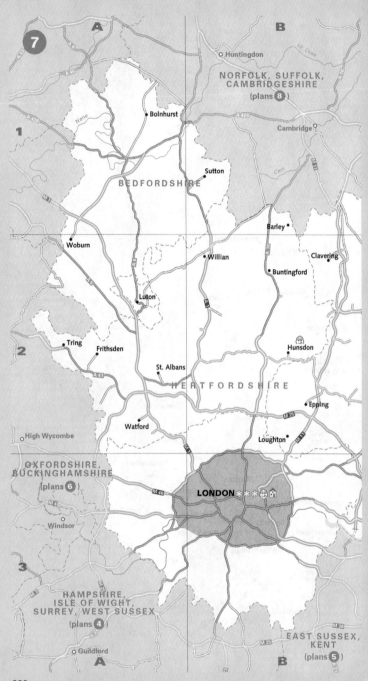

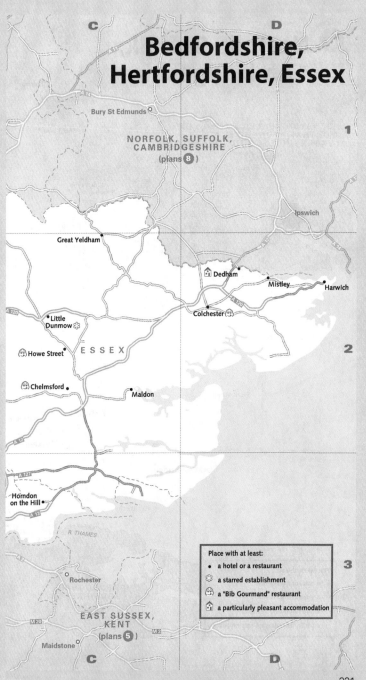

Bedfordshire, Hertfordshire, Essex

C   D

Bury St Edmunds

NORFOLK, SUFFOLK, CAMBRIDGESHIRE
(plans 8)

Ipswich

Great Yeldham

🏠 Dedham

Mistley   Harwich

Colchester 😊

Little Dunmow 🌸

😊 Howe Street   **E S S E X**

😊 Chelmsford

Maldon

Horndon on the Hill

R. THAMES

Rochester

Place with at least:
- a hotel or a restaurant
- 🌸 a starred establishment
- 😊 a "Bib Gourmand" restaurant
- 🏠 a particularly pleasant accommodation

EAST SUSSEX, KENT
(plans 5)

Maidstone

C   D

1

2

3

8 # Norfolk, Suffolk, Cambridgeshire

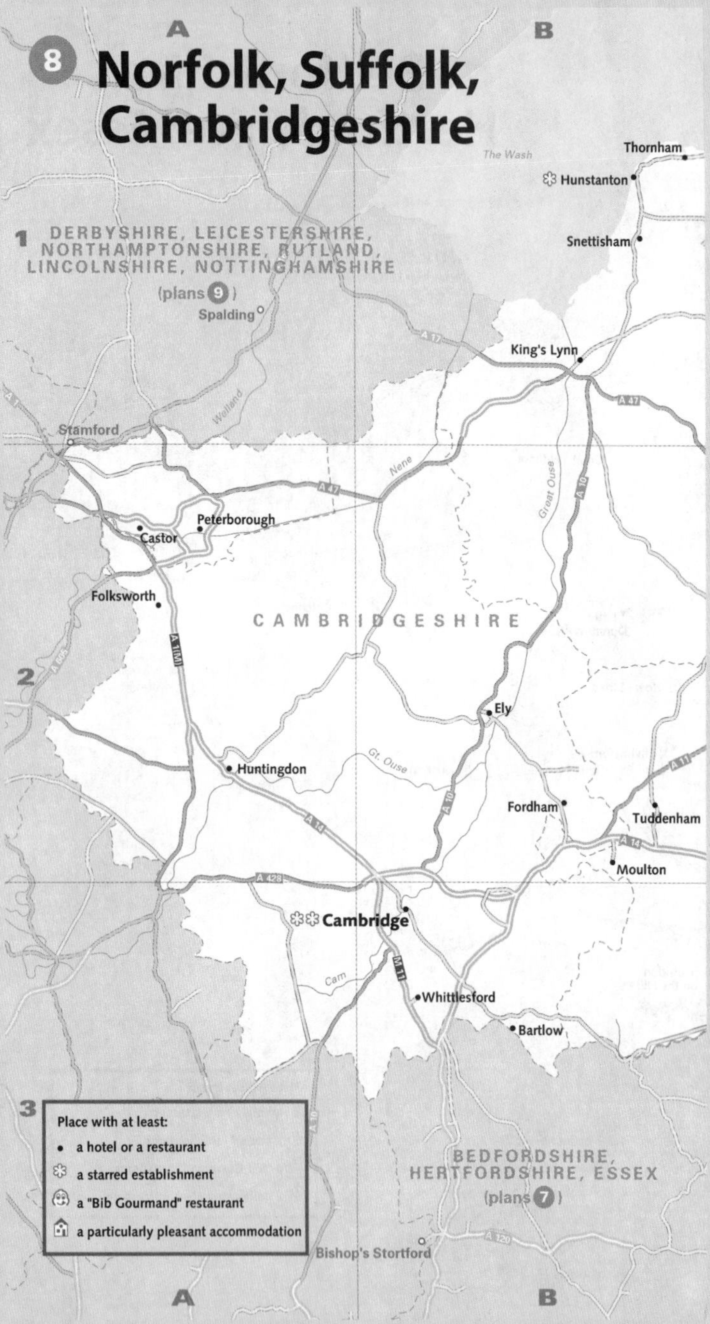

The Wash

Thornham

❄ Hunstanton •

1 DERBYSHIRE, LEICESTERSHIRE, NORTHAMPTONSHIRE, RUTLAND, LINCOLNSHIRE, NOTTINGHAMSHIRE

Snettisham •

(plans **9**)

Spalding ○

King's Lynn •

Stamford •

Nene

Peterborough •

• Castor

CAMBRIDGESHIRE

Folksworth •

2

Gt. Ouse

• Ely

• Huntingdon

Fordham •

• Tuddenham

Moulton •

❄❄ **Cambridge** •

Cam

•Whittlesford

• Bartlow

3

Place with at least:

•   a hotel or a restaurant

❄   a starred establishment

☺   a "Bib Gourmand" restaurant

⌂   a particularly pleasant accommodation

BEDFORDSHIRE, HERTFORDSHIRE, ESSEX

(plans **7**)

Bishop's Stortford ○

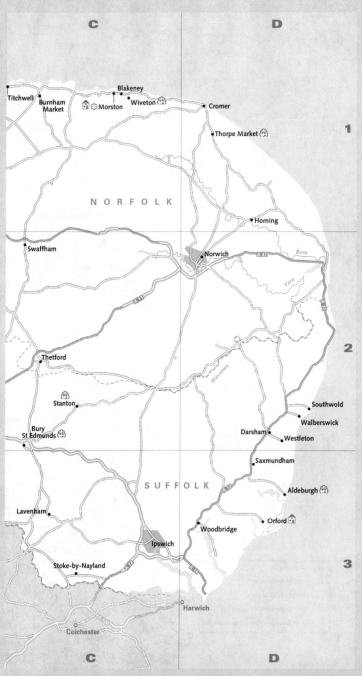

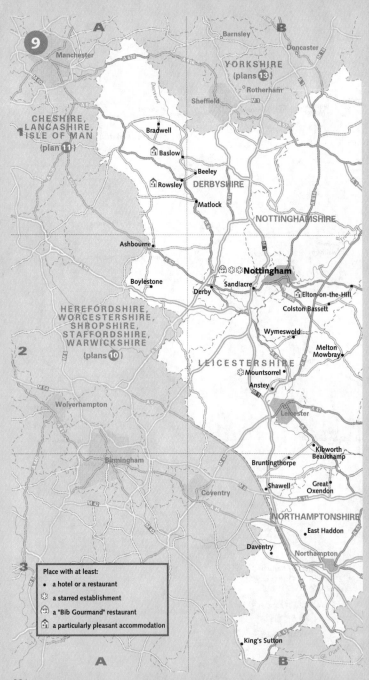

Place with at least:
- • a hotel or a restaurant
- ❀ a starred establishment
- 🙂 a "Bib Gourmand" restaurant
- 🏠 a particularly pleasant accommodation

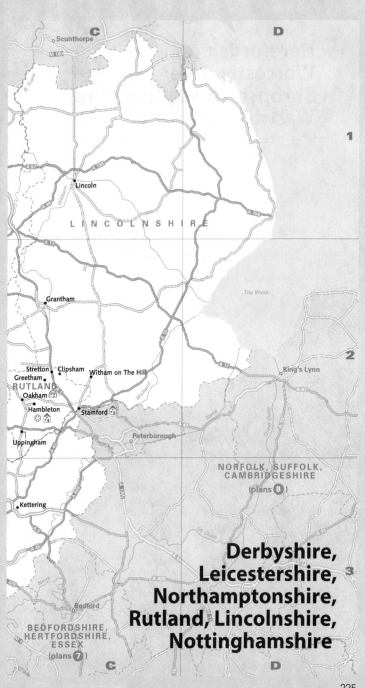

**Derbyshire,
Leicestershire,
Northamptonshire,
Rutland, Lincolnshire,
Nottinghamshire**

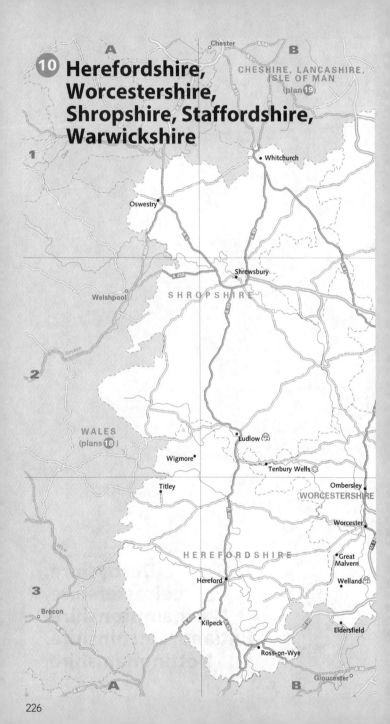

Herefordshire, Worcestershire, Shropshire, Staffordshire, Warwickshire

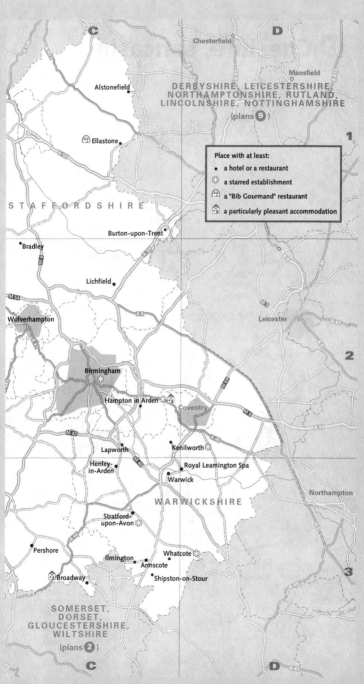

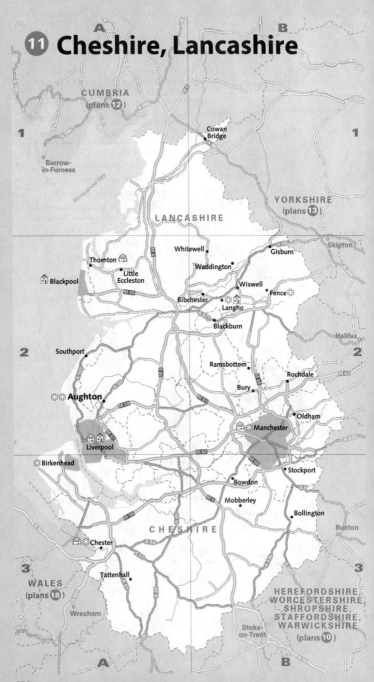

A   B

CUMBRIA
(plans 12)

1   1

Cowan
Bridge

Barrow-
in-Furness

YORKSHIRE
(plans 13)

Morecambe Bay

Skipton

LANCASHIRE

Whitewell   Gisburn

Thornton   Waddington

Little   Wiswell
Eccleston   Fence

Blackpool   Ribble   Langho

Ribchester

Blackburn

Halifax

2   Southport   2

Ramsbottom
Rochdale

Bury

Aughton   Oldham

Manchester

Liverpool

Birkenhead   Stockport

Bowdon

Mobberley

Bollington

CHESHIRE   Buxton

Chester

3   3
WALES
(plans 18)   Tattenhall

Wrexham   HEREFORDSHIRE,
WORCESTERSHIRE,
SHROPSHIRE,
STAFFORDSHIRE,
WARWICKSHIRE
Stoke-   (plans 10)
on-Trent

A   B

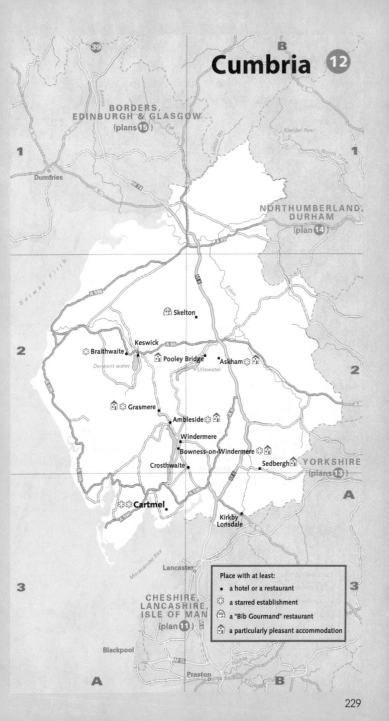

Cumbria 12

BORDERS,
EDINBURGH & GLASGOW
(plans 15)

NORTHUMBERLAND,
DURHAM
(plan 14)

Skelton

Keswick
Braithwaite
Pooley Bridge
Askham

Derwent water
Ullswater

Grasmere
Ambleside
Windermere
Bowness-on-Windermere
Crosthwaite
Sedbergh

YORKSHIRE
(plans 13)

Cartmel

Kirkby
Lonsdale

Dumfries

Lancaster

CHESHIRE,
LANCASHIRE,
ISLE OF MAN
(plan 11)

Blackpool

Preston

Place with at least:
- a hotel or a restaurant
- a starred establishment
- a "Bib Gourmand" restaurant
- a particularly pleasant accommodation

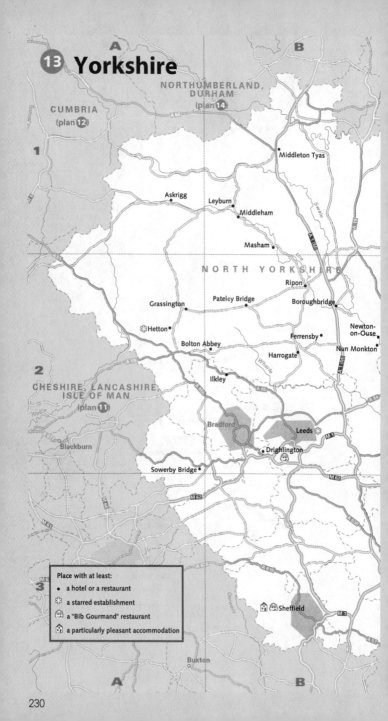

13 Yorkshire

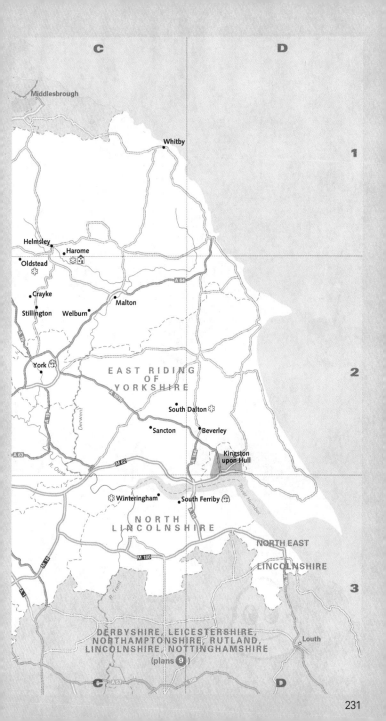

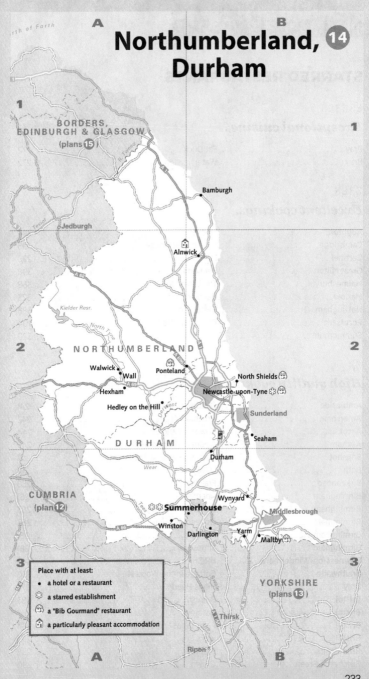

Northumberland, Durham

14

STARRED RESTAURANTS

Exceptional cuisine...

Excellent cooking...

High quality cooking...

Michelin

BIB GOURMAND RESTAURANTS ⊕

Good quality, good value cooking

Restaurant Nathan Outlaw, Port Isaac

... ON THE NEW MICHELIN STARS: THE ANGEL, HETTON

Acclaimed chef Michael Wignall and his wife, Johanna, took over The Angel in September 2018, in partnership with James and Jo Wellock, former owners of Wellocks food suppliers. Just over a year later, The Angel has achieved One Star in the Michelin Guide Great Britain & Ireland 2020.

Michael achieved his first Michelin Star at the age of 25 and has held Stars at no less than six restaurants; two of them at Two-Star level, so it is no great surprise that his new venture has won a Star so quickly. But what is it about The Angel that makes it so special?

This pretty inn, situated deep in the Yorkshire Dales National Park, dates from the 15th century but was made famous in the 1980s by the late Denis Watkins – the 'Godfather of the Gastropub' – when it became renowned for its fresh, flavoursome and good value cooking. It is widely regarded as having helped to transform the standard of cooking in British pubs.

When Michael was head chef at the nearby Devonshire Arms in Bolton Abbey (2002-2007), James became his fruit and vegetable supplier. As Michael moved around the country, working in

Michelin / The Angel

Michelin / The Angel

different restaurants, James continued to supply him and, over the years, the two have become firm friends. When they learned that The Angel was for sale, they jumped at the chance to buy it; closing for a short time to stamp their own mark on it, and plan the all-important new menus.

Being situated in the Yorkshire Dales means that local produce is of the highest quality; Michael likes to shoot game and cook with it, so is in his element here. Dishes like 'local Yorkshire duck breast, croquette, Asian cabbage, spring onion and squash' and 'Skrei cod, haricot blanc, sea vegetables and gnocchi cassoulet' are confidently cooked and immensely enjoyable, with a subtle modernity and vibrant, perfectly balanced flavours.

It is delightful to see this inn once again delivering the high standards of hospitality and cooking for which it was previously known. More exciting changes are planned at The Angel – including improvements to the bedrooms – and we can't wait to see what the future has in store for this iconic Yorkshire inn!

ENGLAND

ABBOTS RIPTON – Cambridgeshire → See Huntingdon

ALDEBURGH
Suffolk – Regional map n° **8**–D3

🕸 Lighthouse 🛜 AC 🌀
MEDITERRANEAN CUISINE · BISTRO X Popular, long-standing, split-level eatery with bright yellow décor, amiable service and a laid-back feel. Menus change constantly, featuring fish from the boats 200m away and local, seasonal meats and vegetables. Cooking is rustic and flavoursome, and dishes arrive generously proportioned.
Specialities: Lighthouse fish soup with rouille and croutons. Pan-fried sea bass with tarragon braised puy lentils. Boozy banana pancake with toffee crunch ice cream.
Menu £17 (lunch) – Carte £22/40
77 High Street ⊠ IP15 5AU – ℰ 01728 453377 – www.lighthouserestaurant.co.uk – Closed 6-17 January

⫯⃝ Sea Spice 🛗 AC 🅿
INDIAN · ELEGANT XX Hidden in a hotel is this dark, moody restaurant with period lighting and contrastingly bright, patterned crockery. Freshly ground spices and local fish, meat and game feature; try the muntjac vindaloo and the delicious rasmalai.
Menu £13 (lunch) – Carte £24/36
White Lion Hotel, Market Cross Place ⊠ IP15 5BJ – ℰ 01728 452720 – www.seaspice.co.uk – Closed Tuesday

ALFRISTON
East Sussex – Regional map n° **5**–A3

⫯⃝ Tasting Room 🆕 ⇚ ⇐ 🛋 🛗 🕤 🅿
MODERN BRITISH · CONTEMPORARY DÉCOR XX The upper floor of the Rathfinny Winery houses a narrow restaurant boasting lovely vineyard views. Simple lunches are followed by 3 set dinner menus: Land, Sea and Garden. Cooking has a creative element and is informed by seasonal Sussex produce. There's also a terrace for drinks and bedrooms in a nearby farmhouse.
Menu £30 (lunch)/65
Rathfinny Wine Estate ⊠ BN26 5TU – ℰ 01323 870022 – www.rathfinnyestate.com/tasting-room – Closed Sunday dinner, Monday, Tuesday

ALNWICK
Northumberland – Regional map n° **14**–B2

🏠 Cookie Jar 🕤 🛋 🖨 🛗
TOWNHOUSE · DESIGN This former convent is now a stylish hotel. Every bedroom comes with a 'smart' speaker and a jar of homemade cookies; the Chapel Suite has original stained glass windows and a shower where the altar used to be. Enjoy afternoon tea in the beautifully secluded terraced garden. The bistro opens Thurs-Sat.
11 rooms ⊊ – 👫 £165/335
12 Bailiffgate ⊠ NE66 1LU – ℰ 01665 510465 – www.cookiejaralnwick.com

ALSTONEFIELD
Staffordshire – Regional map n° **10**–C1

⫯⃝ The George 🛋 🛜 🕤 🅿
TRADITIONAL CUISINE · PUB X The moment you walk into this 18C pub on the village green, feel the warmth from the roaring fires and start to soak up the relaxed, cosy atmosphere, you just know it's going to be good. It's simply furnished, with stone floors and scrubbed wooden tables, and cooking is well-priced and down-to-earth.
Carte £28/50
⊠ DE6 2FX – ℰ 01335 310205 – www.thegeorgeatalstonefield.com

240

AMBERLEY
West Sussex – Regional map n° **4**–C2

ⅈ○ Queen's Room   🍴 ⇄ **P**

MODERN BRITISH · ELEGANT XXX Within the walls of a stunning 12C castle is this elegant dining room with a barrel-vaulted ceiling, lancet windows and an open fire. Ambitious modern dishes arrive artfully presented. Henry VIII's wives all visited, hence its name.

Menu £29 (lunch), £54/67

Amberley Castle Hotel ⊠ BN18 9LT – ℰ 01798 831992 – www.amberleycastle.co.uk

🏨 Amberley Castle   ⚐ ⍦ 🍴 🐎 **P**

LUXURY · HISTORIC Stunning 12C castle displaying original stonework, battlements and evidence of a moat. The charming grounds consist of lovely gardens, lakes and a croquet lawn, and are matched inside by a characterful array of rooms. Sumptuous bedrooms have a palpable sense of history; those in the main castle are the best.

19 rooms ⚏ – ♀♀ £245/345 – 6 suites

Amberley Castle ⊠ BN18 9LT – ℰ 01798 831992 – www.amberleycastle.co.uk

ⅈ○ **Queen's Room** – See restaurant listing

AMBLESIDE
Cumbria – Regional map n° **12**–A2

🍃 Old Stamp House (Ryan Blackburn)

MODERN CUISINE · INTIMATE XX The Old Stamp House is as quirky as its name implies. It sits in the centre of Ambleside – which in turn sits within the heart of the Lake District National Park – inside the cellars of an old house where William Wordsworth used to work as the Distributor of Stamps for Westmorland. It's a tiny place, split over two low-ceilinged rooms which are hung with local art.

It's owned by the Blackburn brothers: Ryan heads up the kitchen, while Craig looks after the service. Menus provide plenty of flexibility, with both an à la carte and tasting menus on offer, and the skilfully prepared, carefully balanced dishes have been well-thought-through and are packed with flavour. The Cumbrian larder is the star of the show, with local rabbit, deer and beef popular choices. The iconic Herdwick hogget and outstanding cheeses are must-tries.

Specialities: Potted shrimps with cauliflower, curry and mead sauce. Yew Tree Farm Herdwick hogget with wood blewits, confit potato and anchovy & mint emulsion. Cumbrian gingerbread with panna cotta and rhubarb.

Menu £29 (lunch), £40/70 – Carte £29/50

Church Street ⊠ LA22 0BU – ℰ 015394 32775 – www.oldstamphouse.com –
Closed Sunday, Monday, Tuesday lunch

ⅈ○ The Samling   ⇐ 🍴 ⅃ **P**

MODERN CUISINE · DESIGN XXX A stunning glass and slate extension to a superbly set hotel – its full-length windows offer wonderful lake and country views. Elaborate modern cooking showcases garden ingredients in eye-catching dishes. Start with drinks on the terrace or in the stylish lounge.

Menu £25 (lunch), £65/85

The Samling Hotel, Ambleside Road ⊠ LA23 1LR – ℰ 015394 31922 –
www.thesamlinghotel.co.uk

ⅈ○ Drunken Duck Inn   ⇐ ⇐ 🍴 **P**

WORLD CUISINE · PUB X This picture-postcard pub sits in the heart of the beautiful Lakeland countryside. Simple brunches are followed by elaborate dinners with subtle global influences. Cooking is generous, service is attentive and the ales are brewed on-site. Some of the boutique country bedrooms have terraces with fell views.

Carte £22/47

Barngates ⊠ LA22 0NG – ℰ 015394 36347 – www.drunkenduckinn.co.uk –
Closed 25-26 December

🍴 Lake Road Kitchen

CREATIVE · SIMPLE Wooden planks line the walls and fleeces cover the chairs at this intimate restaurant. The passionate chef-owner uses only ingredients grown in the same climate as The Lakes and his experience with preservation techniques allows him to use seasonal ingredients year-round. Creative dishes have natural flavours.

Menu £65/145

Lake Road ⊠ LA22 0AD – ℰ 015394 22012 – www.lakeroadkitchen.co.uk –
Closed Sunday lunch, Monday, Tuesday, Wednesday - Saturday lunch

🏠 The Samling

COUNTRY HOUSE · CONTEMPORARY A former farmhouse and outbuildings perched on the hillside; the outdoor hot tub is the perfect spot to take in the stunning lake and fell views. Both the guest areas and the bedrooms have a stylish, contemporary look; the latter come in neutral tones and their bathrooms have underfloor heating.

7 rooms ⊊ – 👫 £230/310 – 5 suites

Ambleside Road ⊠ LA23 1LR – ℰ 015394 31922 – www.thesamlinghotel.co.uk
🍴 **The Samling** – See restaurant listing

AMERSHAM (OLD TOWN)
Buckinghamshire – Regional map n° **6**–D2

❀ **Artichoke** (Laurie Gear)   AC 🛈♥ ⇄

MODERN BRITISH · ELEGANT ✕✕ The Artichoke is located in a 16C red-brick house set at the centre of a picturesque town. It's a bijou place, with a heavily timbered interior and a contemporary, design-led style. The narrow beamed main room leads through to a modern Scandic-style extension with a semi-open kitchen and glass screens etched with branches – and neutral shades give it a laid back, 'natural' feel.

Self-taught chef-owner Laurie Gear has completed 'stages' at The Fat Duck and Noma, and brings his experiences together in an array of menus. Accomplished modern British dishes are confidently prepared and well-measured flavour combinations have an understated complexity. The English larder is kept to the fore: lamb is reared locally, venison is from the Woburn Estate and seafood from Brixham is a particular highlight. Relaxed, super-friendly service completes the picture.

Specialities: Hop-smoked sea trout tartare with apple, pickled mooli, and beetroot sorbet. Rump of rose veal with artichokes, orzo pasta, almond and lemon thyme sauce. Yorkshire rhubarb '2 ways'.

Menu £30 (lunch), £50/80

9 Market Square ⊠ HP7 0DF – ℰ 01494 726611 – www.artichokerestaurant.co.uk –
Closed 12-20 April, 16-31 August, 24 December-7 January, Sunday, Monday

ANSTEY
Leicestershire – Regional map n° **9**–B2

🍴 **Sapori** 🅝   ૐ AC

ITALIAN · FAMILY ✕ Don't be put off by its plain look, as this former Victorian Working Men's Club is now run by a passionate Italian family who proudly deliver refined, authentic cooking. Dishes centre around their home city of Naples and everything is homemade. Service – from the chef's brother-in-law – is charming.

Menu £19 – Carte £24/51

40 Stadon Road ⊠ LE7 7AY – ℰ 0116 236 8900 – www.sapori-restaurant.co.uk –
Closed 26 December-9 January, Sunday, Monday

ARLINGHAM
Gloucestershire – Regional map n° **2**–C1

🍽️○ **Old Passage**

SEAFOOD · **FRIENDLY** XX Sit out on the terrace or beside the window, surrounded by colourful art, and watch the famous Severn bore travel up the estuary. Concise seafood menus offer everything from a fish pie to a fruits de mer platter or lobster direct from their saltwater tank. Simply furnished modern bedrooms share the view.

Menu £22 (lunch) – Carte £37/60

Passage Road ⊠ *GL2 7JR* – ℰ *01452 740547 – www.theoldpassage.com –*
Closed Sunday dinner, Monday

ARMSCOTE

Warwickshire – Regional map n° **10**–C3

🍽️○ **Fuzzy Duck**

TRADITIONAL CUISINE · **PUB** X Siblings Adrian and Tania – also owners of toiletries company Baylis & Harding – took this place from boarded up boozer to welcoming, fashionably attired dining pub. Seasonal British dishes use great quality local and sustainable ingredients. Stylish boutique bedrooms complete the picture.

Menu £23/30 – Carte £25/50

Ilmington Road ⊠ *CV37 8DD* – ℰ *01608 682635 – www.fuzzyduckarmscote.com –*
Closed Sunday dinner, Monday

ARUNDEL

West Sussex – Regional map n° **4**–C2

🍽️○ **Parsons Table**

MODERN BRITISH · **FRIENDLY** XX Tucked away in a little courtyard is this lovely restaurant with a fresh modern feel. Flavoursome dishes have a hint of modernity and are as seasonal and local as the quality of the produce will allow. Service comes with a smile.

Menu £19 (lunch), £31/48 – Carte £19/48

2 & 8 Castle Mews, Tarrant Street ⊠ *BN18 9DG* – ℰ *01903 883477 –*
www.theparsonstable.co.uk – Closed 17-24 February, 24 August-2 September,
24-28 December, Sunday, Monday

🍽️○ **Town House** 🔚

MODERN CUISINE · **ELEGANT** XX If you're a fan of Renaissance architecture, head for this early 17C townhouse, where you'll find a gilt walnut panelled ceiling which was originally installed in the Medici Palace in Florence. Cooking is assured; if there's local crab on the menu, be sure to choose it. Comfy bedrooms include four-posters.

Menu £23 (lunch) – Carte £32/48

65 High Street ⊠ *BN18 9AJ* – ℰ *01903 883847 – www.thetownhouse.co.uk –*
Closed 1-17 March, 8-24 November, Sunday, Monday, Tuesday, Friday lunch

at Burpham Northeast: 3 mi by A27

🍽️○ **The George at Burpham**

MODERN BRITISH · **PUB** X Beside the cricket pitch you'll find this characterful village pub where smart furnishings sit alongside old beams, open fires and a smugglers' wheel. Honest, well-priced dishes always include 'Pie of the Day' and some of the produce comes from the Arundel Estate, whose castle can be seen in the distance.

Carte £25/44

Main Street ⊠ *BN18 9RR* – ℰ *01903 883131 – www.georgeatburpham.co.uk*

ASCOT

Windsor and Maidenhead – Regional map n° **6**–D3

❀ Coworth Park   🍴 🛱 & 🎦 🕼 ⇄ 🅿

MODERN CUISINE · ELEGANT XXX A chic, luxurious 18C property set in 246 acres of grounds plays host to this elegant, intimate restaurant. As you enter, the striking ceiling sculpture is the first thing to catch your eye; it's named 'Autumn' – to match the colours of the room – and comprises copper oak leaves and acorns. The service might be structured but the atmosphere is relaxed, and the large main room has a bright, contemporary look; for the best view ask for a seat in the conservatory, overlooking the manicured gardens.

Chef Adam Smith spent a number of years at The Ritz, before moving to the Devonshire Arms in Yorkshire, which explains both his classical cooking and his love of the countryside. His à la carte, 'Best of British' and 7 course tasting menus reflect this, with simply cooked, beautifully presented dishes paying the utmost respect to natural British ingredients. Cooking is assured and technically skilled, and dishes display real depth and finesse.

Specialities: Caviar tart with Cornish crab, yuzu and cucumber. Salt-aged beef with smoked sweetbreads, sprouting broccoli and Baron Bigod. Valrhona chocolate with hazelnut and tonka bean ice cream.

Menu £35 (lunch), £50/110

Coworth Park Hotel, Blacknest Road ✉ *SL5 7SE – ☎ 01344 876600 –*
www.dorchestercollection.com – Closed Sunday dinner, Monday, Tuesday,
Wednesday - Thursday lunch

⭑○ Ascot Grill   🛱 🎦

MEATS AND GRILLS · ELEGANT XX Neighbourhood restaurant with a slick, minimalistic interior featuring leather, silk and velvet; full-length windows open onto a pleasant pavement terrace. Wide-ranging modern grill menu offers steak and seafood. Good value lunches.

Carte £24/52

6 Hermitage Parade, High Street ✉ *SL5 7HE – ☎ 01344 622285 –*
www.ascotgrill.co.uk – Closed Sunday dinner, Monday

⭑○ Bluebells   🛱 & 🎦 ⇄ 🅿

MODERN CUISINE · CONTEMPORARY DÉCOR XX A striking dark green interior with glitzy rose gold panelling and distinctive tiling sets this elegant restaurant apart. Menus offer an appealing range of beautifully-presented European dishes, which are delicately crafted using modern techniques. Sit overlooking the fire pit or in the airy conservatory.

Menu £32 (lunch), £43/51

London Road ✉ *SL5 0PU – ☎ 01344 622722 –*
www.bluebells-restaurant.com – Closed 1-16 January, Sunday dinner, Monday,
Tuesday

🏨 Coworth Park   ⭑ ⬥ ⬅ 🛏 🖼 🕉 ⋙ 🗝 ⬆ & 🎦 ♨ 🅿

COUNTRY HOUSE · GRAND LUXURY A luxurious 18C property set in 246 acres, with stylish, contemporary guest areas and beautiful bedrooms featuring bespoke furniture, marble bathrooms and excellent facilities; those in main house are the largest. Dine in the elegant restaurant or more casual brasserie, overlooking their championship polo fields. The superb spa has a 'living roof' of herbs and flowers.

70 rooms ☲ – 👫 £435/995 – 6 suites

Blacknest Road ✉ *SL5 7SE – ☎ 01344 876600 – www.dorchestercollection.com*
❀ **Coworth Park** – See restaurant listing

ASHBOURNE

Derbyshire – Regional map n° **9**–A2

at Shirley Southeast: 5 mi by A515 and off A52

🏵️○ **Saracen's Head**

TRADITIONAL BRITISH · PUB 🕽 A rustic, open-plan dining pub opposite the village church, in a remote, picturesque village. Menus are chalked on blackboards above the open fire and offer an eclectic mix of generously portioned pub and restaurant-style classics.

Carte £ 21/43

Church Lane ⊠ *DE6 3AS –* ℰ *01335 360330 – www.saracens-head-shirley.co.uk*

ASHENDON

Buckinghamshire – Regional map n° **6**–C2

🏵️ **The Hundred of Ashendon** ⇦ 🍴🛏️ 🄿

REGIONAL CUISINE · PUB 🕽 In Saxon times, shires were divided into 'hundreds' for military and judicial purposes. This charming 17C inn keeps the concept alive by sourcing its produce from within its 'hundred'. Great value dishes arrive in hearty portions, packed full of flavour – and influences from Matt's time at St John are clear to see. Modest bedrooms are continually being upgraded.

Specialities: Pork belly with pickled chicory, apple and beer mustard. Ray wing with tomato, little gem and aioli. Baked egg custard with shortbread.

Carte £ 27/35

Lower End ⊠ *HP18 OHE –* ℰ *01296 651296 – www.thehundred.co.uk –*
Closed 1-8 January, Sunday dinner, Monday - Tuesday lunch

ASKHAM

Cumbria – Regional map n° **12**–B2

🏵️ **Allium at Askham Hall** 🛏️ 🍴💠 🄿

MODERN BRITISH · INTIMATE 🕽🕽 Relax by the fire in the sitting room of this 11C castle, while you enjoy canapés and peruse the hugely impressive wine selection from the estate cellars; then head through to the modish, country kitchen style restaurant with its unique tiled floor, views over the mature gardens and elegant private room. Service is charming and it's worth taking the advice of the experienced team.

Locally born chef Richard Swales oversees the kitchen, offering a concise menu with just two choices at each course. These dishes are driven by the seasons and the availability of produce from the Lowther Estate, in which the castle sits. The gardener plays an important part in guiding the menu, advising which ingredients are at their peak and what to plant next. Accomplished dishes have a certain simplicity to them but also focus on complementary textures and tastes.

Specialities: Askham reared chicken with smoked shallots, onion and beetroot. Loin & shoulder of Cumbrian lamb with goat's curd, lamb fat potatoes and mint. Caramel tart with damson, candied walnuts and sorrel ice cream.

Menu £ 55/70

Askham Hall Hotel ⊠ *CA10 2PF –* ℰ *01931 712350 – www.askhamhall.co.uk –*
Closed 2 January-11 February, 24-26 December, Sunday, Monday, Tuesday -
Saturday lunch

🏨 **Askham Hall** 🏵️🛏️🍴⚒️🄿

COUNTRY HOUSE · CLASSIC At the edge of the Lowther Estate you'll find this fine, family-run castle dating from the 1200s and surrounded by beautiful gardens. It's been stylishly yet sympathetically refurbished and its spacious rooms are full of original features and old family furnishings. Opt for a bedroom in the Pele Tower.

18 rooms � - 🛏️🛏️ £ 150/320

⊠ *CA10 2PF –* ℰ *01931 712350 – www.askhamhall.co.uk –*
Closed 2 January-11 February

🏵️ **Allium at Askham Hall** – See restaurant listing

ASKRIGG

North Yorkshire – Regional map n° **13**–A1

ⅠⅠ◯ **Yorebridge House**   🛏 🛖 ♻ **P**

MODERN BRITISH · DESIGN XX Romantic restaurant set within an old school-master's house and offering lovely countryside views. Concise menus evolve with the seasons and feature locally sourced produce; dishes are modern, flavoursome and attractively presented.

Menu £60

Yorebridge House Hotel, Bainbridge ⊠ *DL8 3EE* – ℰ *01969 652060 –*
www.yorebridgehouse.com

🏠 **Yorebridge House**   🛏 **P**

COUNTRY HOUSE · CONTEMPORARY Stylish former schoolmaster's house in a lovely Dales setting, with a snug bar and great country views. Bold modern bedrooms are themed around the owner's travels; those in the old schoolhouse have riverside patios and hot tubs.

12 rooms ⌸ – ♟ £220/410

Bainbridge ⊠ *DL8 3EE* – ℰ *01969 652060 – www.yorebridgehouse.com*
ⅠⅠ◯ **Yorebridge House** – See restaurant listing

AUGHTON

Lancashire – Regional map n° **11**–A2

✿✿ **Moor Hall** (Mark Birchall)   😄 ⟵ 🛏 ♿ **AC** ♻ **P**

MODERN BRITISH · DESIGN XXX Charming grounds with a lake and a fountain lead up to this 16C house with Tudor origins and Victorian extensions. Inside it's an appealing mix of the old and the new: cosy lounges feature ornately carved dark wood panelling and squashy sofas set in front of roaring fires, which contrast with an ultra-modern glass-fronted restaurant with sleek blond wood furnishings and an impressive open kitchen.

Mark Birchall brings his knowledge and experience together in a style of his own, where skilfully executed dishes combine the classic flavours of the region with modern techniques and a light touch. The produce leads the menu and he only uses ingredients at their peak; as well as tasting delicious individually, each has its part to play when a dish is eaten as a whole, contributing maybe earthiness, acidity or herbal tones. Local gingerbread is often a feature and the pacing of the meal is well-judged.

Spacious bedrooms have a contemporary feel.

Specialities: Turnip and crab with anise hyssop and sunflower seeds. Grilled langoustine with smoked marrow and green tomato. Green strawberries with sweet cicely and cream cheese.

Menu £70 (lunch)/135

Prescot Road ⊠ *L39 6RT* – ℰ *01695 572511 – www.moorhall.com –*
Closed 1-16 January, 5-20 August, Monday, Tuesday, Wednesday lunch
ⅠⅠ◯ **The Barn** – See restaurant listing

ⅠⅠ◯ **The Barn**   🛏 🛖 ♿ ⅠⓋ **P**

TRADITIONAL BRITISH · RUSTIC XX In the grounds of Moor Hall you'll find this rustic barn and terrace overlooking a lake. The ground floor houses the ageing rooms; head upstairs to dine, while watching the chefs. Well-sourced produce underpins carefully prepared, familiar British dishes. The hay-aged sirloin cooked over wood is a speciality.

Menu £23 (lunch) – Carte £29/52

Moor Hall, Prescot Road ⊠ *L39 6RT* – ℰ *01695 572511 – www.moorhall.com –*
Closed 2-15 January, 22 January, 29 January, Monday, Tuesday

AXMINSTER

Devon – Regional map n° **1**–D2

ⅠⅠ◯ River Cottage Canteen   🅖

REGIONAL CUISINE · RUSTIC ✗ Busy restaurant, deli and coffee shop owned by Hugh Fearnley-Whittingstall. The slightly stark rear room was once a dance hall. Menus change twice-daily and offer gutsy, flavoursome country dishes which showcase local produce.

Menu £12 (lunch) – Carte £25/39

Trinity Square ⊠ EX13 5AN – ℰ 01297 631715 –
www.rivercottage.net/restaurants/axminster – Closed Sunday dinner

AYLESBURY

Buckinghamshire – Regional map n° **6**-C2

🏚🏚🏚 Hartwell House 

HISTORIC · TRADITIONAL An impressive palatial house set in 90 acres of parkland: the erstwhile residence of Louis XVIII, exiled King of France, and now owned by the National Trust. It boasts ornate furnishings, luxurious lounges, an intimate spa and magnificent antique-filled bedrooms. The formal restaurant offers traditional country house cooking and afternoon tea is a speciality.

48 rooms – 🛉🛉 £250/610 – 10 suites

Oxford Road ⊠ HP17 8NR – ℰ 01296 747444 –
www.hartwell-house.com

BAGSHOT

Surrey – Regional map n° **4**-C1

☸ Matt Worswick at The Latymer   🚪 & 🄰🄲 🅿

MODERN CUISINE · CLASSIC DÉCOR ✗✗✗ Guests have always been drawn to this impressive 19C manor house for its superb spa facilities, but increasingly they are also coming for the top-class dining.

Matt Worswick is a chef who eats, sleeps and breathes cooking and his passion, determination and hard work swiftly led to success. Inspired initially by his grandmother, and then a host of other chefs, he is now, himself, a mentor for the next generation.

Rather than constantly searching for new techniques, he believes, first and foremost, that he must honour the craft he was taught, and he brings prime luxury ingredients to life in deceptively simple-looking dishes which have superb depth and show a great understanding of complementary flavours.

The room's traditional dark wood panels and beams are offset by colourful, boldly printed fabrics, giving it an elegant, contemporary feel.

Specialities: Poached Colchester oyster, pickled apple, Oscietra caviar and marigold. Rack of Herdwick hogget, Wye Valley asparagus, smoked ewe's curd and wild garlic pesto. Dark chocolate délice, salted caramel and yoghurt sorbet.

Menu £49 (lunch), £69/105

Pennyhill Park Hotel, London Road ⊠ GU19 5EU – ℰ 01276 471774 –
www.exclusivehotels.co.uk – Closed 1-15 January, Monday, Tuesday, Wednesday -
Friday lunch

🏚🏚🏚🏚 Pennyhill Park 

LUXURY · CLASSIC An impressive 19C manor house set in 123 acres and boasting one of Europe's best spas. Both the guest areas and the bedrooms are spacious, with period furnishings and modern touches; feature bathrooms come with rain showers or glass baths. Dine in the elegant restaurant or stylish brasserie.

124 rooms ⊡ – 🛉🛉 £295/485 – 10 suites

London Road ⊠ GU19 5EU – ℰ 01276 471774 –
www.exclusivehotels.co.uk – Closed 1-15 January

  ☸ **Matt Worswick at The Latymer** – See restaurant listing

BAMBURGH

Northumberland – Regional map n° **14**–B1

ⅠⅠ○ **Potted Lobster**

SEAFOOD · FRIENDLY ⅹ A sweet, homely bistro hung with dramatic local seascapes; sit outside for a view of the majestic castle. Classic dishes come in large portions. Check the blackboard for the latest catch; the squid and oysters are must-tries.

Carte £23/60

3 Lucker Road ⊠ NE69 7BS – ℰ 01668 214088 –
www.thepottedlobsterbamburgh.co.uk

BAMPTON

Devon – Regional map n° **1**–D1

ⅠⅠ○ **Swan**

TRADITIONAL BRITISH · PUB ⅹ The Swan's history can be traced back to 1450, when it provided accommodation for craftsmen working on the village church – and its original inglenook fireplace and bread oven still remain. Neatly presented, unfussy pub classics showcase local farm produce. Smart, modern bedrooms are on the 2nd floor.

Carte £27/43

Station Road ⊠ EX16 9NG – ℰ 01398 332248 – www.theswan.co

BARLEY

Hertfordshire – Regional map n° **7**–B1

ⅠⅠ○ **Fox & Hounds** Ⓝ 🛖 ⅆ 🅿

BRITISH CONTEMPORARY · PUB ⅹ The 17C Fox & Hounds oozes character, with its cosy bar, impressive inglenook fireplace, rustic restaurant and charming terrace. Cooking is hearty and satisfying, with ingredients sourced from within 30 miles and an emphasis on rare breed meats. The appealing menu mixes pub classics and modern British fare.

Menu £19 (lunch) – Carte £26/42

High Street ⊠ SG8 8HY – ℰ 01763 802505 – www.foxandhoundsbarley.com –
Closed Sunday dinner, Monday

BARNSLEY – Gloucestershire ➜ See Cirencester

BARTLOW

Cambridgeshire – Regional map n° **8**–B3

ⅠⅠ○ **The Three Hills**

MODERN BRITISH · PUB ⅹ It's named after a nearby Roman burial site and has 15C origins but it wasn't until the 1840s that The Three Hills first opened as an ale house. Seasonal modern menus mix pub and restaurant style dishes and there's a pizza oven on the charming terrace. Bedrooms are chic and comfy.

Carte £30/41

Dean Road ⊠ CB21 4PW – ℰ 01223 890500 – www.thethreehills.co.uk –
Closed Monday

BARWICK – Somerset ➜ See Yeovil

BASLOW

Derbyshire – Regional map n° **9**–A1

🍴 Fischer's at Baslow Hall ⇦ 🍴 📍 🚪 🅿

MODERN CUISINE · ELEGANT XxX A fine Edwardian manor house with a classic country house feel and impressive formal grounds plays host to two dining rooms with lovely ornate ceilings. Menus offer a mix of classic and more original modern dishes; sit at the 'Kitchen Tasting Bench' to be part of the action. Bedrooms are charming.

Menu £34 (lunch), £79/88

Calver Road ✉ DE45 1RR – ☎ 01246 583259 – www.fischers-baslowhall.co.uk – Closed Monday

🍴 The Gallery ⇐ 🍴 🅿

MODERN BRITISH · ELEGANT XxX A striking modern restaurant in an elegant hotel – sit below antique oil paintings looking out over the grounds. Well-presented, contemporary British dishes use estate produce; for a ringside seat book the chef's table.

Menu £55

Cavendish Hotel, Church Lane ✉ DE45 1SP – ☎ 01246 582311 – www.cavendishbaslow.co.uk

🍴 Rowley's 🍴 ⅋ 🅿

MODERN BRITISH · BRASSERIE X Stone-built former blacksmith's; now a contemporary bar-restaurant with a small terrace and friendly service. Dine in the buzzy ground floor bar or more intimate upstairs rooms. Hearty, satisfying dishes have classic French roots.

Menu £19 (lunch), £26/38 – Carte £19/38

Church Lane ✉ DE45 1RY – ☎ 01246 583880 – www.rowleysrestaurant.co.uk – Closed Sunday dinner

🏠 Cavendish ☆ ⇐ 🍴 ⅋ 🛁 🅿

TRADITIONAL · PERSONALISED Set on the edge of the Chatsworth Estate is this fine stone building with superb parkland views. Delightful bedrooms are full of period charm and many are styled by national designers and the Duchess of Devonshire herself. Enjoy drinks in the plush bar-cum-sitting room or afternoon tea in the Garden Room.

28 rooms – 👫 £230/289 – ☲ £20 – 1 suite

Church Lane ✉ DE45 1SP – ☎ 01246 582311 – www.cavendishbaslow.co.uk

🍴 **The Gallery** – See restaurant listing

BATH

Bath and North East Somerset – Regional map n° **2**–C2

Top tips!

Bath is known for its Georgian architecture and Roman Baths and is one of England's calmer cities: a place to relax and rejuvenate. Start with an open-top bus tour to get acquainted with the city's wonderful buildings – and be sure to stop off at No. 1 Royal Crescent, now a museum, furnished as the property would have been in the late 1700s.

Stroll around the Abbey, which has 7C origins, before enjoying afternoon tea and live music in the striking neo-classical Pump Rooms, which overlook the Roman Bath's hot spring. A tour around the baths is not to be missed, followed by a relaxing soak at the nearby Thermae Bath Spa.

Worth a visit is one of the longest running farmer's markets in the UK – held every Saturday in Green Park. For dining out, try informal small plates in a wine shop setting at Bib Gourmand **Beckford Bottle Shop**, or splash out with a meal at Michelin-Starred **Olive Tree**.

Restaurants

⮶ Olive Tree

MODERN CUISINE · INTIMATE ✕✕ The Queensbury comprises a series of Georgian townhouses, which sit in one of the oldest parts of the city – and is run by a friendly team. Start with a drink in the charming wood-panelled lounge, the cool bar – which boasts an extensive array of unusual spirits – or on the enclosed rear terrace, then head down to the surprisingly airy basement restaurant spread over three modern rooms.

Talented young chef Chris Cleghorn has worked in some high profile restaurants and while these experiences clearly inform his cooking, his dishes also display plenty of his own personality. His confidently executed dishes may appear simple at first glance, but that's all part of their skilful make-up. Colours, textures and flavours are used to full effect in refined, creative combinations which have plenty of depth.

Funky, individually designed bedrooms boast designer touches and a host of extras.

Specialities: Raw Orkney scallop, horseradish, pink grapefruit and dill. Duck, barbecue beetroot, sea beet, hazelnut and blackcurrant. Bahibé chocolate, Gaelic tobacco and milk jam.

Menu £33 (lunch), £68/85 – Carte £55/60

Town plan C1-x – *Queensberry Hotel, Russel Street* ⊠ *BA1 2QF* – ℰ *01225 447928* – *www.olivetreebath.co.uk* – *Closed 20-26 January, 20-26 April, 3-9 August, Monday, Tuesday – Thursday lunch*

⮷ Beckford Bottle Shop ⓝ

MODERN BRITISH · WINE BAR ✕ It's now a wine shop and bistro but the building was formerly a tea merchant's and a grocer's, and many period features remain, including an old cast-iron range in the intimate basement lounge. The atmosphere is relaxed, the creative small plates offer great value for money and the wine selection is extensive.

Specialities: Anchovies, parsley and shallots on toast. Crispy Bath Chaps with apple sauce. Dark chocolate mousse with hazelnut praline.

Carte £16/35

Town plan C1-e – *5-8 Saville Row* ⊠ *BA1 2QP* – ℰ *01225 809302* – *www.beckfordbottleshop.com* – *Closed Sunday dinner, Monday*

⅋O Menu Gordon Jones

MODERN CUISINE · INTIMATE ✕✕ This tiny restaurant has a relaxed, cheerful feel – a reflection of its easy-going owner-chef – and the room is dominated by an open kitchen, where you can watch him preparing creative, complex dishes. The daily changing surprise menu delivers punchy flavour combinations and interesting textural contrasts.

Menu £55 (lunch)/60

Town plan A2-e – *2 Wellsway* ⊠ *BA2 3AQ* – ℰ *01225 480871* – *www.menugordonjones.co.uk* – *Closed Sunday, Monday*

⅋O Acorn

VEGETARIAN · INTIMATE ✕ A sweet, intimate, split-level restaurant set within one of Bath's oldest buildings. Modern vegetarian dishes are full of colour and show a great understanding of flavours. Wines are carefully chosen to match the food.

Menu £25 (lunch), £40/60 – Carte £25/28

Town plan D2-a – *2 North Parade Passage* ⊠ *BA1 1NX* – ℰ *01225 446059* – *www.acornrestaurant.co.uk*

⅋O Circus

TRADITIONAL BRITISH · NEIGHBOURHOOD ✕ The small pavement terrace of this neighbourhood bistro is the perfect spot for people-watching in the historic heart of the city. Unfussy dishes use West Country produce and have a Mediterranean slant. Wines come from small growers.

Menu £25 (lunch), £31/40 – Carte £25/40

Town plan C1-c – *34 Brock Street* ⊠ *BA1 2LN* – ℰ *01225 466020* – *www.thecircusrestaurant.co.uk* – *Closed 21 December-10 January, Sunday*

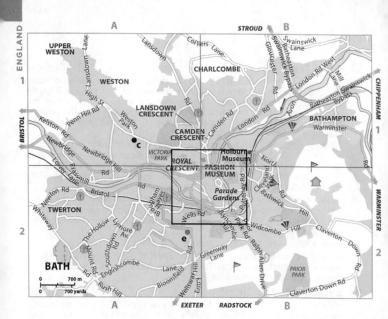

🍴 Henry's

🏮 🔟

MODERN BRITISH · NEIGHBOURHOOD ⚔ A laid-back bistro in a pretty pedestrianised street. It's simple yet appealing, with wooden furnishings and pictures of local scenes. Original modern dishes include some interesting vegetarian options.
Menu £20 (lunch)/50 – Carte £25/50

Town plan C1-n – *4 Saville Row* ✉ BA1 2QP – ☏ 01225 780055 –
www.henrysrestaurantbath.com – *Closed 20 December-15 January, Sunday, Monday*

🍴 Marlborough Tavern

🏮

TRADITIONAL BRITISH · PUB ⚔ This well-run neighbourhood pub sits on the edge of Victoria Park, surrounded by grand terraced properties, and despite its traditional appearance, is surprisingly chic and fashionable inside. Carefully sourced ingredients feature in a mix of accomplished pub classics and more adventurous British dishes.
Carte £24/42

Town plan C1-z – *35 Marlborough Buildings* ✉ BA1 2LY – ☏ 01225 423731 –
www.marlborough-tavern.com

Hotels

🏨 Royal Crescent

☆ ≼ 🛏 🔲 ⧖ ⅃⅋ 🔄 ⏁ AC ⚄ 🛎

HISTORIC · ELEGANT An elegantly refurbished Grade I listed building in a magnificent sweeping terrace. Ornate plasterwork, pastel shades and gilt-framed portraits evoke feelings of the Georgian era, and bedrooms are plush and luxurious. The lovely spa is in the old gothic chapel. Dine on attractive modern dishes.
45 rooms 🍽 – 👥 £330/645 – 12 suites

Town plan C1-a – *16 Royal Crescent* ✉ BA1 2LS – ☏ 01225 823 333 –
www.royalcrescent.co.uk

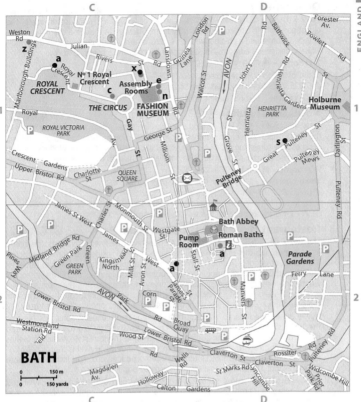

BATH

0   150 m
0   150 yards

🏨 Gainsborough Bath Spa

THERMAL SPA · ELEGANT Set within two listed buildings, this hotel boasts a state-of-the-art spa whose three thermal pools tap into the city's original springs. Bedrooms are elegantly understated and three have thermal water piped directly to their baths. Enjoy afternoon tea in the Canvas Room and seasonal dishes in the restaurant.

99 rooms – ♥♥ £260/450 – ☑ £30

Town plan C2-a – Beau Street ✉ BA1 1QY –
℘ 01225 358888 –
www.thegainsboroughbathspa.co.uk

🏨 Bath Priory

COUNTRY HOUSE · ELEGANT Two adjoining Georgian houses with formal gardens, an outdoor pool and an intimate spa. Country house guest areas are filled with antiques and oil paintings and luxurious bedrooms blend the traditional with the modern. Dine in the elegant restaurant, the more informal Pantry or out on the terrace.

33 rooms ☑ – ♥♥ £215/900 – 6 suites

Town plan A1-c – Weston Road ✉ BA1 2XT –
℘ 01225 331922 –
www.thebathpriory.co.uk

Queensberry

TOWNHOUSE · CONTEMPORARY A series of Georgian townhouses in one of the oldest parts of the city, run by a friendly team. Guest areas include a charming wood-panelled lounge and a chic bar with an extensive array of unusual spirits. Funky, individually designed bedrooms boast designer touches and a host of extras.

29 rooms – †† £99/495 – ☲ £18

Town plan C1-x – *Russel Street* ✉ BA1 2QF –
☎ 01225 447928 – www.thequeensberry.co.uk

🍃 **Olive Tree** – See restaurant listing

No.15 Great Pulteney

TOWNHOUSE · ELEGANT Behind the Georgian façade there's a dramatic fusion of the elegant and the contemporary. Chic, restful bedrooms have top quality bedding and bespoke furnishings. Café No. 15 serves light lunches and dinner Wednesday-Saturday, while the chic cocktail bar is so popular you have to book at weekends.

40 rooms – †† £94/506 – ☲ £20

Town plan D1-s – *13-15 Great Pulteney Street* ✉ BA2 4BS –
☎ 01225 807015 – www.no15greatpulteney.co.uk

at Colerne Northeast: 6. 5 mi by A4 – Regional map n° **2**-C2

✺ Restaurant Hywel Jones by Lucknam Park

MODERN BRITISH · ELEGANT XxxX A mile-long tree-lined drive sets the scene as you approach this grand Palladian mansion – and inside it doesn't disappoint. Rich, elegant décor, luxurious furnishings and sumptuous fabrics feature throughout, from the classically appointed bedrooms to the lounges and drawing rooms where pre-meal drinks and canapés are enjoyed while perusing the menus. This is country house dining at its finest – opulent, formal and sophisticated – and it suits the grand environment it sits within; a meal here is not one you'll soon forget.

Hywel Jones, who learnt his trade from a number of culinary icons, has been at the helm since 2004 and his experience shows. Expertly crafted, sophisticated dishes rely on classic techniques but have a light, modern style, which provides a pleasing contrast to the grandeur of the surroundings. Hywel is a proud Welshman, so alongside British and kitchen garden produce you'll find ingredients from his homeland. The tasting menus are the most popular choice.

Specialities: Citrus-cured salmon with crispy Porthilly oyster, Exmoor caviar and sea vegetables. Lamb '2 ways' with Heritage carrot and cumin granola. Manjari chocolate crémeux with raspberry, caramelised peanut and milk sorbet.

Menu £87/115

Off plan – *LuckNam Park Hotel* ✉ SN14 8AZ –
☎ 01225 742777 – www.lucknampark.co.uk – Closed Monday, Tuesday,
Wednesday - Saturday lunch

🍽 Brasserie

INTERNATIONAL · CONTEMPORARY DÉCOR XX A stylish brasserie in a beautiful courtyard within Lucknam Park's state-of-the-art spa. There's a spacious bar-lounge and an airy dining room with full-length windows. Precise, modern cooking arrives in well-judged combinations and many healthy options are available. Dine on the charming terrace in summer.

Menu £29 (lunch) – Carte £34/50

Off plan – *Lucknam Park Hotel* ✉ SN14 8AZ – ☎ 01225 742777 –
www.lucknampark.co.uk

Lucknam Park

GRAND LUXURY · ELEGANT A grand Palladian mansion with a mile-long tree-lined drive, rich, elegant décor, luxurious furnishings and sumptuous fabrics. Bedrooms are classically appointed and extremely comfortable. Top class facilities include an impressive spa, a renowned equestrian centre and a cookery school.

42 rooms – †† £260/685 – ☲ £32 – 5 suites

Off plan – ✉ SN14 8AZ – ☎ 01225 742777 – www.lucknampark.co.uk

✺ **Restaurant Hywel Jones by Lucknam Park** · 🍽 **Brasserie** – See restaurant listing

BAUGHURST

Hampshire – Regional map n° **4**–B1

⫟○ Wellington Arms ⇐ 🛏 🏠 **P**

TRADITIONAL CUISINE · PUB XX At this smart cream pub they have their own herb and vegetable beds, keep sheep, pigs, chickens and bees, and source the rest of their meats from within 20 miles. Menus feature 6 dishes per course – supplemented by a selection of specials – and cooking is generous and satisfying. Smart, rustic bedrooms come with slate floors, sheepskin rugs and big, comfy beds.

Menu £20 (lunch) – Carte £30/52

Baughurst Road ⊠ RG26 5LP – ℰ 0118 982 0110 – www.thewellingtonarms.com – Closed Sunday dinner

BEACONSFIELD

Buckinghamshire – Regional map n° **6**–D3

⫟○ No 5 London End ♿ 🄰🄲

MODERN BRITISH · BISTRO X A welcoming, modern-day bistro with a faux-distressed interior and a mix of banquettes and burnished leather seats. Creative menus are highly seasonal and textures and flavours are well thought out; influences are wide-ranging with a Mediterranean slant. Service is friendly and passionate.

Menu £21 – Carte £24/33

London End ⊠ HP9 2HN – ℰ 01494 355500 – www.no5londonend.co.uk

🏠 Crazy Bear 🍽 🌫 🄰🄲 🕭 **P**

BOUTIQUE HOTEL · DESIGN A unique hotel with sumptuous, over-the-top styling. Moody, masculine bedrooms blend original features with rich fabrics and idiosyncratic furnishings (some slightly less flamboyant bedrooms are located over the road). The lavishly styled 'English' restaurant uses produce from their farm shop, while sexy, extravagant 'Thai' serves Asian cuisine.

45 rooms – †† £289/429

75 Wycombe End ⊠ HP9 1LX – ℰ 01494 673086 – www.crazybeargroup.co.uk

BEAMINSTER

Dorset – Regional map n° **2**–B3

⫟○ Ollerod ⓝ 🛏 🏠 🍴 **P**

MODERN CUISINE · FRIENDLY XX Set within a hotel, Ollerod has a relaxed, friendly air and offers plenty of choice: you can eat in the bar, the dining room, out on the terrace or in the garden. Alongside the à la carte is a small plates menu; cooking is accomplished and makes good use of produce from the South West.

Carte £37/46

Ollerod Hotel, 3 Prout Bridge ⊠ DT8 3AY – ℰ 01308 862200 – www.theollerod.co.uk

⫟○ Brassica

MEDITERRANEAN CUISINE · BISTRO X A pretty little 16C house set on the small town square plays host to this laid-back restaurant, whose tasty, rustic cooking is full of flavour. Influences are Mediterranean, with a particular focus on Spain and Italy. Opposite, in another attractive Grade II listed property, is their homeware shop.

Menu £20 (lunch) – Carte £25/38

3-4 The Square ⊠ DT8 3AS – ℰ 01308 538 100 – www.brassicarestaurant.co.uk – Closed 6-13 January, 25-27 December, Sunday dinner-Tuesday

🏠 Ollerod

HISTORIC BUILDING · CONTEMPORARY A friendly team welcome you to this hotel; its name is the regional word for cowslip and its 13C walls are built from local Hamstone. It's a characterful place with low-beamed ceilings and an ingle-nook fireplace in the lounge but modern colours also bring a stylish feel. Pretty gardens add to its appeal.

13 rooms – 🛏 £125/285

3 Prout Bridge ⊠ DT8 3AY – ☏ 01308 862200 –
www.theollerod.co.uk

🍽 **Ollerod** – See restaurant listing

BEAULIEU

Hampshire – Regional map n° **4**–B2

🍽 The Terrace

MODERN BRITISH · TRADITIONAL XXX This elegant dining room is found at the heart of an alluring 18C inn; start with a drink on the terrace to take in views across the lovely gardens. This is a chef who really understands how to pair fla-vours and everything is on the plate for a reason. Service is enthusiastic and per-sonable.

Menu £30 (lunch)/90 – Carte £48/77

Montagu Arms Hotel, Palace Lane ⊠ SO42 7ZL – ☏ 01590 612324 –
www.montaguarmshotel.co.uk – Closed Monday, Tuesday

🏨 Montagu Arms

INN · CLASSIC With its characterful parquet floors and wood panelling, this 18C inn has a timeless elegance. Traditional country house bedrooms marry antique furniture with modern facilities, and the conservatory and terrace overlook the lovely gardens. Dine on updated classics in the dining room or pub classics in Monty's.

24 rooms ⊊ – 🛏 £179/349 – 5 suites

Palace Lane ⊠ SO42 7ZL – ☏ 01590 612324 – www.montaguarmshotel.co.uk

🍽 **The Terrace** – See restaurant listing

BEAUMONT – Jersey → See Channel Islands (Jersey)

BEELEY

Derbyshire – Regional map n° **9**–B1

🍽 Devonshire Arms

TRADITIONAL BRITISH · PUB X This stone inn boasts a hugely characterful low-beamed bar and a modern glass extension with views of the stream. A few pub favourites sit alongside some more interesting dishes and estate produce is used to the full. Choose a cosy bedroom in the inn or a modern room in the old dove-cote or nearby cottages.

Carte £30/40

Devonshire Square ⊠ DE4 2NR – ☏ 01629 733259 – www.devonshirebeeley.co.uk

BERRICK SALOME

Oxfordshire – Regional map n° **6**–B2

🍽 Chequers

TRADITIONAL BRITISH · PUB X This delightful 17C pub has a spacious garden and a welcoming interior with fresh flowers and candles on the tables and warm-ing open fires in the grates. Hearty menus list a mix of pub classics and more res-taurant-style dishes; chef-owner Mark is particularly proud of his fish dishes.

Carte £24/42

⊠ OX10 6JN – ☏ 01865 891118 – www.chequersberricksalome.co.uk – Closed Sunday dinner, Tuesday

BEVERLEY
East Riding of Yorkshire – Regional map n° **13**–D2

⭕ Westwood   🏠 ⅙ ⇔ 🅿

MODERN BRITISH · **BRASSERIE** XX The twins who own this smart modern brasserie clearly share the same vision. Appealing menus offer unfussy, recognisable dishes and the meats cooked 'a la plancha' are a hit. It sits in the wing of an impressive Georgian courthouse.

Menu £23/25 – Carte £29/50

New Walk ⊠ HU17 7AE – ℰ 01482 881999 – www.thewestwood.co.uk –
Closed 24 December-7 January, Sunday dinner, Monday

⭕ Whites

CREATIVE · **NEIGHBOURHOOD** XX An enthusiastic chef-owner runs this small restaurant beside the old city walls, where black furnishings and eye-catching art stand out against a plain backdrop. Ambitious modern cooking is delivered in 4 and 9 course surprise menus.

Menu £28 (lunch), £30/58

12a North Bar Without ⊠ HU17 7AB – ℰ 01482 866121 –
www.whitesrestaurant.co.uk – Closed 28 July-6 August, 24 December-3 January,
Sunday, Monday, Tuesday - Friday lunch

BEXHILL
East Sussex – Regional map n° **5**–B3

⭕ The Driftwood   ⇦ ⅙ 🅰🅲

ASIAN · **CONTEMPORARY DÉCOR** X Not far from the De La Warr pavilion is this surprisingly stylish little high street bistro. Together with her husband, the chef-owner creates authentic, vibrantly flavoured dishes that span Asia – including Chinese dumplings, Thai curries and Malaysian rendang. Above, comfy boutique bedrooms await.

Carte £19/31

40 Sackville Road ⊠ TN39 3JE – ℰ 01424 732584 – www.thedriftwoodbexhill.co.uk
– Closed Sunday dinner, Monday, Tuesday - Friday lunch

BIDBOROUGH
Kent – Regional map n° **5**–B2

⭕ Kentish Hare   🏠 ⅙ 🅿

MODERN CUISINE · **PUB** X Behind a grey and white clapboard façade are walls adorned with old photos of the village, which attest to the pub's history. Head through stylish rooms to the extension to watch the chefs cooking steaks on two Big Green Eggs. Care is taken both in sourcing and cooking, and dishes are tasty and well-presented.

Menu £23/27 – Carte £23/65

95 Bidborough Ridge ⊠ TN3 0XB – ℰ 01892 525709 – www.thekentishhare.com –
Closed Sunday dinner, Monday

BIDDENDEN
Kent – Regional map n° **5**–C2

⭕ The Three Chimneys   ⇦ 🛏 🏠 🅿

CLASSIC CUISINE · **PUB** X A delightful pub which dates back to 1420 and boasts dimly lit low-beamed rooms with an old world feel, a contrasting airy conservatory and a charming terrace. Traditional British dishes are accompanied by local wines, ciders and ales. Bedrooms are at the end of the garden and open onto a private terrace.

Carte £25/39

Hareplain Road ⊠ TN27 8LW – ℰ 01580 291472 – www.thethreechimneys.co.uk

BIDDENDEN

ⅱ◯ West House ◁ⓘ◎ ℙ

MODERN BRITISH · RUSTIC 𝕏 Two 16C cottages in a picturesque village; the heavily timbered interior hung with contemporary art is a mirror of the food, where classically based dishes are given a modern twist. The vegetarian tasting menu provides plenty of appeal, service is refreshingly unpretentious and bedrooms have stylish themes.

Menu £29 (lunch), £48/65 – Carte £29/48

28 High Street ✉ TN27 8AH – ℰ 01580 291341 –
www.thewesthouserestaurant.co.uk – Closed 1-17 September,
21 December-2 January, Sunday dinner, Monday, Tuesday, Saturday lunch

BINFIELD HEATH

Oxfordshire – Regional map n° **6**–C3

ⅱ◯ Bottle & Glass Inn 🍴🏠🕭 ℙ

MODERN BRITISH · PUB 𝕏 This pretty thatched pub sits in a lovely rural spot. The original part is the most characterful, while the restaurant is more up-to-date. Modern British cooking is refined but unfussy and has an appealing simplicity.

Menu £19 – Carte £25/40

Bones Lane ✉ RG9 4JT – ℰ 01491 412625 – www.bottleandglassinn.com –
Closed Sunday dinner

BIRKENHEAD

Merseyside – Regional map n° **11**–A3

☃ Fraiche (Marc Wilkinson)

CREATIVE · INTIMATE 𝕏𝕏𝕏 The tiny Victorian village of Oxton – now a conservation area – is home to this unique and intimate restaurant with seating for just 10. Chef-owner Marc Wilkinson cooks alone and devises everything from the daily changing tasting menu to the music playlist and the video images which are projected onto the walls of the cosy bar – anything from seasonal clips and aerial cityscapes to excerpts from Charlie and The Chocolate Factory.

Guests arrive at the same time for an aperitif before heading through to the boldly decorated restaurant or tiny conservatory; while you wait you can watch the chef at work through the kitchen window. Cooking is innovative, often playful, and the well-textured dishes have several layers of flavour. Presentation is impressive and both the colours of the ingredients and the shape and style of the crockery play their part. Service is friendly and confident and adds to the personal experience.

Specialities: Artichoke ice cream with passion fruit and pickled ginger. Salt-aged lamb cooked over fire with soy-braised aubergine and courgette cream. Poached pineapple with coconut cake and rosemary ice.

Menu £48 (lunch), £90/95

11 Rose Mount, Oxton ✉ CH43 5SG – ℰ 0151 652 2914 – www.restaurantfraiche.com
– Closed 12 July-3 August, 24 December-6 January, Monday, Tuesday,
Wednesday - Saturday lunch

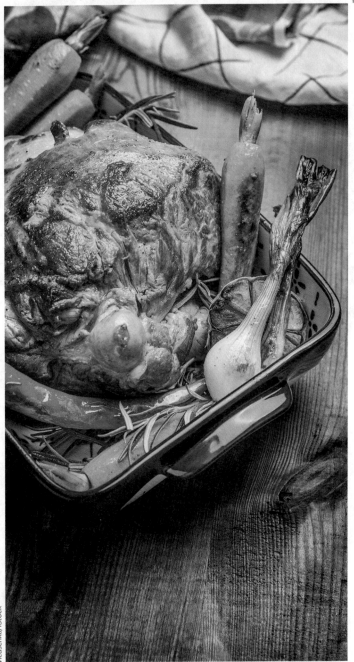

259

BIRMINGHAM

West Midlands – Regional map n° **10**–C2

Top tips!

The UK's 'Second City' is a vibrant place known for its cars, chocolate and network of canals; the latter a nod to its past as an industrial powerhouse. Development of the city centre continues at a rapid pace and there's always something to see or do.

The Birmingham Museum and Art Gallery is worth a visit for its pre-Raphaelite masterpieces alone, while Cadbury World continues to draw chocolate-lovers of all ages. The Bullring – with its 800 year old history – and the newer Mailbox provide excellent shopping opportunities, while Broad Street and Brindley Place really come alive at night. A diverse range of restaurants complete the picture, from modern Indian **Opheem** to sophisticated **Purnell's** and innovative **Carters of Moseley**, which all hold Michelin-Stars.

And things are set to get even more exciting as Birmingham prepares to host the 2022 Commonwealth Games.

Restaurants

✿ Simpsons (Andreas Antona and Luke Tipping)

🛋 🚗 ☂ ᴋ ᴀᴄ 🍷 ✧ **P**

MODERN CUISINE · DESIGN XxX Simpsons celebrated 25 years in 2018 and, although it has never stood still, it has always been an unwavering part of the local culinary scene, with many talented chefs having passed through its kitchens. It's housed in a Georgian mansion in the suburbs and behind its walls you'll find three contemporary bedrooms, a cookery school and a sleek restaurant. The décor is a clever balance of period Georgian and modern Nordic, courtesy of solid stone walls, ornate plasterwork, blonde wood beams and windows looking into the kitchen.

Chef-owner Luke Tipping cooks with confidence and his skill and experience shows through in dishes such as beautifully moist quail with creamy spelt risotto. The classically based cooking has a clean, Scandic style and the harmonious combinations take on a pared-back, understated approach. As well as being very visually pleasing, the seasonal dishes are packed full of powerful flavours. Their signature tapenade bread rolls are a hit, as are their soufflés.

Specialities: Sea bream tartare with wasabi ice cream. Rump of lamb with smoked cod's roe and tamarillo. Lemon meringue pie soufflé with hazelnut ice cream.

Menu £45 (lunch)/70

Town plan A2-e – *20 Highfield Road, Edgbaston ⊠ B15 3DU –*
☏ 0121 454 3434 – www.simpsonsrestaurant.co.uk –
Closed Monday

✿ Adam's (Adam Stokes)

✿✿ ᴋ ᴀᴄ ✧

MODERN CUISINE · ELEGANT XxX Adam Stokes' elegant restaurant feels like it's been around for years. Enjoy a drink in the smart cocktail bar then move on to the plush dining room with its subtle retro feel. The basement, as well as being home to the open kitchen, plays host to a glass wine cave bursting with top names and one of the most beautiful horseshoe chef's tables in the country.

Classical cooking has a subtle simplicity. Luxurious ingredients are the order of the day, although there's also a cheaper fixed price menu which employs simpler produce. A great selection of homemade breads and butters are followed by accurately prepared, well-balanced dishes showcasing top Scottish ingredients such as scallops or venison (from Adam's trusted suppliers established during his time at Glenapp Castle). Flavours are pronounced but true to the ingredients' natural tastes and there are appealing contrasts in texture and taste. Service is knowledgeable and the Coravin system allows you to try top quality wines by the glass.

Specialities: Cornish crab, apple, dashi and lobster tempura. Wagyu brisket and sirloin with chimichurri, grelot and chive. Valrhona 64% Manjari, teriyaki caramel, peanut and mascarpone.

Menu £40 (lunch), £65/95

Town plan E2-c – *New Oxford House, 16 Waterloo Street ⊠ B2 5UG –*
☏ 0121 643 3745 – www.adamsrestaurant.co.uk –
Closed 5-13 April, 25 August-6 September, 23 December-8 January, Sunday, Monday

✿ Purnell's (Glynn Purnell)

ᴋ ᴀᴄ ✧

MODERN CUISINE · DESIGN XxX Glynn Purnell really is 'Mr Birmingham': a larger-than-life character who is a proud ambassador for the city, which he has helped put on the culinary map. A friendly young team assist him at Purnell's; let one of them serve you a drink in the comfy lounge, then follow them past the wine display and through the oak door into the spacious, vibrantly decorated dining room.

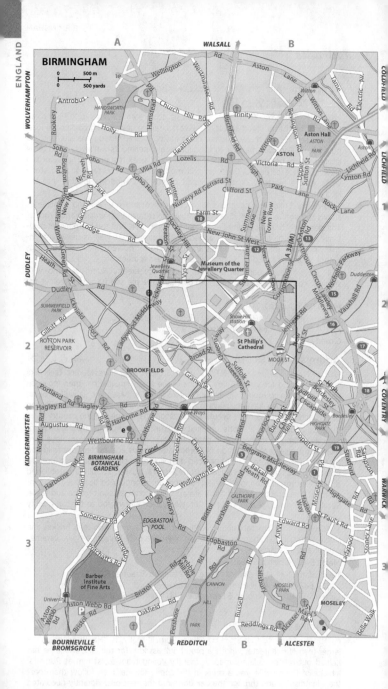

Menus range from an à la carte to a 10 course tasting option and include some of his signature dishes from the 'Great British Menu'. The sophisticated cooking ranges from British to Scandic in style and uses a mix of classic and modern techniques. Flavours and textures marry perfectly and he shows his personality through some of his more playful dishes. Rather than a chef's table, he has the 'Living Room', where he offers a selection of small plates entitled 'Brummie Tapas'.

Specialities: Cheese and pineapple - emotions of 'soixante-dix'. Sirloin of beef with smoked carrot. Opalys Valrhona white chocolate, mango and lime.

Menu £45 (lunch), £68/95

Town plan E1-b – *55 Cornwall Street ✉ B3 2DH – ℰ 0121 212 9799 – www.purnellsrestaurant.com – Closed 12-20 April, 24 December-4 January, Sunday-Tuesday lunch*

✿ Carters of Moseley (Brad Carter)   ✆ ⚍ 🄰🄲 🕼🕉

MODERN BRITISH · NEIGHBOURHOOD XX This lovely little restaurant sits in a small parade of shops and comes with black ash tables and a glass-fronted wine cabinet running down one wall. It's run by a friendly, engaging team, who will turn your visit into a real event, and is led by passionate self-taught chef-owner Brad Carter.

The set menu changes daily, offering a different number of courses throughout the week, and each dish is made up of just three or four well-balanced key components, which demonstrates Brad's skill and confidence. He has a keen interest in the historical elements of cooking, so while his dishes are modern and creative, they also champion heritage ingredients. Wines are natural and bio-dynamic and the home-produced charcuterie is something of a feature. In order to reduce the restaurant's carbon footprint, he sources as much local produce as possible.

Specialities: Razor clams with Old Winchester and pepper dulse. Belted Galloway with wasabi and turnip. Cider soaked Tamworth fat cake with cream cheese.

Menu £50/90

Town plan B3-a – *2c St. Mary's Row, Wake Green Road ✉ B13 9EZ – ℰ 0121 449 8885 – www.cartersofmoseley.co.uk – Closed 1-16 January, 4-20 August, Sunday, Monday, Tuesday - Thursday lunch*

✿ Opheem (Aktar Islam)   🍽 ⚍ 🄰🄲 🕼🕉 ⟷

INDIAN · ELEGANT XX There's no denying this large, modern Indian restaurant makes a statement – and not just in its bold decorative style. Aston-born chef-owner Aktar Islam, who grew up working in his father's restaurant, has created something quite unique and his pride in having his name above the door is palpable.

The 'Progressive Indian cooking' involves the kitchen grinding its own spices and using techniques like pickling and fermenting to produce visually arresting dishes with distinct, defined flavours. Some dishes are the result of research from The Ni'matnama, a 15C collection of recipes, while others are his own family's favourites passed down by his mother. Many Indian regions are represented, along with occasional Persian and Arabian influences. The tasting menu is the best way to experience the kitchen's full repertoire.

Specialities: Soft shell crab with caraway seed tempura and crab shami. Herdwick lamb pavé with confit shoulder, charred broccoli and bone marrow sauce. Passion fruit with Manjari chocolate.

Menu £30 (lunch), £40/70

Town plan D2-c – *48 Summer Row ✉ B3 1JJ – ℰ 0121 201 3377 – www.opheem.com – Closed 1-3 January, 25-28 December, Sunday, Monday*

🕼 Asha's   🍽 ⚍ 🄰🄲 🕼🕉 ⟷

INDIAN · EXOTIC DÉCOR XX A stylish, passionately run Indian restaurant with exotic décor; owned by renowned artiste/gourmet Asha Bhosle. Extensive menus cover most parts of the Subcontinent, with everything cooked to order. Tandoori kebabs are a speciality.

Menu £18 (lunch)/50 – Carte £29/55

Town plan E2-m – *12-22 Newhall Street ✉ B3 3LX – ℰ 0121 200 2767 – www.ashasuk.co.uk – Closed Sunday lunch, Saturday lunch*

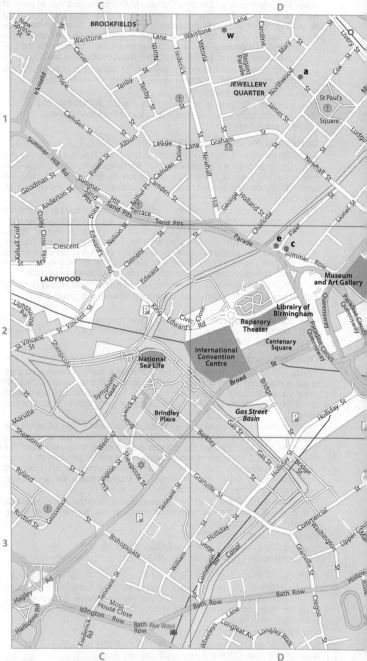

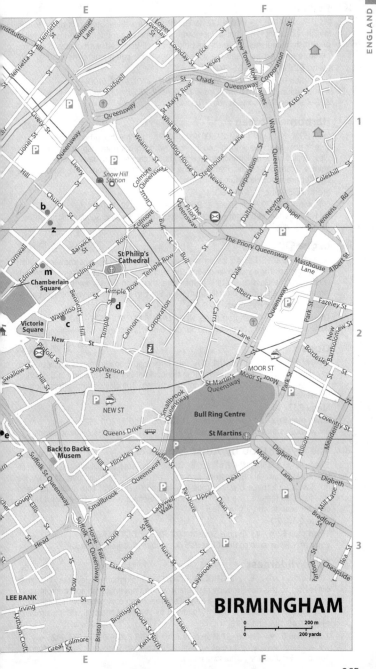

BIRMINGHAM

0   200 m
0   200 yards

ⅈ◯ Folium   ＆ AC

MODERN BRITISH · INTIMATE XX The historic Jewellery Quarter is home to this stylish restaurant. The chef-owner carefully prepares a modern menu which relies on British ingredients. Flavours are bold and well-balanced, with contrasts in temperature and texture – and the wine pairings really complement the food.

Menu £28 (lunch), £55/70

Town plan D1-a – 8 Caroline Street ✉ B3 1TR – ℰ 0121 638 0100 – www.restaurantfolium.com – Closed 12-22 April, 26 July-12 August, 22 December-8 January, Sunday-Tuesday

ⅈ◯ Harborne Kitchen   AC

MODERN BRITISH · NEIGHBOURHOOD XX This neighbourhood restaurant is surprisingly spacious – long and narrow, with an open kitchen at its heart; the tiles depicting a bull harking back to its butcher's shop days. Modern dishes have a Scandic feel and feature some unusual combinations. The seats at the counter are a popular choice.

Menu £35 (lunch), £40/80

Off plan – 175-179 High Street ✉ B17 9QE – ℰ 0121 439 9150 – www.harbornekitchen.com – Closed 31 December-4 January, Sunday, Monday, Tuesday - Wednesday lunch

ⅈ◯ Legna

ITALIAN · DESIGN XX An Italian restaurant reinvented, Legna is modern, stylish and glitzy; ask for a seat overlooking the kitchen or the canal. Dishes are modern versions of the classics. Pasta is homemade, the wood-fired oven is a feature and ingredients are sourced directly from Italy. Start in the impressive cocktail bar.

Menu £20 (lunch) – Carte £20/55

Town plan D2-e – 1 Islington Gates ✉ B3 1JH – ℰ 0121 201 3525 – www.legnarestaurant.com – Closed Sunday dinner, Monday

ⅈ◯ Opus

MODERN CUISINE · DESIGN XX A very large and popular restaurant with floor to ceiling windows; enjoy an aperitif in the cocktail bar before dining in the stylish main room or at the chef's table in the kitchen. The daily menu offers modern brasserie dishes.

Menu £33/38

Town plan E1-z – 54 Cornwall Street ✉ B3 2DE – ℰ 0121 200 2323 – www.opusrestaurant.co.uk – Closed 10-13 April, 23 December-3 January, Sunday

ⅈ◯ The Oyster Club by Adam Stokes   ＆ AC

SEAFOOD · CONTEMPORARY DÉCOR XX The name says it all: this is a place that's passionate about oysters, and they arrive here from all over the UK. It's not just about these bivalves though – a good variety of top quality fish and shellfish also feature. The room is bright and elegant, with marble-topped tables, counter seating and a plush feel.

Carte £30/70

Town plan E2-d – 43 Temple Street ✉ B2 5DP – ℰ 0121 643 6070 – www.the-oyster-club.co.uk – Closed 25 December-15 January, Monday

ⅈ◯ The Wilderness   ＆

MODERN CUISINE · NEIGHBOURHOOD XX Birmingham's Jewellery Quarter plays host to this dark, moody restaurant with an open kitchen and pumping music. Interesting set menus have a playful approach and could open with snacks such as a 'Big Mac' or 'Custard Cream', followed by lamb and charcoal with cucumber.

Menu £40 (lunch), £75/100

Town plan D1-w – Unit B, 27 Warstone Lane ✉ B18 6JQ – ℰ 0121 233 9425 – www.wearethewilderness.co.uk – Closed 22 December-3 January, Sunday, Monday, Tuesday, Wednesday - Thursday lunch

Hotels

Malmaison ✿ ⋔ Ⅼゟ ⊡ 㐆 ⅢⓀ 🐾

BUSINESS · CONTEMPORARY A stylish hotel with dark, moody décor, set on the site of the old Royal Mail sorting office beside designer clothing and home-ware shops. Bedrooms are spacious and the boldly decorated Nirvana suite comes with a mirror-tiled jacuzzi. Dine from an accessible British menu in the bustling brasserie.

192 rooms – †† £100/199 – ☲ £17 – 2 suites

Town plan E2-e – *Mailbox, 1 Wharfside Street ⊠ B1 1RD – ℰ 0121 246 5000 –* *www.malmaison.com*

BLACKBURN
Blackburn with Darwen – Regional map n° **11**–B2

at Langho North: 4. 5 mi on A666 – Regional map n° **11**–B2

✿ Northcote 🐾 ⇦㐆 Ⅲ ⅓Ⓘ⇔ Ⅾ

MODERN BRITISH · CONTEMPORARY DÉCOR ✕✕✕ This extensively refurbished Victorian house sits on the edge of the picturesque Ribble Valley and comes with a lovely fire-lit lounge and a bright, glitzy bar. Despite it being a hotel, you'll find that many people are here more for the food, with a night in one of the stylish, sophisticated bedrooms being all part of the experience.

The reputation of the elegant restaurant is forged on their relationship with nu-merous local biodynamic and organic suppliers – who have now become almost as famous as the restaurant itself – and as much produce as possible is also taken from the kitchen garden. Head Chef Lisa Goodwin-Allen's refined, sophisticated cooking shows real depth of flavour and a lightness of touch, along with plenty of originality. The accompanying wine list is outstanding.

You can watch the chefs close-up from the glass-walled kitchen table and they also run a cookery school on-site.

Specialities: Onion with Wilja potato and ash. Duck with smoked bacon, turnip and parsley. Blood orange 'Jaffa' with whipped toffee and rosemary.

Menu £36 (lunch), £70/90 – Carte £52/90

Northcote Hotel, Northcote Road ⊠ BB6 8BE – ℰ 01254 240555 – *www.northcote.com*

Northcote ⇦㐆 Ⅲ 🐾 Ⅾ

COUNTRY HOUSE · ELEGANT This well-run Victorian house sits on the edge of the Ribble Valley. Individually designed bedrooms are spacious, stylish and so-phisticated – all have queen or king-sized beds and some have garden terraces. Enjoy afternoon tea beside the fire in the lounge, followed by drinks in the bright, glitzy bar.

26 rooms ☲ – †† £215/375 – 1 suite

Northcote Road ⊠ BB6 8BE – ℰ 01254 240555 – www.northcote.com

✿ **Northcote** – See restaurant listing

BLACKPOOL
Blackpool – Regional map n° **11**–A2

Number One St Lukes ⇦ Ⅾ

TOWNHOUSE · DESIGN A boutique guesthouse set close to the promenade and the Pleasure Beach and run by a very charming owner. Bedrooms are named af-ter the town's piers: 'North' has an African feel and 'Central' has a white half-tes-ter and a more feminine touch. There's also an outdoor hot tub and a mini pitch and putt green!

3 rooms – †† £110/140

1 St Lukes Road ⊠ FY4 2EL – ℰ 01253 343901 – www.numberoneblackpool.com

at Thornton Northeast: 5. 5 mi by A584 - on B5412 – Regional map n° **11**–A2

⊛ **Twelve** 🍸 🏠 ♿

MODERN BRITISH · DESIGN ✗✗ This passionately run cocktail bar and restaurant sits beside one of Europe's tallest working windmills. Dine in the main room, on the mezzanine or in the bar, surrounded by exposed brick walls, reclaimed wood and graffiti art. Hearty, wholesome cooking has a refined edge; the à la carte menu is the most innovative.

Specialities: "Chicken livers on toast" parfait with date purée, toasted sourdough. Hake with wild garlic, miso, Jersey Royals and broccoli. Pear and parsnip millefeuille.

Menu £23 – Carte £26/47

Marsh Mill, Fleetwood Road North ⊠ FY5 4JZ – ℰ 01253 821212 –
www.twelve-restaurant.co.uk – Closed 1-13 January, Monday, Tuesday - Saturday lunch

BLAKENEY

Norfolk – Regional map n° **8**–C1

⇞○ **Wiveton Farm Café** ⩽ 🏠 **P**

REGIONAL CUISINE · FRIENDLY ✗ An extension of a farm shop, set down a dusty track and run by a smiley young team. Light breakfasts and tasty, salad-based lunches; weekends see 'Norfolk' tapas in the evenings. Take in glorious farm and sea views from the terrace.

Carte £22/32

1 Marsh Lane ⊠ NR25 7TE – ℰ 01263 740515 – www.wivetonhall.co.uk –
Closed 20 December-31 March

at Morston West: 1. 5 mi on A149 – Regional map n° **8**–C1

⊛ **Morston Hall** (Galton Blackiston) 🖴 **P**

MODERN BRITISH · ELEGANT ✗✗ Galton Blackiston – a distant relative of acclaimed anthropologist Sir Francis Galton – hoped to make his name on the cricket pitch; that was until he discovered where he really excelled: in the kitchen. He worked under John Tovey at Miller Howe, rising to Head Chef, and it was here that he met his wife to be, Tracy. They then set up their own restaurant, in an attractive 19C country house in a coastal hamlet.

Galton has always been enthused by the quality of Norfolk produce and many of his ingredients are plucked from the kitchen garden or foraged from the local beaches at Morston and Blakeney. Dishes are clean, fresh and well-crafted, with familiar flavour combinations leading the way. You might find Brancaster mussels, venison from Holkham Hall or Wagyu beef from Earl Stoneham.

Guests arrive early for drinks and canapes in the lounges, then are seated at 8pm for a 7 course set menu. The conservatory, with its lovely garden outlook, is the best place to sit. Those staying the night can choose from contemporary country house bedrooms or more luxurious garden rooms.

Specialities: Asparagus with Comté and morels. Suckling pig with burnt apple and sauce Robert. Wild strawberry tartlet.

Menu £95

Morston Hall Hotel, The Street ⊠ NR25 7AA – ℰ 01263 741041 –
www.morstonhall.com – Closed 1-24 January, 24-27 December, Monday - Saturday lunch

🏠 **Morston Hall** 🕭 🐾 🖴 **P**

COUNTRY HOUSE · PERSONALISED Set in a small coastal hamlet, an attractive, personally run country house with manicured gardens and keen, friendly service. Comfy guest areas feature antiques and paintings. Bedrooms are split between the main house and an annexe – the latter are larger, with subtle modern touches. Prices include dinner.

13 rooms � – ♥♥ £390/430

The Street ⊠ NR25 7AA – ℰ 01263 741041 – www.morstonhall.com –
Closed 1-24 January, 24-27 December

⊛ **Morston Hall** – See restaurant listing

at Wiveton South: 1 mi by A149 on Wiveton Rd – Regional map n° **8**–C1

🌸 **Wiveton Bell** ⬅ 🏠 **P**

TRADITIONAL BRITISH · PUB 🗙 Modernised pub featuring beams, stripped floors and wood-burning stoves; with picnic tables out the front and a beautifully landscaped rear terrace. Seasonal menu offers pub classics, carefully crafted from quality local ingredients. Stylish, cosy bedrooms have smart bathrooms; continental breakfasts.

Specialities: Cromer crab croquette, spiced fish soup, apple and fennel remoulade. Norfolk hogget, roast short saddle, belly, carrots, barley and wild garlic. Trifle, macerated strawberries, pistachio and Chantilly cream.

Menu £23/28 – Carte £26/43

Blakeney Road ✉ *NR25 7TL –* ☎ *01263 740101 – www.wivetonbell.com*

BLEDINGTON – Gloucestershire ➜ See Stow-on-the-Wold

BOLLINGTON

Cheshire East – Regional map n° **11**–B3

🍴 **Tapa** 🈸

MODERN CUISINE · RUSTIC 🗙 As its name suggests, this appealing restaurant serves small plates designed for sharing. Interesting cooking uses a diverse range of ingredients and has global influences; the fish dishes are usually a highlight.

Menu £18/22

22 High Street ✉ *SK10 5PH –* ☎ *01625 575058 – www.tapawinebar.co.uk – Closed 1-2 January, 25-26 December, Sunday dinner, Monday - Saturday lunch*

BOLNHURST

Bedford – Regional map n° **7**–A1

🍴 **Plough at Bolnhurst** 🐝 🍴 🏠 **P**

MODERN BRITISH · PUB 🗙 Charming whitewashed pub with a rustic bar, a modern restaurant, a lovely garden and a bustling atmosphere. Menus change with the seasons but always feature 28-day aged Aberdeenshire steaks, dishes containing Mediterranean ingredients like Sicilian black olives, and a great selection of wines and cheeses.

Menu £26 – Carte £35/45

Kimbolton Road ✉ *MK44 2EX –* ☎ *01234 376274 – www.bolnhurst.com – Closed 26 December-11 January, Sunday dinner, Monday*

BOLTON ABBEY

North Yorkshire – Regional map n° **13**–B2

🍴 **The Burlington** 🐝 ⬅ 🍴 ♿ 🎬 ⇔ **P**

MODERN BRITISH · ELEGANT 🗙🗙🗙 An antique-filled hotel dining room hung with impressive oils; sit in the conservatory overlooking the Italian garden. Restrained modern dishes utilise just a handful of complementary ingredients, with many coming from the kitchen garden and estate. The wine cellar is one of the best in northern England.

Menu £75

Devonshire Arms Hotel & Spa ✉ *BD23 6AJ –* ☎ *01756 718100 – www.thedevonshirearms.co.uk – Closed 24-26 December, Sunday lunch, Monday, Tuesday - Saturday lunch*

🏨 **Devonshire Arms H. & Spa** 🐎 🦢 ⬅ 🍴 🖼 🧖 🎭 🛁 ♿ 🏋 **P**

LUXURY · ELEGANT A charming coaching inn and spa on the Duke and Duchess of Devonshire's 30,000 acre estate in the Yorkshire Dales. Comfy lounges display part of the owners' vast art collection and dogs are welcome. Bedrooms in the wing are bright, modern and compact; those in the inn are more characterful.

40 rooms 🛏 – 👫 £139/250 – 2 suites

✉ *BD23 6AJ –* ☎ *01756 718100 – www.thedevonshirearms.co.uk*

🍴 **The Burlington** – See restaurant listing

BOROUGHBRIDGE
North Yorkshire – Regional map n° **13**–B2

ⅠО **thediningroom**
MODERN BRITISH · INTIMATE ✗✗ Characterful bow-fronted cottage concealing an opulent bar-lounge and an intimate beamed dining room. Wide-ranging menus offer boldly flavoured, Mediterranean-influenced dishes and chargrilled meats. In summer, head for the terrace.
Menu £20/40 – Carte £27/47
20 St. James's Square ⊠ YO51 9AR – ℰ 01423 326426 –
www.thediningroomonline.co.uk – Closed Sunday dinner, Monday, Tuesday -
Saturday lunch

BORROWDALE – Cumbria ➜ See Keswick

BOURNEMOUTH
Bournemouth – Regional map n° **2**–D3

ⅠО **Arbor**
MODERN CUISINE · CONTEMPORARY DÉCOR ✗✗ Arbor is located in an eco-friendly hotel and comes complete with a feature tree, FSC timbered floors and low energy induction cookers. Modern menus display innovative touches and produce is local and sustainable. You can also dine alfresco at the centre of the eco-garden.
Menu £25/35 – Carte £30/45
Green House Hotel, 4 Grove Road ⊠ BH1 3AX – ℰ 01202 498900 –
www.arbor-restaurant.co.uk

🏠 **Green House**
BUSINESS · DESIGN This bright, eco-friendly hotel is set within a small Grade II listed property and comes with an eco-garden and two electric car charging points. Furnishings are reclaimed and wallpapers are printed using vegetable ink. They even generate their own electricity!
32 rooms ☲ – ♥♥ £89/180
4 Grove Road ⊠ BH1 3AX – ℰ 01202 498900 – www.thegreenhousehotel.com
ⅠО **Arbor** – See restaurant listing

at Southbourne East: 3. 75 mi. by A 35 on B 3059

ⅠО **Roots** Ⅰ🏵
MODERN BRITISH · NEIGHBOURHOOD ✗✗ In an ordinary-looking parade of shops, behind frosted glass, is this bright, modern restaurant with 9 tables and a jovial, laid-back feel. Dishes are attractively prepared, delicately constructed and encompass a contrast of textures, temperatures and flavours; some even mix savoury and sweet.
Menu £35 (lunch), £39/66
141 Belle Vue Road ⊠ BH6 3EN – ℰ 01202 430005 – www.restaurantroots.co.uk –
Closed 23 December-8 January, Monday, Tuesday, Wednesday - Thursday lunch

BOURTON-ON-THE-WATER
Gloucestershire – Regional map n° **2**–D1

at Lower Slaughter Northwest: 1. 75 mi by A429 – Regional map n° **2**–D1

🏠 **Slaughters Manor House**
LUXURY · PERSONALISED A beautiful part-17C manor house built from Cotswold stone and surrounded by delightful grounds. Elegant bedrooms are split between the house and stables – the former are individually styled, the latter more up-to-date – and guest areas are stylish. The formal restaurant offers modern fare.
19 rooms – ♥♥ £195/388
⊠ GL54 2HP – ℰ 01451 820456 – www.slaughtersmanor.co.uk

at Upper Slaughter Northwest: 2. 5 mi by A429

🏠 Lords of the Manor

LUXURY · CLASSIC A charming 17C rectory in a pretty Cotswold village, with beautiful gardens, a superb outlook and a real sense of tranquility. Country house style bedrooms have subtle contemporary touches. Enjoy an aperitif in one of two luxurious sitting rooms then dine in the traditional Dining Room or intimate Atrium.

26 rooms ⌷ – 👫 £180/460 – 3 suites

✉ GL54 2JD – ☏ 01451 820243 – www.lordsofthemanor.com

BOW

Devon – Regional map n° **1**–C2

🏠 Paschoe House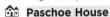

COUNTRY HOUSE · ELEGANT This elegant 19C country house blends classic and contemporary styles. It has a lovely tiled reception room and a modern bar offering far-reaching views over the well-tended grounds. Bedrooms come with hot water bottles and a map of local walks – and wellies are in the boot room. Cooking is modern and refined.

9 rooms ⌷ – 👫 £189/360

✉ EX17 6JT – ☏ 01363 84244 – www.paschoehouse.co.uk

BOWDON

Greater Manchester – Regional map n° **11**–B3

🍴 Borage &

MODERN CUISINE · NEIGHBOURHOOD XX An airy neighbourhood restaurant in a pleasant village. Well-presented, colourful European dishes showcase Polish ingredients and are full of flavour. The homemade breads are a highlight, as is the chocolate mousse.

Menu £24 (lunch), £28/38 – Carte £28/38

7 Vale View, Vicarage Lane ✉ WA14 3BD – ☏ 0161 929 4775 –
www.boragebowdon.co.uk – Closed 1-15 January, Monday, Tuesday, Wednesday, Thursday - Saturday lunch

BOWNESS-ON-WINDERMERE – Cumbria ➜ See Windermere

BOYLESTONE

Derbyshire – Regional map n° **9**–A2

🍴 Lighthouse & P

MODERN BRITISH · DESIGN XX It may not be near the coast but the Lighthouse does attract your attention. The self-taught chef prepares ambitious dishes with great combinations of flavours and textures; a good selection of keenly priced wines accompanies.

Menu £60

New Road (Behind Rose & Crown public house) ✉ DE6 5AA – ☏ 01335 330658 –
www.the-lighthouse-restaurant.co.uk – Closed 1-15 January, Sunday, Monday, Tuesday, Wednesday - Saturday lunch

BRADFORD-ON-AVON

Wiltshire – Regional map n° **2**–C2

🍴 Bunch of Grapes

FRENCH · PUB X The Bunch of Grapes is the oldest operating pub in this historic town and has an appealingly bijou, brocante feel. Have a beer and a pub classic in the ground floor bar or head to the upstairs restaurant for more refined modern dishes; the tasting menu showcases the chef's talent to the full.

Menu £23 (lunch), £30/45 – Carte £23/45

14 Silver Street ✉ BA15 1JY – ☏ 01225 938088 – www.thebunchofgrapes.com –
Closed Sunday dinner, Monday

BRADLEY
Staffordshire – Regional map n° **10**–C2

⅋O **The Red Lion**   🛏 🏠 **P**

TRADITIONAL CUISINE · PUB ⅋ An airy bar and conservatory opens onto a dining room hung with photos of the pub through the ages. Menus offer plenty of choice, with hearty, flavoursome dishes ranging from whole roast witch sole to curried chicken Kiev.

Carte £24/42

Smithy Lane ⊠ ST18 9DZ – ℰ 01785 780297 – www.redlionbradley.co.uk

BRADWELL
Derbyshire – Regional map n° **9**–A1

⅋O **Samuel Fox Country Inn**   🔄 🏠 **P**

MODERN BRITISH · PUB ⅋ An attractive, light-stone pub with smart, cosy bedrooms and a dramatic, hilly backdrop: named after the inventor of the steel-ribbed umbrella, who was born in the village. Flavourful classic dishes have modern touches and make good use of seasonal local produce. Popular 7 course tasting menu.

Menu £24/36

Stretfield Road ⊠ S33 9JT – ℰ 01433 621562 – www.samuelfox.co.uk –
Closed 2-16 January, 1-8 August, Sunday dinner, Monday, Tuesday, Wednesday -
Saturday lunch

BRAITHWAITE – Cumbria ➜ See Keswick

BRAY
Windsor and Maidenhead – Regional map n° **6**–C3

✿✿✿ **Waterside Inn** (Alain Roux)   ⅋ 🔄 ≼ 🎞 🕐 🔄 **P**

CLASSIC FRENCH · ELEGANT ⅋⅋⅋ This illustrious restaurant sits in a glorious spot on a bank of the River Thames. It was opened in 1972 by brothers Michel and Albert Roux and is now in the hands of Michel's son Alain. It remains the longest-standing Starred restaurant in the UK, having been awarded One Star in 1974, Two Stars in 1977 and Three Stars in 1985.

Michel set the bar high and luxury is at every turn. Tables are superbly laid with the finest crockery and glassware, an abundance of staff cater for guests' every whim, and menus are packed with top quality ingredients. Carefully considered classical French menus are a calendar for the seasons and dishes arrive in perfectly judged, sophisticated combinations. The lobster and rabbit are specialities, the Challandais duck for 2 is a seminal dish and the cheese trolley and the soufflé of the day are not to be missed.

Bedrooms are fittingly chic and sumptuous.

Specialities: Tronçonnettes de homard poêlées minute au porto blanc. Filets de lapereau grillés sur un fondant de céleri-rave, sauce à l'armagnac et aux marrons glacés. Soufflé chaud à la rhubarbe teinté de framboises.

Menu £64 (lunch)/172 – Carte £127/175

Ferry Road ⊠ SL6 2AT – ℰ 01628 620691 – www.waterside-inn.co.uk –
Closed 26 December-30 January, Monday, Tuesday

✿✿✿ **Fat Duck** (Heston Blumenthal)   ⅋ 🎞 **P**

CREATIVE · ELEGANT ⅋⅋⅋ Tables at this iconic restaurant are released several months in advance, so you'll need to plan ahead if you have a special date in mind. Once you arrive, a dedicated Story Teller will guide you through your journey, from "breakfast" through to "dinner". Heston's aim is to evoke memories of childhood and to recreate the child-like anticipation and excitement felt in your formative years.

Both the décor and the table settings are understated, allowing you to fully immerse yourself in the theatrical, multi-sensory experience. The innovative cooking is detailed, playful and perfectly judged, and the textures and flavours are harmonious. Elaborate, interactive presentation and a truly engaging service team further heighten the experience and every dish will leave you eagerly anticipating the next.

Specialities: Sound of the sea. Mock turtle soup. Botrytis cyneria.

Menu £325

High Street ✉ SL6 2AQ – ✆ 01628 580333 – www.thefatduck.co.uk – Closed 23 December-10 January, Sunday, Monday

✿ Hinds Head 🍸 A/C Ⓥ ⊡ 🅿

TRADITIONAL BRITISH • HISTORIC ✕ The Hinds Head is a quintessentially English inn that is never less than bustling and the characterful interior provides the perfect backdrop for the historic British dishes. Start with a cocktail in the Royal Lounge – surrounded by some unusual taxidermy – before heading for the characterful 15C restaurant with its wood-panelling, exposed timbers and open fires.

Sophisticated dishes celebrate time-honoured British recipes that have been carefully researched, but Heston Blumenthal's creative influences are also evident, as the dishes have been restructured in a subtle modern style. The execution is precise, the combinations work beautifully, and different textures and temperatures play their part. Don't miss the Quaking Pudding, which changes flavour with the seasons. The friendly serving team have excellent knowledge of the different dishes.

Specialities: Scotch egg with pea and ham soup. Oxtail and kidney pudding. Treacle tart.

Menu £30 (lunch)/47 – Carte £65/95

High Street ✉ SL6 2AB – ✆ 01628 626151 – www.hindsheadbray.com – Closed Sunday dinner

🍽 Caldesi in Campagna ⛱

ITALIAN • INTIMATE ✕✕ Passionate Montepulciano-born owner-cum-food-author Giancarlo Caldesi and his wife Katie run this chic, sophisticated restaurant. It comes with a cosy conservatory and a lovely covered terrace complete with a wood-fired oven. Flavoursome Italian dishes feature Tuscan and Sicilian specialities.

Carte £35/57

Old Mill Lane ✉ SL6 2BG – ✆ 01628 788500 – www.caldesi.com – Closed Sunday dinner, Monday

🍽 Crown 🌳 ⛱ 🅿

TRADITIONAL BRITISH • PUB ✕ Charmingly restored 16C building; formerly two cottages and a bike shop! Drinkers mingle with diners, and dark columns, low beams and roaring fires create a cosy atmosphere. Carefully prepared British dishes are robust and flavoursome.

Carte £29/55

High Street ✉ SL6 2AH – ✆ 01628 621936 – www.thecrownatbray.com

🍽 Royal Oak 🍇 🌳 ⊡ 🅿

TRADITIONAL BRITISH • PUB ✕ It might be a pub but the Royal Oak is a place with an air of formality and a sense of occasion. Classic British dishes follow the seasons – and you definitely won't leave hungry! In summer, pick a spot in the tranquil garden; in winter, cosy up by the fire in the characterful bar.

Menu £20 (lunch) – Carte £35/47

Paley Street ✉ SL6 3JN – ✆ 01628 620541 – www.theroyaloakpaleystreet.com – Closed Sunday dinner, Monday

🏨 Monkey Island Ⓝ 🏠 ⋞ 🌳 Spa 🚲 🏋 🅿

COUNTRY HOUSE • PERSONALISED This charming hotel has a fairytale setting on a private island: check in at the Boathouse and cross the bridge to the two Grade I listed pavilions, originally commissioned as a fishing retreat in 1723 by the third Duke of Marlborough. Unwind in the lovely terrace cocktail bar or the unique floating spa.

30 rooms – 👫 £275/325 – ☕ £25

✉ SL6 2EE – ✆ 01628 623400 – www.monkeyislandestate.co.uk

BRIDPORT

Dorset – Regional map n° **2**–B3

ⅈ〇 **Dorshi**

ASIAN · FRIENDLY X A bohemian-style restaurant with a laid-back feel: the ground floor is lively while upstairs it's more intimate. Asian street food inspired small plates are perfect for sharing and their flavours pack a punch; the dumplings are a highlight. Cocktails are creative and at weekends there's a house party vibe.

Menu £10 (lunch) – Carte £20/30

Bartholomews Hall, 6 Chancery Lane ⊠ *DT6 3PX* – ℰ *01308 423221* –
www.dorshi.co.uk – *Closed Sunday, Monday*

at Burton Bradstock Southeast: 2 mi by B3157

ⅈ〇 **Seaside Boarding House**

TRADITIONAL BRITISH · CONTEMPORARY DÉCOR XX Stunningly located on the clifftop, this old hotel has a fresh, new look. The bright, airy restaurant has a subtle maritime theme and there's a lovely terrace with sea views. Menus offer everything from fish soup to plaice with lemon and caper butter. Classically understated bedrooms come with claw-foot baths and there's a pleasant bar and library for residents.

Menu £15 (lunch) – Carte £24/42

Cliff Road ⊠ *DT6 4RB* – ℰ *01308 897205* – *www.theseasideboardinghouse.com*

BRIGHTON AND HOVE

Brighton and Hove – Regional map n° **5**–A3

Top tips!

You're never too far from a party in this south coast jewel. This is a city that knows how to have fun – and does it incredibly well: it's colourful, lively, experimental and pioneering, and that goes for the people too.

Take a stroll down the promenade to the Pier or travel 162 metres up the BA i360 observation tower to take in far-reaching coastal views. Then head inland to the Royal Pavilion and 'The Lanes' – a lively neighbourhood brimming with jewellery and antique shops and cool, quirky restaurants. Here you'll find ground-breaking cuisine at Bib Gourmand **64°** and a great vegetarian selection at **Terre à Terre**.

A ten minute stroll away in North Laine are yet more chilled restaurants. If you're after Indian, Bib Gourmand awarded **Chilli Pickle** is a fabulous place; if seafood's your thing, make for **Little Fish Market**; and if the name starts with '**Ginger**', you can be sure it's a safe bet.

Restaurants

Chilli Pickle

INDIAN · SIMPLE X A laid-back restaurant with a buzzy vibe and friendly service. The passionate chef uses good quality ingredients to create authentic Indian dishes with vibrant colours and flavours. Go for a thali at lunch and a kebab, grill or curry at dinner. Beside the terrace they also have a cart selling street food.

Specialities: Tandoori horseradish paneer with fenugreek mayo and green mango salad. Lamb shank with Persian biryani rice, smoked aubergine and green chilli mint pickle. Pistachio kulfi.

Menu £24/28 – Carte £16/34

Town plan C2-z – *17 Jubilee Street* ✉ *BN1 1GE* – ✆ *01273 900383* – *www.thechillipickle.com*

Cin Cin

ITALIAN · SIMPLE X This former single-car garage is hidden away in the North Laine area. It's a modest, quirky little place and seats 21 around a horseshoe counter. The food is Italian, with fresh ingredients cooked simply and natural flavours allowed to shine. Enjoy tasty small plates and delicious homemade pastas.

Specialities: Rabbit crochette with basil emulsion. Pea and smoked ham hock agnolotti. Affogato.

Menu £20 (lunch) – Carte £26/30

Town plan C2-n – *13-16 Vine Street* ✉ *BN1 4AG* – ✆ *01273 698813* – *www.cincin.co.uk* – *Closed Sunday, Monday*

The Set

MODERN BRITISH · RUSTIC X A quirky little hotel eatery. To the front is a café and to the rear is a restaurant – along with a kitchen counter where they serve a surprise tasting menu. Cooking is rustic with international influences and packs plenty of flavour. Exposed wood, brick, iron and reclaimed furnishings set the scene.

Specialities: Crumpet with Marmite-glazed ox tongue, pickled cockles and turnip. Trout with leeks, clotted cream and crab bisque. Rhubarb and custard eclair.

Carte £23/32

Town plan B2-e – *Artist Residence Hotel, 33 Regency Square* ✉ *BN1 2GG* – ✆ *01273 324302* – *www.thesetrestaurant.com*

64°

MODERN BRITISH · SIMPLE X Hidden away in The Lanes is this stylish, laid-back restaurant, comprising 3 tables and a kitchen counter where you can interact with the chefs. The pared-back menu offers 'Fish', 'Veg' and 'Meat' small plates. Fresh, flavoursome dishes use just a handful of ingredients and deliver well-judged contrasts.

Specialities: Highland beef tartare with black sesame mayonnaise, radish and bric pastry. Fillet of turbot, roast chicken, butter sauce and tarragon oil. Spiced rhubarb crème brûlée with coconut and white chocolate crumb.

Menu £42 – Carte £23/30

Town plan B2-c – *53 Meeting House Lane* ✉ *BN1 1HB* – ✆ *01273 770115* – *www.64degrees.co.uk* – *Closed 24-27 December*

etch. by Steven Edwards

MODERN BRITISH · NEIGHBOURHOOD X This compact neighbourhood restaurant is a hit with the locals. Ask to sit in one of the booths in the bay window then choose how many courses you'd like from the set menu – go for the 9 course option at dinner. Cooking captures flavours to the full.

Menu £55 (lunch), £65/75

Town plan A1-h – *216 Church Rd, Hove* ✉ *BN3 2DJ* – ✆ *01273 227485* – *www.etchfood.co.uk* – *Closed Sunday, Monday, Tuesday, Wednesday lunch*

BRIGHTON AND HOVE

Ginger Dog

MODERN BRITISH · PUB ✕ A charming Victorian pub with a pleasingly shabby-chic feel. Ornately carved woodwork sits comfortably alongside more recent additions like bowler hat lampshades. Menus list pub staples alongside some more interesting dishes with a subtle modern style. The dessert cocktails are worth a try.

Menu £16/20 – Carte £25/41

Town plan C2-s – *12 College Place* ✉ *BN2 1HN* – ✆ *01273 620990* – *www.gingermanrestaurants.com*

Gingerman

MODERN CUISINE · NEIGHBOURHOOD ✕ There's a smart Scandic feel to the decoration and an intimacy to the atmosphere at this long-standing neighbourhood restaurant. Lunch is fairly classical while dinner features more elaborate, innovative combinations.

Menu £20 (lunch), £45/60

Town plan B2-a – *21a Norfolk Square* ✉ *BN1 2PD* – ✆ *01273 326688* – *www.gingermanrestaurants.com* – *Closed 1-15 January, Monday*

Ginger Pig

TRADITIONAL BRITISH · PUB ✕ You enter into this striking mock-Tudor building via a beautiful antique revolving door. The original, highly seasonal menu has a European accent and gives the odd nod to North Africa; Sussex produce is to the fore and vegetarians are well catered for. Modern, loft-style bedrooms have comfy Hypnos beds.

Menu £18 (lunch) – Carte £26/60

Town plan A2-e – *3 Hove Street, Hove* ✉ *BN3 2TR* – ✆ *01273 736123* – *www.gingermanrestaurants.com*

Isaac At

MODERN BRITISH · SIMPLE ✕ You have to buy a 'ticket' in advance for dinner at this modest little 20-seater restaurant. Watch the young kitchen team on the TV screen or from the two counter spaces. Sussex produce is showcased in 8 daily changing dishes which have an understated modern style and rely on natural flavours.

Menu £40/59

Town plan C2-f – *2 Gloucester Street* ✉ *BN1 4EW* – ✆ *07765 934740* – *www.isaac-at.com* – *Closed 20 September-5 October, 22 December-15 January, Sunday, Monday, Tuesday - Friday lunch*

Little Fish Market

SEAFOOD · SIMPLE ✕ Fish is the focus at this simple restaurant, fittingly located in a converted fishmonger's opposite the old Victorian fish market. The owner cooks alone and his set 6 course menu offers refined, interesting modern seafood dishes.

Menu £69

Town plan B2-m – *10 Upper Market Street, Hove* ✉ *BN3 1AS* – ✆ *01273 722213* – *www.thelittlefishmarket.co.uk* – *Closed 25 April-6 May, 26 September-6 October, Sunday, Monday, Tuesday - Saturday lunch*

Murmur

MODERN BRITISH · BISTRO ✕ The sister of 64° sits in a pleasant spot on the seafront. It's a colourful, laid-back place, built into the arches of the promenade, and has a lovely beachside terrace for sunny days. Modern classics are supplemented by blackboard specials; the lobster croquettes are a signature dish.

Menu £25 (lunch) – Carte £25/40

Town plan B2-u – *91-96 Kings Road Arches* ✉ *BN1 2FN* – ✆ *01273 711900* – *www.murmur-restaurant.co.uk* – *Closed 24-27 December, Sunday dinner*

⇊○ Terre à Terre   ⌂ ♿ AC 🍸

VEGETARIAN · NEIGHBOURHOOD ✗ Relaxed, friendly restaurant decorated in warm burgundy colours. Appealing menu of generous, tasty, original vegetarian dishes which include items from Japan, China and South America. Mini épicerie sells wine, pasta and chutney.

Menu £35 – Carte £29/37

Town plan C2-e – 71 East Street ✉ BN1 1GE – ✆ 01273 729051 – www.terreaterre.co.uk

⇊○ Wild Flor Ⓝ

MODERN BRITISH · BISTRO ✗ Four friends have realised their ambition at this appealingly relaxed neighbourhood restaurant. Three of them work out front and their pride is palpable; the fourth skilfully prepares dishes with great depth of flavour and an unfussy style. The room has bare brick walls and a modern bistro feel.

Menu £22 (lunch)/33 – Carte £31/40

Town plan A2-g – 42 Church Road ✉ BN3 2FN – ✆ 01273 329111 – www.wildflor.com – Closed Sunday dinner, Tuesday, Wednesday

Hotels

🏨 Hotel du Vin   ⌂ AC ♨

BUSINESS · CONTEMPORARY Made up of various different buildings; the oldest being a former wine merchant's. Kick-back in the cavernous, gothic-style bar-lounge or out on the terrace. Bedrooms are richly decorated and have superb monsoon showers. The relaxed brasserie, with its hidden courtyard, serves French bistro classics.

49 rooms ⌂ – � £89/399

Town plan B2-a – 2-6 Ship Street ✉ BN1 1AD – ✆ 01273 718588 – www.hotelduvin.com

🏠 Artist Residence   ⌂ ⊞

TOWNHOUSE · QUIRKY These two townhouses look over Regency Square to the West Pier. Their style is shabby-chic, with bedrooms featuring reclaimed furnishings and named after the artists who furnished them; choose one with a balcony and a sea view. Unwind with a game of table tennis or a drink in the cocktail shack.

25 rooms – ♟ii £135/310 – ⌂ £11

Town plan B2-s – 33 Regency Square ✉ BN1 2GG – ✆ 01273 324302 – www.artistresidence.co.uk

🍽 **The Set** – See restaurant listing

BRILL

Buckinghamshire – Regional map n° **6**-C2

⇊○ The Pointer   ⇦ 🍴 ⌂

MODERN BRITISH · PUB ✗ Find a spot in the characterful bar-lounge, in the beamed dining room or out in the garden of this delightful pub. Choose from pub classics or more modern dishes with European influences – and be sure to take something home from their butcher's shop. Stylish bedrooms are situated in the cottage opposite.

Menu £18/40 – Carte £18/52

27 Church Street ✉ HP18 9RT – ✆ 01844 238339 – www.thepointerbrill.co.uk

281

BRISTOL

City of Bristol - Regional map n° **2**–C2

Top tips!

The unofficial capital of the West Country is a bohemian city with an interesting maritime history and a vibrant cultural scene, yet it retains the friendly feel of a smaller town.

Once busy with trade, the old docks are now home to attractive modern developments filled with shops and restaurants – and, at the weekend, they buzz with the sound of markets. Visit Brunel's SS Great Britain, hire a bike or a paddle board, take part in a Banksy tour (this was his hometown), or even cross the Clifton Suspension Bridge to take in the view.

You'll find a fittingly eclectic range of restaurants to suit all tastes and wallets. Michelin Stars come in the form of creative **Casamia**, modern **wilks**, neighbourhood-style **Bulrush** and lively **Paco Tapas**, while Wapping Wharf plays host to the likes of laid-back **Tare** and Bib Gourmand awarded **BOX-E** and **Root** – all located in shipping containers.

NXiao/iStock

Restaurants

☸ **Casamia** (Peter Sanchez-Iglesias)   &

CREATIVE · DESIGN XX Casamia sits in an impressive Grade II listed former Victorian hospital on the harbour-side, overlooking Bathurst Basin. You enter through double glass doors, under an arch and through into a pared-down Scandic-style room with just a handful of grey-washed oak tables and two seats at the pastry counter. Vaulted arches give it a light, airy feel and the state-of-the-art open kitchen acts as the focal point.

The menu is delivered in a 'surprise' format, with dishes being presented by a charming, professional team and finished off at your table by the chefs themselves. Top quality seasonal ingredients guide the menu and cooking is modern with Scandic overtones; the simplicity of the presentation belying the huge amount of work that has gone into the execution. Diners are also offered a tour of the kitchen.

Specialities: Parmesan tartlet. Rainbow trout with langoustine. Passion fruit and tarragon.

Menu £48 (lunch)/118

Town plan C2-e – *The General, Lower Guinea Street* ✉ *BS1 6FU* – ☎ *0117 959 2884* – *www.casamiarestaurant.co.uk* –
Closed 1-7 January, 22-27 April, 24-27 June, 23-26 September, Sunday, Monday, Tuesday, Wednesday lunch

☸ **wilks** (James Wilkins)

MODERN BRITISH · FRIENDLY XX A striking mural of a whale stands out against grey walls at this appealingly elegant yet unpretentious neighbourhood restaurant, where the precisely laid tables are well spaced out. It's run by an experienced couple – James and Christine Wilkins: he takes charge of the kitchen, while she looks after the service.

James is well-travelled and skilfully balances different textures with flavours from around the globe. Top quality French and British ingredients jostle with one another on the menu and all of the fish is wild, from the turbot to the John Dory. Dishes are crafted using carefully honed techniques and a light touch, and they show plenty of James' personality. Puddings are elegantly presented and packed full of flavour and the imported French cheeses are worthy of note.

Specialities: Scallop tartare with wasabi, apple, ginger and sesame. Squab pigeon with liver parfait, confit leg, salt-baked celeriac and thyme jus. Cocoa meringue sphere with almond & vanilla milk mousse and coffee bean ice cream.

Menu £34 (lunch), £64/88

Town plan A1-d – *1 Chandos Road* ✉ *BS6 6PG* –
☎ *0117 973 7999* –
www.wilksrestaurant.co.uk –
Closed 2-21 August, 23 December-15 January, Monday, Tuesday, Wednesday - Thursday lunch

☸ **Bulrush** (George Livesey)   🍽️👁️ 🔄

MODERN BRITISH · NEIGHBOURHOOD X It might appear modest from the outside but this sweet neighbourhood restaurant is run by a friendly, professional team and has an appealingly relaxed, cosy atmosphere. It's set over two floors; stay downstairs to soak up the atmosphere from the on-view kitchen run by the keen young team.

Seasonal ingredients are foraged or organic, and preserving and pickling play a key role. The imaginative, well-balanced and deftly prepared tasting menu is the most popular choice among guests. The ingredients are top-notch; the combinations are original and provide plenty of contrasts; and the flavours are clear and natural.

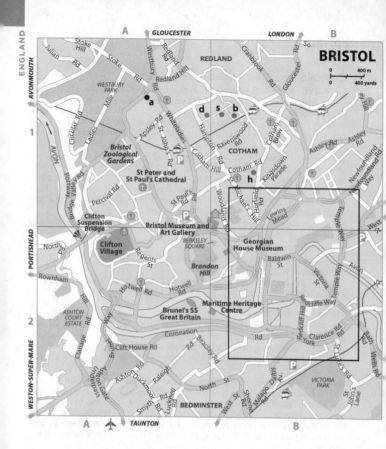

Service is polite and friendly and the chef-owner, George Livesey, often delivers a dish or two to the table himself.

Specialities: Roast quail, asparagus and morels. Middlewhite pork, chicory marmalade and loquat. Truffle ice cream, croissant mousse and caramelised apples.

Menu £55/60 – Carte £34/42

Town plan B1-h – *21 Cotham Road South* ✉ *BS6 5TZ* –
☏ *0117 329 0990* –
www.bulrushrestaurant.co.uk –
Closed 17-26 May, 16 August-1 September, 22 December-7 January, Sunday, Monday, Tuesday - Wednesday lunch

✿ **Paco Tapas**   A/C 🍽

SPANISH · TAPAS BAR 🍴 This buzzy tapas bar shoehorned in the corner of a vast development is the younger sister of Casamia and is named after the head of the family who own it, Mr Sanchez-Iglesias Senior. Sit on the terrace for nibbles accompanied by one of their fine Spanish wines or head for the 8-seater counter set around the large open grill. The décor might be simple, with period grey tiles and a few Spanish prints, but it's the food that will steal your focus here.

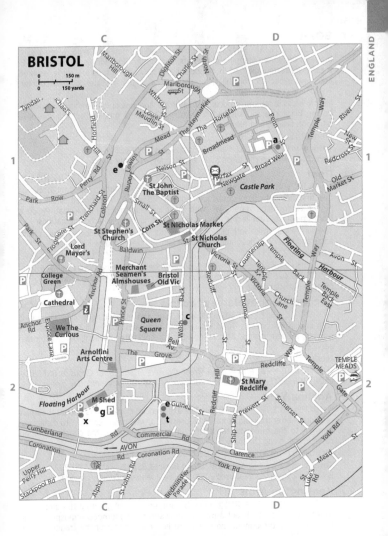

Appealing menus provide plenty of choice and include all the favourites. The authentic, skilfully prepared dishes are packed with flavour and the passion with which they are made is palpable. The "Chef's Menu" will take you on a best-of-the-best tour of Spain with the likes of clams, jamón croquettes and wood-roast gambas, and be sure to try the fire-cooked bread – it will have you in raptures.

They offer a great range of Spanish wines too, with chilled sherries served straight from the cask.

Specialities: Jamón croquetas. Stuffed quail. Crema Catalana.

Menu £50 – Carte £20/50

Town plan C2-t – *The General, 3A Lower Guinea Street ⊠ BS1 6FU –*
𝒞 0117 925 7021 – www.pacotapas.co.uk –
Closed Sunday, Monday, Tuesday - Thursday lunch

⊛ BOX-E

MODERN BRITISH · SIMPLE X Wapping Wharf is home to Cargo, a retail yard made of converted shipping containers, and on the first floor is intimate BOX-E, a compact restaurant clad in chipboard and plywood. Dishes are rustic, assured and flavour-packed; for the tasting menu, book the 4-seater kitchen counter. The panna cotta is a must!

Specialities: Sprouting broccoli with burrata and preserved lemon. Roast cauliflower, black rice and smoked paprika oil. Chocolate mousse, extra virgin olive oil, blood orange and hazelnuts.

Menu £45 – Carte £26/31

Town plan C2-x – *Unit 10, Cargo 1, Wapping Wharf* ✉ *BS1 6WP* – *www.boxebristol.com* – *Closed Sunday, Monday, Tuesday lunch*

⊛ Root

MODERN BRITISH · SIMPLE X This busy, welcoming little restaurant occupies five first floor shipping containers on the old wharf. Well-priced small plates have their focus on vegetables, with meat and fish taking a back seat. Produce from small local suppliers is used in simple yet flavour-packed combinations.

Specialities: Beetroot with blueberry, hazelnuts and seaweed. Gnocchi, garlic, chard, apple and sage. Ring doughnut with carrot jam and cream cheese ice cream.

Carte £17/32

Town plan C2-x – *Unit 9, Cargo 1, Gaol Ferry Steps, Wapping Wharf* ✉ *BS1 6WP* – ✆ *0117 930 0260* – *www.eatdrinkbristolfashion.co.uk/root/* – *Closed Sunday, Monday-Tuesday lunch*

ⅰ○ Second Floor at Harvey Nichols

MODERN CUISINE · DESIGN XxX A spacious and elegant light-filled restaurant with stylish gold décor. Good value lunch menu and concise à la carte offering original, modern dishes. Chic lounge bar for cocktails and light bites. Attentive service.

Menu £22/25 – Carte £38/48

Town plan D1-a – *27 Philadelphia Street, Quakers Friars, Cabot Circus* ✉ *BS1 3BZ* – ✆ *0117 916 8898* – *www.harveynichols.com* – *Closed Sunday - Monday dinner*

ⅰ○ Adelina Yard

MODERN CUISINE · INTIMATE X The experienced chef-owners named their first restaurant after their old home. Well-presented, well-balanced modern dishes are brought to the tables by the chefs. Sit at the far end of the simple L-shaped room, overlooking the quay.

Menu £18 (lunch)/59 – Carte £37/50

Town plan C2-c – *3 Queen Quay, Welsh Back* ✉ *BS1 4SL* – ✆ *0117 911 2112* – *www.adelinayard.com* – *Closed 24 December-7 January, Sunday, Monday*

ⅰ○ Kensington Arms

MODERN BRITISH · PUB X It might be painted 'stealth' grey but this smart Victorian-style pub stands out a mile for its warm neighbourhood atmosphere. The menu evolves throughout the week and is a curious mix of the traditional and the modern.

Menu £15 (lunch) – Carte £26/34

Town plan B1-b – *35-37 Stanley Road* ✉ *BS6 6NP* – ✆ *0117 944 6444* – *www.thekensingtonarms.co.uk*

ⅰ○ Tare

MODERN BRITISH · TRENDY X Tare is set in a block of converted shipping containers and named after the term for their empty weight. It's run by two young chefs and their charming team, and has just 10 tables inside and a few more outside. The menu is equally concise and the creative, flavourful dishes are attractively presented.

Menu £40

Town plan C2-g – *Unit 14, Museum Street, Wapping Wharf* ✉ *BS1 6ZA* – ✆ *0117 929 4328* – *www.tarerestaurant.co.uk* – *Closed 24-27 December, Sunday, Monday, Tuesday, Wednesday - Friday lunch*

⫶○ Wilsons

MODERN BRITISH · RUSTIC ⅹ Wilsons really fits the bill of being a proper neighbourhood restaurant. Vodkas infused with various fruits sit on the bar and large blackboards list the day's dishes. Highly seasonal cooking is gutsy, generous and flavoursome and some of the ingredients come from their own smallholding.

Carte £ 45/50

Town plan B1-s – 24 Chandos Road ⊠ BS6 6PF – 𝒞 0117 973 4157 – www.wilsonsrestaurant.co.uk – Closed 20-27 April, 10-24 August, 23 December-4 January, Sunday-Tuesday lunch

Hotels & guesthouses

🏨 Hotel du Vin

BUSINESS · DESIGN Characterful 18C former sugar refinery with classical Hotel du Vin styling and a wine-theme running throughout. Dark-hued bedrooms and duplex suites boast Egyptian cotton linen – one room has twin roll-top baths. Cosy lounge-bar; French brasserie with a pleasant courtyard terrace for bistro classics.

40 rooms ⌑ – †† £99/289

Town plan C1-e – The Sugar House ⊠ BS1 2NU – 𝒞 0117 403 2979 – www.hotelduvin.com

🏨 Number 38 Clifton

TOWNHOUSE · PERSONALISED Built in 1820, this substantial townhouse overlooks both the city and the Clifton Downs. Boutique bedrooms have coloured wood-panelled walls, Roberts radios and smart bathrooms with underfloor heating; the most luxurious are the loft suites, complete with copper baths. The rear terrace makes a great suntrap.

11 rooms ⌑ – †† £130/255

Town plan A1-a – 38 Upper Belgrave Road ⊠ BS8 2XN – 𝒞 0117 946 6905 – www.number38clifton.com

at Long Ashton Southwest: 2. 5 mi by A370 off B3128

⫶○ Bird in Hand

MODERN BRITISH · PUB ⅹ A tiny country pub with three small but smartly decorated rooms; quirky touches include an antelope's head and a wall covered in pages from Mrs Beeton's Book of Household Management. British dishes mix pub classics from the blackboard with some more ambitious modern creations.

Menu £18 (lunch) – Carte £26/38

Off plan – 17 Weston Road ⊠ BS41 9LA – 𝒞 01275 395222 – www.bird-in-hand.co.uk – Closed Sunday dinner

BRITWELL SALOME

Oxfordshire – Regional map n° **6**–C2

⫶○ Olivier at The Red Lion P

FRENCH · PUB ⅹ Grab one of just a few tables by the bar to enjoy snacks like breaded pigs' trotters or head through to the dining room for carefully prepared classical French dishes like 12-hour Aga-cooked oxtail in pastry or Cornish fish with champagne sauce. Cooking is rich and delicious, from an experienced hand.

Menu £23 (lunch) – Carte £27/45

⊠ OX49 5LG – 𝒞 01491 613140 – www.olivierattheredlionbritwellsalome.co.uk – Closed 6-28 July, 30 December-14 January, Sunday dinner-Tuesday

BROADSTAIRS

Kent – Regional map n° **5**–D1

✿ **Stark** (Ben Crittenden)

MODERN BRITISH · SIMPLE ※ Their slogan, 'Good food, laid bare', sums up this sweet, bijou restaurant, where ladders and rope lights hang beside rustic wood-panelled walls and there's seating for just 10 guests. For chef-owner Ben Crittenden it is the realisation of a lifelong dream and a real labour of love – to get it up and running he spent over a year refurbishing it with his dad's help – and his wife Sophie continues to support him every step of the way.

Ben's cooking, too, has a stripped-back style, with top quality products skilfully prepared to create refined, boldly flavoured dishes. Each night, he knows how many guests he is cooking for and his zero waste policy means that you'll never find any extra ingredients going spare in the fridge. Interesting dishes come with plenty of personality and the matching wine flights are good value.

Specialities: Crab with carrot and yolk. Beef with celeriac and walnut. Rhubarb with pistachio and goat's curd.

Menu £60

1 Oscar Road ✉ CT10 1QJ – ℰ 01843 579786 – www.starkfood.co.uk –
Closed 20-30 December, Sunday, Monday, Tuesday, Wednesday - Saturday lunch

⫯○ **Wyatt & Jones**

MODERN BRITISH · BISTRO ※ Follow the narrow road under the arch and towards the beach; here you'll find 3 old fishermen's cottages with pleasant sea views. From this vantage point you can watch the boats landing their speciality – lobster. Appealing modern blackboard menus keep things regional, with a firm focus on seafood.

Carte £30/50

23-27 Harbour Street ✉ CT10 1EU – ℰ 01843 865126 – www.wyattandjones.co.uk –
Closed Sunday dinner, Monday, Tuesday

⌂ **Belvidere Place**

TOWNHOUSE · QUIRKY Centrally located Georgian house with a charming owner, green credentials and an eclectic, individual style. Bohemian, shabby-chic lounge boasts a retro football table. Spacious bedrooms mix modern facilities with older antique furnishings.

6 rooms – ♥♥ £160/180

Belvedere Road ✉ CT10 1PF – ℰ 01843 579850 – www.belvidereplace.co.uk

BROADWAY

Worcestershire – Regional map n° **10**–C3

⫯○ **Buckland Manor**

MODERN BRITISH · INTIMATE ※※ A formal restaurant set within a country house hotel. The elegant room has wood-panelled walls hung with oil paintings and offers views over the gardens – and there are cosy lounges in which to begin and end your meal. Time-honoured dishes have clean flavours and are brought up-to-date in their presentation.

Menu £25 (lunch), £50/80

Buckland Manor Hotel, Buckland ✉ WR12 7LY – ℰ 01386 852626 –
www.bucklandmanor.com

⫯○ **The Back Garden**

MODERN BRITISH · ELEGANT ※※ A stylish hotel houses this chic, understated restaurant which offers great country views. Sustainability and seasonality are key and cooking is delicate, exacting and full of flavour. Unique combinations are well-balanced and complementary and showcase garden vegetables and rare-breed meats.

Menu £50

Dormy House Hotel, Willersey Hill ✉ WR12 7LF – ℰ 01386 852711 –
www.dormyhouse.co.uk – Closed Monday - Saturday lunch

🍴○ **Lygon Bar & Grill** **P**

TRADITIONAL BRITISH · BISTRO XX The Lygon Arms' Great Hall houses this spacious dining room and smart cocktail bar. Dramatic stag antler chandeliers hang above well-spaced marble-topped tables and faux-leather banquettes. The appealing menu lists everything from quinoa salad to well-hung steaks, and the ingredients are top quality.

Carte £31/60

Lygon Arms Hotel, High Street ✉ *WR12 7DU – ℰ 01386 852255 – www.lygonarmshotel.co.uk*

🍴○ **Russell's**

MODERN BRITISH · CONTEMPORARY DÉCOR XX An attractive Cotswold stone house in the centre of the village, with a smart brasserie-style interior and both a front and rear terrace. Choose from a constantly evolving selection of modern British dishes. Service is relaxed and friendly and bedrooms are stylish – there's even a spacious suite!

Menu £24 (lunch)/35 – Carte £29/53

20 High Street ✉ *WR12 7DT – ℰ 01386 853555 – www.russellsofbroadway.co.uk*

🏠 **Buckland Manor**

HISTORIC · CLASSIC With its 13C origins, beautiful gardens and peaceful setting, this is one of England's most charming country houses. The elegant interior comprises tastefully appointed country house bedrooms and traditionally furnished guest areas featuring parquet floors, wood panelling and big open fires.

15 rooms � – 👫 £225/670

Buckland ✉ *WR12 7LY – ℰ 01386 852626 – www.bucklandmanor.co.uk*

🍴○ **Buckland Manor** – See restaurant listing

🏠 **Dormy House**

LUXURY · CONTEMPORARY Behind the old farmhouse façade you'll find a modern interior and luxurious spa. The odd beam and fireplace remain beside bold contemporary fabrics and designer furnishings; wood and stone play a big part and the atmosphere is laid-back. Dine in the informal bistro, sophisticated Back Garden or intimate MO.

38 rooms ⊐ – 👫 £269/470 – 10 suites

Willersey Hill ✉ *WR12 7LF – ℰ 01386 852711 – www.dormyhouse.co.uk*

🍴○ **The Back Garden** – See restaurant listing

🏠 **Lygon Arms**

HISTORIC · ROMANTIC A sympathetic refurbishment has retained this historical hotel's period charm, which comes courtesy of open fires, wonky ceilings and antique furnishings. The small wine bar serves Italian small plates and afternoon tea is popular in the pretty Terrace Room. Bedrooms in the courtyard are the most spacious.

86 rooms – 👫 £165/375 – ⊐ £20 – 27 suites

High Street ✉ *WR12 7DU – ℰ 01386 852255 – www.lygonarmshotel.co.uk*

🍴○ **Lygon Bar & Grill** – See restaurant listing

BROCKENHURST
Hampshire – Regional map n° **4**-A2

🍴○ **The Pig**

TRADITIONAL BRITISH · BRASSERIE XX A smart manor house, which follows a philosophy of bringing nature indoors, plays host to this delightful, eclectically furnished conservatory dotted with plants. The gardener and forager supply what's best from within a 25 mile radius and cooking is unfussy and wholesome. Bedrooms are characterful.

Carte £28/42

✉ *SO42 7QL – ℰ 01590 622354 – www.thepighotel.com*

BROMESWELL – Suffolk ➜ See Woodbridge

BRUNTINGTHORPE
Leicestershire – Regional map n° **9**–B3

ⅈ◯ **The Joiners**

TRADITIONAL BRITISH · PUB 𝕏 Beams and a tiled floor bring 17C character to this dining pub but designer wallpaper and fresh flower displays give it a chic overall feel. There's plenty of choice on the menus, with the likes of pork rillettes or pot-roast pheasant.

Menu £17 (lunch) – Carte £27/38

Church Walk ⊠ LE17 5QH – ☎ 0116 247 8258 – www.thejoinersarms.co.uk – Closed Sunday dinner, Monday

BRUTON
Somerset – Regional map n° **2**–C2

ⅈ◯ **Roth Bar & Grill**

TRADITIONAL BRITISH · DESIGN 𝕏 The converted outbuildings of a working farm now house this charming restaurant with its striking modern art exhibitions. Beef, pork and lamb from the farm are aged in their salting room. Be sure to try the caramelised lemonade.

Carte £18/50

Durslade Farm, Dropping Lane ⊠ BA10 0NL – ☎ 01749 814700 – www.rothbarandgrill.co.uk – Closed Sunday dinner, Monday, Tuesday - Wednesday dinner

ⅈ◯ **At The Chapel**

MEDITERRANEAN CUISINE · DESIGN 𝕏 A stylish, informal restaurant in a former 18C chapel, with a bakery to one side and a wine shop to the other. Daily menus offer rustic Mediterranean-influenced dishes; specialities include wood-fired breads, pizzas and cakes. Bedrooms are luxurious – Room 8 even has its own terrace.

Carte £22/44

High Street ⊠ BA10 0AE – ☎ 01749 814070 – www.atthechapel.co.uk

BRYHER – Isles of Scilly → See Scilly (Isles of)

BUNTINGFORD
Hertfordshire – Regional map n° **7**–B2

ⅈ◯ **The Falcon** ◍

MODERN BRITISH · COSY 𝕏𝕏 A 17C building houses this intimate restaurant which marries stained glass screens with burnished leather banquettes and old timbers. The experienced chef-owner sources the best local ingredients and his unfussy, modern British dishes are confidently executed with clear flavours. Desserts are a highlight.

Menu £19 (lunch) – Carte £27/45

69 High Street ⊠ SG9 9AE – ☎ 01763 890028 – www.falconrestaurant.co.uk – Closed 3-26 August, Sunday dinner, Monday, Tuesday, Wednesday

BURCHETT'S GREEN
Windsor and Maidenhead – Regional map n° **6**–C3

✿ **Crown** (Simon Bonwick)

REGIONAL CUISINE · PUB 𝕏 The endearingly friendly Crown sits in a pretty village opposite a 300 year old oak tree and is very proudly and passionately run by the Bonwick family; dad takes charge in the kitchen, while the children keep things running smoothly in the small bar and two intimate, open-fired dining rooms.

The concise selection of deftly prepared dishes is decided upon daily; the options are diverse and all are equally appealing and flavoursome, with defined flavours and a refined touch. The warm bread rolls are delicious and to follow you could find anything from spiced pot-roasted pig cheek to honey-smoked trout with beetroot and horseradish grown in their garden.

The experienced chef-owner takes his cooking very seriously, so much so that he closes the pub on a Monday in order to go to the market and visit his suppliers personally.

Specialities: 'Memory of Cairo'. Beef fillet on a string with 'a rather nice sauce'. Bitter brittle chocolate with walnut blancmange and coffee ice cream.

Carte £24/42

✉ SL6 6QZ – ✆ 01628 824079 – www.thecrownburchettsgreen.com –
Closed 19-31 August, 23 December-8 January, Sunday dinner, Monday, Tuesday, Wednesday lunch

BURFORD

Oxfordshire – Regional map n° **6**–A2

🏠 Lamb Inn   ✿ 🛏 **P**

INN · COSY Character and rusticity abound at this 15C inn. Bedrooms are a pleasing mix of the traditional and the modern and some feature four-poster beds. Guest areas include comfy low-ceilinged lounges and there's a hidden gem of a garden to the rear. Dine on pub classics or more ambitious British dishes.

17 rooms ☑ – 👫 £150/280

*Sheep Street ✉ OX18 4LR – ✆ 01993 823155 –
www.cotswold-inns-hotels.co.uk/the-lamb-inn*

at Swinbrook East: 2. 75 mi by A40

🍴 Swan Inn   ⇦ 🛏 🛖 **P**

MODERN BRITISH · PUB 🍴 Wisteria-clad, honey-coloured pub on the riverbank, boasting a lovely garden filled with fruit trees. The charming interior displays an open oak frame and exposed stone walls hung with old lithographs and handmade walking sticks. The daily menu showcases the latest local produce and features modern takes on older recipes. Well-appointed bedrooms have a luxurious feel.

Carte £24/35

✉ OX18 4DY – ✆ 01993 823339 – www.theswanswinbrook.co.uk

BURNHAM MARKET

Norfolk – Regional map n° **8**–C1

🍴 Socius   🛖 & 🏧

MODERN BRITISH · DESIGN 🍴🍴 One meaning of the Latin word Socius is 'sharing' – and it is all about sharing at this smart, Scandic-style restaurant. Sit up on the steel-framed mezzanine level or on the ground floor to watch the chefs hard at work. Unfussy modern small plates feature on a flexible, constantly evolving menu.

Menu £20 (lunch) – Carte £25/40

*11 Foundry Place ✉ PE31 8LG – ✆ 01328 738307 – www.sociusnorfolk.co.uk –
Closed 5-24 January, 11-17 November, Sunday dinner, Monday, Tuesday*

🍴 North Street Bistro   🛖

TRADITIONAL BRITISH · BISTRO 🍴 An old flint chapel set just off the village green; inside it's small and simply decorated, with high ceilings and a relaxed feel. Cooking is fresh and unfussy, with local produce well used. Flavours are clear and textures are complementary. It's proudly run by Dan, Holly and their charming young team.

Menu £20 (lunch) – Carte £20/36

*20 North Street ✉ PE31 8HG – ✆ 01328 730330 – www.20northstreet.co.uk –
Closed 6-26 January, Sunday dinner, Monday, Tuesday, Wednesday lunch*

BURPHAM – West Sussex ➜ See Arundel

BURTON BRADSTOCK – Dorset ➜ See Bridport

BURTON-UPON-TRENT

Staffordshire – Regional map n° **10**–C1

ⅈ◯ **99 Station Street**

TRADITIONAL BRITISH · **NEIGHBOURHOOD** ҳ Amongst the vast brewing towers is this bright, boldly decorated neighbourhood restaurant, run by two experienced locals. They make everything on the premises daily and showcase regional ingredients; try the mature rare breed meats.

Menu £17 (lunch) – Carte £26/37

99 Station Street ⊠ DE14 1BT – ℰ 01283 516859 – www.99stationstreet.com –
Closed Sunday dinner, Monday, Tuesday, Wednesday lunch

BURY

Greater Manchester – Regional map n° **11**–B2

ⅈ◯ **Bird at Birtle**

TRADITIONAL BRITISH · **BISTRO** ҳ A very popular restaurant in a modernised pub. Start with a cocktail on a comfy sofa or out on the terrace then head upstairs to the stylish dining room with its balcony and fell views. Classic dishes are given a modern touch.

Carte £23/38

Bury and Rochdale Old Road ⊠ OL10 4BQ – ℰ 01706 540500 –
www.thebirdatbirtle.co.uk

BURY ST EDMUNDS

Suffolk – Regional map n° **8**–C2

⊛ **Pea Porridge**

MODERN BRITISH · **BISTRO** ҳ A charming former bakery in two 19C cottages, with its original bread oven still in situ. Tasty country cooking is led by the seasons and has a Mediterranean bias; many dishes are cooked in the wood-fired oven. It has a stylish, rustic look and a homely feel – its name is a reference to the old town green.

Specialities: Lightly curried duck hearts with butternut squash and spinach. Confit guinea fowl leg, gratin dauphinoise, turnip tops and crispy shallots. Tarte Tatin.

Menu £20/29 – Carte £28/35

28-29 Cannon Street ⊠ IP33 1JR – ℰ 01284 700200 – www.peaporridge.co.uk –
Closed 27 December-8 January, Sunday, Monday, Tuesday - Wednesday lunch

ⅈ◯ **Maison Bleue**

FRENCH · **NEIGHBOURHOOD** ҳҳ A passionately run town centre restaurant in a converted 17C house, complete with wooden panelling and impressive fish sculptures. Cooking is classically French at heart but has modern and Asian touches. Seafood is a strength and you must try the excellent French cheeses.

Menu £21 (lunch)/37 – Carte £43/57

30-31 Churchgate Street ⊠ IP33 1RG – ℰ 01284 760623 – www.maisonbleue.co.uk
– Closed 23 December-14 January, Sunday, Monday

ⅈ◯ **1921**

MODERN CUISINE · **INTIMATE** ҳҳ A fine period house located at 19-21 Angel Hill; its smart, modern facelift complements the original beams and red-brick inglenook fireplace. Cooking displays a modern flair and features some interesting combinations.

Menu £21 – Carte £33/50

19-21 Angel Hill ⊠ IP33 1UZ – ℰ 01284 704870 – www.nineteen-twentyone.co.uk –
Closed 23 December-7 January, Sunday, Monday

Eaterie

TRADITIONAL BRITISH · BRASSERIE ⅹ An airy two-roomed bistro set within an attractive 15C coaching inn where Dickens once stayed. There's an impressive modern chandelier and a display of the owner's contemporary art. Tasty British brasserie dishes use local produce.

Carte £22/49

Angel Hotel, 3 Angel Hill ⊠ IP33 1LT – ℰ 01284 714000 – www.theangel.co.uk

🏨 **Angel** 🔄 ⅋ ⚒ 🅿

HISTORIC · PERSONALISED The creeper-clad Georgian façade hides a surprisingly stylish hotel. Relax in the atmospheric bar or smart lounges. Individually designed bedrooms offer either classic four-poster luxury or come with funky décor and iPod docks.

77 rooms ⊋ – †† £139/189

3 Angel Hill ⊠ IP33 1LT – ℰ 01284 714000 – www.theangel.co.uk

🍴 **Eaterie** – See restaurant listing

CAMBER

East Sussex – Regional map n° **5**–C2

🏨 **Gallivant** 🔾 🅿

BOUTIQUE HOTEL · SEASIDE A laid-back hotel set opposite the beach and run by a friendly team. Relax by the fire in the New England style lounge. Bedrooms come in blues and whites, with distressed wood furniture, bespoke beds and modern facilities – those to the rear have decked terraces.

20 rooms ⊋ – †† £95/295

New Lydd Road ⊠ TN31 7RB – ℰ 01797 225057 – www.thegallivant.co.uk

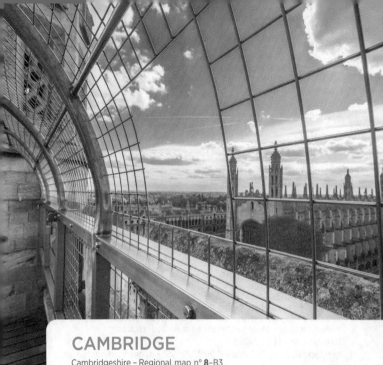

CAMBRIDGE

Cambridgeshire – Regional map n° **8**-B3

Top tips!

This attractive, bustling city has stood on the banks of the River Cam since Roman times, with the world-famous university only appearing relatively recently in the 13C. The Fitzwilliam Museum of arts and antiquities is definitely worth a visit, as is the late Gothic King's College Chapel with its vast fan-vaulted ceiling and ornate stained glass windows – and when the weather's right, a punt on the river, via the Bridge of Sighs, is the perfect way to while away an afternoon.

If you're looking to celebrate your graduation, book a table at Two-Starred **Midsummer House** – a beautiful Victorian property overlooking Midsummer Common towards the river. For classic British dishes in a historic location (a restaurant has stood on this site since 1834), head for **Parker's Tavern**, a buzzy hotel brasserie overlooking Parker's Piece, where the rules of football were devised.

Restaurants

✿✿ **Midsummer House** (Daniel Clifford)

MODERN CUISINE · ELEGANT XX A beautiful Victorian house with a lovely conservatory extension plays host to this stylish restaurant. It's set in an idyllic location overlooking Midsummer Common and the delightful first floor lounge and terrace make the perfect spot for drinks, as they look out over the garden and the River Cam.

Experienced chef-owner Daniel Clifford has run this restaurant for over 20 years and his experience shines through. Never a chef to rest on his laurels, his dishes continually evolve and, although they have a classic base, are packed full of personality and originality. Daniel's travels inform many of his newer creations and the inventive vegetarian dishes are much more than just an afterthought. Flavours are measured, there's an appealing range of different textures and many of the dishes are finished off at the table using modern techniques.

Specialities: Scallop with Granny Smith, celeriac and truffle purée. Saddle of suckling pig with braised cheek, stuffed onion and rocket salad. Coriander white chocolate dome with coconut, mango and jasmine rice.

Menu £50 (lunch)/135

Town plan B1-a – *Midsummer Common* ✉ CB4 1HA – ☎ 01223 369299 – *www.midsummerhouse.co.uk* – *Closed 21 December-8 January, Sunday, Monday, Tuesday*

○ **Cotto**

MODERN CUISINE · INTIMATE XX A stylish, sophisticated hotel restaurant set in a modern glass extension. The experienced chef skilfully prepares a wide range of dishes which are made up of many different components; the chocolate desserts are a highlight.

Menu £70/80

Town plan B3-c – *Gonville Hotel, Gonville Place* ✉ CB1 1LY – ☎ 01223 302010 – *www.cottocambridge.co.uk* – *Closed 1-16 January, 14-22 April, 11 August-2 September, Sunday, Monday, Tuesday - Saturday lunch*

○ **Navadhanya**

INDIAN · CONTEMPORARY DÉCOR XX This former pub is home to a well-regarded restaurant with white décor and a contemporary look. Dishes take their influences from around India and exhibit a modern style, while at the same time respecting tradition.

Carte £33/58

Off plan – *73 Newmarket Road* ✉ CB5 8EG – ☎ 01223 300583 – *www.navadhanya.co.uk* – *Closed Monday - Friday lunch*

○ **Parker's Tavern**

MODERN BRITISH · BRASSERIE XX Start with a signature cocktail in the hotel bar then head through to this buzzy brasserie overlooking Parker's Piece, where the rules of football were devised. The menu has a classic British heart and flavours are bold and satisfying. A restaurant has stood on this site since 1834.

Carte £26/49

Town plan B3-n – *University Arms Hotel, Regent Street* ✉ CB2 1AD – ☎ 01223 606266 – *www.parkerstavern.com*

○ **Restaurant Twenty-Two**

MODERN CUISINE · INTIMATE XX This long-standing restaurant in a converted Victorian townhouse is now run by a young couple, Sam and Alex, who have given it a contemporary makeover with a monochrome theme. Ambitious modern cooking features plenty of contrasting textures and tastes; most diners opt for the tasting menus.

Menu £25 (lunch), £50/60 – Carte £42/50

Town plan B1-c – *22 Chesterton Road* ✉ CB4 3AX – ☎ 01223 351880 – *www.restaurant22.co.uk* – *Closed Sunday, Monday, Tuesday - Wednesday lunch*

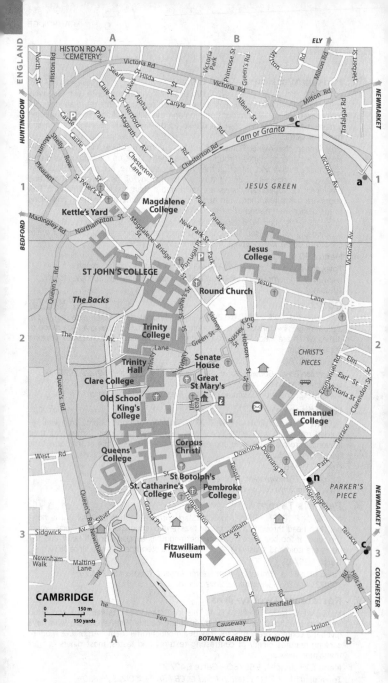

Hotels

🏨 University Arms ⓝ   ✿ 🖼 ⊟ ♿ AC 🏊

BUSINESS · CONTEMPORARY The classical porte-cochère and impressive lobby of this landmark hotel really make a statement. It was refurbished by architect John Simpson and designer Martin Brudnizki and its understated modern bedrooms and white marble bathrooms bring it into the 21C. Book a room with a balcony overlooking Parker's Piece.

192 rooms – ♥♥ £159/550 – ⊊ £16

Town plan B3-n – *Regent Street* ✉ *CB2 1AD* – ℰ *01223 606066* – *www.universityarms.com*

🍽️ **Parker's Tavern** – See restaurant listing

🏨 Gonville   ✿ 📶 🕥 ⊟ ♿ AC 🏊 P

BUSINESS · CONTEMPORARY A long-standing, family-owned hotel, just 5mins from the city centre. Well-appointed modern bedrooms come with iPads; the best are the stylish annexe rooms in Gresham House. Relax in the small spa, borrow a bike or enjoy a tour in the vintage Bentley. Dine in the brasserie or more sophisticated restaurant.

84 rooms ⊊ – ♥♥ £165/320

Town plan B3-c – *Gonville Place* ✉ *CB1 1LY* – ℰ *01223 366611* – *www.gonvillehotel.co.uk*

🍽️ **Cotto** – See restaurant listing

at Horningsea Northeast: 4 mi by A1303 and B1047

🍽️ Crown & Punchbowl   ⇦ 📶 P

MODERN BRITISH · PUB ✗ Watch your head on the beams as you enter the bar, then take your pick from several different seating areas. Start with rustic bread and zingy olive oil then move on to modern seasonal dishes or one of the wide-ranging specials chalked on the fish board. Bedrooms are cosy and welcoming.

Menu £22 – Carte £26/43

Off plan – *High Street* ✉ *CB25 9JG* – ℰ *01223 860643* – *www.thecrownandpunchbowl.co.uk*

CANTERBURY
Kent – Regional map n° **5**-D2

🍽️ The Goods Shed   P

TRADITIONAL BRITISH · RUSTIC ✗ Daily farmers' market and food hall in an early Victorian locomotive shed, selling an excellent variety of organic, free range and homemade produce. Hearty, rustic, daily changing dishes are served at scrubbed wooden tables.

Carte £24/37

Station Road West, St Dunstans ✉ *CT2 8AN* – ℰ *01227 459153* – *www.thegoodsshed.co.uk* – *Closed 1-2 January, Sunday dinner, Monday*

🏨 The Pig ⓝ   ✿ 🌿 ⇦ 📶 P

COUNTRY HOUSE · CONTEMPORARY This ultra-stylish 17C country house sits in stunning grounds and has a pleasingly laid-back feel. Fabulous lodges are dotted about the place and the treatment rooms are in the old potting sheds. Dine on garden produce in the bright restaurant. The pretty terrace is the perfect spot to sample some local wines.

29 rooms – ♥♥ £110/425 – ⊊ £16

Bourne Park Road, Bridge ✉ *CT4 5LF* – ℰ *01227 830208* – *www.thepighotel.com*

at Fordwich Northeast : 2. 75 mi by A28 – Regional map n° **5**–D1

⸙ **Fordwich Arms** (Daniel Smith) 🏠 **P**

MODERN CUISINE · PUB ⋇ England's smallest town is a pretty little place that plays host to this elegant Arts and Crafts style pub, which boasts an impressive bar and a wood-panelled dining room looking out over the river. It's been given a new lease of life by its three proud young owners: Guy enthusiastically looks after their guests, while Dan and Tash can be found hard at work in the kitchen – they previously worked at The Clove Club and this influence can be seen in their cooking.

The provenance of ingredients is key for the chefs, who do everything they can to deliver great natural flavours: they butcher whole beasts, cure meats, churn butter and bake bread on-site. Pared-down dishes are perfectly balanced and each element plays a pivotal role both in terms of flavour and texture. The pheasant dumplings, which use every part of the bird, are something of a hit.

Specialities: Duck liver parfait, clementine, Sauternes and doughnuts. Roast Blackface lamb, Jerusalem artichoke, curds and crisp potato. Rice pudding, Bramley apple and crumble.

Menu £35 (lunch), £65/95 – Carte £49/60

King Street ⊠ CT2 0DB – ℰ 01227 710444 – www.fordwicharms.co.uk – Closed Sunday dinner, Monday

CARTMEL

Cumbria – Regional map n° **12**–A3

⸙⸙ **L'Enclume** (Simon Rogan) 🕸 ⇦ 🍴 AC

CREATIVE · HISTORIC ⋇⋇⋇ Opened in 2002 by Simon Rogan and his wife, L'Enclume has become as synonymous with this sleepy Lakeland village as sticky toffee pudding. Indeed, it's been so successful, that the couple also opened the more relaxed Rogan & Co, as well as stylish bedrooms which are spread about the village.

The characterful old building still displays evidence of its 'smithy' days and its location next to a brook makes it a truly charming spot on a warm summer's evening. 16 or so courses make up the well-balanced, perfectly paced tasting menu and produce from their 12 acre farm guides the fiercely seasonal dishes, which are passionately prepared, innovative and full of interest. Flavours are natural and harmonious and an array of textures stimulates the palate. For those wanting to immerse themselves further, the development kitchen, Aulis, opens at weekends.

Specialities: Scallop, smoked pike perch and roe. Cabbage, mushroom, truffle and wasabi leaf. Frozen Tunworth with malt and verbena.

Menu £59 (lunch)/155

Cavendish Street ⊠ LA11 6PZ – ℰ 015395 36362 – www.lenclume.co.uk – Closed 1-7 January, Monday

⸙ **Rogan & Co** ♿

CREATIVE BRITISH · COSY ⋇⋇ L'Enclume's laid-back cousin sits in the centre of the village and is housed within a pretty cottage by a stream. It has a pleasingly easy-going feel courtesy of a cosy, open-plan interior – which features dark wood beams, welcoming open fires and walls hung with Lakeland photography – and a friendly serving team who bring every dish to the table with a smile.

Simon Rogan's influence is clear to see on the appealing menu, which lists skilfully prepared, understated dishes that make great use of creative ingredient and flavour combinations. His clean, uncomplicated approach keeps the focus firmly on the main ingredient, with top quality produce coming from his own farm in the Cartmel Valley or carefully sourced from trusted Lake District suppliers. The weekly changing set priced lunch is great value.

Specialities: Mackerel tartare, turnip and horseradish. Short rib of beef, creamed potato and bone marrow. Vanilla ice cream, almond, pear, honeycomb and fudge.

Menu £29 (lunch) – Carte £39/45

Devonshire Square ⊠ LA11 6QD – ℰ 015395 35917 – www.roganandco.co.uk – Closed 1-7 January, Sunday dinner, Tuesday

CASTLE COMBE
Wiltshire – Regional map n° **2**–C2

❀ Bybrook

MODERN BRITISH · ELEGANT XX This fine 14C manor house sits within 365 acres of formal gardens and parkland in a picture-postcard village. A sweeping drive leads up to the main building and its immensely charming interior features characterful oak panelling and a host of cosy open-fired lounges.

Dining here is a very formal experience: drinks and nibbles are served in the bar before dinner in the cavernous dining room with its large feature wall, flower arrangements, leather chairs and immaculately laid solid oak tables.

Local and kitchen garden produce plays a pivotal role in the cooking, which closely follows the seasons. Refined, carefully prepared dishes arrive in tried-and-tested combinations but have modern overtones, and presentation is very precise.

Luxurious bedrooms are split between the house and mews cottages.

Specialities: Fillet of mackerel with crab, avocado, charred cucumber and Exmoor caviar. Pot-roast belly of pork with creamed potato, caramelised apple and cider sauce. Chocolate délice with pistachio and Morello cherry sorbet.

Menu £75/95

Manor House Hotel and Golf Club ✉ SN14 7HR – ✆ 01249 782206 –
www.exclusive.co.uk – Closed Monday - Saturday lunch

🏨 Manor House H. and Golf Club 🏡 🐾 🖫 📶 ら 🛁 🅿

LUXURY · ELEGANT Fine period manor house in 365 acres of formal gardens and parkland. The interior exudes immense charm, with characterful oak panelling and a host of open-fired lounges. Luxurious bedrooms are split between the main house and mews cottages. Book ahead for one of the event days.

50 rooms ☷ – 🛏 £230/350 – 8 suites
✉ SN14 7HR – ✆ 01249 782206 – www.exclusive.co.uk
❀ **Bybrook** – See restaurant listing

CASTOR
Peterborough – Regional map n° **8**–A2

🍴 Chubby Castor 🏡 🏮 🕸 🅿

MODERN BRITISH · INTIMATE XX Having spent most of his life in London, Adebola Adeshina found a new home in this 400 year old thatched pub. Inside it's surprisingly modern, with a smart lounge and an intimate linen-laid dining room. Time-honoured recipes are reworked, with flavourful dishes presented in a restrained modern vein.

Menu £20 (lunch), £22/28 – Carte £34/60

Fitzwilliam Arms, 34 Peterborough Road ✉ PE5 7AX – ✆ 01733 380801 –
www.thechubbycastor.com – Closed 6-20 January, Sunday dinner, Monday

CHAGFORD
Devon – Regional map n° **1**–C2

🍴 Gidleigh Park 🏵 ≤ 🏡 ら 🕼 🅿

MODERN CUISINE · ELEGANT XXX Within a grand Edwardian house you'll find these three intimate dining rooms, where produce from the kitchen garden is used in dishes which focus on just two or three ingredients. Cooking has a traditional base but displays a lightness of touch and a few modern twists.

Menu £65 (lunch), £125/145

Gidleigh Park Hotel ✉ TQ13 8HH – ✆ 01647 432367 – www.gidleigh.co.uk

🏨 Gidleigh Park 🏡 🐾 ≤ 🏡 ら 🅿

LUXURY · ELEGANT A stunningly located and truly impressive Arts and Crafts house with lovely tiered gardens and Teign Valley views. Luxurious sitting and drawing rooms have a classic country house feel but a contemporary edge; wonderfully comfortable bedrooms echo this, with their appealing mix of styles.

24 rooms ☷ – 🛏 £275/800 – 1 suite
✉ TQ13 8HH – ✆ 01647 432367 – www.gidleigh.co.uk
🍴 **Gidleigh Park** – See restaurant listing

CHANNEL ISLANDS

Jersey

Top tips!

There's an incredibly relaxing air to the Channel Islands;
here, time seems to slow down and, when the sun shines,
there are few prettier destinations to enjoy a meal alfresco.
Seafood is the natural choice, with lobsters, chancre crabs
and ormers (a local sea snail delicacy) topping the list. Also
not to be missed are the sweet Jersey Royals and the rich
burnt butter – a combination of apple, cider and spice.
For an even more peaceful escape, take the boat over to
car-free Sark; here you can hire a bike and ride to 'La
Coupée' causeway, then head on to the personally run 16C
farmhouse **La Sablonnerie**; now a restaurant with rooms.
If you're dining on Jersey there's Michelin-Starred **Bohemia**,
Bib Gourmand **Mark Jordan at the Beach**, or **Green Island**,
with its wonderful suntrap terrace; while the fish cannot get
much fresher than at **Le Nautique**, set on the quayside in
Guernsey's St Peter Port.

I. Murray /age fotostock

GUERNSEY – Regional map n° **3**–A2

St Peter Port – Regional map n° **3**–A2

ⅠⅠ○ **Le Nautique**

CLASSIC CUISINE · **MEDITERRANEAN** XX An old sailmaker's warehouse on the quayside, with a stylish nautical interior and a pleasant marina view – ask for a window seat. The large menu offers classic dishes and the fish specials are worth considering.

Menu £19 (lunch) – Carte £24/47

Quay Steps ✉ *GY1 2LE –* ✆ *01481 721714 – www.lenautiquerestaurant.co.uk – Closed Sunday, Saturday lunch*

ⅠⅠ○ **The Hook**

MEATS AND GRILLS · **CLASSIC DÉCOR** X Start with a cocktail on the 3rd floor then head for the sushi bar or the buzzy restaurant with harbour views. Dishes arrive in satisfying portions – steaks are a speciality, with larger 'sharing' cuts featured on the blackboard.

Menu £18 – Carte £25/55

North Plantation (1st Floor) ✉ *GY1 2LQ –* ✆ *01481 701373 – www.thehook.gg – Closed Sunday*

ⅠⅠ○ **Slaughterhouse**

TRADITIONAL BRITISH · **CONTEMPORARY DÉCOR** X Old meat hooks hanging from the ceiling of this chic, buzzy bar and brasserie hint at its past as the island's former slaughterhouse. Dine on the mezzanine for the best views. Extensive menus list fresh, tasty dishes.

Carte £24/50

Castle Pier ✉ *GY1 1AU –* ✆ *01481 712123 – www.slaughterhouse.gg*

⌂ **Old Government House H. & Spa**

HISTORIC BUILDING · **CLASSIC** Fine, classically furnished 18C building, with many of its original features restored, including a glorious ballroom. Individually styled bedrooms have padded walls, modern bathrooms and a personal touch. Relax in the well-equipped spa or outdoor pool. Authentic Indian cooking in The Curry Room. The smart yet informal brasserie has a delightful terrace.

62 rooms – 🛏 £195/495 – 1 suite

St Ann's Place ✉ *GY1 2NU –* ✆ *01481 724921 – www.theoghhotel.com*

JERSEY Jersey – Regional map n° **3**–B2

Beaumont – Regional map n° **3**–B2

☺ **Mark Jordan at the Beach**

MODERN CUISINE · **NEIGHBOURHOOD** XX Modern brasserie with a small lounge and bar; a paved terrace with bay views; and a dining room with heavy wood tables, modern seashore paintings and animal ornaments. Menus showcase island produce and fish from local waters. Cooking is refined but hearty, mixing tasty brasserie and restaurant style dishes.

Specialities: Prawn cocktail with Marie Rose espuma. Confit duck leg, creamy mash, caraway cabbage and fine beans. Coconut soufflé with homemade pineapple sorbet.

Menu £23/28 – Carte £33/50

La Plage, La Route de la Haule ✉ *JE3 7YD –* ✆ *01534 780180 – www.markjordanatthebeach.com – Closed 1-14 January*

Gorey

Ⅰ○ Sumas ≤ 斎 AC

MODERN CUISINE · FRIENDLY XX A well-known restaurant in a whitewashed house, with a smart heated terrace affording lovely harbour views. Modern European dishes feature island produce. The monthly changing lunch and midweek dinner menus represent good value.

Menu £23/28 – Carte £27/48

Gorey Hill ⊠ JE3 6ET – ℰ 01534 853291 – www.sumasrestaurant.com –
Closed 21 December-18 January, Sunday dinner

Ⅰ○ Bass and Lobster 斎 AC

TRADITIONAL CUISINE · BISTRO X This simply furnished 'Foodhouse' sits close to the beach. Menus offer plenty of choice and you can watch fresh seafood, meats and vegetables from around the island being prepared through the kitchen window.

Menu £15 (lunch)/19 – Carte £27/46

Gorey Coast Road ⊠ JE3 6EU – ℰ 01534 859590 – www.bassandlobster.com –
Closed Sunday dinner, Monday

Green Island

Ⅰ○ Green Island 斎

MEDITERRANEAN CUISINE · FRIENDLY X Friendly, personally run restaurant with a terrace and beachside kiosk; the southernmost restaurant in the British Isles. Mediterranean-influenced dishes and seafood specials showcase island produce. Flavours are bold and perfectly judged.

Menu £19 (lunch) – Carte £28/45

St. Clement ⊠ JE2 6LS – ℰ 01534 857787 – www.greenisland.je –
Closed 1 January-5 February, Sunday dinner, Monday

La Pulente - Regional map n° **3**-B2

Ⅰ○ Ocean 器♔ ≤ 🚘 斎 P

MODERN CUISINE · LUXURY XXX Perched in a hotel high above St Ouen's Bay, is this smart, understated restaurant with crisply laid tables; ceiling fans and shuttered windows add a slightly colonial feel. The experienced chef creates modern menus which showcase the best of the island's produce – seafood is a highlight.

Menu £28 (lunch)/55 – Carte £60/73

Atlantic Hotel, Le Mont de la Pulente ⊠ JE3 8HE – ℰ 01534 744101 –
www.theatlantichotel.com – Closed 2 January-5 February

🏨 Atlantic ⭐🐾≤🚘🏊🍿⤢🛗♨️P

LUXURY · CONTEMPORARY Set in a superb spot overlooking St Ouen's Bay, this understatedly elegant hotel strikes the perfect balance with its service, which is polished and professional yet warm and welcoming. Stone and wood feature in the laid-back guest areas and many bedrooms look out over the lovely pool and terrace to the sea.

49 rooms � – ††£150/350 – 1 suite

Le Mont de la Pulente ⊠ JE3 8HE – ℰ 01534 744101 – www.theatlantichotel.com –
Closed 2 January-5 February

Ⅰ○ **Ocean** - See restaurant listing

St Brelade's Bay

Ⅰ○ Oyster Box  ≤ 斎 ⅃ AC

SEAFOOD · BRASSERIE X Glass-fronted eatery with pleasant heated terrace, set on the promenade and affording superb views over St Brelade's Bay. Stylish, airy interior hung with sail cloths and fishermen's floats. Laid-back, friendly service. Accessible seasonal menu features plenty of fish and shellfish; oysters are a speciality.

Menu £30 – Carte £21/50

La Route de la Baie ⊠ JE3 8EF – ℰ 01534 850888 – www.oysterbox.co.uk

St Helier – Regional map n° **3**–B2

✿ **Bohemia**

MODERN CUISINE · **ELEGANT** XxX A stylish modern hotel plays host to this marble-fronted restaurant, where the smart, well-drilled team are on the button. Start with a cocktail in the chic, lively bar, then head through to the intimate dining room, which is equally suited for a romantic dinner as a glammed-up night out. Low-slung hanging lamps illuminate the tables and the atmosphere is easy-going and relaxed.

The emphasis here is on tasting menus, with both pescatarian and vegetarian options available, although there is also an à la carte. The chef uses his wealth of experience to create assured modern dishes with plenty of vibrancy and a lightness of touch, and original texture and flavour combinations feature. Classical techniques are skilful and well-rehearsed, presentation is highly creative, and well-sourced ingredients come from the Island, the UK and France, depending on what's best.

Service is detailed and some of the sauces are poured at the table.

Specialities: Seared scallop with celeriac and truffle purée. Cumbrian lamb with Jerusalem artichoke. Popcorn parfait.

Menu £35 (lunch), £69/105

Club Hotel & Spa, Green Street ✉ *JE2 4UH* – ✆ *01534 880588* – *www.bohemiajersey.com* – *Closed 24-30 December, Sunday*

ⅡO **Banjo**

INTERNATIONAL · **BRASSERIE** XX Substantial former gentlemen's club with an ornate façade; the banjo belonging to the owner's great grandfather is displayed in a glass-fronted wine cellar. The appealing, wide-ranging menu features everything from brasserie classics to sushi. Stylish bedrooms have Nespresso machines and Bose sound systems.

Menu £21 – Carte £21/54

8 Beresford Street ✉ *JE2 4WN* – ✆ *01534 850890* – *www.banjojersey.com* – *Closed Sunday*

ⅡO **Samphire**

MODERN CUISINE · **DESIGN** XX This buzzy all-day brasserie deluxe comes with a pavement terrace and a striking colour scheme which takes in blue velour banquettes and yellow leather chairs. Cooking takes on a modern approach and influences come from around the globe. Naturally, local seafood is a highlight.

Menu £29/35 – Carte £35/70

7-11 Don Street ✉ *JE2 4TQ* – ✆ *01534 725100* – *www.samphire.je* – *Closed Sunday*

⌂ **Club Hotel & Spa**

BUSINESS · **CONTEMPORARY** A modern hotel with stylish guest areas, an honesty bar and a split-level breakfast room. Contemporary bedrooms have floor to ceiling windows and good facilities. Relax in the smart spa or on the terrace beside the small outdoor pool.

46 rooms ⊅ – †† £99/209 – 4 suites

Green Street ✉ *JE2 4UH* – ✆ *01534 876500* – *www.theclubjersey.com*

✿ **Bohemia** – See restaurant listing

St Saviour – Regional map n° **3**–B2

ⅡO **Longueville Manor**

MODERN CUISINE · **ELEGANT** XxX Set within a charming manor house; dine in the characterful 15C oak-panelled room, the brighter Garden Room or on the terrace. Daily menus champion island produce; seafood is a feature and many ingredients come from the impressive kitchen garden. Classic dishes have a modern edge.

Menu £28 (lunch), £55/92

Longueville Manor Hotel, Longueville Road ✉ *JE2 7WF* – ✆ *01534 725501* – *www.longuevillemanor.com* – *Closed 6-22 January*

🏠🏠🏠 Longueville Manor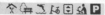

LUXURY · CONTEMPORARY An iconic 13C manor house, which is very personally and professionally run. Comfy, country house guest areas have a modern edge and the well-equipped bedrooms are a mix of classic and contemporary styles. Relax in the lovely pool, on the charming terrace or in the delightful gardens.

28 rooms ⌂ – †† £200/550 – 2 suites

Longueville Road ✉ JE2 7WF – ℰ 01534 725501 – www.longuevillemanor.com –
Closed 6-22 January

🍴 **Longueville Manor** – See restaurant listing

SARK – Regional map n° **3**–A2

🍴 La Sablonnerie

SEAFOOD · COSY XX A charming 16C whitewashed farmhouse with beautiful gardens and a cosy beamed interior; start with an aperitif in the comfy lounge. The regularly changing 5 course dinner menu displays a classic style of cooking and uses produce from the island and their own farm. Lunch is best enjoyed on the terrace. Bedrooms are neat and tidy – No. 14, in the old stables, is the best.

Carte £34/50

Little Sark ✉ GY9 0SD – ℰ 01481 832061 – www.lasablonnerie.com –
Closed 2 October-26 February

🏠🏠🏠 Stocks

COUNTRY HOUSE · PERSONALISED A personally run former farmhouse whose formal gardens boast a split-level swimming pool and a jacuzzi. Bedrooms are sleek, contemporary and well-equipped. Dine on garden and island produce in the panelled dining room, the bistro or out on the terrace. The fantastic wine cellar was built during the war and the harbourmaster also brews country wines and liqueurs here.

23 rooms – †† £280/300 – 5 suites

✉ GY10 1SD – ℰ 01481 832001 – www.stockshotel.com –
Closed 2 January-28 February

CHARWELTON – Northamptonshire → See Daventry

CHELMONDISTON – Suffolk → See Ipswich

CHELMSFORD
Essex – Regional map n° **7**–C2

🍴 The Windmill Chatham Green

CLASSIC CUISINE · PUB X Friendly young couple Mick and Lydia have transformed this whitewashed inn into a smart dining pub. Concise menus constantly evolve as the latest seasonal produce arrives. Dishes are refined versions of British and pub classics. Larger parties can book to eat in the base of the village's old windmill.

Specialities: Great Garnetts pork Scotch egg with mustard mayonnaise. Slow-cooked breast of guinea fowl, ham and leek pie, truffle mash. Belgian chocolate fondant with pistachio ice cream.

Menu £28 – Carte £28/40

Chatham Green ✉ CM3 3LE – ℰ 01245 910910 –
www.thewindmillchathamgreen.com – Closed 1-14 January, Sunday dinner,
Monday, Tuesday, Wednesday - Thursday lunch

robynmac/iStock

CHELTENHAM

Gloucestershire – Regional map n° **2**-C1

Top tips!

This pretty spa town on the edge of the Cotswolds is renowned for its splendid Regency buildings as much as for its horseracing, and a walk around the shops of Montpellier is sure to help you work up an appetite.

There's a profusion of Indian restaurants here, ranging from the friendly basement **East India Café** with its incredibly satisfying Anglo-Indian cuisine to **Prithvi**, which offers ambitious Indian dishes within the charming setting of **No. 38 The Park**, a very originally styled townhouse hotel.

For a bit of fun try **Daffodil** – located in a converted cinema brimming with art deco appeal – or the on-trend **No. 131**, with its lively, easy-going vibe, great cocktail list and superb steaks. At the latter, you can also stay the night in a marvellously opulent bedroom.

Win or lose on the horses, dining in Cheltenham is always a safe bet.

Restaurants

☆ **Le Champignon Sauvage** (David Everitt-Matthias) [A/C]

MODERN CUISINE · INTIMATE XxX For over 30 years, David and Helen Everitt-Matthias' brightly decorated restaurant has provided a 'special occasion' spot in the historic spa town of Cheltenham. The couple make a great team: Helen is in charge of the décor and keenly oversees the service, while David can be found behind the stoves day-in-day-out.

David enthusiastically seeks out the best of British ingredients to showcase in classically based French dishes which employ modern techniques and exhibit some original elements. There is a lightness of touch to many, like fillet of Cornish mackerel with kohlrabi and avocado, while others display bold, robust flavours, such as Brecon venison with parsnip purée and bitter chocolate. The seasons mean everything here and he isn't afraid to use some lesser-known ingredients. Desserts are a highlight and the set priced menu is great value.

Specialities: Scallops with pumpkin and spiced crumbs. Venison with parsnip purée, black pudding and bitter chocolate. Blueberry cannelloni with wood sorrel cream and yoghurt sorbet.

Menu £ 35/85

Town plan A2-a – 24-28 Suffolk Road ✉ GL50 2AQ – ☎ 01242 573449 – www.lechampignonsauvage.co.uk – Closed 7 June-3 July, 22 December-6 January, Sunday-Tuesday

ⅼ○ **Daffodil**

MODERN BRITISH · BRASSERIE XX A delightful 1920s art deco cinema: the tables are in the old stalls, the kitchens are in the screen area and the stylish lounge is up on the balcony. A slick team serve classic brasserie dishes, including steaks from the Josper grill. At weekends lunch is accompanied by live jazz.

Menu £16 – Carte £31/59

Town plan A2-u – *18-20 Suffolk Parade* ⊠ *GL50 2AE* –
☏ *01242 700055* – *www.thedaffodil.com* – *Closed Sunday dinner, Monday lunch, Tuesday, Wednesday - Thursday lunch*

ⅼ○ **Bhoomi**

INDIAN · ROMANTIC XX You'll receive a warm welcome at his luxurious restaurant. You won't find all the usual curries but you will discover original, refined, modern dishes with a focus on southeast India. They also offer a tasting menu and wine pairings.

Menu £49 – Carte £33/49

Town plan A2-b – *52 Suffolk Road* ⊠ *GL50 2AQ* –
☏ *01242 222010* – *www.bhoomi.co.uk* – *Closed 25 December-14 January, Sunday, Monday*

ⅼ○ **Curry Corner**

BANGLADESHI · NEIGHBOURHOOD XX Long-standing, family-run restaurant in a smart Regency townhouse. Authentic, flavoursome dishes take their influences from across Bangladesh, India and Persia. Imported spices are ground and roasted every morning.

Carte £27/44

Town plan B1-a – *133 Fairview Road* ⊠ *GL52 2EX* –
☏ *01242 528449* – *www.thecurrycorner.com* – *Closed Sunday lunch, Monday, Tuesday - Saturday lunch*

ⅼ○ **East India Cafe**

INDIAN · FRIENDLY XX Steep candlelit steps leads down into a magical basement setting, where you're greeted by lovely aromas. Anglo-Indian cooking features home-grown herbs, home-ground spices and prime local meats. They also make their own gin.

Menu £20 (lunch), £37/56

Town plan A1-y – *103 Promenade* ⊠ *GL50 1NW* –
☏ *01242 300850* – *www.eastindiacafe.com* – *Closed Sunday, Monday, Tuesday - Thursday lunch*

ⅼ○ **Lumière**

MODERN CUISINE · INTIMATE XX Friendly, personally run restaurant; its unassuming exterior concealing a long, stylish room decorated with mirrors. Seasonal dishes are modern and intricate with the occasional playful twist – desserts are often the highlight.

Menu £35 (lunch)/70

Town plan B1-z – *Clarence Parade* ⊠ *GL50 3PA* –
☏ *01242 222200* – *www.lumiere.cc* – *Closed 1-8 January, 2-11 June, 22 July-8 August, Sunday, Monday, Tuesday, Wednesday - Thursday lunch*

ⅼ○ **Prithvi**

INDIAN · DESIGN XX This smart Indian restaurant is a refreshing break from the norm, with its ambitious owner, detailed service and refined cooking. Reinvented Indian and Bangladeshi dishes are presented in a sophisticated manner.

Menu £23 (lunch)/59 – Carte £44/50

Town plan B1-x – *No 38 The Park Hotel, 38 Evesham Road* ⊠ *GL52 2AH* –
☏ *01242 226229* – *www.prithvirestaurant.com* – *Closed 25 December, Sunday, Monday, Tuesday - Thursday lunch*

ⅱ◯ No. 131

MODERN CUISINE · BISTRO ⅹ This columned 1820s property overlooks an attractive park. Inside, original features remain but it now has a cool, contemporary style. Bedrooms are individually designed and tastefully furnished. The menu lists deftly-prepared modern dishes, with steaks cooked on the Josper grill a feature.

Carte £24/57

Town plan A1-e – *131 Promenade* ✉ *GL50 1NW* – ☏ *01242 822939* – *www.no131.com*

ⅱ◯ Koj

JAPANESE · SIMPLE ⅹ This intimate little restaurant is both fun and great value. There's no sushi, just a selection of authentic appetisers, buns and grazing plates. Accompany these with Japanese beers, sake and cocktails and you will leave with a smile.

Menu £20 – Carte £18/28

Town plan B1-k – *3 Regent Street* ✉ *GL50 1HE* – ☏ *01242 580455* – *www.kojcheltenham.co.uk* – *Closed Sunday, Monday, Tuesday - Friday lunch*

ⅱ◯ Purslane

MODERN BRITISH · INTIMATE ⅹ A stylishly minimalistic neighbourhood restaurant with relaxed, efficient service. Fresh seafood from Cornwall and Scotland is combined with good quality, locally sourced ingredients to produce interesting, original dishes.

Menu £17 (lunch), £20/60 – Carte £37/41

Town plan B1-p – *16 Rodney Road* ✉ *GL50 1JJ* – ☏ *01242 321639* – *www.purslane-restaurant.co.uk* – *Closed 19 January-4 February, 24-27 December, Sunday, Monday*

Hotels

⌂⌂⌂⌂ Ellenborough Park

LUXURY · ELEGANT A part-15C timbered manor house with stone annexes, an Indian-themed spa and large grounds stretching down to the racecourse. Beautifully furnished guest areas have an elegant classical style. Nina Campbell designed bedrooms have superb bathrooms, the latest mod cons and plenty of extras. Dine on elaborate dishes in the restaurant or pub fare in the brasserie.

61 rooms ⌕ – ♙♙ £146/550

Off plan – *Southam Road* ✉ *GL52 3NH* – ☏ *01242 545454* – *www.ellenboroughpark.com*

⌂ No 38 The Park

TOWNHOUSE · DESIGN Behind the attractive Georgian façade is a very original, tastefully designed hotel with a relaxed atmosphere and supremely comfortable furnishings. Bedrooms come with coffee machines and vast walk-in showers or feature baths.

13 rooms ⌕ – ♙♙ £120/325

Town plan B1-x – *38 Evesham Road* ✉ *GL52 2AH* – ☏ *01242 248656* – *www.no38thepark.com*

CHESTER

Cheshire West and Chester – Regional map n° **11**–A3

Top tips!

There is evidence of Chester's Roman origins all around the city; not least, its two miles of ancient walls, which are Grade I listed and one of the best-preserved examples in the country. There are plenty of other historic sites too, including 'Roodee' Racecourse – the oldest in the UK – and the lovely Victorian Grosvenor Park, set on the banks of the River Dee and boasting an open-air theatre.

Chester is also known for its black & white half-timbered buildings, like the Grade II listed **Chester Grosvenor** hotel – home to city ambassador **Simon Radley**'s Michelin-Starred restaurant.

Chester Town Hall hosts a food market on the third Saturday of each month entitled 'The Taste of Cheshire Farmers' – and you'll find numerous cheese shops selling Cheshire cheese. Coffee shops and tea rooms abound, and if it's great value you're after, Bib Gourmand bistro **Joseph Benjamin** is hard to beat.

Restaurants

❄️ **Simon Radley at Chester Grosvenor**

MODERN CUISINE · LUXURY Stylish bedrooms, a buzzy lounge and a lovely spa hide behind this 19C hotel's grand black and white timbered façade – along with a stylish cocktail lounge, an impressive wine cellar and Simon Radley's classically elegant restaurant. The height of luxury and sophistication, this is a beacon in northwest England, and is the place to come when celebrating a special occasion.

Simon celebrated 20 years at the helm in 2018 and his Head Chef Ray Booker has been here almost as long. Their confident cooking shows great respect for top quality ingredients, bringing together clean, clear flavours in sophisticated dishes that display interesting, innovative modern touches. Presentation is elegant and the bread trolley is a feature. The extensive wine list offers a good range of price options and the service is formal and highly detailed.

Specialities: Yellowfin tuna with white almond gazpacho, green tomatoes and fried sprats. Pyrenean lamb with wild garlic, morels, crispy curds and faggot gravy. Turkish delight with sweet curd, Cheshire saffron cake, lemon and rose.

Menu £75/99

Town plan B2-a – *Chester Grosvenor Hotel, Eastgate* ✉ *CH1 1LT* – ✆ *01244 895618* – *www.chestergrosvenor.com* – *Closed Sunday, Monday, Tuesday - Saturday lunch*

🟤 **Joseph Benjamin**

MODERN CUISINE · BISTRO This personally and passionately run bistro is named after its owners, Joe and Ben. The light, simple décor mirrors the style of cooking and the monthly menu offers tasty, well-judged dishes. They serve breakfast, lunch, coffee and homemade pastries and, from Thursday to Saturday, intimate candlelit dinners.

Specialities: Pan-fried duck livers, duck ham, rhubarb, date labneh and smoked almonds. Fillet of sea bass, squid ink risotto, crispy octopus and samphire. Affogato.

Carte £21/35

Town plan A1-u – *134-140 Northgate Street* ✉ *CH1 2HT* – ✆ *01244 344295* – *www.josephbenjamin.co.uk* – *Closed 25 December-2 January, Sunday dinner, Monday, Tuesday - Wednesday dinner*

🍽️ **Upstairs at the Grill**

MEATS AND GRILLS · INTIMATE Smart restaurant offering prime quality steaks – including porterhouse and bone-in fillet or rib-eye; the 5 week dry-aged cuts are from premium Welsh beef. Eat in the moody cocktail bar or downstairs amongst the cow paraphernalia.

Carte £27/60

Town plan A2-n – *70 Watergate Street* ✉ *CH1 2LA* – ✆ *01244 344883* – *www.upstairsatthegrill.co.uk*

🍽️ **Chef's Table** AC

MODERN BRITISH · SIMPLE A cosy, intimate city centre bistro tucked away down a narrow street; it has a loyal following and a pleasingly laid-back vibe. Monthly menus list colourful, artfully presented dishes. Vegetables are from a local grower who cultivates one of the oldest organic fields in England.

Menu £18 (lunch)/22 – Carte £28/44

Town plan A1-e – *4 Music Hall Passage* ✉ *CH1 2EU* – ✆ *01244 403040* – *www.chefstablechester.co.uk* – *Closed Sunday dinner, Monday lunch*

🍽️ **Covino** AC

BRITISH CONTEMPORARY · WINE BAR This small, intimate establishment with high level seating is more than just a wine bar. Charcuterie and small plates sit alongside some more substantial dishes on the appealing menu – and are a perfect match for the organic and low-intervention wines.

Carte £25/35

Town plan A1-f – *118 Northgate Street* ✉ *CH1 2HT* – ✆ *01244 347727* – *www.covino.co.uk* – *Closed Monday*

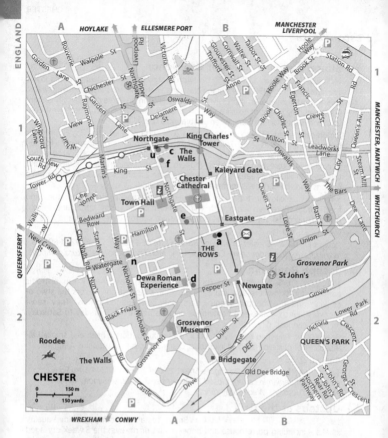

CHESTER

0 — 150 m
0 — 150 yards

🍴 Da Noi

AC

ITALIAN · FAMILY 🍴 Da Noi is an intimate little place in the heart of the city, where the owner and chef do everything they can to please their guests. Chef Valentina is a native of Italy and offers up freshly made, authentic dishes from the northwest of the country. The rustic sauces are homemade and the lasagne is a hit.

Menu £15 (lunch) – Carte £27/44

Town plan A2-d – *63 Bridge Street* ✉ *CH1 1NG* –
📞 *01244 317793* –
www.danoichester.co.uk –
Closed 1-10 January, Sunday dinner, Monday

🍴 Hypha

VEGAN · SIMPLE 🍴 This cute little restaurant sits atop the historic city walls. It's simply furnished, with good eco-credentials, and plenty of reclaimed timber and fauna on display. Unfussy vegan small plates have subtle Asian touches and fermentation techniques create some interesting flavour contrasts.

Carte £19/30

Town plan A1-c – *5 City Walls* ✉ *CH1 2JG* –
📞 *01244 312490* –
www.hypha.restaurant –
Closed Monday, Tuesday, Wednesday

ⅠⅠ○ **Porta**

SPANISH · TAPAS BAR ✗ Close to the city wall, behind a narrow terrace, is this cosy, characterful little tapas bar. It has no reservation system, but it does offer generous, tasty dishes which are served by a friendly young team.

Carte £15/25

Town plan A1-u – *140 Northgate Street* ⊠ *CH1 2HT* – ℰ *01244 344295* – *www.portatapas.co.uk* – *Closed 25 December-2 January, Sunday - Saturday lunch*

Hotels

🏨 **Chester Grosvenor**

LUXURY · CLASSIC Behind this 19C hotel's grand black and white timbered façade are a buzzy lounge and stylish bedrooms which blend traditional furnishings with contemporary fabrics. Unwind in the lovely spa, then dine on French classics in the appealing brasserie or more sophisticated fare in the restaurant.

80 rooms – 👫 £135/200 – ⊇ £29 – 12 suites

Town plan B2-a – *Eastgate* ⊠ *CH1 1LT* – ℰ *01244 324024* – *www.chestergrosvenor.com*

❀ **Simon Radley at Chester Grosvenor** – See restaurant listing

CHEW MAGNA
Bath and North East Somerset – Regional map n° **2**-C2

❀ **Pony & Trap** (Josh Eggleton)

MODERN BRITISH · PUB ✗ Chef-owner Josh bought the Pony & Trap back in 2006 and he is as passionate about it now as ever. He has continually developed the place over the years and today it boasts its own soft fruit cage, a polytunnel and even an orchard. You can dine in any of the areas: the characterful front bar, the rustic rear room or out on the terrace – the latter two choices offer wonderful country views.

A daily changing menu sees herbs and fruits from the garden come together with West Country meats and fish. Accomplished British dishes are bold and gutsy and range from great snacks, such as a mini game pie with apple chutney, to tasty pub classics, dry-aged steaks and more refined offerings like seaweed-baked cod with herb risotto. Puddings are satisfying and you're just as welcome for a pint and a snack as for the full tasting menu with wine pairings.

Specialities: Barbecued, tartare and parfait of mackerel with sorrel and cucumber & charcoal mayonnaise. Rack and breast of lamb with kidneys and wild garlic. Apple trifle with thyme custard, crab apple cream and warm apple cake.

Menu £50/65 – Carte £27/53

Knowle Hill, Newtown ⊠ *BS40 8TQ* – ℰ *01275 332627* – *www.theponyandtrap.co.uk* – *Closed Monday*

CHICHESTER
West Sussex – Regional map n° **4**-C2

at Funtington Northwest: 4. 75 mi by B2178 on B2146

ⅠⅠ○ **Hallidays**

CLASSIC CUISINE · INTIMATE ✗✗ Characterful thatched cottage comprising a series of interconnecting rooms with low beams. The chef knows a thing or two about sourcing good ingredients and his menu changes regularly. Cooking is skilful and classically based.

Menu £23 (lunch)/39 – Carte £35/39

Watery Lane ⊠ *PO18 9LF* – ℰ *01243 575331* – *www.hallidays.info.co.uk* – *Closed 8-14 April, 12-25 August, Sunday dinner, Monday, Tuesday, Saturday lunch*

at Mid Lavant North: 2 mi on A286

⫠○ **Earl of March**

TRADITIONAL CUISINE · PUB Ⅹ This 18C inn offers the perfect blend of contemporary styling and relaxed country character. Good quality seasonal produce is showcased in British-based dishes. Find a spot on the terrace to take in the amazing South Downs views.

Menu £28 – Carte £32/41

✉ PO18 0BQ – ☏ 01243 533993 – www.theearlofmarch.com

at Tangmere East: 2 mi by A27

⫠○ **Cassons**

MODERN CUISINE · RUSTIC ⅩⅩ Passionately run restaurant with exposed brick, wooden beams and a rustic feel. Boldly flavoured dishes are generously proportioned. Cooking is classically based but employs modern techniques. The regular gourmet evenings are a hit.

Menu £33/42

Arundel Road ✉ PO18 0DU – ☏ 01243 773294 – www.cassonsrestaurant.co.uk – Closed 24-30 December, Sunday dinner, Monday, Tuesday, Wednesday - Saturday lunch

at West Ashling Northwest: 4. 5 mi by B2178 and B2146

⫠○ **Richmond Arms** ⇐ 🛖 🅿

INTERNATIONAL · PUB Ⅹ Appealing, laid-back country pub opposite a duck pond in a lovely little village. The menu offers an appealing mix, from freshly sliced hams and local steaks to game from the family estate in Anglesey; many meats are cooked on the rotisserie or the Japanese robata grill. Two luxurious bedrooms are above.

Carte £28/45

Mill Road ✉ PO18 8EA – ☏ 01243 572046 – www.therichmondarms.co.uk – Closed 15-22 April, 21-29 July, 19 December-16 January, Sunday dinner-Tuesday

CHILCOMPTON
Somerset – Regional map n° **2**–C2

⫠○ **Redan Inn** ⇐ 🍴 🛖 ✿ 🅿

MODERN BRITISH · PUB Ⅹ An impressive collection of old curios and enamel signs decorate this pub, where they cure their own fish and meat, make their own sausages and use fruit and veg from the garden. Cooking is accomplished: choose from the 'Classics' selection or more adventurous à la carte. Bedrooms have a stylish rustic feel.

Menu £45 – Carte £26/43

Fry's Well ✉ BA3 4HA – ☏ 01761 258560 – www.theredaninn.co.uk – Closed Sunday dinner

CHINNOR
Oxfordshire – Regional map n° **6**–C2

at Sprigg's Alley Southeast: 2. 5 mi by Bledlow Ridge rd

⫠○ **Sir Charles Napier**

MODERN BRITISH · COSY ⅩⅩ Enjoy an aperitif in the delightful garden or beside the log fire in this quirky restaurant, where animal sculptures peer out from every corner. British cooking is modern yet unfussy and the wine list is a labour of love.

Menu £22/27 – Carte £40/60

Sprigs Holly ✉ OX39 4BX – ☏ 01494 483011 – www.sircharlesnapier.co.uk – Closed 2-14 January, Sunday dinner, Monday

CHIPPING CAMPDEN
Gloucestershire – Regional map n° **2**–D1

🏠 Cotswold House H. and Spa   🏃 🍴 🧖 AC ⚒ P

TOWNHOUSE · CONTEMPORARY A set of stylish Regency townhouses with lovely gardens, boldly decorated lounges hung with eclectic modern art, and a beautiful staircase winding upwards towards luxurious modern bedrooms. Relax in the spa our outdoor hot tub then enjoy sophisticated modern dishes amongst Regency columns.

28 rooms 🖵 – 🛏 £130/230 – 3 suites
The Square ✉ *GL55 6AN – ☎ 01386 840330 –*
www.cotswoldhouse.com

at Ebrington East: 2 mi by B4035

🍴 Ebrington Arms   ⇦ 🍴 🏡 P

MODERN CUISINE · PUB 🍴 Set in a charming chocolate box village, a proper village local with a beamed, flag-floored bar at its hub. Choose from pub classics on the blackboard or more elaborate dishes on the à la carte. Be sure to try one of the ales brewed to their own recipe. Bedrooms have country views and thoughtful extras.

Carte £28/38
✉ *GL55 6NH – ☎ 01386 593223 – www.theebringtonarms.co.uk*

at Paxford Southeast: 3 mi by B 4035

🍴 Churchill Arms   ⇦ 🏡

TRADITIONAL BRITISH · PUB 🍴 This charming 17C inn sits in a residential spot in a delightful Cotswold village and the intimate bar is hung with photos of local scenes taken by the owner himself. The menu offers everything from unfussy classics to more modern dishes. Bedrooms are comfy and well-appointed.

Carte £29/50
✉ *GL55 6XH – ☎ 01386 593159 –*
www.churchillarms.co – Closed 6-12 January

CHIPPING NORTON
Oxfordshire – Regional map n° **6**–A1

🍴 Wild Thyme

TRADITIONAL BRITISH · COSY 🍴 A keen husband and wife team run this cosy restaurant with rustic tables; number 10, in the window, is the best. Wholesome regional British cooking has Mediterranean influences, with tasty homemade breads and game in season.

Menu £20 (lunch), £32/40
10 New Street ✉ *OX7 5LJ – ☎ 01608 645060 –*
www.wildthymerestaurant.co.uk – Closed Sunday, Monday, Tuesday - Wednesday lunch

CHOBHAM
Surrey – Regional map n° **4**–C1

🍴 Stovell's   🏡 AC ⇔ P

MODERN BRITISH · INTIMATE 🍴🍴🍴 This characterful 16C farmhouse has put Chobham firmly on the culinary map. Creative, often intricate dishes use top quality ingredients. Highlights include dishes from the wood-fired grill and the 'Taste of Mexico' tasting menu, where chef-owner Fernando celebrates his roots.

Menu £24 (lunch), £48/75
125 Windsor Road ✉ *GU24 8QS – ☎ 01276 858000 –*
www.stovells.com – Closed 19-25 August, Sunday dinner, Monday, Tuesday - Wednesday lunch

CHRISTCHURCH
Dorset – Regional map n° **2**–D3

⑩ **Jetty**

MODERN BRITISH · DESIGN ❌❌ Set within the grounds of the Christchurch Harbour hotel, this contemporary, eco-friendly restaurant offers fantastic water views. Appealing menus reflect what's available locally, with fish from nearby waters and game from the forest.

Menu £27 – Carte £30/47

Christchurch Harbour Hotel, 95 Mudeford ✉ *BH23 3NT –* ☎ *01202 400950 – www.thejetty.co.uk*

CHURCHILL
Oxfordshire – Regional map n° **6**–A1

⑩ **Chequers**

TRADITIONAL CUISINE · PUB ❌ This welcoming Cotswold stone pub sits in the heart of the village and is a vital part of the local community. Owners Sam and Georgie have got the formula just right. The bar is stocked with local ales and the cooking is gutsy and traditional; steaks are cooked on the Josper grill.

Carte £23/36

Church Road ✉ *OX7 6NJ –* ☎ *01608 659393 – www.thechequerschurchill.com*

CIRENCESTER
Gloucestershire – Regional map n° **2**–D1

⑩ **Jesse's Bistro** 🗔 ♻

TRADITIONAL CUISINE · COSY ❌ This rustic bistro is hidden away in a little courtyard behind the Jesse Smith butcher's shop. Local meat and veg feature alongside Cornish fish and good use is made of the wood-fired oven. Beams and flagstones give it a cosy feel.

Menu £20 (lunch) – Carte £17/28

14 Blackjack Street ✉ *GL7 12AA –* ☎ *01285 641497 – www.jessesbistro.co.uk – Closed Sunday dinner, Monday*

at Barnsley Northeast: 4 mi by A429 on B4425 – Regional map n° **2**–D1

⑩ **Village Pub** ⇔ 🗔 🅿

TRADITIONAL BRITISH · PUB ❌ With an interior straight out of any country homes magazine, this place has the cosy, open-fired, village pub vibe down to a tee. It has four intimate rooms and a carefully manicured terrace. Appealing modern British dishes and irresistible nibbles feature locally sourced meats, charcuterie from Highgrove and comforting desserts. Bedrooms are tastefully styled.

Carte £26/38

✉ *GL7 5EF –* ☎ *01285 740421 – www.thevillagepub.co.uk*

🏠 **Barnsley House**

HISTORIC · PERSONALISED A 17C Cotswold manor house with a wonderfully relaxed vibe, set in the midst of beautiful gardens styled by Rosemary Verey. The chic interior blends original features with modern touches; there's also a spa and even a cinema in the grounds. The kitchen gardens inform what's on the menu.

18 rooms ⌒ – ♟ £229/509 – 8 suites

✉ *GL7 5EE –* ☎ *01285 740000 – www.barnsleyhouse.com*

CLANFIELD
Oxfordshire – Regional map n° **6**–A2

‖○ **Cotswold Plough**　　　　　　　⇔ 帝 帝 **P**

TRADITIONAL BRITISH · FRIENDLY XX Set within a 16C hotel, a lovely three-roomed restaurant with relaxed service, a gin pantry and a comfortingly traditional feel. Classic menus provide plenty of appeal and all wines are available by the glass or carafe.

Menu £21 (lunch), £23/40 – Carte £21/40

Cotswold Plough Hotel, Bourton Road ✉ OX18 2RB – ℰ 01367 810222 –
www.cotswoldploughhotel.com – Closed 23-27 December

CLAVERING
Essex – Regional map n° **7**–B2

‖○ **Cricketers**　　　　　　　　　⇔ 帝 **P**

MEDITERRANEAN CUISINE · PUB X This long-standing pub has built up quite a name for itself. The characterful main bar has extremely low ceilings and timbers hung with horse brasses. Menus offer plenty of choice and include lots of British classics. Bedrooms are set over three different buildings (the keys come attached to cricket balls!)

Menu £19 (lunch) – Carte £25/45

✉ CB11 4QT – ℰ 01799 550442 – www.thecricketers.co.uk – Closed 25-26 December

CLIPSHAM
Rutland – Regional map n° **9**–C2

‖○ **Olive Branch & Beech House**　　🐝 ⇔ 帝 ⅋ 🛈 **P**

TRADITIONAL BRITISH · PUB X Characterful village pub made up of a series of small rooms which feature open fires and exposed beams. The selection of rustic British dishes changes daily, reflecting the seasons and keeping things fiercely local. These are accompanied by real ales, homemade lemonade and vodka made from hedgerow berries. Bedrooms are cosy and thoughtfully finished.

Menu £19 (lunch)/40 – Carte £28/50

Main Street ✉ LE15 7SH – ℰ 01780 410355 – www.theolivebranchpub.com

COLCHESTER
Essex – Regional map n° **7**–D2

🛞 **grain** 🄽　　　　　　　　　帝 ⅋ 📠 ⇔

MODERN CUISINE · RUSTIC X Its former use as a joinery and its décor comprising reclaimed wood panelling and tables made from scaffold boards give this tucked away restaurant its name. Carefully crafted, well-presented small plates are inspired by the owners' travels and have well-judged flavours. 3-4 dishes each is about right.

Specialities: Asparagus with morels, smoked egg yolk and Jersey butter. Gloucester Old Spot pork, ham and potato terrine with rhubarb and mustard. Jerusalem artichoke and coffee stout tiramisu.

Menu £18 (lunch) – Carte £26/40

11A North Hill ✉ CO1 1DZ – ℰ 01206 570005 – www.grain-colchester.co.uk –
Closed 1-13 January, 22-30 December, Sunday, Monday, Tuesday lunch

‖○ **Church Street Tavern**　　　　🍸 ⅋ 🄰🄲 🛈 🐾

TRADITIONAL BRITISH · BRASSERIE X Set down a narrow city centre street, this modern brasserie sits within an attractive 18C building and is run in a relaxed, efficient manner. The trendy, shabby-chic bar serves cocktails and light bites, while the upstairs restaurant offers British classics with Mediterranean influences.

Menu £16/21 – Carte £25/38

3 Church Street ✉ CO1 1NF – ℰ 01206 564325 – www.churchstreettavern.co.uk –
Closed 1-5 January, Sunday dinner, Monday, Tuesday

COLERNE – Wiltshire ➜ See Bath

COLSTON BASSETT
Nottinghamshire – Regional map n° **9**–B2

Ⅰ○ **The Martins Arms** ⎔ ⌂ **P**
TRADITIONAL CUISINE · PUB ⅹ Creeper-clad pub in a charming village, with a cosy fire-lit bar and period furnished dining rooms. The menu has a meaty, masculine base, with a mix of classical and more modern dishes –and plenty of local game in season.

Carte £30/45

School Lane ⊠ NG12 3FD – ℰ 01949 81361 – www.themartinsarms.co.uk –
Closed Sunday dinner

COMPTON BASSETT
Wiltshire – Regional map n° **2**–D2

Ⅰ○ **White Horse Inn** ⇐ ⎔ ⌂ **P**
TRADITIONAL BRITISH · PUB ⅹ The White Horse dates back over a century: the cosy bar is where you'll find the regulars, while most diners head for the rustic room next door. For traditionalists there are pub classics; for those with more adventurous tastes there's the à la carte. Beyond the large garden are 8 snug bedrooms.

Menu £18 (lunch) – Carte £25/42

⊠ SN11 8RG – ℰ 01249 813118 – www.whitehorse-comptonbassett.co.uk

COOKHAM
Windsor and Maidenhead – Regional map n° **6**–C3

Ⅰ○ **White Oak** ⎔ ⌂ **P**
TRADITIONAL BRITISH · PUB ⅹ One could argue whether this is a contemporary pub or a pubby restaurant, as it's set up quite formally, but what is in no doubt is the warmth of the welcome and the affection in which the place is held by its regulars. Cooking is hearty and full of flavour; the set menu is great value.

Menu £16/19 – Carte £24/33

Pound Lane ⊠ SL6 9QE – ℰ 01628 523043 – www.thewhiteoak.co.uk

CORTON DENHAM
Somerset – Regional map n° **2**–C3

Ⅰ○ **Queens Arms** ⇐ ⌂ ⎔
MODERN BRITISH · PUB ⅹ This hub-of-the-village pub hosts plenty of events and comes with plush bedrooms. The menu lists food 'metres' rather than miles and much of the produce is from their smallholding and local shoots. Choose from small plates, pub classics and more elaborate dishes; the bar is also topped with tempting treats.

Menu £28 – Carte £30/50

⊠ DT9 4LR – ℰ 01963 220317 – www.thequeensarms.com

COWAN BRIDGE
Lancashire – Regional map n° **11**–B1

Ⅰ○ **Hipping Hall** ⇐ ⎔ ⌂ **P**
MODERN CUISINE · ROMANTIC ⅹⅹ A charming part-15C blacksmith's named after the stepping stones over the beck. The elegant restaurant has a superb beamed ceiling, a minstrel's gallery and a medieval feel. Creative, original dishes feature on two tasting menus and come with wine pairings. The best bedrooms are in the outbuildings.

Menu £29 (lunch)/70

on A 65 ⊠ LA6 2JJ – ℰ 015242 71187 – www.hippinghall.com – Closed Monday,
Tuesday, Wednesday lunch

COWLEY
Gloucestershire – Regional map n° **2**–C1

🏠 Cowley Manor ❀ 🏊 🛒 🍸 🖼 🕸 📶 🛁 ⊕ 🚭 🅿

LUXURY · CONTEMPORARY Impressive Regency house in 55 acres, with beautiful formal gardens, a superb spa, and lake views from some of the bedrooms. Original features and retro furnishings mix with bold colours and modern fittings to create a laid-back, understated vibe. The carved wood panelling in the restaurant is a feature.

30 rooms ⌂ – 👫 £ 205/675 – 8 suites

✉ GL53 9NL – ☎ 01242 870900 – www.cowleymanor.com

CRAYKE

North Yorkshire – Regional map n° **13**–C2

🍴◯ **Durham Ox** ⇔ 🖼 🕚 ⇩ 🅿

TRADITIONAL BRITISH · PUB 𝕏 A 300 year old pub in a sleepy hamlet; in summer, head for the lovely courtyard. Menus focus on honest, homely cooking, with everything made on-site; choose a blackboard special – often game or seafood accompanied by something 'wild'. Cosy bedrooms feature original brickwork and quarry tiling.

Carte £ 27/46

Westway ✉ YO61 4TE – ☎ 01347 821506 – www.thedurhamox.com

CROMER

Norfolk – Regional map n° **8**–D1

🍴◯ **No1 Cromer** 🖼 ⇐ 🏖 🆚

FISH AND CHIPS · SIMPLE 𝕏 This is fish and chips with a difference: looking out over the beach and pier and offering everything from fresh fish and battered local sausages to cockle popcorn and mushy pea fritters. Potatoes are from their farm and the varieties change throughout the year. Head up to the bistro for some tasty fish tapas.

Carte £ 19/29

1 New Street ✉ NR27 9HP – ☎ 01263 515983 – www.no1cromer.com

CROSTHWAITE

Cumbria – Regional map n° **12**–A2

🍴◯ **Punch Bowl Inn** ⇔ ⇐ 🖼 🅿

TRADITIONAL BRITISH · PUB 𝕏 The picturesque Lyth valley plays host to this charming 17C inn, where a cosy beamed bar doubles as the village post office. Have a pint of local beer and some homemade pork scratchings or fresh, carefully cooked classics like cheese soufflé. Bedrooms are luxurious – one even has twin baths!

Carte £ 25/50

✉ LA8 8HR – ☎ 015395 68237 – www.the-punchbowl.co.uk

CRUDWELL – Wiltshire ➜ See Malmesbury

CRUNDALE

Kent – Regional map n° **5**–C2

😊 **Compasses Inn** 🛒 🖼 🅿

MODERN CUISINE · PUB 𝕏 This hugely characterful 1420s pub is run by an enthusiastic young couple who have a genuine desire to please. The small front bar has hop-hung beams and inglenook fireplaces and the dining room opens out onto the garden. Menus mix well-prepared comfort dishes with those with a little more finesse.

Specialities: Sweet-soused herring with Jersey Royals, pickled shallots and dill emulsion. Roast rump of lamb, confit shoulder, potato terrine and wild garlic. Chocolate and caramel macaron with malt and barley ice cream.

Menu £ 18 (lunch)/23 – Carte £ 27/41

Sole Street ✉ CT4 7ES – ☎ 01227 700300 – www.thecompassescrundale.co.uk – Closed Sunday dinner, Monday, Tuesday

DARLEY ABBEY – Derby → See Derby

DARLINGTON
Darlington – Regional map n° **14**-B3

at Hurworth-on-Tees South: 5. 5 mi by A167

⅋○ **The Orangery**　　　　　　　　⊞ & ⑩ P

MODERN CUISINE · INTIMATE ╳╳ A striking country house plays host to this elegantly refurbished orangery. Each carefully crafted, well-presented dish features just a handful of ingredients and focuses on using them in their natural state. There is an à la carte but go for the tasting menu for the best experience. Service is engaging.

Menu £55

Rockcliffe Hall Hotel ✉ DL2 2DU – ℰ 01325 729999 – www.rockliffehall.com – Closed Sunday - Saturday lunch

⅋○ **Bay Horse**　　　　　　⊞ 🏠 & ⑩ ⇄ P

MODERN CUISINE · PUB ╳ A good-looking pub with an elegant feel and plenty of appeal; the jewel in its crown is its lovely garden and terrace. Appealing modern menus include the likes of pan-fried halibut with a glazed chicken wing, red wine salsify and purple potatoes. The caramelised rice pudding is something of a speciality.

Menu £21 (lunch)/28 – Carte £25/66

45 The Green ✉ DL2 2AA – ℰ 01325 720663 – www.thebayhorsehurworth.com

🏨 **Rockcliffe Hall**　🎿 🐎 ⊞ ▣ 🖼 🌐 ⑭ 🎛 🔁 & 🔤 🎿 P

LUXURY · CONTEMPORARY An impressive manor house set in 375 acres of grounds, complete with a championship golf course, extensive leisure facilities and an Alice in Wonderland outdoor adventure area. The original Victorian house has grand guest areas and characterful bedrooms; rooms in the extensions are more modern. Dining options range from classics and grills to ambitious modern dishes.

61 rooms ⌧ – ❢❢ £190/540

✉ *DL2 2DU – ℰ 01325 729999 – www.rockliffehall.com*

⅋○ **The Orangery** – See restaurant listing

at Summerhouse Northwest: 6. 5 mi by A68 on B6279 – Regional map n° **14**-B3

❀❀ **Raby Hunt** (James Close)　　　⇔ ⑩ P

MODERN BRITISH · INTIMATE ╳╳ This former drovers' inn in a rural hamlet was originally part of the Raby Estate and its name refers to it being a favourite finishing point for the old hunt. It's owned by the Close family, with son James – a self-taught chef – heading up the kitchen. His interest in food was sparked as a youngster, and he would ask his parents to order certain dishes in restaurants so he could try new things – he even kept notebooks of his discoveries.

Now inspired by his travels and the landscape around him, he favours a classic base with modern overtones and an international style. His ingredients are first-class and, while his ethos is one of simplicity, every dish has originality and flavours are sublime. His drive and passion also lead him to continually refine and enhance his dishes – he is never a man to stand still.

Stay the night in a contemporary bedroom.

Specialities: Chūtoro tuna with white truffle. Wagyu with smoked aubergine and caviar. Mango tart with yuzu and coconut ice cream.

Menu £150/180

✉ *DL2 3UD – ℰ 01325 374237 – www.rabyhuntrestaurant.co.uk – Closed 19-28 April, 24 August-9 September, 20 December-8 January, Sunday, Monday, Tuesday, Wednesday - Thursday lunch*

DARSHAM
Suffolk – Regional map n° **8**-D2

⭑○ **Darsham Nurseries Café**

COUNTRY COOKING · SIMPLE ⭑ In 2014 the owners of this nursery opened a smart gift shop and this sweet little café. Expect colourful, richly flavoured small plates of locally sourced organic and garden produce, with vegetarian and vegan dishes making up a large proportion of the menu. On Sundays they only serve brunch.

Menu £20 – Carte £24/33

Main Road ✉ IP17 3PW – ☏ 01728 667022 –
www.darshamnurseries.co.uk –
Closed Sunday - Thursday dinner

DARTMOUTH

Devon – Regional map n° **1**-C3

⭑○ **The Angel** ❶

MODERN BRITISH · INTIMATE ⭑⭑ This smart yet informal riverside restaurant was where Joyce Molyneux rose to fame for her modern British cooking in the 1970s. Elly Wentworth is now aiming to follow in her footsteps, by creating accomplished dishes that deliver bold flavours and showcase the best produce from within a 30 mile radius.

Menu £30 (lunch) – Carte £40/65

2 South Embankment ✉ TQ6 9BH – ☏ 01803 833488 –
www.theangeldartmouth.co.uk –
Closed 1-15 January, Sunday, Monday, Tuesday lunch

⭑○ **Seahorse**

SEAFOOD · CHIC ⭑⭑ A smart restaurant in a lovely spot on the embankment; sit outside looking over the estuary or inside beside the glass-walled kitchen. Seafood-orientated menus have a Mediterranean bias, with Josper-grilled whole fish and fresh pastas the favourites. Start with a cocktail in the lovely Joe's Bar.

Menu £20/35 – Carte £22/63

5 South Embankment ✉ TQ6 9BH – ☏ 01803 835147 –
www.seahorserestaurant.co.uk –
Closed 24-27 December, Sunday dinner, Monday

🏨 **Dart Marina**

TRADITIONAL · DESIGN Once an old boat works and chandlery, now a relaxed, modern hotel with a small spa and leisure centre. Smart, contemporary bedrooms have lovely outlooks over either the river or marina – many also boast balconies. The stylish, formal restaurant offers up-to-date versions of British classics.

53 rooms ⌂ – 👫 £180/250 – 4 suites

Sandquay Road ✉ TQ6 9PH – ☏ 01803 832580 –
www.dartmarina.com

at Strete Southwest: 4. 5 mi on A379 – Regional map n° **1**-C3

🏠 **Strete Barton House**

HISTORIC · PERSONALISED Attractive part-16C manor house in a quiet village, with partial views over the rooftops to the sea. The contemporary interior has a personal style; bedrooms come with bold feature walls and modern facilities. Homemade cake is served on arrival and top quality local ingredients feature at breakfast.

6 rooms – 👫 £105/175

Totnes Road ✉ TQ6 0RU – ☏ 01803 770364 –
www.stretebarton.co.uk –
Closed 1-31 January

DAVENTRY
Northamptonshire – Regional map n° **9**–B3

at Charwelton South : 6. 25 mi by A 45 on A 361

🍴○ **Fox & Hounds** 　　　　　　　　　　　🔲 **P**

TRADITIONAL BRITISH · PUB 〤 The Fox & Hounds has been a fixture in Charwelton since 1871 and is now owned by the villagers themselves. The lunch menu offers pub classics, while dinner sees British dishes with some European influences. Whole beasts are butchered on-site and every part of the animal is used.

Menu £18 – Carte £25/50

Banbury Road ✉ NN11 3YY – 𝒞 01327 260611 –
www.foxandhoundscharwelton.co.uk – Closed 1-5 January, Sunday dinner, Tuesday

DAYLESFORD – Gloucestershire → See Stow-on-the-Wold

DEAL
Kent – Regional map n° **5**–D2

🍴○ **Frog and Scot** 　　　　　　　　　　　🦽

MODERN BRITISH · BISTRO 〤 A quirky bistro with yellow canopies and mismatched furnishings; its unusual name refers to its French and Scottish owners. Large blackboard menus list refined, innately simple dishes which let the ingredients do the talking.

Menu £18/27 – Carte £18/49

86 High Street ✉ CT14 6EG – 𝒞 01304 379444 – www.frogandscot.co.uk –
Closed Sunday dinner, Monday, Tuesday

DEDHAM
Essex – Regional map n° **7**–D2

🍴○ **Le Talbooth** 　　　　　　🎿 🍷 🔲 🦽 🏳 **P**

MODERN BRITISH · RUSTIC 〤〤〤 This superbly characterful restaurant on the riverbank belongs to the charming Maison Talbooth hotel; if you're staying the night, you can be chauffeured over. Inside it has a stylish, rustic-chic design; most tables afford a river view. Cooking has classic roots but is given subtle modern touches.

Menu £39 (lunch) – Carte £51/66

Maison Talbooth Hotel, Gun Hill ✉ CO7 6HP – 𝒞 01206 323150 –
www.milsomhotels.com – Closed Sunday dinner

🍴○ **Sun Inn** 　　　　　　🎿 🍷 🔲 🏳 **P**

ITALIAN · PUB 〤 Characterful yellow inn with an appealing shabby-chic style, located in a picturesque spot in the heart of Constable Country. The monthly menu offers generous Italian-inspired dishes and the well-chosen wine list offers plenty by the glass. Bedrooms are cosy – two have a modern New England style.

Menu £23 – Carte £24/38

High Street ✉ CO7 6DF – 𝒞 01206 323351 – www.thesuninndedham.com

🏨 **Maison Talbooth** 　　　　🏹 🌿 ⛷ 🍷 🔲 **P**

LUXURY · CONTEMPORARY A charming part-Georgian house in rolling countryside, with a modern country house feel and views over the river valley. Luxurious bedrooms boast quality furnishings and come in a mix of classic and contemporary styles. Seek out the tennis court and the year-round heated outdoor pool and hot tub.

12 rooms ☲ – 🍴 £295/375

Stratford Road ✉ CO7 6HN – 𝒞 01206 322367 – www.milsomhotels.com
🍴○ **Le Talbooth** – See restaurant listing

DERBY
Derby – Regional map n° **9**–B2

322

at Darley Abbey North: 2. 5 mi off A6

⊙ **Darleys** 🛱 🗚 🎯 🅿

MODERN CUISINE · FRIENDLY ✕✕ A popular weir-side restaurant, located in the old canteen of a 19C silk mill. Start with drinks in the modern bar-lounge or on the attractive terrace. Good value lunches are followed by more ambitious European dishes in the evening.

Menu £25 (lunch) – Carte £40/47

Darley Abbey Mill ⊠ DE22 1DZ – 𝄢 01332 364987 – www.darleys.com –
Closed 25 December-10 January, Sunday dinner, Monday

DOGMERSFIELD

Hampshire – Regional map n° **4**–C1

🏨 **Four Seasons** 🏌 🐎 🔽 🛏 🔲 ⬢ 🐾 🗡 ⬆ 👍 🗚 🕷 🅿

LUXURY · CLASSIC An attractive part-Georgian house in 350 acres of parkland where, along with relaxing in the superb spa, you can try your hand at all manner of outdoor pursuits. Luxurious bedrooms are well-equipped and boast marble bathrooms. Rotisserie meats are a speciality in the stylish bar and brasserie.

133 rooms – 👫 £340/350 – 🍽 £30 – 21 suites

Dogmersfield Park, Chalky Lane ⊠ RG27 8TD – 𝄢 01252 853000 –
www.fourseasons.com/hampshire

DONHEAD-ST-ANDREW

Wiltshire – Regional map n° **2**–C3

🕸 **The Forester** 🛏 🛱 🅿

TRADITIONAL BRITISH · PUB ✕ A gloriously rustic 13C thatched pub, hidden down narrow lanes in a delightful village. Exposed stone walls and vast open fires feature throughout. Daily changing menus showcase well-prepared, flavoursome dishes with a classical country base and a refined edge; Brixham fish features highly.

Specialities: Provençal fish soup with rouille and homemade bread. Barnsley chop with mash, swede and carrots. Sticky toffee pudding with vanilla ice cream.

Carte £28/34

Lower Street ⊠ SP7 9EE – 𝄢 01747 828038 –
www.theforesterdonheadstandrew.co.uk – Closed Sunday dinner, Monday

DORCHESTER

Dorset – Regional map n° **2**–C3

⊙ **Sienna** 🗚

MODERN CUISINE · COSY ✕✕ This unassuming high street restaurant is run by a keen young chef who cooks alone in the kitchen. Concise menu descriptions belie the complexity of the dishes, which are modern and ambitious both in flavour and presentation. It has just five tables, so book ahead.

Menu £25 (lunch), £35/70

36 High West Street ⊠ DT1 1UP – 𝄢 01305 250022 – www.siennadorchester.co.uk –
Closed Sunday, Monday, Tuesday lunch

⊙ **Yalbury Cottage** 🡸 🛏 🅿

TRADITIONAL BRITISH · RUSTIC ✕✕ This very proudly and personally run restaurant is set within an old thatched cottage and has a snug beamed interior. Cooking is traditional, gutsy and flavoursome. Produce is sourced from within 9 miles and the menu evolves as new ingredients become available. Well-kept cottagey bedrooms are located in a wing.

Menu £35/40

Lower Bockhampton ⊠ DT2 8PZ – 𝄢 01305 262382 – www.yalburycottage.com –
Closed 23 December-17 January, Sunday dinner, Monday, Tuesday - Saturday lunch

DORKING
Surrey – Regional map n° **4**–D2

✿ **Sorrel** (Steve Drake)

MODERN BRITISH · ELEGANT XX A fine 300 year old building in the centre of Dorking houses this delightful restaurant, which is named after chef-owner Steve Drake's favourite herb. Having worked in the area for many years he really understands what the locals are looking for, and here, he has got it just right. Sit on the cosy ground floor or in the intimate upstairs room, where beams divide the area into three and a glass-walled kitchen – which guests are encouraged to visit – provides a pleasing modern contrast.

Local ingredients form the backbone of menus which echo the seasons and display great balance. The creative modern dishes are precisely prepared and flavours work together in harmony; as well as being colourful, they are sometimes playfully presented. Portion sizes are well-judged and dishes are served at an even pace by the knowledgeable team.

Specialities: Scallop, seaweed lettuce, oyster and lemon thyme emulsion. Etherley Farm duck with Moroccan spices. Blackberry Waldorf.

Menu £ 45 (lunch), £ 65/95

77 South Street ⊠ RH4 2JU – ☏ 01306 889414 – www.sorrelrestaurant.co.uk – Closed 9-19 August, 23 December-8 January, Sunday, Monday

DREWSTEIGNTON
Devon – Regional map n° **1**–C2

⫶○ **Old Inn**

MODERN BRITISH · INTIMATE XX An old 17C pub in the centre of a lovely village. It has two small, cosy dining rooms, and a parquet–floored lounge with a wood-burning stove in its inglenook fireplace and modern art for sale on the walls. The concise menu offers assured, seasonal modern dishes. Bedrooms are simply furnished.

Menu £ 38 (lunch), £ 54/61

⊠ EX6 6QR – ☏ 01647 281276 – www.old-inn.co.uk – Closed Sunday, Monday, Tuesday, Wednesday - Saturday lunch

DRIGHLINGTON
West Yorkshire – Regional map n° **13**–B2

⛁ **Prashad**

INDIAN VEGETARIAN · NEIGHBOURHOOD XX Stylish former pub with wooden panels from India fronting the bar; head upstairs to admire the huge picture of a Mumbai street scene. Authentic vegetarian dishes range from enticing street food to more original creations, with influences from Southern India and Gujarat; be sure to try the dosas.

Specialities: Open samosa of asafoetida and mango-infused mixed beans. Seasonal greens and paneer dough balls with caraway infused tomato sauce. Roast wheat flour with jaggery, sesame seeds and star anise.

Carte £ 27/37

137 Whitehall Road ⊠ BD11 1AT – ☏ 0113 285 2037 – www.prashad.co.uk – Closed Monday, Tuesday - Friday lunch

DULVERTON
Somerset – Regional map n° **2**–A2

⫶○ **Woods**

MODERN BRITISH · PUB X Former bakery, with a cosy, hugely characterful interior. Tasty, carefully prepared dishes offer more than just the usual pub fare. Provenance is taken seriously, with quality local ingredients including meat from the owner's farm.

Carte £ 22/38

4 Banks Square ⊠ TA22 9BU – ☏ 01398 324007 – www.woodsdulverton.co.uk

DURHAM

Durham – Regional map n° **14**–B3

⭐ **Finbarr's**

🛖 ♻ **P**

MODERN BRITISH · BISTRO 𝗫𝗫 Finbarr's sits in an attractively converted farm building on the edge of the city and comes with a contented buzz. Menus offer plenty of choice and the hearty brasserie cooking suits the area well. If the weather's good, start with a drink in the lovely inner courtyard.

Menu £19 (lunch), £22/25 – Carte £27/45

Aykley Heads House, Aykley Heads ✉ *DH1 5TS –* ℰ *0191 307 7033 –*
www.finbarrsrestaurant.co.uk

EAST CHISENBURY

Wiltshire – Regional map n° **2**–D2

⭐ **Red Lion Freehouse** (Guy Manning)

⇦ 🛏 🛖 ♻ **P**

CLASSIC CUISINE · PUB 𝗫 The Red Lion sits on the edge of Salisbury Plain and although it's not a spot for passing trade, its owners need not worry, as it's become a real destination in itself. With its thatched roof and welcoming look, it immediately draws you in; although you'll probably want to stay out in the pretty garden when the weather's right.

The daily à la carte is a roll-call of carefully prepared classics which arrive fully garnished and packed with flavour; these could include Cornish crab tart or rib of Wiltshire beef for two to share. The fixed price menu is great value, the colourful modern puddings are a highlight, and the well-chosen wine list offers a good selection by the glass.

Smart, well-equipped bedrooms are set opposite and have private terraces overlooking the river.

Specialities: Cornish crab tart with dressed fennel and dill. Chateaubriand with hand-cut chips and sauce béarnaise. Truffle pain perdu with salted honey ice cream.

Menu £24/28 – Carte £40/60

✉ *SN9 6AQ –* ℰ *01980 671124 – www.redlionfreehouse.com – Closed 2-14 January, Sunday dinner, Monday, Tuesday*

EAST END

Hampshire – Regional map n° **4**–A3

⭐ **East End Arms**

⇦ 🛖 **P**

TRADITIONAL BRITISH · PUB 𝗫 This traditional country pub is owned by John Illsley of Dire Straits and boasts a great display of photos from his personal collection in its shabby bar and pine-furnished dining room. Concise menus feature local produce in satisfying British dishes. Modern cottage-style bedrooms provide a smart contrast.

Carte £25/40

Lymington Road ✉ *SO41 5SY –* ℰ *01590 626223 – www.eastendarms.co.uk*

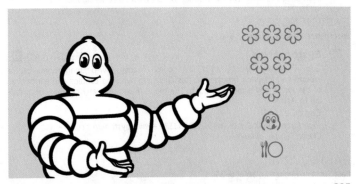

EAST GRINSTEAD

West Sussex – Regional map n° **4**–D2

🕸 **Gravetye Manor**

MODERN BRITISH · TRADITIONAL XxX This quintessential country house is surrounded by 35 acres of glorious gardens; it was, after all, once home to pioneering gardener William Robinson. Ornate Elizabethan ceilings and fireplaces feature in beautiful lounges, while the restaurant sits within a contemporary extension and balances tradition with modernity.

The architect has been a regular guest for over 30 years and his design brings the gardens inside using natural colours and lots of glass. The kitchen garden provides the restaurant's heartbeat – if it's not in season, you simply won't find it on the menu – and chef George Blogg really knows how to get the best out of his produce. Carefully crafted dishes appeal to both the taste buds and the eyes, with their vibrant flavours and appealingly colourful presentation. Service is personalised and the bedrooms are luxurious.

Specialities: Roasted quail with pickled quince, liver parfait and seeded granola. Newhaven turbot with parsnip, black truffle and roast chicken sauce. Forced rhubarb soufflé with stem ginger ice cream.

Menu £48 (lunch), £80/95

Gravetye Manor Hotel, Vowels Lane ✉ *RH19 4LJ –* ☎ *01342 810567 –*
www.gravetyemanor.co.uk

🏘 **Gravetye Manor**

LUXURY · CLASSIC A quintessential English country house set in a forest and surrounded by 35 acres of glorious gardens. Ornate Elizabethan ceilings and fireplaces dominate beautifully furnished lounges, which provide the perfect spot for afternoon tea. Bedrooms are luxurious and the service is personalised and detailed.

17 rooms ⊑ – ♦♦ £295/650 – 1 suite

Vowels Lane ✉ *RH19 4LJ –* ☎ *01342 810567 – www.gravetyemanor.co.uk*
🕸 **Gravetye Manor** – See restaurant listing

EAST HADDON

Northamptonshire – Regional map n° **9**–B3

🍽 **Red Lion**

TRADITIONAL CUISINE · PUB X A thatched, honey-stone inn at the heart of an attractive village, with a pleasing mix of exposed wood, brick and slate, a pretty garden and chic, cosy bedrooms. The good value, seasonal menu offers generously proportioned dishes; the scotch egg is a favourite. Service is smiley and enthusiastic.

Carte £22/36

Main Street ✉ *NN6 8BU –* ☎ *01604 770223 – www.redlioneasthaddon.co.uk*

EAST HENDRED

Oxfordshire – Regional map n° **6**–B3

🍽 **Eyston Arms**

TRADITIONAL CUISINE · PUB X A series of cosy, low-beamed rooms centre around an inglenook fireplace at this charming pub, and candles and caricatures of the locals add a modern touch. The menu draws on many cuisines, from Italian to Asian.

Carte £23/45

High Street ✉ *OX12 8JY –* ☎ *01235 833320 – www.eystonarms.co.uk –*
Closed Sunday dinner

EASTBOURNE

East Sussex – Regional map n° **5**–B3

🏨 Grand ✿ ⬦ 📶 ⛵ 🎐 ♨ 🎣 ⬇ ♿ 🏊 P

GRAND LUXURY · CLASSIC Built in 1875 and offering all its name promises, the Grand retains many original features including ornate plasterwork, columned corridors and a Great Hall. The delightful gardens feature a superb outdoor pool and sun terrace. Bedrooms are spacious and classical – it's worth paying extra for a sea view. Dine in formal Mirabelle or the more accessible Garden Restaurant.

152 rooms 🖵 – 👬 £150/345 – 14 suites

King Edward's Parade ✉ BN21 4EQ – 𝒞 01323 412345 –
www.grandeastbourne.com

EBRINGTON – Gloucestershire ➜ See Chipping Campden

ECKINGTON – Worcestershire ➜ See Pershore

EGHAM
Surrey – Regional map n° **4**–C1

✿ **Tony Parkin at The Tudor Room** 📶 ♿ P

MODERN CUISINE · INTIMATE 🍴🍴 This striking Elizabethan manor was built as a hunting lodge for Henry VIII and boasts 50 acres of stunning gardens which include a beautiful parterre and an amphitheatre. The charming interior displays characterful original detailing and the dining room comes with attractive mullioned windows; it's an intimate space with just seven tables and they never serve more than 20 guests a night.

The restaurant bears the name of head chef Tony Parkin, who has been given free rein to make it his own, so he has as much say in the service as in the cooking. His classically based menus are intentionally concise to allow for maximum consistency, and dishes are accomplished and well-balanced, with a lightness of touch. The kitchen garden provides many of the ingredients and natural flavours are to the fore.

Bedrooms have a flamboyant touch.

Specialities: Asparagus with morels, Parmesan, lemon, wild garlic and cured pork jowl. Turbot with Granny Smith, celeriac, truffle and nasturtium. Gariguette strawberry with lemon verbena, crème fraiche and yuzu.

Menu £45 (lunch)/95

Great Fosters Hotel, Stroude Road ✉ TW20 9UR – 𝒞 01784 433822 –
www.alexanderhotels.co.uk – Closed 2-15 January, 6-16 April, Monday, Tuesday,
Wednesday, Saturday lunch

🏨 Great Fosters ✿ 📶 ⛵ ♿ 🏊 P

BUSINESS · ELEGANT A striking Elizabethan manor built as a hunting lodge for Henry VIII, boasting 50 acres of gardens, a beautiful parterre and an amphitheatre. The charming interior displays characterful original detailing. Bedrooms come with feature beds and a flamboyant touch; those in the annexes are more modern. Dine on steaks from the Josper grill or more formally in the Tudor Room.

43 rooms 🖵 – 👬 £155/355 – 3 suites

Stroude Road ✉ TW20 9UR – 𝒞 01784 433822 – www.alexanderhotels.co.uk

✿ **Tony Parkin at The Tudor Room** – See restaurant listing

ELDERSFIELD
Worcestershire – Regional map n° **10**–B3

🍴 **Butchers Arms** 📶 P

MODERN BRITISH · PUB 🍴 A thick wooden door salvaged from an old ship leads you into this sweet rural inn where hop bines vie for space with the locals' tankards on low exposed beams. Food is a mix of the classical and the modern, flavours are honest and portions are satisfying. Ales are served straight from the keg.

Menu £25 – Carte £32/50

Lime Street ✉ GL19 4NX – 𝒞 01452 840381 – www.thebutchersarms.net –
Closed 26 December-6 January, Sunday dinner, Monday, Tuesday - Thursday lunch

ELLASTONE
Staffordshire – Regional map n° **10**–C1

☺ Duncombe Arms

TRADITIONAL BRITISH · PUB X A stylish dining pub owned by the Hon. Johnny Greenall and his wife – a descendant of the Duncombe family. There are several cosy rooms to choose from, each with their own identity, and menus mix pub classics with more ambitious restaurant-style dishes. Luxurious bedrooms overlook the countryside.

Specialities: Wye Valley asparagus with cured duck ham, crispy hen's egg and hollandaise sauce. Roast cod with brown shrimps, tenderstem broccoli, crushed potatoes and beurre blanc. Pistachio soufflé, blood orange sorbet.

Menu £19/22 – Carte £27/47

Main Road ✉ DE6 2GZ – ℰ 01335 324275 – www.duncombearms.co.uk

ELTON-ON-THE-HILL
Nottinghamshire – Regional map n° **9**–B2

⌂ The Grange
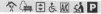

FAMILY · COSY What better way to start your holiday than in this charming Georgian farmhouse with a slice of homemade cake? The owners are lovely, the gardens are delightful and the country views are superb. Bedrooms are homely and come with good facilities and thoughtful touches; one is accessed via a spiral staircase.

3 rooms – †† £85/89

✉ NG13 9LA – ℰ 07887 952181 – www.thegrangebedandbreakfastnotts.co.uk

ELY

Cambridgeshire – Regional map n° **8**–B2

⌂ Poets House

BUSINESS · CONTEMPORARY A series of 19C townhouses set opposite the cathedral. Spacious, boutique bedrooms come with beautiful bathrooms, good extras and a moody feel. The modern bar overlooks the pretty walled garden and also offers afternoon tea. Dine on ambitious dishes, which include plenty of vegetarian options.

21 rooms ☑ – †† £170/270

St Mary's Street ✉ CB7 4EY – ℰ 01353 887777 – www.poetshouse.uk.com

EMSWORTH
Hampshire – Regional map n° **4**–B2

▯○ 36 on the Quay

MODERN BRITISH · INTIMATE XX A quayside cottage plays host to this intimate restaurant, which affords lovely harbour views – and the sheltered terrace is a hit come summer. Modern dishes display a wealth of different flavours and textures and have the occasional international leaning. Bedrooms are cosy and stylish.

Menu £28 (lunch) – Carte £33/59

47 South Street, The Quay ✉ PO10 7EG – ℰ 01243 375592 –
www.36onthequay.co.uk – Closed 1-18 January, 20-28 May, Sunday, Monday

▯○ Fat Olives

MODERN BRITISH · RUSTIC X This sweet 17C fisherman's cottage sits in a characterful coastal town, in a road leading down to the harbour. It's run by a charming couple and has a rustic modern feel, courtesy of locally crafted tables and upholstered chairs. Classic British dishes have a modern edge and rely on small local suppliers.

Menu £24 (lunch) – Carte £30/45

30 South Street ✉ PO10 7EH – ℰ 01243 377914 – www.fatolives.co.uk –
Closed 1-7 January, 14 June-8 July, Sunday, Monday

EPPING

Essex – Regional map n° **7**–B2

ⅼ○ Haywards   ♿ 🆒 ⇔ **P**

MODERN CUISINE · INTIMATE XX This proudly run restaurant is the realisation of a couple's dream. It's set in the old stables of their family's pub and boasts a hammer-beam ceiling, cherry wood tables and canvases of local forest scenes. Appealing dishes follow the seasons and flavours are well-balanced. Service is extremely welcoming.

Menu £ 36 (lunch), £ 49/65

111 Bell Common ⌧ CM16 4DZ – ℰ 01992 577350 – www.haywardsrestaurant.co.uk – Closed 1-21 January, Sunday dinner, Monday, Tuesday, Wednesday lunch

EPSOM

Surrey – Regional map n° **4**–D1

ⅼ○ Le Raj

BANGLADESHI · ELEGANT XxX This passionately-run restaurant has been welcoming guests since 1989 and has become a local institution. Dine on freshly made, authentic Bangladeshi dishes and superb breads, surrounded by wooden panels picked out in gold leaf.

Carte £ 27/45

211 Fir Tree Rd, Epsom Downs ⌧ KT17 3LB – ℰ 01737 371371 – www.lerajrestaurant.co.uk

ERMINGTON

Devon – Regional map n° **1**–C2

ⅼ○ Plantation House   ⇔ 🛏 🏡 **P**

MODERN CUISINE · INTIMATE XX Georgian former rectory in a pleasant country spot, with a small drinks terrace, an open-fired lounge and two dining rooms: one formal, with black furnishings; one more relaxed, with polished wood tables. Interesting modern menus feature local produce. Stylish bedrooms come with fresh milk and homemade cake.

Menu £ 39/49

Totnes Road ⌧ PL21 9NS – ℰ 01548 831100 – www.plantationhousehotel.co.uk – Closed Sunday - Saturday lunch

EVERSHOT

Dorset – Regional map n° **2**–C3

🏨 Summer Lodge   🏇 🐾 🛏 🏊 🌀 ⅃⅃ ♿ 🆒 **P**

LUXURY · ELEGANT An attractive former dower house in mature gardens, featuring a smart wellness centre, a pool and a tennis court. Plush, individually designed bedrooms come with marble bathrooms and country house guest areas display heavy fabrics and antiques – the drawing room was designed by Thomas Hardy. Dine formally from a classic menu, which is accompanied by a superb wine list.

24 rooms – ♥♥ £ 215/530 – 4 suites

9 Fore Street ⌧ DT2 0JR – ℰ 01935 482000 – www.summerlodgehotel.com

EWELL

Surrey – Regional map n° **4**–D1

🕸 Dastaan

INDIAN · NEIGHBOURHOOD X Two friends who worked in London's Gymkhana own this simple restaurant in a parade of shops. Its name means 'story' – their story – and they even made the tables and benches themselves! Great value cooking is mainly northern Indian and ranges from street food and classics to some more unusual choices.

Specialities: Kasoori chicken chops with mint chutney. Lamb rogan josh. Pistachio kulfi.

Carte £ 19/34

Town plan Ewell6 C6-d *– 447 Kingston Road ⌧ KT19 0DB – ℰ 020 8786 8999 – www.dastaan.co.uk – Closed Monday, Tuesday - Friday lunch*

EXETER

Devon – Regional map n° **1**-D2

🏠 **Southernhay House**

TOWNHOUSE · CONTEMPORARY Attractive Georgian townhouse with original ceiling roses and ornate coving. Smart, compact guest areas include a stylish lounge and a bar with bright blue furniture. Warmly decorated bedrooms have sumptuous beds, luxurious fabrics and chic bathrooms. The small dining room offers British-based menus.

11 rooms – 🛉🛉 £95/240 – ☲ £16

36 Southernhay East ⊠ EX2 1NX – ℰ 01392 435324 – www.southernhayhouse.com

FAIRFORD

Gloucestershire – Regional map n° **2**-D1

🍴 **The Bull**

TRADITIONAL CUISINE · PUB 🗡 The 14C Bull sits in the marketplace of an attractive little town and is a hit with fishermen courtesy of its mile of fishing rights. The main bar is characterful and cosy, while the two smaller dining rooms have a quirky feel. Menus offer plenty of choice, from antipasti, pizza and pasta to hearty British dishes. Bedrooms come with exposed timbers and designer touches.

Menu £19 (lunch)/23 – Carte £29/42

Market Place ⊠ GL7 4AA – ℰ 01285 712535 – www.thebullhotelfairford.co.uk

FALMOUTH

Cornwall – Regional map n° **1**-A3

at **Maenporth Beach** South: 3. 75 mi by Pennance Rd

🍴 **Cove**

MODERN CUISINE · CONTEMPORARY DÉCOR 🗡 A bright, stylish restaurant in a smart glass-fronted building overlooking the beach, the cove and St Anthony's Head. The modern dining room leads through to a lovely split-level terrace with a retractable roof. Menus are contemporary, with a strong seafood base and some Asian influences.

Menu £22/27 – Carte £21/40

Maenporth Beach ⊠ TR11 5HN – ℰ 01326 251136 – www.thecovemaenporth.co.uk – Closed 7-31 January, Monday

FAVERSHAM

Kent – Regional map n° **5**-C1

🍴 **Read's**

MODERN BRITISH · ELEGANT 🗙🗙 An elegant Georgian manor house in landscaped grounds, with traditional country house styling, antique furnishings and lovely oil paintings. Classically based dishes have subtle modern touches and make use of seasonal produce from the walled kitchen garden and the nearby quay. Comfortable bedrooms are full of period charm and thoughtful extras provide a sense of luxury.

Menu £32 (lunch)/60

Macknade Manor, Canterbury Road ⊠ ME13 8XE – ℰ 01795 535344 – www.reads.com – Closed 1-16 January, Sunday, Monday

FENCE

Lancashire – Regional map n° **11**-B2

⚘ **White Swan** (Tom Parker)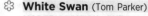

MODERN BRITISH · PUB 🗙 The sign might proclaim 'The White Swan' but to the locals this traditional-looking pub will always be the Mucky Duck – so-called because the coal miners used to stop here for a pint on their way home from work.

It's owned by Timothy Taylor's brewery, so you're always guaranteed a good pint – and the food is just as satisfying. Tom oversees the kitchen while Gareth looks after things out front. Jars of maturing homemade fruit liqueurs and gins, which they use in their cocktails, sit behind the bar, and a blackboard highlights their upcoming 'guest chef' evenings.

Concise menus allow the kitchen to concentrate on preparing good value dishes from small batches of locally sourced seasonal produce. Dishes might appear simple at first but have complementary textures and tastes and an impressive depth of flavour; you'll find some have a playful element too. The cheeseboard with homemade crackers and English truffle honey is a must and there are some interesting wines available by the glass.

Specialities: Organic salmon with English wasabi, buttermilk, apple and dill. Burholme Farm Lonk lamb with charred lettuce, onions and wild garlic. Alphonso mango with white chocolate, toasted coconut and passion fruit.

Menu £35/60

300 Wheatley Lane Road ⊠ BB12 9QA – 𝒞 01282 611773 –
www.whiteswanatfence.co.uk – Closed 1-8 January, Sunday dinner, Monday

FERRENSBY

North Yorkshire – Regional map n° **13**–B2

ⓘ○ **General Tarleton**

TRADITIONAL BRITISH · **COSY** XX Characterful 18C coaching inn with low beams and exposed stone walls; most sit in the main room but there's also a glass-roofed courtyard and a large terrace for warmer days. Hearty dishes champion Yorkshire produce. Bedrooms feature solid oak furnishings and come with home-baked biscuits.

Carte £26/35

Boroughbridge Road ⊠ HG5 0PZ – 𝒞 01423 340284 –
www.generaltarleton.co.uk

FILKINS

Oxfordshire – Regional map n° **6**–A2

ⓘ○ **Five Alls**

TRADITIONAL BRITISH · **PUB** X Like its curious logo, this pub has it all: an open-fired bar where they serve snacks and takeaway burgers, a locals bar stocked with fine ales, three antique-furnished dining rooms, and a lovely terrace and garden. The menu is satisfyingly traditional and bedrooms are modern and cosy.

Carte £21/44

⊠ GL7 3JQ – 𝒞 01367 860875 –
www.thefiveallsfilkins.co.uk – Closed Sunday dinner

FIVEHEAD

Somerset – Regional map n° **2**–B3

ⓘ○ **Langford Fivehead**

MODERN CUISINE · **INTIMATE** XX A beautiful, personally run country house with 13C origins, set in 7 acres of well-tended gardens – with its antique panelling, old stone fireplaces and mullioned windows, it conveys a real sense of history. Well-balanced modern menus are highly seasonal and feature lots of kitchen garden ingredients. Bedrooms are tastefully furnished and many have four-poster beds.

Menu £30 (lunch), £38/45

Lower Swell ⊠ TA3 6PH – 𝒞 01460 282020 –
www.langfordfivehead.co.uk – Closed 20 July-9 August, 21 December-4 January,
Sunday-Tuesday lunch, Saturday lunch

FOLKESTONE
Kent – Regional map n° **5**–D2

⫲◯ **Rocksalt**

SEAFOOD · DESIGN XX An impressive harbourfront eco-building with a curvaceous wood façade. Full-length windows give every table a view and the terrace extends over the water. Seafood-orientated menus also offer local meats. The semi-open upstairs bar serves lighter dishes. Stylish bedrooms – in an annexe – have a loft-like feel.

Menu £25 (lunch) – Carte £33/43

4-5 Fish Market ⊠ CT19 6AA – ℰ 01303 212070 – www.rocksaltfolkestone.co.uk – Closed Sunday dinner

FOLKSWORTH
Cambridgeshire – Regional map n° **8**–A2

⫲◯ **The Fox at Folksworth**

MODERN CUISINE · PUB X The Fox's dining room is hung with chandeliers and its light, bright bar is filled with designer furniture and has sliding doors which open onto a huge terrace. Dine on pub favourites or more creative modern dishes.

Carte £26/39

34 Manor Road ⊠ PE7 3SU – ℰ 01733 242867 – www.foxatfolksworth.co.uk

FONTMELL MAGNA
Dorset – Regional map n° **2**–C3

⫲◯ **Fontmell**

MODERN CUISINE · PUB X A stylish dining pub in a delightfully rural spot, with a cosy bar and a restaurant straddling the beck – keep an eye out for otters. The eclectic modern menu offers something for all tastes, from British to Mediterranean and Asian; try their own rare breed Old Spot pork. Bedrooms are chic and well-appointed.

Carte £29/41

Crown Hill ⊠ SP7 0PA – ℰ 01747 811441 – www.thefontmell.com

FORDHAM
Cambridgeshire – Regional map n° **8**–B2

⫲◯ **White Pheasant**

MODERN CUISINE · SIMPLE X An enthusiastic chef-owner runs this cosy former pub in the centre of the village. Cooking is all-encompassing, including everything from well-presented classics to creative modern dishes.

Carte £29/45

21 Market Street ⊠ CB7 5LQ – ℰ 01638 720414 – www.whitepheasant.com – Closed Sunday dinner, Monday

FORDWICH – Kent → See Canterbury

FOWEY
Cornwall – Regional map n° **1**–B2

⫲◯ **Q**

MODERN CUISINE · INTIMATE XX Ask for a window seat or head to the terrific waterside terrace of this romantic hotel restaurant. Dinner is the main event, with modern takes on old classics: presentation is colourful and provenance is key.

Menu £45 – Carte £28/31

Old Quay House Hotel, 28 Fore Street ⊠ PL23 1AQ – ℰ 01726 833302 – www.theoldquayhouse.com

🍴 Fitzroy

MODERN BRITISH · BISTRO 𝕏 Having already established three neighbourhood restaurants in London, owners David Gingell and Jeremie Cometto-Lingenheim turned their attention to an old bank building in Cornwall. Their deep-rooted local and sustainable philosophy remains the same, except here the small plates have more of a seafood slant.

Carte £21/38

2 Fore Street ⊠ PL23 1AQ – ☎ 01726 932934 –
www.fitzroycornwall.com – Closed Monday, Tuesday lunch

🏨 Fowey Hall

COUNTRY HOUSE · PERSONALISED A striking 19C manor house with an ornate lounge and a mix of traditional and modern bedrooms. It's set high above the village and has lovely views. Families are well-catered for and an informal feel pervades. There's an oak-panelled restaurant reserved for adults and a conservatory for those with children.

36 rooms � – ♟ £139/249

Hanson Drive ⊠ PL23 1ET – ☎ 01726 833866 –
www.foweyhallhotel.co.uk

🏠 Old Quay House

TOWNHOUSE · CONTEMPORARY A 19C seamen's mission in a pretty harbour village; now a boutique hotel with a laid-back feel and a lovely riverside terrace. Bedrooms have an understated modern style; most have balconies and water views.

13 rooms ⊡ – ♟ £150/200

28 Fore Street ⊠ PL23 1AQ – ☎ 01726 833302 –
www.theoldquayhouse.com – Closed 1-16 January
🍴 **Q** – See restaurant listing

FREATHY

Cornwall – Regional map n° **1**–C2

🍴 The View

MODERN BRITISH · SIMPLE 𝕏 A charming converted café perched on the clifftop and affording commanding coastal views; if the weather's right, find a spot on the terrace. It has a relaxed daytime vibe and is more atmospheric in the evening. Assured, confident, cooking arrives in generous portions; the homemade bread is tasty.

Menu £20 (lunch) – Carte £33/45

⊠ PL10 1JY – ☎ 01752 822345 –
www.theview-restaurant.co.uk – Closed Monday, Tuesday

FRILSHAM – West Berkshire ➜ See Yattendon

FRITHSDEN

Hertfordshire – Regional map n° **7**–A2

🍴 Alford Arms

TRADITIONAL BRITISH · PUB 𝕏 An attractive Victorian pub beside the village green. The menu follows the seasons and offers a broad array of dishes, so alongside British classics you'll find dishes with more global leanings such as imam bayildi.

Carte £23/43

⊠ HP1 3DD – ☎ 01442 864480 –
www.alfordarmsfrithsden.co.uk

FROME
Somerset – Regional map n° **2**–C2

🏠 Babington House ⭐ ☁ 🛁 🏊 🖼 🕸 🛎 🌿 ♨ **P**

LUXURY · TRENDY Behind this country house's classic Georgian façade is a cool, fashionable hotel with bold colour schemes, understated bedrooms and a bohemian feel. Unwind in the luxurious lounges or in the beautiful spa with its superb fitness area and pool. The Orangery offers an accessible menu of Mediterranean-influenced dishes which showcase ingredients from the walled garden.

33 rooms – 🛏 £350/615 – ⌑ £17 – 11 suites

Babington ✉ BA11 3RW – ℰ 01373 812266 – www.babingtonhouse.co.uk

FUNTINGTON – West Sussex → See Chichester

FYFIELD
Oxfordshire – Regional map n° **6**–B2

🍴○ White Hart ♿ 🌿 **P**

TRADITIONAL BRITISH · PUB X An intriguing 15C chantry house with a cosy open-fired bar, a minstrels' gallery and an impressive three-storey high vaulted dining room; not forgetting a pleasant terrace. Seasonally driven dishes are guided by produce from the kitchen garden. Save room for one of the excellent desserts.

Menu £23 (lunch)/32 – Carte £30/43

Main Road ✉ OX13 5LW – ℰ 01865 390585 – www.whitehart-fyfield.com – Closed Monday

GERRARDS CROSS
Buckinghamshire – Regional map n° **6**–D3

🕸 Three Oaks ♿ 🌿 **P**

MODERN BRITISH · PUB X An appealing, well-run pub in a rural location, comprising several different areas: dine in the brighter room overlooking the terrace and pretty garden. Cooking is tasty, satisfying and seasonal, and they offer particularly good value set lunch and dinner menus. The bright young staff are eager to please.

Specialities: Whipped chicken liver parfait with apple and beer chutney. Red wine-marinated chicken, mushroom, pancetta, pickled onions and bacon mayo. Milk chocolate crémeux with salted caramel and cherry sorbet.

Menu £16 (lunch), £19/23 – Carte £29/42

Austenwood Lane ✉ SL9 8NL – ℰ 01753 899016 – www.thethreeoaksgx.co.uk – Closed Sunday dinner

GISBURN
Lancashire – Regional map n° **11**–B2

🍴○ La Locanda

ITALIAN · NEIGHBOURHOOD X A charming low-beamed, flag-floored restaurant run by a keen couple: a little corner of Italy in Lancashire. Extensive menu of hearty homemade dishes; try the tasty pastas. Top quality local and imported produce; well-chosen wine list.

Carte £24/37

Main Street ✉ BB7 4HH – ℰ 01200 445303 – www.lalocanda.co.uk – Closed Monday - Thursday lunch

GOREY – Jersey → See Channel Islands (Jersey)

GORING
Oxfordshire – Regional map n° **6**–B3

ⅼ◯ Miller of Mansfield

TRADITIONAL BRITISH · PUB ⅼ According to the poem, the Miller of Mansfield provided a lost Henry VIII with food and a bed for the night; in keeping with this tale, this pub's cheery team provide great hospitality. Unfussy lunches are followed by more ambitious dinners and the homemade bread is a highlight. Bedrooms are bright and cosy.

Carte £36/46

High Street ✉ RG8 9AW – 𝒞 01491 872829 –
www.millerofmansfield.com

GRANTHAM

Lincolnshire – Regional map n° **9**–C2

ⅼ◯ Harry's Place ▣P

TRADITIONAL BRITISH · COSY ⅼⅼ Long-standing, intimate restaurant in a former farmhouse: it consists of just 3 tables and is personally run by a dedicated and delightful husband and wife team. Warm, welcoming feel, with fresh flowers, candles and antiques. Classically based menus offer 2 choices per course. Good cheese selection.

Carte £60/73

17 High Street, Great Gonerby ✉ NG31 8JS –
𝒞 01476 561780 –
Closed 1-15 August, 25 December-7 January, Sunday, Monday

GRASMERE

Cumbria – Regional map n° **12**–A2

⁘ Forest Side

MODERN BRITISH · DESIGN ⅼⅼ This restored Victorian mansion has a modern country house style and a laid-back feel; find a spot in the elegant lounge and admire the view over deer-filled grounds towards the mountains. The beautifully furnished restaurant features deep leather armchairs and, at its centre, an impressive glass table supported by a huge tree root reflects the natural philosophy of the place.

Their strapline 'inspired by the Cumbrian landscape' is spot on: the stunning Victorian kitchen garden supplies many of the vegetables, and foraged herbs are a recurring theme in the creams and ice creams. Creative modern dishes have a Scandic style, with bold flavours and complex composition; to start, you're invited for snacks at the kitchen counter.

Contemporary bedrooms complete the picture.

Specialities: Scorched cod with oyster and tarragon salsa. Will & Emma's Herdwick hogget. Flowering currant with sorrel and caramel.

Menu £40 (lunch), £80/105

Forest Side Hotel, Keswick Road ✉ LA22 9RN – 𝒞 015394 35250 –
www.theforestside.com –
Closed Monday, Tuesday, Wednesday lunch

⌂ Forest Side

COUNTRY HOUSE · CONTEMPORARY Enjoy afternoon tea in the elegant fire-lit lounge while admiring the view over the deer-filled grounds towards the mountains. Both the guest areas and bedrooms have a modern country house style and there's a laid back feel throughout.

20 rooms ⌑ – ♀♀ £329/459

Keswick Road ✉ LA22 9RN – 𝒞 015394 35250 –
www.theforestside.com

⁘ **Forest Side** – See restaurant listing

GRASSINGTON
North Yorkshire – Regional map n° **13**–A2

⑪○ **Grassington House** ⇦ 🏠 AC P

MODERN BRITISH · BRASSERIE XX This attractive Grade II listed Georgian house sits overlooking a cobbled square in the heart of the Yorkshire Dales. Home-bred pork and many other home-smoked items feature on the Mediterranean-inspired menu, and afternoon tea has become something of a feature. Bedrooms are smart and modern.

Menu £18/20 – Carte £27/42

5 The Square ✉ *BD23 5AQ – 𝒞 01756 752406 – www.grassingtonhouse.co.uk*

GREAT MALVERN
Worcestershire – Regional map n° **10**–B3

at Welland Southeast: 5 mi on B4208 – Regional map n° **10**–B3

⑳ **The Inn at Welland** 🏠 🏠 ㊅ ⑩Ⓥ P

TRADITIONAL BRITISH · PUB X Take in delightful views of the Malvern Hills from the charming terrace of this country inn, or sit on plush chairs at large wooden tables, surrounded by flower-filled vases. The menu has something for one and all and the carefully prepared dishes are packed full of flavour. Service is friendly and efficient.

Specialities: Oak-smoked Godminster cheddar soufflé with figs and rosemary cream. Loin of cod with saffron potatoes, broccoli, poached egg and dill hollandaise. Warm treacle tart, blood orange curd and crème fraîche sorbet.

Carte £27/46

Hook Bank ✉ *WR13 6LN – 𝒞 01684 592317 – www.theinnatwelland.co.uk –
Closed Sunday dinner, Monday*

GREAT MILTON – Oxfordshire → See Oxford

GREAT OXENDON
Northamptonshire – Regional map n° **9**–B3

⑪○ **The George** ⇦ 🏠 🏠 ㊅ P

MODERN BRITISH · CLASSIC DÉCOR X An experienced chef has transformed this roadside inn by creating a modern country house lounge and a lovely New England style dining room complete with glass doors opening onto the pretty terrace and garden. Classically based British dishes have an unfussy modern style. Bedrooms are bright and contemporary.

Carte £27/38

Harborough Road ✉ *LE16 8NA – 𝒞 01858 452286 –
www.thegeorgegreatoxendon.co.uk – Closed 25 December*

GREAT TEW
Oxfordshire – Regional map n° **6**–B1

🏠 **Soho Farmhouse** ⇧ 🐾 🏠 ⚒ 🔲 🕥 ⑭ ⅃⅁ ㊅ P

RESORT · DESIGN Set in 110 acres of rolling countryside, this exclusive resort offers everything you could want. Luxurious self-contained cabins are dotted about the estate and come with wellies and bikes. Unwind in the stunning spa or the outside pool set within a lake, then choose from a range of dining options.

44 rooms – 🚻 £400/2000 – ⊡ £13 – 18 suites

✉ *OX7 4JS – 𝒞 01608 691000 – www.sohofarmhouse.com –
Closed 1 May-31 August*

GREAT YELDHAM
Essex – Regional map n° **7**–C2

⫞○ White Hart ⟵ 🛏 🏠 🅿

MODERN BRITISH · ROMANTIC XX Charming 16C house with a characterful interior. The open-fired bar with its wonky floors and exposed beams serves unfussy favourites, while the elegant restaurant (open later in the week) offers a refined modern menu of skilfully prepared dishes. Bedrooms are stylish and comfortable.

Carte £23/49

Poole Street ⊠ CO9 4HJ – ℰ 01787 237 250 – www.whitehartyeldham.co.uk – Closed 1-19 January

GREEN ISLAND – Jersey → See Channel Islands (Jersey)

GREETHAM
Rutland – Regional map n° **9**–C2

⫞○ Wheatsheaf Inn 🛏 🏠 🅿

TRADITIONAL BRITISH · PUB X The aroma of fresh bread greets you at this simple, family-friendly country pub. Cooking is unfussy and traditional; cheaper cuts keep prices sensible and desserts are a must. It's run by a charming couple.

Menu £19 (lunch) – Carte £26/34

1 Stretton Road ⊠ LE15 7NP – ℰ 01572 812325 – www.wheatsheaf-greetham.co.uk – Closed 2-19 January, Monday

GURNARD – Isle of Wight → See Wight (Isle of)

HAMBLETON – Rutland → See Oakham

HAMPTON IN ARDEN
West Midlands – Regional map n° **10**–C2

✿ Peel's 🛏 & 🕭 ⇆ 🅿

CREATIVE BRITISH · ELEGANT XXX Set in 45 acres of grounds is this family-owned, Victorian Gothic-style manor house which was built for Sir Robert Peel's son. Characterful original features blend with contemporary décor in the various lounges and there's a lovely sitting room with an Italianate feel. The elegant formal dining room boasts beautiful plasterwork, oak panelling and hand-painted Chinoiserie wallpaper – and at its centre is a long, chunky table crafted from one of the estate's oak trees.

Creative modern dishes come from a confident kitchen and feature refined, original combinations with some playful elements. Flavours are pure and unadulterated and ingredients taste exactly of what they should. They are keen to serve English and Welsh wines and also keep natural and organic options to the fore.

Service is pitched perfectly and bedrooms are modern and spacious.

Specialities: Crab XO with white beetroot, coriander and lime. Longhorn beef, St George's mushrooms, kidneys and parsley. Chocolate, sherry and vanilla.

Menu £75/95

Hampton Manor Hotel, Shadowbrook Lane ⊠ B92 ODQ – ℰ 01675 446080 – www.hamptonmanor.com – Closed 22 December-3 January, Sunday, Monday, Tuesday - Saturday lunch

🏠 Hampton Manor ⇭ 🛏 & 🆎 🛁 🅿

HISTORIC · GRAND LUXURY An early Victorian Gothic-style manor house set in 45 acres of mature grounds – it was built for Sir Robert Peel's son. Contemporary décor blends with characterful original plasterwork and wood panelling in various lounges and drawing rooms. Spacious bedrooms have a smart modern style and superb bathrooms.

15 rooms ⌂ – †† £170/310 – 3 suites

Shadowbrook Lane ⊠ B92 ODQ – ℰ 01675 446080 – www.hamptonmanor.com – Closed 24-26 December

✿ **Peel's** – See restaurant listing

HAMPTON POYLE
Oxfordshire – Regional map n° **6**–B2

‡○ Bell at Hampton Poyle ⟨⟩ 🏠 ♿ **P**
MEDITERRANEAN CUISINE · PUB X A passionately run pub with several comfy lounge areas and a chic restaurant. The open kitchen adds a buzz and the pizza oven and glass meat ageing fridge draw your eye. The menu covers many bases and has strong Mediterranean undertones. Stylish bedrooms are located above the bar and in a cottage.

Menu £18 – Carte £26/47

11 Oxford Road ✉ OX5 2QD – 𝒞 01865 376242 –
www.thebellathamptonpoyle.co.uk

HAROME - North Yorkshire ➔ See Helmsley

HARROGATE
North Yorkshire – Regional map n° **13**–B2

‡○ Horto 🏠 🏠 ♿ 🆎 **P**
MODERN BRITISH · DESIGN XX This smart restaurant is set in Rudding Park's spa and has floor to ceiling windows overlooking the hotel's grounds. Choose between three different tasting menus, where classic dishes are made up of just a few complementary ingredients; much of the produce is picked from the garden each morning.

Menu £69 – Carte £51/62

Rudding Park Hotel, Rudding Park, Follifoot ✉ HG3 1JH – 𝒞 01423 871350 –
www.ruddingpark.co.uk – Closed Sunday lunch, Monday, Tuesday, Wednesday -
Saturday lunch

‡○ Stuzzi 🕸 🏠
ITALIAN · RUSTIC X A great little place comprising a deli, a café and an osteria, and serving homemade cakes, topped focaccia and fresh, authentic Italian small plates. It's run with passion by a young but experienced team and it's great value too.

Carte £20/30

46b King's Road ✉ HG1 5JW – 𝒞 01423 705852 – Closed Monday, Tuesday

🏨 Rudding Park 🏠 🏠 📷 🌐 🛗 🖼 ♿ 🎿 **P**
LUXURY · CONTEMPORARY A substantial hotel set in 250 acres; its listed manor house is popular for events. The superb spa has outdoor hot tubs, rooftop terraces and an infinity pool, while the best of the sleek bedrooms have their own jacuzzis or saunas. Dine on modern British dishes in Clocktower or those crafted from garden produce in Horto.

90 rooms ☲ – 🛏 £217/553 – 6 suites

Rudding Park, Follifoot ✉ HG3 1JH – 𝒞 01423 871350 – www.ruddingpark.co.uk
‡○ **Horto** - See restaurant listing

HARWICH
Essex – Regional map n° **7**–D2

‡○ The Pier 🍸 ⟨⟩ ⟨ 🏠 ♿ 🆎 ⟨⟩ **P**
SEAFOOD · CONTEMPORARY DÉCOR XX This stylish first floor brasserie boasts a terrific balcony with North Sea views. Seafood forms the foundation of the menu, with much landed locally, and the chic bar has an impressive gin library. Ask for a bedroom with an estuary view.

Carte £28/48

The Quay ✉ CO12 3HH – 𝒞 01255 241212 – www.milsomhotels.com

HASTINGS AND ST LEONARDS
East Sussex – Regional map n° **5**–B3

Old Rectory

TOWNHOUSE · QUIRKY A delightful Georgian house with beautiful tiered gardens, set next to the church at the bottom of the hill, not far from the sea. No expense has been spared inside, with hand-painted feature walls, bespoke designer furnishings and luxurious styling. They cure the bacon and make their own sausages on-site.

8 rooms – ♦♦ £110/175

Harold Rd, Old Town ✉ TN35 5ND – ☎ 01424 422410 –
www.theoldrectoryhastings.co.uk – Closed 2-15 January, 22-30 December

HAYWARDS HEATH

West Sussex – Regional map n° **4**–D2

℔ Jeremy's at Borde Hill

MODERN CUISINE · FRIENDLY ✕✕ Converted stable block with exposed rafters, contemporary sculptures, vivid artwork and delightful views towards the Victorian walled garden. Interesting, modern European dishes and a good value 'menu of the day'. Regular gourmet nights.

Menu £24/29 – Carte £35/50

Borde Hill Gardens ✉ RH16 1XP – ☎ 01444 441102 – www.jeremysrestaurant.co.uk –
Closed 2-16 January, Sunday dinner, Monday

HECKFIELD

Hampshire – Regional map n° **4**–C1

℔ Marle ⓝ

MODERN BRITISH · CONTEMPORARY DÉCOR ✕✕ Within a Georgian country house you'll find this charming orangery-style dining room looking out over a lake and parkland. Provenance is everything, with many of the ingredients coming from the estate's own farm. The presentation might be modern but at its heart, cooking relies on honest, natural flavours.

Menu £32 (lunch) – Carte £44/65

Heckfield Place Hotel ✉ RG27 0LD – ☎ 0118 932 6868 – www.heckfieldplace.com

Heckfield Place ⓝ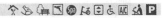

COUNTRY HOUSE · GRAND LUXURY This lovingly restored Georgian country house has an atmosphere more akin to that of a house party than a hotel. It has a stylish blend of modern and period furnishings and the owner's prized collection of post-war art adorns the walls. Kick back in the plush cinema or cellar bar before dining on home-grown produce – some cooked over the wood fire.

45 rooms ⌥ – ♦♦ £350/700 – 4 suites

✉ RG27 0LD – ☎ 0118 932 6868 – www.heckfieldplace.com
℔ **Marle** – See restaurant listing

HEDLEY ON THE HILL

Northumberland – Regional map n° **14**–A2

℔ Feathers Inn

TRADITIONAL BRITISH · PUB ✕ This warm, welcoming pub is set on a steep hill in the heart of a characterful village and is a hub of the local community. The shelves are crammed with cookbooks and the walls are hung with pictures of their suppliers. Constantly evolving menus highlight Northumbrian produce and everything is made in-house.

Carte £27/43

✉ NE43 7SW – ☎ 01661 843607 – www.thefeathers.net – Closed 1-16 January,
Monday lunch, Tuesday, Wednesday lunch

HELMSLEY

North Yorkshire – Regional map n° **13**–C1

⅋○ Gallery   🕸 ⌂🕭⌗ **P**

MODERN BRITISH · BRASSERIE ✕✕ Bright, modern restaurant within a historic 15C coaching inn; its walls are filled with artwork for sale and at dinner, the plate becomes the canvas. Attractive, modern dishes have a classical base; the tasting menu is a highlight.

Carte £37/55

Black Swan Hotel, Market Place ⊠ YO62 5BJ – ☏ 01439 770466 –
www.blackswan-helmsley.co.uk

🏚 Feversham Arms H. & Verbena Spa

🍴 ⌂ 🛋 🕭 🛏 🔌 🔯 **P** 🚗

TRADITIONAL · CONTEMPORARY 19C former coaching inn with a lovely stone façade. Relax on the terrace beside the outdoor pool; the spa is superb and boasts a salt vapour room and an ice cave. Be sure to book one of the stylish newer bedrooms; many have stoves or fires.

33 rooms ⊊ – � £100/300 – 20 suites

1-8 High Street ⊠ YO62 5AG – ☏ 01439 770766 – www.fevershamarmshotel.com

---

at Harome Southeast: 2. 75 mi by A170 – Regional map n° **13**–C1

✵ Star Inn at Harome (Andrew Pern)   🕸 ⌂🕭& ⌂ **P**

MODERN BRITISH · PUB ✕✕ This 14C thatched building oozes character with its low beamed ceilings and fires burning in the grates. While the restaurant side has a plush, luxurious feel, it's still very much the village local and you'll find the regulars supping on a pint of bespoke 'Two Chefs' beer in the characterful bar.

This is a place that proudly champions its home county, with fish sourced from Whitby, game from the Yorkshire Moors and vegetables from the kitchen garden, and Head Chef Steve Smith uses them to create rich, gutsy, flavour-driven dishes with a classical base and modern overtones. The wine list, meanwhile, offers bottles from some lesser-known producers and growers.

Across the road are a series of sympathetically converted farm buildings with ultra-stylish bedrooms – one boasts a snooker table; another, a bed suspended on ropes.

Specialities: Ravioli of lobster with ham hock, apple, mustard and pea velouté. Milk-fed & pot-roasted pigeon, Jerusalem artichoke and blue Wensleydale. Yorkshire rhubarb soufflé with Pontefract cake ice cream and vanilla custard.

Menu £25 – Carte £32/61

High Street ⊠ YO62 5JE – ☏ 01439 770397 – www.starinntheharbour.co.uk –
Closed Sunday dinner, Monday lunch

⅋○ Pheasant   ⌂🕭⌗ **P**

MODERN BRITISH · ELEGANT ✕✕ Elegant hotel dining room with both classical and contemporary touches – along with a less formal conservatory and a lovely terrace overlooking the village duck pond. Appealing menus of seasonal dishes with a classical base and a modern touch. Skilful, knowledgeable cooking; smooth, assured service.

Carte £40/62

Pheasant Hotel, Mill Street ⊠ YO62 5JG – ☏ 01439 771241 –
www.thepheasanthotel.com

🏚 Pheasant   🍴⌂ 🔲 **P**

TRADITIONAL · PERSONALISED An attractive hotel in a picturesque hamlet, with a delightful duck pond and a mill stream close by. Beautiful, very comfortable lounges and spacious, well-furnished bedrooms; Rudland – running the width of the building and with views of the pond – is one of the best. Pleasant service. Excellent breakfasts.

16 rooms ⊊ – ♦♦ £180/270

Mill Street ⊠ YO62 5JG – ☏ 01439 771241 – www.thepheasanthotel.com
⅋○ **Pheasant** – See restaurant listing

🏠 **Cross House Lodge** 🛗 🅿️

COUNTRY HOUSE · DESIGN These sympathetically converted farm buildings have a rustic ski-chalet style and ultra-stylish, individually decorated bedrooms; one boasts a snooker table; another, a bed suspended on ropes. Relax in the open-plan, split-level lounge; excellent breakfasts are taken in the dramatic beamed 'Wheelhouse'.

9 rooms ⌂ – ♔♔ £150/270

High Street ⌂ YO62 5JE – ℰ 01439 770397 – www.thestaratharome.co.uk

❀ **Star Inn at Harome** – See restaurant listing

at Scawton West : 5 mi. by B 1257

🍴 **The Hare** 🔄 ♿ 🅿️

MODERN CUISINE · COSY ✗✗ Exposed bricks and wooden beams give this passionately run, part-13C inn a characterful feel and two comfy bedrooms complete the picture. The self-taught chef offers 2 set menus of creative, accomplished dishes which are attractively presented, full of flavour and have some Asian influences.

Menu £55/70

⌂ YO7 2HG – ℰ 01845 597769 – www.thehare-inn.com – Closed 14-30 June, 24 December-31 January, Sunday, Monday, Tuesday, Wednesday - Saturday lunch

HELSTON
Cornwall – Regional map n° **1**–A3

at Trelowarren Southeast: 4 mi by A394 and A3083 on B3293

🍴 **New Yard** 🔓 🅿️

MODERN BRITISH · RUSTIC ✗ This converted 17C stable building adjoins a craft gallery hidden in the grounds of the Trelowarren Estate. Rusticity abounds in the spacious timber-walled room and its doors open onto a lovely terrace. Local produce guides the seasonal menu, with some produce grown on or foraged from the estate.

Menu £29 (lunch), £38/64

Trelowarren Estate ⌂ TR12 6AF – ℰ 01326 221595 – www.newyardrestaurant.co.uk – Closed 1 January-12 February, Sunday dinner, Monday

HENFIELD
West Sussex – Regional map n° **4**–D2

🍴 **Ginger Fox** 🎇 🔓 🏠 🎐 ⇆ 🅿️

CLASSIC CUISINE · PUB ✗ Look out for the thatched fox running across the roof of this long-standing pub, then head under the fruiting vine into a lovely garden with hidden bee hives. Menus mix refined, delicate dishes with those of a more hearty nature; the vegetarian tasting plate is a hit and the playful desserts are a must.

Menu £20 (lunch) – Carte £29/45

Muddleswood Road, Albourne ⌂ BN6 9EA – ℰ 01273 857888 – www.gingermanrestaurants.com

HENLADE – Somerset → See Taunton

HENLEY – West Sussex → See Midhurst

HENLEY-IN-ARDEN
Warwickshire – Regional map n° **10**–C3

🍴 **Cheal's of Henley** ⇆

MODERN CUISINE · ELEGANT ✗✗ A 400 year old house on the high street, which has been smartly refurbished yet retains plenty of character – it's owned by a local couple and run by their son. Complex modern cooking relies on classic flavour combinations.

Menu £33 (lunch), £44/77

64 High Street ⌂ B95 5BX – ℰ 01564 793856 – www.chealsofhenley.co.uk – Closed 1-9 January, 13-21 April, 3-18 August, Sunday dinner-Tuesday

🍴 **Bluebell**

MODERN BRITISH · PUB 🗙 This early 16C pub in a busy market town is run by a brother and sister: he cooks and she looks after the service. Modern dishes have bold, distinctive flavours – the Aubrey Allen steaks are popular and desserts are a highlight.

Carte £27/50

93 High Street ⊠ B95 5AT – ℰ 01564 793049 – www.thebluebell-henley.co.uk – Closed Monday

HENLEY-ON-THAMES

Oxfordshire – Regional map n° **6**-C3

🍴 **Shaun Dickens at The Boathouse** 🌣 �& 🅰🅲

MODERN BRITISH · FRIENDLY 🗙🗙 This modern restaurant is sure to please with its floor to ceiling glass doors and decked terrace overlooking the Thames. The young chef-owner offers an array of menus; attractively presented dishes centre around local ingredients.

Menu £34 (lunch), £30/75 – Carte £40/50

Station Road ⊠ RG9 1AZ – ℰ 01491 577937 – www.shaundickens.co.uk – Closed Monday, Tuesday

at Shiplake South: 2 mi on A4155

🍴 **Orwells** 🌣 🅿

MODERN BRITISH · RUSTIC 🗙🗙 This 18C building may look like a rural inn but inside it has a modern, formal feel. Creative cooking uses top quality produce and flavours are pronounced. It's named after George Orwell, who spent his childhood in the area.

Menu £30 (lunch), £35/40 – Carte £53/70

Shiplake Row ⊠ RG9 4DP – ℰ 0118 940 3673 – www.orwellsrestaurant.co.uk – Closed 1-15 January, 24 August-9 September, Sunday dinner-Tuesday

HEREFORD

Herefordshire – Regional map n° **10**-B3

🏠 **Castle House** 🌣 ᝥ �& 🅿

TOWNHOUSE · CONTEMPORARY This elegant Georgian house sits close to the cathedral. An impressive staircase leads to warmly furnished bedrooms of various sizes; some overlook the old castle moat. More contemporary rooms can be found in nearby 'Number 25'.

24 rooms � – 👫 £155/260

Castle Street ⊠ HR1 2NW – ℰ 01432 356321 – www.castlehse.co.uk

HETHE

Oxfordshire – Regional map n° **6**-B1

🍴 **Muddy Duck** 🌣 ᝥ ᝥ ᝥ 🅰🅲 🅿

MODERN CUISINE · PUB 🗙 It might have been modernised but this welcoming local retains plenty of rustic character. Choose from pub staples or more adventurous dishes, with steaks hung in a unique salt-ageing chamber and specials from the wood-fired oven in summer. The friendly team always welcome you with a smile.

Carte £24/52

Main Street ⊠ OX27 8ES – ℰ 01869 278099 – www.themuddyduckpub.co.uk – Closed Sunday dinner

HETTON

North Yorkshire – Regional map n° **13**-A2

The Angel (Michael Wignall)

MODERN CUISINE · INN XX The Angel sits deep within the Yorkshire Dales National Park and, with its 15C origins, delivers all the character and rusticity you'd expect. Those after a light snack can eat in the bar, while the appealing beamed dining rooms bring a little more formality to proceedings.

Co-owner Michael Wignall has a fine pedigree and is a mature and grounded chef. His cooking is accomplished and while his dishes respect the classics, they are delivered with a well-judged modern touch. Flavours are natural yet vivid and the combinations of both texture and flavour are perfectly balanced, with every ingredient on the plate for a reason. Local produce features heavily and he is particularly passionate about game.

Classical bedrooms are found in the Barn Lodgings and more modern rooms in Sycamore Bank.

Specialities: Suckling pig with parsnip purée, bark, cider and pork crackling. Poached turbot with charred white asparagus, wild garlic emulsion and fermented asparagus juice. Hazelnut parfait with dark chocolate and namelaka.

Carte £40/55

✉ BD23 6LT – ℰ 01756 730263 –
www.angelhetton.co.uk – Closed 2-16 January, Tuesday, Wednesday

HEXHAM

Northumberland – Regional map n° **14**–A2

Rat Inn

TRADITIONAL BRITISH · PUB X Set in a small hillside hamlet is this traditional 18C drovers' inn with wooden beams, an open range and a multi-level garden boasting arbours and Tyne Valley views. The daily changing menu showcases good quality produce in interesting dishes; the Northumberland rib of beef 'for two or more' is a must.

Menu £20 – Carte £24/44

Anick ✉ NE46 4LN – ℰ 01434 602814 –
www.theratinn.com – Closed Sunday dinner

HINTON ST GEORGE

Somerset – Regional map n° **2**–B3

Lord Poulett Arms

MODERN BRITISH · PUB X Characterful pub with open fires and beams fringed with hop bines; outside it's just as charming, with a lavender-framed terrace, a boules pitch and a secret garden. Creative cooking has a British base but also displays a wide range of influences. Stylish bedrooms come with feature beds and Roberts radios.

Menu £20 – Carte £27/42

High Street ✉ TA17 8SE – ℰ 01460 73149 –
www.lordpoulettarms.com

HOLLINGBOURNE

Kent – Regional map n° **5**–C2

The Windmill

TRADITIONAL BRITISH · PUB X With its giant inglenook fireplace and low-slung beams, the Windmill is as characterful as they come. You'll find tempting bar snacks, sharing roasts on Sundays and, alongside the hearty British classics, some more refined dishes too.

Menu £17 (lunch) – Carte £28/46

32 Eyhorne Street ✉ ME17 1TR – ℰ 01622 889000 –
www.thewindmillhollingbourne.co.uk – Closed Sunday dinner

HONITON
Devon – Regional map n° **1**–D2

⅏○ **Holt**

REGIONAL CUISINE · PUB ⅄ A rustic, family-run pub, where their passion for food is almost palpable. The regularly changing menu features regional and homemade produce, with meats and fish smoked and cured on-site. Try the 3 or 5 ale tasting rack – thirds of pints of Otter Brewery ales from their nearby family brewery.

Carte £30/40

178 High Street ⊠ EX14 1LA – ℰ 01404 47707 – www.theholt-honiton.com – Closed 25 December-2 January, Sunday, Monday

🏠 **The Pig**　　　　　　　　　　🛇 🐾 ⪡ 📶 **P**

COUNTRY HOUSE · CONTEMPORARY A hugely impressive Elizabethan mansion set down a winding drive. Its traditional interior has been stylishly redesigned and service is relaxed. Bedrooms in the house boast wonderful country views; those in the old stables still have their original partitions. The laid-back restaurant offers unfussy classics.

30 rooms – ♟♟ £145/325 – 🍽 £18

Gittisham ⊠ EX14 3AD – ℰ 01404 540400 – www.thepighotel.com

HORLEY
Surrey – Regional map n° **4**–D2

🏠 **Langshott Manor**　　　　　🛇 🐾 📶 **P**

HISTORIC · PERSONALISED Characterful 16C manor house set amidst roses, vines and ponds. The traditional exterior contrasts with contemporary furnishings and many of the bedrooms have fireplaces, four-posters or balconies. Afternoon tea is a feature.

22 rooms – ♟♟ £169/299 – 1 suite

Langshott ⊠ RH6 9LN – ℰ 01293 786680 – www.alexanderhotels.co.uk

HORNDON ON THE HILL
Thurrock – Regional map n° **7**–C3

⅏○ **Bell Inn**　　　　　　　　　　⪢ 🛖 **P**

TRADITIONAL BRITISH · PUB ⅄ The Bell was built in the first half of the 15C and positively oozes history; keep an eye out for the hot cross bun collection! Cooking has a pleasingly classical edge and a modern touch. Two neighbouring Georgian buildings house contemporary bedrooms and the Ostlers restaurant (open Fri and Sat nights).

Carte £27/45

High Road ⊠ SS17 8LD – ℰ 01375 642463 – www.bell-inn.co.uk

HORNING
Norfolk – Regional map n° **8**–D1

⅏○ **Bure River Cottage**

SEAFOOD · FRIENDLY ⅄ Friendly restaurant tucked away in a lovely riverside village that's famed for its boating. Informal, L-shaped room with modern tables and chairs. Blackboard menu features fresh, carefully cooked fish and shellfish; much from Lowestoft.

Carte £26/51

27 Lower Street ⊠ NR12 8AA – ℰ 01692 631421 – www.burerivercottagerestaurant.co.uk – Closed 12 December-14 February, Sunday, Monday, Tuesday - Saturday lunch

HORNINGSEA – Cambridgeshire → See Cambridge

HORSHAM
West Sussex – Regional map n° **4**–D2

ⓈⓈ **Restaurant Tristan** (Tristan Mason)

MODERN BRITISH · RUSTIC ⅄ Restaurant Tristan sits on the first floor of a 16C town centre property and comes with a characterful original oak-beamed ceiling, exposed hanging lightbulbs and a bright, airy feel. It is also one of those all-too-hard-to-find places where the atmosphere is refreshingly relaxed, helped along in no small part by the friendly, enthusiastic serving team; it's no wonder then, that it celebrated its 10th anniversary in 2018.

Committed chef-owner Tristan Mason can always be found behind the stoves and he wisely offers a good variety of well-priced menus to keep the locals coming back time and again. Excellent quality ingredients feature in creative, carefully crafted dishes that are delivered with a modern touch, and flavours and textures are distinct and well-matched. Breakfast and lunch are served in the ground floor café but it's the tasting menus at dinner that are the ones to go for.

Specialities: Scallops with cauliflower, tonka bean and Montgomery cheddar. Lamb, kid and goat with Jerusalem artichoke, trompette and bergamot. Passion fruit soufflé with chamomile crumb and vanilla yoghurt granita.

Menu £30 (lunch), £50/90

3 Stans Way, East Street ⊠ RH12 1HU – ℰ 01403 255688 –
www.restauranttristan.co.uk – Closed 2-11 January, 4-8 August, Sunday, Monday

at Rowhook Northwest: 4 mi by A264 and A281 off A29

🍴○ **Chequers Inn**   🍴 🛋 **P**

TRADITIONAL BRITISH · PUB ⅄ Part-15C inn with a charming open-fired, stone-floored bar and an unusual dining room extension. The chef-owner grows, forages for or shoots the majority of his produce. Classical menus.

Carte £30/42

⊠ RH12 3PY – ℰ 01403 790480 – www.thechequersrowhook.com – Closed Sunday dinner

HOWE STREET

Essex – Regional map n° **7**–C2

Ⓢ **Green Man**   🍴 🛋 ♿ 🆒 🔄 **P**

TRADITIONAL BRITISH · PUB ⅄ A friendly team offer a warm welcome at this lovely pub. The original 14C building offers all the rustic charm you'd expect but there's also a modern barn extension and riverside garden. Classic British dishes are carefully constructed and full of flavour; those cooked in the wood oven are their speciality.

Specialities: Old Spot Scotch egg with mustard and pickled onions. Roast auber-gine, charred spring onions, cumin yoghurt and smoked tomatoes. Salted caramel tart and almond milk ice cream.

Menu £15 (lunch), £17/21 – Carte £27/45

Main Road ⊠ CM3 1BG – ℰ 01245 408820 – www.galvingreenman.com

HUNSDON

Hertfordshire – Regional map n° **7**–B2

Ⓢ **Fox & Hounds**   🍴 🛋 **P**

TRADITIONAL BRITISH · PUB ⅄ A welcoming high street pub with contempo-rary styling. The chef's ethos is to let good quality ingredients speak for them-selves. Alongside homemade pasta dishes you'll find meats cooked on the Josper grill and plenty of local game. Flavours are pronounced, combinations are classi-cal and portions are hearty.

Specialities: Normandy black pudding with mushrooms and fried egg. Day-boat lemon sole, Jersey Royals and brown shrimps. Treacle tart and clotted cream.

Menu £24 – Carte £24/40

2 High Street ⊠ SG12 8NH – ℰ 01279 843999 –
www.foxandhounds-hunsdon.co.uk – Closed Sunday dinner, Monday

HUNSTANTON
Norfolk – Regional map n° **8**–B1

✿ The Neptune (Kevin Mangeolles)

MODERN CUISINE · INTIMATE XX In 2007 a couple bought this old roadside inn on the main route to the North Norfolk coast and set about transforming it into a smart destination restaurant complete with stylishly understated bedrooms.

The restaurant is only open for dinner and your evening starts with drinks and canapés in the bar while choosing from the ever-evolving menu. The experienced chef, Kevin, works alone in the kitchen, making everything from the bread to the ice cream, and his skilfully crafted, unfussy dishes allow the natural flavours of top quality local produce to shine. Meats and vegetables are from the surrounding countryside and seafood is from the nearby coast – Brancaster mussels are often a feature.

Dishes are brought to the table by Jacki, Kevin's chatty, friendly and equally enthusiastic wife.

Specialities: Norfolk quail with pickled sultanas and cauliflower. Loin and braised haunch of hare with celeriac tart and carrots. Agen prune and Armagnac parfait with tea meringue.

Menu £62/80

85 Old Hunstanton Road, Old Hunstanton ⊠ PE36 6HZ – ℰ 01485 532122 – www.theneptune.co.uk – Closed 1-31 January, 11-19 May, Monday, Tuesday - Saturday lunch

HUNSTRETE
Bath and North East Somerset – Regional map n° **2**–C2

⅋○ The Pig ⚘ ☕ ⌂ 🏠 & ♻ P

TRADITIONAL CUISINE · BRASSERIE XX This rustic hotel conservatory takes things back to nature with pots of fresh herbs placed on wooden tables and chimney pots filled with flowering shrubs. The extremely knowledgeable team serve dishes which showcase ingredients from their extensive gardens, along with produce sourced from within 25 miles.

Carte £32/45

The Pig Hotel ⊠ BS39 4NS – ℰ 01761 490490 – www.thepighotel.com

🏠 The Pig ✿ ☽ ⪻ ⌂ & P

COUNTRY HOUSE · PERSONALISED Nestled in the Mendip Hills, with deer roaming around the parkland, this Grade II listed house is all about getting back to nature. It has a relaxed, friendly atmosphere and extremely comfortable bedrooms which feature handmade beds and fine linens; some are in converted sheds in the walled vegetable garden.

29 rooms – ♦♦ £155/330 – ⌂ £18

⊠ BS39 4NS – ℰ 01761 490490 – www.thepighotel.com

⅋○ **The Pig** – See restaurant listing

HUNTINGDON
Cambridgeshire – Regional map n° **8**–A2

Abbots Ripton North: 6. 5 mi by B1514 and A141 on B1090

⅋○ Abbot's Elm

TRADITIONAL BRITISH · PUB X A modern reconstruction of an attractive 17C pub, with a spacious open-plan layout, homely touches and a vaulted, oak-beamed roof. Extensive menus offer hearty, flavoursome cooking; the wine list is a labour of love and the cosy, comfy bedrooms come with fluffy bathrobes and complimentary mineral water.

Menu £18 (lunch) – Carte £25/45

Moat Lane ⊠ PE28 2PD – ℰ 01487 773773 – www.theabbotselm.co.uk – Closed Sunday dinner

HURLEY

Windsor and Maidenhead – Regional map n° **6**–C3

🍴⃝ **Hurley House**

MODERN BRITISH · PUB ✗ Hurley House is a stylish place: outside you'll find a charming canopied terrace with patio heaters and its own bar, while inside smart furnishings sit amongst exposed bricks, beams and flagstones. Well-sourced ingredients underpin modern British dishes, which confidently blend contrasting tastes and textures. Well-appointed bedrooms pay great attention to detail.

Menu £23 (lunch) – Carte £31/55

Henley Road ✉ *SL6 5LH – 𝒞 01628 568500 – www.hurleyhouse.co.uk*

HURWORTH-ON-TEES – Darlington → See Darlington

ICKHAM

Kent – Regional map n° **5**–D2

🍴⃝ **Duke William** ⇦⃝ 🏠 ⅙

MODERN BRITISH · PUB ✗ The smart exterior of this pub has more of a city than a country look but inside it has a good old neighbourhood vibe. Keenly priced menus list time-honoured classics everyone knows and loves. Cosy up on fur throw covered benches by the fire, then stay the night in one of the smart yet casual bedrooms.

Carte £22/53

The Street ✉ *CT3 1QP – 𝒞 01227 721308 – www.thedukewilliamickham.com – Closed Sunday dinner*

ILFRACOMBE

Devon – Regional map n° **1**–C1

🌸 **Thomas Carr @ The Olive Room** ⇦⃝ 🍴ⓥ

SEAFOOD · RUSTIC ✗ Don't let the unremarkable exterior of this 19C townhouse put you off – it might be a simple place but it's homely and welcoming and the food is top notch. It's run by experienced local chef Thomas Carr, who learnt his trade with Nathan Outlaw and he has drawn on Nathan's ethos to inform the cooking here at The Olive Room.

Ultra-fresh seafood is the focus, with dishes only confirmed once the day boat deliveries come in. Each dish comprises just 4 or 5 accurately prepared ingredients of the highest quality and the cooking is creative with distinct flavours and complementary textures. Menus offer a good variety of dishes and represent good value when considering the use of some more luxurious items, such as lobster.

Bedrooms have a pleasant period feel and some offer great views out over the town.

Specialities: Beetroot-cured salmon and smoked mackerel pâté, crispy salmon skin. Hake, crab and sweetcorn pancake with crab bisque. Chocolate tart, chocolate textures and praline ice cream.

Menu £55/75

56 Fore Street ✉ *EX34 9DJ – 𝒞 01271 867831 – www.thomascarrdining.co.uk – Closed Sunday, Monday, Tuesday, Wednesday - Thursday lunch*

🍴 **The Antidote** ⇦⃝

MODERN BRITISH · FRIENDLY ✗ A sweet glass-fronted former shop set just off the quayside and run by a friendly couple; brown paper covered tables contribute to the cool, modish feel. Thoughtfully prepared menus list well-judged dishes with plenty of flavour and prices are kept low. Bedrooms are modern – one even has a small terrace.

Specialities: Pigs on toast, sherry, tarragon and mustard. Roast hake and crab with saffron butter, spiced potatoes, tomato jam and aioli. Chocolate, salted caramel and orange.

Carte £24/30

20 St James Place ✉ *EX34 9BJ – 𝒞 01271 865339 – www.theantidoteilfracombe.co.uk – Closed Sunday, Monday, Tuesday - Saturday lunch*

ILKLEY
West Yorkshire – Regional map n° **13**–B2

⃝ **Box Tree**   A/C ⟡

MODERN BRITISH · CLASSIC DÉCOR XxX This iconic Yorkshire restaurant was established back in 1962. It's set in two charming sandstone cottages and has a plush, antique-furnished lounge and two luxurious dining rooms. Cooking has a classical French base with subtle modern touches and dishes are light and delicate.
Menu £ 45/85

37 Church Street ⊠ LS29 9DR – ℰ 01943 608484 – www.theboxtree.co.uk –
Closed 1-8 January, 26-30 December, Sunday dinner, Monday, Tuesday,
Wednesday - Thursday lunch

⃝ **Host** Ⓝ   ⍝ ⍢

MODERN CUISINE · BISTRO X Stylishly understated Host is a great match for the pretty spa town of Ilkley. The likeable chef makes everything on-site, creating a nicely varied selection of unfussy small plates which arrive in generous portions. 4 or 5 to share is about right – be sure to try the buttermilk chicken.
Carte £ 21/37

60 The Grove, ⊠ LS29 9PA – ℰ 01943 605337 – www.hostilkley.co.uk –
Closed Sunday dinner, Monday, Tuesday, Wednesday lunch

ILMINGTON
Warwickshire – Regional map n° **10**–C3

⃝ **Howard Arms**   ⇐ ⍤ ⍝ ⅙ A/C P

MODERN BRITISH · PUB X Built from golden stone quarried in the village itself, The Howard Arms really is part of the local community. Hearty flavours are the order of the day and pub favourites are listed alongside dishes of a more global bent; Tuesday is pie night – and great value. Bedrooms come in a variety of styles.
Carte £ 25/40

Lower Green ⊠ CV36 4LT – ℰ 01608 682226 – www.howardarms.com

IPSWICH
Suffolk – Regional map n° **8**–C3

⃝ **Trongs**   A/C

CHINESE · FRIENDLY XX Loyal locals are always a good sign, and this sweet little restaurant has plenty. One brother cooks and the other looks after the service. Authentic dishes include spicy Hunanese specialities – ask and they will adjust the heat.
Menu £ 30 – Carte £ 14/37

23 St. Nicholas Street ⊠ IP1 1TW – ℰ 01473 256833 – Closed Sunday, Monday -
Saturday lunch

at Chelmondiston Southeast : 6 mi by A 137 on B 1456

⃝ **Red Lion**   ⍝ ⅙ ⟡ P

TRADITIONAL CUISINE · BISTRO X Smartly refurbished former pub with a few comfy chairs in the bar and two dining rooms furnished with dark wood tables and Lloyd Loom chairs. Menus offer a broad range of dishes and daily specials. The bubbly owner leads the service.
Carte £ 22/32

Main Street ⊠ IP9 1DX – ℰ 01473 780400 – www.chelmondistonredlion.co.uk –
Closed Sunday, Monday

KELMSCOTT
Oxfordshire – Regional map n° **6**–A2

ⅠⓄ Plough 　　　　　　🍽 👐 🏠 👐

TRADITIONAL CUISINE · PUB Ⅹ The 16C Plough has all the character you would expect of a pub its age, with rough stone walls, open fires and a cottage-style garden. Traditional menus list dishes you'll know and love, from twice-baked Double Gloucester soufflé to cottage pie or flat iron steak. Comfortable bedrooms exceed expectations.

Carte £27/42

✉ GL7 3HG – ✆ 01367 253543 –
www.theploughinnkelmscott.com –
Closed Sunday dinner, Monday

KENILWORTH

Warwickshire – Regional map n° **10**-C2

❀ The Cross at Kenilworth (Adam Bennett) 　🏠 & 🅰🅲 ⅠⓋ 👐 🅿

CLASSIC CUISINE · PUB Ⅹ When you first catch sight of this pub's smart exterior, you'll just know that they take things seriously here – and when an eager member of staff greets you, settles you in and explains the menu, this initial impression is confirmed. Further proof comes on your plate: skilfully executed, classical dishes showcase prime seasonal ingredients, and dishes not only look impressive but deliver on flavour too. This is, after all, a mature and confident kitchen team who know how to treat their produce with respect.

If you're seated in the back room, which opens onto the terrace, you get to watch the kitchen team in action; the bright, airy room next door used to be a classroom – a fact alluded to by the eye-catching wall lamps shaped like hand bells. The front bar, meanwhile, with its adjoining snug and wood burning stove, makes a cosy place for a beer and a homemade sausage roll.

Specialities: Crispy duck egg with cured ham, celeriac purée and chicken jus. Roast loin of lamb with Jersey Royals, seaweed butter and lamb jus. Hazelnut praline soufflé, blood orange ice cream and caramelised white chocolate sauce.

Menu £29 (lunch)/75 – Carte £48/58

16 New Street ✉ CV8 2EZ –
✆ 01926 853840 –
www.thecrosskenilworth.co.uk –
Closed Sunday dinner, Monday

KENTISBURY

Devon – Regional map n° **1**-C1

ⅠⓄ Coach House by Michael Caines 　🏠 & 🅿

MODERN CUISINE · DESIGN ⅩⅩ This smart hotel restaurant has a lovely walnut and marble bar counter, a funky lounge under the eaves and an elegant dining room featuring plush blue velvet booths. Flavoursome modern dishes use local meats and south coast fish.

Menu £28 (lunch)/50

Kentisbury Grange Hotel ✉ EX31 4NL – ✆ 01271 882295 –
www.kentisburygrange.co.uk

🏠 Kentisbury Grange 　　　　🌱 👐 🅿

COUNTRY HOUSE · DESIGN This Victorian country house may have a Grade II listing but it's been smartly decked out with designer fabrics and furnishings in the colours of its original stained glass windows. Go for one of the chic, detached Garden Suites.

20 rooms ⌂ – 🛉 £110/375

✉ EX31 4NL – ✆ 01271 882295 –
www.kentisburygrange.co.uk

ⅠⓄ **Coach House by Michael Caines** – See restaurant listing

KENTON
Devon – Regional map n° **1**-D2

○ Rodean

TRADITIONAL BRITISH · NEIGHBOURHOOD ※※ This family-run restaurant sits overlooking a tiny village green and started life as a butcher's shop. The two dining rooms blend modern furnishings with wooden beams, exposed stone and dark wood panelling. Constantly evolving menus have a classic base and modern overtones.

Menu £26 – Carte £40/50

The Triangle ⊠ EX6 8LS – 𝒞 01626 890195 – www.rodeanrestaurant.co.uk –
Closed 1-10 January, Sunday dinner, Monday, Tuesday - Friday lunch

KESWICK
Cumbria – Regional map n° **12**–A2

at Borrowdale South : 5. 5 mi on B 5289

○ Leathes Head

MODERN BRITISH · CONTEMPORARY DÉCOR ※※ Enjoy an aperitif on the terrace of this Lakeland hotel and take in magnificent mountain views; in colder weather the Graphite Bar with its impressive slate-topped counter provides a stylish alternative. The constantly evolving modern menu sees natural flavours feature in well-judged combinations.

Menu £50

Leathes Head Hotel, Borrowdale ⊠ CA12 5UY – 𝒞 017687 77247 –
www.leatheshead.co.uk – Closed 3-25 January, Sunday - Saturday lunch

⌂ Leathes Head

COUNTRY HOUSE · CONTEMPORARY The beautiful fells and mountains of Borrowdale provide the backdrop for this traditional slate-built hotel and its attractive gardens. Both the bedrooms and guest areas mix the classic and the contemporary; an original tiled floor contrasts with a stylish bar and an attractive modern dining room.

11 rooms ⊡ – ♛♛ £180/195

⊠ CA12 5UY – 𝒞 017687 77247 – www.leatheshead.co.uk – Closed 3-25 January
○ **Leathes Head** – See restaurant listing

at Braithwaite West: 2 mi by A66 on B5292 – Regional map n° **12**–A2

✿ Cottage in the Wood

MODERN BRITISH · ROMANTIC ※※ As you leave the small hamlet of Braithwaite, the narrow road rises steeply towards the Whinlatter Forest and Pass. Here, you'll find a small black and white roadside inn run by a friendly team. It really is a cosy little place: in winter sit in the dining room; in summer take in the view over the fells and valley from the conservatory.

Chef Ben Wilkinson has made the place his own and there is a quiet confidence to his cooking. Top quality ingredients and classic techniques take the lead, and there is a certain sophistication to the well-balanced flavour pairings – and while skilfully making the dishes look eye-catching, he manages to avoid over-elaboration. Like the food, the service is natural and honest, and you leave feeling that they really do care about every little detail here.

Contemporary bedrooms complete the picture.

Specialities: Scallop with Jerusalem artichoke, sea purslane and hazelnut. Loin of Herdwick hogget with asparagus, Jersey Royals, roast sweetbread, anchovy and almond. Forest gateau.

Menu £30 (lunch), £50/70

Magic Hill, Whinlatter Forest ⊠ CA12 5TW – 𝒞 017687 78409 –
www.thecottageinthewood.co.uk – Closed 5-24 January, Sunday, Monday,
Tuesday - Wednesday lunch

KETTERING
Northamptonshire – Regional map n° **9**–C3

at Rushton Northwest : 3. 5 mi by A 14 and Rushton Rd

🏠 **Rushton Hall** ⌂ 🦢 🛋 🖼 🌐 🎿 ♨ 📶 🛗 ♿ 🏊 **P**

COUNTRY HOUSE · HISTORIC An imposing 15C house with stunning architecture, set in 28 acres of countryside. The Grand Hall features huge stained glass windows and an impressive fireplace, and the classically furnished bedrooms are luxurious. Dine in the brasserie or on more elaborate dishes in the elegant restaurant.

51 rooms – 👫 £180/400 – 3 suites

✉ NN14 1RR – ☎ 01536 713001 – www.rushtonhall.com

KIBWORTH BEAUCHAMP
Leicestershire – Regional map n° **9**–B2

🍴 **Lighthouse** 🏮

SEAFOOD · NEIGHBOURHOOD 🍴 With its array of nautical knick-knacks, the Lighthouse is a fitting name. The flexible menu has a seafood emphasis and offers many dishes in two different sizes; the 'Nibbles' are a popular choice.

Menu £16/19 – Carte £19/37

9 Station Street ✉ LE8 0LN – ☎ 0116 279 6260 – www.lighthousekibworth.co.uk – Closed Sunday, Monday, Tuesday - Saturday lunch

KILNDOWN
Kent – Regional map n° **5**–B2

🍴 **The Small Holding** 🆕 🛋 🍧 🎱 **P**

MODERN BRITISH · RUSTIC 🍴 Two brothers run this former village pub, which has a rustic farmhouse feel. The focus here is on self-sufficiency, and they grow fruit and veg and raise chickens and rare breed pigs. Rustic British meets Nordic cooking on the tasting menus and dishes have bold, well-balanced flavours and lots of personality.

Menu £ 30 (lunch)/60

Ranters Lane ✉ TN17 2SG – ☎ 01892 890105 – www.thesmallholding.restaurant – Closed 26 December-2 January, Sunday dinner, Monday, Tuesday

KILPECK
Herefordshire – Regional map n° **10**–A3

🍴 **Kilpeck Inn** ⇔ 🍧 ♿ **P**

TRADITIONAL CUISINE · PUB 🍴 A popular pub which narrowly escaped being turned into private housing thanks to the villagers' valiantly fought 'Save Our Pub' campaign. Its spacious interior and bedrooms are smart, modern and characterful, with impressive green credentials. Menus offer locally sourced meats and old fashioned puddings.

Menu £15 (lunch) – Carte £24/40

✉ HR2 9DN – ☎ 01981 570464 – www.kilpeckinn.com – Closed Sunday dinner, Monday lunch

KINGHAM
Oxfordshire – Regional map n° **6**–A1

🍴 **Kingham Plough** ⇔ 🍧 ♿ **P**

MODERN BRITISH · PUB 🍴 Set on the green of an unspoilt village, this pub delivers all the rusticity you'd hope for along with some subtle modern touches. Sit out on the terrace, in the stylish dining room or beside locals and their dogs in the bar. Fiercely seasonal British dishes exude freshness and simplicity. Bedrooms are comfy.

Carte £25/46

The Green ✉ OX7 6YD – ☎ 01608 658327 – www.thekinghamplough.co.uk – Closed Sunday dinner

⑪○ **The Wild Rabbit** ◁ 🏠 & ♻ 🅿

MODERN BRITISH · PUB 🗡 Just down the road from the Daylesford Farm Shop is the Bamford family's stylishly modernised country pub. Accomplished modern dishes have plenty of appeal, with the natural flavours of their farm's superb organic ingredients underpinning the menu. Luxurious bedrooms are delightfully understated.

Carte £43/57

Church Street ⊠ OX7 6YA – ℰ 01608 658389 – www.thewildrabbit.co.uk – Closed Monday, Tuesday

KING'S LYNN
Norfolk – Regional map n° **8**–B1

⑪○ **Goldings** ◁

TRADITIONAL BRITISH · COSY 🗡 The traditional-looking Goldings is a smart but pleasingly laid-back pub, where they serve local ales and dogs are welcome. Classically based menus offer plenty of choice – including platters for two – and portions are substantial. Modern bedrooms and a deli complete the picture.

Menu £20/27

8-9 Saturday Market Place ⊠ PE30 5DQ – ℰ 01553 602388 – www.goldingskl.co.uk

KING'S SUTTON
Northamptonshire – Regional map n° **9**–B3

⑪○ **White Horse** 🏠 🅿

MODERN BRITISH · PUB 🗡 A pretty sandstone pub run by a keen young couple. The self-taught chef crafts the creative modern dishes from scratch and always tries to exceed guests' expectations. Produce is local and follows a 'when it's gone, it's gone' approach. The 'Taste of The White Horse' menu fully demonstrates his talents.

Menu £16/18 – Carte £23/40

2 The Square ⊠ OX17 3RF – ℰ 01295 812440 – www.whitehorseks.co.uk – Closed Monday

KINGSTON - UPON - HULL
Kingston upon Hull – Regional map n° **13**–D2

⑪○ **Tapasya @ Marina** & 🆎 🕼 ♻

INDIAN · BRASSERIE 🗡🗡 Tapasya sits on the harbourside, looking out over the bobbing boats. It's a large place, split over two floors, and has an airy brasserie feel. Authentic Indian dishes are freshly prepared and full of flavour. The lunch menu is great value, the naan breads are delicious and high tea has some great twists.

Menu £20 (lunch) – Carte £25/30

9 Humber Dock Street ⊠ HU1 1TB – ℰ 01482 242607 – www.tapasyarestaurants.co.uk

KIRKBY LONSDALE
Cumbria – Regional map n° **12**–B3

⑪○ **Sun Inn** ◁ 🕼

TRADITIONAL BRITISH · PUB 🗡 After a riverside stroll head for this charming 17C pub. Enjoy a local beer in the characterful stone-walled bar then dine in the smart restaurant. Lunch sees small plates and pub classics, while dinner steps up a gear with more elaborate dishes. Cosy bedrooms blend original features with modern furnishings.

Carte £20/34

6 Market Street ⊠ LA6 2AU – ℰ 015242 71965 – www.sun-inn.info – Closed Monday lunch

KNOWSTONE
Devon – Regional map n° **1**–C1

✿ **Masons Arms** (Mark Dodson) 🍴 🛏 **P**

CLASSIC FRENCH · PUB 🕱 This pretty thatched pub sits in a secluded village in the beautiful foothills of Exmoor and is run by a husband and wife. It was built in the 13C by the masons who constructed the village church and with its cosy beamed bar and inglenook fireplace, exudes plenty of rural charm. Pick a spot in the series of inviting beamed rooms or dine beneath a Grecian ceiling mural in the bright rear dining room while enjoying delightful views over the rolling hills towards Exmoor.

The food is more sophisticated than you'd expect to find in a pub, with canapés and petit fours served alongside attractively presented British and French classics. Cooking is refined and flavours are pronounced and assured; the chef, Mark Dodson, has plenty of experience and employs the finest local produce to full effect. The service is charming and attentive and a perfect match for the food.

Specialities: Scallops, squid and fregola with bisque style sauce. Breast of guinea fowl with crumbed mousse sausage, fennel, potato fondant, morel cream sauce. Trio of raspberry desserts.

Menu £ 28 (lunch) – Carte £ 45/55

✉ EX36 4RY – ✆ 01398 341231 – www.masonsarmsdevon.co.uk –
Closed 16-25 February, 23 August-2 September, 26 December-7 January, Sunday, Monday

LA PULENTE – Jersey ➔ See Channel Islands (Jersey)

LANGFORD

Oxfordshire – Regional map n° **6**-A2

🏵 **Bell Inn** 🛏 🛖 **P**

TRADITIONAL BRITISH · PUB 🕱 The Bell Inn's rustic charm is hard to resist with its cosy bar, impressive inglenook fireplace and 16C origins. The large menu offers everything from a homemade burger to a muntjac, cep and bacon pie, and the wood-fired garlic, parsley and bone marrow flatbread is a must. Bedrooms are nicely furnished.

Specialities: Cotswold IPA rarebit with soldiers and pickles. Calf's liver with mash, pancetta, onion gravy and sage. Custard tart with poached rhubarb.

Carte £ 15/37

✉ GL7 3LF – ✆ 01367 860249 – www.thebelllangford.com

LANGHO – Lancashire ➔ See Blackburn

LAPWORTH

– Regional map n° **10**-C2

🍴 **Boot Inn** 🍴 🛖 **P**

TRADITIONAL BRITISH · PUB 🕱 A big, buzzy pub boasting a large terrace, a traditional quarry-floored bar and a modern restaurant. Dishes range from sandwiches, picnic boards and sharing plates to more sophisticated specials. You can eat in a tepee in the summer!

Menu £ 16 – Carte £ 25/43

Old Warwick Road ✉ B94 6JU – ✆ 01564 782464 – www.lovelypubs.co.uk

LAVENHAM

Suffolk – Regional map n° **8**-C3

🍴 **Great House** 🛏 🛖

CLASSIC FRENCH · ELEGANT 🕱🕱🕱 Passionately run restaurant on the main square of an attractive town; its impressive Georgian façade concealing a timbered house with 14C origins. Choose between two dining rooms and a smart enclosed terrace. Concise menus offer ambitious dishes with worldwide influences and a French heart. Stylish, contemporary décor blends well with the old beams in the bedrooms.

Menu £ 28 (lunch), £ 38/58 – Carte £ 44/54

Market Place ✉ CO10 9QZ – ✆ 01787 247431 – www.greathouse.co.uk –
Closed 2 January-1 February, Sunday dinner, Monday, Tuesday lunch

LEATHERHEAD
Surrey – Regional map n° **4**-D1

ᵗ⃝ **Dining Room**

JAPANESE · HISTORIC XX Have a drink in the elegant Parrot Bar of this historic country house before heading for the delightful dining room with its bold décor, impressive ceiling and huge windows overlooking the estate. Extensive Japanese menus mix the classic with the modern and the flavours provide plenty of interest.

Menu £60/95 – Carte £22/85

Beaverbrook Hotel, Reigate Road ⊠ *KT22 8QX –* ℰ *01372 375532 –*
www.beaverbrook.co.uk – Closed Sunday dinner, Monday lunch

🏚 **Beaverbrook**

HISTORIC BUILDING · CONTEMPORARY This neo-classical Victorian mansion set in 475 acres was once the country home of Lord Beaverbrook – a close friend of Churchill. Charming bedrooms are spread about the place and it has a laid-back feel. Take in delightful country views from the many terraces or relax in huge guest areas which evoke memories of yesteryear. Dine on British, Italian or Japanese fare.

35 rooms – ⚥ £265/450 – ⌕ £25

Reigate Road ⊠ *KT22 8QX –* ℰ *01372 571300 – www.beaverbrook.co.uk*

ᵗ⃝ **Dining Room** – See restaurant listing

355

LEEDS

West Yorkshire – Regional map n° **13**–B2

Top tips!

Its central location makes Leeds one of the most accessible cities in the region. A former mill town, famed for its cloth making, it's now known as the 'Knightsbridge of the North' – and you'll find shops and restaurants located in both old industrial buildings as well as newer retail spaces.

Must-sees include the Royal Armouries Museum (go when the jousting is on), Roundhay Park, with its 700 acres of lakes and parkland, and County Arcade – a stunning Victorian masterpiece.

There are also some great markets – Kirkgate is one of the largest indoor venues in Europe – and while the old art deco Tetley building may not be brewing beers anymore, it's worth visiting for its contemporary art exhibitions.

You can't go wrong enjoying a cocktail with a view in the DoubleTree hotel, and if it's a memorable night you're after, head for Michelin-Starred **The Man Behind The Curtain** for unique modern cuisine.

R. Harding/hemis.fr

Restaurants

⁂ **The Man Behind The Curtain** (Michael O'Hare)

CREATIVE · DESIGN ✗✗ Michael O'Hare has never been a conventional chef and this idiosyncratic basement restaurant matches his cooking style perfectly. It's a spacious place characterised by polished concrete, black marble and a rather disorientating array of mirrored pillars, and is decorated with skateboard decks, a surfboard and even a motorbike. A meal here constitutes an 'experience', the likes of which few restaurants can achieve, so securing a reservation here is often a challenge.

Accomplished, highly skilled cooking showcases some very original, creative combinations and the artful presentation is equally striking. You choose 6 or 10 courses at lunch and 10 or 14 at dinner from a 'collection' of dishes, some of which are a mouthful, others of which are larger – and from these your surprise dinner will be created; many, like 'Emancipation' have already established themselves as classics. Equal thought has gone into the drinks pairings, which are well worth choosing.

Specialities: Veal sweetbread slider and XO. 'Emancipation'. 'Lemon Top'.

Menu £55 (lunch), £75/100

Town plan B2-c – *68-78 Vicar Lane (Lower ground floor)* ⊠ *LS1 7JH* – ℰ *0113 243 2376* – *www.themanbehindthecurtain.co.uk* – *Closed Sunday, Monday, Tuesday - Thursday lunch*

⑩ **Crafthouse**

MODERN CUISINE · DESIGN ✗✗ A bright, chic restaurant in the Trinity shopping centre, with great rooftop views and a wraparound terrace. Creative, elaborate dishes showcase a huge array of ingredients. The open kitchen and marble counter take centre stage. Start with a cocktail in all-day Angelica.

Menu £14/24 – Carte £31/65

Town plan A2-a – *Trinity Leeds (5th Floor), 70 Boar Lane* ⊠ *LA1 6HW* – ℰ *0113 897 0444* – *www.crafthouse-restaurant.co.uk*

⑩ **HOME**

MODERN BRITISH · ELEGANT ✗✗ HOME is a buzzy place with a stylish feel. It's unusually set in an old Victorian fish market, above the shops on a pedestrianised street; ascend the original stairs and emerge in a spacious lounge-bar. Pre-paid tasting menus see interesting combinations of British ingredients full of texture contrasts.

Menu £45 (lunch), £65/85

Town plan B2-z – *16/17 Kirkgate* ⊠ *LS1 6BY* – ℰ *0113 430 0161* – *www.homeleeds.co.uk* – *Closed 1-8 January, 3-18 August, Sunday dinner, Monday, Tuesday, Wednesday - Thursday lunch*

⑩ **Issho**

JAPANESE · DESIGN ✗✗ This chic eatery in Victoria Gate serves modern Japanese cooking in a stylish setting, including sushi, tempura and dishes from the robata grill. Enjoy cocktails in the bar and city skyline views from the rooftop terrace.

Menu £25 – Carte £22/57

Town plan B2-r – *Victoria Gate* ⊠ *LS2 7AU* – ℰ *0113 426 5000* – *www.issho-restaurant.com* – *Closed Sunday dinner, Monday*

⑩ **Matt Healy X The Foundry** ⓝ

MODERN BRITISH · RUSTIC ✗✗ Exposed brickwork and period features set the scene at this former foundry, which has a smart, rustic feel and a large courtyard terrace for warmer days. The frequently changing menu offers both modern and classical dishes in a mix of sizes. Don't miss the wonderful crème brûlée.

Carte £31/46

Town plan A2-k – *1 Saw Mill Yard* ⊠ *LS11 5WH* – ℰ *0113 245 0390* – *www.mhfoundry.co.uk* – *Closed Sunday dinner, Monday, Tuesday lunch*

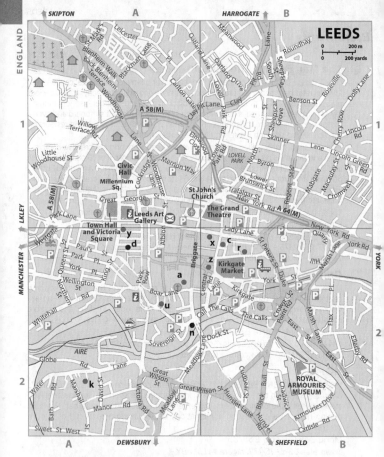

🍴 Stockdales of Yorkshire   🕭 AC ⇄

MEATS AND GRILLS · CLASSIC DÉCOR XX Here, it's is all about showcasing the county's best ingredients in attractively presented dishes, with Josper-cooked beef – including Yorkshire Wagyu – a speciality. Sit in the comfy lounge-bar or attractive basement restaurant.

Menu £23 (lunch) – Carte £27/66

Town plan A2-y – *8 South Parade* ✉ *LS1 5QX* –
☎ *0113 204 2460* – *www.stockdales-restaurant.com* –
Closed 24-26 December, Sunday dinner

🍴 Black Market 🆕   🪑 AC 🍽 ⇄

BRITISH CONTEMPORARY · BISTRO X A pleasant city suburb is home to this bright, modern bistro run by a cheerful owner. The menu is a mix of small plates – some familiar and others offering something a little different – and cooking is honest and full of flavour. Come at the weekend for brunch; on Sundays they play old vinyl at lunch.

Menu £20/25 – Carte £20/38

Off plan – *5 Stainbeck Lane* ✉ *LS7 3PJ* –
☎ *0113 262 2531* – *www.blackmarketleeds.co.uk* –
Closed Monday, Tuesday lunch

⁑○ HanaMatsuri

SUSHI · SIMPLE ⚹ Suburban Leeds is home to this very intimate restaurant, which seats just 7 guests and must be booked at least 24hrs in advance. Japanese memorabilia and shelves of sake fill the room. The chef-owner serves a wide range of sushi and sashimi crafted from good quality imported ingredients.

Menu £20 (lunch), £45/90 – Carte £20/90

Off plan – *580 Meanwood Road* ✉ *LS6 4AZ* – ℰ *0113 295 5920* –
www.sushibarhanamatsuri.co.uk – *Closed 29 July, 25 December-3 January, Monday, Tuesday*

⁑○ Ox Club 　　　　　　　　　　　　　　　　　AC

BARBECUE · SIMPLE ⚹ A former mill houses this multi-floor venue comprising a beer hall, cocktail bar, event space and restaurant. The latter boasts a wood-fired grill imported from the USA; rustic, smoky-flavoured dishes showcase Yorkshire ingredients.

Menu £20/23 – Carte £24/43

Town plan B2-x – *Bramleys Yard, The Headrow* ✉ *LS1 6PU* – ℰ *07470359961* –
www.oxclub.co.uk – *Closed 1-2 January, Sunday dinner, Monday, Tuesday - Friday lunch*

⁑○ Tharavadu 　　　　　　　　　　　　　　AC

INDIAN · EXOTIC DÉCOR ⚹ A simple-looking restaurant with seascape murals. The extensive menu offers superbly spiced, colourful Keralan specialities and refined street food – the dosas are a hit. Service is friendly and dishes arrive swiftly.

Menu £9 (lunch) – Carte £16/40

Town plan A2-u – *7-8 Mill Hill* ✉ *LS1 5DQ* – ℰ *0113 244 0500* –
www.tharavadurestaurants.com – *Closed 22-27 December, Sunday*

Hotels

🏨 Dakota Deluxe 　　　　　　　⚒ ⊟ ⅙ AC 🛎

BUSINESS · CONTEMPORARY Its location in the heart of the business district and its stylish, well-equipped bedrooms make this design hotel ideal for business travellers. It's tucked away in a pedestrianised square and its dark, intimate décor provides a calming influence. The bar is a popular spot, as is the seductive restaurant.

84 rooms ⌂ – ♙♙ £121/293 – 1 suite

Town plan A2-d – *8 Russell Street* ✉ *LS1 5RN* – ℰ *0113 322 6261* –
www.leeds.dakotahotels.co.uk

🏨 Malmaison 　　　　　　　　　⚒ ⊟ AC 🛎

BUSINESS · DESIGN A chic boutique hotel in the former offices of the city's tram and bus department. Generously sized bedrooms have warm colour schemes and good comforts; for special occasions book the stylish suite. Smart, intimate guest areas include a relaxing bar and a modern take on a brasserie.

100 rooms ⌂ – ♙♙ £79/200 – 1 suite

Town plan A2-n – *1 Swinegate* ✉ *LS1 4AG* – ℰ *0113 426 0047* –
www.malmaison.com

LETCOMBE REGIS
Oxfordshire – Regional map n° **6**-B3

⁑○ Greyhound Inn 　　　　　⇦ 🍴 🛏 ⅙ ⟳ P

MODERN BRITISH · PUB ⚹ Two villagers stepped in to save this 18C pub from redevelopment and the locals are clearly thankful. Its original character is still visible through its beams and lovely inglenook fireplace but it's also been subtly modernised. Menus range from pub favourites to more sophisticated dishes. Bedrooms are cosy.

Menu £28 – Carte £26/41

Main Street ✉ *OX12 9JL* – ℰ *01235 771969* – *www.thegreyhoundletcombe.co.uk* –
Closed 6-16 January, Monday lunch

LEWANNICK
Cornwall – Regional map n° **1**–B2

ⅼ○ Coombeshead Farm

COUNTRY COOKING · RUSTIC X Set on a working farm, in 66 acres of meadows and woodland, this former farmhouse and dairy offers the ultimate field to fork experience. Techniques include curing, pickling and cooking over wooden embers. The home-bred Mangalitsa pork and home-baked sourdough are hits. Bedrooms have a cosy farmhouse style.

Menu £65

✉ PL15 7QQ – ☏ 01566 782009 – www.coombesheadfarm.co.uk –
Closed 3 January-13 February, Monday, Tuesday, Wednesday, Thursday - Saturday lunch

LEWDOWN
Devon – Regional map n° **1**–C2

🏠 Lewtrenchard Manor

HISTORIC · ELEGANT Hugely impressive Grade II listed Jacobean manor house in mature grounds. The characterful antique-furnished interior features huge fireplaces, ornate oak panelling, intricately designed ceilings and mullioned windows. Bedrooms are spacious and well-equipped; those in the coach house are the most modern.

14 rooms ⌸ – ♥♥ £140/240 – 1 suite
✉ EX20 4PN – ☏ 01566 783222 – www.lewtrenchard.co.uk

LEYBURN
North Yorkshire – Regional map n° **13**–B1

ⅼ○ Sandpiper Inn

TRADITIONAL BRITISH · PUB X A friendly Yorkshire welcome is extended at this characterful, stone-built, part-16C pub just off the main square. Subtle, refined cooking offers a modern take on the classics and the skilled kitchen prides itself on the provenance of its ingredients. Two country-chic style bedrooms offer excellent comforts.

Carte £26/37

Market Place ✉ DL8 5AT – ☏ 01969 622206 – www.sandpiperinn.co.uk –
Closed 1-14 January, Monday

LICHFIELD
Staffordshire – Regional map n° **10**–C2

ⅼ○ The Boat Inn

MODERN BRITISH · PUB X This old roadside hostelry was once backed by a canal and its walls are filled with black and white photos of the area's locks. Refined modern dishes are colourful and eye-catching, and the chef likes to make local, organic ingredients the stars of the show – including their home-raised chickens and pigs.

Menu £19 (lunch)/65 – Carte £36/44

Walsall Road ✉ WS14 0BU – ☏ 01543 361692 – www.theboatinnlichfield.com –
Closed Sunday dinner, Monday, Tuesday

LICKFOLD – West Sussex ➔ See Petworth

LINCOLN
Lincolnshire – Regional map n° **9**–C1

Ⅲ○ Jews House ⌂

MODERN CUISINE · COSY XX At the bottom of a steep cobbled hill is this cosy stone house dating from 1150; reputedly Europe's oldest surviving dwelling. Bold, ambitious dishes display an eclectic mix of influences – the tasting menu is a hit. Service is charming.

Menu £26 (lunch) – Carte £35/49

15 The Strait ⌧ LN2 1JD – ℰ 01522 524851 – www.jewshouserestaurant.co.uk – Closed 1-29 January, 1-10 July, Sunday, Monday, Tuesday

LITTLE BEDWYN – Wiltshire → See Marlborough

LITTLE DUNMOW
Essex – Regional map n° **7**-C2

⌘ Tim Allen's Flitch of Bacon ⇦ ⌂ & P

MODERN BRITISH · NEIGHBOURHOOD XX This restaurant's unusual name originates from the 12C Dunmow Flitch Trials, which awarded a flitch of bacon to married couples who could swear not to have regretted their marriage for a year and a day! It's a pretty place, set in an equally attractive village, and is run by experienced chef-owner Tim Allen.

Head past the local drinkers in the bar and into the long, narrow dining room. Concise menus showcase top quality produce from Cornwall (the seafood) and the West Coast of Scotland, and the creative modern dishes have a refined yet unfussy style. To really get close to the action, book the two-seater kitchen counter.

Two Big Green Eggs cater for summer BBQs on the enclosed rear terrace and the old Citroën van is a fully-stocked bar. Contemporary bedrooms are boldly decorated and come with wet rooms.

Specialities: Flitch of bacon with black treacle, miso, mooli and toasted sesame. Monkfish with crispy chicken wing, mussel cream, puffed rice and sea herbs. Bitter chocolate tart with buckwheat caramel and maple verjus ice cream.

Menu £32 (lunch), £60/70

The Street ⌧ CM6 3HT – ℰ 01371 821660 – www.flitchofbacon.co.uk – Closed 1-7 January, 27 July-11 August, Sunday dinner-Tuesday

LITTLE ECCLESTON
Lancashire – Regional map n° **11**-A2

ⅢО Cartford Inn ⇦ ⌂ ⌂ P

TRADITIONAL CUISINE · PUB X The Cartford Inn stands next to a small toll bridge on the River Wyre and comes complete with a deli and farm shop. Cooking is gutsy and satisfying and many of the tried-and-tested classics come with a twist. The owner played a big part in the interior design, particularly the bold, boutique bedrooms.

Carte £28/54

Cartford Lane ⌧ PR3 0YP – ℰ 01995 670166 – www.thecartfordinn.co.uk – Closed Monday lunch

LITTLEHAMPTON
West Sussex – Regional map n° **4**-C3

⌂⌂⌂ Bailiffscourt H. & Spa ⌂ ⌂ ⌂ ⌂ ⌂ spa ⌂ ⌂ ⌂ P

COUNTRY HOUSE · HISTORIC Charming, reconstructed medieval manor in immaculately kept gardens. Bedrooms are split between the main house and the outbuildings; the newer rooms are in the grounds and are more suited to families. Beautiful spa facility. Classic country house cooking served in the formal dining room.

39 rooms ⌧ – ⌗ £245/765

Climping Street, Climping ⌧ BN17 5RW – ℰ 01903 723511 – www.hshotels.co.uk

⊛ Pilgrim ℕ   🛖 AC 🍴

SPANISH · SIMPLE ✕ Trendy Duke Street Market is home to this Spanish restaurant, whose name refers to those who walk the Camino del Norte across Cantabria and Galicia. Vibrant, colourful small plates are formed around recipes and produce originating from these regions – and the chargrill is put to good use.

Specialities: Coal-roasted courgette with courgette flowers, truffled sheep's cheese and seeds. Cured brill with smoked broad beans, walnuts and spruce oil. Chocolate, sea salt and olive oil mousse.

Carte £26/38

34 Pilgrim Street ✉ L1 5AS – www.pilgrimrestaurant.com – Closed Sunday dinner, Monday, Tuesday

○ The Art School   🔥 AC 🍴 🛇 ⇄

MODERN BRITISH · ELEGANT ✕✕✕ Bright red chairs contrast with crisp white tablecloths at this elegant restaurant, where a huge glass roof floods the room with light. The experienced local chef carefully prepares a bewildering array of colourful modern dishes.

Menu £34/75

1 Sugnall Street ✉ L7 7DX – ✆ 0151 230 8600 – www.theartschoolrestaurant.co.uk – Closed 1-7 January, 2-10 August, Sunday, Monday

○ Panoramic 34   ⩽ 🔥 AC

MODERN BRITISH · CHIC ✕✕✕ On the 34th floor of the city's highest skyscraper you'll find this elegant restaurant with under-lit tables and fabulous 360° views. Ambitious dishes arrive swiftly and are attractively presented; the lunch menu offers good value.

Menu £35/79 – Carte £35/49

West Tower, Brook Street (34th Floor) ✉ L3 9PJ – ✆ 0151 236 5534 – www.panoramic34.com – Closed Monday

○ Röski   🛇

MODERN CUISINE · COSY ✕✕ An amalgamation of the owners' names, Röski is a small modern restaurant decorated in grey tones. Modern tasting menus list complex, carefully crafted dishes which feature many different ingredients and are eye-catchingly presented. Local produce is cleverly used to give dishes a regional slant.

Menu £25 (lunch), £55/75

16 Rodney Street ✉ L1 2TE – ✆ 0151 708 8698 – www.roskirestaurant.com – Closed Sunday, Monday, Tuesday lunch

○ 60 Hope Street   AC 🍷 ⇄

REGIONAL CUISINE · BRASSERIE ✕✕ This long-standing restaurant might be located in a Grade II listed house but it certainly moves with the times, with its modern brasserie and chic basement wine bar. Local produce is used in refined versions of classic comfort dishes.

Menu £25/30 – Carte £35/60

60 Hope Street ✉ L1 9BZ – ✆ 0151 707 6060 – www.60hopestreet.com

○ Spire   AC

MODERN BRITISH · BISTRO ✕ Two experienced, enthusiastic brothers run this homely neighbourhood restaurant in the Penny Lane area of the city. Well-priced menus list modern British dishes which are full of flavour and rely on regional ingredients.

Menu £21 (lunch)/24 – Carte £28/46

1 Church Road ✉ L15 9EA – ✆ 0151 734 5040 – www.spirerestaurant.co.uk – Closed 1-7 January, Sunday, Monday - Tuesday lunch

🏨 Hard Days Night ⌖ ▣ ♿ ⒶⒸ ⚐

LUXURY · DESIGN The world's only Beatles-themed hotel sits adjacent to the Cavern Club – in a Grade II listed building dating from 1884 – and is packed to the rafters with photos, memorabilia and specially commissioned artwork; the two suites are themed around Lennon and McCartney. Modern brasserie fare is served in Blakes.

110 rooms – 👫 £84/330 – 🖵 £10 – 2 suites

Central Buildings, North John Street ✉ L2 6RR – 𝒞 0151 236 1964 – www.harddaysnighthotel.com

🏨 Hope Street ⌖ ♨ ▣ ♿ ⚐

TOWNHOUSE · DESIGN A minimalist hotel set over two adjoining buildings: bedrooms in the old carriage works have a rustic edge, while those in the former police station are more contemporary – and the top floor suites afford stunning skyline views. Large shards of glass divide the spacious restaurant, which offers modern fare.

89 rooms – 👫 £89/295 – 🖵 £19

40 Hope Street ✉ L1 9DA – 𝒞 0151 709 3000 – www.hopestreethotel.co.uk

🏠 2 Blackburne Terrace Ⓟ

LUXURY · ELEGANT A delightful Georgian house with plenty of personality – the owners are charming and there is a playful element to the place. Individually styled bedrooms come with top quality beds, free-standing baths and extras such as fresh fruit and cut flowers. Modern art features in the large sitting room.

4 rooms – 👫 £180/300

2 Blackburne Terrace ✉ L8 7PJ – 𝒞 0151 708 5474 – www.2blackburneterrace.com – Closed 16 December-19 January

LONG ASHTON - North Somerset → See Bristol

LONG CRENDON

Buckinghamshire - Regional map n° **6**-C2

🍴 Mole & Chicken ⇔ 🏠 🏠 ♿ Ⓟ

TRADITIONAL BRITISH · PUB ⓧ A charming pub built in 1831 as part of a local farm workers' estate, with low wonky ceilings, open fires and a large garden offering commanding country views. The menu features classic British dishes and heartwarming puddings. Staff are friendly and there are five cosy bedrooms in the adjoining house.

Menu £20 – Carte £24/38

Easington ✉ HP18 8EY – 𝒞 01844 208387 – www.themoleandchicken.co.uk

LONG SUTTON

Somerset - Regional map n° **2**-B3

🍴 Devonshire Arms ⇔ 🏠 🏠 ⬥ Ⓟ

REGIONAL CUISINE · PUB ⓧ A striking Grade II listed hunting lodge overlooking the green. Wing-back chairs sit by an open fire and panelled walls are broken up by bold wallpaper; there's also a lovely split-level garden. Appealing menus follow the seasons and keep refined pub classics to the fore. Modern bedrooms are well-furnished.

Carte £23/35

✉ TA10 9LP – 𝒞 01458 241271 – www.thedevonshirearms.com

LONG ROCK

Cornwall - Regional map n° **1**-A3

🍴 Mexico Inn

TRADITIONAL CUISINE · PUB ⓧ This roadside inn is run by an experienced local couple, who host regular quiz and live music nights. It has a touch of the shabby-chic about it, with a wood-burner in the bar and a sunnier room to the rear – and there's a lovely suntrap terrace too. Classic pub dishes are gusty and flavourful.

Carte £22/30

4 Riverside ✉ TR20 8JD – 𝒞 01736 710625 – www.themexicoinn.com

LOOE

Cornwall – Regional map n° **1**–B2

Sardine Factory ⓝ &

SEAFOOD · CONTEMPORARY DÉCOR XX A converted sardine factory on the quayside plays host to this laid-back first floor restaurant which affords views across the harbour to East Looe. The extensive menu champions Cornish seafood, including mussels from Fowey and fish from Looe itself – much of it cooked on the bone.

Specialities: Smoked haddock Scotch egg with curried mayonnaise. Monkfish with purple sprouting broccoli, black olive caramel and almonds. White chocolate blondie with Caramac, peanut and chocolate ice cream.

Carte £25/38

Quay Road, West Looe ✉ PL13 2BX – ✆ 01503 770262 –
www.thesardinefactorylooe.com – Closed 1-2 January, Monday, Tuesday

LOSTWITHIEL

Cornwall – Regional map n° **1**–B2

ⅰ◯ Asquiths

MODERN CUISINE · INTIMATE XX Smartly converted shop with exposed stone walls hung with modern Cornish art, funky lampshades and contemporary styling. Confidently executed dishes feature some original flavour combinations. The atmosphere is relaxed and intimate.

Carte £33/43

19 North Street ✉ PL22 0EF – ✆ 01208 871714 – www.asquithsrestaurant.co.uk –
Closed 1-15 January, 24-30 December, Sunday, Monday, Tuesday - Saturday lunch

LOUGHTON

Essex – Regional map n° **7**–B2

ⅰ◯ Tom, Dick & Harry's ⓝ

MODERN CUISINE · BRASSERIE XX If you're after a fun, lively atmosphere, you're in the right place at this laid-back brasserie with a quirky contemporary style. The experienced chef sources good quality ingredients and the charcoal oven is used to good effect. Global menus include brunch on Saturdays – and it has a playful cocktail list too.

Carte £30/37

153 High Road ✉ IG10 4LF – ✆ 020 3327 3333 – www.tomdickandharrys.co.uk –
Closed Monday

LOWER BEEDING

West Sussex – Regional map n° **4**–D2

✿ Interlude ⓝ

CREATIVE · INTIMATE XXX The 240 acre, Grade I listed Leonardslee Lakes and Gardens were first planted in 1801 and are today famous for their azaleas, rhododendrons and even a wallaby colony. They are now run by the owner of a South African vineyard, who has also restored the Grade II listed Italianate mansion where you'll find this intimate ten-table restaurant.

Both the Executive Chef and the Head Chef hail from South Africa but the two surprise tasting menus keep their focus firmly on the local area, with produce foraged from the garden or sourced from nearby. Skilfully crafted dishes show good balance in their textures and flavours, and take on a creative, original style.

They produce their own gin for the aperitifs and offer wines from their Benguela Cove Lagoon Wine Estate in The Cape.

Specialities: Scallop with green almonds, apple and nettle. Halibut with watercress and seaweed. Sheep's milk with birch tree.

Menu £90/120

Leonardslee Gardens, Brighton Road ✉ RH13 6PS – ✆ 01403 289490 –
www.restaurant-interlude.co.uk – Closed Sunday, Monday, Tuesday, Wednesday -
Saturday lunch

║○ Tom Kemble at The Pass ⓝ 🍴🔥&🕮🕪Ⓟ

MODERN CUISINE · INTIMATE XX The Pass is South Lodge Hotel's most unique, intimate restaurant, with just a glass partition separating it from all the action going on in the kitchen. The tasting menus offer a mix of two different types of dishes: Asian and classical French – the latter stand out as the best.

Menu £50 (lunch), £70/105

South Lodge H. & Spa, Brighton Road ⊠ RH13 6PS – ☏ 01403 891711 – www.exclusive.co.uk – Closed 1-15 January, Monday, Tuesday, Wednesday - Friday lunch

║○ Crabtree 🍴🔥&Ⓟ

TRADITIONAL CUISINE · PUB X A family-run affair with a cosy, lived-in feel, warming fires and cheery, helpful staff. Traditional English dishes come with a touch of refinement and plenty of flavour, and the wine list is well-priced and full of helpful information.

Menu £16/20 – Carte £30/40

Brighton Road ⊠ RH13 6PT – ☏ 01403 892666 – www.crabtreesussex.com – Closed Sunday dinner

🏨 South Lodge H. & Spa 🏌🐾≤🍴🔥🎿🖼🌐🛁🔲&🏊Ⓟ

LUXURY · HISTORIC Intricate carved fireplaces and ornate ceilings are proudly on display in this Victorian mansion, which affords superb South Downs views from its 93 acres. Bedroom are beautifully appointed. Relax in the luxurious spa with its lovely pool and outdoor swim pond, then dine in one of three restaurants.

85 rooms ⊠ – ♔♔ £265/859 – 4 suites

Brighton Road ⊠ RH13 6PS – ☏ 01403 891711 – www.exclusive.co.uk

║○ **Tom Kemble at The Pass** – See restaurant listing

LOWER SLAUGHTER – Gloucestershire → See Bourton-on-the-Water

LUDLOW
Shropshire – Regional map n° **10**–B2

🍴 Charlton Arms ⇔≤🔥&Ⓟ

TRADITIONAL BRITISH · PUB X This pub sits in a commanding position on the banks of the River Teme and is owned by Claude Bosi's brother Cedric and Cedric's wife, Amy. Menus offer something for everyone and the carefully prepared dishes are good value and full of flavour. Most of the bedrooms have river outlooks.

Specialities: Spiced Elwy Valley lamb Scotch egg with paprika mayonnaise. Pan-seared fillet of hake with crushed new potatoes, asparagus and mussel broth. Sticky toffee pudding with vanilla ice cream.

Carte £24/33

Ludford Bridge ⊠ SY8 1PJ – ☏ 01584 872813 – www.thecharltonarms.co.uk

║○ Forelles ≤🍴🔥&🕪Ⓟ

MODERN CUISINE · INTIMATE XX An appealing conservatory restaurant offering lovely views over the hotel gardens and named after the pear tree just outside. Attractively presented dishes use local produce and modern techniques, and feature some unusual flavour and texture combinations.

Menu £34 (lunch), £55/79

Fishmore Hall Hotel, Fishmore Road ⊠ SY8 3DP – ☏ 01584 875148 – www.fishmorehall.co.uk – Closed 2-13 January, Sunday, Monday lunch

║○ Mortimers 🕪⇌

MODERN BRITISH · ELEGANT XX A local forest gives this 16C townhouse restaurant its name. It has plenty of character, courtesy of exposed stone, sloping floors and lovely wood panelling. Concise set menus offer classically rooted dishes with a personal touch.

Menu £25 (lunch), £55/65

17 Corve Street ⊠ SY8 1DA – ☏ 01584 872325 – www.mortimersludlow.co.uk – Closed 26 January-3 February, 27 September-6 October, Sunday, Monday

⬤ Old Downton Lodge

MODERN CUISINE · RURAL XX Set on a 5,500 acre estate, these supremely characterful farm buildings date from medieval to Georgian times. Dining takes place in the 13C stone and timber barn and cooking is contemporary and original with a Scandic style. Bedrooms combine period features with modern amenities.

Menu £30 (lunch), £65/80

Downton on the Rock ⊠ SY8 2HU – ℰ 01568 771826 – www.olddowntonlodge.com – Closed 16 February-2 March, Sunday, Monday, Tuesday - Wednesday lunch

🏠 Fishmore Hall

COUNTRY HOUSE · DESIGN A whitewashed Georgian mansion in half an acre of mature gardens, set just out of town. Original features mix with modern fittings to create a boutique country house feel. Smart bedrooms have bold wallpapers, stylish bathrooms and good views. The lovely spa features an outdoor hot tub.

15 rooms ⌑ – ♥♥ £175/275

Fishmore Road ⊠ SY8 3DP – ℰ 01584 875148 – www.fishmorehall.co.uk – Closed 2-13 January

⬤ **Forelles** – See restaurant listing

LURGASHALL

West Sussex – Regional map n° **4**–C2

⬤ Noah's Ark Inn

TRADITIONAL CUISINE · PUB X A quintessentially English pub in a picturesque village green location; its garden overlooks the cricket pitch. The gloriously rustic interior features a bar, a baronial-style room with cosy sofas and 'The Restaurant' with its large inglenook fireplace. Generous dishes keep things in the traditional vein.

Carte £22/40

The Green ⊠ GU28 9ET – ℰ 01428 707346 – www.noahsarkinn.co.uk – Closed Sunday dinner

LUTON

Luton – Regional map n° **7**–A2

🏛 Luton Hoo

GRAND LUXURY · HISTORIC Stunning 18C house in over 1,000 acres of gardens; some designed by Capability Brown. The main mansion boasts an impressive hallway, numerous beautifully furnished drawing rooms and luxurious bedrooms. The marble-filled Wernher restaurant offers sophisticated classic cuisine. The old stable block houses the smart spa and casual, contemporary brasserie.

228 rooms ⌑ – ♥♥ £210/320 – 23 suites

The Mansion House ⊠ LU1 3TQ – ℰ 01582 734437 – www.lutonhoo.co.uk

LYDFORD

Devon – Regional map n° **1**–C2

⬤ Dartmoor Inn

MODERN BRITISH · PUB X A rustic roadside pub with spacious bedrooms and a shabby-chic style; low ceilings add a cosy feel, while the artwork provides a modern touch. Satisfying classics are full of flavour and there's an emphasis on local produce. Specialities include Devon Ruby Red beef and dishes from the charcoal grill.

Carte £28/52

Moorside ⊠ EX20 4AY – ℰ 01822 820221 – www.dartmoorinn.com – Closed Sunday dinner, Monday

LYMINGTON

Hampshire – Regional map n° **4**–A3

ⅰ○ Elderflower

MODERN CUISINE · FAMILY XX Their motto is 'quintessentially British, with a sprinkling of French', and that's just what you'll find at this proudly run restaurant. Cooking is playful and imaginative – as well as an à la carte they also serve small plates. Bedrooms are simply appointed and the quay is just a stone's throw away.

Menu £45/65

4-5 Quay Street ⊠ *SO41 3AS –* ℰ *01590 676908 –*
www.elderflowerrestaurant.co.uk – Closed Sunday dinner, Monday, Tuesday

LYMPSTONE

Devon – Regional map n° **1**–D2

✿ Lympstone Manor (Michael Caines)

MODERN CUISINE · ELEGANT XxX This tastefully restored Georgian country house sits in peaceful grounds which stretch down to the estuary and its pretty veranda is the perfect spot to admire the view. It's a luxurious place, owned by local chef Michael Caines, and its elegant restaurant looks out over the Exe Estuary and Lyme Bay. The airy Berry Head room offers views over the headland and is a great place for lunch, while the Powderham room is ideal for cosying up in the intimate booths in the evening.

Sophisticated cooking is well-balanced and boldly flavoured and while it has classical undertones, presentation is modern and elaborate. The 8 course 'Signature' tasting menu best demonstrates the team's abilities or there's the 'Estuary' option for pescatarians.

Bedrooms are beautifully furnished; opt for a Garden Room with a fire and a hot tub on the terrace.

Specialities: Langoustine cannelloni with sauce vierge, fennel purée and langoustine bisque. Fillet of beef with horseradish and shallot confit, celeriac purée and red wine sauce. White chocolate candle with rose and raspberry sorbet.

Menu £48 (lunch), £135/155

Lympstone Manor Hotel, Courtlands Lane ⊠ *EX8 3NZ –* ℰ *01395 202040 –*
www.lympstonemanor.co.uk

🏠 Lympstone Manor

COUNTRY HOUSE · ELEGANT A tastefully restored Georgian country house set in peaceful grounds which stretch down to the estuary – the pretty veranda is the perfect spot to admire the view. Luxurious bedrooms are beautifully furnished and have a stylish, modern feel; opt for a Garden Room with a fire and hot tub on the terrace.

21 rooms ⊡ – ♔♔ £385/1139

Courtlands Lane ⊠ *EX8 3NZ –* ℰ *01395 202040 –*
www.lympstonemanor.co.uk

✿ **Lympstone Manor** – See restaurant listing

LYNDHURST

Hampshire – Regional map n° **4**–A2

ⅰ○ Hartnett Holder & Co

ITALIAN · ELEGANT XX Elegant restaurant in an impressive Georgian mansion, offering a relaxed, clubby feel and views over the delightful grounds. The main menu lists Italian favourites like pizzetta, pastas and risottos as well as authentic fish and meat dishes. The sharing menu offers the likes of whole duck 'family-style'.

Menu £28 (lunch) – Carte £50/60

Lime Wood Hotel, Beaulieu Road ⊠ *SO43 7FZ –* ℰ *023 8028 7177 –*
www.limewood.co.uk

🏛️ Lime Wood   ☆ 🐾 ⇆ 🛏 🖼 ⓢ ⌂ 🛋 ⊟ ♿ 🅿️

LUXURY · ELEGANT Impressive Georgian mansion with a stunning spa topped by a herb garden roof. Stylish guest lounges have quality fabrics and furnishings; one is set around a courtyard and features a retractable glass roof. Beautifully furnished bedrooms boast luxurious marble-tiled bathrooms, and many have New Forest views.

33 rooms – 🛏 £385/510 – ⌲ £25 – 14 suites

Beaulieu Road ✉ SO43 7FZ – ✆ 023 8028 7177 – www.limewoodhotel.co.uk

🕸 **Hartnett Holder & Co** – See restaurant listing

LYNTON
Devon – Regional map n° **1**–C1

at Martinhoe West: 4. 25 mi via Coast rd (toll) – Regional map n° **1**–C1

🏠 Old Rectory   ☆ 🐾 🛏 🅿️

COUNTRY HOUSE · ELEGANT Built in the 19C for a rector of Martinhoe's 11C church, this quiet country retreat sits in a charming spot and has a well-tended 3 acre garden with a cascading brook. Bedrooms are bright and modern yet retain period touches: Heddon and Paddock are two of the best. Prices include simple home-cooked dinners.

11 rooms – 🛏 £190/290

✉ EX31 4QT – ✆ 01598 763368 – www.oldrectoryhotel.co.uk –
Closed 1 November-28 March

MAENPORTH BEACH – Cornwall ➜ See Falmouth

MALDON
Essex – Regional map n° **7**–C2

🕸 Rubino Kitchen   🏠 🅿️

MODERN BRITISH · COSY XX Hidden away on Chigborough Farm is this tiny, intimate restaurant – a former fisherman's lodge – decorated with fishing memorabilia. Flavour-packed cooking mixes English and Italian influences. At dinner, choose 2-5 courses from a monthly changing menu of 9 dishes.

Menu £25/46 – Carte £18/24

*Chigborough Farm, Chigborough Rd, Heybridge ✉ CM9 4RE – ✆ 01621 855579 –
www.rubinokitchen.co.uk – Closed 25 December-8 January, Monday, Tuesday*

MALMESBURY
Wiltshire – Regional map n° **2**–C2

❀❀ The Dining Room   ❀ 🛏 ♿ 🕸 🅿️

ASIAN INFLUENCES · ELEGANT XxxX Twelve acres of formal gardens surround this charming Cotswold stone house, which dates back to 1802 and offers lovely views over the countryside. Head Chef Niall Keating oversees both the elegant brasserie and the intimate dining room; the latter is the best place to sample dishes packed full of his personality. Here, the room is neutral and serene, and that keeps the focus where it matters: firmly on the food.

Accomplished modern cooking has a well-measured originality and many Asian elements (inspired by Niall's travels) feature on the appealing multi-course set menus. To start, you are invited into the kitchen for snacks. Service is charming and attentive, and the enthusiastic sommelier offers some creative suggestions, with organic, bio-dynamic and natural wines to the fore.

Luxurious modern bedrooms come with sumptuous bathrooms.

Specialities: 'Risotto', chorizo, scallop. Salmon, aloe vera, yeast beurre blanc. Chocolate crémeux, olive oil, nasturtium.

Menu £95 (lunch)/125

*Whatley Manor Hotel, Easton Grey ✉ SN16 0RB – ✆ 01666 822888 –
www.whatleymanor.com – Closed Sunday lunch, Monday, Tuesday, Wednesday, Thursday lunch*

🍴○ Grey's Brasserie 🛏🏠&🅿

MODERN BRITISH · BRASSERIE XX The slightly less formal alternative to What-ley Manor's 'Dining Room' is this elegant grey-hued brasserie; ask for a booth or dine in the garden in the summer months. Salad and vegetables from the kitchen garden feature on modern menus with a British bias.

Menu £25 (lunch) – Carte £31/52

Whatley Manor Hotel, Easton Grey ⊠ SN16 0RB – ℰ 01666 822888 –
www.whatleymanor.com

🏨 Whatley Manor 🛏🌳⟨🛏🖼🕥⿴🔊⎗&�%🅿

LUXURY · CONTEMPORARY A charming Cotswold stone house built in 1802 and set in 12 acres of formal gardens. Guest areas include a delightful wood-pa-nelled sitting room, a stunning spa, a top class business centre and a cinema. Lux-urious, individually decorated bedrooms have sumptuous bathrooms and a con-temporary feel.

23 rooms ⊡ – ♥♥ £249/549 – 8 suites

Easton Grey ⊠ SN16 0RB – ℰ 01666 822888 – www.whatleymanor.com

   ❀❀ **The Dining Room** · 🍴○ **Grey's Brasserie** – See restaurant listing

at Crudwell North: 4 mi on A429

🍴○ Potting Shed 🛏🏠♻🅿

REGIONAL CUISINE · PUB X Spacious, light-filled pub with contemporary décor, exposed beams and a relaxing feel. Monthly changing menus offer wholesome, satisfying dishes, with vegetables and herbs from their garden.

Carte £23/35

The Street ⊠ SN16 9EW – ℰ 01666 577833 – www.thepottingshedpub.com

MALTBY
Stockton-on-Tees – Regional map n° **14**-B3

❀ Chadwicks Inn 🛏🏠🍴○🅿

MODERN CUISINE · PUB X Well-prepared dishes, a wide-ranging wine list and smartly attired staff add a touch of formality to this village pub; although you can still come just for a drink in the bar. Pub classics sit alongside more modern creations; all are colourful and eye-catching and show a clear understanding of flavours.

Specialities: Ham hock pressing, quail's egg, pease pudding and pineapple relish. Loin of halibut, lobster ravioli, butter sauce and seashore vegetables. Salted cara-mel custard tart, maple ice cream and pecan praline.

Menu £20 (lunch)/28 – Carte £26/51

High Lane ⊠ TS8 0BG – ℰ 01642 590300 – www.chadwicksinnmaltby.co.uk –
Closed Sunday dinner, Monday

MALTON
North Yorkshire – Regional map n° **13**-C2

🍴○ New Malton 🍴○

TRADITIONAL BRITISH · PUB X 18C stone pub with open fires, reclaimed furni-ture and photos of old town scenes. A good-sized menu offers hearty pub clas-sics with the odd more adventurous dish thrown in; cooking is unfussy and fla-voursome with an appealing Northern bias.

Carte £21/32

2-4 Market Place ⊠ YO17 7LX – ℰ 01653 693998 – www.thenewmalton.co.uk

🏨 The Talbot 🌳🛏&🔊🅿

BOUTIQUE HOTEL · HISTORIC This early 17C hunting lodge is owned by the Fitzwilliam Estate and features an impressive wooden staircase and stylish shabby-chic guest areas. Contemporary bedrooms have smart marble bathrooms. Dine from a menu of modern classics – the Garden Room is the most comfortable.

26 rooms ⊡ – ♥♥ £120/295

Yorkersgate ⊠ YO17 7AJ – ℰ 01653 639096 – www.talbotmalton.co.uk

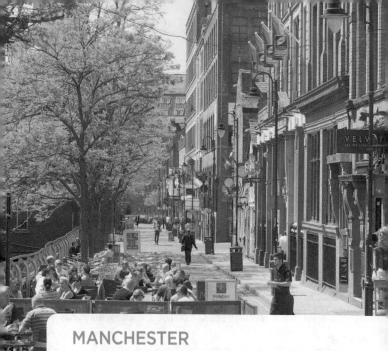

MANCHESTER

Greater Manchester – Regional map n° **11**-B2

Top tips!

The Manchester dining scene has exploded in recent years and with many opportunities presented by the opening of huge new residential and retail developments in the city's former warehouses, it now offers a great degree of vibrancy and diversity.

The Science and Industry Museum sits on the site of the world's first intercity railway, now a heritage site, and looks to both the past and the future; while the historic John Rylands Library still fulfils its original purpose – as well as attracting visitors interested in its striking Gothic architecture.

Markets include Altrincham and Castlefield – the latter with a strong foodie focus – where must-tries include Bury black pudding and Manchester tart; **20 Stories** does a great version of the latter, accompanied by a super city view. Vegans are well-catered for at **The Allotment**; **Tast** offers tasty Catalan food; and **Adam Reid** focuses on bold, modern cooking.

P. Frilet/hemis.fr

Restaurants

⍟ Mana ⓝ (Simon Martin)   AC

CREATIVE BRITISH · CONTEMPORARY DÉCOR XX There is so much to love about Mana, not least of which is the service; the team create a relaxed atmosphere, while at the same time letting you know that this is a place that's serious about its food. Chef Simon Martin has spent years garnering experience and ideas from restaurants around the world and now brings this knowledge to Manchester. The room is modern, with an impressively high ceiling and immaculately laid tables set with bespoke earthenware and china.

The smartly fitted open-kitchen is a reflection of Simon's clear, unadulterated vision; here the chefs create exciting modern British dishes with Nordic influences. These are packed with originality and, while at first they might appear simple, are complex in their delivery. The menu is a 12-16 course surprise which unfolds throughout the evening and is perfectly paced.

Specialities: Beef tartare with rhubarb and oxalis. Seaweed-fed hogget with ramsons and salad. Baked pear with sheep's milk and sorrel.

Menu £50 (lunch)/105

Off plan – *42 Blossom Street* ✉ *M4 6BF* – ☎ *0161 392 7294* – *www.manarestaurant.co.uk* – *Closed 12-22 April, 1-8 July, 22 December-3 January, Sunday, Monday, Tuesday, Wednesday - Friday lunch*

⍟ El Gato Negro

SPANISH · TAPAS BAR X The buzzy 'Black Cat' sits in a pedestrianised street. The ground floor houses a bar, the first floor plays host to an industrial-style dining room and the top floor is home to a private events space with a retractable roof. Appealing tapas dishes include meats from the Josper grill.

Specialities: Catalan bread with olive oil, garlic and tomato. Chargrilled lamb skewers with spiced chickpea purée and harissa. Creme Catalan.

Menu £15 (lunch) – Carte £20/35

Town plan A2-e – *52 King Street* ✉ *M2 4LY* – ☎ *0161 694 8585* – *www.elgatonegrotapas.com* – *Closed Monday lunch*

❍ Adam Reid at The French

MODERN BRITISH · ELEGANT XXX An intimate hotel restaurant created in the Belle Époque age and brought up-to-date with a moody colour scheme, striking chandeliers and booths down the centre of the room. Boldly flavoured modern dishes focus on one main ingredient and the chefs present and explain the dishes themselves. Desserts are playful.

Menu £65/90

Town plan A2-x – *Midland Hotel, Peter Street* ✉ *M60 2DS* – ☎ *0161 932 4780* – *www.the-french.co.uk* – *Closed 10-24 August, Sunday, Monday, Tuesday - Thursday lunch*

❍ Asha's

INDIAN · ELEGANT XX Start in the intimately lit basement cocktail bar then move up to the exotic, glamorous restaurant. The modern Indian menu offers both 'Classic' and 'Creative' curries; kebabs are a specialty, as is the traditional masala recipe.

Menu £32/40 – Carte £28/50

Town plan A2-c – *47 Peter Street* ✉ *M2 3NG* – ☎ *0161 832 5309* – *www.ashasrestaurant.co.uk* – *Closed Monday*

❍ Restaurant MCR ⓝ   AC

MODERN BRITISH · CHIC XX Restaurant MCR sits on the second floor of a tower in the heart of Spinningfields. Start with a drink on the terrace before heading for the bright, industrial-style dining room with its large open kitchen. Complex modern dishes feature on set and tasting menus. Don't miss the Manchester tart.

Menu £35 (lunch), £50/75

Town plan A2-u – *18-22 Bridge Street* ✉ *M3 3BZ* – ☎ *0161 835 2557* – *www.restaurantmcr.com* – *Closed 1-13 January, 28 July-12 August, Sunday-Tuesday lunch*

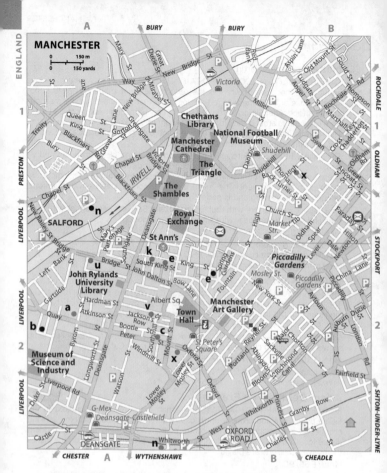

MANCHESTER

🍴○ **63 Degrees**   🛋 ♿ A/C

FRENCH · NEIGHBOURHOOD XX The bustling Northern Quarter is home to this family-run restaurant. The experienced owner-chef hails from France and his classic dishes are cooked with pride and passion using both local and imported French produce. The set lunch represents good value.

Menu £16 (lunch)/28 – Carte £40/60

Town plan B1-x – *104 High Street* ⊠ *M4 1HQ* – ℰ *0161 832 5438* – *www.63degrees.co.uk* – *Closed 22 December-2 January, Monday*

🍴○ **Tast** 🆕   A/C 🍽 🍷

SPANISH · BISTRO XX Tast is housed on the first two floors of this three-storey operation; ask for a seat on the lower level to watch the chefs behind the counter. Uncomplicated Catalan dishes are executed to a high level and are tasty and satisfying. A set menu is served in top floor Enxaneta Tast.

Carte £23/29

Town plan A2-k – *20-22 King Street* ⊠ *M2 6AG* – ℰ *0161 806 0547* – *www.tastcatala.com* – *Closed Monday*

⅋○ 20 Stories

MODERN BRITISH · DESIGN XX Set on the 19th floor, in the old cotton mill area, is this huge design-led restaurant. A central cocktail bar divides the room and there's a glass-walled terrace with super views. Modern British menus offer everything from homely classics to refined restaurant dishes and most produce is from within 50 miles.

Menu £28 (lunch) – Carte £30/64

Town plan A2-a – *No. 1 Spinningfields, 1 Hardman Square* ⌂ *M3 3EB* – ℰ *0161 204 3333* – *www.20stories.co.uk*

⅋○ Wood Manchester

MODERN BRITISH · DESIGN XX The old Gaythorn Gas Works redevelopment is home to this large modern restaurant run by MasterChef winner Simon Wood. There's a lively buzz to the place, which could best be described as 'industrial-chic' in looks. Carefully crafted dishes are modern and creative.

Menu £28 – Carte £35/57

Town plan A2-n – *Jack Rosenthal Street, First Street* ⌂ *M15 4RA* – ℰ *0161 236 5211* – *www.woodmanchester.com* – *Closed Sunday, Monday*

⅋○ Allotment

VEGAN · BISTRO X A basement in the heart of the city plays host to this spacious modern restaurant with a rustic bar and a dining room adorned with monochrome photographs. Flavour-packed vegan dishes take on a modern approach and are prepared with skill and care; the cauliflower 3 ways is very tasty.

Menu £10 (lunch)/65 – Carte £30/36

Town plan A2-v – *16 Lloyd Street* ⌂ *M2 5WA* – ℰ *0161 478 1331* – *www.allotmentvegan.co.uk*

Hotels

Lowry

LUXURY · DESIGN Modern and hugely spacious, with excellent facilities, an impressive spa and a minimalist feel: art displays and exhibitions feature throughout. Stylish bedrooms with oversized windows; some have river views. The airy first floor restaurant serves a wide-ranging menu.

165 rooms – ⅋⅋ £119/299 – ⌂ £19 – 7 suites

Town plan A1-n – *50 Dearmans Pl, Chapel Wharf, Salford* ⌂ *M3 5LH* – ℰ *0161 827 4000* – *www.thelowryhotel.com*

Hotel Gotham

LUXURY · ELEGANT This Grade II listed former bank has something of a Manhattan-style exterior, hence its name. Stylish modern bedrooms have black and white prints of Manchester and New York on the walls and some have projected 'wonderwalls' instead of windows. The delightful all-day dining room serves English classics.

60 rooms – ⅋⅋ £250/450 – ⌂ £15

Town plan B2-e – *100 King Street* ⌂ *M2 4WU* – ℰ *0161 413 0000* – *www.hotelgotham.co.uk*

Great John Street

HISTORIC · CONTEMPORARY This stylish, boutique hotel was once a wonderful Victorian schoolhouse; you can hold a meeting in the old Headmaster's study! All of the bedrooms are duplex suites with roll-top baths. Relax on the roof terrace with its cocktail bar and hot-tub. There's no restaurant but they do offer room service.

30 rooms – ⅋⅋ £250/450 – ⌂ £18

Town plan A2-b – *Great John Street* ⌂ *M3 4FD* – ℰ *0161 831 3211* – *www.greatjohnstreet.co.uk*

MARAZION
Cornwall – Regional map n° **1**–A3

🍴 **Ben's Cornish Kitchen**   ♿

MODERN CUISINE · SIMPLE 🍴 Rustic family-run eatery; sit upstairs for views over the rooftops to St Michael's Mount. Unfussy lunches are followed by sophisticated dinners, which feature some interesting flavour combinations. They offer 25 wines by the glass.

Menu £28/34

West End ⊠ TR17 0EL – ℰ 01736 719200 – www.benscornishkitchen.com – Closed 22 December-16 January, Sunday, Monday

at Perranuthnoe Southeast: 1. 75 mi by A394 – Regional map n° **1**–A3

🏠 **Ednovean Farm**

FAMILY · PERSONALISED 17C granite barn in a tranquil spot overlooking the bay and surrounded by 22 acres of sub-tropical gardens and paddocks. Individually styled bedrooms feature local toiletries; the Blue Room has a French bed, a roll-top bath and a terrace. Complimentary sherry is left in the hall. Have a range-cooked breakfast at the oak table or a continental selection in bed.

3 rooms – 🛏 £100/150

⊠ TR20 9LZ – ℰ 01736 711883 – www.ednoveanfarm.co.uk – Closed 1 December-31 January

MARGATE
Kent – Regional map n° **5**–D1

🍴 **Angela's** 🆕

SEAFOOD · FRIENDLY 🍴 A friendly team run this understated little bistro set just off the esplanade. Their ethos is fiercely local and sustainable and even the tables are made of compressed recycled plastic. The concise blackboard menu lists sustainable fish and a vegetarian option – no meat – and cooking is pleasingly unfussy.

Menu £18 (lunch) – Carte £23/40

21 The Parade ⊠ CT9 1EX – ℰ 01843 319978 – www.angelasofmargate.com – Closed Sunday dinner, Monday, Tuesday

🍴 **Bottega Caruso** 🆕

ITALIAN · FRIENDLY 🍴 A fresh-looking former pub plays host to this sweet little deli-cum-osteria offering southern Italian fare. The pastas are made fresh every day and most of the artisanal ingredients come from the owner's family and friends back in her home region of Campania. Service is engaging and heartfelt.

Carte £27/35

2-4 Broad Street ⊠ CT9 1EW – ℰ 01843 297142 – www.bottegacaruso.com – Closed Sunday dinner-Wednesday, Thursday dinner, Saturday dinner

🍴 **Hantverk & Found**

SEAFOOD · SIMPLE 🍴 The owner of this bohemian café and adjoining wine bar is passionate about art, so you'll find an exhibition by local artists in the cellar. Choose from the blackboard or have the daily menu, where seafood from the Kent coast features in unfussy dishes bursting with freshness and flavour.

Carte £25/40

16-18 King Street ⊠ CT9 1DA – ℰ 01843 280454 – www.hantverk-found.co.uk – Closed 22 December-5 January, Sunday dinner, Monday, Tuesday, Wednesday

MARLBOROUGH
Wiltshire – Regional map n° **2**–D2

🍴 **Rick Stein**

SEAFOOD · ELEGANT ✕✕ An attractive double-fronted townhouse where 5 charming rooms spread over 2 floors make you feel like you're dining privately. The daily menu offers the best value; for those pushing the boat out, try the turbot on the bone.

Menu £25 (lunch) – Carte £27/57

Lloran House, 42a High Street ⊠ SN8 1HQ – ℰ 01672 233333 –
www.rickstein.com

at Little Bedwyn East: 9. 5 mi by A4

🍴 **Harrow at Little Bedwyn**   🕸 🏠 🕸

MODERN CUISINE · INTIMATE ✕✕ This former pub is tucked away in a small village and has an intimate, understated, neighbourhood style. Cooking has a classical base but exhibits some modern elements; choose between several set menus. The comprehensive wine list champions the New World and there's a good selection by the glass.

Menu £40 (lunch), £60/85

⊠ SN8 3JP – ℰ 01672 870871 –
www.theharrowatlittlebedwyn.com –
Closed 23 December-8 January, Sunday, Monday, Tuesday

at West Overton West: 4 mi on A4

🍴 **Bell**   🏠 ♿ **P**

MODERN BRITISH · PUB ✕ A simple, friendly pub, rescued from oblivion by a local couple, who hired an experienced pair to run it. The menu mixes pub classics with Mediterranean-influenced dishes; presentation is modern but not at the expense of flavour.

Carte £25/36

Bath Road ⊠ SN8 1QD – ℰ 01672 861099 –
www.thebellwestoverton.co.uk –
Closed Sunday dinner, Monday

MARLOW

Buckinghamshire – Regional map n° **6**-C3

✿✿ **Hand and Flowers** (Tom Kerridge)   ⇔ ⇕ **P**

MODERN BRITISH · PUB ✕✕ Norfolk-born Tom Kerridge has successfully turned this characterful beamed pub into a world-renowned destination – and as such, you'll need to book well in advance. Arrive early for a drink beside the log-burning stove in the appealing bar, then head through to the smart, rustic restaurant with low beams, flagged floors and nooks and crannies aplenty.

Refined British dishes are elevated to new heights yet remain reassuringly familiar, and the chefs aren't afraid to push the boundaries while at the same time knowing when to hold back. Sourcing of ingredients is given due reverence, execution is confident and presentation is first-rate. The playful dishes are often the best. For an extra-special occasion book The Shed, an intimate dining space with a special menu prepared by a dedicated team.

The luxurious bedrooms are dotted about the town.

Specialities: Glazed omelette of smoked haddock and parmesan. Fillet of Stokes Marsh Farm beef with Hand & Flowers chips and béarnaise sauce. Vanilla crème brûlée.

Menu £30 (lunch) – Carte £51/75

126 West Street ⊠ SL7 2BP – ℰ 01628 482277 –
www.thehandandflowers.co.uk –
Closed Sunday dinner

⌘ **The Coach**

MODERN BRITISH · PUB Ⅹ If you can't get a booking at the Hand and Flowers, worry not, as there's usually room at its more casual counterpart – and here they don't take reservations. It's a cosy, pleasingly unpretentious kind of a place, with studded red leather chairs and a comfortingly traditional air. The zinc-topped counter is the best place to sit, with its views of the rotisserie and open kitchen, and there's a good chance the chefs will deliver dishes themselves here too.

Breakfast could include kedgeree or a waffle with truffle honey, and you can come later in the morning just for coffee and cake. The main menu of small plates is headed 'Meat', 'No Meat' and 'Sweet', allowing you to compose your meal how-ever you wish; 3 plates is probably about right or let the knowledgeable serving team guide you. Dishes are refined, detailed and packed with flavour – be sure to save room for dessert.

Specialities: Mussels marinière with warm stout and brown bread. Beef biltong chilli with Monterey Jack and lime. The Coach profiteroles with soured vanilla cream and chocolate sauce.

Carte £22/34

3 West Street ⊠ SL7 2LS –
℘ 01628 481704 – www.thecoachmarlow.co.uk

Ⅰ○ **Sindhu**

INDIAN · CONTEMPORARY DÉCOR ⅩⅩ This hotel restaurant is named after one of the longest rivers in the world and sits in a great spot beside a gushing weir. South Indian recipes are given a sophisticated modern makeover to cre-ate refined, subtly spiced dishes. Atul Kochhar is the consultant and cooks here twice a week.

Menu £22 (lunch) – Carte £42/74

Compleat Angler Hotel, Marlow Bridge, Bisham Road ⊠ SL7 1RG –
℘ 01628 405405 – www.sindhurestaurant.co.uk

MARTINHOE - Devon ➜ See Lynton

MASHAM
North Yorkshire – Regional map n° **13**–B1

Ⅰ○ **Vennell's**

TRADITIONAL BRITISH · INTIMATE ⅩⅩ This personally run restaurant has pur-ple walls, boldly patterned chairs and a striking feature wall – at weekends, sit downstairs surrounded by local art. Seasonal menus offer 4 choices per course and cooking has a modern edge.

Menu £38

7 Silver Street ⊠ HG4 4DX –
℘ 01765 689000 – www.vennellsrestaurant.co.uk – Closed 1-9 January,
24 August-3 September, Sunday, Monday, Tuesday, Wednesday - Saturday lunch

🏚 **Swinton Park**

HISTORIC · CLASSIC A 17C castle with Georgian and Victorian additions, set on a 22,000 acre estate; try your hand at shooting, riding or falconry or relax in the state-of-the-art spa. The grand interior features open fires, ornate plas-terwork, oil portraits and antiques. Dine in the relaxed brasserie or impressive dining room.

32 rooms – 🛏 £185/495 – 6 suites

Swinton ⊠ HG4 4JH –
℘ 01765 680900 – www.swintonestate.com

MATFIELD
Kent – Regional map n° **5**–B2

The Poet at Matfield

MODERN CUISINE · PUB This unassuming-looking dining pub (named after local resident and war poet Siegfried Sassoon), has a modest rustic style and an atmospheric little dining room with an inglenook fireplace. 'Flavoursome, fresh and careful' is the South African chef's mantra and his dishes are modern and sophisticated.

Menu £23 – Carte £36/64

Maidstone Road ⊠ TN12 7JH – ℰ 01892 722416 – www.thepoetatmatfield.co.uk – Closed Sunday dinner, Monday

MATLOCK
Derbyshire – Regional map n° **9**–B1

Stones

MODERN BRITISH · NEIGHBOURHOOD Negotiate the steep steps down to this small riverside restaurant and head for the front room with its floor to ceiling windows. Unfussy, modern British dishes are attractively presented and display the odd Mediterranean touch.

Menu £25 (lunch), £36/40

1c Dale Road ⊠ DE4 3LT – ℰ 01629 56061 – www.stones-restaurant.co.uk – Closed 25 December-2 January, Sunday, Monday

MAWGAN PORTH – Cornwall → See Newquay

MELLS
Somerset – Regional map n° **2**–C2

Talbot Inn

TRADITIONAL BRITISH · PUB This 15C coaching inn's cobbled courtyard leads through to a series of rustic rooms: there's a cosy open-fired sitting room, a snug bar offering real ales and an elegant Grill Room which opens at weekends. Gutsy cooking is seasonal, modern and full of flavour. Comfy bedrooms have an understated style

Carte £25/42

Selwood Street ⊠ BA11 3PN – ℰ 01373 812254 – www.talbotinn.com

MELTON MOWBRAY
Leicestershire – Regional map n° **9**–B2

Stapleford Park

COUNTRY HOUSE · PERSONALISED Beautiful stately home in 500 acres of landscaped grounds, with grand drawing rooms, exceedingly comfortable bedrooms and an ornate rococo dining room. British designers have styled the rooms in keeping with their original features; look out for the impressive Grinling Gibbons wood carvings.

55 rooms ⊇ – †† £170/320 – 3 suites

⊠ LE14 2EF – ℰ 01572 787000 – www.staplefordpark.com – Closed 1-5 January

MID LAVANT – West Sussex → See Chichester

MIDDLEHAM
North Yorkshire – Regional map n° **13**–B1

The Saddle Room

TRADITIONAL BRITISH · PUB Located within an area of parkland close to the 'Forbidden Corner', is this converted stable decked out with equine paraphernalia – ask for a table in a stall! Unfussy menus offer the usual pub favourites alongside more interesting dishes like sticky pig cheeks. Stylish bedrooms are named after racehorses.

Carte £22/54

Tupgill Park, Coverdale ⊠ DL8 4TJ – ℰ 01969 640596 – www.thesaddleroom.co.uk – Closed Sunday dinner

MIDDLETON TYAS
North Yorkshire – Regional map n° **13**–B1

Ⅰ○ **The Coach House at Middleton Lodge**
⇦ ╒═ ☂ & 🕦 ⇔ **P**

MODERN BRITISH · DESIGN XX A stylishly converted coach house to the Georgian mansion where the owner grew up. The bar is where the coaches once parked and the laid-back all-day restaurant is in the former stables. There's also a more formal restaurant serving sophisticated tasting menus. Bedrooms are contemporary.

Carte £26/46

Kneeton Lane ⊠ *DL10 6NJ – 𝒞 01325 377977 – www.middletonlodge.co.uk*

MIDHURST
West Sussex – Regional map n° **4**–C2

at Henley North: 4. 5 mi by A286

Ⅰ○ **Duke of Cumberland Arms**
╒═ ☂ **P**

TRADITIONAL BRITISH · PUB X A hidden gem, nestled in pretty tiered gardens with trickling streams, trout ponds and splendid South Downs views. Sit in the cosy bar or more modern dining area which opens onto a terrace. Appealing menus offer carefully prepared seasonal dishes: lunch sees pub classics and dinner shifts things up a gear.

Carte £33/48

⊠ *GU27 3HQ – 𝒞 01428 652280 – www.dukeofcumberland.com*

MILFORD-ON-SEA
Hampshire – Regional map n° **4**–A3

ⅠO **Verveine**
&

SEAFOOD · FRIENDLY X Behind this attractive-looking fishmonger's is a bright and airy New England style restaurant with an open kitchen. Breads are baked twice-daily, veg is from the raised beds and smoking takes place on-site. The focus is on wonderfully fresh fish and cooking is original with the odd playful twist.

Menu £17 (lunch), £44/90

98 High Street ⊠ *SO41 0QE – 𝒞 01590 642176 – www.verveine.co.uk –*
Closed 24 December-15 January, Sunday, Monday

MILTON ABBOT – Devon → See Tavistock

MINSTER LOVELL
Oxfordshire – Regional map n° **6**–A2

ⅠO **Old Swan**
⇦ ╒═ ☂ & **P**

TRADITIONAL CUISINE · PUB X A quintessential country inn set in a lovely riverside village. Dine in the charming garden or in one of the open-fired front rooms with their beams and flagged floors. Menus blend hearty pub favourites with more restaurant-style dishes. Characterful bedrooms have a romantic feel.

Carte £27/47

⊠ *OX29 ORN – 𝒞 01993 774441 – www.oldswanminstermill.co.uk*

MISTLEY
Essex – Regional map n° **7**–D2

ⅠO **Mistley Thorn**
⇦ 🕦

SEAFOOD · FRIENDLY X An appealing bistro with a homeware shop and cookery school. The focus is on sourcing local, seasonal ingredients and then showing them off. Local seafood is to the fore and most of the fish and meat is grilled over wood. Bedrooms are stylishly understated; some have river views.

Menu £18 – Carte £27/41

High Street ⊠ *CO11 1HE – 𝒞 01206 392821 – www.mistleythorn.co.uk*

MOBBERLEY
Cheshire East – Regional map n° **11**–B3

ⅱ○ **Church Inn** 🍴🏠♿🅿

TRADITIONAL CUISINE · PUB 🗙 18C brick pub beside the bowling green, offering lovely views of the 12C church from its terrace. Regularly changing menus reflect the seasons, with light dishes in summer and hearty stews in winter. Hand-pumped local beers feature.

Carte £26/45

Church Lane ⊠ WA16 7RD – ℰ 01565 873178 – www.churchinnmobberley.co.uk

MORETONHAMPSTEAD
Devon – Regional map n° **1**–C2

ⅱ○ **The Horse** 🏠♿

MEDITERRANEAN CUISINE · PUB 🗙 Behind its unassuming façade, this rustic pub conceals an appealing flag-floored dining room and a sunny Mediterranean-style courtyard. The unfussy cooking has more than a hint of the Mediterranean about it, with authentic thin-crust pizzas baked in a custom-built oven and tapas served in the evening.

Carte £21/42

7 George Street ⊠ TQ13 8PG – ℰ 01647 440242 – www.thehorsedartmoor.co.uk – Closed Sunday lunch, Monday

MORETON-IN-MARSH
Gloucestershire – Regional map n° **2**–D1

ⅱ○ **Mulberry** 🍴♿🆎🅿

MODERN BRITISH · DESIGN 🗙🗙 A formal restaurant with an enclosed walled garden, set within a part-16C manor house. Cooking is modern and adventurous and features some challenging combinations – choose between a 4 course set menu and an 8 course tasting menu.

Menu £45/65

Manor House Hotel, High Street ⊠ GL56 0LJ – ℰ 01608 650501 – www.cotswold-inns-hotels.co.uk – Closed Monday - Saturday lunch

MORSTON – Norfolk → See Blakeney

MOULTON
Suffolk – Regional map n° **8**–B2

ⅱ○ **Packhorse Inn** ⇦🍴🏠♿♿🅿

MODERN CUISINE · PUB 🗙 A smart modern pub set near the green in a pretty village and named after the 15C flint bridge which spans the river. Cooking keeps things classical, with the focus firmly on the ingredients' natural flavours. Ultra-stylish bedrooms have plush furnishings and roll-top baths.

Menu £19 (lunch) – Carte £26/45

Bridge Street ⊠ CB8 8SP – ℰ 01638 751818 – www.thepackhorseinn.com

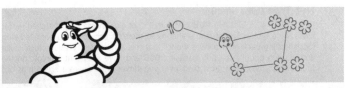

MOUNTSORREL

Leicestershire – Regional map n° **9**–B2

සි **John's House** (John Duffin)   **P**

MODERN CUISINE · RUSTIC XX The 4,000 acre Duffin family farm plays host to a 16C farmhouse – where the eponymous John was born and now cooks – along with a shop, a café, a petting farm and a motor museum. It's a real family affair, with his parents, brother and sister all involved.

Cooking doesn't get more 'farm to plate' than this, with the surrounding fields supplying most of the ingredients, from herbs, vegetables and fruits to sheep, pigs and cattle. Butchery takes place on-site and they use every part of the animal; rare breeds are a feature and include Leicester Longwool sheep and Gloucester Old Spot and Tamworth pigs.

The talented chef has a great appreciation for his ingredients and knows what it takes to get the best out of them. His accomplished, interesting dishes show a real understanding of both flavours and textures and feature some original combinations. Lunch sees a concise, great value menu and there's a 7 course tasting menu for those who want to experience the full extent of the kitchen's talents.

Specialities: Bradgate Park venison tartare with lovage, artichoke and smoked confit egg yolk. Lightly salted fillet of cod with brawn, aubergine, passion fruit and curry spices. Carrot sorbet with yoghurt, liquorice and mint.

Menu £30 (lunch), £48/79

Stonehurst Farm, 141 Loughborough Road ✉ LE12 7AR – ☎ 01509 415569 – www.johnshouse.co.uk – Closed 22 December-7 January, Sunday, Monday

MOUSEHOLE

Cornwall – Regional map n° **1**–A3

⁙◯ **Old Coastguard**   ⊗ ⇦ ⇇ ⌂ 🏠 ♿ **P**

MEDITERRANEAN CUISINE · BISTRO X Old coastguard's cottage in a small fishing village, with a laid-back, open-plan interior, a sub-tropical garden and views towards St Clement's Isle. Well-presented brasserie dishes display a Mediterranean edge; great wine selection. Individually styled bedrooms – some with balconies, most with sea views.

Menu £24 (lunch)/27 – Carte £29/38

The Parade ✉ TR19 6PR – ☎ 01736 731222 – www.oldcoastguardhotel.co.uk

⁙◯ **2 Fore Street**   🏠

SEAFOOD · FRIENDLY X Friendly café-cum-bistro with a delightful courtyard terrace and garden. All-day menus offer everything from coffee and cake to a full meal, with brunch a feature at weekends. Tasty, unfussy dishes are guided by the day's catch.

Carte £25/42

2 Fore Street ✉ TR19 6PF – ☎ 01736 731164 – www.2forestreet.co.uk – Closed 3 January-10 February

MURCOTT

Oxfordshire – Regional map n° **6**–B2

සි **Nut Tree** (Mike North)   ⇦ 🏠 **P**

TRADITIONAL BRITISH · PUB X With its 15C origins and smartly thatched roof it looks like a typical English pub – and inside there's a cosy beamed bar filled with locals kicking back after a day's work – but this is no ordinary village local. Mike and Imogen bought the pub back in 2006 and have since put Murcott on the foodie map; they even grow their own vegetables and rear rare breed pigs out the back.

It's a friendly, welcoming place: the rear extension has more of a restaurant feel, while the lively front bar is the place to be if you like a bit of atmosphere. You'll always find a couple of refined pub classics on the menu but it comprises mainly of satisfying, full-flavoured restaurant-style dishes – maybe confit leg of Barbary duck followed by raspberry soufflé. For a quick snack try the Bar & Garden menu or for the full experience go for the 8 course tasting menu.

Specialities: Veal sweetbreads with maple glaze and celeriac purée. Best end & braised shoulder of lamb 'en crépinette' with herb aioli and braising juices. Passion fruit soufflé with passion fruit sorbet.

Menu £75 – Carte £37/68

*Main Street ⊠ OX5 2RE – ℰ 01865 331253 – www.nuttreeinn.co.uk –
Closed 27 December-10 January, Sunday dinner, Monday*

NAILSWORTH
Gloucestershire – Regional map n° **2**-C1

○ **Wilder**
MODERN CUISINE · INTIMATE XX Everyone arrives at 7. 30pm for a 3-hour surprise menu accompanied by optional matching wines. Humble ingredients are used in well-balanced, ambitious combinations. Service is structured but passionate.

Menu £70

*Market Street ⊠ GL6 0BX – ℰ 01453 835483 – www.dinewilder.co.uk –
Closed Sunday, Monday, Tuesday, Wednesday - Saturday lunch*

○ **Wild Garlic**
MODERN BRITISH · INTIMATE X This attractive little restaurant has a friendly, laid-back feel. Modern bistro dishes include artisan pastas, which are something of a speciality – the 5 spice pulled pork tagliatelle is a hit. Enjoy lunch on the south-facing terrace and brunch at weekends. Bedrooms are stylish and well-equipped.

Carte £25/45

*3 Cossack Square ⊠ GL6 0DB – ℰ 01453 832615 – www.wild-garlic.co.uk –
Closed Sunday dinner, Monday, Tuesday*

NETHER WESTCOTE – Gloucestershire → See Stow-on-the-Wold

NEW ALRESFORD
Hampshire – Regional map n° **4**-B2

⊛ **Pulpo Negro**
SPANISH · TAPAS BAR X A characterful, laid-back restaurant in an old townhouse; its name translates as 'Black Octopus'. The stylish interior features exposed brick, rough floorboards and an open kitchen. The chef-owner hails from Barcelona and his tasty, authentic tapas is accompanied by a good choice of Spanish wines.

Specialities: Catalan tomato bread. Chicken thighs with almonds and capers. Whiskey tart.

Carte £16/44

*28 Broad Street ⊠ SO24 9AQ – ℰ 01962 732262 – www.pulponegro.co.uk –
Closed Sunday, Monday*

NEW MILTON
Hampshire – Regional map n° **4**-A3

○ **The Kitchen**
MODERN BRITISH · TRENDY X A striking new build with an impressive kitchen garden and a greenhouse beside it; set at the entrance of the Chewton Glen hotel. Brasserie menus showcase local and garden produce. The glass-fronted cookery school is popular.

Carte £17/44

*Chewton Glen Hotel, Christchurch Road ⊠ BH25 6QS – ℰ 01425 282212 –
www.chewtonglen.com/the-kitchen*

🏨 Chewton Glen   ✿ 🦢 ⪡ 🛏 ▮ 🗔 🗖 💯 🈺 🛝 🖭 🛗 AK 🕍 P

GRAND LUXURY · CLASSIC A professionally run country house with an impressive spa, set in 130 acres of New Forest parkland – try a host of outdoor pursuits, including croquet, archery and clay pigeon shooting. Luxurious bedrooms range from classic to contemporary; opt for one with a balcony or terrace, or try a unique Treehouse suite. Dine in the traditional restaurant or modern brasserie.

72 rooms – 🛉🛉 £325/725 – 🖵 £25 – 18 suites

Christchurch Road ✉ BH25 6QS – ☎ 01425 275341 – www.chewtonglen.com

🍴⃝ **The Kitchen** – See restaurant listing

NEWBURY

West Berkshire – Regional map n° **6**-B3

✿ **The Woodspeen** (John Campbell)   🍸🍷 🛏 🍴 🛗 ♻ P

MODERN CUISINE · CONTEMPORARY DÉCOR XX Despite being set in an old pub, this neighbourhood eatery has a contemporary feel, courtesy of its bright wood and glass extension which comes with a thatched roof, a vaulted larch ceiling and modern Scandic styling. Sit by the open-plan kitchen to watch the smooth efficiency of the chefs or book the chef's table in the smart cookery school opposite to observe close-up the precision and accuracy with which the dishes are prepared.

Mouth-watering menus centre on the seasons and bring together ingredients from their garden and the local area. Flavour is paramount and dishes have a comforting, modern classic style; there are even some dishes for two to share. Experienced chef-owner John Campbell leads the confident kitchen team and the service is charming and structured.

Specialities: Seafood risotto with garden herbs, crispy shrimps and lemon. Pan-fried sea bream with fennel, pickled shallots, mussels and seaweed broth. Banana mousse, lime caramel, praline ganache and sheep's yoghurt ice cream.

Menu £28 (lunch) – Carte £36/68

Lambourn Road, Bagnor ✉ RG20 8BN – ☎ 01635 265070 –
www.thewoodspeen.com – Closed Sunday dinner

✿ **Blackbird** (Dom Robinson)   🛏 P

CLASSIC CUISINE · PUB X This delightful inn sits in an equally charming hamlet and is the backbone of the local community. The experienced chef-owner Dom Robinson spent time working in London and Dubai before fulfilling his lifelong ambition of opening a place of his own, but he's keen to keep this a proper pub that the locals can be proud of. Freshly baked loaves sit on the bar, the staff are amiable and music from the '60s, '70s and '80s plays in the background.

Top-notch ingredients feature in dishes with a classical French base and their unfussy, back-to-basics style belies the precise, well-honed techniques involved in their preparation. The various elements of each dish blend together seamlessly and the flavours are superb. Start with maybe a cheese soufflé, followed by poached halibut Véronique or Spring lamb Provençal, and finish off with rhum baba or prune and Armagnac tart.

Specialities: Roast foie gras with a ragout of haricot beans. Fillet of turbot with creamed leeks and sauce Véronique. Poached pear 'Belle Hélène' with caramelised white chocolate and almonds.

Menu £29 (lunch) – Carte £43/56

Bagnor ✉ RG20 8AQ – ☎ 01635 40005 – www.theblackbird.co.uk –
Closed 23-27 December, 30 December-1 January, Sunday, Monday

🍴⃝ **The Vineyard**   🛏 🍴 🛗 AK 🎦 P

MODERN CUISINE · ELEGANT XXX Smart hotel restaurant split over two levels. Accomplished dishes are attractively presented; choose between a set and two tasting menus. They offer over 100 wines by the glass – some from their own Californian vineyard.

Menu £29 (lunch), £69/89

Vineyard Hotel, Stockcross ✉ RG20 8JU – ☎ 01635 528770 –
www.the-vineyard.co.uk – Closed Sunday dinner, Monday, Tuesday

⅋○ Henry & Joe's

MODERN BRITISH · FRIENDLY X What started as a pop-up and a dream is now an appealing modern bistro that's winning everyone's hearts. Joe is a charmer and works the room with aplomb, while Henry conjures up interesting, adventurous dishes. The lunch and early evening menu is great value; don't miss the freshly baked bread.

Menu £21 – Carte £33/48

17 Cheap Street ⊠ RG14 5DD – ℰ 01635 581751 –
www.henryandjoes.co.uk – Closed 2-18 September, 22 December-7 January,
Sunday-Tuesday

The Vineyard ⌂ ⊆ ⬛ ⬚ ⑂ ⅃⊾ ⊟ ⒶⒸ ⅍ ⯐

BUSINESS · CLASSIC This extended former hunting lodge displays a collection of over 1,000 pieces of art. Some bedrooms have a country house style, while others are more contemporary, and all boast smart marble bathrooms. The owner also has a vineyard in California, hence the stunning wine vault and wine-themed bar.

49 rooms ⌑ – †† £118/178 – 32 suites

Stockcross ⊠ RG20 8JU – ℰ 01635 528770 –
www.the-vineyard.co.uk

⅋○ **The Vineyard** – See restaurant listing

NEWCASTLE UPON TYNE

Tyne and Wear – Regional map n° **14**-B2

❀ House of Tides (Kenny Atkinson) ⅟ ⓥ

MODERN CUISINE · INTIMATE XX This characterful Grade I listed merchant's house sits on the historic quayside. It's a vast place, with a rustic ground floor bar featuring flagged floors, cast iron pillars and exposed brickwork, and an upstairs restaurant characterised by sloping floors, wonky ceilings and carved beams.

Passionate chef-owner Kenny Atkinson fell in love with the place at first sight and wants a visit here to be a real experience from start to finish. He is helped along by an engaging, knowledgeable serving team and a sommelier who recommends some great wine matches for the well-balanced tasting menus. Accomplished, creative dishes evolve as ingredients come into season, with only top quality produce being used. The attractively presented dishes are well-thought-out and flavours have plenty of depth – and there's the occasional playful touch in evidence too.

Specialities: Roast scallop with pork belly, sweetcorn and lardo. Herdwick lamb with shallots, black garlic and lovage. Apple parfait, almond biscuit and compressed apple with marigold & baked croissant ice cream.

Menu £55 (lunch), £65/95

28-30 The Close ⊠ NE1 3RF – ℰ 0191 230 3720 –
www.houseoftides.co.uk – Closed 23 December-8 January, Sunday, Monday,
Tuesday - Thursday lunch

❀ Broad Chare ⒶⒸ

TRADITIONAL BRITISH · PUB X Sit in the snug ground floor bar or more comfortable upstairs dining room of this quayside pub. Choose from a snack menu of 'Geordie Tapas', an appealing 'on toast' selection, hearty daily specials and tasty nursery puddings. They also offer over 40 ales, including some which are custom-made for the pub.

Specialities: Haggis and fried egg on toast with HP sauce. Roast halibut with monk's beard and Shetland mussels. Ginger sponge with milk ice cream and butterscotch.

Carte £22/40

25 Broad Chare ⊠ NE1 3DQ – ℰ 0191 211 2144 –
www.thebroadchare.co.uk – Closed Sunday dinner

Route 🛈 ⛩ 🗊

COUNTRY COOKING · BISTRO X This simple bistro sits on a steep city centre street that once formed the route from the castle to the quayside. It has a concrete floor, a breeze block wall and an open kitchen to the rear. Regularly changing menus offer well-priced, gutsy small plates with punchy flavours and a British heart.

Specialities: White onion soup, Winslade and wild garlic. Simonburn lamb chops with chicory and mint. Rhubarb & custard with pistachios.

Menu £15 – Carte £22/35

35 Side ⊠ NE1 3JE – ☏ 0191 222 0973 – www.routenewcastle.co.uk – Closed 1-14 January, 1-14 June, Sunday dinner, Monday lunch, Tuesday, Wednesday - Friday lunch

Violets 🛈 🗊

MODERN BRITISH · SIMPLE X The vibrant historic quayside plays host to this friendly little café run by the House of Tides team. Come for a tasty breakfast or brunch, or later in the evening for carefully thought through, skilfully prepared small plates. The latter have a British base and some interesting touches.

Specialities: Potato & goat's cheese terrine with apple, kohlrabi and walnuts. Beef cheek, with pease pudding, smoked bacon and chestnut mushrooms. Rosewater panna cotta with rhubarb and strawberry.

Carte £21/35

5-7 Side ⊠ NE1 3JE – www.violetscafe.co.uk – Closed Monday, Tuesday, Wednesday

Dobson & Parnell

MODERN CUISINE · DESIGN XX This elegant restaurant is an iconic address in the city and is named after Victorian architects John Dobson and William Parnell. Cooking has a classic style, with the occasional international influence, and dishes are colourful and satisfying. At lunch the menu is made up of a selection of small plates.

Menu £25 – Carte £20/51

21 Queen Street ⊠ NE1 3UG – ☏ 0191 221 0904 – www.dobsonandparnell.co.uk – Closed Monday

21 🍷 & 🆎 🛈 🔄

MODERN BRITISH · BRASSERIE XX Start with a gin from the large selection behind the zinc-topped counter then head through to the smart red and black brasserie. Menus offer a comprehensive array of confidently cooked classics; the 'menu du jour' is good value.

Menu £25 (lunch)/26 – Carte £33/62

Trinity Gardens ⊠ NE1 2HH – ☏ 0191 222 0755 – www.21newcastle.co.uk

Bistro Forty Six ⛩

BRITISH CONTEMPORARY · NEIGHBOURHOOD X A refreshingly honest bistro with a homely interior. The self-taught chef hunts and forages, using the local larder to full effect. Passionately seasonal dishes will appeal to one and all; check the blackboard for the daily specials.

Menu £16 (lunch)/19 – Carte £28/40

46 Brentwood Ave, Jesmond ⊠ NE2 3DH – ☏ 0191 281 8081 – www.bistrofortysix.co.uk – Closed Sunday dinner, Monday, Tuesday - Wednesday lunch

The Patricia & 🗊

MODERN BRITISH · NEIGHBOURHOOD X This simply furnished bistro sits in the vibrant suburb of Jesmond and is named after the owner's grandmother. Tasty cooking displays Mediterranean influences and the wine list is good value. They also open at the weekend for lunch – Saturday sees a selection of well-priced small plates.

Menu £25 – Carte £30/44

139 Jesmond Rd, Jesmond ⊠ NE2 1JY – ☏ 0191 281 4443 – www.the-patricia.com – Closed Sunday dinner, Monday, Tuesday, Wednesday - Thursday lunch

Träkol

MODERN BRITISH • RUSTIC X An assortment of shipping containers in an enviable waterside location make up this on-trend eatery which comes complete with its own microbrewery. Its name is Swedish for 'charcoal' and cooking takes place over an open fire. Bold, hearty dishes range from small plates to feasting options for two to share.

Carte £26/44

Hillgate Quays, Gateshead ✉ NE8 2BH – ✆ 0191 737 1120 – www.bytheriverbrew.co – Closed Sunday dinner

Jesmond Dene House

LUXURY • CONTEMPORARY Stone-built Arts and Crafts house in a peaceful city dene; originally owned by the Armstrong family. Characterful guest areas with wood panelling, local art and striking original fireplaces. Individually furnished bedrooms have bold feature walls, modern facilities and smart bathrooms with underfloor heating.

40 rooms – †† £109/209 – ☕ £18

Jesmond Dene Road ✉ NE2 2EY – ✆ 0191 212 3000 – www.jesmonddenehouse.co.uk

at Ponteland Northwest: 8. 25 mi by A167 on A696 – Regional map n° **14**-A2

Haveli

INDIAN • BRASSERIE XX Haveli means 'grand house' and this neighbourhood restaurant is certainly very smart. Influences come from all over India; try one of the chef's signature curries. Staff combine personality with professionalism.

Specialities: Coconut and chilli marinated Indian Ocean king prawns. Lamb shank jungle curry with chilli, garlic, onions and cloves. Royal Hyderabadi bread and butter pudding with saffron & cardamom infused milk.

Menu £15/18 – Carte £23/34

3-5 Broadway, Darras Hall ✉ NE20 9PW – ✆ 01661 872727 – www.haveliponteland.com – Closed Sunday lunch, Monday, Tuesday - Saturday lunch

NEWLYN

Cornwall – Regional map n° **1**-A3

Tolcarne Inn

SEAFOOD • PUB X An unassuming pub set behind the sea wall; inside it's narrow and cosy, with 18C beams, a wood-burning stove and a long bar. Appealing, flavoursome dishes centre around fresh fish and shellfish, most of which is landed at the adjacent harbour – go for the turbot if it's on the menu.

Carte £26/42

Tolcarne Place ✉ TR18 5PR – ✆ 01736 363074 – www.tolcarneinn.co.uk

NEWPORT – Isle of Wight ➜ See Wight (Isle of)

NEWQUAY

Cornwall – Regional map n° **1**-A2

at Mawgan Porth Northeast: 6 mi by A3059 on B3276

Scarlet

BOUTIQUE HOTEL • PERSONALISED Eco-centric, adults only hotel set high on a cliff and boasting stunning coastal views. Modern bar and lounges, and a great spa offering extensive treatments. Bedrooms range from 'Just Right' to 'Indulgent' and have unusual open-plan bathrooms and a cool, Scandic style – every room has a terrace and sea view.

37 rooms ☕ – †† £250/545

Tredragon Road ✉ TR8 4DQ – ✆ 01637 861800 – www.scarlethotel.co.uk – Closed 12-18 January

at Watergate Bay Northeast: 3 mi by A3059 on B3276

🕪 **Fifteen Cornwall**

ITALIAN · BRASSERIE 🕱🕱 A lively beachfront restaurant with fabulous bay views; the profits go towards training disengaged adults to become chefs. Unfussy Italian menus have a Cornish twist and feature homemade pastas and steaks from the Josper grill. At lunch they also serve antipasti at the unbookable bar counter.

Carte £35/54

On The Beach ✉ TR8 4AA – ℰ 01637 861000 – www.fifteencornwall.co.uk – *Closed 5-20 January*

NEWTON-ON-OUSE
North Yorkshire – Regional map n° **13**–B2

🕪 **Dawnay Arms**

MODERN BRITISH · PUB 🕱 A handsome pub with stone floors, low beams, open fires and all manner of bric-a-brac – its delightful dining room has views over the garden and down to the river. Gutsy, well executed British dishes include plenty of local game.

Menu £18 – Carte £21/45

✉ YO30 2BR – ℰ 01347 848345 – www.thedawnayatnewton.co.uk – *Closed Sunday dinner, Monday*

NOMANSLAND
Wiltshire – Regional map n° **2**–D3

🕪 **Les Mirabelles**

CLASSIC FRENCH · FRIENDLY 🕱🕱 This bright, modern restaurant overlooks the common and is enthusiastically run by a welcoming Frenchman. The well-balanced menu features unfussy, classic Gallic dishes and the superb wine selection lists over 3,000 bins!

Menu £24 – Carte £32/51

Forest Edge Road ✉ SP5 2BN – ℰ 01794 390205 – www.lesmirabelles.co.uk – *Closed 22 December-15 January, Sunday, Monday*

NORTH BOVEY
Devon – Regional map n° **1**–C2

🏨 **Bovey Castle**

HISTORIC · CLASSIC An impressive manor house on an extensive country estate, beautifully set within the Dartmoor National Park. Bedrooms have contemporary touches but still retain their traditional edge, and there's a relaxed, homely feel throughout. Dine on either seasonal modern dishes or British classics.

60 rooms ☑ – 🛉🛉 £190/800 – 6 suites

✉ TQ13 8RE – ℰ 01647 445000 – www.boveycastle.com

NORTH MARSTON
Buckinghamshire – Regional map n° **6**–C2

🕪 **The Pilgrim**

MODERN CUISINE · PUB 🕱 A friendly community pub filled with heavy timbers; find a spot by the wood-burning stove in the cosy bar-lounge. Proper home-cooking relies on local, sustainable produce. Every Tuesday the menu changes for 'Village Night'.

Carte £23/31

25 High Street ✉ MK18 3PD – ℰ 01296 670969 – www.thepilgrimpub.co.uk – *Closed 1-9 January, Sunday dinner, Monday, Tuesday lunch*

NORTH SHIELDS
Tyne and Wear – Regional map n° **14**–B2

Staith House

⌂ & P

TRADITIONAL BRITISH · PUB ⅄ A stone's throw from market stalls overflowing with crab, lobster and Craster kippers, is this smart quayside pub. Photos of the old docks line the walls of numerous dining areas and it has a pleasingly cluttered feel. Daily changing dishes showcase Northumberland's latest yield; the fish is smoked on-site.

Specialities: Breaded herring with kohlrabi and Granny Smith slaw. Naturally smoked haddock with Isle of Lewis mussel and spring vegetable broth. Lemon posset with blueberry compote and almond biscotti.

Menu £20 (lunch) – Carte £23/35

57 Low Lights ⊠ NE30 1HF –
℘ 0191 270 8441 – www.thestaithhouse.co.uk – Closed Sunday dinner

River Cafe on the Tyne

TRADITIONAL BRITISH · BISTRO ⅄ A laid-back restaurant run by a friendly local team, set above a pub in the North Shields fish quay. The daily changing à la carte offers unfussy bistro-style dishes of fresh local produce; ask for a window table to see the fish being landed. The 3 course set lunch and early dinner menu is a steal.

Menu £9/10 – Carte £20/35

51 Bell Street, Fish Quay ⊠ NE30 1HF –
℘ 0191 296 6168 – www.rivercafeonthetyne.co.uk – Closed Sunday dinner, Monday, Tuesday lunch

NORTHMOOR

Oxfordshire – Regional map n° **6**-B2

Red Lion

⇛ ⌂ P

TRADITIONAL BRITISH · PUB ⅄ Extremely welcoming pub owned by the villagers and run by an experienced young couple and a friendly team. Low beams, open fires and fresh flowers abound and the menu is a great mix of pub classics and more modern daily specials.

Carte £16/36

Standlake Road ⊠ OX29 5SX –
℘ 01865 300301 – www.theredlionnorthmoor.com – Closed Sunday dinner, Monday

NORWICH

Norfolk – Regional map n° **8**-D2

Roger Hickman's

AC ⇼

MODERN CUISINE · TRADITIONAL ⅄⅄ Personally run restaurant in a historic part of the city, with soft hues, modern art and romantic corners. Service is attentive yet unobtrusive. Cooking is modern, intricate and displays respect for ingredients' natural flavours.

Menu £21 (lunch), £39/48

79 Upper St Giles Street ⊠ NR2 1AB –
℘ 01603 633522 – www.rogerhickmansrestaurant.com –
Closed 31 December-10 January, Sunday, Monday

Benedicts

⇼

MODERN CUISINE · BISTRO ⅄ A huge window lets in lots of light and white wood panelling keeps things suitably down-to-earth. Tried-and-tested combinations are given subtle modern touches and show respect for good quality Norfolk ingredients.

Menu £22 (lunch), £39/62

9 St Benedicts Street ⊠ NR2 4PE –
℘ 01603 926080 – www.restaurantbenedicts.com – Closed 1-7 January,
28 July-12 August, Sunday, Monday

⁀○ Farmyard ⓝ   AC

BRITISH CONTEMPORARY · BISTRO ⅹ As its name suggests, the cooking at
this spacious bistro centres on unadulterated local ingredients. At the heart of
the open kitchen is a Big Bertha charcoal oven, which adds plenty of flavour to
the various meats and fish. For dessert, try the Farmyard Chocolate Bar. The
lunch menu is good value.

Menu £21 (lunch)/26 – Carte £29/34

25 St Benedicts Street ⊠ NR2 4PF – ℰ 01603 733188 –
www.farmyardrestaurant.co.uk – Closed Sunday, Monday lunch

⁀○ Georgian Townhouse   ⇦ 🛏 🛖 ⅆ AC ⇿ P

TRADITIONAL CUISINE · PUB ⅹ Laid-back pub with a flexible menu: choose
small plates to start or to share; dishes 'for the table' for 2 or 4; or something
for yourself 'from the store'. Fruit and veg is home-grown and they home-smoke
cheese and spit-roast and flame-grill meats. Bold, retro-style bedrooms have
fridges and coffee machines.

Carte £24/40

30-34 Unthank Road ⊠ NR2 2RB – ℰ 01603 615655 –
www.thegeorgiantownhousenorwich.com

at Stoke Holy Cross South: 5. 75 mi by A140

⁀○ Stoke Mill   🛏 AC ⇿ P

TRADITIONAL CUISINE · HISTORIC ⅹⅹ Characterful 700 year old mill spanning
the River Tas; the adjoining building is where the Colman family started making
mustard in 1814. Confidently prepared, classically based dishes use good ingredients and flavours are distinct.

Menu £18 (lunch), £22/28 – Carte £28/44

*Mill Road ⊠ NR14 8PA – ℰ 01508 493337 – www.stokemill.co.uk – Closed Sunday
dinner, Monday, Tuesday*

NOTTINGHAM

Nottingham – Regional map n° **9**–B2

✿✿ Restaurant Sat Bains   ⇦ 🛏 AC 🍷 ⇿ P

CREATIVE · INTIMATE ⅹⅹⅹ The location beneath a flyover on the fringes of the
city might be a little incongruous but don't let that put you off, as once at your
table, the world outside will be forgotten. Flagged floors and deer skin covered
tables blend with contemporary artwork and the atmosphere is smart yet casual.

At lunch a 7 course menu is offered in 3 intimate locations: the 'Chef's Table', the
'Kitchen Bench' or the development kitchen 'Nucleus'. In the latter, the Head Chef
cooks for you personally, precisely preparing premium ingredients in dishes with
plenty of originality; all the while answering your questions.

At night, the main room comes alive. 7 and 10 course tasting menus incorporate
the five tastes – salt, sweet, sour, bitter and umami. Cooking is highly technical
with good balance and a delicate style, and presentation is creative. Their urban
kitchen garden provides many of the herbs and leaves.

Spacious modern bedrooms complete the picture.

Specialities: Smoked eel with apple, Périgord truffle, pickled turnip and truffle velouté. Barbecued Anjou pigeon with carrot, Moroccan spices and pastilla. Honey
jelly with chamomile, pollen and grains.

Menu £95 (lunch), £105/135

Trentside, Lenton Lane ⊠ NG7 2SA – ℰ 0115 986 6566 –
*www.restaurantsatbains.com – Closed 9-26 August, 22 December-9 January,
Sunday, Monday, Tuesday*

✿ alchemilla (Alex Bond)   🍷

MODERN BRITISH · RUSTIC ⅹⅹ Alchemilla occupies six red-brick vaulted arches
of a Victorian carriage house once owned by wealthy lace merchants. Despite its
rustic look, it's a modern place; ask for a seat by the open kitchen to get in on the
action or a table under the arches for a more intimate feel.

A living wall and roof garden set the scene for inspired, exciting cooking where plant-based ingredients are kept to the fore, and the chef Alex Bond has an admirable attitude towards finding ingredients with strong sustainable and ethical qualities. As well as injecting plenty of his own personality into the dishes, he has an innate skill for bringing together sweet, sour, salty and citrus elements in wonderful harmony, with the highly original combinations of flavours and textures arranged in layers. The sommelier offers an esoteric list with a bias towards natural wines.

Specialities: Risotto of grains with roasted yeast, artichoke and truffle. Aged sirloin with barbecued leek and fermented garlic. Chocolate with beetroot, salted liquorice and spent coffee porridge.

Menu £65/90

192 Derby Road ✉ *NG7 1NF –* ☏ *0115 941 3515 – www.alchemillarestaurant.uk – Closed 4-18 August, 24 December-6 January, Sunday-Tuesday lunch*

Ibérico World Tapas

MEDITERRANEAN CUISINE · TRENDY X A well-run restaurant with a vaulted ceiling, colourful Moorish tiles and ornate fretwork, hidden in the basement of the old city law courts and jail. Tapas-style sharing dishes are listed under 'Nibbles', 'Meat', 'Fish' and 'Veg'. Skilful cooking is full of flavour and displays some Japanese influences.

Specialities: Flamed edamame, garlic butter and shichimi. Marinated tuna with charred cucumber and moro miso. Sourdough treacle tart with burnt milk ice cream and blood orange.

Menu £15 – Carte £15/27

The Shire Hall, High Pavement ✉ *NG1 1HN –* ☏ *0115 941 0410 – www.ibericotapas.com – Closed 1-2 January, Sunday, Monday, Tuesday - Friday lunch*

MemSaab

INDIAN · EXOTIC DÉCOR XX Professionally run restaurant with eye-catching artwork and a wooden 'Gateway of India'. Original, authentic cooking has a distinct North Indian influence. Spicing is well-judged and dishes from the charcoal grill are a highlight.

Menu £22/38 – Carte £22/38

12-14 Maid Marian Way ✉ *NG1 6HS –* ☏ *0115 957 0009 – www.mem-saab.co.uk – Closed Sunday - Saturday lunch*

World Service

MODERN CUISINE · EXOTIC DÉCOR XX Hidden in the extension of a Georgian property and accessed via an Indonesian-inspired courtyard garden. It has a clubby, colonial feel, with panelled walls and cases of archaeological artefacts. Appealing dishes have global influences.

Menu £28 (lunch)/32 – Carte £30/54

Newdigate House, Castlegate ✉ *NG1 6AF –* ☏ *0115 847 5587 – www.worldservicerestaurant.com – Closed 1-2 January, 3-4 August, Sunday dinner*

Bar Ibérico

MEDITERRANEAN CUISINE · TAPAS BAR X A buzzy, laid-back tapas bar with a large pavement terrace. The wide-ranging menu is designed for sharing, from charcuterie and cheese to pintxos from the Josper grill and tapas inspired by Spain and the Mediterranean.

Menu £12 (lunch) – Carte £14/22

17-19 Carlton Street ✉ *NG1 1NL –* ☏ *0115 988 1133 – www.baribericotapas.com*

Larder on Goosegate

TRADITIONAL BRITISH · RUSTIC X This appealing restaurant sits on the first floor of a listed Victorian building. It was the first branch of Boots the Chemists and the floor to ceiling windows displayed their wares; ask to sit beside them for a view of the street below. Dishes are unfussy, good value and tasty; the steaks are a hit.

Menu £17/20 – Carte £26/40

16-22 Goosegate (1st Floor) ✉ *NG1 1FE –* ☏ *0115 950 0111 – www.thelarderongoosegate.co.uk – Closed 15-22 August, Sunday, Monday, Tuesday - Thursday lunch*

🏨 Hart's ✿ ≤ 🛏 🖎 & 🛗 🅿

BUSINESS · DESIGN A sophisticated boutique-style hotel built on the ramparts of a medieval castle. Compact bedrooms have modern bathrooms and a high level of facilities; ask for one with a garden terrace. Unwind in the cosy bar or out in the courtyard. Breakfast includes bread and pastries from their own bakery.

32 rooms – 🛉🛉 £139/279 – ☑ £15 – 2 suites

Standard Hill, Park Row ✉ NG1 6FN – ☎ 0115 988 1900 –
www.hartsnottingham.co.uk

at Plumtree Southeast: 5.75 mi by A60 off A606

🍽️○ Perkins Bar & Bistro ⇐ 🛏 🗚 🅿

MODERN BRITISH · FRIENDLY XX This red-brick Victorian railway station is now a bright family-run bistro; pick a seat overlooking the railway line. Modern British menus evolve daily and feature home-smoked fish, game and cheese; their Sleeper Boards are a hit. Stay in a cosy shepherd's hut overlooking the fields – one has a roll-top bath!

Menu £16 (lunch)/25 – Carte £26/39

Old Railway Station, Station Road ✉ NG12 5NA – ☎ 0115 937 3695 –
www.perkinsrestaurant.co.uk – Closed Sunday dinner

at Ruddington South: 5.5 mi on A 60

🍽️○ Ruddington Arms 🛏 & 🅿

TRADITIONAL CUISINE · PUB X This dramatically refurbished, faux-industrial style pub is found in a sleepy village. Flavoursome dishes cater for one and all, with everything from pub classics to more adventurous offerings. Tasty marmalades and chutneys are for sale.

Carte £22/40

56 Wilford Road ✉ NG11 6EQ – ☎ 0115 984 1628 – www.theruddingtonarms.com

at West Bridgford Southeast: 1.75 mi by A60

🍽️○ escabeche 🛏 🗚 🍴

MEDITERRANEAN CUISINE · FRIENDLY X Informal, modern, Mediterranean-inspired restaurant with a sunny front terrace. The broad main menu lists vibrant, well-presented tapas dishes, offering a great variety of flavours. Excellent value set menu.

Menu £12/27 – Carte £18/27

27 Bridgford Road ✉ NG2 6AU – ☎ 0115 981 7010 – www.barescatapas.co.uk

NUN MONKTON

North Yorkshire – Regional map n° **13**–B2

🍽️○ Alice Hawthorn Inn 🛏 🛏 & 🐕 🅿

REGIONAL CUISINE · PUB X This smart, stylish pub sits on a picturesque village green complete with a duck pond, grazing cattle and the country's tallest maypole. Well-presented dishes have classical roots and showcase local and garden produce.

Carte £26/47

The Green ✉ YO26 8EW – ☎ 01423 330303 – www.thealicehawthorn.com –
Closed Monday, Tuesday

OAKHAM

Rutland – Regional map n° **9**–C2

🏠 Hitchen's Barn

MODERN BRITISH · FRIENDLY 𝕏 When their lease came to an end, the owners of the Berkeley Arms in Wymondham upped and moved to this pretty little stone barn. It has a shabby chic bar and a rustic dining room and is run by a bubbly young team. The appealing menu of modern British dishes is fiercely seasonal and can change up to twice a day.

Specialities: Brixham crab on toast. Fillet of hake with Jersey Royals, asparagus and samphire. Blood orange and rhubarb trifle.

Menu £19 (lunch)/23 – Carte £29/46

12 Burley Road ✉ LE15 6DH –
☏ 01572 722255 – www.hitchensbarn.co.uk – Closed 25 December-15 January, Sunday dinner, Monday, Tuesday

at Hambleton East: 3 mi by A606 – Regional map n° **9**–C2

⚜ Hambleton Hall

CLASSIC CUISINE · COUNTRY HOUSE 𝕏𝕏𝕏 There aren't many independently owned country house hotels left but this truly beautiful Victorian manor house with grounds sloping down to Rutland Water is one of them. Antique furnishings and heavy fabrics feature throughout, welcoming open fires burn in the grates and bedrooms come with a host of thoughtful extras.

Enjoy drinks in the bar or on the terrace before taking in superb views over Rutland Water from the traditional dining room. Head Chef Aaron Patterson has headed the kitchen since 1992 and his passion and commitment remain palpable.

Accomplished cooking marries together top quality seasonal ingredients in a 'less is more' approach and flavours are fresh and clearly defined, and while for the most part the dishes are classically based, they also display the occasional modern touch. The delicious bread is from their artisan bakery.

Specialities: Marinated scallops with ginger, apple, crème fraîche and caviar. Launde Farm lamb with Mediterranean vegetables and goat's curd. A taste of Gariguette strawberries with champagne and hibiscus meringue.

Menu £40 (lunch), £78/98

Hambleton Hall Hotel ✉ LE15 8TH –
☏ 01572 756991 – www.hambletonhall.com

🏰 Hambleton Hall

LUXURY · CLASSIC A beautiful Victorian manor house in a peaceful location, with mature grounds sloping down to Rutland Water. Classical country house drawing rooms boast heavy drapes, open fires and antiques. Good-sized bedrooms are designed by the owner herself and come with a host of thoughtful extras. Service is engaging.

16 rooms ☲ – 👫 £295/480 – 1 suite
✉ LE15 8TH – ☏ 01572 756991 – www.hambletonhall.com
⚜ **Hambleton Hall** – See restaurant listing

OLD BURGHCLERE
Hampshire – Regional map n° **4**–B1

🍴 Dew Pond

CLASSIC FRENCH · COSY 𝕏𝕏 A part-16C farmhouse with well-tended gardens leading down to a dew pond. The longstanding restaurant is family owned and run and serves classic French cooking; enjoy an aperitif on the terrace, overlooking the real Watership Down.

Menu £36/44

✉ RG20 9LH – ☏ 01635 278408 – www.dewpond.co.uk – Closed 1-14 August, 23 December-6 January, Sunday, Monday, Tuesday - Saturday lunch

OLDHAM
Greater Manchester – Regional map n° **11**–B2

⫶◯ White Hart Inn

MODERN BRITISH · PUB X The original part of this stone-built inn dates from 1788 but there's always something new going on here. With its brasserie, formal restaurant, private dining room, large function room and smart bedrooms, it can be a busy place. The menu offers a good range of refined dishes, many with a Mediterranean slant.

Menu £23 – Carte £27/52

51 Stockport Road, Lydgate ⊠ OL4 4JJ – ℰ 01457 872566 – www.thewhitehart.co.uk

OLDSTEAD
North Yorkshire – Regional map n° **13**–C2

🕸 Black Swan (Tommy Banks)

CREATIVE BRITISH · RUSTIC XX Hidden away down country lanes, the Black Swan is owned by a family who've farmed in the area for generations. It's set around a characterful little pub with exposed beams, a flagged floor and an open fire: downstairs is the setting for aperitifs and coffee, while upstairs is the simply but pleasantly furnished restaurant with candlelit tables and a laid-back feel.

Appealing modern menus are driven by produce from their farm and garden and they use an array of preservation techniques to ensure that these ingredients last. This results in dishes with bold contrasts, plenty of depth and a Scandinavian feel. Preparation is highly skilled and the dishes are attractively presented. The wine list also provides plenty of interest and every wine is available by the glass.

The antique-furnished bedrooms come with private patios.

Specialities: Scallop with razor clam and rhubarb. Aged sirloin with onion and lovage. Root vegetable toast.

Menu £98/125

⊠ YO61 4BL – ℰ 01347 868387 – www.blackswanoldstead.co.uk – Closed Sunday - Friday lunch

OMBERSLEY
Worcestershire – Regional map n° **10**–B3

⫶◯ Venture In

TRADITIONAL BRITISH · COSY XX A hugely characterful black and white timbered house with 15C origins and a large inglenook fireplace in the bar. Cooking is classically based but has modern overtones and there's always a good choice of specials available.

Menu £36 (lunch), £45/50

Main Street ⊠ WR9 0EW – ℰ 01905 620552 – www.theventurein.co.uk – Closed 13-21 March, 8-16 June, 3-18 August, 25 December-4 January, Sunday dinner, Monday

ORFORD
Suffolk – Regional map n° **8**–D3

🏠 Crown and Castle

HISTORIC · PERSONALISED It is thought that the original 12C inn which stood on this site was built into the walls of Orford Castle. The latest incarnation, a Tudor-style house, is run in a pleasantly laid-back manner. Most bedrooms are in chalets and many have terraces and distant sea views. The bistro offers seasonal fare.

21 rooms ⌂ – †† £140/250 – 1 suite

⊠ IP12 2LJ – ℰ 01394 450205 – www.crownandcastle.co.uk

🍴○ Sebastians

TRADITIONAL CUISINE · COSY XX Housed in three characterful 17C cottages, Sebastians is a long-standing restaurant with an open fire, lots of beams and bags of charm. Cooking uses good ingredients and is classically based, and you'll be well looked after by the team. Many of the cosy, characterful bedrooms are set around a courtyard.

Menu £49

45 Willow Street ⊠ *SY11 1AQ –* ☎ *01691 655444 – www.sebastians-hotel.com –*
Closed 22-30 December, Sunday lunch, Monday, Tuesday, Wednesday - Saturday lunch

🍴○ Townhouse

MODERN BRITISH · BRASSERIE XX Contemporary restaurant in a Georgian townhouse. There's a flamboyant cocktail bar, a sunny terrace and an airy dining room featuring glitzy chandeliers. Classical cooking has a modern edge and dishes are attractively presented.

Menu £17 – Carte £24/38

35 Willow Street ⊠ *SY11 1AQ –* ☎ *01691 659499 – www.townhouseoswestry.com –*
Closed Monday

OXFORD

Oxfordshire – Regional map n° **6**–B2

Top tips!

You can't mention Oxford without thinking about the historic university, but there's more to the City of Dreaming Spires than academia. The Ashmolean Museum, founded in 1683, has exhibits on art and archaeology, while the Blenheim Palace and Gardens world heritage site boasts over 300 years of history; and what could be more calming than a punt along the River Cherwell on a summer's day? The city is home to a diverse population and the dining options offer a similarly eclectic mix of influences. Michelin-Starred **Oxford Kitchen** in pretty Summertown offers exacting, innovative cuisine, while around the corner is **Pompette**, a lovely French brasserie run by a husband and wife team. The Bib Gourmand awarded **Magdalen Arms**, meanwhile, is a great spot for anything from coffee and cakes to a 3 course meal.

For a real treat, head out of the city to the iconic Two-Starred **Belmond Le Manoir aux Quat Saisons**.

Restaurants

✿ Oxford Kitchen

MODERN BRITISH · MINIMALIST ✗✗ Hidden away in trendy Summertown is this bright, modern neighbourhood restaurant. It's split over two levels: the ground floor has exposed brick walls, intimate booths and a simple bistro style, while the first floor houses a plush dining room that opens less frequently.

The owners have wisely left the kitchen in the capable hands of Paul Welburn, whose knowledge and skill are standing him in good stead. His vast experience shows though in assured, well-balanced, deftly prepared dishes, where classical flavour combinations are given innovative modern touches. Sourcing focuses on top-notch produce – be it from near or far – portion sizes are well-judged, and the speed of the service is just right. In a nice touch, they even offer a special Locals' Lunch so as not to price out their regulars.

Specialities: Gin & tonic cured trout with dill, cucumber and treacle. Irish Hereford sirloin with black garlic, broccoli and Yorkshire Blackout. Amalfi lemon, honey cake, fennel jam and limoncello.

Menu £29 (lunch), £45/65

Town plan A1-e – *215 Banbury Road, Summertown ✉ OX2 7HQ – ☏ 01865 511149 – www.theoxfordkitchen.co.uk – Closed 1-17 January, Sunday, Monday*

☺ Magdalen Arms

TRADITIONAL BRITISH · PUB ✗ Locals and visitors flock to this large pub to enjoy the lively, easy-going atmosphere. It opens at 10am for tea and cake and even hosts a monthly flea market. The experienced chef-owner creates gutsy, flavoursome dishes with wide-ranging influences and the menu can change up to twice a day.

Specialities: Whole globe artichoke with goat's cheese and olive crumbs. Slow-cooked shoulder of lamb, gratin dauphinoise and pickled red cabbage. Raspberry and almond tart with vanilla ice cream.

Carte £28/32

Town plan B2-s – *243 Iffley Road ✉ OX4 1SJ – ☏ 01865 243159 – www.magdalenarms.co.uk – Closed Monday lunch*

☺ Oli's Thai

THAI · FRIENDLY ✗ This lovely little restaurant is set off the beaten track, in an up-and-coming residential area. Start with a drink on the patio then make for the cool, relaxed restaurant; if you haven't booked, try for a seat at the counter. The concise menu offers fresh, meticulously prepared, vibrantly flavoured dishes.

Specialities: Crispy chickpea salad. Panang confit duck. Custard tart.

Carte £20/27

Town plan B2-r – *38 Magdalen Road ✉ OX4 1RB – ☏ 01865 790223 – www.olisthai.com – Closed 11-28 April, Sunday, Monday, Tuesday dinner, Saturday dinner*

❄ Pompette

FRENCH · BRASSERIE ✗✗ An experienced chef and his welcoming wife proudly run this modern French brasserie. Freshly prepared dishes are based around Gallic classics, with the occasional Mediterranean or North African influence thrown in, and cooking is honest, unfussy and full of flavour. There's also a bar for all-day snacks.

Menu £20 (lunch) – Carte £32/50

Town plan A1-n – *7 South Parade, Summertown ✉ OX2 7JL – ☏ 01865 311166 – www.pompetterestaurant.co.uk – Closed 10-13 April, 24-27 December, Sunday dinner, Monday*

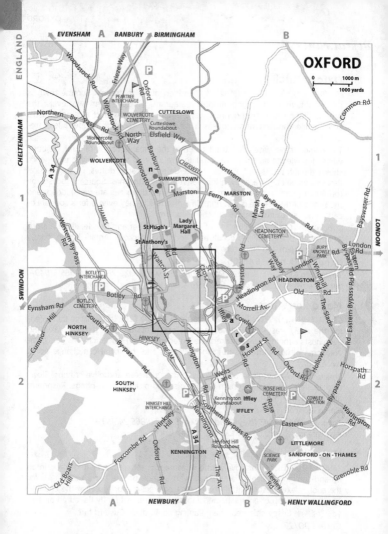

OXFORD

ⅱ◯ Arbequina   ㅊ 〓

SPANISH · NEIGHBOURHOOD ⅹ A simply furnished, bohemian tapas bar: sit downstairs by the vintage stainless steel counter or upstairs in the bay window. The concise menu offers tasty, authentic, filling tapas dishes; 3 plus dessert is about right.

Carte £10/35

Town plan B2-a – 74 Cowley Road ⊠ OX4 1JB –
℘ 01865 792777 – www.arbequina.co.uk –
Closed 21 December-3 January, Sunday, Monday - Thursday lunch

✿✿✿, ✿✿, ✿, 😋 & ⅱ◯

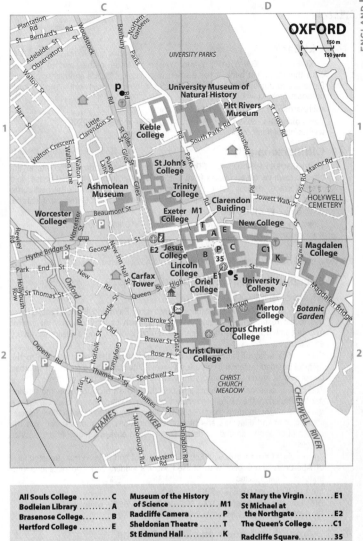

OXFORD

0   150 m
0   150 yards

University Parks

University Museum of Natural History

Pitt Rivers Museum

Keble College

St John's College

Trinity College

Clarendon Building

Exeter College   M1

New College

Ashmolean Museum

Worcester College

Beaumont St

Jesus College

Brasenose B

Radcliffe Square 35

Lincoln College

Magdalen College

St Edmund Hall K

Carfax Tower

Oriel College

University College

Corpus Christi College

Merton College

Botanic Garden

Christ Church College

CHRIST CHURCH MEADOW

HOLYWELL CEMETERY

THAMES RIVER

CHERWELL RIVER

All Souls College C	Museum of the History of Science M1	St Mary the Virgin E1
Bodleian Library . . . . A	Radcliffe Camera . . . . P	St Michael at the Northgate E2
Brasenose College . . . . B	Sheldonian Theatre . . . . . . T	The Queen's College C1
Hertford College . . . . E	St Edmund Hall . . . . K	Radcliffe Square 35

Hotels

Old Bank

☆ 🖃 ⬧ ⬧ 🅰🄲 ⬧ 🅿

LUXURY · CONTEMPORARY Warm, welcoming hotel in the heart of the city: once the area's first bank. It has a smart neo-classical façade and plenty of style. Elegant bedrooms have modern furnishings and eclectic artwork – those higher up boast great views.

42 rooms – ♥♥ £190/480 – ⬧ £16 – 1 suite

Town plan D2-s – *92-94 High Street* ✉ *OX1 4BN* – ☎ *01865 799599* – *www.oldbankhotel.co.uk*

Old Parsonage

☆ ⬧ 🅰🄲 🅿

TOWNHOUSE · PERSONALISED This ivy-clad sandstone parsonage sits in the historic town centre and dates from the 1660s. Enter into the original house via a pretty terrace; inside it's chic and modern – light hues feature in the bedrooms, along with the latest mod cons. Appealing menus offer classic British comfort food.

35 rooms – ♥♥ £190/480 – ⬧ £16

Town plan C1-p – *1 Banbury Road* ✉ *OX2 6NN* – ☎ *01865 310210* – *www.oldparsonagehotel.co.uk*

at **Great Milton** Southeast: 12 mi by A40 off A329 – Regional map n° **6**-C2

✿✿ **Belmond Le Manoir aux Quat' Saisons** (Raymond Blanc)

🕸 ⬧⬧ ⬧ 🅰🄲 🕩 ⬧ 🅿

FRENCH · LUXURY XxxX Legendary French chef Raymond Blanc presides over this iconic restaurant in a quintessentially English country house. You cannot help but fall in love with the place: the setting is divine and a feeling of luxury envelops you.

Enjoy a fine array of canapés in a sumptuous lounge then head through to the magical beamed restaurant comprising several interconnecting rooms; in summer, be sure to sit in the conservatory for views over the manicured gardens.

Top quality seasonal ingredients and beautifully fresh produce from the kitchen garden underpin the skilfully executed cooking – which has a classical French base and a light, modern touch – and the main menu is fittingly entitled 'Spécialités du Moment'. Flavours are intense, combinations are sophisticated and the presentation shows an eye for detail. Desserts are always a highlight and service is polished.

Specialities: Cornish crab with kaffir lime, coconut and passion fruit. Roasted fillet of Aberdeen Angus beef with braised Jacob's ladder. Dark chocolate cup with textures of cappuccino.

Menu £105 (lunch), £175/190

Off plan – *Church Road* ✉ *OX44 7PD* – ☎ *01844 278881* – *www.belmond.com* – *Closed Monday - Wednesday lunch*

Belmond Le Manoir aux Quat' Saisons

☆ ⬧ ⬧⬧ ⬧ 🅰🄲 ⬧ 🅿

COUNTRY HOUSE · ELEGANT This quintessential English country house part-dates from the 15C and is surrounded by majestic gardens. Guest areas are sumptuous, bedrooms are luxurious (ask for one in the Garden Wing) and service is top-class. Enjoy drinks on the delightful terrace overlooking the grounds.

32 rooms ⬧ – ♥♥ £695/1335 – 14 suites

Off plan – *Church Road* ✉ *OX44 7PD* – ☎ *01844 278881* – *www.belmond.com/lemanoir*

✿✿ **Belmond Le Manoir aux Quat' Saisons** – See restaurant listing

PADSTOW

Cornwall – Regional map n° **1**–B2

✿ Paul Ainsworth at No.6

MODERN CUISINE · INTIMATE XX A delightful Georgian townhouse on a narrow harbour backwater plays host to Paul Ainsworth's restaurant. The small first floor bar-lounge has a clubby, masculine feel, while the cosy, intimate dining room has a slightly funky vibe. All of the tables have a view into the kitchen and diners are encouraged to step inside and talk to the chefs after their meal. Service is friendly and enthusiastic and the well-versed team strive to make your visit a memorable one.

Paul's creative, original cooking is founded on well-honed classic techniques; he likes to play with traditional recipes and give them a contemporary twist. Dishes arrive attractively presented, ingredients are first class and flavours are robust and clearly defined.

Nearby, six luxurious, individually styled suites come with top quality linens and bespoke toiletries.

Specialities: Smoked haddock quiche Lorraine. Chicken tournedos Rossini with spring ragout roasting juices. 'A fairground tale'.

Menu £34 (lunch) – Carte £60/89

6 Middle Street ⊠ PL28 8AP – ℰ 01841 532093 – www.paul-ainsworth.co.uk –
Closed 11 January-6 February, 24-26 December, Sunday, Monday

☺ Rick Stein's Café ⇦ 🏠

INTERNATIONAL · BISTRO X A deceptively large café hidden behind a tiny shop front on a side street. The concise, seasonally changing menu offers tasty, unfussy dishes which display influences from Thailand, Morocco and the Med. The homemade bread is worth a try, as is the good value set dinner menu. Bedrooms are comfy and simply furnished; have breakfast in the café or small courtyard garden.

Specialities: Vietnamese poached chicken salad with peanuts, mint and coriander. Fillets of lemon sole with stir-fried wild garlic, asparagus and red peppers. Sticky toffee pudding with Cornish clotted cream.

Menu £26 – Carte £23/41

10 Middle Street ⊠ PL28 8AP – ℰ 01841 532700 – www.rickstein.com

⯈○ Seafood ⇦ ♿ A/C P

SEAFOOD · ELEGANT XXX Stylish, laid-back, local institution – dominated by a large pewter-topped bar. Daily menus showcase fresh fish and shellfish. Classic dishes sit alongside those influenced by Rick Stein's travels; perhaps Singapore chilli crab or Madras fish curry. New England style bedrooms boast good quality furnishings; some have terraces or balconies and estuary views.

Menu £45 (lunch) – Carte £39/105

Riverside ⊠ PL28 8BY – ℰ 01841 532700 – www.rickstein.com

⯈○ Appleton's ⇦ 🏠 ♿ P

MEDITERRANEAN CUISINE · FRIENDLY X A striking modern building plays host to this bright, spacious, first floor restaurant overlooking the 11,000+ vines of the Trevibban Mill Vineyard. Enjoy wines, ciders and apple juices made on-site while gazing down the valley and dining on original Italian-influenced dishes. The terrace makes the perfect spot for Sunday brunch and the serving team are charming.

Carte £25/45

Trevibban Mill, Dark Lane ⊠ PL27 7SE – ℰ 01841 541355 –
www.appletonsatthevineyard.com – Closed Sunday dinner, Monday, Tuesday,
Wednesday - Thursday dinner

⯈○ Prawn on the Lawn

SEAFOOD · TAPAS BAR X If you like seafood then you'll love this modern fishmongers-cum-seafood bar with its beautiful display of super-fresh fish out front and its tasty tapas-style sharing plates of shellfish and fish. It's cosy, with some counter seating.

Carte £21/43

11 Duke Street ⊠ PL28 8AB – ℰ 01841 532223 – www.prawnonthelawn.com –
Closed 12 January-3 February, Monday

Rojano's in the Square

ITALIAN · BRASSERIE X A bright, modern restaurant geared up to family dining, with a small cocktail bar, two floors for dining and a glass-enclosed terrace. Italian dishes are hearty and full of flavour and Cornish ingredients are to the fore.
Menu £19/25 – Carte £23/47
9 Mill Square ⊠ PL28 8AE – ℰ 01841 532796 – www.paul-ainsworth.co.uk – Closed 6-13 January

St Petroc's Bistro

MEDITERRANEAN CUISINE · BISTRO X An attractive townhouse on a steep hill, just a stone's throw from the harbour, with an oak-furnished bistro and terraces to the front and rear. The menu offers simply prepared classics with a Mediterranean slant and an emphasis on seafood and grills. Smart, well-appointed bedrooms are split between the house and an annexe.
Menu £20 (lunch) – Carte £30/53
4 New Street ⊠ PL28 8EA – ℰ 01841 532700 – www.rickstein.com

Padstow Townhouse

TOWNHOUSE · ELEGANT Everything's been thought of at this beautiful 18C townhouse. Six luxurious, individually styled suites come with top quality linens and bespoke toiletries made by local company St Kitts. There's an honesty bar in the kitchen pantry; breakfast is taken in your room or at their nearby restaurant.
6 rooms ⊡ – ♯♯ £300/380
16-18 High Street ⊠ PL28 8BB – ℰ 01841 550950 – www.paul-ainsworth.co.uk – Closed 11 January-6 February, 23-27 December
❀ Paul Ainsworth at No.6 – See restaurant listing

PATELEY BRIDGE
North Yorkshire – Regional map n° 13–B2

Yorke Arms

MODERN CUISINE · COUNTRY HOUSE XX This charming 17C inn sits on the green of a small hamlet and champions all things Yorkshire. Choose between the laid-back 'Little Dining Room' and the more formal 'Restaurant' where good quality local ingredients inform modern cooking. Stylish bedrooms also display Yorkshire themes.
Menu £75/105 – Carte £40/57
Ramsgill-in-Nidderdale ⊠ HG3 5RL – ℰ 01423 755243 – www.theyorkearms.co.uk – Closed 6-20 January

PAXFORD – Gloucestershire ➜ See Chipping Camden

PENN
Buckinghamshire – Regional map n° 6–D2

Old Queens Head

TRADITIONAL BRITISH · PUB X Legend has it that Lord Penn inherited this characterful country pub when he won a game of cards against Charles II. Robust, satisfying dishes follow the seasons and have a British heart. The sunny terrace is a popular spot.
Carte £23/46
Hammersley Lane ⊠ HP10 8EY – ℰ 01494 813371 – www.oldqueensheadpenn.co.uk

PENZANCE
Cornwall – Regional map n° 1–A3

ⅼ○ Harris's

CLASSIC CUISINE · INTIMATE XX Long-standing, split-level restaurant with a spiral staircase and an unusual Welsh black metal plate ceiling; run by a keen husband and wife. Classical cooking uses seasonal Cornish produce; try the steamed lobster when it's in season.

Carte £35/45

46 New Street ⊠ TR18 2LZ – ℰ 01736 364408 – www.harrissrestaurant.co.uk – Closed 12-26 January, 3-20 November, Sunday, Monday

ⅼ○ Shore

SEAFOOD · INTIMATE XX The name refers to the cooking rather than the location of this small bistro. The experienced chef works alone: his produce is ethically sourced and many of his precisely prepared dishes have Mediterranean or Asian influences.

Menu £59

13-14 Alverton Street ⊠ TR18 2QP – ℰ 01736 362444 – www.theshorerestaurant.uk – Closed 23 December-20 January, Sunday, Monday, Tuesday - Saturday lunch

🏠 Chapel House

TOWNHOUSE · CONTEMPORARY A smartly refurbished 18C house with a pretty walled garden. Sumptuous lounges are filled with modern art and there's a fabulous basement dining room where they serve breakfast and pre-booked weekend meals. Bedrooms have a cool, understated elegance and sea views: all feature fresh flowers and hand-crafted oak furnishings and one has a bathroom with a retractable roof!

8 rooms ⊑ – ♛♛ £160/220

Chapel Street ⊠ TR18 4AQ – ℰ 01736 362024 – www.chapelhouse.pz.co.uk

PERRANUTHNOE – Cornwall ➡ See Marazion

PERSHORE
Worcestershire – Regional map n° **10**-C3

at Eckington Southwest: 4 mi by A4104 on B4080

ⅼ○ Eckington Manor

MODERN CUISINE · DESIGN XX You'll find this proudly run 13C manor house and its characterful, converted barns on a 300 acre farm. The constantly evolving set priced menu offers refined, classical dishes which feature plenty of farm produce. For those who want to get more involved there's a cookery school, as well as stylish bedrooms.

Menu £21 (lunch)/48

Manor Farm, Hammock Road (Via Drakes Bridge Road) ⊠ WR10 3BJ – ℰ 01386 751600 – www.eckingtonmanor.co.uk – Closed Sunday dinner, Monday, Tuesday

PETERBOROUGH
Peterborough – Regional map n° **8**–A2

ⅼ○ Prévost

CREATIVE BRITISH · DESIGN XX You enter via an alleyway into a bright, spacious room, where local artists' work is displayed on the walls and the tables overlook a small kitchen garden. Lunch sees a good value 3 course set menu, while dinner offers 3, 5 or 9 courses. Attractive dishes have a creative Scandic style.

Menu £20 (lunch), £35/75

20 Priestgate ⊠ PE1 1JA – ℰ 01733 313623 – www.prevostpeterborough.co.uk – Closed 1-16 January, 27 July-10 August, Sunday-Tuesday lunch

PETWORTH
West Sussex – Regional map n° **4**-C2

at Lickfold Northwest: 6 mi by A 272

⫟○ Lickfold Inn ⛲ &. **P**

MODERN BRITISH · COSY ⅩⅩ A pretty Grade II listed brick and timber pub with a characterful lounge-bar serving small plates and a formal first floor restaurant. Terse descriptions hide the true complexities of the innovative dishes, which echo the seasons and are given a touch of theatre. Staff are friendly and eager to please.

Menu £ 30 (lunch) – Carte £ 42/56

Highstead Lane ✉ GU28 9EY – ☏ 01789 532535 – www.thelickfoldinn.co.uk – Closed Sunday dinner, Monday, Tuesday

PLUMTREE – Nottinghamshire → See Nottingham

PLYMOUTH
Plymouth – Regional map n° **1**-C2

⫟○ Greedy Goose 🛖

MODERN BRITISH · ELEGANT ⅩⅩ Smart restaurant housed in a delightful building dating from 1482 and named after the children's book 'Chocolate Mousse for Greedy Goose'. Cooking is modern and flavoursome and the local beef is superb. Sit in the 'quad' in summer.

Menu £ 13 – Carte £ 27/47

Prysten House, Finewell Street ✉ PL1 2AE – ☏ 01752 252001 – www.thegreedygoose.co.uk – Closed 22-30 December, Sunday, Monday

⫟○ Barbican Kitchen &. 🅰🅒 🕼 🕲 ⇄

INTERNATIONAL · BRASSERIE Ⅹ An informal eatery in the Plymouth Gin Distillery (where gin was once distilled for the Navy). Brasserie menus offer a good choice of simply cooked dishes, with classic comfort food to the fore; vegetarians are well catered for.

Menu £ 16 (lunch)/19 – Carte £ 25/59

Plymouth Gin Distillery, 60 Southside Street ✉ PL1 2LQ – ☏ 01752 604448 – www.barbicankitchen.com – Closed Sunday

⫟○ Fig Tree @ 36 🛖

MODERN BRITISH · FRIENDLY Ⅹ A young local couple run this inviting neighbourhood restaurant near Royal William Yard; it's named after a tree they found in the small rear courtyard. Alongside these fruits, you'll find regional produce and fish landed just down the road. Fresh, unfussy cooking lets the ingredients speak for themselves.

Menu £ 20/25 – Carte £ 25/45

36 Admiralty Street ✉ PL1 3RU – ☏ 01752 253247 – www.thefigtreeat36.co.uk – Closed Sunday dinner, Monday, Tuesday lunch

PONTELAND – Northumberland → See Newcastle upon Tyne

POOLE
Poole – Regional map n° **2**-C3

⫟○ Rick Stein ⟨ &. 🅰🅒 🕼

SEAFOOD · CHIC ⅩⅩ Rick may be expanding his empire but he's keeping his fishy theme. The large menu offers everything from cod and chips to seafood platters and all his classics are there, including turbot hollandaise and plaice alla carlina. Start with a drink in the sleek bar then enjoy superb sea views from the restaurant.

Menu £ 26 (lunch) – Carte £ 32/102

10-14 Banks Rd, Sandbanks ✉ BH13 7QB – ☏ 01202 283000 – www.rickstein.com

POOLE

ENGLAND

⼘○ **Guildhall Tavern**

SEAFOOD · BISTRO ⅩⅩ Proudly run restaurant opposite the Guildhall, with a bright, cheery interior and a nautical theme. Tasty, classical French dishes are generously proportioned and largely seafood-based. They also host monthly gourmet evenings.

Menu £21/30 – Carte £30/55

15 Market Street ⊠ BH15 1NB –
☏ 01202 671717 – www.guildhalltavern.co.uk – Closed 1-14 April,
24 December-6 January, Sunday, Monday

POOLEY BRIDGE

Cumbria – Regional map n° **12**–B2

⼘○ **Sharrow Bay Country House**

CLASSIC CUISINE · ELEGANT ⅩⅩⅩ A charming country house in an idyllic lakeside location. Enjoy an aperitif by the fire in the sitting room then head through to one of two dining rooms – Lakeside offers stunning views. Well-judged dishes have a classical base and subtle modern touches; save room for their renowned sticky toffee pudding.

Menu £25 (lunch)/68

Sharrow Bay Country House Hotel, Ullswater ⊠ CA10 2LZ –
☏ 017684 86301 – www.sharrowbay.co.uk

🏠 **Sharrow Bay Country House**

COUNTRY HOUSE · CLASSIC This iconic English country house sits in a stunning spot on the shore of Lake Ullswater and has the Lakeland hills as its backdrop. It has a charmingly traditional style and a tranquil feel; take in views of the water while enjoying afternoon tea. Bedrooms are elegant and luxurious.

17 rooms ⌂ – ♛ £165/395

Ullswater ⊠ CA10 2LZ –
☏ 017684 86301 – www.sharrowbay.co.uk
⼘○ **Sharrow Bay Country House** – See restaurant listing

at Watermillock Southwest 2. 5 mi by B5320 on A592

🏠 **Another Place, The Lake**

FAMILY · TRENDY A stunning spot on the shore of Lake Ullswater plays host to this stylishly understated, activity-led hotel, which has a laid-back atmosphere and caters well for children. The Living Space is ideal for an informal drink and a pub-style dish, while more sophisticated Rampsbeck serves a menu of classics.

40 rooms ⌂ – ♛ £170/289 – 2 suites
⊠ CA11 0LP – ☏ 017684 86442 – www.another.place

PORT GAVERNE

Cornwall – Regional map n° **1**–B2

⼘○ **Pilchards**

SEAFOOD · SIMPLE Ⅹ Park in Port Isaac and walk over to this modern timber and glass building with a large terraced garden, which overlooks the bay where the famous Cornish pilchards were once landed. The seafood-orientated menu offers both small and large plates, with whole fish grilled over charcoal a speciality.

Carte £25/31

⊠ PL29 3SQ – ☏ 01208 880891 – www.pilchardsatportgaverne.co.uk –
Closed 1 January-12 April, Monday, Tuesday

PORTHLEVEN
Cornwall – Regional map n° **1**–A3

Kota

ASIAN INFLUENCES · RUSTIC XX Welcoming harbourside granary with thick stone walls, a tiled floor and an array of wood furnishings; its name means 'shell-fish' in Maori. Menus mix unfussy and more elaborate dishes and display subtle Asian influences courtesy of the owner's Chinese and Malaysian background. Many of the ingredients are foraged. Bedrooms are simply furnished – one over-looks the harbour.

Specialities: Mackerel with celeriac remoulade and pickled beets. Five spice roasted duck with teriyaki orange glaze and duck croquette. Chocolate fondant with miso caramel and caramelised banana.

Menu £28 – Carte £27/45

Harbour Head ⊠ TR13 9JA – ℰ 01326 562407 – www.kotarestaurant.co.uk –
Closed 1-31 January, Sunday, Monday, Tuesday - Saturday lunch

Rick Stein

SEAFOOD · COLOURFUL XX This old harbourside clay store has been trans-formed into a smart restaurant with floor to ceiling windows and a first floor ter-race. Top quality seafood small plates are inspired by Rick Stein's travels and sharing is encouraged.

Menu £23 (lunch) – Carte £26/48

Mount Pleasant Road ⊠ TR13 9JS – ℰ 01326 565636 – www.rickstein.com

Square

MODERN CUISINE · SIMPLE X In summer, bag a table on the terrace of this small harbourside bistro; in winter, cosy up and watch the waves crash on the harbour wall. Coffee and cakes give way to snacks and sharing platters, followed by well-prepared modern classics with punchy flavours. They have a deli and ice cream shop next door.

Carte £21/38

7 Fore Street ⊠ TR13 9HQ – ℰ 01326 573911 – www.thesquareatporthleven.co.uk

PORT ISAAC
Cornwall – Regional map n° **1**–B2

Restaurant Nathan Outlaw (Nathan Outlaw)

SEAFOOD · INTIMATE XX He might not be Cornish by birth but Nathan Outlaw has certainly made Cornwall his home and he has been warmly welcomed by the locals. His smart yet relaxed restaurant sits in a great position on the head-land, just a stone's throw from the harbour, and the views from the first floor din-ing room are stunning. If you'd rather keep your attention solely on the food though, there's a Chef's Table on the ground floor.

There is no other chef in the country who understands and executes seafood cookery so well and his name has become synonymous with ultra-fresh fish and shellfish. His set menus are guided by the daily catch, landed just down the road at Port Isaac, and the carefully crafted dishes feature classical combinations which keep the focus firmly on the main ingredient. Service strikes the perfect balance of professional yet personable.

Specialities: Raw scallops with cucumber and chilli. John Dory with Porthilly sauce. Rhubarb ice cream sandwich.

Menu £140

6 New Road ⊠ PL29 3SB – ℰ 01208 880896 – www.nathan-outlaw.com –
Closed 21 December-5 February, Sunday, Monday, Tuesday, Wednesday lunch

Outlaw's Fish Kitchen

SEAFOOD · INTIMATE X The characterful Cornish fishing village of Port Isaac is known around the globe as the setting for TV series Doc Martin, but it's also well-known in the culinary world as the home of this intimate 15C fisherman's cot-tage with low ceilings, wonky walls and tasty seafood menus. It sits right on the harbourside, where you can watch the day boats unloading their catch shortly before it arrives at the restaurant's doors.

Quality and sustainability are the watchwords here and the menu is dictated not only by the seasons but by the weather too. This is a place where it's all about small plates designed for sharing, with 4-5 between two about the right amount. Combinations are kept simple but pair together bold flavours – these really bring the dishes alive yet cleverly manage to keep the fish as the star of the show.

Specialities: Cured brill with anchovy, pistachio, mint and coriander dressing. Tandoori monkfish with pickled fennel and coriander yoghurt. Chocolate, peanut and lime 'baked Alaska'.

Menu £50 – Carte £35/50

1 Middle Street ✉ *PL29 3RH –* ✆ *01208 881183 –*
www.nathan-outlaw.com/outlaws-fish-kitchen – Closed 22 December-5 February, Sunday, Monday

🍴 Stargazy Inn

CREATIVE BRITISH · CONTEMPORARY DÉCOR ✗ This detached Victorian house sits in an elevated spot; start with a drink on the terrace and enjoy the impressive coastal view. The ambitious chef prepares interesting snacks, excellent homemade bread and deceptively creative dishes with stimulating textures and flavours. Some of the bedrooms share the view.

Carte £32/75

The Terrace ✉ *PL29 3SG –* ✆ *01208 811516 – www.stargazyinn.co.uk – Closed 1 January-1 March, Monday, Tuesday*

PORTLOE
Cornwall – Regional map n° **1**-B3

🏠 Lugger

INN · COSY This 17C smugglers' inn sits in a picturesque fishing village and affords dramatic views over the rugged bay. It's snug and cosy, with open fires, low ceilings and friendly service. Have a drink on the terrace and dinner in the clean-lined, Scandic-style dining room, which serves seafood fresh from the bay.

24 rooms ☎ – 👫 £165/320

✉ *TR2 5RD –* ✆ *01872 501322 – www.luggerhotel.co.uk*

PORTSCATHO
Cornwall – Regional map n° **1**-B3

🍴 Driftwood

MODERN CUISINE · DESIGN ✗✗ A bright New England style restaurant located in an attractive hotel, in a peaceful clifftop setting; it's delightfully run by a friendly team and boasts superb views out to sea. Unfussy modern dishes follow the seasons and are pitched perfectly for the hotel's laid-back style.

Carte £70/100

Driftwood Hotel, Rosevine ✉ *TR2 5EW –* ✆ *01872 580644 – www.driftwoodhotel.co.uk – Closed 11 December-1 February*

🏠 Driftwood

COUNTRY HOUSE · PERSONALISED A charming clifftop hotel looking out over mature grounds, which stretch down to the shore and a private beach. Stylish, contemporary guest areas are decorated with pieces of driftwood. Smart bedrooms – in the main house and annexed cottages – have a good level of modern facilities; some have decked terraces.

15 rooms ☎ – 👫 £210/295

Rosevine ✉ *TR2 5EW –* ✆ *01872 580644 – www.driftwoodhotel.co.uk – Closed 11 December-1 February*

🍴 **Driftwood** – See restaurant listing

PORTSMOUTH AND SOUTHSEA

Portsmouth – Regional map n° **4**–B3

⫶○ **Restaurant 27** 🅥

MODERN BRITISH · NEIGHBOURHOOD XX This elegant restaurant is professionally and passionately run. Attractively presented, contemporary dishes have a slight Scandic style; they only serve tasting menus, supplemented by a set priced Sunday lunch.

Menu £49/59

27a South Par, Southsea ⊠ PO5 2JF – ℰ 023 9287 6272 – www.restaurant27.com – Closed Sunday dinner, Monday, Tuesday, Wednesday - Saturday lunch

PRESTON CANDOVER

Hampshire – Regional map n° **4**–B2

⫶○ **The Purefoy** Ⓝ 🛏 ⛩ 🅥 🅿

MODERN BRITISH · PUB X Across the road from the church is this village pub with exposed stone walls, welcoming open fires and a small garden. A range of menus offers everything from keenly priced pub classics to more modern, innovative combinations and even a tasting menu. The simpler dishes are often the best.

Menu £25/42 – Carte £25/42

Alresford Road ⊠ RG25 2EJ – ℰ 01256 389777 – www.thepurefoyarms.co.uk – Closed Sunday dinner, Monday

RADNAGE

Buckinghamshire – Regional map n° **6**–C2

⫶○ **The Mash Inn** ⇦ 🛏 ⛩ 🅿

MODERN BRITISH · PUB X Characterful 18C pub with flagged floors, exposed timbers, hand-crafted oak tables, and great country views from the terrace. Top quality local and garden ingredients lead the daily menu and the bespoke wood-fired chargrill is used to great effect. Bedrooms are modern and simply furnished.

Menu £25 (lunch), £60/95

Horseshoe Rd, Bennett End ⊠ HP14 4EB – ℰ 01494 482440 – www.themashinn.com – Closed Sunday dinner, Monday, Tuesday

RAMSBOTTOM

Greater Manchester – Regional map n° **11**–B2

⫶○ **Hungry Duck** Ⓝ

TRADITIONAL BRITISH · BISTRO X Black and white photos adorn the walls of this sweet neighbourhood bistro, which is split over two levels and run with plenty of purpose by its owner, Joe. Hearty, seasonal dishes are cooked with care and full of flavour. Everything is homemade – including the ice cream – and the cheese pie is a hit.

Menu £21 – Carte £22/44

76 Bridge Street ⊠ BL0 9AG – ℰ 01706 550899 – www.hungry-duck.co.uk

⫶○ **Levanter**

SPANISH · TAPAS BAR X Joe has a passion for all things Spanish – he's even a trained flamenco guitarist – so, unsurprisingly, his sweet little tapas bar has an authentic feel. The menu is dictated by market produce; be sure to try some of the freshly sliced Iberico ham. He also owns the nearby Basque-style Baratxuri pintxo bar.

Carte £19/29

10 Square Street ⊠ BL0 9BE – ℰ 01706 551530 – www.levanterfinefoods.co.uk – Closed Monday, Tuesday, Wednesday lunch

RAMSGATE

Kent – Regional map n° **5**–D1

Arya

MODERN CUISINE · FRIENDLY X This hidden gem sits in the heart of town. There's a delightful bar downstairs; upstairs is a dining room with a lively hum. It's proudly run by a brother and sister: she keeps things running smoothly out front while he prepares interesting small plates with modern European influences.

Specialities: Grilled prawns with pak choi and paella rice. Beef shin, gnocchi and Parmesan. Buttermilk panna cotta with blueberry and hazelnut.

Carte £23/35

54-56 King Street (Above The Ravensgate Arms) ✉ *CT11 8NY –* 𝒞 *07943 628357 –* *www.aryaramsgate.co.uk – Closed Sunday dinner, Monday, Tuesday, Wednesday -* *Friday lunch*

READING

Reading – Regional map n° **6**–C3

🏠 Roseate

TOWNHOUSE · DESIGN An impressive former civic hall overlooking Forbury Square Gardens; now a smart townhouse hotel where contemporary designs meet with original features. Luxurious bedrooms come with coffee machines, fridges and top electronics. The chic bar and restaurant offer modern menus.

55 rooms ♅ – ⚥ £150/250

26 Forbury ✉ *RG1 3EJ –* 𝒞 *0118 952 7770 – www.roseatehotels.com*

at Shinfield South: 4. 25 mi on A327 – Regional map n° **6**–C3

🌸 L'Ortolan

MODERN FRENCH · INTIMATE XxX Hidden under a creeper cloak and surrounded by beautiful grounds is L'Ortolan, a truly fine example of a Georgian rectory. It's a comfortable place with stylish modern décor and plenty of space: dine in one of several private dining rooms, the contemporary main room or in the conservatory overlooking the garden. This was one of the first restaurants to have a chef's table, so if you're in a party of four, sitting here in the heart of the kitchen is always a good bet.

Modern French dishes exhibit a pleasing array of colours, textures and flavours, and many have a certain surprise element to them too. Flavours are gutsy and pronounced and head chef Tom Clarke aims to bring together all of the tastes – bitter, sweet, salty, sour, umami – in complementary combinations. For the ultimate dining experience, book the 'Discovery' menu – a multi-course tasting menu written specifically for your group. Service is attentive and professional.

Specialities: Steak tartare with nasturtium and charcoal. Guinea fowl with peas and broad beans. Toffee apple and pecan.

Menu £42/105

Church Lane ✉ *RG2 9BY –* 𝒞 *0118 988 8500 – www.lortolan.com –* *Closed 24 December-3 January, Sunday, Monday*

at Sonning-on-Thames Northeast: 4. 25 mi by A4 on B4446

ⅰ○ French Horn

TRADITIONAL BRITISH · ELEGANT XxX A beautifully located, 200 year old coaching inn, set on a bank of the Thames fringed by weeping willows; on sunny days head for the splendid terrace. The formal dining room has delightful views over the river and gardens and offers a classical menu of dishes from yesteryear – a gueridon trolley adds to the theatre. Cosy bedrooms are also traditionally appointed.

Menu £35 – Carte £57/87

✉ *RG4 6TN –* 𝒞 *0118 969 2204 – www.thefrenchhorn.co.uk*

RIBCHESTER
Lancashire – Regional map n° **11**–B2

⅏○ **Angels**
MODERN CUISINE · INTIMATE XxX Smartly converted roadside pub with a cocktail bar and comfy lounge seating. Two formally dressed dining rooms offer a comfortable, intimate dining experience. Classic dishes with a modern edge are tasty, well-balanced and good value.

Menu £25 – Carte £38/49

Fleet Street Lane ⊠ PR3 3ZA – 𝒞 01254 820212 – www.angelsribchester.co.uk – Closed Monday, Tuesday, Wednesday - Saturday lunch

RIMPTON
Somerset – Regional map n° **2**–C3

⅏○ **White Post**
CLASSIC CUISINE · PUB X A smart dining pub set on the Dorset/Somerset border and affording stunning West Country views. Pub classics sit alongside more imaginative dishes, some with quirky touches like the piggy nibbles and, every carnivore's dream, the Sunday roast board. Bedrooms are comfortable – 'Dorset' has the best views.

Carte £28/50

⊠ BA22 8AR – 𝒞 01935 851525 – www.thewhitepost.com – Closed Sunday dinner, Monday, Tuesday

RIPLEY
Surrey – Regional map n° **4**–C1

✿ **Clock House**
MODERN CUISINE · INTIMATE XxX Occupying a delightful Georgian building in the centre of the village, this restaurant takes its name from the double-sided clock above the door. Inside it has been beautifully restored and fuses original architectural splendour with a modern air. The panelled bar with Queen Anne origins leads through to an elegant timbered dining room overlooking a delightful garden and terrace – and the service is as charming as the setting itself.

Having started here in 2012, Fred Clapperton rose through the ranks to become Head Chef in 2016 and in that time developed a creative personal style based on natural tastes. Bold flavours come together in well-balanced combinations with a refined, understated style and dishes are accurately prepared and display plenty of finesse. The seasonal tasting menus are a great way to see the diversity of his cooking.

Specialities: Cured venison with hay custard. Short-rib with sweetbreads, brassicas and mustard. Blackberries with hibiscus, apple and shortbread.

Menu £40 (lunch), £70/90

High Street ⊠ GU23 6AQ – 𝒞 01483 224777 – www.theclockhouserestaurant.co.uk – Closed 6-14 April, 17-31 August, Sunday, Monday, Tuesday

✿ **Anchor**
MODERN BRITISH · PUB X A smart yet rustic pub with a 400 year history, polished slate floors and on-trend grey walls. Despite its name, it's nowhere near the water, but it is close to a famous cycle route, which explains the bicycle-themed interior. Restaurant-style dishes are carefully executed and bursting with flavour.

Specialities: Grilled mackerel escabeche with garlic and saffron mayonnaise. Roast guinea fowl with charred cabbage and Sarlardaise potatoes. Mango soufflé with lime and white chocolate sorbet.

Menu £28 (lunch) – Carte £30/40

High Street ⊠ GU23 6AE – 𝒞 01483 211866 – www.ripleyanchor.co.uk – Closed Monday

🏠 Broadway Barn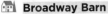

TOWNHOUSE · DESIGN This charming double-fronted house spent time as an antiques shop before being converted into a guesthouse. The large open-fired lounge leads to a conservatory breakfast room which overlooks a well-tended garden. Bedrooms display good attention to detail and come with thoughtful extras.

4 rooms – 👫 £125

High Street ⊠ GU23 6AQ – ℰ 01483 223200 –
www.broadwaybarn.com

RIPON

North Yorkshire – Regional map n° **13**–B2

🏠 Grantley Hall ⓝ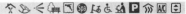

HISTORIC · GRAND LUXURY This impressively restored 17C hall is fronted by attractive gardens and the River Skell runs through its charming grounds. Bedrooms are elegant and luxurious and many come with original features and stunning views. Unwind in the smart spa or fitness centre then dine in one of three restaurants.

47 rooms – 👫 £270/650 – 3 suites

⊠ HG4 3ES – ℰ 01765 620070 –
www.grantleyhall.co.uk

ROCHDALE

Lancashire – Regional map n° **11**–B2

🍴 Nutters

MODERN BRITISH · FRIENDLY 🕸 Enthusiastically run restaurant in a beautiful old manor house – a popular spot for afternoon tea. Appealing menus list modern British dishes with international influences. Can't decide? Go for the 6 course 'Surprise' menu.

Menu £23 (lunch)/48 – Carte £35/45

Edenfield Road, Norden ⊠ OL12 7TT – ℰ 01706 650167 –
www.nuttersrestaurant.com –
Closed Monday

ROCK

Cornwall – Regional map n° **1**–B2

🍴 Dining Room

MODERN BRITISH · NEIGHBOURHOOD 🕸 Immaculately kept, understated restaurant with modern seascapes on the walls; run by a friendly, family-led team. Flavoursome, classically based cooking features local seasonal produce. Everything is homemade, including the butter.

Menu £48

Pavilion Buildings, Rock Road ⊠ PL27 6JS – ℰ 01208 862622 –
www.thediningroomrock.co.uk –
Closed 5 January-14 February, Sunday lunch-Tuesday, Wednesday-Saturday lunch

🍴 Mariners ⓝ

TRADITIONAL CUISINE · PUB 🕸 The setting is wonderful, with the terrace affording stunning views over the Camel Estuary, and there's no doubting the passion put into both the cooking and the service. The British pub menu brims with local produce and they also offer small plates, breakfasts and cream teas.

Carte £27/44

Slipway ⊠ PL27 6LD – ℰ 01841 532093 –
www.paul-ainsworth.co.uk – Closed 19-29 January

ROMSEY
Hampshire – Regional map n° **4**–A2

⑩ **Three Tuns** ⌂ P

TRADITIONAL BRITISH · PUB X Cosy 300 year old pub off the market square. Original features include oak beams and a central bar which divides the place in two – head left if you want to dine. Classic pub dishes are generously proportioned and full of flavour.

Carte £22/36

58 Middlebridge Street ⊠ SO51 8HL – ℰ 01794 512639 –
www.the3tunsromsey.co.uk

ROSS-ON-WYE
Herefordshire – Regional map n° **10**–B3

at Upton Bishop Northeast: 3 mi by A40 on B4221

⑩ **Moody Cow** ⌂ P

TRADITIONAL BRITISH · PUB X A traditional country pub serving classic dishes to match the surroundings. What the food may lack in originality, it makes up for with quality ingredients, careful cooking and distinct flavours. Friendly owners run the place with passion.

Menu £30 (lunch) – Carte £30/44

⊠ HR9 7TT – ℰ 01989 780470 – www.moodycowpub.co.uk – Closed 1-16 January,
Sunday dinner, Monday, Tuesday

ROWHOOK – West Sussex → See Horsham

ROWSLEY
Derbyshire – Regional map n° **9**–A1

⑩ **Peacock** ⌂ ⊞ ℐ℔ P

MODERN CUISINE · INTIMATE XX An elegant hotel restaurant where old mullioned stone windows, oak 'Mousey Thompson' furnishings and antique oil paintings are juxtaposed with modern lighting and contemporary art. Modern cooking is ingredient-led and has fresh, clean flavours; alongside, they offer some more traditional 'Classics'.

Menu £25 (lunch)/75 – Carte £46/68

Peacock Hotel, Bakewell Road ⊠ DE4 2EB – ℰ 01629 733518 –
www.thepeacockatrowsley.com – Closed 6-25 January

🏠 **Peacock** ⌂ ⊞ P

COUNTRY HOUSE · PERSONALISED A characterful 17C Dower House of the Duchess of Rutland, with gardens leading down to the river. There's a snug open-fired sitting room and a characterful bar with stone walls, wood-panelling and a large peacock mural. Bedrooms mix antique furnishings with modern facilities and service is top-notch.

15 rooms ⊡ – ⑩ £225/310

Bakewell Road ⊠ DE4 2EB – ℰ 01629 733518 – www.thepeacockatrowsley.com
⑩ **Peacock** – See restaurant listing

ROYAL LEAMINGTON SPA
Warwickshire – Regional map n° **10**–D3

🏠 **Mallory Court** ⌂ ⊞ 🐎 ⊞ ℐ℔ ⊞ P

COUNTRY HOUSE · PERSONALISED A part-Edwardian house in Lutyens' style, with lovely gardens, a smart spa and classical lounges displaying fine antiques. Fresh flowers feature in the bedrooms: those in the main house are characterful, those in Orchard House are contemporary and those in the Knight's Suite have a more corporate feel. Dine from modern menus in the elegant dining room or brasserie.

43 rooms – ⑩ £129/450

Harbury Ln, Bishop's Tachbrook ⊠ CV33 9QB – ℰ 01926 330214 –
www.mallory.co.uk

ROYAL TUNBRIDGE WELLS

Kent – Regional map n° **5**-B2

Ⅰ○ **Thackeray's**

MODERN BRITISH · INTIMATE XXX A softly illuminated clapboard house; the oldest in town and once home to the eponymous author. Classic dishes have modern elements and feature lots of different ingredients. The moody first floor private rooms showcase local art.

Menu £20 (lunch)/55

85 London Road ✉ *TN1 1EA –* ✆ *01892 511921 – www.thackerays-restaurant.co.uk – Closed Sunday dinner, Monday*

Ⅰ○ **The Warren**

MODERN BRITISH · INTIMATE XX This large, multi-roomed restaurant is set above the High Street shops and its quirky, eclectic décor includes gold walls, brightly coloured linen and various objets d'art. Ambitious modern cooking showcases meats from their 650 acre estate.

Menu £25 – Carte £31/54

5a High Street (1st Floor) ✉ *TN1 1UL –* ✆ *01892 328191 – www.thewarren.restaurant – Closed Sunday dinner, Monday, Tuesday*

Ⅰ○ **The Old Fishmarket**

SEAFOOD · SIMPLE X This small black and white building in The Pantiles was once the town's fish market, so it's fitting that it's now an intimate seafood restaurant. The menu focuses on oysters, fruits de mer platters and the daily catch.

Menu £15 (lunch) – Carte £30/65

19 The Upper Pantiles ✉ *TN2 5TN –* ✆ *01892 511422 – www.sankeys.co.uk – Closed Sunday dinner, Monday*

at Southborough North : 2 mi on A 26

Ⅰ○ **The Twenty Six** ╬

CREATIVE · RUSTIC X A very homely, rustic restaurant with a welcoming wood-burning stove, set overlooking the village green; it has 26 seats and 26 light bulbs hanging from the ceiling. They style themselves as a 'Test Kitchen'. Menus change daily and creative modern cooking offers stimulating contrasts in texture and flavour.

Carte £20/37

15a Church Road ✉ *TN4 0RX –* ✆ *01892 544607 – www.thetwenty-six.co.uk – Closed Sunday - Wednesday dinner*

RUDDINGTON – Nottinghamshire → See Nottingham

RUSHTON – Northamptonshire → See Kettering

RYE

East Sussex – Regional map n° **5**-C2

Ⅰ○ **Tuscan Kitchen**

ITALIAN · RUSTIC X Owner Franco hails from Tuscany, which is the inspiration for everything in this sweet little house. It resembles an osteria and the walls are filled with Florentine artefacts. Cooking too is based on recipes of the region; homemade pasta is a strength and olive oil comes from their farm in San Gimignano.

Carte £25/40

8 Lion Street ✉ *TN31 7LB –* ✆ *01797 223269 – www.tuscankitchenrye.co.uk – Closed 1 January-1 February, Monday, Tuesday, Wednesday lunch*

🏠 George in Rye

INN · DESIGN A deceptively large, centrally located coaching inn offering an attractive blend of the old and the new. Stylish bedrooms have bold colour schemes and good facilities. There's a characterful beamed bar, a cosy wood-panelled lounge and a modern grill restaurant where Josper-cooked steaks are a highlight.

34 rooms ☲ – ♥♥ £135/165

98 High Street ✉ TN31 7JT – ℰ 01797 222114 – www.thegeorgeinrye.com

ST ALBANS

Hertfordshire – Regional map n° **7**–A2

⑪ THOMPSON St Albans

MODERN CUISINE · INTIMATE ✕✕ Thompson's three contemporary dining rooms feature bold artwork from the local gallery – and the dishes are equally attractive. The weekday fixed price menu offers the best value but for the full experience opt for either the 5 or 7 course tasting menu, accompanied by some lesser-known wines by the glass.

Menu £19 (lunch), £25/47

2 Hatfield Road ✉ AL1 3RP – ℰ 01727 730777 – www.thompsonstalbans.co.uk – Closed 2-10 January, Sunday dinner, Monday, Tuesday lunch

ST AUSTELL

Cornwall – Regional map n° **1**–B2

🏠 Anchorage House

TOWNHOUSE · PERSONALISED A contemporary guesthouse run by lovely owners – one is an ex-American Navy Commander! Charming, antique-filled bedrooms boast modern fabrics, state-of-the-art bathrooms and plenty of extras. There's a lovely indoor pool with a sauna and a hot tub, along with a chill-out lounge. Afternoon tea is a hit.

3 rooms – ♥♥ £130/140

Nettles Corner, Boscundle ✉ PL25 3RH – ℰ 01726 814071 – www.anchoragehouse.co.uk – Closed 1 June-15 July, 1 October-20 April

ST HELIER – Jersey ➜ See Channel Islands (Jersey)

ST IVES

Cornwall – Regional map n° **1**–A3

⑪ Porthgwidden Beach Café

MODERN CUISINE · NEIGHBOURHOOD ✕ Tucked away by the beach, this super-friendly all-day café offers fantastic views over the bay to the lighthouse. The appealing menu comprises unfussy Mediterranean-influenced dishes, including plenty of seafood from St Ives, Looe and Mevagissey; be sure to have the Panang curry if it's on the specials list.

Carte £23/34

Porthgwidden Beach ✉ TR26 1PL – ℰ 01736 796791 – www.porthgwiddencafe.co.uk

⑪ Porthminster Beach Café

SEAFOOD · BISTRO ✕ A charming 1930s beach house in a superb location overlooking Porthminster Sands. It's hung with Cornish artwork, has a nautical style and leads out onto a glass-walled heated terrace. The seasonal seafood menu offers unfussy, vibrantly flavoured dishes with Asian influences. Service is relaxed and friendly.

Carte £26/45

Porthminster Beach ✉ TR26 2EB – ℰ 01736 795352 – www.porthminstercafe.co.uk

⁙○ Porthmeor Café Bar   ⩽ 斋 ⛾

MODERN CUISINE · NEIGHBOURHOOD ※ A popular beachfront café where you can sit inside, on the terrace or in heated pods. They offer breakfast, cakes, Mediterranean small plates and a few more substantial dishes too. Every table has a great view, especially at sunset.

Carte £22/34

Porthmeor Beach ⊠ TR26 1JZ – ℰ 01736 793366 – www.porthmeor-beach.co.uk

⁙○ Porthminster Kitchen   ⛾ ⩽ 斋 ⛾

MODERN CUISINE · NEIGHBOURHOOD ※ Follow the narrow staircase up to this contemporary bistro and you'll be rewarded with glorious harbour views from both the restaurant and terrace. The all-day menu offers light, fresh, global cuisine with a focus on local seafood.

Carte £26/42

The Wharf ⊠ TR26 1LG – ℰ 01736 799874 – www.porthminster.kitchen

⌂ Trevose Harbour House   P

TOWNHOUSE · CONTEMPORARY The experienced owners have decorated this stylish townhouse themselves, so you'll find lots of personal touches alongside an unusual mix of designer and upcycled furnishings. Breakfast features local produce and is a real highlight. They have 3 parking spaces reserved at the nearby station.

6 rooms – ⋔ £170/295

*22 The Warren ⊠ TR26 2EA – ℰ 01736 793267 – www.trevosehouse.co.uk –
Closed 14 November-18 March*

ST KEW

Cornwall – Regional map n° **1**-B2

⁙○ St Kew Inn   ⭄ 斋 P

TRADITIONAL BRITISH · PUB ※ A characterful country pub with flagged floors and wooden beams, set in a quintessentially English location. Menus offer a wide range of appealing, good value dishes and on summer Sundays joints are cooked in the garden on the Big Green Egg. Be sure to order a beer from the wooden casks behind the bar.

Carte £27/41

⊠ PL30 3HB – ℰ 01208 841259 – www.stkewinn.co.uk

ST MAWES

Cornwall – Regional map n° **1**-B3

⁙○ Idle Rocks   ⩽ 斋 ⅋ ⓥ

MODERN CUISINE · CHIC ※※ This relaxed restaurant – running the entire length of the Idle Rocks hotel – offers superb bay views, and the water laps at its fabulous terrace. Refined, eye-catching dishes exhibit a wealth of flavours and textures, and the vegetarian dish of the day showcases produce from the Lost Gardens of Heligan.

Menu £35 (lunch)/60

Idle Rocks Hotel, Harbourside ⊠ TR2 5AN – ℰ 01326 270270 – www.idlerocks.com

⁙○ Watch House   ⩽ ⅋

MEDITERRANEAN CUISINE · SIMPLE ※ Old Customs and Excise watch house on the quayside, with a nautically styled interior, friendly service and harbour views. Light lunches and substantial dinners; unfussy cooking follows a Mediterranean theme – try the tasty fish specials.

Menu £25 (lunch) – Carte £28/48

*1 The Square ⊠ TR2 5DJ – ℰ 01326 270038 – www.watchhousestmawes.co.uk –
Closed Sunday dinner*

🏚️ Hotel Tresanton

LUXURY · SEASIDE Set in a collection of old fishermen's cottages and a former yacht club. Elegant, nautically themed guest areas include an intimate bar and a movie room. Understated bedrooms – some in cottages – have a high level of facilities and superb sea views. The lovely split-level terrace shares the outlook.

26 rooms ☷ – 👫 £225/435 – 4 suites

27 Lower Castle Road ⊠ TR2 5DR – ℰ 01326 270055 – www.tresanton.com

🏚️ Idle Rocks

BOUTIQUE HOTEL · SEASIDE This boutique hotel sits on the water's edge and affords fabulous views over the harbour and estuary. The décor is personalised and tasteful and local art is displayed throughout. Comfortable modern bedrooms are well-equipped and show good attention to detail; ask for one at the front.

19 rooms ☷ – 👫 £220/475

Harbourside ⊠ TR2 5AN – ℰ 01326 270270 – www.idlerocks.com

🍴○ Idle Rocks – See restaurant listing

🏚️ St Mawes

BOUTIQUE HOTEL · CONTEMPORARY A smart refurbishment has given this classic harbourside hotel a cool and trendy vibe. Bedrooms are understated and immaculately kept, the lounge boasts squashy sofas and opens onto a small balcony, and there's even a small cinema. The lively restaurant serves fresh seafood and wood-fired pizzas.

7 rooms – 👫 £195/320

Harbourside ⊠ TR2 5DN – ℰ 01326 270270 – www.stmaweshotel.com

ST PETER PORT – Guernesey → See Channel Islands (Guernsey)

ST SAVIOUR – Jersey → See Channel Islands (Jersey)

ST TUDY
Cornwall – Regional map n° **1**–B2

🅰️ St Tudy Inn

MODERN BRITISH · PUB 🍴 A lovingly restored pub in a pretty village – inside there's a labyrinth of cosy rooms with fresh flowers, open fires and rustic, modish overtones. Beautifully presented dishes are unfussy, seasonal and satisfying; meats are from Launceston and seafood is from Padstow. The chef is passionate, service is friendly and modern bedrooms complete the picture.

Specialities: Scallop mousse with gruyère and wild herbs. Cornish duck breast, radicchio, fondant potato and sea beets. Vanilla panna cotta with coconut and blackberry ice cream.

Carte £25/45

Churchtown ⊠ PL30 3NN – ℰ 01208 850656 – www.sttudyinn.com –
Closed 25-27 December, Sunday dinner, Monday

SALTWOOD
Kent – Regional map n° **5**–D2

🍴○ Hide and Fox

MODERN BRITISH · CONTEMPORARY DÉCOR 🍴🍴 This stylish restaurant was once the village shop and the original shelves and drawers add character to the room. Cooking showcases the best seasonal ingredients and exhibits a sound understanding of technique. The carefully compiled wine list offers old favourites alongside those that are lesser-known.

Menu £29 (lunch) – Carte £40/54

The Green ⊠ CT21 4PS – ℰ 01303 260915 – www.hideandfox.co.uk –
Closed 8-14 January, 14-20 October, Sunday dinner, Monday, Tuesday

SANCTON
East Riding of Yorkshire – Regional map n° **13**–C2

🍴○ **The Star Inn** 🏡 ♿ ⑩ **P**

MODERN CUISINE · PUB ✗ Personally run pub in a small village, with a cosy bar, two smart dining rooms and a smiley team. The bar menu offers hearty, boldly flavoured dishes, while the à la carte has some imaginative twists.

Menu £20 (lunch) – Carte £26/53

King Street ⊠ YO43 4QP –
☎ 01430 827269 – www.thestaratsancton.co.uk –
Closed 1-6 January, Monday

SANDIACRE
Derbyshire – Regional map n° **9**–B2

🍴○ **La Rock** ♿ 🅰🅲

MODERN BRITISH · RUSTIC ✗✗ Charming, personally run restaurant with an airy feel – it was once a butcher's. Exposed brick walls and antler chandeliers feature. Cooking combines classical flavours with modern techniques; home-grown fruits are well utilised.

Menu £36 (lunch) – Carte £38/57

4 Bridge Street ⊠ NG10 5QT –
☎ 0115 939 9833 – www.larockrestaurant.co.uk –
Closed 22 December-8 January, Sunday dinner, Monday, Tuesday, Wednesday lunch

SANDSEND – North Yorkshire → See Whitby

SANDWICH
Kent – Regional map n° **5**–D2

🍴○ **The Salutation** ⇐ 🍴 🏡 ⑩ **P**

MODERN BRITISH · CONTEMPORARY DÉCOR ✗✗ Book a table in the 'Tasting Room' – in the old servants' quarter of this impressive Lutyens-designed house – to watch the chefs through a glass wall. Modern dishes comprise many different ingredients and provide plenty of contrasts. A surprise tasting menu is available. Bedrooms are stylish.

Carte £46/63

The Salutation Hotel, Knightrider Street ⊠ CT13 9EW –
☎ 01304 619919 – www.the-salutation.com –
Closed Monday - Saturday lunch

SAXMUNDHAM
Suffolk – Regional map n° **8**–D3

🍴○ **The Bell at Sax'** ⇐

TRADITIONAL BRITISH · TRADITIONAL ✗ The Bell sits at the centre of the community: it's a favourite haunt of the Rotary Club and the market takes place next door. It's comfy and cosy inside, from the well-kept bedrooms to the homely dining rooms. The experienced chef has a great understanding of flavours and his dishes are carefully priced.

Carte £20/45

31 High Street ⊠ IP17 1AF –
☎ 01728 602331 – www.thebellatsax.co.uk –
Closed Monday

ENGLAND

SCAWTON – North Yorkshire ➜ See Helmsley

SCILLY (ISLES OF)
Cornwall

Bryher – Regional map n° **1**-A1

🏠 Hell Bay

BOUTIQUE HOTEL · PERSONALISED Several charming, New England style buildings arranged around a central courtyard, with a contemporary, nautical-style interior displaying an impressive collection of modern art. Immaculately kept bedrooms come with plenty of thoughtful extras. The fabulous coastal location allows for far-reaching views.

25 rooms ⌷ – ♔♔ £190/630 – 14 suites

✉ TR23 0PR – ☏ 01720 422947 –
www.hellbay.co.uk – Closed 26 October-16 March

Tresco

🍴 Ruin Beach Café

MEDITERRANEAN CUISINE · RUSTIC ✕ Relaxed beachside restaurant in an old smugglers cottage – part of an aparthotel. The rustic room is decorated with striking Cornish art and opens onto a terrace with superb St Martin views. Colourful Mediterranean dishes have big, bold flavours; seafood and pizzas from the wood-burning oven are a hit.

Carte £26/45

Sea Garden Cottages Hotel, Old Grimsby ✉ TR24 0QQ – ☏ 01720 424849 –
www.tresco.co.uk – Closed 1 November-13 March

🏠 Sea Garden Cottages

BOUTIQUE HOTEL · CONTEMPORARY A smart aparthotel divided into New England style 'cottages'. Each has an open-plan kitchen and lounge with a terrace; the first floor bedroom opens onto a balcony offering stunning views over Old Grimsby Quay and Blockhouse Point.

9 rooms – ♔♔ £305/350 – ⌷ £16

Old Grimsby ✉ TR24 0QQ – ☏ 01720 422849 – www.tresco.co.uk –
Closed 1 November-13 March

🍴 **Ruin Beach Café** – See restaurant listing

SEAHAM
Durham – Regional map n° **14**-B2

🏠 Seaham Hall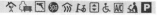

LUXURY · CONTEMPORARY An imposing part-18C mansion which combines grand original features with striking modern styling. Spacious bedrooms have luxurious touches and comfy sitting areas; many have coastal views and some have hot tubs. There's also a great games room, a chic lounge, two restaurants and an impressively equipped spa.

21 rooms – ♔♔ £245/355 – 5 suites

Lord Byron's Walk ✉ SR7 7AG – ☏ 0191 516 1400 – www.seaham-hall.com

SEASALTER – Kent ➜ See Whitstable

SEAVIEW – Isle of Wight ➜ See Wight (Isle of)

SEDBERGH
Cumbria – Regional map n° **12**-B2

🏠 The Malabar   🕭 ⪪ 🍽 **P**

FAMILY · PERSONALISED A stylishly converted stone barn surrounded by roll-ing hills. The hands-on owners provide a warm welcome: Graham previously lived on an Indian tea plantation, so there's always a good choice of teas. Smart bed-rooms mix antique furnishings with modern facilities. Cumbrian produce features at breakfast.

6 rooms ⌂ – 🛏 £140/195

Garths ✉ LA10 5ED – 𝒞 015396 20200 – www.themalabar.co.uk

SHAWELL

Leicestershire – Regional map n° **9**–B3

ⅈ○ White Swan   🛜 ⅋ 🆎 🎰 **P**

MODERN BRITISH · PUB ⅄ This welcoming village pub really is a place of two halves, with a bar and two cosy rooms at the front and a contrasting smart res-taurant extension to the rear. Dishes are modern and sophisticated, and they even offer a vegan tasting menu.

Menu £65 – Carte £33/55

Main Street ✉ LE17 6AG – 𝒞 01788 860357 – www.whiteswanshawell.co.uk – Closed 26 December-9 January, Sunday dinner, Monday - Saturday lunch

SHEFFIELD

South Yorkshire – Regional map n° **13**–B3

😊 Jöro   ⅋ 🍽 🎰

MODERN CUISINE · SIMPLE ⅄ A simple but stylish place housed in the Krynkl shipping container development and run by a keen chef-owner. Daily changing small plates with unusual flavour combinations draw on a mix of modern British, New Nordic and Asian cuisine. Book the Chef's Bench to really feel part of the action.

Specialities: Scottish mackerel with English wasabi and yuzu. Goosnargh chicken with lemon and thyme. Yorkshire rhubarb with sweet cheese ice cream.

Menu £29 (lunch), £55/65 – Carte £24/33

0.2-0.5 Krynkl, 294 Shalesmoor ✉ S3 8US – 𝒞 0114 299 1539 – www.jororestaurant.co.uk – Closed 1-16 January, 5-11 April, 6-12 June, Sunday, Monday, Tuesday, Wednesday lunch

ⅈ○ Old Vicarage   🎐 🍽 **P**

MODERN CUISINE · FAMILY ⅄⅄ A delightful former vicarage in a semi-rural spot on the city's edge. Two fixed price menus offer sophisticated dishes with as-sured flavours and subtle modern influences; the 'Prestige' best showcases the chef's abilities.

Menu £60/70

Ridgeway Moor ✉ S12 3XW – 𝒞 0114 247 5814 – www.theoldvicarage.co.uk – Closed 6-14 April, 27 July-10 August, Sunday, Monday, Tuesday lunch, Saturday lunch

ⅈ○ Rafters   🆎

MODERN BRITISH · CLASSIC DÉCOR ⅄⅄ A long-standing city institution; the owners stamped their own identity on it by using Sheffield cutlery and Yorkshire tweed covered chairs. Refined cooking sees well-judged flavour combinations presented in an attractive manner.

Menu £38/50

220 Oakbrook Road, Nether Green ✉ S11 7ED – 𝒞 0114 230 4819 – www.raftersrestaurant.co.uk – Closed 24-30 August, 23-30 December, Sunday, Monday, Tuesday - Saturday lunch

ⅈ◯ Juke + Loe

BRITISH CONTEMPORARY · BISTRO ✗ Brothers Luke and Joe have come to-gether to run this laid-back eatery in a bustling part of the city. Seasonal cooking mixes the traditional with the modern and every dish is equally appealing; preparation is skilful and flavours are big and bold. Start with a cocktail in the small bar.

Menu £25 (lunch) – Carte £20/45

617 Ecclesall Road ⊠ S11 8PT – ℰ 0114 268 0271 – www.jukenadloe.com –
Closed 1-8 January, 7-14 April, 3-11 August, Sunday, Monday, Tuesday lunch

ⅈ◯ Brocco Kitchen

MODERN BRITISH · BISTRO ✗ A bright, laid-back 'urban kitchen' in a stylish hotel. As well as lunch and dinner they serve breakfast, coffee and cakes, and afternoon tea. The well-priced menu comprises a selection of small plates listed under the headings 'The Hunter', 'The Fisher' and 'The Gardener' – and these include some great salads.

Carte £20/35

Brocco on the Park Hotel, 92 Brocco Bank ⊠ S11 8RS – ℰ 0114 266 1233 –
www.brocco.co.uk/kitchen – Closed Sunday dinner

🏠 Brocco on the Park

TOWNHOUSE · CONTEMPORARY Brocco's claim to fame is that Picasso once stayed here! It's a compact place, overlooking a park, and has plenty of style and individuality, albeit set by a roundabout. Bedrooms have a chic modern feel courtesy of light colour schemes, quality furnishings and great attention to detail.

8 rooms – ♥♥ £115/245 – ☟ £10

92 Brocco Bank ⊠ S11 8RS – ℰ 0114 266 1233 – www.brocco.co.uk
ⅈ◯ **Brocco Kitchen** – See restaurant listing

SHERBORNE
Dorset – Regional map n° **2**–C3

😊 The Green

MODERN CUISINE · BISTRO ✗ A pretty listed stone property with an enclosed garden terrace. Mediterranean-style dishes are full of flavour; the 'Zakuski' (snacks) are great for sharing and the menu du jour (Tues-Thurs) is a steal. The chef-owner hails from the Russian foothills of the Caucasus Mountains and the team are super-friendly.

Specialities: Dorset scallops with black pudding brandy snap, pea & mint velouté. Chargrilled Cornish hake with wild garlic and squid ink vinaigrette. Rhubarb and almond tart with 'green marmalade' ice cream.

Menu £23 (lunch) – Carte £28/43

3 The Green ⊠ DT9 3HY – ℰ 01935 813821 – www.greenrestaurant.co.uk –
Closed 1-14 January, Sunday dinner, Monday

SHINFIELD – Wokingham → See Reading

SHIPLAKE – Oxfordshire → See Henley-on-Thames

SHIPSTON-ON-STOUR
Warwickshire – Regional map n° **10**–C3

ⅈ◯ Bower House

MODERN BRITISH · BRASSERIE ✗ This smart brasserie occupies two former shops in the heart of a small but characterful town. Appealing dishes are attractively presented and have a modern edge. Sit in the larger room with its comfy banquettes and copper-topped tables. Spacious bedrooms come with Hungarian-tiled bathrooms.

Carte £22/35

Market Place ⊠ CV36 4AG – ℰ 01608 663333 – www.thebowerhouseshipston.com
– Closed Sunday dinner, Monday, Tuesday

SHIRLEY – Derbyshire → See Ashbourne

SHREWSBURY

Shropshire – Regional map n° **10**–B2

○ **The Walrus** N

MODERN BRITISH · INTIMATE XX Young chef-owners Ben and Carla run this two-floored restaurant in Ben's hometown; sit downstairs to watch them in action in the open kitchen. Ambitious modern cooking delivers an intriguing blend of pronounced flavours and contrasting textures, and makes great use of Shropshire's larder.

Menu £35/50

5 Roushill ✉ SY1 1PQ –
℘ 01743 240005 – www.the-walrus.co.uk – Closed 1-16 January, Sunday, Monday, Tuesday, Wednesday - Saturday lunch

at Upton Magna East : 6 mi by A 5064 off B 4380

○ **The Haughmond**

MODERN BRITISH · PUB X A stylish dining pub with a village shop and a recurring stag theme. Lunchtime sees a good value set priced menu of ambitious modern dishes; evening menus include an à la carte and a creative, sophisticated tasting menu. Bedrooms are smart and modern – the Red Room has a terrific country outlook.

Menu £23 (lunch)/49 – Carte £28/50

✉ SY4 4TZ –
℘ 01743 709918 – www.thehaughmond.co.uk – Closed Sunday dinner, Monday

SIDFORD – Devon → See Sidmouth

SIDLESHAM

West Sussex – Regional map n° **4**–C3

○ **Crab & Lobster**

SEAFOOD · PUB X This sympathetically modernised inn is superbly located within the striking landscape of Pagham Harbour Nature Reserve. Well-presented, seafood-focused dishes are at the restaurant end of the scale, although lunch also sees sandwiches and salads. Comfortable bedrooms have a modern, minimalist style.

Menu £23 (lunch) – Carte £32/71

Mill Lane ✉ PO20 7NB –
℘ 01243 641233 – www.crab-lobster.co.uk

SIDMOUTH

Devon – Regional map n° **1**–D2

at Sidford North : 2 mi

○ **Salty Monk**

REGIONAL CUISINE · INTIMATE XX Set in an old 16C salt house, a proudly run restaurant which pleasantly blends the old and the new. Dine from a menu of refined, classically based dishes in the Abbots Den or the Garden Room; or come for coffee and cake or afternoon tea. Bedrooms have good extras and there's a gym and hot tub in the garden.

Carte £29/50

Church Street ✉ EX10 9QP –
℘ 01395 513174 – www.saltymonk.com – Closed Sunday, Monday, Tuesday - Saturday lunch

SKELTON

Cumbria – Regional map n° **12**–B2

Dog and Gun Inn

TRADITIONAL BRITISH · PUB X Beams, an open fire and Lizzie's greeting give this modest pub a welcoming feel. Ben is an experienced hand in the kitchen and recognises that the locals want hearty, familiar dishes, so he takes pub classics, refines them and elevates them to new heights; they're not only delicious but good value too.

Specialities: Saffron and mozzarella arancini, Romesco sauce and salsa verde. Venison suet pudding, triple cooked chips, spring greens and black truffle vinaigrette. Cumbrian honey parfait with rhubarb and honeycomb.

Carte £23/30

✉ CA11 9SE – ✆ 017684 84301 – www.dogandgunskelton.co.uk – Closed Sunday dinner, Monday, Tuesday, Wednesday, Thursday - Saturday lunch

SNETTISHAM

Norfolk – Regional map n° **8**–B1

The Old Bank

MODERN BRITISH · BISTRO X A friendly young couple run this laid-back restaurant. Cooking is modern and sophisticated, with well-crafted dishes keeping local produce to the fore, from Norfolk asparagus to Cromer crab. Lunch is good value and dinner sees the use of more luxurious ingredients.

Menu £22 (lunch) – Carte £30/45

10 Lynn Road ✉ PE31 7LP – ✆ 01485 544080 – www.theoldbankbistro.co.uk – Closed 1-15 January, 4-13 May, Sunday dinner, Monday, Tuesday, Wednesday lunch

Rose and Crown

TRADITIONAL CUISINE · PUB X 14C pub featuring a warren of rooms with uneven floors and low beamed ceilings. Gutsy cooking uses locally sourced produce, with globally influenced dishes alongside trusty pub classics. Impressive children's adventure fort. Modern bedrooms are decorated in sunny colours, and offer a good level of facilities.

Carte £20/40

Old Church Road ✉ PE31 7LX – ✆ 01485 541382 – www.roseandcrownsnettisham.co.uk

SONNING-ON-THAMES – Wokingham → See Reading

SOUTH DALTON

East Riding of Yorkshire – Regional map n° **13**–C2

Pipe and Glass (James Mackenzie)

MODERN BRITISH · PUB XX This charming 15C pub was originally the gatehouse of Dalton Park and its passionate owners have nurtured it from scruffy pub to destination dining inn; look out for the church spire to help you navigate through the maze of country lanes.

It's a cosy, characterful place where you'll find locals in the bar – and usually a table or two for those who haven't made a reservation – and a country house style restaurant with views over the garden and estate.

Kate oversees the friendly, efficient service, while experienced chef James Mackenzie is in charge of the kitchen. He champions regional ingredients in unfussy, instantly recognisable dishes which are packed with flavour and exhibit subtle modern touches. Whether it's a ploughman's or parkin-crusted deer, he takes the same amount of care with the preparation.

Bedrooms are luxurious and have private patios overlooking the estate.

Specialities: Salt beef hash cake with rhubarb ketchup, fried quail's egg and crispy pickled onion rings. Yorkshire Barnsley chop with devilled kidneys, confit lamb boulangère and mint & nettle sauce. 'Five reasons to love chocolate'.

Carte £30/57

West End ⊠ HU17 7PN – ℰ 01430 810246 – www.pipeandglass.co.uk –
Closed 2-16 January, Sunday dinner, Monday

SOUTH FERRIBY
North Lincolnshire – Regional map n° **13**–C3

Hope & Anchor   ⇔ ≼ 🏠 ఈ 🕦 **P**

TRADITIONAL BRITISH · PUB X A rustic, nautically-themed pub with Humber views. Tasty British dishes display touches of originality and showcase fish from Grimsby, fruit and veg from their smallholding and meats from the Lake District – which are aged in a glass-fronted drying cabinet. Bedrooms are modern; some have estuary views.

Specialities: Celery soup with walnut & Lincolnshire Poacher crouton. Risotto of wild garlic with wild mushrooms and asparagus. Tahitian vanilla panna cotta with salted caramel and coconut ice cream.

Carte £25/36

Sluice Road ⊠ DN18 6JQ – ℰ 01652 635334 – www.thehopeandanchorpub.co.uk –
Closed Monday

SOUTH POOL
Devon – Regional map n° **1**–C3

Millbrook Inn   🏠

TRADITIONAL CUISINE · PUB X You'll find this appealingly worn pub squeezed in between the houses on a narrow street. It really is a part of the village and hosts various events such as good value 'Village Table' nights and BBQs (which coincide with the tides). It also has two pleasant terraces and a lovely boutique apartment.

Carte £17/60

⊠ TQ7 2RW – ℰ 01548 531581 – www.millbrookinnsouthpool.co.uk

SOUTHAMPTON
Southampton – Regional map n° **4**–B2

Jetty   🍸 ≼ 🏠 ఈ 🕮 🕦 **P**

MODERN BRITISH · DESIGN XX The sister of the Jetty in Christchurch sits within a striking glass hotel. It's a stylish, elegant place with floor to ceiling windows and a great terrace offering spectacular views of the Ocean Village marina. Boldly flavoured, generously proportioned modern classics have a seafood bias.

Menu £26 (lunch) – Carte £45/95

Southampton Harbour Hotel, 5 Maritime Walk, Ocean Village ⊠ SO14 3QT –
ℰ 02381 103 777 – www.southampton-harbour-hotel.co.uk

SOUTHBOROUGH – Kent → See Royal Tunbridge Wells

SOUTHBOURNE – Bournemouth → See Bournemouth

SOUTH LEIGH
Oxfordshire – Regional map n° **6**–B2

The Mason Arms   ⇔ 🛏 🏠 **P**

TRADITIONAL BRITISH · PUB X This attractive thatched pub might look traditional but inside it's quirky and idiosyncratic. Flagged floors and antique signs are juxtaposed with intriguing modern art. The only classic part is the cooking, which has a satisfying British heart. Bedrooms blend mod cons with shabby-chic styling.

Carte £28/47

Station Road ⊠ OX29 6XF – ℰ 01993 656238 – www.themasonarms.co.uk

SOUTHPORT

– Regional map n° **11**–A2

⅛○ **Bistrot Vérité**

CLASSIC FRENCH · FRIENDLY ✗ A friendly, experienced husband and wife team run this bustling neighbourhood bistro in a pretty parade. Expect gutsy French dishes with a classic base, punchy flavours and the occasional British touch; the 2 course lunch is good value.

Menu £27 (lunch) – Carte £27/47

7 Liverpool Road, Birkdale ⊠ *PR8 4AR* – ℰ *01704 564199 –*
www.bistrotverite.co.uk – Closed 16-24 February, 16-24 August, Sunday, Monday, Tuesday lunch

SOUTHROP

Gloucestershire – Regional map n° **2**–D1

⅛○ **Ox Barn** Ⓝ

MODERN BRITISH · RUSTIC ✗✗ This delightful barn conversion is part of the Thyme complex and no expense has been spared in its stunning restoration. Beautifully pared-back, flavour-packed dishes follow a nature-to-plate philosophy and showcase ingredients from their kitchen gardens and farm. On Sundays they also offer brunch.

Menu £27 (lunch) – Carte £38/49

Thyme Hotel, Southrop Manor Estate ⊠ *GL7 3NX* – ℰ *01367 850174 –*
www.thyme.co.uk – Closed Sunday dinner, Monday, Tuesday, Wednesday lunch

⅛○ **Swan** ⇔

TRADITIONAL BRITISH · PUB ✗ A delightful Virginia creeper clad inn set in a quintessential Cotswold village in the Leach Valley. With its characterful low-beamed rooms and charming service, it's popular with locals and visitors alike. Dishes are mainly British-based and feature garden produce; try the delicious homemade bread.

Carte £25/40

⊠ *GL7 3NU* – ℰ *01367 850205 – www.theswanatsouthrop.co.uk*

🏠 **Thyme** Ⓝ

COUNTRY HOUSE · ELEGANT A series of restored barns and Cotswold stone properties come together here to form a 'village within a village', comprising luxurious bedrooms, a spa, dining venues and a cookery school. It has strong eco-credentials and an understatedly elegant feel. Don't miss after-dinner cocktails in the charming bar.

31 rooms ⊠ – 🛏 £350/410

Southrop Manor Estate ⊠ *GL7 3NX* – ℰ *01367 850174 – www.thyme.co.uk*
⅛○ **Ox Barn** – See restaurant listing

SOUTHWOLD

Suffolk – Regional map n° **8**–D2

🏠 **Swan**

HISTORIC BUILDING · CONTEMPORARY This iconic coaching inn sits in the heart of town beside the Adnams Brewery, who own the place. Its origins may be 17C but its brightly furnished interior brings it into the 21C; ask for a bedroom in the lovely garden wing. The restaurant serves refined British classics; start with an Adnams ale in the bar.

35 rooms – 🛏 £200/420

Market Place ⊠ *IP18 6EG* – ℰ *01502 722186 – www.theswansouthwold.co.uk*

SOWERBY BRIDGE

West Yorkshire – Regional map n° **13**–A2

🍴 Moorcock Inn   🛋 🏡 **P**

CREATIVE BRITISH · PUB 🗙 A substantial yet cosy stone pub in the industrial heartland. Blackboards list homemade charcuterie and appealing snacks, while the daily set menu focuses on ingredients from Yorkshire's fields and coasts. They use lots of preservation techniques and the age of the produce informs the accompaniments.

Menu £39 – Carte £24/40

*Moorbottom Lane, Norland ✉ HX6 3RP – ℰ 01422 832103 –
www.themoorcock.co.uk – Closed Sunday dinner, Monday, Tuesday, Wednesday -
Friday lunch*

SPARSHOLT – Hampshire → See Winchester

SPRIGG'S ALLEY – Oxfordshire → See Chinnor

STADHAMPTON
Oxfordshire – Regional map n° **6**–B2

🏠 Crazy Bear   🏠 🛋 ♨ **P**

LUXURY · CONTEMPORARY Wacky converted pub with a London bus reception, a characterful bar, a smart glasshouse and even a Zen garden. Sumptuous, quirky bedrooms are spread about the place; some have padded walls and infinity baths. Eat in 'Thai' or flamboyant 'English', with its mirrored walls and classic British and French dishes.

18 rooms ☑ – 🛏 £249/449

Bear Lane ✉ OX44 7UR – ℰ 01865 890714 – www.crazybeargroup.co.uk

STALISFIELD
Kent – Regional map n° **5**–C2

🍴 Plough Inn   ⇦ 🛋 🏡 **P**

TRADITIONAL BRITISH · PUB 🗙 The term 'rustic' could have been invented for this 15C pub, with its thick walls, farming implements, exposed beams and hop bines. You'll find the usual suspects on the bar menu and more ambitious dishes on the à la carte – along with an impressive range of Kentish real ales. Bedrooms are modern and stylish.

Menu £27 – Carte £24/36

*✉ ME13 0HY – ℰ 01795 890256 – www.theploughinnstalisfield.co.uk –
Closed Sunday dinner, Monday*

STAMFORD
Lincolnshire – Regional map n° **9**–C2

🍴 The Oak Room   🕸 🛋 🏡 **P**

TRADITIONAL BRITISH · CLASSIC DÉCOR 🗙🗙🗙 Smart dress is required in this lovely oak-panelled dining room, which is found at the heart of an equally charming 16C coaching inn. Classical menus are largely British based with a few international influences. Alongside their speciality beef carving trolley, there are also 'cheese' and 'sweet' trolleys.

Menu £32 (lunch) – Carte £38/90

*George of Stamford Hotel, 71 St. Martins ✉ PE9 2LB – ℰ 01780 750750 –
www.georgehotelofstamford.com*

🏠 George of Stamford   🏠 🛋 🅰🅲 ♨ **P**

INN · ELEGANT This characterful coaching inn dates back over 500 years and, despite its bedrooms having a surprisingly contemporary feel, it still offers good old-fashioned hospitality. There are plenty of bars and lounges to relax in and both of the restaurants spill out into the lovely courtyard in summer.

45 rooms ☑ – 🛏 £225/380 – 1 suite

71 St. Martins ✉ PE9 2LB – ℰ 01780 750750 – www.georgehotelofstamford.com
🍴 **The Oak Room** – See restaurant listing

STANTON
Suffolk – Regional map n° **8**–C2

Leaping Hare ⛿ 🛱 & **P**

MODERN BRITISH · RUSTIC X This beautiful 17C timber-framed barn sits at the centre of a 7 acre vineyard. Carefully judged cooking relies on well-sourced seasonal ingredients – many from their own farm. Sit on the lovely terrace and choose from the good value Vintners menu or pick something more refined from the à la carte.

Specialities: Smoked chalk stream trout with lemon crème fraîche. Wild Wyken venison haunch with smoked mash, wild garlic and fine beans. St Emilion au chocolat, salted caramel ice cream.

Menu £22 (lunch) – Carte £27/37

Wyken Vineyards ✉ IP31 2DW – ☎ 01359 250287 – www.wykenvineyards.co.uk – Closed 25 December-4 January, Sunday - Thursday dinner

STILLINGTON
North Yorkshire – Regional map n° **13**–C2

🍴 Bay Tree ⛿ 🛱

TRADITIONAL BRITISH · PUB X Enthusiastic couple Ed and Harri run this homely village pub. Sit by the fire, in the cosy snug or in the conservatory dining room and enjoy a traditional pub dish or more adventurous daily special. They have a real passion for gin, with 110 varieties offered, along with the likes of gin-cured salmon.

Carte £12/38

Main Street ✉ YO61 1JU – ☎ 01347 811394 – www.thebaytreeyork.co.uk – Closed Monday, Tuesday, Wednesday lunch

STOCKBRIDGE
Hampshire – Regional map n° **4**–B2

🍴 Greyhound on the Test ⟵ ⛿ 🛱 **P**

MODERN BRITISH · PUB X Mustard-coloured pub with over a mile of River Test fishing rights to the rear. Low beams and wood burning stoves abound and elegant décor gives it a French bistro feel. The appealing range of dishes includes modern small plates, a selection 'on toast' and a classical daily menu; the chef will also cook your catch. Homely bedrooms have large showers and quality bedding.

Menu £20 (lunch) – Carte £27/55

31 High Street ✉ SO20 6EY – ☎ 01264 810833 – www.thegreyhoundonthetest.co.uk

STOCKPORT
Greater Manchester – Regional map n° **11**–B3

🍴 Where The Light Gets In 🕅

MODERN BRITISH · RUSTIC X This large, loft-style restaurant is located on the top floor of a Victorian coffee warehouse and its open kitchen forms part of the room. The surprise menu is formed from whatever they have foraged that day and beasts are brought in whole and fully utilised. Matching wine flights focus on natural wines.

Menu £65/90

7 Rostron Brow ✉ SK1 7JY – ☎ 0161 477 5744 – www.wtlgi.co – Closed Sunday, Monday, Tuesday, Wednesday - Friday lunch

STOKE BY NAYLAND
Suffolk – Regional map n° **8**–C3

⅋○ Crown

REGIONAL CUISINE · PUB ⅀ Smart, relaxed pub in a great spot overlooking the Box and Stour river valleys. Globally influenced menus feature produce from local farms and estates, with seafood from the east coast. Well-priced wine list with over 25 wines by the glass. Large, luxurious, superbly equipped bedrooms with king or super king sized beds; some have French windows and terraces.

Carte £30/44

✉ CO6 4SE – ☏ 01206 262001 – www.crowninn.net

STOKE HOLY CROSS – Norfolk ➜ See Norwich

STOKE POGES

Buckinghamshire – Regional map n° **6**–D3

⅏ Stoke Park

LUXURY · CLASSIC This Grade I listed Palladian property was once home to the Penn family, who created England's first country club. Guest areas are characterful, there's an impressive spa and the range of sporting activities is extensive. All of the bedrooms are luxurious, with those in the Pavilion being more contemporary.

49 rooms – ⅋⅋ £240/640 – 2 suites

Park Road ✉ SL2 4PG – ☏ 01753 717171 – www.stokepark.com

STON EASTON

Somerset – Regional map n° **2**–C2

⅏ Ston Easton Park

LUXURY · ELEGANT Striking Palladian mansion in 36 acres of delightful grounds. Fine rooms of epic proportions are filled with antiques, curios and impressive flower arrangements. Many of the bedrooms have coronet or four-poster beds; three are set in a cottage. Classic menus showcase produce from the Victorian kitchen garden.

23 rooms ⅀ – ⅋⅋ £195/345 – 2 suites

✉ BA3 4DF – ☏ 01761 241631 – www.stoneaston.co.uk

STOW-ON-THE-WOLD

Gloucestershire – Regional map n° **2**–D1

⅋○ Old Butchers

CLASSIC CUISINE · FRIENDLY ⅀⅀ An old butcher's shop with quirky décor, colourful chairs and ice bucket and colander lampshades. The menu offers plenty of choice from old favourites to dishes with a Mediterranean slant. The 'bin end' wine list is worth a look.

Carte £30/52

7 Park Street ✉ GL54 1AQ – ☏ 01451 831700 – www.theoldbutchers.com

at Bledington Southeast: 4 mi by A436 on B4450

⅋○ Kings Head Inn

TRADITIONAL BRITISH · PUB ⅀ A charming 16C former cider house on a picturesque village green, bisected by a stream filled with bobbing ducks. Choose from appealing bar snacks, pub classics or some more interesting modern dishes. The large bar has a vast inglenook fireplace and bedrooms are cosy; ask for one in the courtyard.

Carte £29/65

The Green ✉ OX7 6XQ – ☏ 01608 658365 – www.kingsheadinn.net –
Closed 25-27 December

ENGLAND

at Daylesford East: 3. 5 mi by A436

ⅱ○ Café at Daylesford Organic ⊘Ⅱ 🛉 & ⇔ **P**

MODERN BRITISH · CHIC 𝕏 A stylishly rustic eatery attached to a farm shop: dine in the 'Legbar' for charcuterie and nibbles, the 'Old Spot' for pizzas and wood-roasted specials or the main 'Trough Café', where at night, candle-lit suppers step things up a gear. Everything is organic, with much of the produce coming from the farm.

Carte £26/52

✉ GL56 0YG –

𝒫 01608 731700 – www.daylesford.com – Closed Sunday dinner

at Nether Westcote Southeast: 4. 75 mi by A429 and A424

ⅱ○ Feathered Nest 🐾 ⇐ ⇐ 🍴 🛉 & **P**

MODERN CUISINE · INN 𝕏𝕏 This 17C former malt house sits in an idyllic spot overlooking the valley and boasts a characterful flag-floored bar with leather saddle stools and two timbered dining rooms. Refined modern cooking is full of colour and beautifully presented. Well-appointed bedrooms are furnished with antiques.

Menu £45 (lunch), £70/90

✉ OX7 6SD – 𝒫 01993 833030 – www.thefeatherednestinn.co.uk – Closed Monday, Tuesday, Wednesday

STRATFORD-UPON-AVON

Warwickshire – Regional map n° **10**–C3

✿3 Salt (Paul Foster) 🛉

MODERN BRITISH · RUSTIC 𝕏 Set in the heart of town is this lovely little restaurant with whitewashed walls, exposed timbers, flagged floors and a wood-burning stove to keep things cosy in winter. Its simple look and laid-back atmosphere are in perfect harmony with the honesty and purity of the cooking, as is the friendly, fuss-free service.

To really get in on the action sit in the rear of the two rooms, opposite the open kitchen, where you can watch the chef crafting assured, unfussy dishes which showcase precise techniques and restrained originality. First-rate ingredients are carefully sourced and flavours are clear and defined. The weekday lunch is great value and the weekend tasting menus show the chef's creativity to the full.

In warmer weather, arrive early for drinks beside the raised beds in the small courtyard.

Specialities: Carrot cooked in chicken fat with pickled carrot and chicken skin. Barbecued Mangalitsa pork rump with white shallot purée and wild garlic. Baked chocolate délice with peanut parfait and kalamansi.

Menu £28 (lunch), £43/75

8 Church Street ✉ CV37 6HB –

𝒫 01789 263566 – www.salt-restaurant.co.uk – Closed 5-19 August, 22 December-8 January, Sunday dinner-Tuesday

ⅱ○ Woodsman ⓝ 🛉 & ⇔

MEATS AND GRILLS · RUSTIC 𝕏𝕏 This well-run restaurant sits beside the recently restored former Falcon Hotel (now the Indigo). Have a local ale and some snacks beside the open fire or head for the more modern back room. Menus revolve around game cooked over an open fire and simple preparation allows top quality ingredients to shine.

Carte £27/60

4 Chapel Street ✉ CV37 6HA –

𝒫 01789 331535 – www.thewoodsmanrestaurant.com

🍴 **Lambs**

TRADITIONAL CUISINE · RUSTIC 🏶 This attractive 16C house has an interesting history; dine on one of several levels, surrounded by characterful beams and original features – the first floor is a pleasant spot. The classic bistro menu lists simply, carefully prepared favourites and daily fish specials.

Menu £21 – Carte £26/43

12 Sheep Street ⊠ CV37 6EF – ℰ 01789 292554 – www.lambsrestaurant.co.uk – Closed Monday lunch

🍴 **No 9 Church St.**

MODERN BRITISH · BISTRO 🏶 In the heart of Stratford, you'll find this cosy, proudly run restaurant set in a 400 year old townhouse. The experienced chef-owner offers flavoursome British cooking with an original modern twist. Dishes are attractively presented and feature lots of different ingredients.

Menu £21 (lunch)/45 – Carte £30/47

9 Church Street ⊠ CV37 6HB – ℰ 01789 415522 – www.no9churchst.com – Closed Sunday, Monday

🍴 **Rooftop**

MODERN BRITISH · DESIGN 🏶 Set atop the RSC Theatre; a curvaceous restaurant with a superb terrace and lovely views from its window tables. Come for a light lunch, afternoon tea, cocktails and snacks or something from the à la carte. On performance days they offer a pre-theatre set menu.

Menu £26 – Carte £26/36

Royal Shakespeare Theatre, Waterside ⊠ CV37 6BB – ℰ 01789 403449 – www.rsc.org.uk/eat – Closed Sunday dinner

STRETE – Devon ➜ See Dartmouth

STRETTON
Rutland – Regional map n° **9**-C2

🍴 **Jackson Stops Inn**

TRADITIONAL BRITISH · PUB 🏶 A lovely stone and thatch pub comprising several areas, including a small open-fired bar, a cosy barn and several beamed rooms. It's a real family affair, with both the parents and children involved. British classics and pub favourites feature and include some tasty homemade breads and ice creams.

Carte £27/33

Rookery Lane ⊠ LE15 7RA – ℰ 01780 410237 – www.thejacksonstops.com – Closed Monday

STUDLAND
Dorset – Regional map n° **2**-C3

🍴 **Pig on the Beach**

REGIONAL CUISINE · FRIENDLY 🏶 Set within a large, plant-filled conservatory in a delightful country house; a rustic, shabby-chic restaurant where the wonderful kitchen garden informs the menu and additional produce comes from within 25 miles. Cooking is light and fresh and is accompanied by superb views over the lawns to Old Harry Rocks.

Carte £28/48

Pig on the Beach Hotel, Manor Road ⊠ BH19 3AU – ℰ 01929 450288 – www.thepighotel.com

🍴 **Shell Bay**

SEAFOOD · BISTRO 🏶 Every table has a view at this superbly located restaurant on the water's edge, overlooking Brownsea Island. It started life as a shack and retains an appealingly rustic feel – and the terrace is a real hit come summer. The twice daily menu showcases local seafood in a mix of modern and classic dishes.

Carte £23/47

Ferry Road ⊠ BH19 3BA – ℰ 01929 450363 – www.shellbay.net – Closed 1 October-1 February

🏠 Pig on the Beach ☆ ⅋ ⪕ ⪚ ⚶ 🅿

COUNTRY HOUSE · SEASIDE A delightful country house with commanding coastal views and lovely gardens leading down to the sea. It has a relaxed, shabby-chic style and the furnishings are a pleasing mix of the old and the new. For something a little different, stay in an old gardener's bothy or dovecote. Staff are extremely welcoming.

23 rooms – 👫 £155/360 – ⚏ £18

Manor Road ⊠ BH19 3AU – ☎ 01929 450288 – www.thepighotel.com

🍴 **Pig on the Beach** – See restaurant listing

SUMMERHOUSE – Darlington → See Darlington

SUTTON

Central Bedfordshire – Regional map n° **7**–B1

🍴 John O'Gaunt Inn ⪚ 🏠 ⅖ 🅿

TRADITIONAL CUISINE · PUB 🍴 Well-run by experienced owners, this is a cosy, honest village inn with a fire-warmed bar, a smart dining room and delightful gardens overlooking wheat fields. The tried-and-tested menu includes some tasty 'Crumps Butchers' steaks.

Carte £ 29/34

30 High Street ⊠ SG19 2NE – ☎ 01767 260377 – www.johnogauntsutton.co.uk – Closed 1-9 January, Sunday dinner, Monday

SWAFFHAM

Norfolk – Regional map n° **8**–C2

🏠 Strattons ☆ ⪚ 🅿

TOWNHOUSE · PERSONALISED A laid-back, eco-friendly hotel in an eye-catching 17C villa with Victorian additions. Quirky, individually styled bedrooms are spread about the place: some are duplex suites and some have terraces or courtyards. The rustic basement restaurant serves modern British dishes; breakfast is taken in their deli.

14 rooms – 👫 £99/256

4 Ash Close ⊠ PE37 7NH – ☎ 01760 723845 – www.strattonshotel.com – Closed 22-28 December

---

SWINBROOK – Oxfordshire → See Burford

TANGMERE – West Sussex → See Chichester

TAPLOW

Buckinghamshire – Regional map n° **6**–C3

🍴 Roux at Skindles 🅝 ⚘ ⪕ 🏠 ⅖ 🆎 🎦 ⟳ 🅿

FRENCH · CONTEMPORARY DÉCOR 🍴🍴 Michel and Alain Roux of the Waterside Inn own this contemporary brasserie and cocktail bar in a pleasant riverside setting – part of a residential development that was formerly the Skindles Hotel. Arrive early for drinks on the terrace before enjoying classic French dishes cooked with confidence.

Carte £ 31/49

Mill Lane ⊠ SL6 0AG – ☎ 01628 951100 – www.rouxatskindles.co.uk – Closed 26 December-2 January, Sunday dinner, Monday

🏰 Cliveden House ☆ ⅋ ⪕ ⪚ 🏊 🎦 🌐 🍸 ⛱ 🎱 ⚶ 🅿

GRAND LUXURY · HISTORIC A stunning Grade I listed, 17C stately home in a superb location, boasting views over the gardens towards the Thames. The opulent interior boasts sumptuous antique-filled lounges and luxuriously appointed bedrooms. Unwind in the smart spa then kick-back in style with a picnic on one of the vintage launches.

48 rooms ⚏ – 👫 £495/870 – 6 suites

⊠ SL6 0JF – ☎ 01628 607107 – www.clivedenhouse.co.uk

TATTENHALL

Cheshire West and Chester – Regional map n° **11**–A3

🕮 **Allium by Mark Ellis**

MODERN BRITISH · DESIGN XX You can't miss the bow-fronted façade of this former village shop, where you can come for everything from a light lunch or afternoon tea to a tasting menu and cocktails. Some dishes have a playful element and you can even cook your own steak on a lava stone at your table. Bedrooms are fresh and modern.

Carte £24/37

Lynedale House, High Street ✉ CH3 9PX – ℰ 01829 771477 –
www.theallium.co.uk – Closed Sunday dinner, Monday, Tuesday, Wednesday -
Saturday lunch

TAUNTON

Somerset – Regional map n° **2**–B3

🕮 **Castle Bow**

MODERN CUISINE · ELEGANT XX Elegant, art deco style restaurant in the old snooker room of a Norman castle. Regularly changing menus showcase top quality regional produce. Well-balanced dishes are classically based yet refined, and feature some playful modern touches.

Carte £34/52

Castle Hotel, Castle Green ✉ TA1 1NF – ℰ 01823 328328 –
www.castlebow.com – Closed Sunday, Monday, Tuesday, Wednesday - Saturday
lunch

🕮 **Augustus**

MODERN BRITISH · BISTRO X An experienced chef and a bright, breezy team run this welcoming little bistro. Sit in the cosy, intimate dining room or the bright conservatory with sliding glass doors and a retractable roof. Hearty, unfussy cooking mixes French-influenced dishes with updated British classics.

Carte £25/45

3 The Courtyard, St. James Street ✉ TA1 1JR – ℰ 01823 324354 –
www.augustustaunton.co.uk – Closed 22 December-2 January, Sunday dinner,
Monday

🏛 **Castle**

HISTORIC BUILDING · CLASSIC Part-12C, wisteria-clad Norman castle with impressive gardens, a keep and two wells. It's been run by the Chapman family for three generations and retains a fittingly traditional style. Well-kept, individually decorated bedrooms. Castle Bow serves modern dishes; relaxed Brazz offers brasserie classics.

44 rooms ⌂ – †† £130/170

Castle Green ✉ TA1 1NF – ℰ 01823 272671 –
www.the-castle-hotel.com

🕮 **Castle Bow** – See restaurant listing

at Henlade East : 3 mi on A 358

🕮 **Somerset Dining Room** ◍

MODERN CUISINE · COUNTRY HOUSE XX A Regency country house is home to this capacious restaurant featuring ornate plasterwork and a chandelier. Start with canapés in the elegant open-fired bar as you choose from the appealing modern menus. The passionate chef skilfully prepares accomplished dishes with well-thought-through flavours and textures.

Menu £18 (lunch), £35/60

The Mount Somerset Hotel and Spa, Lower Henlade ✉ TA3 5NB – ℰ 01823 442500
– www.themountsomersethotelandspa.com

TAVISTOCK

Devon – Regional map n° **1**–C2

☺ **Cornish Arms**   ⇦ 🏠 &

TRADITIONAL CUISINE · PUB ⅓ A fine selection of St Austell ales sit behind the bar, which provide a clue as to the owners. The knowledgeable team are genuinely warm and welcoming and the mix of drinkers and diners make for a great atmosphere. Appealing dishes mix classic elements with some unusual modern twists – and you'll have to go a long way to beat the sorbets! Bedrooms are bold and modern.

Specialities: Wood mushroom and truffle arancini with wild garlic and chive mayonnaise. Fillet of Cornish hake, cep purée, chicken and mushroom butter sauce. Treacle tart, candied walnuts, muscovado ice cream and clotted cream.

Carte £24/35

15 West Street ⊠ PL19 8AN – ☎ 01822 612145 – www.thecornisharmstavistock.co.uk

at Milton Abbot Northwest: 6 mi on B3362 – Regional map n° **1**–C2

🏠 **Hotel Endsleigh**   ⚘ ⅍ ⇐ 🚪 🅿

HISTORIC · CLASSIC Restored Regency lodge in an idyllic rural setting; spacious guest areas offer wonderful countryside views and have a warm, classical style with a contemporary edge. Comfortable, antique-furnished bedrooms boast an understated elegance; choose one overlooking the magnificent gardens.

18 rooms ⌂ – ♥♥ £225/450 – 6 suites

⊠ *PL19 0PQ – ☎ 01822 870000 – www.hotelendsleigh.com*

TENBURY WELLS

Worcestershire – Regional map n° **10**–B2

✿ **Pensons** Ⓝ (Lee Westcott)   & ⇄ 🅿

MODERN CUISINE · DESIGN ⅩⅩ The 1,200 acre Netherwood Estate sits on the Worcestershire-Herefordshire border and plays host to this delightfully converted barn overlooking arable farmland. Old agricultural artefacts unearthed during its restoration adorn the walls and, while the interior is design-led, it also has a certain rustic charm.

Chef Lee Westcott moved from London and his experience shows in measured, Scandic-style dishes which deliver well-balanced flavours. He uses the finest ingredients, sourced from the kitchen garden and the local area, including rapeseed oil, flour and honey from the estate – and foraging, fermenting and pickling all play their part. Don't be fooled by the understated presentation, as the modern dishes are much more complex than they may first appear. The sourdough with marmite butter and roasted yeast is a hit, and the lunch menu is a steal.

Specialities: Scallop, yeast, apple and monk's beard. Herefordshire Herdwick lamb, potato and turnip. Sheep's yoghurt, apple and dill.

Menu £32 (lunch), £50/75

Pensons Yard, Netherwood Estate, Stoke Bliss ⊠ WR15 8RT – ☎ 01885 410333 – www.pensons.co.uk – Closed 23 December-7 January, Sunday dinner, Monday, Tuesday, Wednesday lunch

TENTERDEN

Kent – Regional map n° **5**–C2

☺ **Swan Wine Kitchen**   🏠 AK ⇄ 🅿

MODERN BRITISH · FRIENDLY ⅩⅩ This rustic modern restaurant sits above the shop in the Chapel Down vineyard and boasts a cosy lounge and a lovely rooftop terrace with views over the vines; naturally, wines from the vineyard feature. Refined cooking is full of flavour and relies on just a few ingredients to do the talking.

Specialities: Gin-cured sea trout, cucumber, fennel and citrus. Breast of guinea fowl with cannellini bean and courgette fricassee. Rhubarb with Chapel Down gin & tonic sorbet, shortbread and lavender meringue.

Menu £25/29

Swan Chapel Down, Small Hythe Road ⊠ TN30 7NG – ☎ 01580 761616 – www.swanchapeldown.co.uk – Closed Sunday - Wednesday dinner

TETBURY
Gloucestershire – Regional map n° **2**-C1

↿○ Conservatory

MODERN BRITISH · CHIC XX Next to the hotel's main entrance is this beautiful conservatory with a chic rustic style. One room overlooks the kitchen and its wood-fired oven; the other looks over the fields. Concise menus offer flavoursome modern dishes which showcase local ingredients – many from their own organically certified farm.

Menu £25 (lunch) – Carte £43/56

Calcot Manor Hotel, Calcot ⊠ GL8 8YJ – ℰ 01666 890391 –
www.calcot.co

↿○ Gumstool Inn

TRADITIONAL CUISINE · PUB X Set in the 700 year old grounds of Calcot Manor; an attractively converted outbuilding with a laid-back pub vibe and plenty of rustic character courtesy of exposed beams and flagged floors. The accessible menu centres on pub favourites. Start with a drink on the appealing terrace.

Menu £23 (lunch) – Carte £24/47

Calcot Manor Hotel, Calcot ⊠ GL8 8YJ – ℰ 01666 890391 –
www.calcot.co

⌂⌂⌂ Calcot Manor

FAMILY · CONTEMPORARY An impressive collection of converted farm buildings in a peaceful countryside setting, comprising ancient barns, old stables and a characterful farmhouse. Comfy lounges and stylish bedrooms have good mod cons; the outbuildings house a kids club, conference rooms and a superb spa complex.

35 rooms ⌂ – ♯♯ £209/299 – 1 suite

Calcot ⊠ GL8 8YJ – ℰ 01666 890391 –
www.calcot.co

↿○ **Conservatory** · ↿○ **Gumstool Inn** – See restaurant listing

THETFORD
Norfolk – Regional map n° **8**-C2

↿○ The Mulberry

MEDITERRANEAN CUISINE · NEIGHBOURHOOD X A bell tinkles as you enter this delightful stone property and the charming owner welcomes you in. The dining room leads through to a conservatory and a walled garden complete with a mulberry tree. Cooking is gutsy and boldly flavoured.

Carte £25/42

11 Raymond Street ⊠ IP24 2EA – ℰ 01842 824122 –
www.mulberrythetford.co.uk – Closed Sunday, Monday, Tuesday - Saturday lunch

THORNHAM
Norfolk – Regional map n° **8**-B1

↿○ Chequers Inn

TRADITIONAL CUISINE · PUB X Sit on the terrace or hire a wooden pavilion and take in the view. Cooking makes use of the local bounty; alongside the main menu there's tapas, such as tempura mussels, and pizzas which are stone-baked using local ingredients.

Carte £27/54

High Street ⊠ PE36 6LY – ℰ 01485 512229 –
www.chequersinnthornham.com

THORNTON – Lancashire → See Blackpool

THORPE MARKET
Norfolk – Regional map n° **8**–D1

Gunton Arms

TRADITIONAL BRITISH · PUB 🍴 This charming inn overlooks the 1,000 acre Gunton Estate deer park. Enjoy a tasty homemade snack over a game of pool or darts in the bar or make for a gnarled wood table by the fireplace in the flag-floored Elk Room. Dishes are fiercely seasonal; some – such as the Aberdeen Angus steaks – are cooked over the fire. Well-equipped bedrooms have a stylish country house feel.

Specialities: Bure Valley goat shawarma with pickled chilli and wild garlic yoghurt. Loin of Gunton fallow deer with truffled mash and Scottish girolles. Sea buckthorn berry posset with seaweed biscuit.

Carte £ 20/38

Gunton Park ⊠ NR11 8TZ – ℘ 01263 832010 –
www.theguntonarms.co.uk

TICEHURST
East Sussex – Regional map n° **5**–B2

Bell

TRADITIONAL BRITISH · PUB 🍴 With top hats as lampshades, tubas in the loos and a dining room called 'The Stable with a Table', quirky is this 16C coaching inn's middle name. Seasonal menus offer proper pub food and the rustic bedrooms and luxurious lodges in the garden share the pub's idiosyncratic charm.

Carte £ 25/35

High Street ⊠ TN5 7AS – ℘ 01580 200300 –
www.thebellinticehurst.com

TISBURY
Wiltshire – Regional map n° **2**–C3

Beckford Arms

TRADITIONAL CUISINE · PUB 🍴 A charming 18C inn with a beamed dining room, a rustic bar and a lovely country house sitting room; there's also a delightful terrace and garden with hammocks and a petanque pitch. Flavour-packed cooking has a modern edge. Bedrooms provide thoughtful comforts; 2 smart duplex suites are a 3min drive away.

Carte £ 22/40

Fonthill Gifford ⊠ SP3 6PX – ℘ 01747 870385 –
www.beckfordarms.com

Pythouse Kitchen Garden

TRADITIONAL BRITISH · SIMPLE 🍴 A charming red-brick potting shed and glass extension, which sit inside an 18C walled garden. The terrace leads down to the kitchen garden and there's a fire-pit where many of the rustic, flavour-packed dishes are cooked. They serve breakfast, lunch, afternoon tea, and dinner Fri and Sat. The monthly event nights are a hit.

Menu £ 25/45

West Hatch ⊠ SP3 6PA – ℘ 01747 870444 –
www.pythousekitchengarden.co.uk – Closed Sunday - Thursday dinner

The Compasses Inn

TRADITIONAL BRITISH · PUB 🍴 Hidden down narrow lanes in the Nadder Valley is this laid-back thatched inn. With 14C origins it's a hugely characterful place and it also has a pleasant terrace and garden. Fresh, tasty dishes have a mix of regional and Mediterranean influences. Bedrooms mix modern and antique furnishings.

Carte £ 23/35

Lower Chicksgrove ⊠ SP3 6NB – ℘ 01722 714318 –
www.thecompassesinn.com – Closed 25-26 December

TITCHWELL

Norfolk – Regional map n° **8**-C1

ⅱ○ **The Conservatory**　　　⇔ 🛏 & AC P

MODERN CUISINE · BRASSERIE XX Titchwell Manor's smart restaurant offers lovely views over the garden. Dinner offers an à la carte of creative modern dishes. Alternatively, you can dine with sea views in the more informal, funky Eating Rooms, where they serve also light lunches.

Carte £35/55

Titchwell Manor Hotel ⊠ PE31 8BB – ℰ 01485 210221 –
www.titchwellmanor.com

🏠 **Titchwell Manor**　　　🕆 ⇔ 🛏 & P

COUNTRY HOUSE · PERSONALISED This attractive brick farmhouse has a stylish interior, where bare floorboards, Chesterfield sofas and seaside photos feature. Bedrooms in the main house have a quirky retro feel, while those in the grounds are modern and colourful. The Potting Shed – a stand-alone room – is a popular choice.

26 rooms ⌑ – 👫 £100/300

⊠ PE31 8BB – ℰ 01485 210221 –
www.titchwellmanor.com

ⅱ○ **The Conservatory** – See restaurant listing

TITLEY

Herefordshire – Regional map n° **10**-A3

ⅱ○ **Stagg Inn**　　　⇐ ⇔ 🛏 ⑩ P

MODERN BRITISH · PUB X Deep in rural Herefordshire, at the meeting point of two drover's roads, sits this part-medieval, part-Victorian pub. Seasonal menus offer tried-and-tested combinations; be sure to open with the home-salted crisps with vinegar dipping foam. The pub bedrooms can be noisy; opt for one in the old vicarage.

Carte £27/40

⊠ HR5 3RL – ℰ 01544 230221 –
www.thestagg.co.uk – Closed 29 June-8 July, 4-20 November, Monday, Tuesday

TOPSHAM

Devon – Regional map n° **1**-D2

ⅱ○ **Salutation Inn**　　　⇐ 🛏 & ⇧ P

MODERN CUISINE · DESIGN XX A 1720s coaching inn with a surprisingly contemporary interior. The glass-covered courtyard serves breakfast, a fixed price lunch and afternoon tea, while the stylish dining room offers nicely balanced weekly 4, 6 and 8 course menus of well-judged modern dishes. Bedrooms are up-to-date and understated.

Menu £21 (lunch), £45/85

68 Fore Street ⊠ EX3 0HL – ℰ 01392 873060 –
www.salutationtopsham.co.uk – Closed 31 January-6 February, Sunday dinner

TORQUAY

Torbay – Regional map n° **1**–C-D2

⌘ **Elephant** (Simon Hulstone)   ൠ

MODERN BRITISH · FRIENDLY ✗ Just across from the harbour is this brightly decorated bistro, which sets out to prove that good food can be enjoyed in simple surroundings. The light, airy room looks out across the harbour and the laid-back atmosphere and down-to-earth prices are a perfect fit for this seaside town.

It's run by Simon Hulstone and his wife Katy, and eighty percent of the produce (everything apart from the cattle) comes from their 96 acre farm situated just across the bay in Brixham. The confidently crafted, eye-catching dishes are ingredient-focused and full of flavour and you'll find the occasional international influence along the way too. The seafood dishes are particularly accomplished – perfect for a restaurant overlooking the sea – and they even offer a dedicated children's menu.

Specialities: Roast scallops with cabbage, sweet onion cream and pancetta. Skrei cod with Jerusalem artichoke, truffle and hazelnuts. Warm chocolate fondant tart with milk ice cream and banana purée.

Menu £25 (lunch)/80 – Carte £33/50

3-4 Beacon Terrace ✉ TQ1 2BH – ℰ 01803 200044 –
www.elephantrestaurant.co.uk – Closed 1-16 January, Sunday, Monday

↺◯ **Orange Tree**

CLASSIC FRENCH · NEIGHBOURHOOD ✗✗ A homely, split-level restaurant set down a narrow town centre backstreet. The seasonally evolving menu is made up of classically based, French-influenced dishes, which are carefully prepared and rely on fresh, local produce.

Carte £30/60

14-16 Parkhill Road ✉ TQ1 2AL – ℰ 01803 213936 –
www.orangetreerestaurant.co.uk – Closed 26-28 December,
31 December-3 January, Sunday, Monday, Tuesday - Saturday lunch

↺◯ **Number 7**   AC

SEAFOOD · BISTRO ✗ A personally run bistro in a terrace of Regency houses. Fish-related photos and artefacts sit alongside extensive blackboard menus of seafood fresh from the Brixham day boats. The simplest dishes are the best. They offer all of their 80+ wines – including some top vintages – by the glass.

Carte £25/47

7 Beacon Terrace ✉ TQ1 2BH – ℰ 01803 295055 – www.no7-fish.com –
Closed 9-27 February, 3-13 November, 22 December-4 January, Sunday, Monday -
Tuesday lunch

TOTNES

Devon – Regional map n° **1**–C2

↺◯ **Gather** ◍

MODERN BRITISH · NEIGHBOURHOOD ✗ Three friends from Exeter College came together with one ambition: to create a welcoming neighbourhood restaurant showcasing the finest produce from the local waters and fields. These seasonal, often foraged ingredients are brought together in original dishes; the tasting menus are the way to go.

Menu £24 (lunch)/55 – Carte £35/42

50 Fore Street ✉ TQ9 5RP – ℰ 01803 866666 – www.gathertotnes.com –
Closed Sunday, Monday

TRELOWARREN – Cornwall → See Helston

TRENT

Dorset – Regional map n° **2**–C3

⫟○ **Rose & Crown** ⟨⇦ 🛏 🎍 ⅋ **P**

MODERN CUISINE · PUB 🅧 Sit in the characterful 'Buffs Bar' or the bright conservatory of this part-thatched 14C pub. Tasty country cooking is the order of the day – bypass the pub classics and go for the likes of pig's head with apple purée or calves' liver with sage fritters. Bedrooms come with patios overlooking the countryside.

Carte £27/45

✉ DT9 4SL – ℰ 01935 850776 – www.theroseandcrowntrent.co.uk

TRESCO – Cornwall ➔ See Scilly (Isles of)

TRING
Hertfordshire – Regional map n° **7**–A2

⫟○ **Crockers Chef's Table** 🆊 ⫟⊘

MODERN BRITISH · DESIGN 🅧🅧 Arrive early for a cocktail in the smart bar before being shown through to a copper-walled room where orange leather stools are set at a large U-shaped counter. Lunch is at 12. 30 and dinner at 7. 30. Seasonal tasting menus feature creative, eye-catching modern dishes with distinct flavours and textures.

Menu £48 (lunch)/90

74 High Street ✉ HP23 4AF – ℰ 01442 828971 – www.crockerstring.co.uk – Closed 14-18 April, 18-29 August, 22 December-2 January, Sunday, Monday, Tuesday dinner

TRURO
Cornwall – Regional map n° **1**–B3

⫟○ **Tabb's** 🕽🗗

MODERN BRITISH · NEIGHBOURHOOD 🅧🅧 Tucked away in the backstreets you'll find this unassuming former pub which comprises a series of homely cream and lilac rooms. The owner works alone in the kitchen, cooking refined, classically based dishes with masculine flavours. Sauces are a strength and the deep-fried courgettes are a must.

Menu £27/38 – Carte £29/38

85 Kenwyn Street ✉ TR1 3BZ – ℰ 01872 262110 – www.tabbs.co.uk – Closed Sunday, Monday

TUDDENHAM
Suffolk – Regional map n° **8**–B2

⫟○ **Tuddenham Mill** ⟨⇦ 🛏 ⫟⊘ ⇄ **P**

MODERN BRITISH · CONTEMPORARY DÉCOR 🅧🅧 A delightful 18C watermill overlooking a millpond; the old workings are still in situ in the stylish bar, above which is a beamed restaurant with black furnishings. Cooking features quality seasonal produce in unusual, innovative combinations. Some of the modern bedrooms are in the attractive outbuildings.

Menu £26 (lunch) – Carte £36/54

High Street ✉ IP28 6SQ – ℰ 01638 713552 – www.tuddenhammill.co.uk

TURNERS HILL
West Sussex – Regional map n° **4**–D2

🏛🏛 **Alexander House** 🌣 🕭 🛏 🔲 🕙 🕉 🎝 🕃 🕭 🎝 **P**

COUNTRY HOUSE · ELEGANT A stunning 18C country house in extensive grounds – once owned by Percy Shelley's family. The superb spa has 21 treatment rooms and a Grecian pool. Spacious bedrooms are well-equipped; the contemporary Cedar Lodge Suites have mood lighting and either a balcony or terrace. Dine in the brasserie or formal AG's.

58 rooms – 🛉🛉 £189/349 – 3 suites

East Street ✉ RH10 4QD – ℰ 01342 714914 – www.alexanderhouse.co.uk

TYTHERLEIGH
Devon – Regional map n° **1**–D2

⑪○ **Tytherleigh Arms** ⑩   ⇦ 🛏 🅿

MODERN BRITISH · INN 🅇 This sympathetically refurbished 16C coaching inn is personally run by experienced owners and its characterful timbered interior features a large inglenook fireplace. Choose from pub classics or boldly flavoured modern British dishes with a European slant. Stylish bedrooms await in the old stables.

Carte £20/44

Chard Road ⊠ EX13 7BE – ℰ 01460 220214 – www.tytherleigharms.com – Closed 2-21 January

---

UPPER SLAUGHTER – Gloucestershire ➜ See Bourton-on-the-Water

UPPER SOUTH WRAXALL
Wiltshire – Regional map n° **2**–C2

⑥ **Longs Arms**   🍴 🛏 ♿ 🅿

TRADITIONAL BRITISH · PUB 🅇 Handsome, bay-windowed, Bath stone pub opposite a medieval church in a sleepy village. Traditional British dishes are full-flavoured, hearty and satisfying; everything is homemade and they smoke their own meats and fish. Dine in the characterful area in front of the bar. Warm, friendly service.

Specialities: Chicken liver parfait with rowan jelly, hazelnuts and sourdough toast. Steamed lamb & mint suet pudding with buttermilk mash and spring greens. Strawberry choc-ice with honeycomb, strawberries and yoghurt.

Carte £21/40

⊠ BA15 2SB – ℰ 01225 864450 – www.thelongsarms.com – Closed 1-19 January, 2-13 September, Sunday dinner, Monday, Tuesday

---

UPPINGHAM
Rutland – Regional map n° **9**–C2

⑪○ **Lake Isle**   🎇 ⇦ 🛏 🅰🅺 ⇔ 🅿

CLASSIC CUISINE · FRIENDLY 🅇🅇 Characterful 18C town centre property accessed via a narrow passageway and very personally run by experienced owners. It has a cosy lounge and a heavy wood-furnished dining room. Light lunches are followed by much more elaborate modern dinners. Bedrooms come with good extras and some have whirlpool baths.

Menu £17 (lunch) – Carte £27/56

16 High Street East ⊠ LE15 9PZ – ℰ 01572 822951 – www.lakeisle.co.uk – Closed Sunday dinner, Monday lunch

---

UPTON
Hampshire – Regional map n° **4**–B1

⑥ **Crown Inn**   🛏 🅿

MODERN BRITISH · PUB 🅇 Set amidst narrow lanes and lush farmland is this truly welcoming pub. It has an open-fired bar with comfy sofas, an antique chess table and a farm shop, and an airy conservatory restaurant. Flavour-packed menus champion the county's produce, following the ethos of 'what grows together, goes together'.

Specialities: Gammon Scotch egg with Lea & Perrins mayonnaise. Braised shoulder of lamb with smoked potato purée, cabbage and onion jus. Honey and lavender crème brûlée with citrus shortbread.

Carte £25/30

⊠ SP11 0JS – ℰ 01264 736044 – www.thecrowninnupton.co.uk – Closed Monday, Tuesday, Wednesday - Friday lunch

---

UPTON BISHOP – Herefordshire ➜ See Ross-on-Wye

UPTON GREY
Hampshire – Regional map n° **4**–B1

⅋○ **Hoddington Arms** ⟨≒ 🛋 & **P**
TRADITIONAL BRITISH · PUB ✕ Find a sofa in the wonderfully atmospheric former barn – which has plenty of rustic character and a laid-back feel – bag a spot in the smart cabana or find a seat in the lovely garden beside the wood-burning oven. Menus mix pub classics and sharing boards with more adventurous dishes.

Menu £27 (lunch) – Carte £27/42

Bidden Road ⊠ RG25 2RL – ℰ 01256 862371 –
www.hoddingtonarms.co.uk

UPTON MAGNA – Shropshire → See Shrewsbury

VENTNOR – Isle of Wight → See Wight (Isle of)

WADDINGTON
Lancashire – Regional map n° **11**–B2

⅋○ **Higher Buck** ⟨⟩ 🛋 & **P**
TRADITIONAL CUISINE · PUB ✕ A smartly refurbished pub with pastel-painted wood panelling and modern furnishings, in a lovely Ribble Valley village. Bag a spot at one of the U-shaped banquettes or on the sunny terrace overlooking the Square and dine on reassuringly robust, seasonal dishes. Service is friendly and stylish bedrooms await.

Carte £24/42

The Square ⊠ BB7 3HZ – ℰ 01200 423226 –
www.higherbuck.com

WADEBRIDGE
Cornwall – Regional map n° **1**–B2

🏠 **Trewornan Manor** ⟨🦋 ⟨ ⟨≒ **P**
COUNTRY HOUSE · ELEGANT Stunning Grade II listed 13C manor house set in 25 acres beside the River Amble, with over 8 acres of delightfully manicured gardens. Sumptuous, ultra-chic bedrooms all have views of the grounds. Welcoming young owners offer cream tea by the fire in the restful sitting room and fresh home-cooked breakfasts.

7 rooms – ♀♀ £130/220

Trewornan Bridge, Street Minver ⊠ PL27 6EX – ℰ 01208 812359 –
www.trewornanmanor.co.uk

WALBERSWICK
Suffolk – Regional map n° **8**–D2

⅋○ **Anchor** 🦋 ⟨⟩ ⟨≒ 🛋 & **P**
TRADITIONAL CUISINE · PUB ✕ A welcoming pub in an Arts and Crafts building; its sizeable garden features a wood-fired oven and leads down to the beach. Dishes are prepared with real care and global flavours punctuate the menu. If you're staying the night, choose a wood-clad chalet in the garden; breakfasts are impressive.

Carte £20/45

Main Street ⊠ IP18 6UA – ℰ 01502 722112 –
www.anchoratwalberswick.com

WALL
Northumberland – Regional map n° **14**-A2

⅃○ **Hjem**  ⇔ ⥱ **P**

SCANDINAVIAN · CONTEMPORARY DÉCOR XX Set within a traditional country inn close to Hadrian's Wall is this small modern restaurant with an open kitchen and a Scandic feel. It's run by an enthusiastic young couple who like to showcase local produce on their Scandic-inspired tasting menus. There are wine – and even juice – flights to match.

Menu £45/75

Hadrian Hotel ⊠ NE46 4EE – ℰ 01434 681232 – www.restauranthjem.co.uk – Closed Sunday, Monday, Tuesday, Wednesday - Saturday lunch

WALWICK
Northumberland – Regional map n° **14**-A2

🏠 **Walwick Hall**  ⇐ ⥱ 🖼 ⅃ ⬆ ⅄ 🆎 **P**

COUNTRY HOUSE · RURAL Hadrian's Wall is almost within touching distance of this charming Georgian country house. While its décor is stylish, it also manages to retain a homely feel. Take in stunning views of the Northumbrian countryside from the 100 acre grounds; produce from the gardens features in modern dishes.

10 rooms ☺ – ♟♟ £195/350

⊠ NE46 4BJ – ℰ 01434 620156 – www.walwickhall.com

WARMINSTER
Wiltshire – Regional map n° **2**-C2

⅃○ **Weymouth Arms** ⇔ 🏠

TRADITIONAL BRITISH · PUB X Grade II listed building with plenty of history. It's immensely characterful, with wood panelling, antiques and lithographs, as well as two fireplaces originally intended for nearby Longleat House. Cooking is fresh and fittingly traditional. Cosy bedrooms have charming original fittings.

Carte £26/44

12 Emwell Street ⊠ BA12 8JA – ℰ 01985 216995 – www.weymoutharms.co.uk – Closed Sunday dinner, Monday - Wednesday lunch

WARWICK
Warwickshire – Regional map n° **10**-C3

⅃○ **Tailors**

MODERN CUISINE · INTIMATE X As well as a tailor's, this intimate restaurant was once a fishmonger's, a butcher's and a casino! It's run by two ambitious chefs, who offer good value modern lunches, and elaborate dinners which feature unusual flavour combinations.

Menu £22 (lunch)/55

22 Market Place ⊠ CV34 4SL – ℰ 01926 410590 – www.tailorsrestaurant.com – Closed 21-31 December, Sunday, Monday, Tuesday lunch

WATERGATE BAY – Cornwall → See Newquay

WATERMILLOCK – Cumbria → See Pooley Bridge

WATFORD
Hertfordshire – Regional map n° **7**-A2

🏛️ Grove   ✿ 🍴 ▣ ⏚ ⬒ 🆂🅿🅰 🐾 ♨ ⬇ ⅙ 🅰🅲 🐾 🅿

BUSINESS · GRAND LUXURY An impressive Grade II listed country house in 300 acres, with elegant lounges and smart, contemporary bedrooms – some with balconies. There's a superb spa and an outdoor pool, as well as tennis, cro-quet, golf and volleyball facilities. Enjoy international cuisine in the Glasshouse or classics in the Stables.

215 rooms – 👫 £275/690 – ⬚ £28 – 6 suites

Chandler's Cross ⊠ WD3 4TG – ℰ 01923 807807 – www.thegrove.co.uk

WELBURN

North Yorkshire – Regional map n° **13**-C2

🍴 **Crown and Cushion**   🛖 ⅙ ♨ 🅿

CLASSIC CUISINE · PUB 🕱 Well run 18C pub two miles from Castle Howard. The menu champions local meats and the kitchen's pride and joy is its charcoal-fired rotisserie. Dishes are hearty, sandwiches are doorstops, and puddings are of the nursery variety.

Carte £20/40

⊠ YO60 7DZ – ℰ 01653 618777 – www.thecrownandcushionwelburn.com

WELLAND – Worcestershire → See Great Malvern

WELLS

Somerset – Regional map n° **2**-C2

🏛️ **Swan**   ✿ ♨ 🐾 ⅙ 🐾 🅿

INN · CONTEMPORARY 15C former coaching inn with a good outlook onto the famous cathedral; its charming interior has subtle contemporary touches, particu-larly in the lounge and bar. Comfortable, stylish, well-equipped bedrooms and an opulent 'Cathedral Suite'. The formal, wood-panelled restaurant serves classic dishes.

50 rooms – 👫 £140/202 – 1 suite

11 Sadler Street ⊠ BA5 2RX – ℰ 01749 836300 – www.swanhotelwells.co.uk

🏠 **Stoberry House**   ⅏ ⪕ 🍴 🅿

TRADITIONAL · PERSONALISED 18C coach house with a delightful walled gar-den, overlooking Glastonbury Tor. Large lounge with a baby grand piano and an-tique furniture. Breakfast is an event, with 7 homemade breads, a porridge menu and lots of cooked dishes. Immaculately kept bedrooms come with fresh flowers, chocolates and a pillow menu.

7 rooms – 👫 £95/215

Stoberry Park ⊠ BA5 3LD – ℰ 01749 672906 – www.stoberryhouse.co.uk – Closed 16 December-9 January

WEST ASHLING – West Sussex → See Chicester

WEST BRIDGFORD – Nottinghamshire → See Nottingham

WEST BYFLEET

Surrey – Regional map n° **4**-C1

🍴 **London House**   ⅙ 🅰🅲

MODERN BRITISH · BISTRO 🕱🕱 A pleasant neighbourhood restaurant set in a busy parade of shops. White walls are hung with modern art and equally colourful modern dishes take their influences from Britain and the Med. Top quality ingredi-ents include local rare breed pork and their superb deli stocks some great cheeses.

Menu £38/45

30 Station Approach ⊠ KT14 6NF – ℰ 01932 482026 – www.restaurantlondonhouse.co.uk – Closed Sunday dinner, Monday, Tuesday – Saturday lunch

WEST BEXINGTON
Dorset – Regional map n° **2**-B3

⬦ **Club House** ⬕ 🛋 🗇 ⅃ **P**

SEAFOOD · BISTRO ⅄ This old clubhouse sits in a superb location atop Chesil Beach, so when the sun's out, head for the terrace. Inside, contemporary décor blends with period nautical touches such as lifebelts and sepia prints. Unfussy modern dishes showcase Exmouth oysters, Weymouth lobster, Portland crab and Brixham fish.

Carte £30/60

Beach Road ⊠ DT2 9DG – ☏ 01308 898302 –
www.theclubhousewestbexington.co.uk – Closed Sunday dinner, Monday

WEST HOATHLY
West Sussex – Regional map n° **4**-D2

⊛ **Cat Inn** ⬅ 🗇 **P**

TRADITIONAL BRITISH · PUB ⅄ Popular with the locals and very much a village pub, with beamed ceilings, pewter tankards, open fires and plenty of cosy corners. Carefully executed, good value cooking focuses on tasty pub classics like locally smoked ham, egg and chips or steak, mushroom and ale pie. Service is friendly and efficient – and four tastefully decorated bedrooms complete the picture.

Specialities: Chicken & duck terrine with pickled carrot, tarragon emulsion and bacon crumb. Steak, mushroom and ale pie with seasonal vegetables. Bakewell tart with clotted cream ice cream.

Carte £23/40

North Lane ⊠ RH19 4PP – ☏ 01342 810369 – www.catinn.co.uk

WEST MALLING
Kent – Regional map n° **5**-B1

⬦ **Amano** ⓝ ⬅ ⅃ 🅰🅲

ITALIAN · BISTRO ⅄ A refurbished pub houses this modern Italian bistro. Enjoy a glass of wine accompanied by cheese and salami in the small bar or head to the glass-roofed restaurant for authentic, unfussy dishes – the homemade pastas and wood-fired pizzas are a highlight. Sleek bedrooms are located above.

Menu £20 (lunch) – Carte £24/40

47 Swan Street ⊠ ME19 6JU – ☏ 01732 600128 – www.amanorestaurant.co.uk

⬦ **Swan** ⅋ 🗇 ⅃ ♺

MODERN CUISINE · CLASSIC DÉCOR ⅄ A 15C coaching inn plays host to this stylish yet characterful restaurant. Start in the chic cocktail bar, then dine in the relaxed front or rear room or on the terrace. Modern day classics feature on an appealing menu and the experienced, hands-on owners keep things running smoothly from morning to night.

Menu £22 – Carte £25/48

35 Swan Street ⊠ ME19 6JU – ☏ 01732 521910 – www.theswanwestmalling.co.uk

WEST MEON
Hampshire – Regional map n° **4**-B2

⬦ **Thomas Lord** ⬅ 🛋 🗇 **P**

TRADITIONAL CUISINE · PUB ⅄ This smart, early 19C pub is named after the founder of Lord's Cricket Ground and decorated with cricketing memorabilia. The atmosphere is warm and welcoming and the menu perfectly balances the classics with some more adventurous offerings. The lovely garden is home to a wood-burning stove, as well as to 4 delightful wooden lodges for those who wish to stay.

Carte £27/39

High Street ⊠ GU32 1LN – ☏ 01730 829244 – www.thethomaslord.co.uk

WESTLETON

Suffolk – Regional map n° **8**-D2

🍴○ **Westleton Crown**　　　　　　　　⇦ 🏠 🛏 ℷ ☺ ⒱ **P**

TRADITIONAL CUISINE · PUB ℷ Good-looking, 17C former coaching inn with an appealing terrace and garden, set in a pretty little village. Welcoming beamed bar with open fires; more modern conservatory. Seasonal menu, with special diets well-catered for. Uncluttered bedrooms are named after birds found on the adjacent RSPB nature reserve.

Carte £ 26/40

The Street ✉ IP17 3AD – ℰ 01728 648777 – www.westletoncrown.co.uk

WHATCOTE

Warwickshire – Regional map n° **10**-C3

❀ **The Royal Oak** (Richard Craven)　　　　　　　　ℷ **P**

MODERN BRITISH · PUB ℷ The Royal Oak started out as a drinks shelter catering for the workmen building the local church and is reputedly one of the oldest pubs in the country – Oliver Cromwell supposedly stayed here before the Battle of Edgehill in 1642. It's a charming place, with a lovely atmosphere and plenty of character, from the cosy, traditional bar to the bright, airy dining room.

Richard Craven has a passion for British produce and the cooking follows a strong 'farm to fork' ethos, with produce coming from small producers in and around the nearby hills and estates. He favours organic and wild ingredients and game is often shot to order. Dishes are created with obvious care and skill and have an unfussy, tried-and-tested style, relying on the quality of the ingredients to do the talking. Richard's charming wife Solanche looks after the service.

Specialities: Pig's head & black pudding lasagna with hazelnuts and cider reduction. Red deer with venison suet pudding, carrot, elderberry and purple sprouting broccoli. Yorkshire rhubarb with caramelised white chocolate and fennel.

Menu £ 29/55 – Carte £ 37/45

The Orchard ✉ CV36 5EF – ℰ 01295 688100 – www.theroyaloakwhatcote.co.uk – Closed 23-26 December, Sunday dinner, Monday, Tuesday, Wednesday - Thursday lunch

WHITBY

North Yorkshire – Regional map n° **13**-C1

🍴○ **The Star Inn The Harbour**　　　　　　　　🏠

MODERN BRITISH · BRASSERIE ℷℷ Andrew Pern has fulfilled a dream by opening this modern brasserie by the harbour in his home town. The extensive menu offers classic British brasserie dishes from the 'Harbourside', the 'Countryside' and the 'Ice Cream Parlour'.

Carte £ 26/45

1 Langborne Road ✉ YO21 1YN – ℰ 01947 821900 – www.starinntheharbour.co.uk

at Sandsend Northwest: 3 mi on A174

🍴○ **Estbek House**　　　　　　　　❀ ⇦

SEAFOOD · FRIENDLY ℷℷ A personally run Regency house close to the beach, with a lovely front terrace and an elegant dining room. The basement bar overlooks the kitchen and doubles as a breakfast room. Menus offer unfussy dishes of sustainable wild fish from local waters. Smart bedrooms come with stylish bathrooms.

Carte £ 39/67

East Row ✉ YO21 3SU – ℰ 01947 893424 – www.estbekhouse.co.uk – Closed 1 January-14 February, Sunday - Saturday lunch

WHITCHURCH

Shropshire – Regional map n° **10**–B1

ᛏO **Docket N°. 33**

MODERN BRITISH · NEIGHBOURHOOD X A sweet little restaurant set in an old market town and run by a friendly couple. The set tasting menu changes weekly and offers modern dishes which are inspired by the restaurant's location and enhanced with some international influences. Appealing drinks pairings complete the picture.

Menu £45

33 High Street ⊠ SY13 1AZ – ☎ 01948 665553 – www.docketrestaurant.com –
Closed Sunday, Monday, Tuesday, Wednesday, Thursday - Saturday lunch

WHITE WALTHAM

Windsor and Maidenhead – Regional map n° **6**–C3

ᛏO **Beehive**

MODERN BRITISH · PUB X A traditional English pub overlooking the cricket pitch, where you'll find local drinkers in the bar and a comfy, light-filled dining room. Eye-catching daily dishes are full of flavour and exhibit a staunch sense of Britishness.

Menu £25 (lunch) – Carte £30/55

Waltham Road ⊠ SL6 3SH – ☎ 01628 822877 –
www.thebeehivewhitewaltham.com – Closed Sunday dinner

WHITEWELL

Lancashire – Regional map n° **11**–B2

🏠 **Inn at Whitewell**

INN · PERSONALISED A 14C creeper-clad inn set high on the banks of the river and affording stunning valley views. Spacious bedrooms are split between the inn and a nearby coach house – some are traditional, with four-posters and antique baths; others more contemporary. Classic menus offer wholesome, regionally inspired dishes.

23 rooms ⊊ – ♦♦ £137/270

Forest of Bowland ⊠ BB7 3AT – ☎ 01200 448222 – www.innatwhitewell.com

WHITSTABLE

Kent – Regional map n° **5**–C1

ᛏO **Whitstable Oyster Company**

SEAFOOD · RUSTIC X A lovely old oyster warehouse with a tremendous view over the estuary. It has a large terrace, two capacious wood-panelled rooms and a trendy first floor lounge-bar. The hand-written menu changes daily depending on the latest catch; the oysters from their own beds are a must-try.

Carte £33/70

Royal Native Oyster Stores, Horsebridge ⊠ CT5 1BU – ☎ 01227 276856 –
www.whitstableoystercompany.com

at Seasalter Southwest: 2 mi by B2205 – Regional map n° **5**–C1

🕸 **The Sportsman** (Stephen Harris)

MODERN BRITISH · PUB X It's long been about food at this wind-blown spot by the sea wall of the Thames Estuary, which has hosted an inn since the 17C and farmland since the 12C. True, it might look like a pub with its traditional furnishings, wood panelling and tiled floor – and you can still drop by just for a pint as many regulars do – but the main draw here is the cooking, and what cooking it is.

It's run by Stephen and Philip Harris – with Stephen overseeing the kitchen and Philip manning the bar – and comes complete with brightly painted bedroom cabins in the garden.

Top local ingredients including fish from the Thames Estuary and vegetables from the kitchen garden make up the core of the menu, which is chalked up on the blackboard. Carefully prepared, confidently executed dishes follow a 'less is more' philosophy, relying on just a few ingredients and their natural flavours to impress. Choose the 5 course daily tasting menu or ask to extend it to 9 courses when you book.

Specialities: Slip sole grilled in seaweed butter. Roast saddle of lamb with mint sauce. Rhubarb soufflé with rhubarb ripple ice cream.

Menu £55/70 – Carte £42/49

Faversham Road ⊠ CT5 4BP – ℰ 0227 273370 –
www.thesportsmanseasalter.co.uk – Closed Sunday dinner, Monday

WHITTLESFORD

Cambridgeshire – Regional map n° **8**–B3

⅋◯ **Tickell Arms**   🛏 🏠 ♿ 🄰🄲 🅿

MODERN BRITISH · PUB 𝖃 A welcoming team run this characterful pub, where constantly evolving menus offer everything from sandwiches to steaks. Fish is delivered 6 days a week and some leaves and fruits come from the garden; the weekday set menu offers good value. Ask for a seat in the orangery-style extension overlooking the pond.

Menu £22 – Carte £26/43

1 North Road ⊠ CB2 4NZ – ℰ 01223 833025 – www.thetickellarms.co.uk

WIGHT (ISLE OF)

Isle of Wight – Regional map n° **4**–B3

Top tips!

England's largest island sits 3 miles from the mainland and can be reached via ferry in less than an hour. It became a fashionable holiday resort in the mid-19C, thanks mostly to Prince Albert, who built an Italianate style villa here.

The island has always been associated with maritime pursuits and each August plays host to Cowes Week, one of the longest-running regattas in the world. The Isle of Wight Festival of British music also draws crowds every June.

A mild climate and plentiful sunlight make it ideal for cultivating a whole range of ingredients – the most famous being their wonderful tomatoes and garlic; you can even pay a visit to the UK's largest specialist Garlic Farm.

The island's beaches are a hit, as is beachside dining; for a laid-back vibe head for **The Hut** in Freshwater or **Little Gloster** in Gurnard – or, for the ultimate waterside spot, the terrace at **The George** hotel in Yarmouth.

FRESHWATER
Isle of Wight

⅋○ **The Hut** 🍸 ⟨ 🏠 �ⅈ ☼

MODERN CUISINE · FRIENDLY ⅋ This laid-back, beach shack style restaurant is superbly set among colourful beach huts and looks over the sea to Hurst Castle. Sit on the terrace or under retractable roofs and enjoy anything from fish tacos to a fruits de mer platter. Most diners arrive by boat (they'll even collect you from your mooring).

Carte £26/55

Colwell Chine Road, Colwell Bay ⊠ PO40 9NP – ℰ 01983 893637 –
www.thehutcolwell.co.uk – Closed 3 November-4 March

GURNARD
Isle of Wight

⅋○ **Little Gloster** ⟨⟩ ⟨ 🏠 🏠 **P**

TRADITIONAL CUISINE · RUSTIC ⅋ Set in a great spot among the beach huts, with lovely views over The Solent. Have a cocktail on the terrace then head inside to the tables by the kitchen or the relaxed, shabby chic dining room. Unfussy, flavoursome cooking uses island produce. Stylish bedrooms have a fresh nautical theme and superb views.

Menu £20 – Carte £27/46

31 Marsh Road ⊠ PO31 8JQ – ℰ 01983 298776 – www.thelittlegloster.com –
Closed 30 December-13 February, Sunday dinner, Monday, Tuesday, Wednesday -
Thursday lunch

NEWPORT
Isle of Wight

⅋○ **Thompson's** & **AC**

MODERN BRITISH · COSY ⅋ A stylish yet relaxed restaurant in the centre of town; try to book one of the three tables in front of the open kitchen. Original cooking makes good use of island ingredients and exhibits some interesting flavour combinations.

Menu £24 (lunch), £47/55

11 Town Lane ⊠ PO30 1JU – ℰ 01983 526118 – www.robertthompson.co.uk –
Closed 23 February-12 March, Sunday, Monday

SEAVIEW
Isle of Wight – Regional map n° **4**-B3

⊛ **Seaview** 🏠 & **AC**

MODERN BRITISH · CLASSIC DÉCOR ⅋⅋ The seafaring décor gives a clue as to the focus at this hotel restaurant. Good value set-priced menus focus on carefully prepared, classical seafood dishes and ingredients are good quality. The 'Naval Mess' and 'Pump Room' provide simpler alternatives; the crab ramekin has become something of an institution.

Specialities: Green Barn Farm goat's cheese soufflé with wild garlic velouté and rapeseed oil. Rump and crispy belly of lamb, peas, broad beans, garlic and salsa verde. Blood orange parfait with honey and yoghurt.

Menu £22 (lunch)/28

Seaview Hotel, High Street ⊠ PO34 5EX – ℰ 01983 612711 –
www.seaviewhotel.co.uk

🏠 **Seaview** ⅋ ⊡ &

TRADITIONAL · QUIRKY A long-standing seaside hotel with a laid-back feel – its interesting interior filled with nautical charts, maritime photos and model ships. Bright, comfy bedrooms come in various styles; some are in annexes and several are suites.

24 rooms ⅏ – ⅋⅋ £99/195 – 1 suite

High Street ⊠ PO34 5EX – ℰ 01983 612711 – www.seaviewhotel.co.uk
⊛ **Seaview** – See restaurant listing

445

VENTNOR

Isle of Wight – Regional map n° **4**–B3

Hillside

COUNTRY HOUSE · UNIQUE Set high above the town, this wonderful thatched Georgian house has a beautiful terrace and superb sea views. The Danish owner has fused period furnishings with clean-lined Scandinavian styling, and displays over 350 pieces of CoBrA and Scandinavian art. Everything is immaculate and the linens are top quality. Frequently changing menus use local and garden produce.

14 rooms ☑ – †† £156/206

151 Mitchell Avenue ⊠ PO38 1DR –
℘ 01983 852271 – www.hillsideventnor.co.uk

YARMOUTH

Isle of Wight

The Conservatory

TRADITIONAL BRITISH · BRASSERIE Hidden at the back of the George hotel is this airy brasserie with a sizeable terrace offering views over a lovely garden which leads down to the water's edge. It opens all day and offers everything from breakfast, snacks and afternoon tea to modern brasserie classics featuring island produce.

Carte £28/54

The George Hotel, Quay Street ⊠ PO41 0PE –
℘ 01983 760331 – www.thegeorge.co.uk

The George

BOUTIQUE HOTEL · DESIGN Set in the shadow of the castle, this cosy 17C inn blends subtle modern touches with characterful period features. Bedrooms vary in shape and style: some are wood-panelled, some have luxurious bathrooms, some open onto the garden or have spacious balconies – and many have excellent Solent views.

17 rooms ☑ – †† £145/385

Quay Street ⊠ PO41 0PE –
℘ 01983 760331 – www.thegeorge.co.uk

  ⇧○ **The Conservatory** – See restaurant listing

WIGMORE

Herefordshire – Regional map n° **10**–A2

⇧○ The Oak Wigmore

MODERN BRITISH · PUB The charming, hands-on owner spent 3 years transforming this 16C coaching inn and outbuildings into the smart, contemporary pub you see before you today. The experienced local chef really knows how to get the best out of his ingredients. Simple, comfortable bedrooms complete the picture.

Carte £28/47

Ford Street ⊠ HR6 9UJ –
℘ 01568 770424 – www.theoakwigmore.com – Closed Sunday dinner, Monday, Tuesday, Wednesday - Friday lunch

WILLIAN

Hertfordshire – Regional map n° **7**–B2

⇧○ Fox

MODERN BRITISH · PUB The Fox sits in the heart of the village and is a pleasingly unpretentious place. Monthly menus present an appealing range of modern British dishes which keep natural flavours to the fore and arrive neatly presented. Service is sweet and friendly, and comfy, contemporary country bedrooms await.

Carte £24/43

⊠ SG6 2AE – ℘ 01462 480233 – www.foxatwillian.co.uk – Closed Sunday dinner

WILMINGTON

Kent – Regional map n° **5**–B1

🏨 Rowhill Grange

COUNTRY HOUSE · CONTEMPORARY An early 19C house set in 15 acres of pretty gardens, with smart modern bedrooms in dark, bold hues. The fantastic spa has 9 treatment rooms, a large gym and a superb swimming pool, along with a separate infinity pool with a waterfall. RG's serves fresh seasonal dishes – try the grills.

38 rooms ☲ – 👫 £115/495

✉ DA2 7QH – ℰ 01322 615136 – www.alexanderhotels.co.uk/rowhill-grange/

WIMBORNE MINSTER

Dorset – Regional map n° **2**–C3

🟙 Tickled Pig 🛱 ໄ

MODERN BRITISH · BISTRO ✗ Charmingly run restaurant in the heart of a pretty market town, with a modern country interior, a lovely terrace and a laid-back feel. Daily brown paper menus feature home-grown veg and home-reared pork; their mantra is 'taking food back to its roots'. Cooking is vibrant, flavourful and unfussy.

Menu £25 (lunch) – Carte £28/37

26 West Borough ✉ BH21 1NF – ℰ 01202 886778 – www.thetickledpig.co.uk – Closed 24-27 December, Sunday dinner

WINCHCOMBE

Gloucestershire – Regional map n° **2**–D1

🟙 5 North St

MODERN BRITISH · COSY ✗✗ This long-standing neighbourhood restaurant, run by a husband and wife, is a hit with the locals; it might be small inside but it's big on character. Concise menus feature regional ingredients in classic combinations.

Menu £32/55

5 North Street ✉ GL54 5LH – ℰ 01242 604566 – www.5northstreetrestaurant.co.uk – Closed 1-14 January, 1-7 August, Sunday dinner-Tuesday lunch

WINCHESTER

Hampshire – Regional map n° **4**–B2

✿ Black Rat 🛱 ♨

MODERN CUISINE · RUSTIC ✗ Don't be put off by the rat sign swinging outside or the roadside location, as you can't help but love this rustic, candlelit former pub with its quirky, bohemian-style interior. It's a truly welcoming place with relaxed shabby-chic styling, an eclectic display of curios and a fire burning in the grate – not forgetting a friendly team. Start with a drink upstairs in the richly decorated bar or outside in one of the lovely heated straw huts on the terrace; as well as some carefully chosen wines and cocktails, they offer a selection of over 30 different gins.

Jon Marsden-Jones and his team carefully prepare refined, innovative British dishes which showcase items that they've foraged or plucked from their allotment. Portions are hearty, flavours really pack a punch there is a beguiling originality to the presentation.

Specialities: Mackerel with cucumber cannelloni, rhubarb and watercress. Ox heart with celeriac, spelt barley, Judas Ears and purple sprouting broccoli. Tonka bean panna cotta with sorrel bavarois and rhubarb.

Menu £34 (lunch) – Carte £40/60

88 Chesil Street ✉ SO23 0HX – ℰ 01962 844465 – www.theblackrat.co.uk – Closed 24 December-10 January, Monday - Friday lunch

⫯○ Chesil Rectory

MODERN CUISINE · HISTORIC XX This double-gabled wattle and daub house dates from the 15C and its characterful interior takes in heavily beamed ceilings and a large inglenook fireplace. Appealing menus offer classic British dishes with the odd Mediterranean touch.

Menu £21 – Carte £29/41

Chesil Street ⊠ SO23 0HU – ℰ 01962 851555 – www.chesilrectory.co.uk

⫯○ Kyoto Kitchen

JAPANESE · INTIMATE XX This sweet little restaurant is a hit with the locals. Authentic Japanese dishes are prepared with care and there's good detail in the execution. The tempura, sushi and sashimi are highlights but don't overlook the small plates.

Carte £25/50

70 Parchment Street ⊠ SO23 8AT – ℰ 01962 890895 – www.kyotokitchen.co.uk – Closed Monday lunch

at Sparsholt Northwest: 3. 5 mi by B3049

⫯○ Avenue

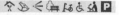

MODERN BRITISH · ELEGANT XX Start with a drink in the cedar wood panelled bar of this country house, then sit amongst oil paintings overlooking the avenue of lime trees which have stood here since 1716. Modern menus champion British produce, with scallops from Orkney, fish from Lymington and game from the New Forest.

Menu £60/80

Lainston House Hotel, Woodman Lane ⊠ SO21 2LT – ℰ 01962 776088 – www.exclusive.co.uk/lainston-house – Closed Monday - Saturday lunch

🏠 Lainston House

COUNTRY HOUSE · CONTEMPORARY An impressive 17C William and Mary manor house with attractive gardens and a striking mile-long avenue of lime trees. Enjoy a game of tennis, croquet or boules, try your hand at falconry, or brush up on your culinary skills at the superb cookery school. Bedrooms are spacious and contemporary.

50 rooms ⊡ – 👫 £162/315 – 3 suites

Woodman Lane ⊠ SO21 2LT – ℰ 01962 776088 – www.exclusive.co.uk/lainston-house

⫯○ **Avenue** – See restaurant listing

WINDERMERE

Cumbria – Regional map n° **12**–A2

⫯○ Holbeck Ghyll

MODERN BRITISH · CLASSIC DÉCOR XX A three-roomed restaurant in a traditional stone Arts and Crafts house; its elegant oak-panelled front room offers superb views over Lake Windermere and the mountains. Concise set menus utilise good quality local ingredients in modern dishes; at dinner there's also an 8 course tasting menu.

Menu £52 (lunch)/72

Holbeck Ghyll Hotel, Holbeck Lane ⊠ LA23 1LU – ℰ 015394 32375 – www.holbeckghyll.com

🏠 Holbeck Ghyll

TRADITIONAL · CLASSIC A charming Arts and Crafts house boasting stunning views over the lake and mountains. Well-equipped bedrooms are spread about the place and range from classical to contemporary; Miss Potter, complete with a hot tub, is the best.

32 rooms ⊡ – 👫 £170/420 – 4 suites

Holbeck Lane ⊠ LA23 1LU – ℰ 015394 32375 – www.holbeckghyll.com

⫯○ **Holbeck Ghyll** – See restaurant listing

at Bowness-on-Windermere South: 1 mi – Regional map n° **12**–A2

🕸 HRiSHi ⊟ 🛱 ⅋ 🛈 🄿

MODERN CUISINE · ELEGANT 🅇🅇🅇 A charming, experienced family run this delightfully modernised country house nestled in the fells. Start with an aperitif in the comfy lounge or chic bar then move on to one of the three intimate dining rooms that make up HRiSHi, where the décor is eye-catching and slightly eclectic – a mirror for Head Chef Hrishikesh Desai's colourfully presented food.

His cooking style pays the utmost respect to classical techniques and features the likes of salt-aging, brining and smoking, and he aims to awaken the senses by using flavours and textures to provoke certain memories. Precisely prepared, original dishes are very attractively presented and some blend local ingredients with subtle Indian or Asian spicing. The vegetarian dishes are packed with flavour too.

Bedrooms range from contemporary country doubles to spacious garden suites with outdoor hot tubs.

Specialities: Scallop ceviche with chilli, ginger and orange dressing. Loin of lamb with Hyderabadi masala braised shoulder and onion Tatin. White chocolate parfait with carrot & cardamom compote and dark chocolate sorbet.

Menu £70/90

Gilpin Hotel & Lake House Hotel, Crook Road ⊠ LA23 3NE – ☎ 015394 88818 – www.thegilpin.co.uk – Closed 6-7 January, Monday - Saturday lunch

🍴 Gilpin Spice ⊟ 🛱 🎋 🛈 ⇄ 🄿

ASIAN · EXOTIC DÉCOR 🅇🅇 Cumbria was a key player in the spice trade and this slate restaurant in the grounds of Gilpin Hotel is inspired by that history. Extensive menus follow the Silk Road from Cumbria to Asia and many dishes are designed for sharing. Enter the colourful rooms via wooden walkways built over stone-filled pools.

Carte £20/40

Gilpin Hotel & Lake House Hotel, Crook Road ⊠ LA23 3NE – ☎ 015394 88818 – www.thegilpin.co.uk – Closed 6-7 January, 25-26 December

🏨 Gilpin Hotel & Lake House 🌣 🦢 ≼ ⊟ 🖼 🕸 🙈 ⅋ 🄿

LUXURY · PERSONALISED A delightful country house hotel run by a charming, experienced family. Bedrooms range from contemporary country doubles to spacious garden suites with outdoor hot tubs. There are even more peaceful, luxurious suites a mile down the road beside a tarn – stay here for exclusive use of the smart spa.

31 rooms ☲ – †† £285/735

Crook Road ⊠ LA23 3NE – ☎ 015394 88818 – www.thegilpin.co.uk – Closed 6-7 January

🕸 HRiSHi · 🍴 Gilpin Spice – See restaurant listing

🏨 Linthwaite House 🌣 🦢 ≼ ⊟ 🏋 🄿

TRADITIONAL · CONTEMPORARY This stylish hotel sits in a peaceful spot overlooking the fells and Lake Windermere and is surrounded by 14 acres of beautiful grounds. Go for one of the suites: four are in the grounds and one has a hot tub with garden views. Simon Rogan is taking over the restaurant.

36 rooms ☲ – †† £199/400 – 6 suites

Crook Road ⊠ LA23 3JA – ☎ 015394 88600 – www.leeucollection.com

WINDSOR

Windsor and Maidenhead – Regional map n° **6**–D3

🍴 Greene Oak 🛱 🆎 🄿

MODERN CUISINE · PUB 🅇 The Greene Oak's modern bar has a pleasingly laid-back feel and the quirky horsebox tables on the terrace add something a little different. Menus use the best of the British larder and offer an appealing mix of dishes. The 45-day aged rare breed steaks are a speciality and the weekend lunch menu is a steal.

Menu £19 (lunch) – Carte £27/52

Oakley Green ⊠ SL4 5UW – ☎ 01753 864294 – www.thegreeneoak.co.uk

Oxford Blue

🛜 ⅃ 🅰🅒 ⇌ 🅿

MODERN CUISINE · PUB X With its contemporary look and smart landscaped grounds, you'd be forgiven for thinking this is a new-build, but it started life as two 19C gamekeepers' cottages and has been a pub for over 100 years. Accomplished classics offer more than their descriptions imply and come with the occasional modern twist.

Menu £ 30 (lunch) – Carte £ 43/58

10 Crimp Hill, Old Windsor ⊠ SL4 2QY – ℰ 01753 861954 –
www.oxfordbluepub.co.uk – Closed 1-8 January, Monday, Tuesday

WINSTON

Durham – Regional map n° **14**–A3

Bridgewater Arms

🛜 🅿

SEAFOOD · PUB X This traditional pub spent the first hundred years of its life as a school; look out for the copperplate alphabet. The chef is known for his seafood and dishes are unashamedly classic, accurately executed and extremely satisfying.

Carte £ 20/70

⊠ DL2 3RN – ℰ 01325 730302 – www.thebridgewaterarms.com –
Closed 1-3 January, 24-27 December, Sunday, Monday

WINTERINGHAM

North Lincolnshire – Regional map n° **13**–C3

Winteringham Fields (Colin McGurran)

⇦ ⇌ 🅿

MODERN CUISINE · INTIMATE XXX This 16C former farmhouse sits in a sleepy village close the Humber Estuary, in an area rich in agriculture. The long-standing owners – Colin and Bex McGurran – also have their own smallholding where they rear animals and grow vegetables, which makes the cooking highly seasonal. Their impeccable ingredients are married with classic techniques, resulting in refined, confidently executed dishes with bags of flavour. Colin was born in Zambia and spent his childhood years in the Middle East, so there are always a few subtle nods to his past too. The best way to fully experience his cooking is the multi-course surprise dinner menu.

Service is professional yet personable and the team work together to create an almost country house style experience. Bedrooms mix classic character with modern comforts, and some have a slightly eclectic style.

Specialities: Wye Valley asparagus with confit egg yolk, herb emulsion and chicken wing. Roast breast of guinea fowl with wild garlic pesto, braised morels and leg ragout dumpling. Vanilla panna cotta.

Menu £ 65 (lunch)/89 – Carte £ 63/78

1 Silver Street ⊠ DN15 9ND – ℰ 01724 733096 – www.winteringhamfields.co.uk –
Closed 22 December-3 January, Sunday, Monday, Tuesday lunch

WISWELL
Lancashire – Regional map n° **11**-B2

ⅡО **Freemasons**   ॐ ⇦ 😤 ᰀ ⇔

MODERN BRITISH · PUB Ⅹ A delightful pub hidden away on a narrow lane. Downstairs it's all flagged floors, low beams and open fires; the antique-furnished upstairs is a little more elegant. Refined, skilful cooking sees modern versions of traditional pub dishes. For a special occasion book the chef's table. Bedrooms are luxurious.

Menu £25/80 – Carte £27/70

8 Vicarage Fold ⊠ BB7 9DF – ☎ 01254 822218 – www.freemasonsatwiswell.com –
Closed Sunday, Monday

WITHAM ON THE HILL
Lincolnshire – Regional map n° **9**-C2

ⅡО **Six Bells**   ⇦ 😤 ᰀ ⅼⓋ Ⓟ

TRADITIONAL CUISINE · PUB Ⅹ This pub's spacious courtyard is an obvious draw and the bright, stylish interior keeps things cheery whatever the weather. Choose hand-crafted pizzas cooked in the wood-burning oven in the bar or something more sophisticated from the main menu. Bedrooms are very stylishly appointed; Hayloft is the best.

Menu £17 (lunch) – Carte £24/38

⊠ PE10 0JH – ☎ 01778 590360 – www.sixbellswitham.co.uk –
Closed 25 December-3 January

WIVETON – Norfolk ➜ See Blakeney

WOBURN
Central Bedfordshire – Regional map n° **7**-A2

ⅡО **Paris House**   ⇮ ⅼⓋ ⇔ Ⓟ

CREATIVE · INTIMATE ⅩⅩ A beautiful mock-Tudor house built in Paris and reassembled in an idyllic parkland location; enjoy a drink on the terrace and watch the deer. Dishes reflect the chef's passion for Asian ingredients and are creative and complex with some challenging flavour combinations. The tasting menus are the way to go.

Menu £51/112 – Carte £46/72

Woburn Park ⊠ MK17 9QP – ☎ 01525 290692 – www.parishouse.co.uk –
Closed 24 December-3 January, Sunday dinner, Monday, Tuesday, Wednesday

WOLVERHAMPTON
Staffordshire – Regional map n° **10**-C2

ⅡО **Bilash**   🅰🅲 🍴 ⇔

INDIAN · FAMILY ⅩⅩ This smart contemporary restaurant is well-established and has several generations of the same family involved. Appealing, original menus offer South Indian and Bangladeshi dishes, crafted only from local and homemade produce.

Menu £16 (lunch) – Carte £15/55

No 2 Cheapside ⊠ WV1 1TU – ☎ 01902 427762 – www.thebilash.co.uk –
Closed Sunday

WOODBRIDGE
Suffolk – Regional map n° **8**-D3

ⅡО **Turk's Head**   ⇮ 😤 ᰀ Ⓟ

MODERN BRITISH · PUB Ⅹ Charming pub with a petanque pitch, lovely gardens and a great terrace with country views. As well as pub classics, the Indian chef creates interesting, cleverly spiced dishes such as paneer steak with curry butter.

Menu £19 (lunch) – Carte £30/49

Low Rd, Hasketon ⊠ IP13 6JGB – ☎ 01394 610343 –
www.theturksheadhasketon.co.uk – Closed Sunday dinner

at Bromeswell Northeast: 2. 5 mi by B1438 off A1152

⫻○ Unruly Pig

MODERN CUISINE · PUB ⊠ This modern dining pub is far from unruly, its owner – a former lawyer – sees to that; and the wood panelling, interesting art and friendly team add a warm feel. The Mediterranean-inspired cooking offers plenty of choice, the set menus are good value and the vegetarian and gluten free options are a hit.

Menu £20 – Carte £27/45

Orford Road ⊠ IP12 2PU – ℰ 01394 460310 –
www.theunrulypig.co.uk

WOODSTOCK
Oxfordshire – Regional map n° **6**–B2

⫻○ Crown

MEDITERRANEAN CUISINE · PUB ⊠ It might have 18C origins but the Crown is not your typical coaching inn, with its bright, almost greenhouse-style dining room complete with an attractive Belgian tiled floor. Fresh, light cooking takes its influences from the Med and makes good use of the wood-fired oven. Bedrooms are beautifully appointed.

Carte £20/40

31 High Street ⊠ OX20 1TE – ℰ 01993 813339 –
www.thecrownwoodstock.com

WOOLACOMBE
Devon – Regional map n° **1**–C1

⫻○ Noel Corston

MODERN BRITISH · INTIMATE ⊠ A rustic restaurant consisting of just 8 seats set around an open kitchen counter. Dinner is served at 7pm and the multi-course tasting menu evolves daily, with skilfully prepared modern dishes showcasing ingredients largely from North Devon's UNESCO Biosphere Reserve. Go for the wine pairings.

Menu £105

South Street ⊠ EX34 7BB – ℰ 01271 871187 – www.noelcorston.com –
Closed 1 October-1 April, Sunday-Wednesday, Thursday-Saturday lunch

WOOLFARDISWORTHY
Devon – Regional map n° **1**–C2

⫻○ Farmers Arms 🆕

MODERN BRITISH · PUB ⊠ A full renovation has left this charming Grade II listed pub with a delightful interior that offers a unique blend of modern design and characterful original features. Menus feature produce from their 70 acre farm and offer pub classics, as well as creative modern dishes Weds-Sat. Sundays see sharing lunches.

Carte £22/45

⊠ EX39 5QS – ℰ 01237 439328 – www.woolsery.com

WOOTTON
Oxfordshire – Regional map n° **6**–B2

⫻○ Killingworth Castle

TRADITIONAL BRITISH · PUB ⊠ A friendly roadside inn dating from the 16C, set just outside the village centre and run by a chatty team. Concise menus have a British heart and champion local and organic produce. This is a place where they bake their own breads, butcher their own meats and brew their own beers. Bedrooms are spacious.

Menu £22 – Carte £26/51

Glympton Road ⊠ OX20 1EJ – ℰ 01993 811401 – www.thekillingworthcastle.com

WORCESTER
Worcestershire – Regional map n° **10**–B3

ⓘ○ Old Rectifying House ♈ 🏠 & ⑩

TRADITIONAL BRITISH · **PUB** ✗ With shabby-chic décor, young chefs hard at work in the open kitchen, a cocktail list and a soundtrack of jazz, blues and soul, this mock-Tudor building overlooking the river brings a hipster vibe to Worcester. Appealing dishes have a British slant and there's a well-thought-out vegan menu too.

Carte £21/47

North Parade ✉ WR1 3NN – ℰ 01905 619622 – www.theoldrec.co.uk –
Closed Monday

WRINGTON
North Somerset – Regional map n° **2**–B2

ⓘ○ The Ethicurean ≤ 🏠 🏠 🅿

MODERN BRITISH · **SIMPLE** ✗ Two rustic, informal glasshouses in a beautifully restored Victorian walled garden; fresh produce leads the daily menu and they strive to be 'ethical' and 'epicurean'. They serve everything from coffee and cake to 5 set courses.

Menu £45 – Carte £27/38

Barley Wood Walled Garden, Long Lane ✉ BS40 5SA – ℰ 01934 863713 –
www.theethicurean.com – Closed Sunday - Monday dinner

WYE
Kent – Regional map n° **5**–C2

ⓘ○ Wife of Bath ⇐ 🏠 🆎 ⑩ 🅿

SPANISH · **RUSTIC** ✗✗ An attractive red-brick house plays host to this understated restaurant where a Spanish tiled floor marries with a wooden bar counter and old timbers. The menu champions northern Spain, with colourful, vibrant dishes including sharing plates and a small range of tapas. Stylish bedrooms come with lots of extras.

Menu £25 (lunch), £45/55

4 Upper Bridge Street ✉ TN25 5AF – ℰ 01233 812232 – www.thewifeofbath.com –
Closed 13-23 January, Sunday dinner, Monday, Tuesday lunch

WYMESWOLD
Leicestershire – Regional map n° **9**–B2

ⓘ○ Hammer & Pincers 🏠 🅿

MODERN BRITISH · **ELEGANT** ✗ Formerly the village forge (the old water pump can still be seen at the back), then a pub, and now a stylish, intimate restaurant. Modern menus have classic British roots; the 7 and 10 course grazing menus are the most creative.

Menu £29 (lunch) – Carte £37/50

5 East Road ✉ LE12 6ST – ℰ 01509 880735 – www.hammerandpincers.co.uk –
Closed Sunday dinner, Monday

WYNYARD
Stockton-on-Tees – Regional map n° **14**–B3

🏰 Wynyard Hall ⚡ 🐾 ≤ 🏠 ⑩ 🏠 ⊡ & 🏋 🅿

COUNTRY HOUSE · **ELEGANT** An impressive Georgian mansion built for the Marquis of Londonderry; its smart spa overlooks a lake. Bedrooms in the main house are traditional, while those in the lodges are more modern. Classic guest areas feature stained glass, open fires and antiques. The formal dining room offers modern classics.

24 rooms – 👫 £210 – 2 suites

✉ TS22 5NF – ℰ 01740 644811 – www.wynyardhall.co.uk

YARM

Stockton-on-Tees – Regional map n° **14**–B3

🍽️ Judges Country House 〰️ 🕙 ⇔ 🅿️

MODERN CUISINE · TRADITIONAL XX A formal two-roomed restaurant in a traditional country house hotel; the conservatory extension has a lovely outlook over the lawns. Modern, well-prepared dishes are straightforward yet full of flavour. Choose from classics, a strong vegetarian selection and some more refined, imaginative dishes.

Carte £45/62

Judges Country House Hotel, Kirklevington Hall,
Kirklevington ⊠ TS15 9LW – ℰ 01642 789000 –
www.judgeshotel.co.uk

🍽️ Muse 🍷 🛖 ♿ 🅰️©️

CLASSIC FRENCH · BRASSERIE X A smart continental café with a bright modern interior and a popular pavement terrace. Extensive international menus list everything from a bacon sandwich to salads, pastas and grills; they also offer a good value set price menu.

Menu £19 – Carte £28/49

104b High Street ⊠ TS15 9AU –
ℰ 01642 788558 – www.museyarm.com –
Closed Sunday dinner

🏨 Judges Country House 🏃 🦢 〰️ ⅃ᶠ 🛁 🅿️

COUNTRY HOUSE · CLASSIC A charming Victorian judge's house with a welcoming atmosphere, filled with wood panelling, antiques and ornaments and set within impressive grounds. Traditional country house bedrooms come with a high level of facilities, bright modern bathrooms and extra touches such as fresh fruit and flowers.

21 rooms ☲ – 🛉🛉 £145/225

Kirklevington Hall, Kirklevington ⊠ TS15 9LW –
ℰ 01642 789000 – www.judgeshotel.co.uk

🍽️ **Judges Country House** – See restaurant listing

YARMOUTH – Isle of Wight → See Wight (Isle of)

YATTENDON

West Berkshire – Regional map n° **6**–B3

🍽️ Royal Oak ⇔ 〰️ 🛖 ⇔

TRADITIONAL BRITISH · PUB X A red-brick pub bursting with country charm, set in a picture postcard village; you'll find a heavily beamed bar with a roaring fire at its hub and plenty of local ales on offer. Menus offer honest British dishes and traditional puddings. Country house style bedrooms come with their own gun cabinets.

Carte £20/30

The Square ⊠ RG18 0UF –
ℰ 01635 201325 – www.royaloakyattendon.co.uk

at Frilsham South: 1 mi by Frilsham rd on Bucklebury rd

🍽️ Pot Kiln ⇔ ⅏ 〰️ 🛖 🅿️

TRADITIONAL BRITISH · PUB X The Pot Kiln is a characterful little country pub owned by the Yattendon Estate. Head for the cosy bar and order a pint, then follow the delicious aromas through to the dining area, where flavoursome British dishes arrive in gutsy portions. Game is a speciality – they even have a game cookery school.

Carte £30/47

⊠ RG18 0XX – ℰ 01635 201366 – www.potkiln.co.uk

YEOVIL

Somerset – Regional map n° **2**–B3

ENGLAND

at Barwick South: 2 mi by A30 off A37

⑩ **Little Barwick House** ⇔ ⌂ AC P

MODERN BRITISH · INTIMATE XX Attractive Georgian dower house on the outskirts of town, run by a hospitable husband and wife team. Relax on deep sofas before heading into the elegant dining room with its huge window and heavy drapes. Cooking is classical, satisfying and full of flavour – a carefully chosen wine list accompanies. Charming, comfortably furnished bedrooms, each with its own character.

Menu £ 32 (lunch)/55

✉ BA22 9TD – ☏ 01935 423902 – www.littlebarwickhouse.co.uk –
Closed 24 December-26 January, Sunday, Monday, Tuesday lunch

YORK

York – Regional map n° **13**–C2

Top tips!

The tourist capital of the North, York is a compact city you can easily walk around. It was founded by the Romans but also has Viking connections, and every cobbled twist and turn reveals another historic building.

The famous Minster is the largest Gothic cathedral in Northern Europe – climb to the top of the tower to be rewarded with a lovely city vista, then wander the narrow streets of The Shambles, which are overhung with old buildings and host a daily market and food court. Finish with a trip around the Jorvik Viking Centre for an interactive insight into the city's past.

Clifford's Tower, now all that remains of William the Conqueror's castle, offers some stunning views – and no visit would be complete without walking the 13C city walls. Nearby you'll find **Skosh**, a contemporary bistro serving international small plates and buzzy brasserie **Star Inn The City**, in the delightful Museum Gardens.

J. Arnold Images/hemis.fr

Restaurants

⊕ Skosh   AC 🍽

MODERN BRITISH · COLOURFUL ✗ Skosh sits in a glass-fronted Grade II listed building close to the 12C Micklegate Bar. Both the décor and the cooking are bright and colourful; sit at the counter to really get involved. Constantly evolving small plates keep Yorkshire produce at their heart but have global – especially Indian – influences.

Specialities: Chawanmushi, asparagus, hazelnut and truffle. Braised hogget shoulder with cauliflower porridge and green herb chutney. 63% Idukki chocolate tart with lime and black olive.

Carte £20/32

Town plan A2-s – *98 Micklegate* ✉ *YO1 6JX* – ✆ *01904 634849* – *www.skoshyork.co.uk – Closed 1-7 January, 27 May-2 June, 22 August-8 September, Sunday dinner-Tuesday*

⍟○ Roots ⓝ   ♿ 🍽 🛇 ⇄

MODERN CUISINE · CONTEMPORARY DÉCOR ✗✗ This attractive former pub – sister to the Black Swan at Oldstead – has been tastefully converted into a contemporary restaurant and spacious lounge-bar. Interesting small plates have sophisticated flavour contrasts and are delivered with a degree of finesse. Menus change style according to the season.

Carte £31/52

Town plan A1-e – *68 Marygate* ✉ *YO30 7BH* – *www.rootsyork.co.uk* – *Closed Tuesday*

⍟○ Arras   ⌂ AC ⇄

MODERN CUISINE · DESIGN ✗✗ A red-brick former coach house with a bright, contemporary interior. Well-priced modern menus offer creative cooking. The bar boasts an unusual white-fronted counter and there's a lovely enclosed terrace hidden to the rear.

Menu £22/49

Town plan B1-x – *The Old Coach House, Peasholme Green* ✉ *YO1 7PW* – ✆ *01904 633737 – www.arrasrestaurant.co.uk – Closed 7-23 July, 22 December-7 January, Sunday, Monday, Tuesday lunch*

⍟○ Hudsons   ♿ AC

MODERN BRITISH · ELEGANT ✗✗ If you're after a sense of occasion, this intimate hotel restaurant with its feature parquet floor is the answer. Choose from two seasonally evolving tasting menus which showcase Yorkshire ingredients. Cooking employs modern techniques and dishes are bold and gutsy with clearly defined flavours.

Menu £55/85

Town plan A2-v – *Grand Hotel & Spa York, Station Rise* ✉ *YO1 6GD* – ✆ *01904 380038 – www.thegrandyork.co.uk/drinking-and-dining/hudsons/ – Closed Sunday, Monday, Tuesday, Wednesday - Saturday lunch*

⍟○ Melton's   AC 🛇 ⇄

MODERN BRITISH · NEIGHBOURHOOD ✗✗ A cosy-looking shop conversion in the suburbs. The walls are covered with murals of ingredients and happy diners, which is fitting as the restaurant is well-regarded and local produce features highly. Cooking is fresh and flavoursome, with a subtle modern style and well-judged contrasts.

Menu £40 (lunch)/50

Town plan A2-c – *7 Scarcroft Road* ✉ *YO23 1ND* – ✆ *01904 634341 – www.meltonsrestaurant.co.uk – Closed 20 December-7 January, Sunday, Monday, Tuesday lunch*

⑩ The Park   A/C 🅿

MODERN CUISINE · INTIMATE XX Adam Jackson has moved his restaurant to a quiet residential suburb of York; it's set within a hotel and is run by a chatty, knowledgeable team. The seasonal set menus feature complex, eye-catching dishes comprising many flavours.

Menu £29 (lunch), £45/65

Town plan A1-s – *Marmadukes Hotel, 4-5 St Peters Grove, Bootham* ⊠ YO30 6AQ – ℰ 01904 540903 – www.theparkrestaurant.co.uk – *Closed 1-14 January, 7-13 April, 4-10 August, Sunday, Monday, Tuesday - Thursday lunch*

⑩ Star Inn The City   🍴 & A/C ⇄

MODERN BRITISH · DESIGN XX A buzzy all-day brasserie set in an old brick engine house, in a delightful riverside spot beside the Museum Gardens. Well-judged dishes are modern yet gutsy and showcase top Yorkshire produce – the chargrilled meats are a highlight.

Carte £31/61

Town plan A1-a – *Lendal Engine House, Museum Street* ⊠ YO1 7DR – ℰ 01904 619208 – www.starinnthecity.co.uk

458

🍴 Le Cochon Aveugle

MODERN CUISINE · BISTRO 🍴 A red neon sign in the window marks out this individual little restaurant. It has just 5 tables, plus 4 seats at the kitchen counter, and the room has a pared-back, contemporary look. A constantly evolving surprise menu showcases boldly flavoured, imaginative combinations created using French techniques.

Menu £70/85

Town plan B2-a – *37 Walmgate* ✉ *YO1 9TX* – ✆ *01904 640222* –
www.lecochonaveugle.uk – *Closed 5-21 January, Sunday, Monday, Tuesday, Wednesday - Friday lunch*

🍴 Mr P's Curious Tavern

TRADITIONAL BRITISH · BISTRO 🍴 This is indeed a curious place; it's set in a Grade I listed house in the shadow of the Minster and has a fun, bohemian style and a lively buzz. Well-priced dishes are full of personality and keep local suppliers to the fore. Cooking mixes British and global influences and the sharing boards are popular.

Menu £20 (lunch)/40 – Carte £32/61

Town plan B1-s – *71 Low Petergate* ✉ *YO1 7HY* – ✆ *01904 521177* –
www.mrpscurioustavern.co.uk – *Closed Sunday dinner, Monday*

Hotels

🏨 Grand H. & Spa York

BUSINESS · CONTEMPORARY Choose a bedroom in the grand William and Mary style former offices of the North Eastern Railway Company or a brighter, more contemporary room with great city views in the adjoining building; all are well-equipped. Relax in the impressive basement spa then enjoy some of the 110 whiskies on offer in the Whisky Lounge. Dine in the smart brasserie or formal restaurant.

208 rooms ⌂ – 🛏 £190/320 – 13 suites

Town plan A2-v – *Station Rise* ✉ *YO1 6GD* – ✆ *01904 380038* –
www.thegrandyork.co.uk

🍴 **Hudsons** – See restaurant listing

ZENNOR

Cornwall – Regional map n° **1**-A3

🍴 Gurnard's Head

MODERN BRITISH · PUB 🍴 Surrounded by nothing but fields and livestock; a dog-friendly pub with shabby-chic décor, blazing fires and a relaxed, cosy feel. Menus rely on regional and foraged produce and the wine list offers some interesting choices by the glass. Compact bedrooms feature good quality linen and colourful throws.

Menu £20 (lunch), £24/29 – Carte £25/38

Treen ✉ *TR26 3DE* – ✆ *01736 796928* – *www.gurnardshead.co.uk*

SCOTLAND

Scotland may be small, but its variety is immense. The vivacity of Glasgow can seem a thousand miles from the vast peatland wilderness of Caithness; the arty vibe of Georgian Edinburgh a world away from the remote and tranquil Ardnamurchan peninsula. Wide golden sands trim the Atlantic at South Harris, and the coastline of the Highlands boasts empty islands and turquoise waters. Meantime, Fife's coast draws golf fans to St Andrews and the more secretive delights of East Neuk, an area of fishing villages and stone harbours. Wherever you travel, a sense of a dramatic history prevails in the shape of castles, cathedrals and rugged lochside monuments to the heroes of old.

Food and drink embraces the traditional too, typified by Speyside's famous Malt Whisky Trail. And what better than Highland game, fresh fish from the Tweed or haggis, neeps and tatties to complement a grand Scottish hike? The country's glorious natural larder yields such jewels as Spring lamb from the Borders, Perthshire venison, fresh fish and shellfish from the Western Highlands and Aberdeen Angus beef.

- Michelin Road maps n° 501, 502 and 713

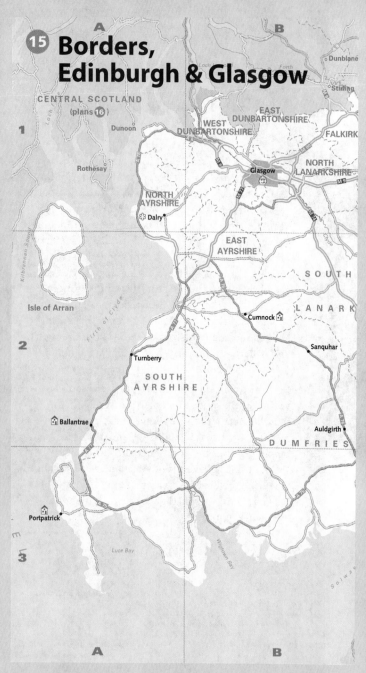

15 **Borders,**
Edinburgh & Glasgow

CENTRAL SCOTLAND
(plans **16**)

1

Loch

Dunblane

Stirling

Dunoon

WEST
DUNBARTONSHIRE

EAST
DUNBARTONSHIRE

FALKIRK

Rothesay

Glasgow

NORTH
LANARKSHIRE

NORTH
AYRSHIRE

Dalry

EAST
AYRSHIRE

Kilbrannan Sound

SOUTH

LANARK

Isle of Arran

Cumnock

Firth of Clyde

2

Turnberry

Sanquhar

SOUTH
AYRSHIRE

Ballantrae

Auldgirth

DUMFRIES

Portpatrick

3

Luce Bay

Wigtown Bay

Solway

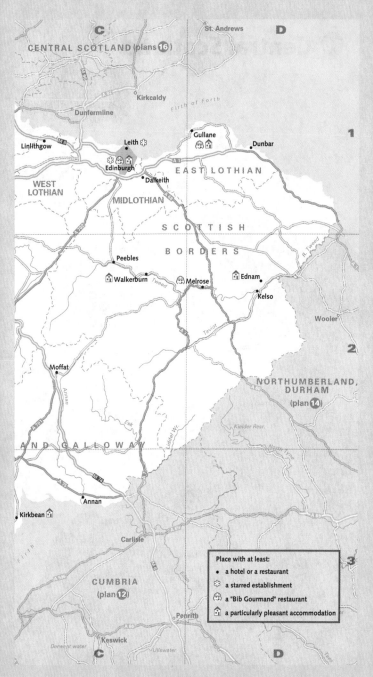

16 Central Scotland

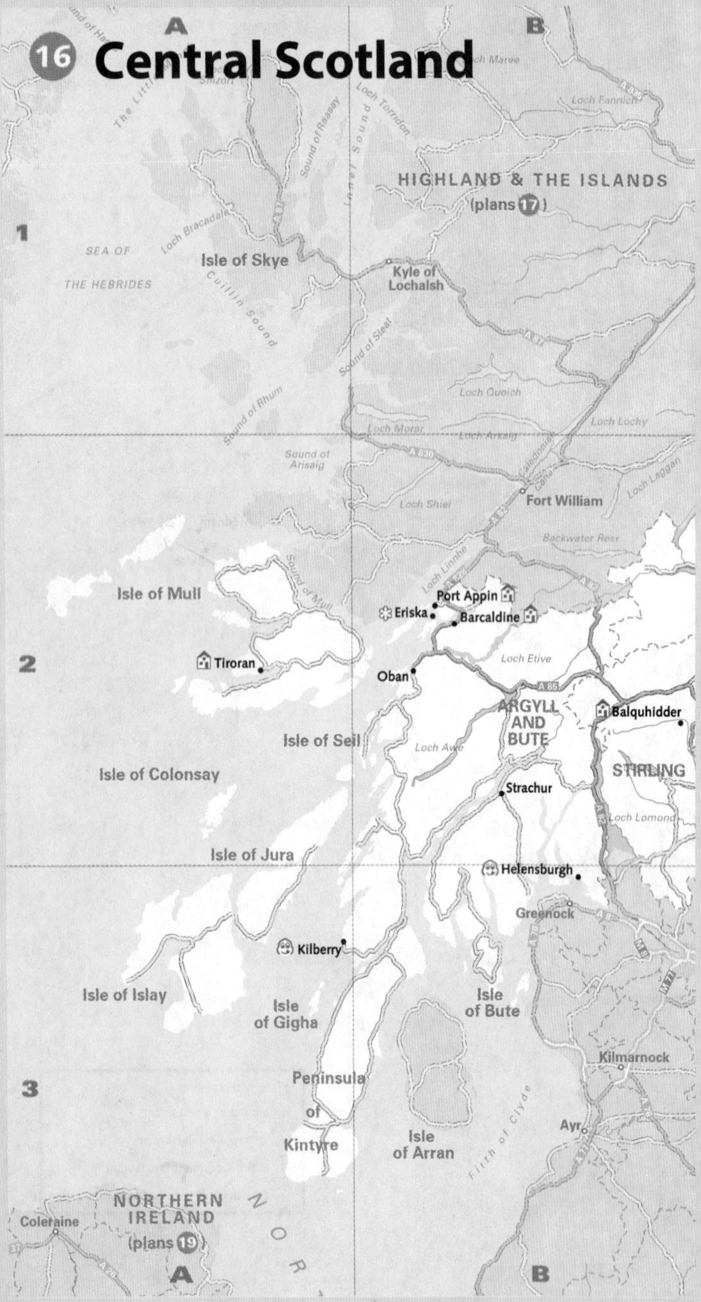

A
B
HIGHLAND & THE ISLANDS
(plans 17)
Loch Fannich
Loch Torridon
Sound of Raasay
Inner Sound
Loch Bracadale
SEA OF
THE HEBRIDES
Isle of Skye
Cuillin Sound
Kyle of
Lochalsh
Sound of Sleat
Loch Quoich
Sound of Rhum
Loch Lochy
Loch Morar
Loch Arkaig
Sound of
Arisaig
Loch Shiel
Fort William
Loch Laggan
Backwater Resr
Loch Linnhe
Sound of Mull
Isle of Mull
Port Appin
Eriska
Barcaldine
Tiroran
Oban
Loch Etive
ARGYLL
AND
BUTE
Balquhidder
Isle of Seil
Loch Awe
STIRLING
Isle of Colonsay
Strachur
Loch Lomond
Isle of Jura
Helensburgh
Greenock
Kilberry
Isle of Islay
Isle
of Gigha
Isle
of Bute
Kilmarnock
Peninsula
of
Kintyre
Isle
of Arran
Firth of Clyde
Ayr
NORTHERN
IRELAND
(plans 19)
Coleraine
1
2
3

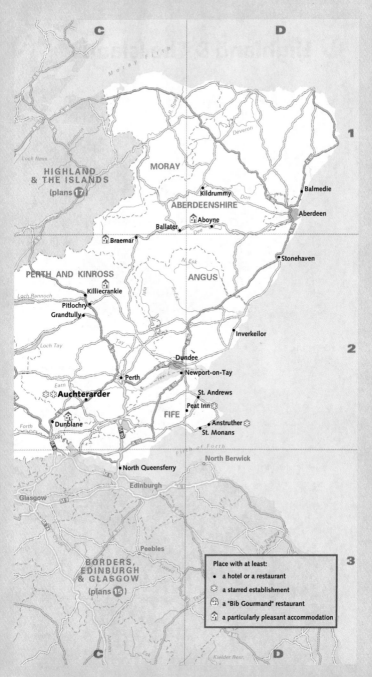

1

Isle of Lewis
and Harris

THE MINCH

OUTER HEBRIDES

West Loch Tarbert

WESTERN ISLES

Grulnard
Bay

Sound of Harris

Loch

2 Isles of Uist

The Little Minch

Loch
Snizort

Sound of Monach

Loch Torridon

⌂
Torridon

Stein ✿

Sound of Raasay

Applecross

Inner Sound

SEA OF

Loch Bracadale

THE HEBRIDES

Isle of Skye

Sleat ⌂

Cuillin Sound

Sound of Barra

Sound of Sleat

Isle of Barra

Loch

3

INNER HEBRIDES

Sound of Rhum

Loch Morar

Sound of
Arisaig

Loch Shiel

Onich

Lochaline

Loch Linnhe

Isle
of Mull

Oban

Firth of Lorn

A **B**

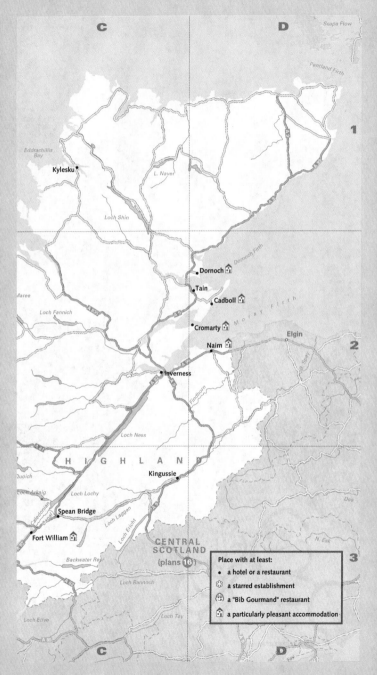

C   D

Scapa Flow

Pentland Firth

1

Eddrachillis
Bay

Kylesku •

L. Naver

Loch Shin

Dornoch Firth

Dornoch 🏠

Tain •

Cadboll 🏠

Maree

Loch Fannich

Moray Firth

Cromarty 🏠

Elgin

Nairn 🏠

2

R. Spey

• **Inverness**

Findhorn

Loch Ness

H I G H L A N D

Quoich

Kingussie •

Dee

Loch Arkaig

Loch Lochy

Spean Bridge •

Loch Laggan

Fort William 🏠

Loch Ericht

CENTRAL
SCOTLAND
(plans **16**)

N. Esk

Backwater Res.

3

Loch Rannoch

Place with at least:
•   a hotel or a restaurant
✷   a starred establishment
🏠   a "Bib Gourmand" restaurant
🏠   a particularly pleasant accommodation

Loch Etive

Loch Tay

C   D

Tay

NOT TO BE MISSED

STARRED RESTAURANTS

Excellent cooking...

High quality cooking...

BIB GOURMAND RESTAURANTS

Good food, good value cooking

ZOOMING IN...

... ON TWO OF SCOTLAND'S TOP RESTAURATEURS

Tom Kitchin – Pub: The Bonnie Badger, Gullane – Michelin Bib Gourmand

He's best known for his Michelin-Starred restaurant, The Kitchin, in Leith and, with his wife and business partner, Michaela, also owns Castle Terrace, The Scran & Scallie and Southside Scran in Edinburgh, but for his latest venture, Tom Kitchin chose to open a pub further along the coast in the East Lothian town of Gullane.

So, why Gullane?

Tom: *As a family we've always been drawn to Gullane and often go for walks along its beaches – it's one of the nicest seaside towns within travelling distance of Edinburgh. So, when we heard a pub was on the market, we had to take a look – as soon as we saw it, we knew it was right for us.*

Marc Millar/Bonnie Badger

Tell us about the food...

Tom: *We adhere as much as possible to the 'Nature to Plate' philosophy, using fresh seasonal, local produce – and the menu we offer features wholesome, classic dishes, the sort that belong in a pub. We also serve a traditional roast beef Sunday lunch cooked on the Green Egg BBQ.*

And the rooms...?

Michaela: *My background is in hotels, so I always wanted us to have a place that offered accommodation. We have 13 bedrooms which range from cosy rooms under the eaves to secluded cottages. We endeavour to promote all things Scottish and our wallpapers, fabrics, linens and toiletries are all sourced from small local businesses.*

Keith Braidwood – Restaurant: Braidwoods, Dalry – One Michelin Star

Not all chefs awarded a Michelin Star go on to become media darlings – in fact, some prefer to stay well and truly out of the limelight. Such a chef is Keith Braidwood, who along with his wife Nicola, has been running Braidwoods since 1994. Their restaurant was awarded a Michelin Star in 2000 and has retained it every year since, making it the longest held Michelin Star in Scotland.

What would you say are the challenges of running a rural restaurant?

It can be difficult attracting customers to the area because, unless they live close by, they either need to drive or pay for a taxi. We have, however, managed to build up a base of loyal regulars who travel over from Troon and Glasgow. When it comes to supplies, sourcing high grade fish can also be a challenge, which is surprising considering our location.

Do you have a trusted circle of suppliers?

We try to use Ayrshire produce where possible and source the majority of our ingredients from Scotland – including lamb and deer – but if the quality isn't there, then we are happy to look further afield.

Have you come across any challenges in being a husband and wife team? *No – we have worked happily together here for 25 years!*

Do you have a signature dish?

Our warm parmesan tart is a permanent fixture on the dinner menu; our customers won't allow us to take it off!

ABERDEEN
Aberdeen City – Regional map n° **16**–D1

ⅰ○ IX ♨ & AC ⇄ P
MODERN BRITISH · DESIGN ✗✗ Pass through The Chester Hotel's moody cocktail bar and up to this chic split-level restaurant, where you can watch the chefs at work in the open kitchen. Creative cooking champions Scottish produce, with Aberdeenshire steaks from the Josper grill the highlight.
Carte £35/72

The Chester Hotel, 59-63 Queens Road ⊠ AB15 4YP – ℰ 01224 327777 – www.chester-hotel.com – Closed Sunday

ⅰ○ Silver Darling ≤ ⇄
SEAFOOD · FRIENDLY ✗✗ Attractively set at the port entrance, on the top floor of the castellated former customs house. Floor to ceiling windows make the most of the superb view. Neatly presented dishes showcase excellent quality seafood.
Carte £28/48

Pocra Quay, North Pier ⊠ AB11 5DQ – ℰ 01224 576229 – www.thesilverdarling.co.uk – Closed Sunday lunch

ⅰ○ Moonfish Cafe
MODERN BRITISH · BISTRO ✗ A high ceiling and mirrored walls give this former toy shop in the Merchant Quarter an airy feel. Concise menus change every 6 weeks; at dinner, choose 2-4 courses from a set priced menu. Descriptions are terse, presentation is colourful and flavours are well-defined.
Menu £30/44 – Carte £24/30

9 Correction Wynd ⊠ AB10 1HP – ℰ 01224 644166 – www.moonfishcafe.co.uk – Closed 1-15 January, Sunday, Monday

ⅿⅿⅿ Malmaison ✿ ⅠⅢ ⅲ & ⅷ P
BUSINESS · DESIGN Set in a smart city suburb and built around a period property; its funky, modern bedrooms are the height of urban chic. The black, slate-floored reception is adorned with bagpipes and kilts and there's a stylish bar with a whisky cellar. The brasserie serves modern dishes, with steaks a speciality.
79 rooms � – ♥♥ £79/299

49-53 Queens Road ⊠ AB15 4YP – ℰ 01224 327370 – www.malmaison.com

ABOYNE
Aberdeenshire – Regional map n° **16**–D1

ⅿⅿ Lys-Na-Greyne ⓝ ⅗ ≤ ⅷ P
COUNTRY HOUSE · ELEGANT You're guaranteed a warm welcome at this elegant riverside guesthouse. Enjoy cake and a wee dram on arrival, then head up to a large, luxurious bedroom with antique furnishings. Beautiful gardens lead down to the water and the chickens provide the eggs for breakfast – which feature alongside Balmoral bread.
6 rooms ⊠ – ♥♥ £130/180

Rhu-Na-Haven Road ⊠ AB34 5JD – ℰ 01339 886502 – www.lys-na-greyne.com – Closed 15 December-15 January

ANNAN
Dumfries and Galloway – Regional map n° **15**–C3

ⅰ○ Del Amitri ≤ & P
MODERN BRITISH · BRASSERIE ✗ Set within a coastal hotel, a cleanly decorated restaurant with views out over the Solway Firth. The extensive menu has a Scottish bias and focuses on classically based dishes which have a modern edge.
Carte £20/40

Powfoot Hotel, Links Ave, Powfoot ⊠ DG12 5PN – ℰ 01461 700300 – www.thepowfoothotel.com

ANSTRUTHER

Fife – Regional map n° **16**–D2

☆ **The Cellar** (Billy Boyter)

MODERN CUISINE · RUSTIC XX Local lad Billy Boyter worked in several of Edinburgh's Starred restaurants before deciding to go it alone in 2014 – and his restaurant is now considered something of an icon in these parts. It's tucked away through an arch on a narrow side street close to the harbour and was previously a smokehouse and a cooperage. Despite its name, it's not a cellar at all but a series of low-ceilinged cottages with exposed beams, stone walls, wood-burning stoves and a cosy, characterful feel.

The room itself might be relaxed and homely but the cooking is contrastingly modern. The multi-course set menus are nicely balanced in terms of both variation and portion size, and the chef's strength is his great understanding of flavours: he likes to blend numerous layers of flavour and while each one stands out by itself, it also complements the others and brings the dish together as a whole.

Specialities: Ox tongue with parmesan and truffle. Halibut with cockles, onion and garlic shoot broth, verbena. Apple and hay custard, sea buckthorn.

Menu £40 (lunch)/70

24 East Green ⊠ KY10 3AA – ℰ 01333 310378 – www.thecellaranstruther.co.uk – Closed 6-13 May, 2-16 September, 23 December-15 January, Monday, Tuesday, Wednesday lunch

APPLECROSS

Highland – Regional map n° **17**–B2

⊕◯ **Applecross Inn** ⇦ ⇐ ⇲ ⌂ & **P**

SEAFOOD · PUB X Unpretentious inn with friendly service and a bustling atmosphere; take the scenic route over the hair-raising, single-track Bealach na Ba, with its stunning views and hairpin bends to reach it. Dine on the freshest of seafood, often caught within sight of the door. Simple bedrooms have marvellous sea views.

Carte £20/50

Shore Street ⊠ IV54 8LR – ℰ 01520 744262 – www.applecrossinn.co.uk

⊕◯ **Applecross Walled Garden** ⇲ ⌂ & **P**

TRADITIONAL CUISINE · FRIENDLY X Set in an old potting shed in a 17C walled garden – where much of the produce is grown. In the daytime come for homemade cake, local langoustines or fresh crab lasagne; at night come for boldly flavoured, original dishes.

Carte £21/35

⊠ IV54 8ND – ℰ 01520 744440 – www.applecrossgarden.co.uk – Closed 24 December-14 February

AUCHTERARDER

Perth and Kinross – Regional map n° **16**–C2

☆☆ **Andrew Fairlie at Gleneagles** ⇲ & AC †⊕ **P**

CREATIVE FRENCH · LUXURY XXXX You'll find this elegant restaurant concealed within the world-famous Gleneagles hotel. It may be windowless, but the classically dressed room is an intimate spot, with contemporary still-life paintings on the walls. Tables are immaculately laid and an air of comfort pervades the room, but that's not to say the atmosphere is in any way stilted or solemn.

Head Chef Stevie McLaughlin leads the way in honouring the memory of Andrew Fairlie. The kitchen works well with the seasons and when you're in this part of the world you don't lack for prime ingredients, whether that's scallops from Mull, Highland lamb or local venison. These ingredients form the focus of the French-based menu and add a sense of luxury and indulgence. Great use is also made of the Victorian walled kitchen garden, which provides plenty of leaves, vegetables and fruits.

Specialities: Home-smoked lobster with lime and herb butter. Roast fillet of rose veal with slow-cooked oxtail and red wine jus. Apple soufflé with gingerbread and Calvados.

Menu £110/155

Gleneagles Hotel ⊠ PH3 1NF – ℰ 01764 694267 – www.andrewfairlie.co.uk – Closed Sunday, Monday - Saturday lunch

🏨 Gleneagles

GRAND LUXURY · CLASSIC Built in 1924, this iconic resort hotel has been redeveloped by its current owners to offer the height of luxury. Its extensive facilities include a world-famous golf course, a state-of-the-art spa, horse riding, fishing and shooting. Kick-back over a whisky or afternoon tea and dine in one of 3 restaurants.

232 rooms – 🛏 £285/785 – 🍽 £35 – 27 suites

✉ PH3 1NF – ☎ 01764 662231 – www.gleneagles.com

❀❀ **Andrew Fairlie at Gleneagles** – See restaurant listing

AULDGIRTH

Dumfries and Galloway – Regional map n° **15**–B2

🍴 Auldgirth Inn

MODERN BRITISH · CONTEMPORARY DÉCOR XX 500 years of history go before this Gothic-style roadside pub, where it's claimed that Robert Burns was once a regular. The eclectic menu ranges from pub favourites to some more adventurous combinations; all are generously proportioned and full of flavour. Smart, modern bedrooms complete the picture.

Menu £19 (lunch) – Carte £26/48

✉ DG2 0XG – ☎ 01387 740250 – www.auldgirthinn.co.uk – Closed Monday lunch

BALLANTRAE

South Ayrshire – Regional map n° **15**–A2

🏨 Glenapp Castle

HISTORIC BUILDING · CLASSIC A long wooded drive leads to this stunning baronial castle with beautifully manicured gardens and Ailsa Craig views; it's personally run and the service is charming. The grand antique-filled interior has oak-panelled hallways, luxurious, impressively proportioned lounges and handsomely appointed bedrooms. The elegant dining room showcases local and garden ingredients.

17 rooms 🍽 – 🛏 £255/835 – 3 suites

✉ KA26 0NZ – ☎ 01465 831212 – www.glenappcastle.com – Closed 2-16 January

BALLATER

Aberdeenshire – Regional map n° **16**–C1

🍴 Rothesay Rooms

MODERN BRITISH · COSY XX The Prince of Wales' restaurant sits beside the Highgrove shop and has the look of a Baronial dining room, with its green walls, tartan fabrics and antique furnishings. Seasonal dishes are classically executed and full of flavour.

Menu £28 (lunch) – Carte £34/52

3 Netherley Place ✉ AB35 5QE – ☎ 01339 753816 – www.rothesay-rooms.co.uk – Closed 1-24 January, Sunday dinner, Monday, Tuesday, Wednesday lunch

🏠 Darroch Learg

COUNTRY HOUSE · CLASSIC This iconic Victorian country house affords superb views over the Dee Valley and the Grampians. It retains much of its period character, with antiques on display in the lounges – although the bedrooms are now modern and stylish. Accomplished dishes are served in the formal conservatory restaurant.

10 rooms 🍽 – 🛏 £160/240

Braemar Road ✉ AB35 5UX – ☎ 01339 755443 – www.darrochlearg.co.uk – Closed 3-21 January, 20-27 December

BALMEDIE

Aberdeenshire – Regional map n° **16**–D1

⅟○ Cock and Bull

TRADITIONAL BRITISH · PUB ✗ Quirky pub with a profusion of knick-knacks; dine in the cosy open-fired lounge, the formal dining room or the airy conservatory. Menus offer a mix of well-presented pub classics and more modern restaurant-style dishes. Spacious, contemporary bedrooms are located in the next door bungalow.

Carte £20/35

Ellon Rd, Blairton ⊠ AB23 8XY –
℘ 01358 743249 – www.thecockandbull.co.uk

🏠 Trump International Golf Links Scotland

LUXURY · CONTEMPORARY Intimate hotel with a Championship links golf course, set on a 2,200 acre estate. The hotel is split between an 18C stone house and a lodge and features plush fabrics and opulent furnishings. Large bedrooms have arabesque furnishings and offer all you could want. The intimate restaurant serves a modern menu.

18 rooms 🖙 – 🛉 £125/195

MacLeod House and Lodge, Menie Estate ⊠ AB23 8YE –
℘ 01358 743300 – www.trumpgolfscotland.com

BALQUHIDDER

Stirling – Regional map n° **16**-B2

🏠 Monachyle Mhor

TRADITIONAL · PERSONALISED A former farmhouse set in a beautiful, very remote glen. Contemporary furnishings blend with original features in the reception, lounge and cosy bar. Bedrooms boast slate-tiled bathrooms with underfloor heating; those in the main house afford great views over the Braes of Balquhidder.

18 rooms 🖙 – 🛉 £195/285

⊠ FK19 8PQ –
℘ 01877 384622 – www.mhor.net – Closed 5-25 January

BARCALDINE

Argyll and Bute – Regional map n° **16**-B2

🏠 Ardtorna

LUXURY · CONTEMPORARY An ultra-modern guesthouse in a stunning spot, with lovely views of the lochs and mountains – and amazing sunsets. Immaculate bedrooms have plenty of space in which to relax, perhaps with a complimentary glass of whisky. Home-baked scones are served on arrival. The charming owners also offer archery lessons.

6 rooms – 🛉 £160/200

Mill Farm ⊠ PA37 1SE –
℘ 01631 720125 – www.ardtorna.co.uk – Closed 1 November-1 April

BRAEMAR

Aberdeenshire – Regional map n° **16**-C2

⅟○ Clunie Dining Room 🅝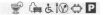

MODERN CUISINE · DESIGN ✗✗ Murano chandeliers hang from the ceiling and a cubistoid mural adorns the walls, while a huge stag stands at the centre of this quirky hotel restaurant. Original modern dishes take Scottish ingredients and add some subtle Nordic influences – the wood fire is used to great effect.

Carte £37/58

Fife Arms Hotel, Mar Road ⊠ AB35 5YN –
℘ 01339 720200 – thefifearms.com – Closed Monday - Saturday lunch

🏨 Fife Arms ⓝ
LUXURY · UNIQUE Original features, a superb collection of artwork and some quirky modern touches – including a neon chandelier – come together in the extensive guest areas of this sizeable Victorian hotel. Bedrooms have a unique vintage style and themes such as nature or poetry; they also afford great mountain views.

42 rooms – 👫 £130/900 – 4 suites

Mar Road ⊠ AB35 5YN – ☎ 01339 720200 – www.thefifearms.com

🍴 **Clunie Dining Room** – See restaurant listing

BROUGHTY FERRY – Dundee City → See Dundee

CADBOLL – Highland → See Tain

COLBOST – Highland → See Skye (Isle of)

CROMARTY
Highland – Regional map n° **17**–D2

🍴 Sutor Creek Cafe
TRADITIONAL CUISINE · FRIENDLY 🗙 A great little eatery hidden away by the harbour in a well-preserved coastal town. Wonderfully seasonal cooking features seafood from the local boats and pizzas from the wood-fired oven. It's run by a friendly, experienced couple.

Carte £23/50

21 Bank Street ⊠ IV11 8YE – ☎ 01381 600855 – www.sutorcreek.co.uk

🏠 Factor's House
LUXURY · PERSONALISED This late Georgian house is very passionately run by a charming owner. It sits in a peaceful spot and offers pleasant sea views from its mature gardens. Tastefully designed bedrooms have a subtle contemporary style and come with good extras. Breakfast and dinner are taken around a farmhouse table.

3 rooms ⊡ – 👫 £135/155

Denny Road ⊠ IV11 8YT – ☎ 01381 600394 – www.thefactorshouse.com

CUMNOCK
East Ayrshire – Regional map n° **15**–B2

🏠 Dumfries House Lodge
COUNTRY HOUSE · PERSONALISED Set at the entrance to the 2,000 acre Dumfries Estate is this stylish country house hotel, formerly a factor's house and steading. Guest areas include two cosy lounges and a billiard room – and some of the furniture is from the original manor house. Bedrooms are designed by the Duchess of Cornwall's sister.

22 rooms ⊡ – 👫 £120/160

Dumfries House ⊠ KA18 2NJ – ☎ 01290 425959 – www.dumfries-house.org.uk – Closed 23-27 December

DALKEITH
Midlothian – Regional map n° **15**–C1

🍴 Sun Inn
TRADITIONAL CUISINE · PUB 🗙 A 17C blacksmith's with two open-fired rooms and a rustic modern extension, where bright wallpapers sit beside stone walls. Extensive menus feature top local produce – lunch keeps things simple but appealing, while dinner is more ambitious. Smart bedrooms boast handmade furniture and Egyptian cotton linen.

Menu £16 – Carte £24/32

Lothian Bridge ⊠ EH22 4TR – ☎ 0131 663 2456 – www.thesuninnedinburgh.co.uk

DALRY
North Ayrshire – Regional map n° **15**–A1

✿ **Braidwoods** (Keith Braidwood)   🅿

CLASSIC CUISINE · INTIMATE ✕✕ It might only be 40mins from the centre of Glasgow but you may well get stuck behind a queue of cattle crossing the road on your way to this whitewashed crofter's cottage set amidst fields and mountains. It's a cosy, intimate place run in a proud yet unassuming manner by husband and wife Keith and Nicola Braidwood; he cooks while she looks after their guests.

The menus favour tried-and-tested classics, where the true flavour of each ingredient is allowed to shine and the techniques are executed with textbook precision. Lunch represents excellent value, while the dinner menu shows a little more ambition and creativity; the warm tart of parmesan is one of their signature dishes and has established itself as a pretty permanent fixture. The international wine list includes some seasonal recommendations.

Specialities: Roast quail and confit of legs with sweetcorn velouté and hoisin jus. Grilled turbot with asparagus risotto and wild garlic oil. Iced caramelised pecan nut and espresso parfait with blood orange syrup.

Menu £30 (lunch)/55

Drumastle Mill Cottage ⊠ KA24 4LN – 𝒞 01294 833544 – www.braidwoods.co.uk – Closed 1 January-1 February, 1-18 September, Sunday dinner-Tuesday

DORNOCH
Highland – Regional map n° **17**–D2

🏠 **Links House**   ✿ 🅖 🅿

LUXURY · CONTEMPORARY This restored 19C manse sits opposite the first tee of the Royal Dornoch Golf Club. Enjoy a dram from the honesty bar in the pine-panelled library or have tea and cake in the antique-furnished sitting room. Some of the beautifully furnished bedrooms feature bespoke tweed fabrics. The elegant orangery boasts an impressive stone fireplace and an elaborate 4 course menu.

15 rooms – 👫 £270/420

Golf Road ⊠ IV25 3LW – 𝒞 01862 810279 – www.linkshousedornoch.com – Closed 6 January-1 April

DUNBAR
East Lothian – Regional map n° **15**–D1

ⅼ○ **Creel**

TRADITIONAL CUISINE · BISTRO ✕ An unassuming, cosy former pub with wood-panelling on the walls and ceiling. The experienced chef creates good value, full-flavoured dishes using seafood fresh from the adjacent harbour. Service is friendly.

Menu £24 (lunch)/30

The Harbour, 25 Lamer Street ⊠ EH42 1HG – 𝒞 01368 863279 – www.creelrestaurant.co.uk – Closed Monday, Tuesday

DUNBLANE
Stirling – Regional map n° **16**–C2

ⅼ○ **Chez Roux**   🚗 🏡 🅖 🅿

FRENCH · BRASSERIE ✕✕ Light and spacious conservatory restaurant in a magnificent country house hotel. Smart, yet relaxed, it's a hit with locals and tourists alike thanks to the enthusiastic service and good value, flavoursome cooking. Classic French dishes might include soufflé Suissesse, chateaubriand or tarte au citron.

Menu £42 (lunch)/45 – Carte £47/87

Cromlix Hotel, Kinbuck ⊠ FK15 9JT – 𝒞 01786 822125 – www.cromlix.com

🏠 **Cromlix**

COUNTRY HOUSE · CONTEMPORARY This grand house, owned by Sir Andy Murray, has elegant sitting rooms, a whisky room, a chapel and a superb games room, as well as a tennis court in its 30 acre grounds. Luxurious, antique-furnished bedrooms display modern touches while also respecting the house's original style.

16 rooms 🖵 – 👫 £375/395 – 5 suites

Kinbuck ⌧ FK15 9JT – ☎ 01786 822125 – www.cromlix.com

🍴 **Chez Roux** – See restaurant listing

DUNDEE

Dundee City – Regional map n° **16**-C2

🍴 **Castlehill**

MODERN CUISINE · INTIMATE XX Both the name and the décor of this intimate restaurant celebrate the city's history. Ambitious modern cooking is formed around seasonal Scottish ingredients. Choose between an à la carte and a surprise tasting menu; the set priced lunch/pre-theatre menu represents good value.

Menu £22 (lunch)/38

22 Exchange Street ⌧ DD1 3DL – ☎ 01382 220008 – www.castlehillrestaurant.co.uk – Closed Sunday, Monday

at Broughty Ferry East : 4. 5 mi by A 930

🍴 **Collinsons**

CLASSIC CUISINE · FRIENDLY XX You can't miss the name etched in large letters across the floor to ceiling windows of this bright modern restaurant. Cooking is classic to the core, with unfussy, wholesome dishes presented in a refined, eye-catching manner.

Menu £25 (lunch)/38

122-124 Brown Street ⌧ DD5 1EN – ☎ 01382 776000 – www.collinsonsrestaurant.com – Closed 1-14 January, Sunday, Monday

🍴 **Tayberry**

MODERN BRITISH · FRIENDLY XX An unassuming roadside property overlooking the mouth of the Tay. The keen young chef offers fresh, tasty cooking with original modern touches and local and foraged ingredients play a key role. Service is engaging and attentive.

Menu £36

594 Brook Street ⌧ DD5 2EA – ☎ 01382 698280 – www.tayberryrestaurant.com – Closed Sunday, Monday

EDINBANE – Highland ➜ See Skye (Isle of)

EDINBURGH

City of Edinburgh – Regional map n° **15**-C1

Top tips!

The Georgians forged Scotland's capital: a mighty city where imposing buildings are arranged in stunning terraces. The port of Leith played a key role at this time (be sure to pay a visit to the Royal Yacht Britannia), as did the railways – and many old railway hotels impress to this day, with the rather grand **Balmoral** occupying a spot beside the terminus on the famed Princes Street; in its basement you'll find Michelin-Starred **Number One**.

The magnificent castle sits in the city centre and provides a worthy backdrop for the Saturday Farmers Market selling local and artisan produce. From the castle, the Royal Mile runs past the cathedral and through the heart of the Old Town to Holyrood House, the Queen's official residence in Edinburgh.

Must-haves include Scottish salmon and haggis, along with local malt whisky, shortbread and the tooth-achingly sweet tablet, a more sugary version of fudge.

P. Hauser/hemis.fr

Restaurants

✿ Number One   🐾 ὧ AC 🍸

MODERN CUISINE · INTIMATE XxxX The Balmoral is one of the top hotels in Scotland and its grand Edwardian façade conceals a traditional interior that has been sympathetically modernised. Start with drinks in Bar Prince or the chic cocktail bar, then head through to the stylish Number One restaurant. It might be set in the basement but its richly upholstered banquettes and red lacquered walls give it a plush, luxurious feel, while the professional serving team bring plenty of personality to the room.

Cooking is classically rooted yet modern and intricate, with combinations designed to complement rather than overpower one other. Prime Scottish ingredients are proudly utilised and the carefully crafted dishes also have a Scottish heart. To finish, there's a rather appealing bon bon trolley to choose from!

Specialities: Roast langoustines with squash, wakame and shell butter. Highland Wagyu beef, beetroot, smoked bone marrow and bitter leaf. Roast pineapple soufflé with coconut and liquorice root.

Menu £90/105

Town plan G2-n – *Balmoral Hotel, 1 Princes Street* ✉ *EH2 2EQ* –
✆ *0131 557 6727* –
www.roccofortehotels.com – *Closed 2-17 January, Sunday - Saturday lunch*

✿ Condita 🆕   AC

MODERN CUISINE · DESIGN XX Just outside the city centre you'll find this smart shop conversion with an understated modern style: seasonally changing banners cover the windows and origami blackbirds sit on branches protruding from the plain white walls. It's a small place, with just six large wooden tables and Mackintosh-inspired chairs.

Chef Conor Toomey offers two surprise menus, where interesting modern dishes are confidently prepared and skilfully presented. Ingredients are British but it's the quality that dictates their origin, not their location. Flavours are honest yet delicate, and are carefully thought-through so that they enhance one another. The well-crafted dishes are delivered with pride and some nice wine pairings with an Italian slant accompany. If you have any questions, Conor is more than willing to find time to talk to you.

Specialities: Haddock sandwich with chicken skin biscuit, confit egg yolk and smoked crème fraîche. Venison with kale, broccoli and fermented wild garlic. Parsnip mousse with cocoa butter, honeycomb and roasted parsnip.

Menu £50/80

Off plan – *15 Salisbury Place* ✉ *EH9 1SL* –
✆ *0131 667 5777* –
www.condita.co.uk – *Closed 6-20 January, Sunday, Monday, Tuesday - Saturday lunch*

🍴 Merienda 🆕   ὧ 🍽

MEDITERRANEAN CUISINE · BISTRO X Merienda is a sweet little place run by a passionate owner and is the perfect fit for the neighbourhood of Stockbridge. The menu changes daily and is formed of around 20 or so small plates with a strong seasonal bent. These are skilfully prepared and mix Scottish and Mediterranean influences.

Specialities: Seared Scottish asparagus with lemon and honey emulsion. Roasted monkfish cheek, courgette ribbons and lobster bisque. Caramelised banana with white chocolate crémeux, streusel and vanilla cream.

Carte £20/32

Town plan F1-m – *30 North West Circus Place, Stockbridge* ✉ *EH3 6TP* –
✆ *0131 220 2020* –
www.eat-merienda.com – *Closed 13-28 January, 14-29 September, Monday, Tuesday*

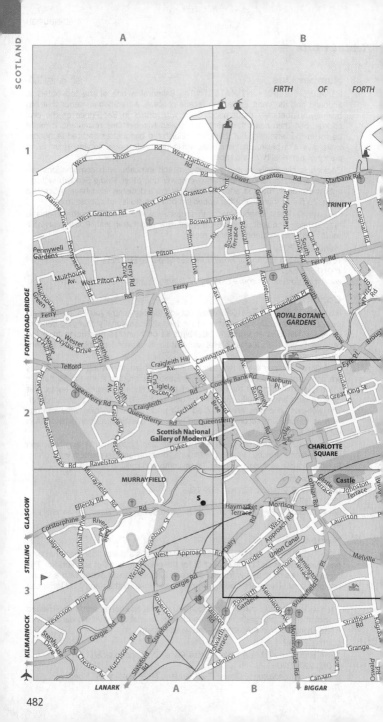

FIRTH   OF   FORTH

TRINITY

West   Shore   Rd
West   Harbour   Rd
Lower   Granton   Rd
Starbank Rd

West   Granton Rd
West Granton   Granton Crescent

Marine Drive
Pennywell
West Granton Rd

Boswall Parkway

Netherby Rd
Clark Rd
South Trinity Rd
Ferry Rd
Craighall Rd

Pennywell
Gardens

Pilton

Boswall
Terrace

Granton

Boswall
Drive

Muirhouse
Av.
West Pilton Av.

Ferry   Rd

Arboretum Rd
Inverleith Pl.

Muirhouse
Green

Ferry

Ferry Rd
Drive

Crewe

East

Inverleith Pl.
Inverleith Pl.

Ferlea

**ROYAL BOTANIC
GARDENS**

Wester
Drylaw Drive

House
O'Hill Rd

Groathill
Rd North

Crewe
Rd

Carrington Rd

Eyre Pl.

Telford

Craigleith Hill
Av.

South

Dundas King St

Queensferry Rd
Craigleith
Hill Crescent

Comely Bank Rd

Raeburn
Pl.

Great King St

Ravelston Dykes Rd
Strachan Rd

South
Groathill
Av.

Craigleith
Hill Crescent

Orchard Rd

Comely
Bank Av.

Comely
Bank Rd

Queensferry

Craigleith

Queensferry   Rd

**Scottish National
Gallery of Modern Art**

Queensferry

Ainslie Pl.

**CHARLOTTE
SQUARE**

Murrayfield Rd

Dykes

Castle
Terrace

Castle

Ravelston   Dykes Rd

Ravelston

MURRAYFIELD

Johnston
Terrace

Lothian Rd

Ellersly Rd

Rd

S

Haymarket
Terrace

Morrison   St

Castle
Terrace

Corstorphine Rd

Riverside
Drive

Roseburn St

West   Approach Rd

Dairy

Dundee

West
Approach Rd

Laurston

Leamington Terrace

Balgreen

Saughtonhall Drive

Stenhouse
Drive

Westfield
Rd

West   Approach   Rd

Union Canal

Gilmore Pl.

Melville

Stevenson   Drive

Gorgie Rd

Robertson Av.

Harrison Rd

Polwarth Gardens

Meadowbank Av.

Brunsfield

Strathearn
Rd

Kilgraston

Chesser Av.

Gorgie Rd

Slateford Rd

Slateford Rd

Polwarth
Terrace

Colinton

Morningside Rd

Grange

Canaan

Lane

LANARK   **BIGGAR**

FORTH-ROAD-BRIDGE

GLASGOW   STIRLING   KILMARNOCK

482

EDINBURGH

0   1000 m
0   1000 yards

C   D

1

LEITH DOCKS

P

P

z

u

e

Commercial St

North Fort St

Ferry Rd

Salamander St

Constitution St

LEITH

ater of Leith

Bonnington Rd

Pilrig

Rd

McDonald Rd

Leith Walk

Great Junction St

Duke St

Seafield

Rd

Rd

Albert St

St Clair St

Lochend

Rd

Restalrig Rd

Seafield

Rd

Nantwich Drive

East

2

Brunswick Rd

Montgomery St

Haddin

Easter Rd

London Rd

Sleigh
Drive

Lochend Rd
South

Sleigh
Drive

Restalrig Drive
Loaning Rd

Craigentinny Rd

Kekewich Av.

Wakefield Av.

Seafield

RESTALRIG

Craigentinny Av.

Calton Hill

Royal
Terrace

Regent Rd

Dalziel
Pl.

Marionville
Rd

Marionville
Av.

Restalrig Av.

London Rd

Piersfield
Terrace

Portobello Rd

HADDINGTON

Calton

Canongate

Holyrood Rd

Abbey and Palace
of Holyroodhouse

Willowbrae

Northfield Rd

Mountcastle Drive

Northfield
Farm Av.

Northfield Rd

BERWICK
-UPON-TWEED

NATIONAL MUSEUM
OF SCOTLAND

astro
uare

HOLYROOD PARK

Queen's Drive

Meadowfield

Duddingston Rd

Mountcastle
Av.

Mountcastle Drive South

Durham Rd

3

St Leonards St

Clark St

rive

iennes Rd

Queens Drive

Drive

Queen's Drive

Old

Church Lane

West

Milton Rd

Rd

West

DUDDINGTON

BERWICK-UPON-
TWEED

r

x

c

Dalkeith Rd

Minto St

Mayfield

Pr

Craigmillar
park

Relugas Rd

West
Savile
Terrace

Peffermill

Rd

Horse

Niddrie

Mains

Rd

Greendykes

Craigmillar
Castle Rd

Greendykes Rd

HADDINGTON

C   PEEBLES   JEDBURGH   D

EDINBURGH

0 — 250 m
0 — 250 yards

Inverleith Terrace

Canonmi
Canon Lane Canon
Glenogle Rd St

East Fettes North Park Terrace Portgower Pl Arboretum Av Reid Terrace Glenogle Rd Brandon Ter Dundas Eyre

Comely Bank Rd Raeburn Pl **s** **h** Henderson Row Clarence St Stephen St Fettes Row Royal Row St

Comely Bank Comely Bank St Comely Bank Row Dean Park Mews Dean Park St Leslie Pl Dean Terrace Saunders St **e** Stephen St Circus Lane Cumberland King Great

Learmonth Grove Learmonth Av Learmonth Gardens South Learmonth Gardens Dean Dean Path Dean Bank Dean Park Crescent Ann St Lennox St Dean Terrace **m** Pl India Doune Terrace Gloucester Lane India Circus Pl Howe St Herlot Row

Buckingham Belgrave Pl Belgrave Crescent Lane Belgrave Crescent Queensferry Rd Clarendon Crescent Eton Terrace Water of Leith Moray Pl Moray Herlot Row STREET Queen St Thistle

Dean Path Belford Bothasay Mews Rothesay Pl Drumsheugh Gardens Bells Brae Ainslie Pl **Georgian House** Queen St **n** Young St Hill St Frederick St Queen St

Douglas Crescent Eglinton Crescent Glencairn Crescent Chester St Manor Pl Melville St Stafford Alva St **CHARLOTTE SQUARE** George St George St Rose St South Lan

West Register House Rose St Rose St South Lane Princes St **v**

Grosvenor Crescent Lansdowne Crescent Palmerston Pl William St Coates Crescent Shandwick Pl Atholl Crescent Atholl Lane West Approach Rd Lothian Pl **x** Princes St PRINCES STREET GARDENS

Castle

West Maitland St Dewar Pl Lane Morrison Gardner's Crescent **f** Castle Terrace Johnston Port

Haymarket Terrace Haymarket Yards Distillery Lane Morrison Link Morrison St Grove St Upper Grove Pl Fountainbridge **Usher Hall** **a** **s** Bread St West Lawson St Lady Lauriston St Lauriston Park Lonsdale Terrace Chalmers

Easter Dalry Rd Olive Terrace Dalry Rd West Approach Rd Dundee St St Fountain Park Yeaman Pl Viewforth Gilmore Pl Union Canal Lochrin Pl Tarvit St Home St Earl Grey Lauriston Gardens Lauriston Park Melville Dr

Dundee Terrace Dorset Gilmore Pl Leamington Terrace Upper Gilmore Pl Leven St Glengyle Terrace Bruntsfield Pl **w** Warrender Par

E F

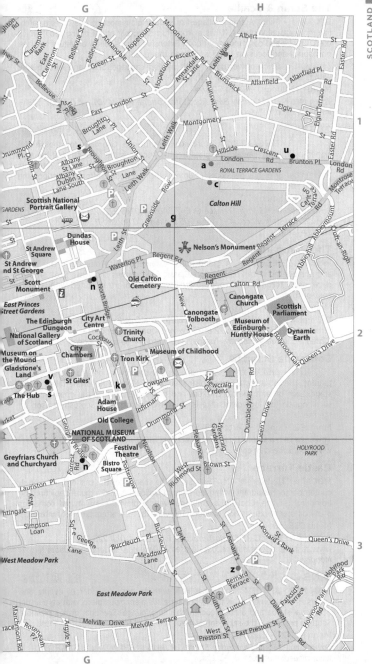

G

H

Albert St

Leith Walk

r

Allanfield Pl

Allanfield Rd

Easter Rd

McDonald St

Annandale St Lane

Hopetoun St

Hopetoun Crescent

Brunswick St

Brunswick Rd

Elgin St

Elgin Terrace

Green St

Bellevue Rd

Bellevue St

Annandale St

Claremont Bank

East Claremont St

Montgomery St

London Rd

Mansfield Pl

Bellevue

East London St

Leith Walk

Hillside Crescent

London Rd

u

Brunton Pl

London Rd

Drummond Pl

Dublin St

s

Broughton Pl

Union St

Broughton St

a

c

ROYAL TERRACE GARDENS

Montrose Terrace

Albany St Lane

Albany St

Dublin St Lane South

Broughton St Lane

Leith Walk

Calton Hill

Scottish National Portrait Gallery

GARDENS

g

Greenside Row

Regent Terrace

Abbeyhill

Dundas House

Leith St

St Andrew Square

Waterloo Pl

Regent Rd

Nelson's Monument

Regent Terrace

Abbey-hill

Fort-an-Righ

St Andrew and St George

Scott Monument

n

North Bridge

Old Calton Cemetery

Regent Rd

Calton Rd

East Princes Street Gardens

New St

Canongate Church

Scottish Parliament

The Edinburgh Dungeon

City Art Centre

Cockburn St

Trinity Church

Canongate Tolbooth

Museum of Edinburgh - Huntly House

Dynamic Earth

National Gallery of Scotland

Museum on the Mound

City Chambers

Tron Kirk

Museum of Childhood

Holyrood Gait

Queen's Drive

Gladstone's Land

v

St Giles'

k

Cowgate

Newcraig Gardens

The Hub

s

Infirmary St

Dumbiedykes Rd

Adam House

Old College

Drummond St

Pleasance

Viewcraig Gardens

HOLYROOD PARK

NATIONAL MUSEUM OF SCOTLAND

Queen's Drive

Greyfriars Church and Churchyard

Festival Theatre

n

Bistro Square

George IV Bridge

Forrest Rd

Nicolson St

West Richmond St

Brown St

Lauriston Pl

Candlemaker Row

St Leonard's Bank

htingale

Simpson Loan

Sq e George Lane

Buccleuch Pl

Buccleuch St

Clerk St

St Leonard's St

Queen's Drive

West Meadow Park

Meadow Lane

z

Bernard Terrace

Holyrood Park Rd

East Meadow Park

Melville Drive

Melville Terrace

Lutton Pl

Parkside Terrace

race

Rosemeath

Marchmont Rd

Argyle Pl

West Preston St

East Preston St

Dalkeith Rd

Holyrood Park Rd

G

H

1

2

3

The Scran & Scallie   丛 AC

SCOTTISH · PUB X A smart, village-like suburb plays host to one of Tom Kitch-in's more casual ventures. It has a wood-furnished bar and a dining room which blends rustic and contemporary décor. Extensive menus follow a 'Nature to Plate' philosophy and focus on the classical and the local.

Specialities: Chicken liver parfait with pickled cabbage. Spelt and lentil burger with chips. Vanilla cheesecake with poached rhubarb.

Menu £19 (lunch) – Carte £28/47

Town plan E1-s – 1 Comely Bank Road, Stockbridge ⊠ EH4 1DT – ℰ 0131 332 6281 – www.scranandscallie.com

21212   ⇔ 丛 AC 🕅 🛇 ⇔

CREATIVE · ELEGANT XxX A stunningly refurbished Georgian townhouse de-signed by William Playfair. The glass-fronted kitchen is the focal point of the styl-ish room. Cooking is innovative and features quirky combinations; '21212' reflects the number of dishes per course. Some of the luxurious bedrooms overlook the Firth of Forth.

Menu £32 (lunch)/70

Town plan H1-c – 3 Royal Terrace ⊠ EH7 5AB – ℰ 0345 222 1212 – www.21212restaurant.co.uk – Closed 5-15 January, 30 August-11 September, Sunday-Tuesday

The Pompadour   丛 AC 🕅 🛇 🐯 P

FRENCH · ELEGANT XxX A grand hotel restaurant which opened in the 1920s and is modelled on a French salon. Classic Gallic dishes showcase Scottish pro-duce, using techniques introduced by Escoffier, and are executed with a light-ness of touch.

Menu £55/70

Town plan F2-x – Waldorf Astoria Edinburgh The Caledonian Hotel, Princes Street ⊠ EH1 2AB – ℰ 0131 222 8975 – www.thepompadour.com – Closed 1-15 January, Monday, Tuesday, Wednesday - Saturday lunch

Southside Scran 🆕   AC

SCOTTISH · BISTRO XX The Southside area of the city is home to this smart res-taurant. The room has a French bistro feel and a Maestro Rotisserie takes centre stage. Legs of lamb, whole chickens and pineapples turn on the open grill, and sit alongside top ingredients like Isle of Skye Scallops and Scottish venison on the menu.

Menu £22 (lunch) – Carte £28/59

Town plan F3-w – 14-17 Bruntsfield Place ⊠ EH10 4HN – ℰ 0131 342 3333 – www.southsidescran.com

Castle Terrace   丛 AC 🕅 🛇 ⇔

MODERN CUISINE · INTIMATE XX Set in the shadow of the castle is this bright, contemporary restaurant with hand-painted wallpapers and a mural depicting the Edinburgh skyline. Cooking is ambitious with a playful element and combines many different textures and flavours. The wine list also offers plenty of interest.

Menu £35/75

Town plan F2-a – 33-35 Castle Terrace ⊠ EH1 2EL – ℰ 0131 229 1222 – www.castleterracerestaurant.com – Closed 22 December-13 January, Sunday, Monday

DINE 🆕   丛 AC 🕅 🛇 🐯

SCOTTISH · BISTRO XX The Usher Hall, with its busy calendar of events and shows, is also home to this buzzy brasserie. It's a spacious place with an unusual octagonal shape and a huge cocktail bar and lounge. Seasonal dishes promote Scottish produce – the set menu is great value and the fishcakes are a must.

Menu £21/27 – Carte £29/46

Town plan F2-f – 10 Cambridge Street (1st floor) ⊠ EH1 2ED – ℰ 0131 218 1818 – www.dineedinburgh.co.uk

SCOTLAND

🕄 The Honours   AC 🕄

CLASSIC CUISINE · BRASSERIE XX Bustling brasserie with a smart, stylish interior and a pleasingly informal atmosphere. Classical brasserie menus have French leanings but always offer some Scottish dishes too; meats cooked on the Josper grill are popular.

Menu £26 – Carte £38/64

Town plan F2-n – *58A North Castle Street* ⊠ *EH2 3LU* – 𝒞 *0131 220 2513* – *www.thehonours.co.uk* – *Closed Sunday, Monday*

🕄 Mono ⓝ   & AC

ITALIAN · CONTEMPORARY DÉCOR XX A friendly team run this smart designer restaurant, decorated in a monochrome theme. A good value set priced lunch is followed by a more ambitious à la carte and tasting menus in the evening. A mix of Scottish and Italian produce is used in modern dishes with an authentic Italian heart.

Menu £25 (lunch) – Carte £40/50

Town plan G2-k – *85 South Bridge* ⊠ *EH1 1HN* – 𝒞 *0131 466 4726* – *www.monorestaurant.co.uk* – *Closed 1-16 January, Monday*

🕄 Ondine   & AC 🕄

SEAFOOD · BRASSERIE XX Smart, lively restaurant dominated by an impressive horseshoe bar and a crustacean counter. Classic menus showcase prime Scottish seafood in tasty, straightforward dishes which let the ingredients shine. Service is well-structured.

Menu £23/29 – Carte £37/78

Town plan G2-s – *2 George IV Bridge (1st Floor)* ⊠ *EH1 1AD* – 𝒞 *0131 226 1888* – *www.ondinerestaurant.co.uk* – *Closed Sunday*

🕄 The Lookout by Gardener's Cottage ⓝ   ≤ & AC

MODERN BRITISH · RUSTIC X Take in some of the best views of the city from the full-length windows of this modern cantilevered building on the top of Calton Hill. The room has a minimalist, almost Scandic feel – and the cooking mirrors this, with contemporary, pared-back dishes which allow each core ingredient to shine.

Menu £27 (lunch)/33 – Carte £28/51

Town plan G1-g – *Calton Hill,* ⊠ *EH7 5AA* – 𝒞 *0131 322 1246* – *www.thelookoutedinburgh.co* – *Closed Monday lunch*

🕄 Timberyard   🏠 & 🕅 🕄 ⇄

MODERN CUISINE · RUSTIC X Trendy warehouse restaurant; its spacious, rustic interior incorporating wood-burning stoves. The Scandic-influenced menu offers 'bites', 'small' and 'large' sizes, with some home-smoked ingredients and an emphasis on distinct, punchy flavours. Cocktails are made with vegetable purées and foraged herbs.

Menu £40 (lunch), £57/79 – Carte £26/31

Town plan F3-s – *10 Lady Lawson Street* ⊠ *EH3 9DS* – 𝒞 *0131 221 1222* – *www.timberyard.co* – *Closed 1-8 January, 31 March-8 April, 20-28 October, Sunday, Monday*

🕄 Aizle   AC 🕅

MODERN CUISINE · SIMPLE X Modest little suburban restaurant whose name means 'ember' or 'spark'. Well-balanced, skilfully prepared dishes are, in effect, a surprise, as the set menu is presented as a long list of ingredients – the latest 'harvest'.

Menu £55

Town plan H3-z – *107-109 St Leonard's Street* ⊠ *EH8 9QY* – 𝒞 *0131 662 9349* – *www.aizle.co.uk* – *Closed 8-18 July, 25 December-21 January, Sunday, Monday, Tuesday, Wednesday - Saturday lunch*

ⅺ○ Baba

MIDDLE EASTERN · MEDITERRANEAN ⅹ Follow a long bar with cosy booths through to the lively dining room decorated in bright colours and hung with kilims. A mix of small and large Middle-Eastern sharing dishes show vibrancy in both their colours and flavours, and can be accompanied by some lesser-known wines from Lebanon and Greece.

Carte £16/30

Town plan F2-v – Principal Hotel, 38 Charlotte Square (Entrance on George Street) ⌧ EH2 4HQ – ℰ 0131 527 4999 – www.baba.restaurant

ⅺ○ Edinburgh Food Studio N

MODERN CUISINE · NEIGHBOURHOOD ⅹ The Edinburgh Food Studio provides a valuable lesson in the less-is-more approach. You dine communally at two long tables and the skilfully prepared, understated dishes are seasonal, natural and harmonious in their flavours. Produce is sourced from the best – and most ethical – Scottish suppliers.

Menu £60 – Carte £25/50

Town plan C3-c – 158 Dalkeith Road ⌧ EH16 5DX – www.edinburghfoodstudio.com – Closed Sunday dinner, Monday, Tuesday, Wednesday lunch

ⅺ○ Fhior

CREATIVE · DESIGN ⅹ A husband and wife team run this appealing Scandic-style restaurant whose name means 'True'. Creative modern cooking showcases Scottish produce, including foraged and home-preserved ingredients. Lunch sees small plates which are ideal for sharing, while dinner offers two surprise tasting menus.

Menu £17 (lunch), £40/65

Town plan G1-s – 36 Broughton Street ⌧ EH1 3SB – ℰ 0131 477 5000 – www.fhior.com – Closed 1-14 January, 25-27 December, Sunday, Monday, Tuesday, Wednesday - Thursday lunch

ⅺ○ Gardener's Cottage

TRADITIONAL CUISINE · RUSTIC ⅹ This quirky little eatery was once home to a royal gardener. Two cosy, simply furnished rooms have long communal tables. Lunch is light and dinner offers a multi-course set menu; much of the produce comes from the kitchen garden.

Menu £15 (lunch), £45/60 – Carte £19/60

Town plan H1-a – 1 Royal Terrace Gardens ⌧ EH7 5DX – ℰ 0131 677 0244 – www.thegardenerscottage.co

ⅺ○ The Little Chartroom

MODERN BRITISH · SIMPLE ⅹ There's a lively buzz to this laid-back little restaurant on Leith Walk, which is run by an experienced young couple and filled with nautical charts. Cooking is fresh and flavoursome. Simple small plates and sharing dishes are followed by a modern menu with a Scottish edge; at weekends they serve brunch.

Menu £16/19 – Carte £32/44

Town plan H1-r – 30-31 Albert Place ⌧ EH7 5HN – ℰ 0131 556 6600 – www.thelittlechartroom.com – Closed 1-15 January, Monday, Tuesday

ⅺ○ Purslane

MODERN CUISINE · NEIGHBOURHOOD ⅹ A cosy, atmospheric basement restaurant made up of just 9 tables. The young chef-owner creates ambitious modern dishes which mix tried-and-tested flavours with contemporary techniques. Lunch is particularly good value.

Menu £15 (lunch), £29/60 – Carte £29/60

Town plan F1-e – 33a St. Stephen Street ⌧ EH3 5AH – ℰ 0131 226 3500 – www.purslanerestaurant.co.uk – Closed Monday

ⅈ○ Rabbit Hole 🆕

TRADITIONAL CUISINE · SIMPLE ⅄ Hidden away in the suburbs is this appealing neighbourhood restaurant with tightly packed tables and paper place mats displaying the menu. Passion oozes from the knowledgeable owners and the appealing dishes show plenty of personality. The classically based puddings are a real highlight.

Menu £16 (lunch) – Carte £28/38

Off plan – *10 Roseneath Street* ✉ *EH9 1JH* – ℰ *0131 229 7953* – *www.therabbitholerestaurant.com* – *Closed Sunday, Monday*

ⅈ○ Taisteal

MODERN BRITISH · NEIGHBOURHOOD ⅄ Taisteal is Irish Gaelic for 'journey' and is the perfect name: photos from the chef's travels line the walls and dishes have global influences, with Asian flavours to the fore. The wine list even has a sake section.

Menu £16 – Carte £26/37

Town plan E1-h – *1-3 Raeburn Place, Stockbridge* ✉ *EH4 1HU* – ℰ *0131 332 9977* – *www.taisteal.co.uk* – *Closed 1-10 January, 31 August-15 September, Sunday, Monday*

Hotels & guesthouses

🏨🏨 Balmoral   🕮 🗋 🕸 🏠 🕍 🖂 ♿ 🅰🅲 🏋 🚗

GRAND LUXURY · CLASSIC A renowned Edwardian hotel which provides for the 21C traveller whilst retaining its old-fashioned charm. Bedrooms are classical with a subtle contemporary edge. Live harp music accompanies afternoon tea and 'Scotch' offers over 500 malts. Dine on a choice of modern dishes or brasserie classics.

188 rooms – ♚♚ £195/725 – ☑ £29 – 20 suites

Town plan G2-n – *1 Princes Street* ✉ *EH2 2EQ* – ℰ *0131 556 2414* – *www.roccofortehotels.com*

❀ **Number One** – See restaurant listing

🏨🏨 Prestonfield   🕮 ☞ ≼ 🕍 🖂 ♿ 🅰🅲 🏋 🅿

LUXURY · PERSONALISED 17C country house in a pleasant rural spot, with an opulent, dimly lit interior displaying warm colours, fine furnishings and old tapestries – it's hugely atmospheric and is one of the most romantic hotels around. Luxurious bedrooms boast a high level of facilities and service is excellent.

23 rooms ☑ – ♚♚ £345/550 – 5 suites

Town plan C3-r – *Priestfield Road* ✉ *EH16 5UT* – ℰ *0131 225 7800* – *www.prestonfield.com*

🏨🏨 Hotel du Vin   🕮 🖂 ♿ 🅰🅲 🏋

LUXURY · DESIGN Boutique hotel located close to the Royal Mile, featuring unique murals and wine-themed bedrooms furnished with dark wood. Guest areas include a whisky snug and a mezzanine bar complete with glass-fronted cellars and a wine tasting room. The traditional bistro offers classic French cooking.

47 rooms ☑ – ♚♚ £150/344

Town plan G3-n – *11 Bristo Place* ✉ *EH1 1EZ* – ℰ *0131 247 4900* – *www.hotelduvin.com/edinburgh*

🏨🏨 Radisson Collection H. Royal Mile Edinburgh

🕮 ≼ 🕍 🖂 ♿ 🅰🅲 🏋

LUXURY · DESIGN Set in a great central location on the historic Royal Mile, a striking hotel with bold colour schemes, stylish furnishings and clever design features. Bedrooms on the upper floors have impressive city skyline views. Enjoy local produce at dinner and honey from the bees they keep on the roof at breakfast.

136 rooms ☑ – ♚♚ £200/400 – 7 suites

Town plan G2-v – *1 George IV Bridge* ✉ *EH1 1AD* – ℰ *0131 220 6666* – *www.radissoncollection.com*

🏠 The Dunstane

TOWNHOUSE · CONTEMPORARY An impressive house which used to be a training centre for the Royal Bank of Scotland. Guest areas retain original Victorian features and the smart bedrooms have designer touches; some are located across a busy road. Light snacks are served all day in the lounge.

35 rooms ⌑ – 👫 £174/294

Town plan A3-s – 4 West Coates ⌧ *EH12 5JQ – ℰ 0131 337 6169 – www.thedunstane.com*

🏠 23 Mayfield

TOWNHOUSE · CLASSIC Lovingly restored Victorian house with a helpful owner, an outdoor hot tub and a rare book collection. Sumptuous bedrooms come with coordinated soft furnishings, mahogany features and luxurious bathrooms. Breakfast is extravagant.

7 rooms – 👫 £125/220

Town plan C3-x – 23 Mayfield Gardens ⌧ *EH9 2BX – ℰ 0131 667 5806 ⤴ www.23mayfield.co.uk*

🏠 Six Brunton Place

TOWNHOUSE · CONTEMPORARY This late Georgian townhouse – run by a charming owner – was once home to Frederick Ritchie, who designed the One O'Clock Gun and Time Ball. Inside you'll find flagged floors, columns, marble fireplaces and a cantilevered stone staircase; these contrast with contemporary furnishings and vibrant modern art.

4 rooms ⌑ – 👫 £159/179

Town plan H1-u – 6 Brunton Place ⌧ *EH7 5EG – ℰ 0131 622 0042 – www.sixbruntonplace.com – Closed 20-28 December*

at Leith – Regional map n° **15**–C1

⠿ Martin Wishart

MODERN CUISINE · ELEGANT ✕✕✕ Martin Wishart spent his formative years working in the kitchens of some of the industry's most stellar names, like Albert Roux and Marco Pierre White, so it's no surprise that his cooking comes with a sound classical French base. But this Edinburgh-born chef is also a proud Scot, so he will always seek out the best ingredients his country has to offer, like Shetland squid and Peterhead skate. He then adds innovative little touches of his own to give his cooking personality and his dishes individuality.

2019 marked the restaurant's 20th birthday and it's easy to see why it has become something of a Leith institution. It is warmly decorated and comfortable without being overly formal. It also offers a choice of menus to suit all occasions, whether you're in for a business lunch or an extended evening celebration.

Specialities: Ceviche of Gigha halibut with mango and passion fruit. John Dory with Jerusalem artichoke, confit potato, parsley and lemon. Strawberries with fennel crémeux and strawberry & yoghurt sorbet.

Menu £35 (lunch), £80/120

Town plan C1-u – 54 The Shore ⌧ *EH6 6RA – ℰ 0131 553 3557 – www.martin-wishart.co.uk – Closed 28 July-4 August, 13-14 October, 31 December-16 January, Sunday, Monday*

⠿ Kitchin (Tom Kitchin)

MODERN CUISINE · DESIGN ✕✕ A smartly converted whisky warehouse provides the perfect setting for this patriotic restaurant. Chef-owner Tom Kitchin was born in Edinburgh and Scottish blood runs through this restaurant's veins. The windswept highlands are brought inside courtesy of walls lined with tree bark, tartan tweed covered chairs, and dry stone walls which divide the room – and the personable serving team dressed in kilts help pull it all together.

This is a restaurant serious about what it does but it is in no way stiff and starchy – just look around and you'll see guests relaxed and having fun. Menus offer a mix of time-honoured classics which have bold flavours and a rustic appearance, and fresh modern dishes where there are fewer ingredients on the plate and skilled preparation allows each one to shine. Prime Scottish produce – particularly vegetables – are the chef's passion.

Specialities: Boned & rolled pig's head with roasted tail of langoustine and crispy ear salad. Loin of roe deer with braised haunch, root vegetables and red wine sauce. Rhubarb crumble soufflé with vanilla ice cream.

Menu £35 (lunch)/80

Town plan C1-z – *78 Commercial Quay* ⊠ *EH6 6LX* – ℰ *0131 555 1755* – *www.thekitchin.com* – *Closed 7-11 April, 21-25 July, 24 December-14 January, Sunday, Monday*

○ **Borough** ⑩   AC ⑩

MODERN CUISINE · **NEIGHBOURHOOD** XX A young but experienced couple run this smart restaurant, which sits on a cobbled street in a residential area near the port. Well-crafted, keenly priced dishes have a clean, modern style. Seasonal Scottish produce is kept to the fore, with usually no more than 4 ingredients featured on each plate.

Menu £19 (lunch)/35

Town plan C1-e – *50-54 Henderson Street* ⊠ *EH6 6DE* – ℰ *0131 554 7655* – *www.boroughrestaurant.com* – *Closed 1-14 January, Sunday dinner, Monday, Tuesday, Wednesday - Thursday lunch*

EDNAM - The Scottish Borders → See Kelso

ELGOL - Highland → See Skye (Isle of)

ERISKA (ISLE OF) Argyll and Bute – Regional map n° **16**-B2

⌘ **Isle of Eriska** ⑩   ⑩ P

SCOTTISH · **COUNTRY HOUSE** XXX This impressive 19C baronial mansion sits in an idyllic spot on a private island and affords fantastic views out over the water. It's a spacious place, where a contemporary style contrasts with original features, and open fires welcome you at every turn. When it comes to dining, there's the choice of the formal main room with garden views, a large conservatory and a smaller anteroom.

Experienced chef Graeme Cheevers spent time working at Martin Wishart and Cameron House, and he brings with him plenty of skill and knowledge. Natural flavours are paramount in his cooking, which perfectly reflects both the season and the area, and his dishes have a pleasingly understated style. He also has the natural ability to bring flavours together in well-balanced, truly harmonious combinations. From the first canapé to the last petit four, the quality remains.

Specialities: Crab with Granny Smith, smoked haddock jelly and seaweed butter. Saddle of roe deer with baked celeriac, spelt and green pepper sauce. Vanilla millefeuille with blackcurrant and crème fraîche sorbet.

Menu £67

Isle of Eriska Hotel, Benderloch ⊠ *PA37 1SD* – ℰ *01631 720371* – *www.eriska-hotel.co.uk* – *Closed Sunday - Saturday lunch*

🏠 **Isle of Eriska**   ⌂ ⊗ ← ⌒ 🖬 🔲 ⑩ ♨ 🛁 & P

COUNTRY HOUSE · **CONTEMPORARY** An impressive 19C baronial mansion set in an idyllic spot on a private island and boasting fantastic views. A contemporary style contrasts with original features in the main house and there are luxurious hilltop lodges in the grounds. Dine on modern dishes featuring garden ingredients in the restaurant or bistro; the latter has stunning views from its balcony.

29 rooms � – ♥♥ £295/525 – 13 suites

Benderloch ⊠ *PA37 1SD* – ℰ *01631 720371* – *www.eriska-hotel.co.uk*
⌘ **Isle of Eriska** – See restaurant listing

FIONNPHORT – Argyll and Bute → See Mull (Isle of)

FORT WILLIAM
Highland – Regional map n° **17**–C3

⫶○ Inverlochy Castle

MODERN CUISINE · LUXURY XxxX Set within a striking castle in the shadow of Ben Nevis is this grand restaurant offering stunning loch views. Choose between two candlelit dining rooms where period sideboards are filled with polished silver. Richly flavoured classic dishes showcase luxurious Scottish produce.

Menu £75/95

Inverlochy Castle Hotel, Torlundy ✉ PH33 6SN – ℰ 01397 702177 – www.inverlochycastlehotel.com – Closed Sunday - Saturday lunch

⫶○ Lime Tree An Ealdhain

MODERN CUISINE · RUSTIC X Attractive 19C manse – now an informally run restaurant and art gallery, where the owner's pieces are displayed and two public exhibitions are held each year. Rustic dining room with exposed beams and an open kitchen; cooking is fresh and modern. Simply furnished bedrooms – ask for one with a view of Loch Linnhe.

Menu £19/29

Achintore Road ✉ PH33 6RQ – ℰ 01397 701806 – www.limetreefortwilliam.co.uk – Closed Sunday - Saturday lunch

🏠 Inverlochy Castle

GRAND LUXURY · CLASSIC A striking castellated house in beautiful grounds, boasting stunning views over the loch to Glenfinnan. The classical country house interior comprises sumptuous open-fired lounges and a grand hall with an impressive ceiling mural. Elegant bedrooms offer the height of luxury; mod cons include mirrored TVs.

18 rooms ☟ – ♥♥ £455/665 – 2 suites

Torlundy ✉ PH33 6SN – ℰ 01397 702177 – www.inverlochycastlehotel.com
⫶○ **Inverlochy Castle** – See restaurant listing

🏠 Grange

TOWNHOUSE · PERSONALISED Take in loch and hills views from this delightful Victorian house and its attractive gardens. Spacious bedrooms are luxuriously appointed. Two are suites; one has a beautiful copper bath in the room and the other is a timber bothy in the garden. The charming owner really knows how to look after her guests.

4 rooms – ♥♥ £155/198

Grange Road ✉ PH33 6JF – ℰ 01397 705516 – www.grangefortwilliam.com

GATTONSIDE – The Scottish Borders → See Melrose

GIGHA (ISLE OF) Argyll and Bute – Regional map n° **16**–A3

⫶○ The Boathouse

SEAFOOD · RUSTIC X This 300 year old boathouse is set on a small community-owned island, overlooking the water. Whitewashed stone walls and beamed ceilings enhance the rustic feel. Menus cater for all, centring around fresh seafood and local meats.

Carte £24/58

Ardminish Bay ✉ PA41 7AA – ℰ 01583 505123 – www.boathouseongigha.com – Closed 30 September-3 April

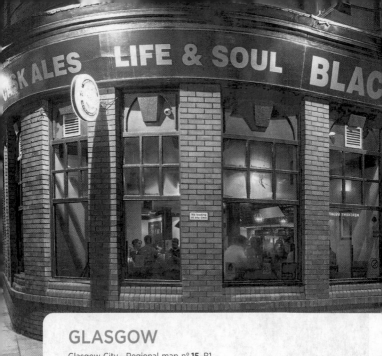

GLASGOW

Glasgow City – Regional map n° **15**–B1

Top tips!

Forget shortbread-tin pictures, Glasgow is the real working man's Scotland; a former industrial powerhouse that has been reborn as a cultural and commercial hub.

To the east of the centre is the Merchant City, one of Glasgow's oldest quarters. In the 1750s it was home to the warehouses of wealthy traders but today it plays host to chic bars, restaurant and boutiques.

To the west of the centre lies Kelvingrove, with its famous art museum and youthful, urban vibe. Try the fun, Bib Gourmand awarded **Ox and Finch** for good value internationally influenced small plates or **The Gannet**, which makes great use of Scotland's larder.

If you're looking for somewhere more iconic, then the **Ubiquitous Chip** offers a great version of venison haggis, champit tatties and neep cream that's been on the menu since its opening in 1971; its younger sister **Stravaigin**, meanwhile, serves local dishes given an Asian makeover.

L. De Simone/AGF Foto/Photononstop

Restaurants

⊛ Monadh Kitchen

MODERN BRITISH · FRIENDLY ⅹ This delightful neighbourhood restaurant has a modern bistro style and is very personally run by a husband and wife. The experienced chef creates a series of appealing, seasonally evolving menus, where classic Scottish cooking is given a contemporary twist; the 2 course lunch is particularly good value.

Specialities: Haggis with potato purée, pickled turnip and red wine sauce. Shetland cod with purple sprouting broccoli, herb gnocchi, golden raisin and mussel sauce. Monadh chocolate cranachan.

Menu £18/23 – Carte £29/36

Off plan – *19 New Kirk Rd, Bearsden* ✉ *G61 3SJ* – ☏ *0141 258 6420* – www.monadhkitchen.co.uk – *Closed Monday*

⊛ Ox and Finch

⟨AC⟩ ▤ ⫯◯ ⟷

MODERN BRITISH · DESIGN ⅹ A bright, breezy team run this likeable rustic restaurant, with its tile-backed open kitchen and wines displayed in a huge metal cage. The Mediterranean small plates tempt one and all: cooking centres around old favourites but with added modern twists – and the flavours really shine through.

Specialities: Tequila-cured sea trout, charred corn, lime and pickled chilli. Confit duck leg, yellow curry, Thai basil and crispy rice. Vanilla custard with poached rhubarb, yoghurt and prosecco granita.

Carte £18/33

Town plan A2-c – *920 Sauchiehall Street* ✉ *G3 7TF* – ☏ *0141 339 8627* – www.oxandfinch.com

⫯◯ Brian Maule at Chardon d'Or

⟨AC⟩ ⫯◯ ⟨⟩ ⟷

MODERN CUISINE · ELEGANT ⅹⅹⅹ Georgian townhouse in the city's heart, with original pillars, ornate carved ceilings and white walls hung with vibrant modern art. Generously proportioned, classical dishes have a modern edge and showcase luxurious ingredients.

Menu £22 (lunch)/26 – Carte £47/63

Town plan C2-b – *176 West Regent Street* ✉ *G2 4RL* – ☏ *0141 248 3801* – www.brianmaule.com – *Closed Sunday, Monday*

⫯◯ Bilson Eleven

⟨AC⟩ ⟷

MODERN CUISINE · INTIMATE ⅹⅹ A bohemian restaurant situated in a small terrace in an eastern suburb; you dine in the house's original drawing room, where the décor blends the old and the new. Cooking is interesting and original with a playful edge.

Menu £39/69

Off plan – *10 Annfield Place, Dennistoun* ✉ *G31 2XQ* – ☏ *0141 554 6259* – www.bilsoneleven.co.uk – *Closed Sunday, Monday, Tuesday, Wednesday - Saturday lunch*

⫯◯ Cail Bruich

⟨AC⟩ ⫯◯ ⟨⟩

MODERN CUISINE · CONTEMPORARY DÉCOR ⅹⅹ Run by two brothers, this smart restaurant's name means 'to eat well', and it won't disappoint. Sit on comfy banquettes or ask for a spot at the counter to keep an eye on what's happening in the kitchen. Cooking is modern and elaborate with some personal twists; the tasting menu is a popular choice.

Menu £30 (lunch), £45/60

Town plan A1-a – *725 Great Western Road* ✉ *G12 8QX* – ☏ *0141 334 6265* – www.cailbruich.co.uk – *Closed 6-14 January, Monday - Tuesday lunch*

DUMBARTON A B STIRLING

Botanic Gardens

Great Western

Dundonald Rd
Observatory Rd
Athole Lane
Victoria Crescent Rd
Dowanside Rd
Highburgh Rd
Havelock St
Elie St
Church St
Dumbarton Rd

Doune Gardens Lane
Wilton St
Kirkland St
Maryhill Rd
Garscube Rd
Raeberry St
Grovepark

Ruskin
Buckingham Terrace
Cecil
Granby Lane
Saltoun Lane
Kersland St
Hillhead
Belmont St
North Woodside Rd
Windsor Terrace
North Woodside Rd
Napiershall St
Maryhill Rd
George

Glasgow Av.
Oakfield
Bank St
Otago St
Kelvinbridge
Barrington Drive
Western
Eldon St
St George's Cross
Prince's St
West Princes St
Great Western Rd

Hunterian Art Gallery
MACKINTOSH HOUSE
University Av.
Hunterian Museum
Park Quadrant
Park Circus Lane
Woodlands Rd
Grant St

KELVINGROVE ART GALLERY AND MUSEUM
Kelvingrove Park
Lynedoch
St Georges Rd
Buccleuch
Tenement House

Old Dumbarton Rd
Yorkhill St
Lumsden St
Haugh Rd
Argyle St
Kelvin Way
Kelvingrove St
Royal Terrace Lane
Fitzroy Lane
Woodside Terrace Lane
Woodside Pl.
Sauchiehall St
Elderslie St
Berkeley St
Bath

DUMBARTON
Eastvale Pl.
Kelvinhaugh St
Stobcross Rd
Pointhouse
Sauchiehall St
Argyle St
Kelvinhaugh St
Vincent St
Kelvinhaugh
Crescent
Minerva Way
Minerva St
Kent Rd
Dover St
Dorset St
St Vincent St
Houldsworth St
Argyle St
M 8

Scottish Exhibition and Conference Center
Minerva Way
Exhibition Centre
Stobcross St
Lancefield St
Hydepark St
Warroch St
Cheapside St
North St
Washington St
Argyle

Science Centre
Govan Rd
Millennium Bridge
Bells Bridge
Congress Rd
Congress Way
Finnieston
Lancefield Quay
Elliot St
M 8
Broomielaw

Imax
BBC Building
Pacific Drive
Clyde Arc
Lancefield Quay
CLYDE

Govan Rd
Brand St
Middleton St
Cessnock
Govan Rd
Pacific Drive
Mavisbank
Govan Rd
Gardens St
Paisley Rd West
Springfield Quay
Paisley Rd
Houston St
Paisley Rd
Morrison
Riverview Drive
Paisley Rd
Wallace

Midlock St
Paisley Rd West
Clifford Lane
Clifford St
M 74
Kinning Park
M 8
Middlesex St
Milnpark St
Stanley St
Admiral St
Seaward St
Shields Road
Scotland
Scotland Street School Museum

M 77
Vermont St
St Andrews Cres
Andrew's Drive
Andrews Cres
West Street
Kil

PAISLEY
Academy Park
Gower St
Maxwell Drive

KILMARNOCK A B

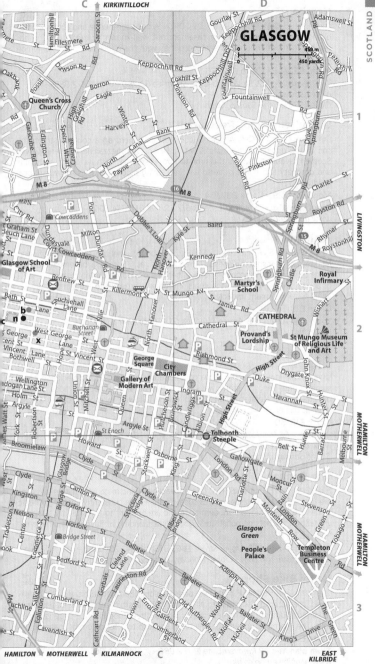

GLASGOW

⅄⃝ Gamba

SEAFOOD · CONTEMPORARY DÉCOR XX A cosy bar-lounge and contemporary dining room, tucked away in a basement but well-known by the locals. The appealing menu offers unfussy seafood dishes with the odd Asian influence; lemon sole is a speciality.

Menu £22/45 – Carte £27/56

Town plan C2-x – *225a West George Street* ✉ *G2 2ND* – ✆ *0141 572 0899* – *www.gamba.co.uk* – *Closed 1-7 January, Sunday lunch*

⅄⃝ Ubiquitous Chip (Restaurant)

SCOTTISH · BISTRO XX A quirky, iconic establishment on a cobbled street; the son of the original owner runs it with passion. The mezzanine brasserie serves Scottish favourites but it's the ground floor restaurant with its ponds, fountains and greenery that is the place to eat. Interesting modern classics showcase local produce.

Menu £24/29 – Carte £37/64

Town plan A1-n – *12 Ashton Lane* ✉ *G12 8SJ* – ✆ *0141 334 5007* – *www.ubiquitouschip.co.uk*

⅄⃝ Alchemilla

MEDITERRANEAN CUISINE · SIMPLE X A bright, friendly restaurant offering Mediterranean-inspired dishes in a range of sizes. There is a basement but the place to sit is on the ground floor – either in the window, on the mezzanine level or at the counter watching the chefs. Ingredients are kept to a minimum but flavours have maximum impact.

Carte £18/35

Town plan A2-a – *1126 Argyle Street* ✉ *G3 8TD* – ✆ *0141 337 6060* – *www.thisisalchemilla.com*

⅄⃝ Cafezique

INTERNATIONAL · BISTRO X Underneath the old Hargan's Dairy sign is this shabby-chic-looking eatery with a contemporary interior. Striking black and white screen prints hang on stone walls and a relaxed, buzzy vibe pervades. All-day breakfasts and Mediterranean light bites are followed by vibrant dishes in two sizes at dinner.

Carte £18/30

Off plan – *66 Hyndland Street* ✉ *G11 5PT* – ✆ *0141 339 7180* – *www.delizique.com* – *Closed Sunday dinner*

⅄⃝ The Gannet

MODERN BRITISH · RUSTIC X This appealingly rustic restaurant makes passionate use of Scotland's larder and as such, its menus are constantly evolving. Classic dishes are presented in a modern style and are brought to the table by a charming team. The chefs demonstrate a good understanding of flavour combinations.

Menu £32/45

Town plan A2-t – *1155 Argyle Street* ✉ *G3 8TB* – ✆ *0141 204 2081* – *www.thegannetgla.com* – *Closed Monday, Tuesday - Wednesday lunch*

⅄⃝ Hanoi Bike Shop

VIETNAMESE · SIMPLE X Old bike parts sit alongside Asian furnishings at this relaxed, characterful bistro; ask to sit in the lighter upstairs room with its fine array of lanterns. Unfussy Vietnamese dishes include street food like rice paper summer rolls. The charming, knowledgeable team are keen to offer recommendations.

Carte £20/28

Town plan A1-s – *8 Ruthven Lane* ✉ *G12 9BG* – ✆ *0141 334 7165* – *www.hanoibikeshop.co.uk*

🍴⃝ Julie's Kopitiam ⃝🍴

MALAYSIAN · SIMPLE 🍴 The young owner has kept the décor simple and the focus firmly on the food at this traditional Malaysian coffee shop; she even visits Malaysia regularly to gather new ideas. Good value street food dishes are vibrant and flavoursome and service is sweet and cheerful. Watch the chefs in the open kitchen.

Menu £15 (lunch), £18/25

Off plan – *1109 Pollokshaws Road* ✉ *G41 3YG* – ℰ *0141 237 9560* – *Closed Monday, Tuesday - Wednesday lunch*

🍴⃝ Six by Nico ⃝🍸

MODERN CUISINE · FRIENDLY 🍴 It's all in the name: the good value 6 course tasting menu changes every 6 weeks and is designed by Italian owner Nico, along with his team. Themes are announced on the website and could be anything from 'Picnic' to 'Vietnamese Street Food'. Dishes are well-executed and a vegetarian menu runs in parallel.

Menu £28

Town plan A2-a – *1132 Argyle Street* ✉ *G3 8TS* – ℰ *0141 334 5661* – *www.sixbynico.co.uk* – *Closed Monday*

🍴⃝ Stravaigin 🏠 ⚹ AC

INTERNATIONAL · SIMPLE 🍴 Their motto here is 'think global, eat local' and you can choose from classical, international and subtly spiced Asian-influenced fare. They make their own haggis and host regular theme nights. On the ground floor is a shabby-chic café-bar; the intimate downstairs restaurant opens evenings and weekends.

Carte £30/48

Town plan B1-z – *28 Gibson Street* ✉ *G12 8NX* – ℰ *0141 334 2665* – *www.stravaigin.co.uk*

Hotels

🏨 Blythswood Square 🏃 🌐 〰 ᴽᵴ ⬆ ⚹ AC 🛁

HISTORIC · DESIGN Stunning property on a delightful Georgian square. Modern décor contrasts with original fittings; bedrooms are dark and moody and the Penthouse Suite features a bed adapted from a snooker table. Afternoon tea is a hit.

114 rooms – 🛏 £120/282 – 3 suites

Town plan C2-n – *11 Blythswood Square* ✉ *G2 4AD* – ℰ *0141 248 8888* – *www.kimptonblythswoodsquare.com/us/en/*

🏨 Hotel du Vin 🏃 ᴽᵴ ⚹ 🛁

TOWNHOUSE · ELEGANT A lovely collection of adjoining townhouses boasting original 19C stained glass, wood panelling and a labyrinth of corridors. It has a bright modern style and a contemporary country house air. Dine on modern dishes in the elegant oak-panelled restaurant; they also offer wine tastings in the cellar.

49 rooms – 🛏 £160/425 – ☶ £18 – 3 suites

Off plan – *1 Devonshire Gardens* ✉ *G12 0UX* – ℰ *0141 378 0385* – *www.hotelduvin.com*

🏨 Dakota Deluxe 🏃 ⬆ ⚹ AC

BUSINESS · CONTEMPORARY With its black brick façade and box hedges, this boutique hotel wouldn't look out of place in NYC. Sleek, spacious bedrooms have good comforts and the professional staff make it feel like a home-from-home. On the first floor there's a champagne bar; in the basement, classics and grills are brought up-to-date.

83 rooms ☶ – 🛏 £135/310 – 1 suite

Town plan B2-h – *179 West Regent Street* ✉ *G2 4DP* – ℰ *0141 404 3680* – *www.glasgow.dakotahotels.co.uk*

🏨 Malmaison

BUSINESS · CONTEMPORARY An impressive-looking former Greek Orthodox Church, with moody, masculine décor. Stylish, boldly coloured bedrooms offer good facilities; the best are the brighter duplex suites. The lively glass-roofed basement bar specialises in craft beers and the vaulted brasserie offers a wide-ranging global menu.

72 rooms – 🛉🛉 £90/320 – ⭐ £18 – 8 suites

Town plan C2-c – *278 West George Street* ✉ *G2 4LL* – ☎ *0141 572 1000* – *www.malmaison.com*

GRANDTULLY

Perth and Kinross – Regional map n° **16**–C2

🍽️ Ballintaggart Farm ⓝ

MODERN BRITISH · SIMPLE 🗙 Formerly a farmhouse and steading, this passionately run restaurant sits in a remote hillside location and comes complete with a cookery school and 4 nicely furnished bedrooms. Local and home-grown produce underpins menus which focus on accomplished, pared-back dishes with natural flavours.

Menu £18 (lunch), £55/65

✉ *PH9 0PX* – ☎ *01887 447000* – *www.ballintaggart.com* – *Closed 23 December-7 January, Monday*

🍽️ The Grandtully Hotel by Ballintaggart ⓝ

TRADITIONAL BRITISH · CONTEMPORARY DÉCOR 🗙 Although you can still stay over in one of 8 individually decorated bedrooms, this former railway hotel, dating from 1866, is now increasingly known for its food. It's a stylish place, with a chic bar and lounge, and the flexible menu offers a good selection of unfussy modern classics.

Carte £21/43

✉ *PH9 0PX* – ☎ *01887 447000* – *www.ballintaggart.com* – *Closed 7-14 January, 23-27 December, Monday*

GULLANE

East Lothian – Regional map n° **15**–D1

🦡 Bonnie Badger ⓝ

MODERN BRITISH · PUB 🗙🗙 Tom and Michaela Kitchin have created their version of a modern pub in a former coaching inn dating from 1836. The bar remains the hub while the dining room offers a menu of refined, boldly flavoured pub classics. Stylish bedrooms showcase Scottish designers and are both cosy and sublimely comfortable.

Specialities: Dressed crab, avocado and toast. Steak pie and bone marrow. Treacle tart with clotted cream.

Menu £17 (lunch) – Carte £27/44

Main Street ✉ *EH31 2AB* – ☎ *01620 621111* – *www.bonniebadger.com*

🍽️ Chez Roux

FRENCH · INTIMATE 🗙🗙 Formal restaurant in a classic country house hotel; enjoy an aperitif in the lounge or delightful Jekyll-designed gardens before dining with a view over the Muirfield golf course. Classical French menus have a Roux signature style and feature tried-and-tested classics with a modern edge.

Menu £45/75 – Carte £21/67

Greywalls Hotel, Duncur Rd, Muirfield ✉ *EH31 2EG* – ☎ *01620 842144* – *www.greywalls.co.uk* – *Closed Sunday - Saturday lunch*

⫛○ La Potinière   ♿ 🅿

TRADITIONAL CUISINE · COSY XX Sweet little restaurant where the two own-ers share the cooking. The regularly changing menu lists two carefully prepared dishes per course; produce is local or home-grown and their homemade bread is renowned.

Menu £27 (lunch)/39

Main Street ⊠ EH31 2AA – ℰ 01620 843214 – www.lapotiniere.co.uk –
Closed 1 January-1 February, Sunday dinner, Monday, Tuesday

⛬ Greywalls   ✿ ⓢ ⫷ 🍴 🏄 🅿

COUNTRY HOUSE · CLASSIC A long-standing Edwardian country house by Lu-tyens, in a superb location beside the Muirfield golf course, overlooking the Firth of Forth. Compact bedrooms are furnished with antiques and the library is partic-ularly cosy. The stunning formal gardens were designed by Jekyll.

23 rooms ⊡ – ♔♔ £295/450

Duncur Rd, Muirfield ⊠ EH31 2EG – ℰ 01620 842144 – www.greywalls.co.uk
⫛○ **Chez Roux** – See restaurant listing

HELENSBURGH

Argyll and Bute – Regional map n° **16**–B3

⊛ Sugar Boat   🛖 ♿

MODERN BRITISH · BISTRO X This appealing all-day bistro is named after the nearby shipwreck. To the front is a café-style area with a marble-topped island bar; behind is the dining room and an enclosed courtyard. Pared-down dishes feature just a handful of carefully prepared ingredients. Flavours are clear and contrasts well-judged.

Specialities: Sardines with tomato and tarragon dressing. Grilled beef with charred cabbage and 'nduja. Ecclefechan tart and clotted cream.

Carte £23/33

30 Colquhoun Square ⊠ G84 8AQ – ℰ 01436 647522 – www.sugarboat.co.uk

INVERKEILOR

Angus – Regional map n° **16**–D2

⫛○ Gordon's   ⫷ 🅿

MODERN CUISINE · CONTEMPORARY DÉCOR XX A long-standing, passion-ately run restaurant where stone walls and open fires contrast with designer touches. The son works in the kitchen and his mother oversees the service. The concise menu lists accomplished classics which showcase the natural flavours of local ingredients. Bedrooms are smart and modern.

Menu £65

32 Main Street ⊠ DD11 5RN – ℰ 01241 830364 – www.gordonsrestaurant.co.uk –
Closed 1 February-1 April, Sunday lunch, Monday, Tuesday, Wednesday - Saturday lunch

INVERNESS

Highland – Regional map n° **17**–C2

⫛○ Chez Roux   ⫷ 🛖 ♿ 🆎 🅿

FRENCH · MINIMALIST XX This smart, modern restaurant comprises three rooms with well-spaced polished tables; their walls hung with photos of the Roux broth-ers' early days. French-inspired menu offers robust, flavoursome dishes and ser-vice is professional. Bedrooms are stylish – some come with hot tubs or saunas.

Menu £40 (lunch)/43 – Carte £43/66

Rocpool Reserve Hotel, 14 Culduthel Road ⊠ IV2 4AG – ℰ 01463 240089 –
www.rocpool.com

🍴 **Rocpool**

MODERN BRITISH · FRIENDLY XX Well-run restaurant on the banks of the River Ness; close to town and popular with the locals. Wide-ranging menus offer vibrant, colourful dishes that are full of flavour and have a distinct Mediterranean edge. The room has a modish feel.

Menu £18 (lunch)/20 – Carte £28/53

1 Ness Walk ⊠ IV3 5NE – ℰ 01463 717274 –
www.rocpoolrestaurant.com – Closed Sunday

ISLAY (ISLE OF) Argyll and Bute – Regional map n° **16**–A3

Port Ellen

🍴 **18** Ⓝ

GRILLS · BRASSERIE XX This bright, airy restaurant sits on the first floor of The Machrie hotel, overlooking the 18th hole of the golf links. The glass-fronted terrace offers some lovely views of the bay and is the perfect spot at sunset. Grill-based cooking includes mature steaks from the island. Finish with a local whisky.

Menu £20 (lunch)/26 – Carte £30/45

The Machrie Hotel, Port Ellen ⊠ PA42 7AN – ℰ 01496 302310 –
www.themachrie.com

🏚 **The Machrie** Ⓝ

HISTORIC · CONTEMPORARY The imposing Machrie hotel sits within Islay's dunes, close to some fabulous beaches, and boasts a pristinely kept golf links designed by Willie Campbell in 1891. The traditional façade conceals a cosy interior with a contemporary style. Unwind in the lovely cinema or the great spa.

47 rooms � – ♦♦ £120/270 – 4 suites

Port Ellen ⊠ PA42 7AN – ℰ 01496 302310 –
www.campbellgrayhotels.com

🍴 **18** – See restaurant listing

KELSO
The Scottish Borders – Regional map n° **15**–D2

at Ednam North: 2. 25 mi on B6461 – Regional map n° **15**–D2

🏠 **Edenwater House**

HISTORIC · CLASSIC This delightful house is run by an equally charming couple. Relax in the lovely garden beside the stream or in one of the antique-filled lounges. Bedrooms are individually styled and tastefully furnished. Dine on traditional dishes overlooking the garden or more informally in the wine cellar.

4 rooms – ♦♦ £120/140

⊠ TD5 7QL – ℰ 01573 224070 –
www.edenwaterhouse.co.uk – Closed 30 November-31 March

KILBERRY – Argyll and Bute ➜ See Kintyre (Peninsula)

KILDRUMMY
Aberdeenshire – Regional map n° **16**–D1

🍴 **Kildrummy Inn**

MODERN BRITISH · COSY X Cosy up beside the fire and sample some local whiskies before enjoying dinner in the intimate dining room or bright conservatory. Dishes are original and creative and the sourcing of ingredients is given top priority. Bedrooms have country views and are popular with fishermen, as the inn has a private beat.

Menu £22 (lunch), £29/37

⊠ AB33 8QS – ℰ 01975 571227 –
www.kildrummyinn.co.uk – Closed 1-31 January, Monday lunch, Tuesday,
Wednesday - Saturday lunch

KILLIECRANKIE – Perth and Kinross → See Pitlochry

KINGUSSIE
Highland – Regional map n° **17**–C3

🍴 **Cross at Kingussie**

MODERN BRITISH · INTIMATE XX 19C tweed mill in four acres of wooded grounds. Enjoy drinks on the terrace or in the first floor lounge then head to the dining room with its low beams, antiques and ornaments. Attractively presented cooking is modern British/Scottish. Pleasant, pine-furnished bedrooms have thoughtful extras.

Menu £30 (lunch), £55/65

Tweed Mill Brae, Ardbroilach Road ✉ *PH21 1LB* – ✆ *01540 661166 – www.thecross.co.uk – Closed 5 January-10 February, Sunday, Monday, Tuesday lunch*

KINTILLO – Perth and Kinross → See Perth

KINTYRE (PENINSULA) Argyll and Bute – Regional map n° **16**–A3

Kilberry – Regional map n° **16**–A3

🏵 **Kilberry Inn**

REGIONAL CUISINE · INN X A remotely set former croft house whose striking red roof stands out against whitewashed walls. Inside you'll find wooden beams, open fires and a mix of bare and linen-laid tables. Classic dishes are crafted from carefully sourced local produce and meat and fish are smoked in-house. Modern bedrooms are named after nearby islands; one has an outdoor hot tub.

Specialities: Fennel, chive and celeriac soup with onion seed breadsticks. Braised lamb with juniper, wild mushrooms and roast squash. Cardamom and rosewater ice cream with pistachio tuiles.

Carte £26/41

✉ *PA29 6YD* – ✆ *01880 770223 – www.kilberryinn.com – Closed 15 December-13 March, Sunday lunch, Monday, Tuesday - Saturday lunch*

KIRKBEAN
Dumfries and Galloway – Regional map n° **15**–C3

🍴 **Cavens**

TRADITIONAL CUISINE · ELEGANT XX Start with drinks by the fire in the sitting room of this 18C country house, before dinner in the elegant candle-lit dining room. Classic dishes are full of flavour and prepared with care. Seafood is from the Dumfriesshire coast, meat from the surrounding fields and game from the local hills.

Menu £35

Cavens Hotel, Cavens Hotel ✉ *DG2 8AA* – ✆ *01387 880234 – www.cavens.com – Closed 1 December-27 February, Sunday - Saturday lunch*

🏠 **Cavens**

COUNTRY HOUSE · PERSONALISED A wealthy merchant built this attractive country house in 1752. It sits in an enviable position, with views stretching over 20 acres to the Solway Firth, and the owners warmly welcome you with afternoon tea beside the fire in the elegant lounge. Choose from a luxurious 'Estate' or simpler 'Country' bedroom.

6 rooms ⌚ – 👫 £200/330

✉ *DG2 8AA* – ✆ *01387 880234 – www.cavens.com – Closed 1 December-27 February*

🍴 **Cavens** – See restaurant listing

KYLESKU

Highland – Regional map n° **17**–C1

ⅺ○ **Kylesku** ⇔ ≤ 🏠

REGIONAL CUISINE · PUB ⅺ Breathtaking views of Loch Glendhu and the mountains make this 17C coaching inn an essential stop-off point. Fresh seafood is the way to go, with langoustines and mussels landed 200 yards away. Relax on the waterside terrace then make for one of the cosy bedrooms; two have balconies with panoramic views.

Carte £24/50

✉ IV27 4HW – ☎ 01971 502231 – www.kyleskuhotel.co.uk –
Closed 25 November-7 February

LEITH – City of Edinburgh → See Edinburgh

LINLITHGOW

West Lothian – Regional map n° **15**–C1

ⅺ○ **Champany Inn** 🍸 ⇔ 🅿

MEATS AND GRILLS · INTIMATE ⅺⅺ Set in a collection of whitewashed cottages – the traditional restaurant was once a flour mill, hence its unusual shape. The focus is on meat and wine, with 21-day aged Aberdeen Angus beef a speciality. There's also a well-stocked wine shop, a more laid-back 'Chop and Ale House' and 16 tartan-themed bedrooms.

Menu £28 (lunch)/45 – Carte £48/75

Champany ✉ EH49 7LU – ☎ 01506 834532 – www.champany.com – Closed Sunday, Saturday lunch

LOCHALINE

Highland – Regional map n° **17**–B3

ⅺ○ **Whitehouse** 🏠 🅿

MODERN BRITISH · COSY ⅺ Adjoining the village shop in a remote coastal hamlet is this unassuming restaurant decorated with nautical memorabilia. A blackboard lists 6 constantly evolving dishes – at lunch pick 2, at dinner 4 or 6. Dishes are accomplished and beautifully presented; ingredients are from the surrounding estate and coast.

Menu £43 (lunch)/56

✉ PA80 5XT – ☎ 01967 421777 – www.thewhitehouserestaurant.co.uk –
Closed 1 January-7 April, Sunday, Monday

MELROSE

The Scottish Borders – Regional map n° **15**–D2

🏵 **Provender** 🆕 ♿

MODERN BRITISH · CONTEMPORARY DÉCOR ⅺ This stylish, family-run restaurant is a perfect match for this lovely Borders town. The chef – a local – spent time in London before returning home, and his time with Pierre Koffmann shows through in well-executed, classically based dishes which deliver plenty of flavour and represent great value for money.

Specialities: Hand-dived scallops with black pudding, apple caramel and bitter leaves. Perthshire venison haunch with braised shoulder pie, confit onions and plum sauce. Priorwood apple soufflé with apple crumble ice cream.

Carte £24/36

West End House, High Street ✉ TD6 9RU – ☎ 01896 820319 –
www.provendermelrose.com – Closed 23 December-20 January, Sunday, Monday -
Tuesday dinner

at Gattonside North: 2 mi by B6374 on B6360

🍴○ **The Hoebridge**

MODERN CUISINE · DESIGN X The self-taught chef grew up in the village and worked here as a youngster. After time spent in NYC, he and his partner moved back to run this simple, stylish restaurant. Monthly menus showcase carefully prepared local ingredients in flavour-packed, internationally influenced dishes.

Carte £30/41

Hoebridge Road East ⊠ TD6 9LZ – ℰ 01896 823082 – www.thehoebridge.com – Closed Sunday, Monday, Tuesday, Wednesday - Saturday lunch

🍴○ **Seasons**

TRADITIONAL CUISINE · NEIGHBOURHOOD X A small Borders village plays host to this friendly restaurant. As its name suggests, cooking is driven by the seasons – the chef works closely with local suppliers and even forages himself. Alongside the ever-changing blackboards they offer a menu of perennial favourites such as chargrilled steaks.

Menu £20 – Carte £22/42

Main Street ⊠ TD6 9NP – ℰ 01896 823217 – www.seasonsborders.co.uk – Closed 1-23 January, Monday, Tuesday, Wednesday - Thursday lunch

MOFFAT

Dumfries and Galloway – Regional map n° **15**-C2

🍴○ **Lime Tree** 🅿

TRADITIONAL CUISINE · COSY XX This small restaurant sits within the old drawing room of a hotel and comes with a feature fireplace, attractive marquetry and a bay window looking down the valley. The short seasonal menu features classically based dishes with rich flavours. Service is friendly and engaging.

Menu £25/31

Hartfell House Hotel, Hartfell Crescent ⊠ DG10 9AL – ℰ 01683 220153 – www.hartfellhouse.co.uk – Closed 1-16 January, 11-22 October, Sunday, Monday, Tuesday - Saturday lunch

MULL (ISLE OF) Argyll and Bute – Regional map n° **16**-A2

Craignure

🍴○ **Pennygate Lodge**

MODERN BRITISH · CONTEMPORARY DÉCOR XX Those arriving on the island by ferry should head straight for this 19C former manse on the shore-side. Island ingredients features on an ambitious modern menu where dishes deliver contrasting flavours, textures and temperatures. Most of the stylishly understated bedrooms have a sea view.

Carte £32/52

Pennygate Lodge ⊠ PA65 6AY – ℰ 01680 812333 – www.pennygatelodge.scot – Closed 25 December-31 January, Monday, Tuesday

Fionnphort

🍴○ **Ninth Wave** 🅿

SEAFOOD · CONTEMPORARY DÉCOR XX This remotely set modern restaurant started life as a crofter's bothy and both the décor and the cooking reflect the owners' travels. Seafood plays a key role, with crab, lobster and other shellfish caught by Mr Lamont himself.

Menu £48/68

Bruach Mhor ⊠ PA66 6BL – ℰ 01681 700757 – www.ninthwaverestaurant.co.uk – Closed 8 October-1 May, Sunday lunch, Monday, Tuesday, Wednesday - Saturday lunch

SCOTLAND

Tiroran – Regional map n° **16**–A2

⌂ Tiroran House

COUNTRY HOUSE · PERSONALISED The beautiful drive over to this remotely set, romantic Victorian house is all part of the charm. Stylish, antique-furnished bedrooms come with plenty of extras and two lovely lounges look out over 56 acres of grounds which lead down to a loch. Dine from a concise à la carte in the conservatory or cosy dining room. The welcoming owner encourages a house party atmosphere.

10 rooms ⌂ – ♥♥ £195/235
✉ PA69 6ES – ✆ 01681 705232 – www.tiroran.com

Tobermory

○ Highland Cottage

TRADITIONAL CUISINE · FAMILY ✕✕ Long-standing, personally run restaurant in an intimate cottage, where family antiques and knick-knacks abound. Classical linen-laid dining room and a homely lounge. Traditional daily menu with a seafood base features plenty of local produce. Bedrooms are snug and individually styled.

Menu £50

Breadalbane Street ✉ PA75 6PD – ✆ 01688 302030 – www.highlandcottage.co.uk – Closed 7 October-14 March, Sunday - Saturday lunch

NAIRN

Highland – Regional map n° **17**–D2

○ Kale Yard Cafe

MODERN CUISINE · RUSTIC ✕ Situated within the walled gardens of the Boath House hotel is this cosy, homely café offering coffee, cakes and a short seasonal menu of flavour-packed dishes which utilise produce from the garden. Cooking is hearty, wholesome and honest. Sourdough pizzas from the wood-fired oven are a feature.

Carte £18/32

Boath House Hotel, Auldearn ✉ IV12 5TE – ✆ 01667 452233 – www.boath-house.com – Closed Monday, Tuesday

⌂ Boath House

HISTORIC · PERSONALISED An elegant 1825 neo-classical mansion framed by Corinthian columns. Inside it cleverly blends original features with contemporary furnishings. Bedrooms are elegant and intimate and some have views over the lake. Dine on traditional Scottish fare in the restaurant or hearty honest dishes in the café.

9 rooms ⌂ – ♥♥ £190/365
Auldearn ✉ IV12 5TE – ✆ 01667 454896 – www.boath-house.com
○ **Kale Yard Cafe** – See restaurant listing

NEWPORT-ON-TAY

Fife – Regional map n° **16**–C2

○ The Newport

MODERN BRITISH · COSY ✕ The Newport is the place to come for cheery, up-beat service in a great waterside location. It serves colourful, imaginative small plates themed around 'land', 'sea', 'garden' and 'ground', which display modern techniques and are presented in an attractive manner.

Menu £55 – Carte £41/58

1 High Street ✉ DD6 8AB – ✆ 01382 541449 – www.thenewportrestaurant.co.uk – Closed 1-9 January, 24-26 December, Sunday dinner, Monday, Tuesday lunch

NORTH QUEENSFERRY

Fife – Regional map n° **16**–C3

⅋○ **The Wee Restaurant**

TRADITIONAL CUISINE · BISTRO ⅃ A likeable quarry-floored restaurant in the shadow of the Forth Rail Bridge; as its name suggests, it's small and cosy. Fresh Scottish ingredients are served in neatly presented, classical combinations. Lunch represents the best value.

Menu £22 – Carte £37/47

17 Main Street ⊠ KY11 1JT –
✆ 01383 616263 – www.theweerestaurant.co.uk –
Closed Sunday, Monday

OBAN

Argyll and Bute – Regional map n° **16**–B2

⅋○ **Baab**

MEDITERRANEAN CUISINE · SIMPLE ⅃⅃ Housed within the Perle Oban and following the hotel's minimalist style is Baab, a Mediterranean-focused restaurant offering great views out to sea. Cooking is flavour-packed: authentic Turkish dishes form the core of menu, with some Greek and Italian influences thrown in.

Carte £15/30

Perle Oban Hotel, Station Square ⊠ PA34 5RT –
✆ 01631 707130 – www.perleoban.com –
Closed Sunday - Saturday lunch

⅋○ **Etive**

MODERN BRITISH · COLOURFUL ⅃⅃ Run by two passionate young owners, this brightly coloured restaurant takes its name from the loch where the business was originally located. Ingredients from the Scottish land and lochs underpin dishes that are carefully cooked, full of flavour and classically based with a subtle modernity.

Menu £38/50

43 Stevenson Street ⊠ PA34 5NA –
✆ 01631 564899 – www.etiverestaurant.co.uk –
Closed Sunday lunch, Monday, Tuesday, Wednesday - Saturday lunch

🏠 **Perle Oban** ⓝ

CHAIN · CONTEMPORARY The Perle Oban sits in a great spot not far from the ferry terminal and close to both the harbourside restaurants and town centre shops. It's a smart place with a modern, minimalist feel and spacious bedrooms – it's worth paying extra for one at the front to take in the wonderful view.

59 rooms – ♟ £99/225 – ⌖ £15 – 2 suites

Station Square ⊠ PA34 5RT –
✆ 01631 700301 – www.perleoban.com
⅋○ **Baab** – See restaurant listing

ONICH

Highland – Regional map n° **17**–B3

⅋○ **Lochleven Seafood Café**

SEAFOOD · SIMPLE ⅃ This laid-back seafood restaurant is part of a family business that started with the neighbouring shellfish shop. It's superbly set on the loch shore and offers stunning water and mountain views. West Coast fish is listed on the blackboards and shellfish comes from the seawater tanks next door.

Carte £21/48

Lochleven ⊠ PH33 6SA –
✆ 01855 821048 – www.lochlevenseafoodcafe.co.uk –
Closed 31 October-15 March

PEAT INN

Fife – Regional map n° **16**–D2

⚛ **The Peat Inn** (Geoffrey Smeddle)

CLASSIC CUISINE · CONTEMPORARY DÉCOR XXX Geoffrey and Katherine Smeddle and their truly charming team might have run this contemporary restaurant since 2006 but the history contained within the walls of this whitewashed inn extends all the way back to the 18C. Start with a drink in the smart lounge, which still boasts its original log fireplace, then head through to one of the three elegant dining rooms – be sure to ask for a table overlooking the floodlit gardens.

Geoffrey brought with him a wealth of experience from his time at the Café Royal and Orrery in London, so there's little wonder that his accomplished cooking is underpinned by classical French techniques. Flavours are bold and harmonious and although some subtle modern touches are in evidence, this is cooking that is free from frippery. Dishes use the finest produce from the region, be that vegetables from the garden or seafood from Anstruther.

Stylish, split-level bedrooms have plenty of extras and breakfast is served in your room.

Specialities: Scallop carpaccio with langoustines, oyster mousse and herb dressing. Loin of roe deer, venison haggis, smoked onion and yoghurt purée. Délice of Scottish 'bean to bar' chocolate, coffee mousse and whisky ice cream.

Menu £25 (lunch), £58/78 – Carte £37/68 ·

✉ KY15 5LH – ☎ 01334 840206 – www.thepeatinn.co.uk – Closed 1-9 January, 22-26 December, Sunday, Monday

PEEBLES

The Scottish Borders – Regional map n° **15**–C2

☲ **Osso**

MODERN CUISINE · FRIENDLY X By day, this is a bustling coffee shop serving a bewildering array of light snacks and daily specials; come evening, it transforms into a more sophisticated restaurant offering a regularly changing menu of tasty, well-presented dishes. Service is friendly and attentive.

Carte £23/41

Innerleithen Road ✉ EH45 8BA – ☎ 01721 724477 – www.ossorestaurant.com – Closed Sunday - Monday dinner

PERTH

Perth and Kinross – Regional map n° **16**–C2

☲ **Deans**

TRADITIONAL CUISINE · CLASSIC DÉCOR XX Two brothers run this classically furnished restaurant on the site of the old Theatre Royal – and pay homage to its past by playing old movies in the comfy bar. Traditional menus offer plenty of choice and include a good value set selection; be sure to try their signature cheese soufflé.

Menu £19/24 – Carte £30/45

77-79 Kinnoull Street ✉ PH1 5EZ – ☎ 01738 643377 – www.letseatperth.co.uk – Closed 6-21 January, Monday, Tuesday

at Kintillo Southeast: 4. 5 mi off A912

☲ **Roost**

MODERN BRITISH · INTIMATE X At the heart of the village you'll find this converted stone hen house: it's a sweet little place with a pleasingly laid-back atmosphere and is run by a passionate owner. Carefully prepared dishes have a classical base and focus on ingredients' natural flavours. The wood-fired steaks are a hit.

Menu £28 (lunch) – Carte £25/61

Forgandenny Road ✉ PH2 9AZ – ☎ 01738 812111 – www.theroostrestaurant.co.uk – Closed 25 December-3 January, Sunday dinner, Monday, Tuesday

PITLOCHRY

Perth and Kinross – Regional map n° **16**–C2

⊫○ **Sandemans**

MODERN CUISINE · INTIMATE XxX Named after the family who built the castle, this intimate wood-panelled hotel restaurant comprises just 9 tables and is the perfect place for celebrating an occasion. The tasting menu showcases top Scottish ingredients from mountain to coast, and cooking has an elaborate modern style.

Menu £85

Fonab Castle Hotel, Foss Road ⊠ *PH16 5ND* – ℰ *01796 470140 –*
www.fonabcastlehotel.com – Closed Sunday, Monday, Tuesday - Saturday lunch

⊫○ **Fonab Brasserie**

MODERN CUISINE · BRASSERIE XX Start with a cocktail in the 'Bar in the Air', then head back down to the chic hotel restaurant and terrace with their panoramic loch views. The concise menu offers modern classics and grills. Service is friendly.

Menu £30 (lunch) – Carte £37/55

Fonab Castle Hotel, Foss Road ⊠ *PH16 5ND* – ℰ *01796 470140 –*
www.fonabcastlehotel.com

🏰 **Fonab Castle**

HISTORIC · GRAND LUXURY This impressive 19C baronial castle sits on the lochside and affords superb views over the water to the hills beyond. Bedrooms in the main building have fittingly traditional undertones. The luxurious Woodland Lodges are more modern and come with terraces or balconies.

42 rooms ⊠ – †† £195/345 – 4 suites
Foss Road ⊠ *PH16 5ND* – ℰ *01796 470140 – www.fonabcastlehotel.com*
⊫○ **Fonab Brasserie** · ⊫○ **Sandemans** – See restaurant listing

---

at Killiecrankie Northwest: 4 mi by A924 and B8019 on B8079 –

Regional map n° **16**–C2

🏠 **Killiecrankie**

TRADITIONAL · CLASSIC A whitewashed house built in 1840 and set in 4. 5 acres of mature rhododendron-filled grounds. There's a charming open-fired lounge, a snug bar and well-appointed bedrooms which offer everything you might want. Choose between light suppers and traditional dinners. Service is excellent.

10 rooms ⊠ – †† £295/360
⊠ *PH16 5LG* – ℰ *01796 473220 – www.killiecrankiehotel.co.uk –*
Closed 3 January-20 March

PORT ELLEN – Argyll and Bute ➜ See Islay (Isle of)

PORTPATRICK

Dumfries and Galloway – Regional map n° **15**–A3

⊫○ **Knockinaam Lodge** ⊗ ≤ ⊊ **P**

MODERN CUISINE · INTIMATE XX Located within a delightful lodge, a traditionally furnished, smartly dressed dining room with delightful sea views. Modern set menus evolve with the seasons and offer good quality produce, often from their own gardens. The Drummore lobster ravioli has become something of a speciality.

Menu £40 (lunch)/73

Knockinaam Lodge Hotel ⊠ *DG9 9AD* – ℰ *01776 810471 –*
www.knockinaamlodge.com

🏠 Knockinaam Lodge

COUNTRY HOUSE · PERSONALISED A charming former hunting lodge in a delightfully secluded private cove, with gardens leading down to the sea. Sample their malts in the wood-panelled bar or relax in the country house style drawing room. Bedrooms are furnished with antiques – 'Churchill' boasts a century-old bathtub. Service is detailed.

10 rooms ⌁ – ♀♀ £310/460

✉ DG9 9AD – ☎ 01776 810471 – www.knockinaamlodge.com

🍴 **Knockinaam Lodge** – See restaurant listing

PORT APPIN

Argyll and Bute – Regional map n° **16**–B2

🍴 Airds

MODERN BRITISH · ELEGANT XX An intimate, candlelit country house restaurant with superb loch and mountain views. Classic dishes are presented with a modern edge and much use is made of west coast seafood and local meats, with game a highlight. Don't miss the Mallaig crab or the scallops – and ensure you ask for a table in the window!

Menu £60 – Carte £24/49

Airds Hotel ✉ PA38 4DF – ☎ 01631 730236 – www.airds-hotel.com –
Closed 24 November-12 December

🏠 Airds

LUXURY · PERSONALISED A characterful former ferryman's cottage fronted by colourful planters and offering lovely loch and mountain views. Two sumptuous, antique-furnished sitting rooms are filled with fresh flowers and magazines. Bedrooms offer understated luxury – ask for one at the front with a waterside view.

11 rooms ⌁ – ♀♀ £295/525

✉ PA38 4DF – ☎ 01631 730236 – www.airds-hotel.com –
Closed 24 November-12 December

🍴 **Airds** – See restaurant listing

PORTREE – Highland ➜ See Skye (Isle of)

ST ANDREWS

Fife – Regional map n° **16**–D2

🍴 Adamson

MEATS AND GRILLS · BRASSERIE XX A stylish brasserie and cocktail bar set within a house once owned by eminent photographer John Adamson (it was also later the town's Post Office). The wide-ranging menu of tasty dishes includes steaks from the Josper grill.

Menu £17 (lunch) – Carte £25/46

127 South Street ✉ KY16 9UH – ☎ 01334 479191 – www.theadamson.com

🍴 Haar

MODERN CUISINE · CONTEMPORARY DÉCOR XX The lively cocktail bar provides a contrast to the intimate dining room at this restaurant – its name a reference to the cold sea fog from the chef-owner's home on the East Coast. His travels inform the menu: combinations are simple but techniques and flavours show skill and understanding.

Menu £30 (lunch)/65 – Carte £38/56

Kinnettles Hotel, 127 North Street ✉ KY16 9AG – ☎ 01334 473387 –
www.haarrestaurant.com – Closed Monday

🍴○ Seafood Ristorante

SEAFOOD · DESIGN XX This striking glass cube offers commanding bay views and is perfect for watching the setting sun. The experienced team bring a modern Italian twist to seafood: choose from cicchetti, fish platters, hearty stews and homemade pastas.

Menu £25 (lunch)/30 – Carte £25/65

Bruce Embankment, The Scores ✉ *KY16 9AB –* ☎ *01334 479475 –*
www.theseafoodristorante.com – Closed 1-2 January, 6-16 January,
24-26 December

🍴○ Grange Inn

TRADITIONAL CUISINE · COSY X A former pub, atop a hill, with great views over the bay. Have an aperitif beside the fire, then head for the stone-walled restaurant with its huge stag's head. The experienced chef serves a menu of tasty, well-prepared classics.

Menu £21 (lunch), £42/55

Grange Road ✉ *KY16 8LJ –* ☎ *01334 472670 – www.thegrangeinn.com –*
Closed 1-29 January, Sunday, Monday

🏨 Old Course H. Golf Resort & Spa
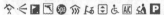

LUXURY · CLASSIC A vast resort hotel with an impressive spa, set on a world-famous golf course overlooking the bay. Luxurious guest areas have a subtle Scottish theme and bedrooms are chic, sumptuous and well-equipped. Try their bespoke ales in the Jigger Inn then dine on modern-classics, Josper-grilled meats or seafood.

144 rooms 🛏 – 👫 £292/427 – 15 suites

Old Station Road ✉ *KY16 9SP –* ☎ *01334 474371 – www.oldcoursehotel.co.uk*

SANQUHAR
Dumfries and Galloway – Regional map n° **15**–B2

🍴○ Blackaddie House

MODERN BRITISH · TRADITIONAL XX A stone-built former manse with 16C origins, set by the river. Lunch offers good value classics, while dinner is more elaborate and features original modern cooking; ingredients are luxurious and dishes are well-presented. Bedrooms are named after game birds – ask for 'Grouse', which has a four-poster bed.

Menu £62/80

Blackaddie Road ✉ *DG4 6JJ –* ☎ *01659 50270 – www.blackaddiehotel.co.uk*

SKYE (ISLE OF)

Highland – Regional map n° **17**-B2

Top tips!

Skye is the largest island of the Inner Hebrides and stretches almost 50 miles north to south, although nowhere is more than 5 miles from the sea. It has a rich history – from Norse invasion to Jacobite uprisings – and is famed for its abundant wildlife; keep an eye out for red deer, golden eagles, dolphins and even whales.

With its rugged landscapes, breathtaking scenery and views over other islands in the archipelago, it's a paradise for walkers, whether wandering the tiny fishing villages or scaling the Cuillin mountains. If appreciating the view over a quick tipple is more your thing, then pay a visit to the Talisker or Torabhaig whisky distilleries.

When exploring the top of the island, enjoy fresh local seafood at the UK's most northerly Michelin Star **Loch Bay**, set in a charming waterside hamlet; if you're in the south, stay at **Kinloch Lodge**, owned by one of the island's oldest clans.

zhuzhu/iStock

COLBOST
Highland

🍴◯ Three Chimneys & The House Over-By

MODERN CUISINE · RUSTIC XX Immaculately kept crofter's cottage in a stunning lochside setting. Contemporary art hangs on exposed stone walls in the characterful low-beamed dining rooms. Modern Scottish menus showcase good regional ingredients and seafood from local waters is a highlight. Spacious, split-level bedrooms are stylishly understated and the residents' lounge has a great outlook.

Menu £42 (lunch), £69/98

✉ IV55 8ZT – ℰ 01470 511258 – www.threechimneys.co.uk –
Closed 15 December-16 January

EDINBANE
Highland

🍴◯ Edinbane Lodge ⓝ

MODERN CUISINE · CONTEMPORARY DÉCOR XX It may have had a modern makeover but Edinbane Lodge dates back to 1543 and is reputedly the oldest inn on Skye. The chef, a native, loves to use the best island and Highland produce, and the imaginative multi-course dinner menu shows a range of techniques. Bedrooms have a subtle Scottish theme.

Menu £32 (lunch)/65

Old Dunvegan Road ✉ IV51 9PW – ℰ 01470 582217 – www.edinbanelodge.com –
Closed Sunday dinner, Monday, Tuesday, Wednesday - Thursday lunch

🍴◯ Edinbane Inn

TRADITIONAL CUISINE · PUB X This traditional-looking former farmhouse is the perfect place to cosy up by the fire on a misty night. Choose a pub favourite or one of the appealing specials. Come on a Wednesday, Friday or Sunday for the popular music sessions, then stay the night in one of the comfy, cosy, Scottish-themed bedrooms.

Carte £27/36

✉ IV51 9PW – ℰ 01470 582414 – www.edinbaneinn.co.uk –
Closed 2 January-10 February

ELGOL
Highland

🍴◯ Coruisk House

CLASSIC CUISINE · SIMPLE X This traditional croft house sits in a remote spot on the west of the island and offers superb views over the hills to the mountains; it's very personally run and seats just 12. Skye produce features in a concise selection of fresh, flavoursome, daily changing dishes. Bedrooms share the stunning outlook.

Menu £49

✉ IV49 9BL – ℰ 01471 866330 – www.coruiskhouse.com –
Closed 1 November-1 March, Sunday - Saturday lunch

PORTREE
Highland

🍴◯ Scorrybreac

MODERN CUISINE · BISTRO X Simply furnished restaurant with distant mountain views and just 8 tables; named after the chef's parents' house, where he ran his first pop-up. Creative modern cooking uses meats from the hills and seafood from the harbour below.

Menu £42

7 Bosville Terrace ✉ IV51 9DG – ℰ 01478 612069 – www.scorrybreac.com –
Closed Monday, Tuesday - Saturday lunch

SLEAT
Highland – Regional map n° **17**–B2

Kinloch Lodge

COUNTRY HOUSE · CLASSIC With a loch in front and heather-strewn moorland behind, this 17C hunting lodge affords fantastic panoramic views. Antique-filled lounges are hung with photos of the Macdonald clan, and bedrooms are cosy and contemporary. Menus mix traditional Scottish elements with some more unusual flavour combinations.

19 rooms – ♥♥ £180/380 – 3 suites

✉ IV43 8QY – ℰ 01471 833214 – www.kinloch-lodge.co.uk

STEIN
Highland – Regional map n° **17**–B2

✿ Loch Bay (Michael Smith)

MODERN CUISINE · SIMPLE X This pretty little crofter's cottage sits in an idyllic spot on the Waternish Peninsula and offers commanding views across the countryside to the mountains. It's a pleasingly simple place, with a wood-burning stove, Harris Tweed covered chairs and a snug feel. Chef-owner Michael Smith worked in several classical restaurants before taking it over in 2016 with his wife, Laurence, who looks after the service.

Skilfully prepared, intensely flavoured Scottish dishes come with French overtones and cooking is well-judged, with minimal seasoning bringing out only the most natural of flavours. Lunch sees a fairly classical menu while dinner is more complex; go for the Loch Bay Seafood tasting menu. Stein started life as a fishing village and to this day, the cold, pure Scottish waters which surround it provide the UK's best habitat for fish and shellfish.

Specialities: Smoky shellfish bree. Loch Bay bourride. Clootie dumpling with whisky cream and custard.

Menu £34 (lunch), £44/70

1-2 Macleods Terrace ✉ *IV55 8GA* – ℰ *01470 592235 –*
www.lochbay-restaurant.co.uk – Closed 3-10 August, 31 December-1 March, Sunday dinner-Tuesday lunch, Saturday lunch

SLEAT - Highland ➜ See Skye (Isle of)

SPEAN BRIDGE
Highland – Regional map n° **17**–C3

⑩ Russell's at Smiddy House

TRADITIONAL BRITISH · INTIMATE XX A friendly, passionately run restaurant with a smart ornament-filled lounge and two intimate dining rooms. Tasty dishes showcase local ingredients, with old Scottish recipes taking on a modern style. Cosy, well-equipped bedrooms come with comfy beds and fine linens; homemade cake is served on arrival.

Menu £35/40

Roybridge Road ✉ *PH34 4EU* – ℰ *01397 712335 – www.smiddyhouse.com –*
Closed 4 January-6 February, 7-26 March, 27 October-12 December, Sunday lunch, Monday, Tuesday - Saturday lunch

STEIN - Highland ➜ See Skye (Isle of)

ST MONANS
Fife – Regional map n° **16**–D2

🍴○ **Craig Millar @ 16 West End**

MODERN CUISINE · INTIMATE ХХ A former pub with an attractive interior and a small terrace; most of the tables afford superb harbour views. Good quality ingredients underpin refined, attractively presented dishes which are full of flavour. 'Land' and 'Sea' tasting menus feature at dinner.

Menu £28 (lunch), £45/65

16 West End ⊠ KY10 2BX – ℰ 01333 730327 –
www.16westend.com – Closed 1-15 January, 8-15 October, Sunday dinner, Monday, Tuesday

STONEHAVEN

Aberdeenshire – Regional map n° **16**–D2

🍴○ **Tolbooth**

SEAFOOD · RUSTIC ХХ Stonehaven's oldest building, located on the harbourside: formerly a store, a sheriff's courthouse and a prison. Classic dishes have modern touches; the emphasis being on local seafood, with langoustine and crab the highlights.

Menu £22 (lunch)/35 – Carte £30/50

Old Pier, Harbour ⊠ AB39 2JU – ℰ 01569 762287 –
www.tolbooth-restaurant.co.uk – Closed 1-23 January, Monday

STRACHUR

Argyll and Bute – Regional map n° **16**–B2

🍴○ **Inver**

MODERN BRITISH · VINTAGE Х A former crofter's cottage and boat store in a beautifully isolated spot on the loch shore. Enjoy afternoon tea sitting in sheepskin covered armchairs in the lounge-bar or take in the view from the vintage-style restaurant, where concise modern menus are led by the finest local and foraged ingredients. Luxurious bothy-style bedrooms in the grounds complete the picture.

Menu £55 – Carte £25/45

Strathlaclan ⊠ PA27 8BU – ℰ 01369 860537 –
www.inverrestaurant.co.uk – Closed 3-16 January, 14-27 December, Monday, Tuesday

TAIN

Highland – Regional map n° **17**–D2

at Cadboll Southeast: 8. 5 mi by A9 and B9165 (Portmahomack rd) off Hilton rd –
Regional map n° **17**–D2

🏠 **Glenmorangie House**

TRADITIONAL · CLASSIC Charming 17C house owned by the famous distillery. Antiques, hand-crafted local furnishings and open peat fires feature; there's even a small whisky tasting room. Luxuriously appointed bedrooms show good attention to detail; those in the courtyard cottages are suites. Communal dining from a classical Scottish menu.

9 rooms ⌫ – 🛉🛉 £310/465

Fearn ⊠ IV20 1XP – ℰ 01862 871671 –
www.theglenmorangiehouse.com – Closed 1-31 January

TIRORAN – Argyll and Bute → See Mull (Isle of)

TOBERMORY – Argyll and Bute → See Mull (Isle of)

TORRIDON

Highland – Regional map n° **17**–B2

 Torridon ⟨icons⟩

TRADITIONAL · CLASSIC A former hunting lodge built in 1887 by Lord Lovelace; set in 40 acres and offering superb loch and mountain views. The delightful interior features wood-panelling, ornate ceilings and a peat fire – and luxury reigns in the bedrooms. The whisky bar has over 350 malts; the dining room offers a modern daily menu.

18 rooms – ♙♙ £175/285 – 2 suites

✉ *IV22 2EY* – ✆ *01445 791242* – *www.thetorridon.com* –
Closed 2 January-6 February

TURNBERRY

South Ayrshire – Regional map n° **15**–A2

Trump Turnberry ⟨icons⟩

GRAND LUXURY · ELEGANT An iconic Edwardian hotel overlooking Ailsa Golf Course. Elegant guest areas have been restored to their former glory and many of the luxurious bedrooms boast enviable sea views; for something different, stay in the lighthouse. Formal 1906 offers classic dishes, while Duel in the Sun serves brasserie-style fare.

204 rooms – ♙♙ £200/550 – ☲ £30 – 5 suites

✉ *KA26 9LT* – ✆ *01655 331000* – *www.trumphotels.com/turnberry*

WALKERBURN

The Scottish Borders – Regional map n° **15**–C2

Windlestraw ⟨icons⟩

LUXURY · ELEGANT An attractive Arts and Crafts property built in 1906, boasting original fireplaces, ornate plaster ceilings and great valley views. Guest areas include a plush lounge and comfy bar and the bedrooms have been stylishly modernised. The attractive wood-panelled dining room offers a daily changing tasting menu.

6 rooms ☲ – ♙♙ £200/290

✉ *EH43 6AA* – ✆ *01896 870636* – *www.windlestraw.co.uk* –
Closed 15 December-1 March

JoeDunckley/iStock

WALES

It may only be 170 miles from north to south, but Wales contains great swathes of beauty, such as the dark and craggy heights of Snowdonia's ninety mountain peaks, the rolling sandstone bluffs of the Brecon Beacons, and Pembrokeshire's tantalising golden beaches. Bottle-nosed dolphins love it here too, arriving each summer at New Quay in Cardigan Bay. Highlights abound: formidable Harlech Castle dominates its coast, Bala Lake has a railway that steams along its gentle shores, and a metropolitan vibe can be found in the capital, Cardiff, home to the Principality Stadium and the National Assembly.

Wales is a country which teems with great raw ingredients and modern-day chefs are employing these to their utmost potential; from succulent slices of Spring lamb farmed on the lush mountains and valleys, through to the humblest of cockles; from satisfying native Welsh Black cattle through to abundant Anglesey oysters, delicious Welsh cheeses and the edible seaweed found on the shores of the Gower and known as laverbread.

- Michelin Road maps n° 501, 502 and 713

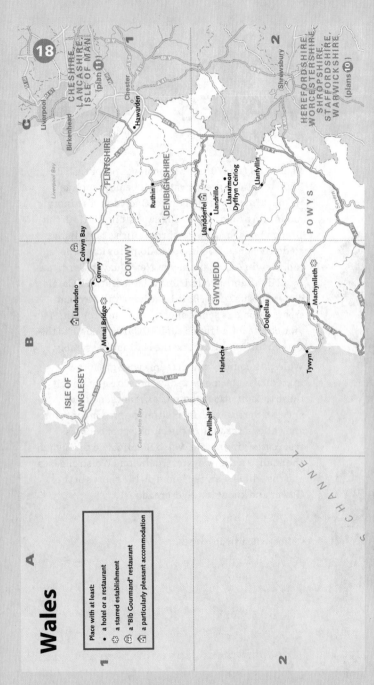

Wales

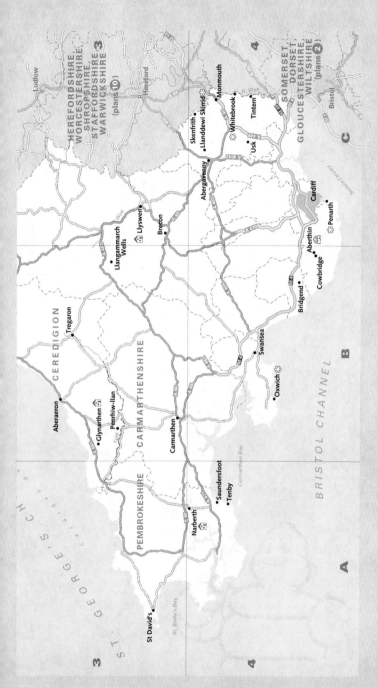

NOT TO BE MISSED

STARRED RESTAURANTS

High quality cooking...

BIB GOURMAND RESTAURANTS 🅶

Good quality, good value cooking

ZOOMING IN...

... ON THE MICHELIN STARS: THE WHITEBROOK, MONMOUTHSHIRE

Chris Harrod took over The Whitebrook in 2013. It won a Michelin Star in 2014 and has retained it every year since. In 2018, chef-owner Chris was one of the four winners of the Great British Menu; his tea and cake dish forming part of the final banquet menu which celebrated 70 years of the NHS. So what is it about his cooking that has helped Chris retain a Star for so many years? And was he pleased with his decision to have taken part in the long-running television programme?

Michelin / Whitebrook

The Whitebrook's location in the Wye Valley is all-important when it comes to the food they serve. Chris describes his cooking as 'environment-led' and likes to source the very best produce available in Monmouthshire – preferably from within 12 miles of the restaurant. The area is blessed with an abundance of excellent producers; Huntsham Farm, for example, provides the pork for Chris' superb dish of suckling pig, with which he won the regional heats of the Great British Menu. He is passionate about

The Whitebrook

using foraged herbs and plants and these are a feature of almost every dish on his menu. He's also keen to promote local Welsh vineyards on his wine list.

The 7 course tasting menu constantly evolves and offers creative, original dishes with well-judged contrasts of texture and flavour. Chris' plates are an object lesson in restraint; this is a chef who knows when to hold back and avoid gilding the lily. The Michelin Inspectors also like the fact that Chris' dishes are all his own, and not a replication of anyone else's style.

Reaching the finals of the Great British Menu seems to have increased Chris' confidence, although this unassuming man remains modest about his success. He feels that taking part in the show was one of the most challenging things he's ever done – citing the time constraints and the judge's criticism as particularly difficult to deal with – but he is glad he took part, as it was useful to discuss dishes and techniques with the other chefs and allowed him to take a fresh look at some of his own dishes.

Business has quadrupled since his appearance on the show – which is impressive, particularly given its location off the beaten track – and Chris feels that people have a better understanding of who he is and what he's trying to achieve at The Whitebrook. People are still talking now about the dishes he made on the show – like the couple who revealed to Chris that they'd come all the way from New York to try his food, having seen him on TV.

ABERAERON • ABER AERON
Ceredigion – Regional map n° **18**-B3

‡○ Harbourmaster

SEAFOOD · PUB ⌶ A vibrant blue inn with a New England style bar-lounge, a modern dining room and lovely harbour views. Choose between an extensive bar menu and a more ambitious evening set price menu. Smart bedrooms, split between the house and a nearby cottage, are brightly decorated and well-equipped; some have terraces.

Menu £35 – Carte £21/35

Quay Parade ⊠ *SA46 0BA – ℰ 01545 570755 – www.harbour-master.com*

ABERGAVENNY • Y - FENNI
Monmouthshire – Regional map n° **18**-C4

⌂ Angel

HISTORIC · PERSONALISED The original Georgian character of this family-run coaching inn remains but it now comes with bold colours and modern furnishings. Contemporary bedrooms display thoughtful touches. Cosy up by the fire in the rustic bar, enjoy afternoon tea in the Wedgewood Room and dine on modern classics in the Oak Room.

35 rooms ⌂ – ♥♥ £109/249 – 5 suites

15 Cross Street ⊠ *NP7 5EN – ℰ 01873 857121 – www.angelabergavenny.com*

at Cross Ash Northeast: 8. 25 mi on B4521

‡○ 1861

TRADITIONAL BRITISH · COSY ⌶⌶ This remotely located, part-timbered former pub is now a cosy restaurant named after the year it was built. Staunchly classical dishes are skilfully prepared and full of flavour, and much of the fruit and veg is grown by the owner's father. An adjacent new-build houses the bedrooms.

Menu £30 (lunch)/39 – Carte £35/50

⊠ *NP7 8PB – ℰ 01873 821297 – www.18-61.co.uk – Closed 26 December-10 January, Sunday dinner, Monday*

at Llanddewi Skirrid Northeast: 3. 25 mi on B4521 – Regional map n° **18**-C4

✿ Walnut Tree (Shaun Hill)

MODERN BRITISH · COSY ⌶ The Walnut Tree is an iconic restaurant with an illustrious past. It was under the leadership of Franco Taruschio for 30 years and now experienced chef Shaun Hill has also broken the two decade mark.

Located in the rolling borderlands of Wales, it's a destination kind of a place, but the loyal band of regulars is testament to the quality of the cooking. The understated bistro-style room suits the food perfectly, as does the relaxed, friendly service.

Shaun's experience and travels inform his cooking, so expect a classical French base with the occasional influence from India or North Africa. Sauces are a strength – ensure you've plenty of buttermilk bread to mop them up – and the flavours just work: this is unfussy, bold, robust cooking using first class ingredients. The fixed price lunch offers good value but for greater choice head for the twice daily changing à la carte. The concise wine list is a connoisseur's selection; look out for modest mark-ups on some of the finer bottles.

Specialities: Scallops with lentil and coriander sauce. Middle White pork loin with black pudding and cromesqui. Orange and almond cake with milk ice cream.

Menu £30 (lunch) – Carte £38/61

⊠ *NP7 8AW – ℰ 01873 852797 – www.thewalnuttreeinn.com – Closed Sunday, Monday*

ABERTHIN
The Vale of Glamorgan – Regional map n° **18**-B4

526

ⓐ Hare & Hounds 🚲 ♿ 🏠 🅿️

TRADITIONAL CUISINE · PUB ✕ The chef's passionate desire to make this 300 year old pub the most seasonal in Wales is laudable. Menus change twice daily and produce is from his 3 acre allotment and family farms; he also hunts and forages, so expect plenty of game, mushrooms and hedgerow berries. Cooking is unfussy yet bursts with flavour.

Specialities: Crispy pig's cheek with chicory, mustard and pickled apple. Roast and braised Torgelly Farm lamb, mint sauce. Forced rhubarb soufflé.

Menu £25 (lunch) – Carte £26/38

Maendy Road ⊠ CF71 7LG – ℰ 01446 774892 – www.hareandhoundsaberthin.com – Closed Sunday dinner, Monday, Tuesday

ANGLESEY (ISLE OF) •

SIR YNYS MÔN Isle of Anglesey – Regional map n° **18**–B1

BEAUMARIS

🏠 The Bull 🔲 ♿ 🛁

INN · PERSONALISED Keep an eye out for the old water clock and ducking stool in the bar of this characterful 1670s coaching inn. Bedrooms in the main house are named after Dickens characters and are traditional; those in the townhouse are more modern and colourful. The former stables house the restaurant.

25 rooms – 🛏️ £100/175

Castle Street ⊠ LL58 8AP – ℰ 01248 810329 – www.bullsheadinn.co.uk

MENAI BRIDGE – Regional map n° **18**–B1

⁜ Sosban & The Old Butchers (Stephen Stevens)

MODERN CUISINE · INTIMATE ✕ Just over Thomas Telford's suspension bridge you'll find this brightly painted restaurant. It's an appealing place, where wooden floors and chairs draped with sheepskins provide a rustic feel, and Welsh slate walls and hand-painted tiles depicting animals point back to its butcher's shop days.

Owners Stephen and Bethan Stevens are the only staff, so to keep standards high, they wisely limit the number of services they do in a week – along with the number of guests they serve each evening.

A well-balanced surprise menu offers boldly flavoured modern dishes with original, personal touches, which demonstrate an innate understanding of cooking techniques and flavour combinations. You'll find a wealth of ingredients from Anglesey and North Wales and the occasional playful note, and the portion sizes and the pacing of the courses are spot on. Service, from Bethan, is warm and friendly and she puts everyone at ease.

Specialities: Dandelion and truffle. Lamb tail with tomato, smoked ricotta and ramsons. Rhubarb with wood sorrel, liquorice and yoghurt.

Menu £50 (lunch)/94

Trinity House, 1a High Street ⊠ LL59 5EE – ℰ 01248 208131 – www.sosbanandtheoldbutchers.com – Closed 1-31 January, 6-26 April, 24-30 August, Sunday-Wednesday, Thursday-Friday lunch

NEWBOROUGH

⁜◯ Marram Grass 🚲 🅿️

MODERN BRITISH · RUSTIC ✕ The flavour-packed dishes at this homely restaurant reflect the area perfectly. They utilise the best of local produce – including laver and Menai mussels – along with home-grown herbs and salad and home-bred chickens and pigs. One brother is in the kitchen and the other looks after the service.

Menu £50 – Carte £32/51

White Lodge ⊠ LL61 6RS – ℰ 01248 440077 – www.themarramgrass.com – Closed Monday, Tuesday, Wednesday

BEAUMARIS – Isle of Anglesey ➜ See Anglesey (Isle of)

BRECON
Powys – Regional map n° **18**–C3

ⅰ○ **Felin Fach Griffin**　　　　　　🏀 ⇦ 🛏 🍴 ⅙ 🅿

MODERN BRITISH · PUB ⅹ Warmth and character abound at this traditional pub. Relax on a sofa beside the fire with a pint of local beer, then head for the Library or Snug, where daily menus feature regional ingredients, including fruit and veg from their garden. Cosy bedrooms come with good extras and are dog friendly.

Menu £24 (lunch)/29 – Carte £25/33

Felin Fach ⊠ LD3 0UB – ℰ 01874 620111 – www.felinfachgriffin.co.uk

BRIDGEND • PEN - Y - BONT
Bridgend – Regional map n° **18**–B4

at Lalestone

ⅰ○ **Leicester's** ⓝ　　　　　　　　🛏 ⇧ 🅿

MODERN BRITISH · HISTORIC ⅹⅹ The atmospheric 16C house in which this restaurant sits was a gift from Elizabeth I to the Earl of Leicester. Pared-back modern cooking uses just a handful of the best local ingredients in each dish and well-judged combinations deliver depth, despite their apparent simplicity.

Menu £22 (lunch) – Carte £27/40

Great House Hotel, High Street ⊠ CF32 0HP – ℰ 01656 657644 – www.great-house-laleston.co.uk – Closed Sunday dinner

529

CARDIFF

Cardiff – Regional map n° **18**-C4

Top tips!

Wales's capital combines a rich history with top events venues and a lively cultural scene. The 2,000 year old castle sits in the centre of the city, just a stone's throw from Welsh rugby's imposing Principality Stadium, and nearby are all manner of restaurants. The Potted Pig offers pleasingly relaxed subterranean dining, while at the other end of the scale, the impressive 19C Park House is an occasion destination.

Cardiff Bay – once a huge port – has been redeveloped and is now home to the National Assembly, the Wales Millennium Centre and Mermaid Quay; a thriving area of houses, shops, restaurants and bars. Be sure to visit the old Coal Exchange to take in its impressive architecture.

The suburb of Pontcanna has also become something of a foodie hotspot, with the eclectic **'Bully's'** and celebrity-chef-owned **Heaneys** sitting alongside neighbourhood bistro **milkwood** and sweet Spanish eatery **La Cuina**.

Restaurants

⅋○ **Park House** ⅋⅋ ⌂

MODERN CUISINE · ELEGANT ✗✗ A striking building overlooking Gorsedd Gardens and designed by William Burgess in the late 1800s; the oak-panelled dining room has a formal air. Ambitious cooking has a strong French base and is flamboyant in its execution. Each dish is matched with a wine from an impressive global list.

Menu £40 (lunch), £55/75 – Carte £45/62

Town plan C1-p – *20 Park Place* ✉ *CF10 3DQ* – ✆ *029 2022 4343* – *www.parkhouserestaurant.co.uk* – *Closed Sunday dinner, Monday*

⅋○ **Asador 44** ⅋⅋ ⅋

SPANISH · ELEGANT ✗✗ A dark, moody restaurant divided into lots of different areas; the best spots are overlooking the Asador, the cheese room or the glass-fronted wine cave. The menu focuses on charcoal-cooked meats which are imported from Galicia, and the wine list is almost exclusively Spanish.

Menu £20 (lunch) – Carte £25/60

Town plan C1-a – *14 Quay Street* ✉ *CF10 1EA* – ✆ *029 2002 0039* – *www.asador44.co.uk* – *Closed Sunday dinner, Monday*

⅋○ **Heaneys** ⓝ ⌂ ⅋ ⒶⒸ 💡 ⅋○ Ⓟ

MODERN CUISINE · NEIGHBOURHOOD ✗✗ Well-known chef Tommy Heaney runs this stylishly laid-back suburban restaurant. Start with a cocktail in the bar then select 2-3 small plates from the menu. These are modern and pared-back in style, with some sophisticated contrasts; the Welsh lamb with sea vegetables is a signature dish.

Menu £21 (lunch) – Carte £21/35

Town plan A1-g – *6-10 Romilly Crescent* ✉ *CF11 9NR* – ✆ *029 2034 1264* – *www.heaneyscardiff.co.uk* – *Closed Sunday dinner, Monday*

⅋○ **Purple Poppadom** ⒶⒸ 💺

INDIAN · COLOURFUL ✗✗ Enter via the glass door between the shop fronts and head up to the smart room with bold purple décor. Classic combinations are cooked in a refined modern style and given a personal twist; the seafood dishes are popular.

Menu £18/48 – Carte £25/35

Town plan B1-n – *185a Cowbridge Road East (1st Floor)* ✉ *CF11 9AJ* – ✆ *029 2022 0026* – *www.purplepoppadom.com* – *Closed Monday, Tuesday - Saturday lunch*

⅋○ **'Bully's** ⒶⒸ

FRENCH · NEIGHBOURHOOD ✗ A proudly and passionately run neighbourhood bistro decorated with an eclectic array of memorabilia. Menus have a French base but also display some British and Mediterranean touches.

Menu £21 (lunch) – Carte £33/49

Town plan A1-x – *5 Romilly Crescent* ✉ *CF11 9NP* – ✆ *029 2022 1905* – *www.bullysrestaurant.co.uk* – *Closed 24-27 December, Monday, Tuesday*

⅋○ **La Cuina** ⒶⒸ 💺

SPANISH · BISTRO ✗ Catalonia comes to Cardiff at this sweet, passionately run neighbourhood restaurant. It is simply styled, with Welsh art on the walls and Spanish pottery for sale. Authentic cooking uses imported ingredients and mixes tapas with more substantial dishes. The unique wine list is Catalonian too.

Carte £23/46

Town plan B1-v – *11 Kings Road* ✉ *CF11 9BZ* – ✆ *029 2019 0265* – *www.lacuina.co.uk* – *Closed Sunday, Monday, Tuesday*

CARDIFF

SWANSEA

Cardiff Rd
Pencisely Rd
Pen-Hill Rd
Clive Rd
Llanfair
Conway Rd
Severn
Pontcanna St
Plasturton Av
Cathedral Rd
Sophia
Walk
North

THOMPSON'S PARK
Romilly Rd
Grove
King's
Wyndham Rd
Ryder
St
Cathedral Rd
Bute Park

Pembroke Rd
Egerton St
Radnor Rd
Glamorgan St
Llandaff Rd
Severn
Talbot St
Hamilton
TAFF

Nottingham St
Glasgow St
Grosvenor St
Intern St
Brunswick St
Cowbridge Rd East
Market Rd East
Leckwith Rd
Theobald Rd
Beda Rd
Rd
Wellington St
Neville
Cowbridge Rd East
De Burgh St
Clare St
Cathedral Rd
Lower Brook St
Cardiff Arms Pa

Lansdowne Rd
Lansdowne Av East
Broad
Atlas Rd
Ninian
Albert St
Wells
St
Park
Craddock
Rd
Tudor
Despenser St
Fitzhamon Embankment
Clare Lane
Tudor Lane

Broadstairs Rd
Broadhaven
Leckwith Av
St
Leckwith
Powderham
Drive
Wedmore Rd
Stafford Rd
Allerton St
Cornwall
Coveny
North
Rd
Mardy St
Pendyris
St

Lawrenny Av
Leckwith Rd
Barkey Wilson Way
Sloper Rd
Virgil St
Clive St
Penarth
Rd
Redlaver St
Stockland St
Penhevad St
Pentrebane St
Llanmaes St
Fagan's St

Leckwith Rd
Hadfield Rd
Whittle Rd
Bessemer Close
Hadfield Rd
Sloper Rd
Penarth Rd
Clive St
Colpora

Lon Cwrt Ynyston
Grangetown Link
Brindley Rd
Coleridge Rd
Freeman Rd Park
Stadium Close
Clive St
Ferry Rd
Holmesdale
Lane
Channel
Clive
Ferry Rd
Ferry Rd

LECKWITH WOODS

CATHAYS Miskin St

Park Pl

CATHAYS
PARK
ALEXANDRA
GARDENS

National Museum
Cardiff

City
Hall

Gorsedd
Gardens

Law
Courts

rdiff
stle

Greyfriars Rd

Military
Museums

Castle
St

St John's
Church

Central Market

llennium
tadium

CARDIFF
CENTRAL

CALLAGHAN
SQUARE

Bute
East
Dock

CARDIFF
BAY

BUTETOWN

Coal
Exchange

Techniquest

Pierhead
Building

Y Senedd

Wales Millennium
Centre

MERMAID
QUAY

Norwegian
Church

CARDIFF BAY

HAMADRYAD
PARK

Windsor Esplanade

CARDIFF BAY
WETLANDS RESERVE

TAFF

ROATH
DOCK

QUEEN
ALEXANDRA DOCK

ⅼ○ Heathcock

MODERN CUISINE · NEIGHBOURHOOD ⅹ Sister to the Hare & Hounds in Aberthin, this modest neighbourhood pub shares its passion for sourcing great ingredients and preparing them with care. The enticing menu changes daily and the delicious homemade breads are a highlight. Wash these down with a local beer or two.

Carte £25/38

Off plan – *58 Bridge Street* ✉ *CF5 2EN –*
⌕ *029 2115 2290 – www.heathcockcardiff.com – Closed Sunday dinner, Monday*

ⅼ○ milkwood   AC

MODERN BRITISH · NEIGHBOURHOOD ⅹ Two experienced chefs own this sweet neighbourhood bistro – a small, bijoux place with friendly service and a laid-back vibe. They cook the type of food they themselves like to eat. Neatly prepared, modern British dishes have clearly defined flavours and tick all the local, seasonal boxes.

Menu £19 (lunch) – Carte £31/37

Town plan A1-d – *83 Pontcanna Street* ✉ *CF11 9HS –*
⌕ *029 2023 2226 – www.milkwoodcardiff.com – Closed Sunday dinner, Monday, Tuesday lunch*

ⅼ○ Potted Pig   🍷 ♿ AC

TRADITIONAL BRITISH · RUSTIC ⅹ Atmospheric restaurant in a stripped back former bank vault, with brick walls, barrel ceilings and a utilitarian feel. Lesser-known products and cuts of meat are used in robust, tasty dishes. The gin cocktails are a speciality.

Menu £17 (lunch) – Carte £26/47

Town plan C1-s – *27 High Street* ✉ *CF10 1PU –*
⌕ *029 2022 4817 – www.thepottedpig.com – Closed 23 December-6 January, Sunday dinner*

Hotels

🏠 Voco St David's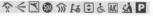

BUSINESS · MINIMALIST This striking waterfront hotel affords lovely 360° views. Good-sized bedrooms have a slightly funky, minimalist feel and most have balconies with sea or quay outlooks. The large spa features seawater pools and a dry floatation tank, and the stylish Australasian-themed brasserie has a superb terrace.

142 rooms ⌑ – 👫 £99/599 – 12 suites

Town plan D3-a – *Havannah Street, Cardiff Bay* ✉ *CF10 5SD –*
⌕ *029 2045 4045 – www.stdavids.vocohotels.com*

CARMARTHEN
Carmarthenshire – Regional map n° **18**-B3

at Nantgaredig East: 5 mi by A4300 on A4310

ⅼ○ Y Polyn   🍴 🛏 ⌂ P

TRADITIONAL BRITISH · PUB ⅹ This well-regarded country pub sits on an old drovers' road and is run by an experienced team. Sit downstairs and admire the tin tiles on the ceiling while supping a locally brewed ale. Confidently prepared local ingredients feature in hearty, daily changing British dishes. The great value lunch menu is hard to resist.

Menu £21 (lunch)/40 – Carte £34/47

✉ *SA32 7LH –* ⌕ *01267 290000 – www.ypolyn.co.uk – Closed Sunday dinner, Monday*

COLWYN BAY • BAE COLWYN

Conwy – Regional map n° **18**–B1

🏵 **Bryn Williams at Porth Eirias**   ⇐ 🏠 ♿ 𝖠𝖢

MODERN BRITISH · DESIGN 𝖷 If you're looking for a relaxed, friendly environment, this striking beachside brasserie with faux industrial styling and blue leather banquettes is the place to come. The owner is proud of his Welsh roots and it shows on the menu. Cooking is pleasingly unfussy and local seafood is to the fore.
Specialities: Salt and pepper squid. Smoked haddock with crushed potatoes, poached egg and butter sauce. Baked Alaska.
Menu £21 (lunch) – Carte £26/37
The Promenade ⊠ *LL29 8HH –* ℰ *01492 577525 – www.portheirias.com –*
Closed Sunday - Tuesday dinner

CONWY

Conwy – Regional map n° **18**–B1

⍩○ **Signatures**   🏠 ♿ 𝖠𝖢 🅿

MODERN CUISINE · DESIGN 𝖷𝖷 Stylish restaurant with elegantly laid tables and a well-versed team – set in a holiday park close to the sea. Brasserie classics and snacks at lunch; more inventive, modern choices at dinner including the chef's 'Signature' dishes.
Carte £27/44
Aberconwy Resort and Spa ⊠ *LL32 8GA –* ℰ *01492 583513 –*
www.signaturesrestaurant.co.uk –
Closed Monday, Tuesday

COWBRIDGE • Y BONT FAEN

The Vale of Glamorgan – Regional map n° **18**–B4

⍩○ **Arboreal**

MEDITERRANEAN CUISINE · RUSTIC 𝖷 There's a lively vibe at this friendly little all-day bar and café, which is run with passion by its hands-on owners. Come for coffee and cake, a light lunch (offering the likes of flatbreads and homemade pies) or a more substantial dinner. Subtle Mediterranean influences reflect the owners' heritage.
Carte £24/36
68 Eastgate ⊠ *CF71 7AB –* ℰ *01446 775093 – www.arboreal.uk.com –*
Closed Monday

CROSS ASH – Monmouthshire ➜ See Abergavenny

DOLGELLAU

Gwynedd – Regional map n° **18**–B2

at Llanelltyd Northwest: 2. 25 mi by A470 on A496

⍩○ **Mawddach**   ⇐ 🏠 🅿

MEDITERRANEAN CUISINE · RUSTIC 𝖷𝖷 Stylish barn conversion run by two brothers and set on the family farm. The terrace and dining room offer superb views of the mountains and estuary. Unfussy Italian-influenced cooking features lamb from the farm and veg from the garden.
Carte £28/40
⊠ *LL40 2TA –* ℰ *01341 421752 – www.mawddach.com –*
Closed 1-31 January, Sunday dinner-Wednesday, Thursday-Saturday lunch

GLYNARTHEN
Ceredigion – Regional map n° **18**–B3

Penbontbren

MANOR HOUSE · COSY A collection of enthusiastically run converted farm buildings, surrounded by an attractive landscaped garden and 35 acres of rolling countryside. Bedrooms are spacious, stylish and well-equipped and most have a sitting room and patio. The boldly decorated stone-walled breakfast room offers an extensive menu.

6 rooms – 🛏 £110/140

✉ SA44 6PE – ☎ 01239 810248 – www.penbontbren.com

HARLECH
Gwynedd – Regional map n° **18**–B2

🍽 Castle Cottage

CLASSIC CUISINE · COSY 🍴 Sweet little cottage behind Harlech Castle, with a cosy yet surprisingly contemporary interior. Start with canapés and an aperitif in the lounge; the table is yours for the evening. Classical menus feature local produce and modern touches. Spacious bedrooms have smart bathrooms and stunning mountain views.

Menu £39/45

Pen Llech ✉ LL46 2YL – ☎ 01766 780479 – www.castlecottageharlech.co.uk – Closed 27 October-18 November, 22 December-4 January, Sunday, Monday, Tuesday, Wednesday - Saturday lunch

HAWARDEN · PENARLÂG
Flintshire – Regional map n° **18**–C1

🍽 Old Grocery ⓝ

MODERN CUISINE · FRIENDLY 🍴 Its name gives a clue as to its previous life but this lovingly restored building has been a restaurant for a while – the owner first worked here back in 1993. Cooking blends local ingredients with international flavours to create some imaginative dishes. Linger awhile in the cosy cocktail bar.

Menu £18/22 – Carte £30/44

68 The Highway ✉ CH5 3DH – ☎ 01244 952989 – www.theoldgrocery.co.uk – Closed 1-14 January, 1-7 June, 1-7 October, Sunday dinner, Monday, Tuesday, Wednesday - Saturday lunch

🍽 Glynne Arms

TRADITIONAL BRITISH · PUB 🍴 This 200 year old coaching inn sits opposite Hawarden Castle and is owned by the descendants of PM William Gladstone. Choose from a range of small and large Mediterranean-inspired dishes, with steaks from the Estate and the odd pub classic thrown in. They host regular event nights and even a cheese club.

Carte £25/45

3 Glynne Way ✉ CH5 3NS – ☎ 01244 569988 – www.theglynnearms.co.uk

LALESTONE – Bridgend ➔ See Bridgend

LLANARMON DYFFRYN CEIRIOG
Wrexham – Regional map n° **18**–C2

🍽 Hand at Llanarmon

TRADITIONAL CUISINE · PUB 🍴 Nestled at the head of the valley, the Hand is ideally located for those who like to get away from it all. Choose a 'Hand Classic' such as mushrooms on toast or pick from 'Today's Choices' like Welsh lamb with black pudding. Bedrooms are modern and there's even a hot tub, a sauna and a small treatment facility.

Carte £30/43

✉ LL20 7LD – ☎ 01691 600666 – www.thehandhotel.co.uk

LLANDDERFEL
Gwynedd – Regional map n° **18**–C2

ⅰ○ **Palé Hall**

MODERN BRITISH · ELEGANT XX Sit in the main room of this hotel restaurant to take in lovely views of the garden. Choose from the classically based à la carte or go for the more creative tasting menus with well-matched wine flights. Dishes are attractively presented.

Menu £25 (lunch), £50/70 – Carte £25/70
Palé Hall Hotel, Palé Estate ✉ *LL23 7PS –*
℘ 01678 530285 – www.palehall.co.uk

Palé Hall

COUNTRY HOUSE · PERSONALISED An impressive Victorian house built for industrialist Henry Robertson; its 1920s hydroelectric generator still heats the water. Spacious, elegant rooms are beautifully appointed and come with wonderful marquetry, antique furnishings and ornate design features. Service is detailed yet discreet.

18 rooms ⌸ – ♥♥ £295/860 – 1 suite
Palé Estate ✉ *LL23 7PS – ℘ 01678 530285 – www.palehall.co.uk*
ⅰ○ **Palé Hall** – See restaurant listing

LLANDDEWI SKIRRID – Monmouthshire → See Abergavenny

LLANDRILLO
Denbighshire – Regional map n° **18**–C2

ⅰ○ **Tyddyn Llan**

CLASSIC CUISINE · ELEGANT XX A husband and wife team own this attractive slate-built former shooting lodge in a pretty valley location. Start with a drink in an antique-filled lounge or on the terrace overlooking the lovely gardens. Wide-ranging menus mix classic and modern dishes and the wine list is appealing. Bedrooms are elegant.

Menu £42 (lunch)/70
✉ *LL21 0ST – ℘ 01490 440264 – www.tyddynllan.co.uk – Closed 12-31 January, Monday, Tuesday, Wednesday - Thursday lunch*

LLANDUDNO
Conwy – Regional map n° **18**–B1

Bodysgallen Hall

COUNTRY HOUSE · HISTORIC A stunning National Trust owned country house in 200 acres of delightful parkland, with a 13C tower and a superb outlook to the mountains beyond. It has a welcoming open-fired hall, a characterful wood-panelled lounge and antique-furnished bedrooms – some in cottages and some affording splendid Snowdon views. The grand dining room serves modern versions of classic dishes.

31 rooms – ♥♥ £200/490 – 21 suites
Royal Welsh Way ✉ *LL30 1RS –*
℘ 01492 584466 – www.bodysgallen.com

LLANELLTYD – Gwynedd → See Dolgellau

LLANFYLLIN

Powys - Regional map n° **18**-C2

Seeds

REGIONAL CUISINE • RUSTIC X Converted 16C red-brick cottages in a sleepy village; run with pride by a friendly husband and wife team. Cosy, pine-furnished room with an old range and a country kitchen feel. Unfussy, classical dishes and comforting homemade desserts.

Menu £23/30 - Carte £18/35

5 Penybryn Cottages, High Street ✉ SY22 5AP - ✆ 01691 648604 - Closed 2 January-1 February, 3-20 June, Sunday, Monday, Tuesday, Wednesday, Thursday lunch

LLANGAMMARCH WELLS

Powys - Regional map n° **18**-B3

Lake Country House and Spa

COUNTRY HOUSE • TRADITIONAL Extended, part-timbered 19C country house in 50 acres of mature gardens and parkland, with a pond, a lake and a river. Comfortable lounges and well-appointed bedrooms with antiques and extras; some are set in a lodge. The impressive spa overlooks the river. Breakfast is in the orangery; the elegant restaurant is perfect for a classical, candlelit dinner.

32 rooms ☕ - 👥 £145/280 - 8 suites

✉ LD4 4BS - ✆ 01591 620202 - www.lakecountryhouse.co.uk

LLYSWEN

Powys - Regional map n° **18**-C3

Llangoed Hall

HISTORIC • PERSONALISED A fine country house beside the River Wye, redesigned by Sir Clough Williams-Ellis in 1910 and restored by the late Sir Bernard Ashley. Delightful sitting rooms and sumptuous bedrooms feature rich fabrics, mullioned windows and antiques; the impressive art collection includes pieces by Whistler. Ambitious modern cooking is led by what's fresh in the kitchen garden.

23 rooms - 👥 £117/770

✉ LD3 0YP - ✆ 01874 754525 - www.llangoedhall.com

MACHYNLLETH

Powys - Regional map n° **18**-B2

Ynyshir (Gareth Ward)

CREATIVE • MINIMALIST XX On the edge of the RSPB nature reserve you'll find this part-Georgian country house with pretty formal gardens, chic bedrooms and an intimate, Scandic-style restaurant. Sheepskins cover the chairs in the rustic bar and the dining room features handmade wooden tables and an open kitchen.

Chef Gareth Ward developed his classical skills at Hambleton Hall and also learnt to think outside of the box working with Sat Bains. The multi-course set menu is served as a series of mouthfuls which pack a punch; it features a huge array of Asian ingredients and foraging and fermenting play their part. He also has a strong passion for Welsh Wagyu beef, which he buys in whole and then matures; digital counters tell the amount time the beasts have been aged - some for over 200 days - and he renders the fat and uses it in soups, spreads and even fudge.

Specialities: 'Not French onion soup'. Welsh Wagyu rib with shiitake and seaweed. Tiramisu.

Menu £180/220

Eglwysfach ✉ SY20 8TA - ✆ 01654 781209 - www.ynyshir.co.uk - Closed 12-21 April, 23 August-8 September, 15 December-7 January, Sunday, Monday, Tuesday, Wednesday - Friday lunch

MENAI BRIDGE - Isle of Anglesey → See Anglesey (Isle of)

MONMOUTH • TREFYNWY

Monmouthshire – Regional map n° **18**–C4

🕯️○ **Stonemill**   🛖 ⓖ 🅿️

REGIONAL CUISINE · RUSTIC 🍴 An attractive 16C cider mill plays host to this rustic restaurant with characterful exposed timbers and an old millstone on display at its centre. Good value set menus offer hearty, classically based dishes, with steaks and sides offered at a supplement. Be sure to start with the home-made bread.

Menu £25 (lunch)/32

Rockfield ⊠ NP25 5SW – ℰ 01600 716273 – www.thestonemill.co.uk –
Closed 1-15 January, Sunday dinner, Monday, Tuesday

at Whitebrook South: 8. 25 mi by A466 – Regional map n° **18**–C4

🕸️ **The Whitebrook** (Chris Harrod)   ⇔ ⓘ🟢 🅿️

CREATIVE BRITISH · INTIMATE 🍴🍴 With its remote valley setting, this is the very definition of a destination restaurant. The isolated woodland feel is all part of its inherent charm and the nature-inspired colour theme and rustic wood flooring suit the location down to a tee.

Modest chef-owner Chris Harrod describes his cooking as 'environment-led' and 90% of his ingredients come from within 12 miles, with a focus on the kitchen garden and local artisan growers. Rare bread meats are from just down the road; seafood is from the Cornish day boats and foraging plays a key part too, with cress, chervil, pennywort, wild garlic and sea vegetables plucked from the valley and the estuary. Descriptions are concise but there's more complexity to the understated modern dishes than first appears.

Bedrooms come in muted tones and follow the theme of bringing nature inside.

Specialities: Asparagus with hogweed, maritime pine and Tintern mead. Suckling pig with caramelised celeriac, pear and sorrel. Violet parfait with blueberries, rose and lemon thyme.

Menu £42 (lunch)/85

⊠ NP25 4TX – ℰ 01600 860254 – www.thewhitebrook.co.uk – Closed 5-17 January,
Monday, Tuesday, Wednesday lunch

NANTGAREDIG – Carmarthenshire → See Carmarthen

NARBERTH

Pembrokeshire – Regional map n° **18**–A4

🕯️○ **Fernery**   ⟨♨ 🛖 ⓖ 🅿️

MODERN CUISINE · ELEGANT 🍴🍴 With a stylish nature-inspired colour scheme and potted ferns dotted about the place, this intimate hotel restaurant brings the outside in. Elaborate, eye-catchingly presented dishes are full of freshness and natural flavours. Some ingredients are from their own garden and the rest are proudly Welsh.

Menu £79/94

Grove Hotel, Molleston ⊠ SA67 8BX – ℰ 01834 860915 –
www.grovenarberth.co.uk – Closed Sunday - Saturday lunch

🏠 **Grove**   🎆 🐾 ⇐ ⟨♨ 🅿️

HISTORIC · PERSONALISED Set in 26 beautiful, rural acres, the Grove comprises a 17C property with Victorian and Arts & Crafts additions, a 15C longhouse and several cottages. Inside, original features blend with designer furnishings; bedrooms are luxurious and service is delightful. The Artisan Rooms, with its wicker wall, serves modern classics. The Fernery offers more sophisticated fare.

26 rooms ⌧ – 🛏️ £160/390 – 7 suites

Molleston ⊠ SA67 8BX – ℰ 01834 860915 – www.thegrovenarberth.co.uk
🕯️○ **Fernery** – See restaurant listing

NEWBOROUGH – Isle of Anglesey → See ANGLESEY (Isle of)

OXWICH

Swansea – Regional map n° **18**–B4

✿ Beach House ← 🏡 ⅃ 🏵 **P**

MODERN CUISINE · DESIGN XX The former coal store of the Penrice Estate is a charming stone building set beside the beach and its lovely terrace affords panoramic views across the bay. The room has a nautical, New England style and local art and pottery feature.

Head Chef Hywel Griffith was born in north Wales and worked at several high profile restaurants around Britain before settling back in Wales again – only this time on the edge of Swansea. A fluent Welsh-speaker, his menus are written in English and Welsh, and his passion for supporting local farmers and fishermen is admirable.

Sophisticated classical cooking is Hywel's focus and his dishes are recognisable and reassuring in their construction. Contrasts in flavours are well-judged and the various components work together to put the spotlight on the main ingredient. His bara brith soufflé is something of a signature.

Specialities: Loin of roe deer with parsley, pickled beetroot and blueberries. Tandoori roasted halibut with crispy pork shoulder, yoghurt, onion and coriander. Bara brith soufflé with tea ice cream.

Menu £ 30 (lunch) – Carte £ 45/60

Oxwich Beach ⊠ *SA3 1LS – ℰ 01792 390965 – www.beachhouseoxwich.co.uk – Closed 9-22 January, Monday, Tuesday*

PENARTH

The Vale of Glamorgan – Regional map n° **18**–C4

✿ James Sommerin ⇦ ← ⅃ ⟳

MODERN CUISINE · CONTEMPORARY DÉCOR XX James Sommerin's eponymous restaurant sits on the esplanade, affording panoramic views over the Severn Estuary, and provides the perfect vantage point when the sun sets over the sea. The room has a contemporary feel courtesy of a striking pale blue banquette, modern artwork and a large window looking into the kitchen; and the laid-back style of the place is refreshing.

The à la carte is supplemented on a Friday and Saturday by two surprise tasting menus. Terse descriptions belie the skill that goes into the well-crafted modern dishes, which exhibit a well-judged blend of complementary textures and flavours, and are delivered to the table by the chefs themselves. First-rate Welsh ingredients are to the fore and the bold, flavoursome sauces are a highlight. If you're planning to stay the night, be sure to book one of the spacious bedrooms facing the estuary.

Specialities: Liquid pea ravioli with serrano ham, sage and parmesan. Monkfish with salsify, kale and coriander. Pineapple, coconut, rum and lime.

Menu £ 75/95 – Carte £ 38/52

The Esplanade ⊠ *CF64 3AU – ℰ 029 2070 6559 – www.jamessommerinrestaurant.co.uk – Closed Monday, Tuesday*

ⅈO Mint and Mustard ⅃ AC 🏵

INDIAN · NEIGHBOURHOOD X A fashionable high street restaurant with bare brick walls, wooden shutters and pictures of Indian scenes. The menu features an extensive selection of vibrantly flavoured curries, tandoor dishes and Keralan-inspired recipes, which range in style from traditional to modern.

Carte £ 20/35

33-34 Windsor Terrace ⊠ *CF64 1AB – ℰ 029 2070 0500 – www.mintandmustard.com*

PENRHIW-LLAN

Ceredigion – Regional map n° **18**–B3

⊗ **The Daffodil** ⓝ 🏠 ♿ **P**

TRADITIONAL CUISINE · **PUB** ✗ As the weather warms up, the daffodils dancing outside draw your eye to this modern dining pub; this is also the time to bag a table on the elevated terrace and take in the view. Top Welsh ingredients feature in tasty, traditional dishes which are generously proportioned. Service is bright and breezy.

Carte £25/45

✉ SA44 5NG – ☎ 01559 370343 – www.thedaffodilinn.co.uk – Closed 2-14 January, Monday, Tuesday

PWLLHELI

Gwynedd – Regional map n° **18**–B2

⊗ **Plas Bodegroes** ❀ ⇦ 🖼 **P**

MODERN CUISINE · **INTIMATE** ✗✗ A charming, Grade II listed Georgian house set in peaceful grounds; inside it's beautifully decorated and features an eclectic collection of modern Welsh art. There's a well-chosen wine list and the kitchen uses the best of the local larder to create classic dishes with a contemporary edge. Understated bedrooms are named after trees and have sleek, modern bathrooms.

Menu £45/50

✉ LL53 5TH – ☎ 01758 612363 – www.bodegroes.co.uk –
Closed 2 January-6 February, Sunday dinner, Monday, Tuesday - Saturday lunch

RUTHIN

Denbighshire – Regional map n° **18**–C1

⊗ **On the Hill** 🏠

TRADITIONAL CUISINE · **RUSTIC** ✗ Immensely charming 16C house in a busy market town; a real family-run business. It has characterful sloping floors, exposed beams and a buzzy, bistro atmosphere. The accessible menu offers keenly priced, internationally-influenced classics.

Menu £21 (lunch) – Carte £26/40

1 Upper Clwyd Street ✉ LL15 1HY – ☎ 01824 707736 –
www.onthehillrestaurant.co.uk – Closed 1-8 January, Sunday, Monday

ST DAVIDS • TYDDEWI

Pembrokeshire – Regional map n° **18**–A3

⊗ **cwtch***

TRADITIONAL BRITISH · **RUSTIC** ✗ Popular, laid-back restaurant; its name meaning 'hug'. The three rustic dining rooms boast stone walls, crammed bookshelves and log-filled alcoves. Classic British dishes arrive in generous portions and service is polite and friendly.

Carte £30/42

22 High Street ✉ SA62 6SD – ☎ 01437 720491 – www.cwtchrestaurant.co.uk –
Closed 1 January-4 February, Sunday dinner, Monday, Tuesday, Wednesday - Saturday lunch

SAUNDERSFOOT

Pembrokeshire – Regional map n° **18**–A4

ⅈ○ Coast

≼ 🛱 🕹 AC P

MODERN CUISINE · CONTEMPORARY DÉCOR ✗✗ A striking beachfront restaurant with a lovely terrace – every table affords stunning views courtesy of floor to ceiling windows. Modern menus have a local seafood bias; start with some snacks and move on to assured, carefully crafted dishes with a classical base. Service is friendly and relaxed.

Menu £29 (lunch) – Carte £42/51

Coppet Hall Beach ⊠ SA69 9AJ – ℰ 01834 810800 –
www.coastsaundersfoot.co.uk – Closed 4-23 January, Monday, Tuesday

🏠 St Brides Spa

✿ ≼ 💯 🛠 ⅃ 🖽 🕹 🐱 P

LUXURY · PERSONALISED Located on the clifftop, overlooking the harbour and the bay, is this nautically styled hotel featuring white wood panelling and contemporary Welsh art. The outdoor infinity pool has a great outlook, as do the restaurant and decked terraces. Smart, well-appointed bedrooms come in white and blue hues.

40 rooms – 🛉🛉 £190/350 – 2 suites

St Brides Hill ⊠ SA69 9NH – ℰ 01834 812304 – *www.stbridesspahotel.com*

SKENFRITH

Monmouthshire – Regional map n° **18**–C4

ⅈ○ Bell at Skenfrith

🕸 ≼ 🍴 🛱 🗘 P

CLASSIC CUISINE · PUB ✗ Well-run pub in a verdant valley, offering hearty, classical cooking with the occasional ambitious twist and using ingredients from the organic kitchen garden. There's an excellent choice of champagnes and cognacs, and service is warm and unobtrusive. Super-comfy bedrooms have an understated elegance.

Carte £31/49

⊠ NP7 8UH – ℰ 01600 750235 – *www.skenfrith.co.uk*

SWANSEA

Swansea – Regional map n° **18**–B4

ⅈ○ Slice

MODERN BRITISH · INTIMATE ✗ Hidden away in the suburbs is this sweet little restaurant run by chef-owners Chris and Adam, who will personally greet you when you arrive and thank you as you leave. Concise menus feature carefully sourced local ingredients and dishes are passionately prepared. The homemade bread is a highlight.

Menu £32 (lunch), £42/55

73-75 Eversley Rd, Sketty ⊠ SA2 9DE – ℰ 01792 290929 –
*www.sliceswansea.co.uk – Closed 6-16 April, 29 June-9 July,
28 September-15 October, Monday, Tuesday, Wednesday, Thursday lunch*

TENBY

Pembrokeshire – Regional map n° **18**–A4

ⅈ○ Rhosyn ℕ

≼ ≼ 🍴 🗘 P

MODERN CUISINE · CONTEMPORARY DÉCOR ✗✗ Rhosyn means 'rose' and there are many of these on display in the gardens of this lovingly restored Strawberry Gothic house. It's a charming place with a calming atmosphere and offers a concise menu of skilfully prepared dishes with pure, natural flavours. Some bedrooms are modern; others, more characterful.

Carte £34/50

Penally Abbey, Penally ⊠ SA70 7PY – ℰ 01834 843033 – *www.penally-abbey.com*
– Closed Sunday - Saturday lunch

Salt Cellar

MODERN CUISINE · FRIENDLY XX Four friends own and run this restaurant. It may be in a hotel basement but it's bright and fresh and its pretty terrace over the road offers glorious coastal views. Refined, well-crafted dishes champion local produce.

Carte £ 35/46

The Esplanade ✉ *SA70 7DU –* ☎ *01834 844005 – www.thesaltcellartenby.co.uk*

TINTERN · TYNDYRN
Monmouthshire – Regional map n° **18**-C4

Parva Farmhouse

MODERN BRITISH · FRIENDLY X A 17C stone farmhouse on a bank of the River Wye, run by a friendly couple. Its simple, rustic interior comprises a spacious lounge and a small 6 table restaurant with an inglenook fireplace. Gutsy modern British cooking has a classic French backbone and the odd Italian or Asian touch. Bedrooms are modest.

Menu £ 42

Riverside ✉ *NP16 6SQ –* ☎ *01291 689411 – www.parvafarmhouse.co.uk –*
Closed Sunday, Monday, Tuesday, Wednesday - Saturday lunch

TREDUNNOCK – Monmouthshire → See Usk

TREGARON
Ceredigion – Regional map n° **18**-B3

Y Talbot

TRADITIONAL CUISINE · PUB X Originally a drover's inn dating back to the 17C; the bar rooms are where the action is, and the best place to sit. Seasonal menus offer full-flavoured traditional dishes made with Welsh produce. Bedrooms are bright and modern: ask for one of the newest. Oh, and there's an elephant buried in the garden!

Carte £ 22/38

✉ *SY25 6JL –* ☎ *01974 298208 – www.ytalbot.com*

TYWYN
Gwynedd – Regional map n° **18**-B2

Salt Marsh Kitchen

TRADITIONAL BRITISH · SIMPLE X This sweet little bistro has a clean, fresh look and a rustic feel. It's run by a proud, hardworking owner who is a keen fisherman and, unsurprisingly, seafood forms the core of the menu. Cooking is honest and generous and Cardigan Bay fish and locally bred meats are a feature.

Carte £ 23/43

6 College Green ✉ *LL36 9BS –* ☎ *01654 711949 – www.saltmarshkitchen.co.uk –*
Closed Sunday - Saturday lunch

USK
Monmouthshire – Regional map n° **18**-C4

at Tredunnock South: 4. 75 mi by Llangybi rd

Newbridge on Usk

MODERN BRITISH · BISTRO X This 200 year inn old stands beside the River Usk. Sit on the terrace for something from the snack menu or find a seat in one of several dining areas for carefully cooked dishes with modern overtones. Herbs and vegetables come from the kitchen garden. Enthusiastic service and smart bedrooms complete the picture.

Menu £ 20 (lunch) – Carte £ 30/50

✉ *NP15 1LY –* ☎ *01633 451000 – www.celtic-manor.com*

WHITEBROOK – Monmouthshire → See Monmouth

IRELAND

NORTHERN IRELAND

Think of Northern Ireland and you think of buzzing Belfast, with its impressive City Hall and Queen's University. But the rest of the Six Counties demand attention too. Forty thousand stone columns of the Giants Causeway step out into the Irish Sea, while inland, Antrim boasts nine scenic glens. County Down's rolling hills culminate in the alluring slopes of Slieve Donard in the magical Mourne Mountains, while Armagh's Orchard County is a riot of pink in springtime. Fermanagh's glassy, silent lakelands are a tranquil attraction, rivalled for their serenity by the heather-clad Sperrin Mountains, towering over Tyrone and Derry.

Rich, fertile land, vast waterways and a pride in traditional crafts like butchery and baking mean that Northern Ireland yields a wealth of high quality produce: tender, full-flavoured beef and lamb, and fish and shellfish from the lakes, rivers and sea, including salmon, oysters, mussels and crabs. You can't beat an eel from Lough Neagh – and the seaweed called Dulse is a local delicacy not to be missed.

- Michelin Road maps n° 712, 713 and 501

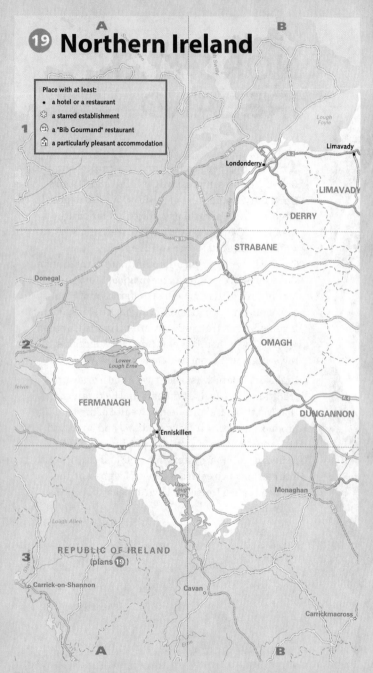

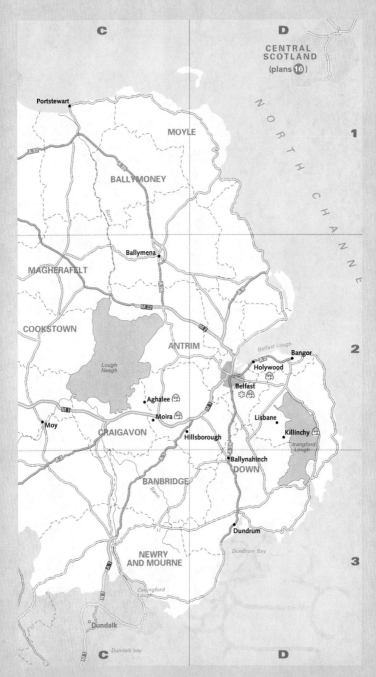

NOT TO BE MISSED

STARRED RESTAURANTS

High quality cooking...

BIB GOURMAND RESTAURANTS 🙂

Good quality, good value cooking

ZOOMING IN...

... ON BELFAST'S NEW MICHELIN STAR — THE MUDDLERS CLUB

Hidden away in the backstreets of the historic Cathedral Quarter, the industrial-looking Muddlers Club might not conform to most people's idea of a Michelin Star, but the dark, moody vibe is bang on-trend and is all part of its appeal.

Its unusual name refers to a group that was formed here in the 1790s, who later became revolutionaries... and on this historic city street, chef-owner **Gareth McCaughey** looks set to be starting a foodie revolution all of his own.

The Muddlers Club first featured in the 2017 edition of the MICHELIN Guide Great Britain and Ireland and since then, the Michelin Inspectors have watched it mature year on year. For the 2020 edition, we are now delighted to award it a Michelin Star.

The lighting is kept low and the rustic tables are constructed from reclaimed floorboards – which give it a refreshingly unpretentious air – and, as they beaver away in the open kitchen which stretches the length of the room, the kitchen team's passion is palpable.

Elaine Hill, The Muddlers Club

Elaine Hill, The Muddlers Club

This is the first restaurant in the city to offer a surprise multi-course tasting menu – and it's going down a storm. The modern dishes are a perfect match for the surroundings and display a pleasing mix of styles: some take on a simpler approach by relying on just a few top quality ingredients, while others have a more ambitious edge – and both are executed equally well.

Gareth started his career by training as a pastry chef, so the desserts are naturally a highlight of the meal.

To complete your experience you'll find an extensive cocktail list and a selection of carefully chosen wines, with many available by the glass courtesy of the Coravin.

Some of the Michelin Inspectors' favourite dishes from the surprise menu include:

- *Goat's cheese and summer truffle*
- *Spring pea, braised short rib and celeriac*
- *Beef, carrot, short rib and bone marrow*
- *Halibut, Romesco sauce and courgette*
- *Rhubarb, orange and yoghurt*
- *Chocolate, coconut and sea salt*

AGHALEE · ACHADH LÍ

Lisburn and Castlereagh – Regional map n° **19**–C2

Clenaghans 　　　　　　　⟨🍴 🏠 � ⊘ P⟩

MODERN BRITISH · COSY ✕ This charming former pub is a hugely characterful place; follow the cobbled path through the garden to the beamed, flagged-floored interior and receive a warm welcome from the friendly team. Reinvented pub classics sit alongside more refined, sophisticated dishes; the lunch menu is great value.

Specialities: Smoked haddock arancini, curry and lime. Beef rib, miso and burnt hispi. Chocolate fondant with milk ice cream.

Menu £20 (lunch) – Carte £24/38

48 Soldierstown Road ⊠ BT67 0ES – ☏ 028 9265 2952 –
www.clenaghansrestaurant.com – Closed 12 July, Sunday dinner, Monday, Tuesday

BALLYMENA · AN BAILE MEÁNACH

Mid and East Antrim – Regional map n° **19**–C2

at Galgorm West: 3 mi on A42

⫶○ River Room 　　　　　　⟨← 🍴 � AC ⊘ P⟩

MODERN BRITISH · LUXURY ✕✕✕ This well-appointed, luxurious restaurant sits within a Victorian manor house – part of an impressive hotel resort – and offers lovely views out over the estate to the river. Cooking showcases the best of Irish ingredients in elaborate dishes with sophisticated flavour contrasts.

Menu £55/65

Galgorm Spa and Golf Resort Hotel, 136 Fenaghy Road ⊠ BT42 1EA –
☏ 028 2588 1001 – www.galgorm.com – Closed Sunday lunch, Monday, Tuesday,
Wednesday - Saturday lunch

Galgorm Spa and Golf Resort

⟨🎾 🍴 🖼 🏞 🛉🛉 🐎 ㅏ⅚ 🔁 ㅕ ㅪ P⟩

GRAND LUXURY · CONTEMPORARY An impressive resort hotel on the banks of the Maine, boasting state-of-the-art bedrooms, a world-class spa and a beautifully landscaped Thermal Village. Dine from an extensive all-day menu in characterful Gillies or on Italian fare in informal Fratelli. Enjoy afternoon tea overlooking the gardens and sample some of nearly 450 gins!

143 rooms ⌴ – 🛉🛉 £175/350 – 3 suites

136 Fenaghy Road ⊠ BT42 1EA – ☏ 028 2588 1001 – www.galgorm.com
⫶○ **River Room** – See restaurant listing

BANGOR · BEANNCHAR

Ards and North Down – Regional map n° **19**–D2

⫶○ Wheathill 　　　　　　　　　⟨ㅏ⅚ AC ⊘⟩

MODERN CUISINE · FRIENDLY ✕ Gray's Hill was once known as Wheathill, as it was the route used to transport wheat to the harbour. Choose from a list of hearty, wholesome classics and a selection of specials on the blackboard. Service is bubbly and the wine list is keenly priced.

Carte £18/42

7 Grays Hill ⊠ BT20 3BB – ☏ 028 9147 7405 – www.thewheathill.com –
Closed Sunday dinner, Monday, Tuesday

BELFAST • BÉAL FEIRSTE

Belfast – Regional map n° **19**–D2

Top tips!

A former industrial hub, Northern Ireland's capital is famous
as the birthplace of the Titanic, and its portside cranes –
Samson and Goliath – dominate the skyline. Visit The Big
Fish to uncover some more of the city's history through its
ceramic tiles, then stop-off at Michelin-Starred **OX** for some
creative, original cuisine.

The east side of the city is home to a wealth of eating and
drinking establishments – try contemporary bistro **Cyprus
Avenue** or Italian small plates at **Il Pirata**. Further, west, the
Cathedral Quarter is also full of trendy bars and eateries
such as market-focussed **Hadskis** and Michelin-Starred
Muddlers Club.

Michael Deane has all bases covered with three restaurants
in the heart of the city, along with **Deanes at Queens** near
the Botanic Gardens. And if you're visiting the Grand Opera
House, be sure to stop in at stunning 1820s gin palace The
Crown Liquor Saloon.

R. Mattes/hemis.fr

Restaurants

✿ **Eipic**   🔥 AC ⓘ 🏛

MODERN CUISINE · ELEGANT XxX Michael Deane is a well-known name locally and Eipic is the flagship restaurant of his mini-empire. You enter through one of his other restaurants, Love Fish, and through into this rather exclusive feeling room with well-spaced tables and large illuminated silver discs on the walls. Chef Alex Greene began his career in 2007 cooking at Deanes then spent time at Pétrus, Claridge's and The Cliff House, before returning to where it all began, once again cooking for Michael.

Aside from an additional Friday lunchtime offering, all menus are tasting menus. Cooking is modern and assured with a creative, original edge and preparation is precise. Flavours are to the fore, with top quality seasonal ingredients sourced as locally as possible – in his spare time Alex also forages. Service is charming and in an interesting twist to the wine pairings, you are presented with the choice of either a glass or a shot.

Specialities: Shorthorn beef, leek, mouli, ponzu and cured yolk. Lamb, wild garlic, peas and broad beans. Chocolate, coconut, yuzu and coffee.

Menu £30 (lunch)/70

Town plan B2-n – *28-40 Howard Street* ✉ *BT1 6PF* – ☎ *028 9033 1134* – *www.deaneseipic.com – Closed 1-22 January, 8-15 April, 8-22 July, Sunday, Monday, Tuesday, Wednesday - Thursday lunch, Saturday lunch*

✿ **OX** (Stephen Toman)   🔥 AC ⓘ

MODERN BRITISH · MINIMALIST XX Stephen Toman likes to keep things moving at this Scandic-style restaurant, which, with its painted bare brick walls and understated design, wouldn't feel out of place in Copenhagen. If you've time to spare, arrive early for an aperitif in their next door Wine Cave (where they also serve snack boards throughout the day).

Top quality produce guides the constantly evolving menus, which are a mix of set-priced and surprise selections created from a list of around 30 or so of the best seasonal ingredients. Skilfully prepared modern dishes capture the true flavours of these ingredients and Stephen's passion for vegetables is clear to see. There's a great balance of different tastes and textures, and cooking has a refined, sophisticated style. Well-matched wines and warm service complete the picture.

Specialities: White asparagus with prosciutto, fig leaf and sorrel. Mourne Mountain lamb with kale, black garlic, and confit onion. 70% chocolate with ginger, shiso and beetroot sorbet.

Menu £22 (lunch), £50/60

Town plan B1-m – *1 Oxford Street* ✉ *BT1 3LA* – ☎ *028 9031 4121* – *www.oxbelfast.com – Closed 12-20 April, 12-26 July, 20 December-1 January, Sunday, Monday, Tuesday lunch*

✿ **The Muddlers Club** (Gareth McCaughey)   🍸 🔥 AC ⓘ

MODERN CUISINE · CONTEMPORARY DÉCOR X Hidden away in the Cathedral Quarter is this modern, industrial-style restaurant named after a 200 year old secret society. It's a simply furnished place with a dark colour scheme and an open kitchen, and the enthusiasm of the young team who run it is palpable.

When it comes to the cooking, chef Gareth McCaughey – formerly the sous chef at nearby OX – likes to keep things fairly straightforward and in a modern vein. His philosophy is to source top ingredients, mainly from Ireland, prepare them well, and not overcomplicate things. His Antrim beef with carrot, short rib and bone marrow is a case in point: the beef is perfectly cooked, the well-crafted sauce is delicious and the accompaniments are suitably unfussy. Gareth started out as a pastry chef, so it's no surprise to find that the desserts are a highlight.

Specialities: Scallop with artichoke and parmesan. Halibut with bisque and greens. Yuzu with Earl Grey and white chocolate.

Menu £45/55 – Carte £30/48

Town plan B1-v – *1 Warehouse Lane (Off Waring Street)* ✉ *BT1 2DX* – ☎ *028 9031 3199 – www.themuddlersclubbelfast.com – Closed 12-20 April, 5-20 July, 29 December-6 January, Sunday, Monday*

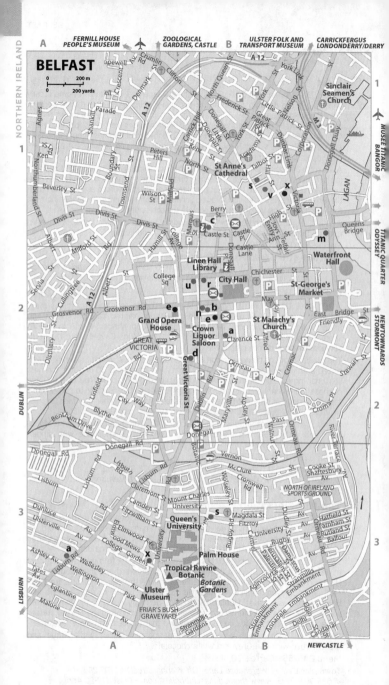

BELFAST

0 — 200 m
0 — 200 yards

ⓐ Deanes at Queens   🍷 🛖 & 👌

MODERN BRITISH · BRASSERIE XX This bustling modern brasserie offers great value, day and night. Those after coffee and cake or a cocktail should make for the bar, while the terrace is a great spot on a sunny day. Refined modern dishes are full of flavour and blackboard specials add to the choice; the Mibrasa charcoal grill is a feature.

Specialities: Beetroot and goat's cheese salad with truffle and multi seed crisp. Roast chicken, potato and cheddar terrine, tarragon and truffle velouté. Jam and custard steamed pudding, ice cream and shortbread.

Menu £24 – Carte £25/43

Town plan A3-x – *1 College Gardens* ⌂ *BT9 6BQ* – *℘ 028 9038 2111 – www.michaeldeane.co.uk* – *Closed 12-13 July, Sunday dinner*

ⓐ Home   & 🗚 🕪 🕸

TRADITIONAL BRITISH · RUSTIC X A relaxed, spacious restaurant with a café to the front and a rustic dining room clad in reclaimed timber to the rear. As its name suggests, cooking focuses on refined versions of British and Mediterranean dishes which are often prepared at home. Menus include gluten free, vegan and 'skinny' options, and dishes are colourful and feature some interesting spicing.

Specialities: Pea and broad bean tartine, avocado butter, feta and poached egg. Braised lamb shoulder, orecchiette pasta, peas, mint, broccoli, parmesan and salsa verde. Coconut rice pudding with clementine compote.

Menu £18/22 – Carte £25/34

Town plan B2-r – *22 Wellington Place* ⌂ *BT1 6GE* – *℘ 028 9023 4946 – www.homebelfast.co.uk* – *Closed 12-13 July, 24-27 December*

ⓘ Deanes Meat Locker   & 🗚 🕸 ⌂

MEATS AND GRILLS · BRASSERIE XX Sit on smart banquettes and look through the large window into the meat fridge, where cubes of pink Himalayan salt gradually dry age the beef. Try the Carlingford rock oysters, followed by a prime Irish cut, cooked on the Asador grill.

Carte £26/61

Town plan B2-n – *28-40 Howard Street* ⌂ *BT1 6PF* – *℘ 028 9033 1134 – www.michaeldeane.co.uk* – *Closed 1-2 January, 13-15 April, 12-14 July, 25-28 December, Sunday*

ⓘ Saphyre   & 🕪

MODERN CUISINE · ELEGANT XX A former church houses an interior design showroom, a boutique and this intimate, opulently styled restaurant. It has quite a formal feel and the cooking is fittingly modern and elaborate; come at lunch to sample sophisticated dishes at a good price – and be sure to save room for dessert.

Menu £20 (lunch) – Carte £42/58

Town plan A3-a – *135 Lisburn Road* ⌂ *BT9 7AG* – *℘ 028 9068 8606 – www.saphyrerestaurant.com* – *Closed Sunday, Monday, Tuesday*

ⓘ Shu   & 🗚 ⌂

CLASSIC CUISINE · BRASSERIE XX A well-established neighbourhood restaurant with a modern look and a lively, vibrant atmosphere. An array of menus provides plenty of choice and cooking is guided by the seasons. Dishes have a classic base and display a mix of British and French influences.

Menu £19 (lunch)/28 – Carte £19/48

Off plan – *253 Lisburn Road* ⌂ *BT9 7EN* – *℘ 028 9038 1655 – www.shu-restaurant.com* – *Closed Sunday*

James St   🕭 ✧

MODERN BRITISH · BRASSERIE X A vibrant modern bistro that's popular with one and all. It's a simple place with red brick walls, a high ceiling and warehouse-style windows. Menus are classic brasserie style. The grill dishes are a hit and the succulent steaks are cooked on the Josper, served on boards and come with a choice of sauces.

Menu £24 – Carte £22/40

Town plan B2-b – *19-21 James Street South* ⊠ *BT2 7GA* –
☏ 028 9560 0700 – www.jamesst.co.uk

Cyprus Avenue   🎪 🕭 AC 🕅

CONTEMPORARY · CONTEMPORARY DÉCOR X You'll find something to please everyone at this contemporary all-day bistro. It's a big, busy place: head to one of the booths to eat or make for the counter for a glass of wine and some snacks. Freshly baked breads come with delicious hop butter and are followed by a wide selection of modern classics.

Carte £21/36

Off plan – *228 Upper Newtownards Road* ⊠ *BT4 3ET* –
☏ 028 9065 6755 – www.cyprusavenue.co.uk

Deanes Deli   🍷 AC 🕭

MODERN BRITISH · BISTRO X Glass-fronted city centre eatery. One side is a smart restaurant offering an appealing menu of classical dishes with some Asian and Mediterranean influences; the other side acts as a coffee shop by day and a buzzy tapas bar by night.

Carte £20/35

Town plan B2-a – *42-44 Bedford Street* ⊠ *BT2 7FF* –
☏ 028 9024 8800 – www.michaeldeane.co.uk –
Closed Sunday dinner

Deanes Love Fish   🕭 AC

SEAFOOD · CONTEMPORARY DÉCOR X If it comes from the sea, they'll serve it here! A glass ceiling makes it light and airy and the décor has a maritime feel. The lunchtime 'Dish of the Day' is good value and the à la carte offers everything from a prawn cocktail and cod croquettes to a seafood platter.

Menu £20 – Carte £23/40

Town plan B2-n – *28-40 Howard Street* ⊠ *BT1 6PF* –
☏ 028 9033 1134 – www.michaeldeane.co.uk –
Closed Sunday

Edō   🍷 🕭 AC 🎴 🕅

MODERN BRITISH · RUSTIC X 'I eat' is a smart, modish brasserie in the heart of the city, with rustic-meets-faux-industrial styling and seats at the long kitchen counter for those who want to get in on the action. The international menu allows for sharing and many dishes are cooked over apple or pear wood in the Bertha oven.

Menu £25/45

Town plan A2-u – *3 Capital House, Unit 2, Upper Queen Street* ⊠ *BT1 6FB* –
☏ 028 9031 3054 – www.edorestaurant.co.uk –
Closed Sunday, Monday

Ginger Bistro   🕭 AC 🕅

TRADITIONAL CUISINE · BISTRO X Close to the Grand Opera House you'll find this neighbourhood restaurant set in an old warehouse; sit in the bar, the traditional bistro or the bright, contemporary room with a glass façade. The chef-owner understands his clientele and delivers classic combinations of simply cooked Irish ingredients.

Carte £27/42

Town plan A2-d – *68-72 Great Victoria Street* ⊠ *BT2 5EE* –
☏ 028 9024 4421 – www.gingerbistro.com –
Closed Sunday, Monday

🕴️⊖ **Hadskis** 🏠 🆎 ⟷

MEATS AND GRILLS · BISTRO 🕽 Hadskis stands in an old building in the up-and-coming Cathedral Quarter. It was once part of the area's Iron Foundry and is named after the owner. The long, narrow room has a modern feel and you can watch the chefs in the open kitchen. Cooking showcases market produce and focuses on the chargrill.

Menu £20 – Carte £25/42

Town plan B1-s – *33 Donegall Street* ✉ *BT1 2NB* – ℰ *028 9032 5444* – *www.hadskis.co.uk*

🕴️⊖ **Molly's Yard** 🏠 ♿ 🎦 🕸️

TRADITIONAL BRITISH · BISTRO 🕽 A former coach house and stables play host to this quirky little eatery and pleasant courtyard, owned by the locally based Hilden Brewing Company; be sure to choose one of their paired ales to match your dish. Simple lunches are followed by more ambitious dinners and cooking is fresh, honest and tasty.

Menu £20/28 – Carte £28/40

Town plan B3-s – *1 College Green Mews, Botanic Avenue* ✉ *BT7 1LW* – ℰ *028 9032 2600* – *www.mollysyard.co.uk* – *Closed Sunday*

🕴️⊖ **Mourne Seafood Bar** ♿ 🆎 🕸️

SEAFOOD · BISTRO 🕽 This well-regarded seafood restaurant comes complete with a small fish shop and a cookery school. Popular choices include the seafood casserole, salt & chilli squid, Carlingford oysters and Strangford Lough mussels. Consider one of the suggested dish and beer pairings from the blackboard.

Carte £26/46

Town plan B1-c – *34-36 Bank Street* ✉ *BT1 1HL* – ℰ *028 9024 8544* – *www.mourneseafood.com*

🕴️⊖ **Il Pirata** ♿ 🆎 🍽️ 🎦

ITALIAN · RUSTIC 🕽 The buzzy suburb of Ballyhackamore is home to this large, stripped-back eatery with a fun, laid-back vibe. The sizeable Italian menu covers all bases, from pasta and pizzetta to arancini and risotto, and the duck ragu has become something of a signature dish. Service is bright and friendly.

Carte £24/40

Off plan – *279-281 Upper Newtownards Road* ✉ *BT4 3JF* – ℰ *028 9067 3421* – *www.ilpiratabelfast.com*

Hotels

🏨 **Grand Central** ⓞ 🍴 ⧀ 🖥️ ♿ 🆎 🏋️

BUSINESS · GRAND LUXURY This modern skyscraper stands in Belfast's Linen Quarter and makes its mark on the city's skyline. Most bedrooms have a view and all offer high standards of modern luxury. Take in stunning 360° views during afternoon tea on the 23rd floor, enjoy modern Irish dishes in Seahorse or dine in the Grand Café.

300 rooms ☑ – 👫 £160/350 – 5 suites

Town plan B2-e – *9 Bedford Street* ✉ *BT2 7FF* – ℰ *028 9023 1066* – *www.grandcentralhotelbelfast.com*

🏨 **Merchant** 🍴 🎏 💆 🖥️ ♿ 🆎 🏋️

LUXURY · ELEGANT The former Ulster Bank HQ has an impressive Victorian façade. Bedrooms come in opulent 'Victorian' and stylish 'Art Deco' themes. The rooftop gym has an outdoor hot tub and a skyline view; relax afterwards in the swish cocktail bar. Enjoy afternoon tea in the plush 'Great Room', modern British dishes in the old banking hall or classic French cuisine in the brasserie.

62 rooms – 👫 £140/420 – ☑ £20 – 2 suites

Town plan B1-x – *16 Skipper Street* ✉ *BT1 2DZ* – ℰ *028 9023 4888* – *www.themerchanthotel.com*

🏠 Fitzwilliam

LUXURY · CONTEMPORARY This stylish hotel by the Grand Opera House has a striking glass façade. Smart bedrooms have bold colour schemes and contemporary furnishings; choose a 'City View' room for extras such as a coffee machine and GHDs. Eat informally in the bar or dine on modern Irish dishes in the first floor restaurant.

145 rooms 🖙 – 👫 £120/350 – 2 suites

Town plan A2-e – *Great Victoria Street* ✉ *BT2 7BQ* –
📞 *028 9044 2080* – *www.fitzwilliamhotelbelfast.com*

DERRY/LONDONDERRY – Derry and Strabane ➜ See Londonderry

DUNDRUM · DÚN DROMA

Newry, Mourne and Down – Regional map n° **19**–D3

🍴 Mourne Seafood Bar ♿

SEAFOOD · BISTRO ✗ On the main street of a busy coastal town you'll find this friendly seafood restaurant. Its décor has a bright, nautical theme and its walls are filled with local art. Start with home-pickled herring or seafood chowder. The Strangford Lough mussels and Carlingford oysters are also particularly good.

Carte £25/45

10 Main Street ✉ *BT33 0LU* –
📞 *028 4375 1377* – *www.mourneseafood.com*

ENNISKILLEN · INIS CEITHLEANN

Fermanagh and Omagh – Regional map n° **19**–A2

🏠 Lough Erne Resort

LUXURY · CONTEMPORARY Vast, luxurious golf and leisure resort on a peninsula between two loughs. Bedrooms have a classical style and are extremely well-appointed; the suites and lodges are dotted about the grounds. Relax in the beautiful Thai spa or the huge pool with its stunning mosaic wall. Ambitious, contemporary dining and lough views in Catalina; steaks and grills in the clubhouse.

120 rooms 🖙 – 👫 £99/319 – 6 suites

Belleek Road ✉ *BT93 7ED* –
📞 *028 6632 3230* – *www.lougherneresort.com*

GALGORM – Mid and East Antrim ➜ See Ballymena

HILLSBOROUGH · CROMGHLINN

Lisburn and Castlereagh – Regional map n° **19**–C2

🍴 hara AC

MODERN BRITISH · CONTEMPORARY DÉCOR ✗✗ An experienced husband and wife run this contemporary restaurant on the high street of a vibrant village. Locally sourced ingredients provide the foundations for dishes that respect the classics yet also demonstrate a subtle modernity in their contrasts of texture and flavour. Lunch is good value.

Menu £20 – Carte £20/32

16 Lisburn Street ✉ *BT26 6AB* –
📞 *028 7116 1467* – *www.harahillsborough.co.uk* – *Closed 20 January-5 February, 6-22 July, Monday, Tuesday, Wednesday - Thursday lunch*

🍴 **Parson's Nose** 🛖 ♿ 𝔸ℂ

TRADITIONAL CUISINE · PUB 𝕏 This characterful Georgian property really is a sizeable place. You can eat anywhere: in the charming bar, the contemporary bistro-style Sunroom or the first floor Attic restaurant. Accessible menus are good value and the bespoke sourdough pizzas cooked in the wood-fired oven are a hit.

Menu £20 – Carte £24/43

48 Lisburn Street ⊠ BT26 6AB – ℰ 028 9268 3009 – www.theparsonsnose.co.uk

HOLYWOOD · ARD MHIC NASCA
Ards and North Down – Regional map n° **19**–D2

😊 **Noble**

MODERN CUISINE · NEIGHBOURHOOD 𝕏 Nestled above a health food shop is this compact little restaurant, where the service is warm and genuine and the room has a happy buzz. Good value dishes showcase carefully handled local ingredients in unfussy combinations that exceed expectations. For dessert have the chocolate delice.

Specialities: Chicken liver parfait, plum chutney and toasted brioche. Suckling pig, sweetheart cabbage and baby turnip. Chocolate délice with peanut and salted caramel ice cream.

Menu £20 – Carte £26/32

27a Church Road ⊠ BT18 9BU – ℰ 028 9042 5655 – www.nobleholywood.com –
Closed 6-15 April, 6-22 July, 23 December-2 January, Monday, Tuesday, Wednesday lunch

🍴 **Fontana**

TRADITIONAL CUISINE · NEIGHBOURHOOD 𝕏𝕏 Accessed via an arch and a passageway, this first floor restaurant has been a favourite with the locals for over 20 years. It's traditionally furnished yet hung with contrasting contemporary art. Classic cooking has subtle Mediterranean and Asian influences and menus offer plenty of choice.

Menu £27 – Carte £26/50

61A High Street ⊠ BT18 9AE – ℰ 028 9080 9908 – www.restaurantfontana.com –
Closed Sunday dinner, Monday

🏰 **Culloden** 🏞 ← 📶 🖼 🧖 ♨ 🔄 ♿ 𝔸ℂ 🎿 🅿

BUSINESS · CLASSIC An extended Gothic mansion overlooking Belfast Lough, with well-maintained gardens and a smart spa. Charming, traditionally furnished guest areas have open fires and fine ceiling frescoes. Bedrooms offer modern luxuries; choose a State Suite. Formal Mitre offers classical menus and good views, while Cultra Inn serves a wide range of traditional dishes.

98 rooms – 👥 £290 – 4 suites

142 Bangor Road ⊠ BT18 0EX – ℰ 028 9042 1066 – www.hastingshotels.com

KILLINCHY
Ards and North Down – Regional map n° **19**–D2

😊 **Balloo House** 🛖 ♿ 𝔸ℂ 🅿

TRADITIONAL BRITISH · PUB 𝕏 A characterful former farmhouse with a rustic dining pub feel and a cosy little bar. Good value menus mix hearty pub classics and dishes with more international leanings. Blackboard specials showcase the latest seasonal ingredients and local seafood is a highlight in the summer months.

Specialities: Homemade black pudding Scotch egg with brown sauce. Honey and soy-glazed duck 'ham', with pineapple chutney, egg and chips. Cinnamon sugar doughnuts, coffee cream and hot chocolate sauce.

Menu £17 (lunch) – Carte £22/38

1 Comber Road ⊠ BT23 6PA – ℰ 028 9754 1210 – www.balloohouse.com

LIMAVADY • LÉIM AN MHADAIDH

Causeway Coast and Glens – Regional map n° **19**–B1

⟨○ **Lime Tree**

TRADITIONAL CUISINE · NEIGHBOURHOOD XX Keenly run neighbourhood restaurant; its traditional exterior concealing a modern room with purple velvet banquettes and colourful artwork. Unfussy, classical cooking features meats and veg from the village; try the homemade wheaten bread.

Menu £13 (lunch)/23 – Carte £17/35

60 Catherine Street ⊠ BT49 9DB – ℰ 028 7776 4300 – www.limetreerest.com – Closed Sunday, Monday, Tuesday - Wednesday lunch, Saturday lunch

LISBANE • AN LIOS BÁN

Ards and North Down – Regional map n° **19**–D2

⟨○ **Poacher's Pocket**   ⛺ & **P**

TRADITIONAL BRITISH · PUB X This modern-looking pub sits on the roadside, in the centre of a small village. Enjoy a pint in the traditional front bar then head through to the two-tiered restaurant extension overlooking the internal courtyard. Wide-ranging menus see pub classics sitting alongside more adventurous offerings.

Carte £21/42

181 Killinchy Road ⊠ BT23 5NE – ℰ 028 9754 1589 – www.poacherspocketlisbane.com

LONDONDERRY/DERRY

Derry and Strabane – Regional map n° **19**–B1

⟨○ **Browns Bonds Hill**   & **AC** ⟨♥⟩

MODERN BRITISH · NEIGHBOURHOOD XX The flagship of the Browns group sits on the east bank of the River Foyle and comes with a plush lounge and an intimate, understated dining room. An à la carte lunch is followed by a fixed price dinner menu. The artful modern cooking is elaborate in its techniques and combinations and represents good value.

Menu £25/35 – Carte £24/28

1 Bonds Hill, Waterside ⊠ BT47 6DW – ℰ 028 7134 5180 – www.brownsbondshill.com – Closed 24-26 December, Sunday dinner, Monday

⟨○ **Browns In Town**   ⛾ & **AC** ⟨♥⟩

MODERN BRITISH · BRASSERIE X Just over the river from the original restaurant in the group is Browns laid-back bigger sister. Great value fixed price menus offer an eclectic range of classic dishes with a modern touch. Staff are friendly and efficient and the cooking is fresh and flavoursome.

Menu £18 (lunch), £21/27

21 Strand Road ⊠ BT48 7BJ – ℰ 028 7136 2889 – www.brownsintown.com – Closed 25 December, Sunday lunch

MOIRA • MAIGH RATH

Lisburn and Castlereagh – Regional map n° **19**–C2

⟨☺⟩ **Wine & Brine**   & **AC** ⟨↔⟩

MODERN CUISINE · BISTRO XX Local chef Chris McGowan has transformed this fine Georgian house into a bright, modern restaurant hung with local art. Top regional ingredients feature in appealing dishes with a comforting feel. Everything is homemade and, as its name implies, some of the meats and fish are gently brined.

Specialities: Hand-dived scallop ceviche with blood orange granita. New season lamb sirloin with wild garlic and smoked yoghurt. Miso caramel tart.

Carte £20/43

59 Main Street ⊠ BT67 0LQ – ℰ 028 9261 0500 – www.wineandbrine.co.uk – Closed 1-15 January, 6-22 July, Sunday dinner, Monday, Tuesday

MOY
Mid Ulster – Regional map n° **19**–C2

⋔○ **Chapter V**

MODERN BRITISH · HISTORIC ✕✕ The oldest property in town sits just off the main Square and provides an interesting backdrop for cooking which is itself rooted in the classical vein. Neatly presented, flavoursome dishes show respect for good local ingredients. Enjoy a fireside aperitif before your meal in the stylish former stables.

Menu £20 – Carte £24/46

5 Killyman Street ⊠ BT71 7SJ – ℰ 028 8778 4521 – www.chaptervrestaurant.com – Closed 9-16 January, 9-16 April, 9-23 July, Monday, Tuesday, Wednesday, Thursday - Saturday lunch

PORTSTEWART • PORT STIÓBHAIRD
Causeway Coast and Glens – Regional map n° **19**–C1

⋔○ **Harry's Shack**

TRADITIONAL CUISINE · RUSTIC ✕ The location is superb: on a sandy National Trust beach, with views across to Inishowen. It's an appealingly simple place with wooden tables and classroom-style chairs. Concise menus wisely let local ingredients speak for themselves.

Carte £27/45

118 Strand Road ⊠ BT55 7PG – ℰ 028 7083 1783

REPUBLIC
OF IRELAND

They say that Ireland offers forty luminous shades of green, but it's not all wondrous hills and down-home pubs: witness the limestone-layered Burren, cut-through by meandering streams, lakes and labyrinthine caves; or the fabulous Cliffs of Moher, looming for mile after mile over the wild Atlantic waves. The cities burst with life: Dublin is one of Europe's coolest capitals, and free-spirited Cork enjoys a rich cultural heritage. Kilkenny mixes a medieval flavour with a strong artistic tradition, while the 'festival' city of Galway is enhanced by an easy, international vibe.

This is a country known for the quality and freshness of its produce, and farmers' markets and food halls yield an array of artisanal cheeses and freshly baked breads. Being an agricultural country, Ireland produces excellent home-reared meat and dairy products and a new breed of chefs are giving traditional dishes a clever modern twist. Seafood, particularly shellfish, is popular – nothing beats sitting on the quayside with a bowl of steaming mussels and the distinctive taste of a micro-brewery beer.

- Michelin Road maps n° 712 and 713

20 Republic of Ireland

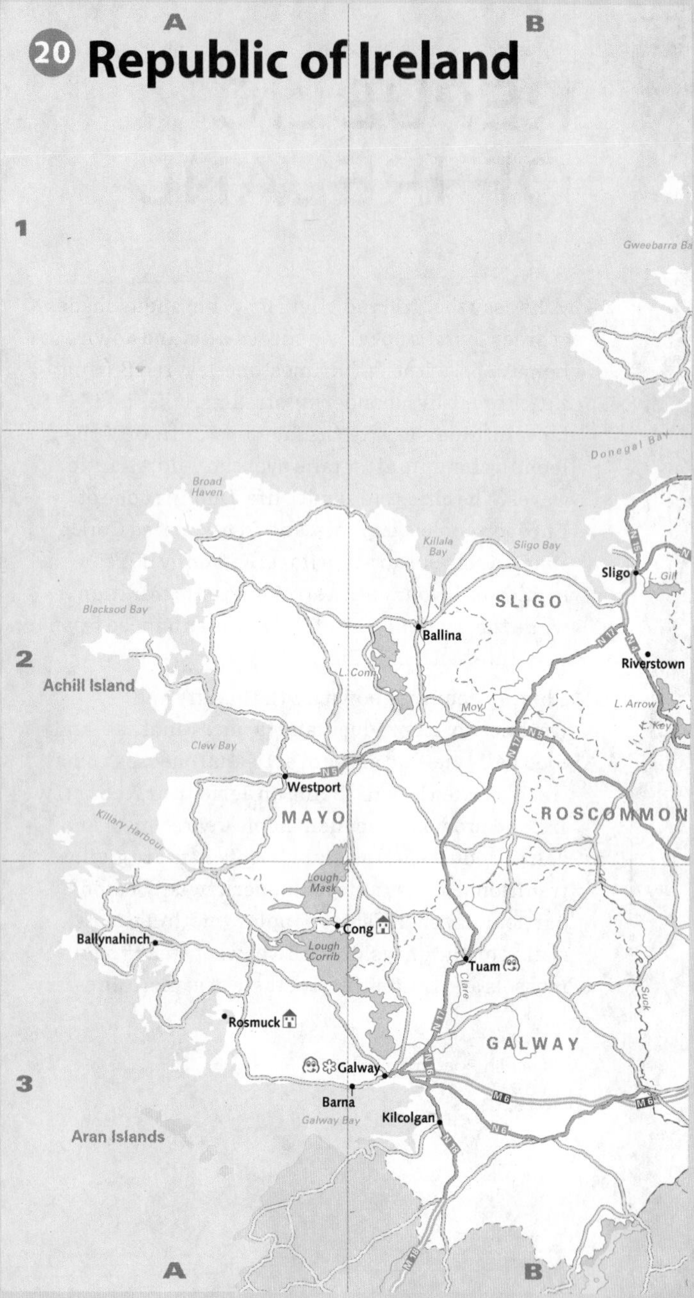

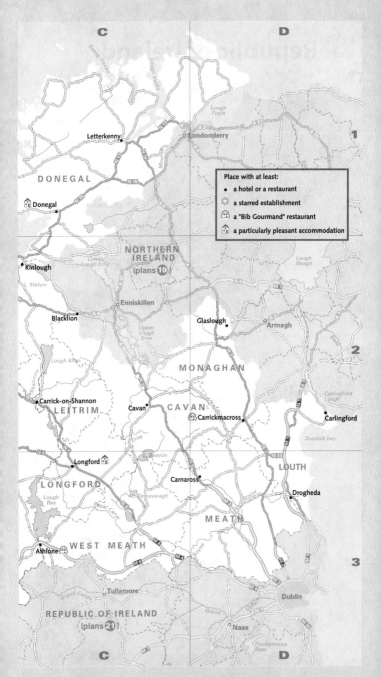

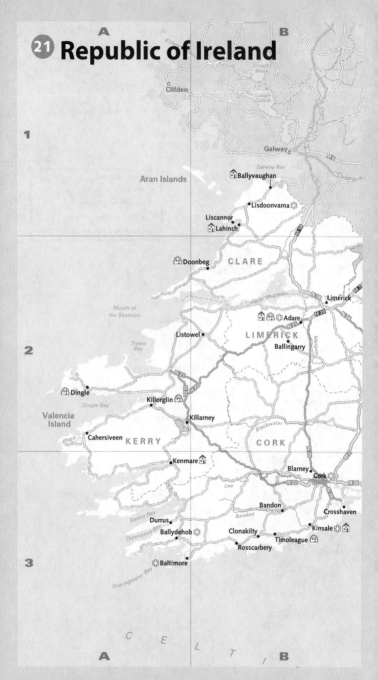

21 Republic of Ireland

Place with at least:
- • a hotel or a restaurant
- ✿ a starred establishment
- 🙂 a "Bib Gourmand" restaurant
- 🏠 a particularly pleasant accommodation

NOT TO BE MISSED

STARRED RESTAURANTS

Excellent cooking, worth a detour!

High quality cooking, worth a stop!

Michelin

Michelin

BIB GOURMAND RESTAURANTS 🏮

Good quality, good value cooking

ZOOMING IN

... ON THE REPUBLIC OF IRELAND'S MICHELIN STARS

Young teams hungry to make their mark mean that the quality of cooking across Ireland just keeps getting stronger and stronger, and a new breed of neighbourhood restaurants – set away from city centres, where costs are lower – are also bringing top quality cuisine to more of the country than ever before.

The diversity of the country's dining scene is reflected in our selection of Michelin Stars, which all offer something different, from the much-loved Dublin institutions that are the elegant **Patrick Guilbaud**, stylish **Chapter One** and legendary **L'Ecrivain** to chic **Liath**, which sits within a bohemian suburban market in the seaside village of Blackrock.

When it comes to dining within hotels there's **House**, with its impressive coastal views, and **Lady Helen**, which proudly show-cases produce from the estate on which it stands. Also offering a place to stay is the **Wild Honey Inn**, which started life in the 1860s as a hotel, and is now a cosy pub with rooms, serving classical French dishes.

Kilkenny's **Campagne** is a sleek neighbourhood spot focusing on refreshingly understated cooking, while County Cork plays host to three very different restaurants: chic Japanese **Ichigo Ichie**, sweet, understated **Chestnut**, which focuses on natural flavours, and intimate **Mews**, where local herbs and seaweeds are a feature.

L'Ecrivain

Galway's Starred restaurants, meanwhile, come at both ends of the design spectrum, with industrial-style basement room **Loam** providing a complete contrast to nature-inspired **Aniar**, which is decked out in wood and stone.

Joining these existing Stars in the 2020 edition of the guide are a whole host of newly Starred restaurants.

Intimate-wine-bar-cum-bistro **Bastion** in Kinsale, and grand manor house dining room **The Oak Room**

Chapter One

in Adare, are promoted to One Michelin Star, while the dynamic, laid-back **Variety Jones** in Dublin – where dishes are cooked over the fire – enters the guide for the first time, also with One Star.

Foraged and preserved produce leads the way at **Aimsir** in Celbridge, which is welcomed into the guide with an impressive Two Michelin Stars and chic, accomplished **Greenhouse** in Dublin also joins the Two-Star category with its promotion from One to Two Stars. At the former, Jordan Bailey brings together overwhelming passion, a great understanding of flavours and supreme craftsmanship. At the latter, Finnish chef Mickael Viljanen creates accomplished, sophisticated dishes which present some very stimulating flavour combinations.

Our Michelin Star selection for 2020 offers discerning diners plenty of choice in terms of atmosphere, style and type of cuisine; a reflection of the Irish dining scene as a whole.

❀ **The Oak Room**   🕸 🛏 ♿ AC 🔄 P

MODERN CUISINE · INTIMATE XxxX The dining room of the impressive 1830s mansion Adare Manor, exhibits all the comfort and grandeur one would expect. It's named after the wood-panelled walls commissioned by architect Augustus Pugin and comes with a dark green colour scheme, period artwork and lavish chandeliers; in summer, ask for a table in the small glass-enclosed terrace for wonderful views over the parterre and 850 acres of grounds.

Michael Tweedie's assured, refreshingly understated modern cooking champions top ingredients from Ireland's artisan producers, and dishes comprise just 3 or 4 ingredients, as he has the experience and courage to know when to hold back. The resulting combinations are refined and well-balanced, with complex flavours and great attention to detail. The wine list is a labour of love and offers a superb range by the glass.

Specialities: Quail with asparagus and walnut. Wild turbot with seaweed, Dooncastle clams and caviar. Jaffa Cake.

Menu € 90/110

Adare Manor Hotel ⊠ V94 W8WR –
𝒞 061 605 200 – www.adaremanor.com –
Closed Sunday - Saturday lunch

🕸 **1826**   🏠

MODERN CUISINE · RUSTIC XX An experienced couple run this pretty little thatched cottage, which was built in 1826 and has a cosy, characterful feel. Interesting, attractively presented dishes use well-sourced ingredients and display subtle modern touches. Several set-priced early bird menus offer the best value.

Specialities: Crisp Dooncastle oysters with shallot and coriander salad. Treacle-braised beef short rib, bone marrow croquette and braising juices. Salted caramel and white chocolate brûlée with hazelnut shortbread.

Menu € 31 (lunch)/36 – Carte € 29/46

Main Street ⊠ V94 R672 –
𝒞 061 396 004 – www.1826adare.ie –
Closed 13 January-5 February, Sunday lunch, Monday, Tuesday, Wednesday - Saturday lunch

🍽○ **Carriage House**   🛏 ♿ AC 🔄 P

MODERN CUISINE · BRASSERIE XX You'd never guess that this smart clubhouse with a plush bar was once the stables of the Adare Manor estate. Lunch is served in the conservatory, with its mosaic tiling and putting green views, and dinner, in the elegant brasserie. Dishes are carefully prepared; steaks from the charcoal grill are a highlight.

Carte € 35/74

Adare Manor Hotel ⊠ V94 W8WR –
𝒞 061 605 200 – www.adaremanor.com

🏚 **Adare Manor**   🎋 🐾 🛏 🖼 🏞 SPA 🏊 Ⅼ↕ 🔌 ♿ AC 🏌 P

GRAND LUXURY · ELEGANT This impressive 1830s Gothic-style mansion sits in 850 acres and offers a host of outdoor activities. Ornate ceilings and superb wood panelling feature throughout and bedrooms have an understated elegance. Enjoy afternoon tea in the cathedral-like 'Gallery'. The Tack Room bar is a fun spot.

104 rooms ⊑ – 👫 € 340/700 – 9 suites

⊠ V94 W8WR – 𝒞 061 605 200 – www.adaremanor.com

❀ **The Oak Room** · 🍽○ **Carriage House** – See restaurant listing

Inishmaan

🍴 **Inis Meáin Restaurant & Suites**   🔄 ‹ 🛏 **P**

REGIONAL CUISINE · FRIENDLY 🟆🟆 Set on a beautiful island, this futuristic stone building is inspired by the surrounding landscapes and features limed walls, sage banquettes and panoramic views. Cooking is modern, tasty and satisfyingly straightforward, showcasing island ingredients including seafood caught in currachs and hand-gathered urchins. Minimalist bedrooms feature natural furnishings.

Menu € 75

✉ *H91 NX86 – ☎ 086 826 6026 – www.inismeain.com – Closed 6 October-1 March, Sunday, Monday, Tuesday - Saturday lunch*

ARDMORE • AIRD MHÓR
Waterford – Regional map n° **21**–C3

🏵 **House**   ‹ 🆎 **P**

MODERN CUISINE · DESIGN 🟆🟆🟆 The Cliff House offers all that its name promises, with its clifftop setting, stunning bay views and stylish décor encompassing slate walls, Irish fabrics and bold colours. The smart modern bedrooms share the wonderful view, as does the restaurant which uses its full-length windows to its advantage.

Dutch born chef Martijn Kajuiter has been here since the very beginning and in that time has made a name for both himself and the hotel. Dishes showcase local ingredients with confidence and maturity, letting the produce speak for itself rather than being overpowered by the techniques. Menus are well-balanced, with the tasting selection offering subtle touches of innovation; flavours are rich and pronounced and the presentation is eye-catching. The team are engaging and personable and the wine list contains a few interesting, lesser-known bottles which are worth a try.

Specialities: Rose veal with Jerusalem artichoke, snails and béarnaise. Lamb with broad beans, marsh samphire, radish, polenta and tomato oil. Sour & preserved cherries with mascarpone, almond and white chocolate.

Menu € 88/110

Cliff House Hotel, Middle Road ✉ P36 AD89 – ☎ 024 87800 – www.cliffhousehotel.ie – Closed 24-26 December, Sunday, Monday, Tuesday - Saturday lunch

🏨 **Cliff House**   ⚡ ‹ 🖼 🕸 🦶 🔁 🆎 🧖 **P**

LUXURY · CONTEMPORARY Stylish cliffside hotel with a superb bay outlook and a lovely spa. Slate walls, Irish fabrics and bold colours feature throughout. Modern bedrooms have backlit glass artwork and smart bathrooms; some have balconies and all share the wonderful view. Choose from an extensive menu in the delightful bar and on the terrace; the restaurant serves more creative dishes.

39 rooms ⌧ – 🛏 € 199/389 – 3 suites

Middle Road ✉ P36 AD89 – ☎ 024 87800 – www.cliffhousehotel.ie – Closed 24-26 December

🏵 **House** – See restaurant listing

ARTHURSTOWN • COLMÁN
Wexford – Regional map n° **21**–D2

🏨 **Dunbrody Country House**   🐾 🛏 💮 **P**

COUNTRY HOUSE · HISTORIC A part-Georgian hunting lodge with a charming period feel, courtesy of original oak floors and open peat fires. It was once owned by the Marquis of Donegal and now celebrity chef Kevin Dundon runs his cookery school here. The restaurant offers seasonal modern dishes and there's a pub in the former stables.

16 rooms – 🛏 € 190/340 – 6 suites

✉ *Y34 R597 – ☎ 051 389 600 – www.dunbrodyhouse.com – Closed 19-26 December*

ATHLONE • BAILE ÁTHA LUAIN

Westmeath – Regional map n° **20**–C3

 Thyme

MODERN CUISINE · FRIENDLY Candles flicker in the windows of this welcoming restaurant set by the river. It's run by a passionate chef-owner and his bright, friendly team, and is a real hit with the locals. Regional ingredients feature in good value dishes which are carefully cooked and full of natural flavours.
Specialities: Ham hock with celeriac velouté, bacon vinaigrette and crispy egg. West Cork Wagyu beef with braised cheek, roast onion and thyme purée. Chocolate fondant with peanut butter ice cream and salted caramel.

Menu € 28/34 – Carte € 35/51

Custume Place, Strand Street – ℰ 090 647 8850 – www.thymerestaurant.ie – Closed 27 January-6 February, Monday - Saturday lunch

Kin Khao

THAI · COSY Hidden down a side street near the castle is this vivid yellow building with red window frames, which plays host to a cosy first floor restaurant decorated with tapestries. The Thai kitchen team prepare authentic dishes which have a subtle North Eastern influence, fresh flavours and gentle spicing.

Menu € 12 (lunch) – Carte € 29/33

Abbey Lane – ℰ 090 649 8805 – www.kinkhaothai.ie – Closed 24-25 December, Monday - Tuesday lunch, Saturday lunch

at Glasson Northeast: 8 km on N55

Wineport Lodge

LUXURY · DESIGN A superbly located hotel where the bedroom wing follows the line of the lough shore and each luxurious room boasts a balcony or a waterside terrace (it's worth paying the extra for the Champagne Suite). The outdoor hot tubs make a great place to take in the view. Extensive menus utilise seasonal produce.

29 rooms ☕ – ♔♔ € 180/350

ℰ 090 643 9010 – www.wineport.ie

BAGENALSTOWN • MUINE BHEAG

Carlow – Regional map n° **21**–D2

Kilgraney Country House

COUNTRY HOUSE · PERSONALISED A Georgian country house which adopts a truly holistic approach. Period features blend with modern, minimalist furnishings and the mood is calm and peaceful. It boasts a small tea room, a craft gallery and a spa with a relaxation room, along with pleasant herb, vegetable, zodiac and monastic gardens. Stay in the original house, the cottage or a self-contained suite.

7 rooms ☕ – ♔♔ € 200/240

ℰ 059 977 5283 – www.kilgraneyhouse.com – Closed 22 June-2 July, 24-31 August, 1 November-31 March

BALLINA • BÉAL AN ÁTHA

Mayo – Regional map n° **20**–B2

Mount Falcon

HISTORIC · ELEGANT Classic former shooting lodge built in 1876, with golf, cycling, fishing and archery available in its 100 acre grounds. Choose between characterful bedrooms in the main house and spacious, contemporary rooms in the extension. The restaurant is located in the old kitchens and serves elaborate modern dishes.

32 rooms ☕ – ♔♔ € 170/280 – 2 suites

Foxford Road – ℰ 096 74472 – www.mountfalcon.com – Closed 24-26 December

BALLINGARRY • BAILE AN GHARRAÍ

Limerick – Regional map n° **21**–B2

🏠 Mustard Seed at Echo Lodge ✿ 🐾 🛋 �🀆 🅿

TRADITIONAL · CLASSIC This cosy former convent is surrounded by well-kept gardens and filled with antique furniture, paintings, books and fresh flowers. Bedrooms in the main house have period styling, while those in the former school house are brighter and more modern. Dinner is an occasion – the two grand rooms are candlelit and have gilt mirrors; cooking is elaborate and boldly flavoured.

16 rooms 🖵 – 🛏 € 180/360

✉ V94 – ☏ 069 68508 – www.mustardseed.ie – Closed 13 January-7 February, 24-27 December

BALLSBRIDGE · DROICHEAD NA DOTHRA – Dublin ➜ See Dublin

BALLYDEHOB · BÉAL AN DÁ CHAB
Cork – Regional map n° **21**-A3

✵ Chestnut (Rob Krawczyk)

MODERN CUISINE · ROMANTIC 🍴 Having travelled the world, locally-born Rob Krawczyk (son of famous charcutier Frank) returned to his roots and, along with his partner Elaine, transformed this run-down old pub in the heart of West Cork into a sweet, intimate restaurant with an elegant style and a relaxed feel. It's a small place, seating just 18, and the bar counter at the front still hints at its past as a pub.

Rob has a great understanding of textures and flavours and his dishes are skilfully prepared yet pleasingly understated, with a focus on pure, natural flavours. The constantly evolving tasting menu champions County Cork and from the turf-smoked butter right through to desserts, his dishes really reflect the local region. The chatty, amiable service – led by Elaine – fits perfectly with the food.

Specialities: Mussels with seaweed and tapioca. Duck with brassicas and beetroot. Sheep's yoghurt with brown butter and wood sorrel.

Menu € 60/85

Staball Hill ✉ P81 X681 – ☏ 028 25766 – www.restaurantchestnutwestcork.ie – Closed 1 January-20 March, 27 September-6 October, Sunday lunch, Monday, Tuesday, Wednesday - Saturday lunch

BALLYFIN · AN BAILE FIONN
Laois – Regional map n° **21**-C1

🏰 Ballyfin ✿ 🐾 ⪍ 🛋 🖼 🀆 🛁 ⮑ ᴃ 🛠 🅿

GRAND LUXURY · HISTORIC An immaculate Regency mansion built in 1820 and set in 600 acres. The interior is stunning, with its cantilevered staircase, breathtaking ceilings and restored antiques. The library features 4,000 books, the drawing room is decorated in gold leaf and the bedrooms are luxurious. Produce grown in the kitchen garden informs the dishes served in the dining room.

21 rooms – 🛏 € 580/1510 – 4 suites

☏ 057 875 5866 – www.ballyfin.com – Closed 5 January-13 February

BALLYMORE EUSTACE · AN BAILE MÓR
Kildare – Regional map n° **21**-D1

🍽 Ballymore Inn 🎪 ᴃ 🆎 🄽 🅿

TRADITIONAL CUISINE · PUB 🍴 Remote village pub with a deli selling homemade breads, pickles, oils and the like. The owner promotes small, artisan producers, so expect organic veg, meat from quality assured farms and farmhouse cheeses. Portions are generous.

Carte € 35/66

✉ W91 – ☏ 045 864 585 – www.ballymoreinn.com

BALLYNAHINCH • BAILE NA HINSE

Galway - Regional map n° **20**–A3

⅋○ Owenmore

≤ 🚐 🏠 ⑩ 🅿

MODERN CUISINE · INTIMATE ✕✕ Within a 17C country house you'll find this bright, elegant restaurant which looks out over the river and the estate. Modern dishes are delicate and subtly flavoured. In winter, end the evening with a drink beside the marble fireplace.

Menu € 70

Ballynahinch Castle Hotel ✉ H91 F4A7 – 𝒞 095 31006 –
www.ballynahinchcastle.com –
Closed Sunday - Saturday lunch

🏠 Ballynahinch Castle

🏂 🐾 ≤ 🚐 ⅊ 🅿

TRADITIONAL · CLASSIC This castellated hotel is dramatically located on the Wild Atlantic Way, amongst 700 acres of woodland, with a salmon fishing river in front and mountains behind. The sitting rooms are cosy and bedrooms have a fitting country house style. Be sure to find time to wander around the pretty walled garden.

45 rooms ⌑ – 👫 € 210/430 – 3 suites

✉ H91 F4A7 – 𝒞 095 31006 –
www.ballynahinchcastle.com

⅋○ **Owenmore** – See restaurant listing

BALLYVAUGHAN • BAILE UÍ BHEACHÁIN

Clare - Regional map n° **21**–B1

⅋○ Gregans Castle

≤ 🚐 🅿

MODERN CUISINE · ELEGANT ✕✕ Have an aperitif in the drawing room of this country house hotel before heading through to the restaurant (ask for a table close to the window, to take in views stretching as far as Galway Bay). Interesting modern dishes have clean, clear flavours and showcase the latest local produce. Service is attentive.

Menu € 79

Gregans Castle Hotel ✉ H91 CF60 – 𝒞 065 707 7005 –
www.gregans.ie –
Closed 1 November-13 February, Sunday - Saturday lunch

🏠 Gregans Castle

🏂 🐾 ≤ 🚐 🅿

FAMILY · PERSONALISED Take in superb views of The Burren and Galway Bay from this well-run country house. The open-fired hall leads to a cosy bar-lounge and elegant sitting room. Bedrooms blend modern styling with antique furnishings: some open onto the garden; one in the old kitchen features a panelled ceiling and a four-poster.

17 rooms ⌑ – 👫 € 240/295 – 4 suites

✉ H91 CF60 – 𝒞 065 707 7005 –
www.gregans.ie – Closed 29 November-13 February

⅋○ **Gregans Castle** – See restaurant listing

BALTIMORE • DÚN NA SÉAD

Cork - Regional map n° **21**–A3

🌸 Mews

MODERN CUISINE · INTIMATE ✕✕ The fishing village of Baltimore plays host to this cosy, intimate restaurant. Exposed stone walls are hung with modern photos and complemented by aged wooden chairs, and there's also a lovely conservatory-style room.

County Cork boasts a wealth of top quality produce and the chef uses it to full effect, by selecting the best seasonal ingredients and showcasing their natural flavours; fish is from the harbour 20 yards away, meat is from the surrounding hills, and vegetables come from just down the road. The appealing modern Irish tasting menu is well-balanced and provides plenty of interest, and local herbs and seaweeds are a feature. It's all brought together perfectly by the engaging, knowledgeable service.

Specialities: Boxty with red mullet. Cod with seaweed and mussel sauce. Milk with honey and pine.

Menu € 95

✉ P81 TC64 – ☏ 028 20572 – www.mewsrestaurant.ie –
Closed 1 January-28 February, Sunday, Monday, Tuesday, Wednesday - Saturday lunch

BANDON • DROICHEAD NA BANDAN
Cork – Regional map n° **21**–B3

🍴○ **Poachers**　　　　　　　　　　　　　　&. 🅰🅲 ⇔ 🅿

TRADITIONAL CUISINE · PUB ✗ Sit in the cosy bar, the small snug or the dining room under the eaves. Dishes are boldly flavoured and local seafood is the star of the show – you'll always find fish landed at Union Hall and crabs from Court-macsherry.

Menu € 32 – Carte € 30/40

Clonakilty Road ✉ P72 – ☏ 023 884 1159 – www.poachers.ie

BARNA • BEARNA
Galway – Regional map n° **20**–B3

🍴○ **West**　　　　　　　　　　　　　　　88 &. 🅰🅲 🅿

MODERN CUISINE · CONTEMPORARY DÉCOR ✗✗ Stylish first floor restaurant in a smart boutique hotel, with a chic champagne bar, booth seating and a moody, intimate feel. Seasonal menus offer ambitious, innovative dishes, show-casing meats and seafood from the 'West' of Ireland.

Menu € 38/65 – Carte € 40/55

Twelve Hotel, Barna Crossroads ✉ H91 Y3KA – ☏ 091 597 000 –
www.westrestaurant.ie – Closed Monday, Tuesday, Wednesday - Saturday lunch

🏨 **Twelve**　　　　　　　　　　　　　🍴 🖭 &. 🅰🅲 🛋 🅿

BUSINESS · CONTEMPORARY An unassuming exterior hides a keenly run bou-tique hotel complete with a bakery, a pizza kitchen and a deli. Stylish, modern bedrooms have large free-standing mirrors, mood lighting and designer seaweed toiletries – and some even boast cocktail bars! Modern European dishes are served in the restaurant.

45 rooms ☲ – ♕♕ € 100/200 – 24 suites

Barna Crossroads ✉ H91 Y3KA – ☏ 091 597 000 – www.thetwelvehotel.ie
🍴○ **West** – See restaurant listing

BLACKLION • AN BLAIC
Cavan – Regional map n° **20**–C2

🍴○ **MacNean House**　　　　　　　　　⇦ 🅰🅲 🕼 ⇔

MODERN BRITISH · ELEGANT ✗✗✗ Renowned Irish chef Neven Maguire owns this smart townhouse restaurant which comprises a chic lounge, a plush dining room and a cookery school. The 8 course tasting menu offers attractively pre-sented, sophisticated dishes which celebrate top quality seasonal Irish ingredi-ents. Bedrooms are a mix of modern and country styles.

Menu € 89

Main Street ✉ F91 – ☏ 071 985 3022 – www.macneanrestaurant.com –
Closed 1-15 January, Monday, Tuesday, Wednesday - Saturday lunch

BLACKROCK – Dún Laoghaire-Rathdown ➜ See Dublin

BLARNEY • AN BHLARNA
Cork – Regional map n° **21**–B3

ⅱ○ **Square Table**

IRISH · COSY XX Sweet restaurant with a warm, welcoming, neighbourhood feel. Menus offer French-influenced dishes crafted from Irish produce; the early evening menu is good value. It's proudly and enthusiastically run by twins Tricia and Martina.

Carte €31/45

5 The Square ⊠ T23 – ☎ 021 438 2825 – www.thesquaretable.ie –
Closed 7 January-7 February, Monday, Tuesday, Wednesday - Saturday lunch

BORRIS • AN BHUIRÍOS
Carlow – Regional map n° **21**–D2

ⅱ○ **Clashganny House** 🛋 🅿

CLASSIC CUISINE · INTIMATE XX Hidden away in a lovely valley, this early Victorian house is the setting for the realisation of one couple's dream. The modern restaurant is split over three rooms; appealing menus balance light options with more gutsy dishes.

Menu €40

Clashganny – ☎ 059 977 1003 – www.clashgannyhouse.com – Closed Sunday dinner, Monday, Tuesday, Wednesday - Saturday lunch

ⅱ○ **1808** 🛋 🅱 🅿

MODERN CUISINE · BISTRO X The Step House hotel's restaurant is an appealing bistro deluxe with lots of mahogany, red leather banquettes and French doors opening onto the garden. Modern menus use the best of Irish produce. Service is relaxed and friendly.

Carte €30/48

Step House Hotel, Main Street ⊠ R95 V2CR – ☎ 059 977 3209 –
www.stephousehotel.ie – Closed 1-6 February, Monday, Tuesday

CAHERSIVEEN • CATHAIR SAIDHBHÍN
Kerry – Regional map n° **21**–A2

ⅱ○ **Quinlan & Cooke** ⇦ 🛖 🅿

SEAFOOD · BRASSERIE X 'QC's, as the locals call it, is an atmospheric restaurant with a nautical theme. Seafood-orientated menus offer unfussy classics and more unusual daily specials; the family also own a local fish wholesalers. Stylish, well-equipped bedrooms are in a townhouse and mews; breakfast is brought to your room.

Carte €27/50

3 Main Street ⊠ V23 WA46 – ☎ 066 947 2244 – www.qc.ie –
Closed 20 January-10 February, Sunday - Saturday lunch

CARLINGFORD • CAIRLINN
Louth – Regional map n° **20**–D2

ⅱ○ **Bay Tree** ⇦ ⟷

MODERN CUISINE · FRIENDLY XX An honest little neighbourhood restaurant on the bustling main street of a small town, just a stone's throw from Carlingford Lough. Carefully prepared, well-balanced dishes feature veg from the garden and seafood from the lough – including its renowned oysters. Bedrooms are simple but warm and cosy.

Carte €35/48

Newry Street ⊠ A91 – ☎ 042 938 3848 – www.belvederehouse.ie – Closed Monday, Tuesday, Wednesday - Saturday lunch

CARNAROSS • CARN NA ROS
Meath – Regional map n° **20**–D3

⑪○ Forge

TRADITIONAL CUISINE · RUSTIC XX Rural Meath plays host to this stone-built former lodge, which has an atmospheric interior comprising warm red décor, flagged floors and exposed rafters hung with farming implements. Produce from nearby farms features in generously proportioned, fairly priced dishes that are a hit with the locals.

Menu €30/40

Pottlereagh – ℰ 046 924 5003 – www.theforgerestaurant.ie –
Closed 20 January-4 February, Sunday dinner, Monday, Tuesday, Wednesday -
Saturday lunch

CARRICKMACROSS • CARRAIG MHACHAIRE ROIS
Monaghan – Regional map n° **20**–D2

⊛ Courthouse

REGIONAL CUISINE · RUSTIC X Relaxed, rustic restaurant featuring wooden floors, exposed ceiling rafters and bare brick; ask for table 20, by the window. Great value menus offer carefully prepared, flavourful dishes which are a lesson in self-restraint – their simplicity being a key part of their appeal. Friendly, efficient service.

Specialities: Roast lamb heart on sourdough. John Dory with brown shrimps, spinach and lemon butter. Warm chocolate tart with vanilla ice cream.

Menu €28 – Carte €31/44

1 Monaghan Street ✉ A81 X066 – ℰ 042 969 2848 – www.courthouserestaurant.ie
– Closed 6-16 January, 1-11 June, Monday, Tuesday, Wednesday - Saturday lunch

CARRICK-ON-SHANNON • CORA DROMA RÚISC
Leitrim – Regional map n° **20**–C2

⑪○ St.George's Terrace

MODERN CUISINE · CLASSIC DÉCOR XX Start with drinks in the plush bar of this imposing Victorian building – formerly a bank – before moving into the boldly decorated main dining room with its high ceiling and chandelier. Well-balanced cooking has seasonal Irish produce at its heart. The basement is home to a cookery school.

Carte €34/49

St George's Terrace – ℰ 071 961 6546 – www.stgeorgesterrace.com –
Closed 12-29 January, Monday, Tuesday, Wednesday - Saturday lunch

⑪○ Oarsman 🛖

TRADITIONAL CUISINE · PUB X A traditional family-run pub set close to the river and filled with pottery, bygone artefacts and fishing tackle – it's a real hit with the locals. Flavoursome cooking uses local produce and all the bread is home-baked; they even have a lager brewed for them. The upstairs restaurant opens later in the week.

Carte €25/45

Bridge Street – ℰ 071 962 1733 – www.theoarsman.com – Closed Sunday, Monday

CASHEL • CAISEAL
South Tipperary – Regional map n° **21**–C2

⑪○ Chez Hans 🅿

TRADITIONAL CUISINE · TRADITIONAL XX An imposing former Synod Hall built in 1861 houses this long-standing, family-owned restaurant. It offers a good value set price menu midweek and a more interesting à la carte of classic dishes at the weekend. Start with a drink in the bar, surrounded by contemporary Irish art.

Menu €35 – Carte €42/60

Rockside, Moor Lane ✉ E25 – ℰ 062 61177 – www.chezhans.net – Closed 6-22 April,
Sunday dinner, Monday, Tuesday, Wednesday - Saturday lunch

ⅈ◯ Café Hans   ⌖✝ AC P ⊅

TRADITIONAL CUISINE · FRIENDLY ⅄ Located just down the road from the Rock of Cashel; a vibrant, popular eatery set next to big sister 'Chez Hans' and run by the same family. Sit at closely set tables amongst an interesting collection of art. Tasty, unfussy dishes are crafted from local ingredients; the express lunch is great value.

Menu € 20 (lunch) – Carte € 23/40

Rockside, Moore Lane ✉ E25 TK65 – ☎ 062 63660 – Closed 31 January-13 February, Sunday, Monday, Tuesday - Saturday dinner

CASTLECOMER
Kilkenny – Regional map n° **21**-C2

ⅈ◯ Lady Anne at Creamery House ⓝ   ⇦ ⇧ P

MODERN CUISINE · ELEGANT ⅩⅩ This restored Georgian house was originally built for Lady Anne Wandersforde, the Countess of Ormond, and later in life became offices for the local creamery co-operative. Its latest incarnation is an elegant restaurant run by a passionate chef-owner, who serves refined, modern, lovingly prepared dishes.

Menu € 60/90

✉ R95 – ☎ 056 440 0080 – www.restaurantladyanne.ie – Closed 21-28 January, Sunday lunch, Monday, Tuesday, Wednesday, Thursday - Saturday lunch

CASTLEMARTYR · BAILE NA MARTRA Cork
Cork – Regional map n° **21**-C3

ⅈ◯ Bell Tower   ⇦ 🛱 ⅋ AC P

CLASSIC CUISINE · LUXURY ⅩⅩⅩ A bright, formally laid restaurant set on the ground floor of a 17C manor house, with traditional décor and plenty of windows overlooking the attractive gardens. Classic dishes with a modern twist from an experienced team.

Carte € 40/52

Castlemartyr Hotel ✉ P25 – ☎ 021 421 9000 – www.castlemartyrresort.ie – Closed Monday - Saturday lunch

🏚 Castlemartyr   ✿ ⅌ ⇐ ⇦ 🖻 🔲 ⑩ ⋔ ♨ ⊟ ⅋ AC ⅍ P

COUNTRY HOUSE · CONTEMPORARY Impressive 17C manor house in 220 acres of grounds, complete with castle ruins, lakes, a golf course and a stunning spa. Luxurious bedrooms have superb marble bathrooms. Look out for the wonderful original ceiling in the Knight's Bar. Franchini's offers an extensive Italian menu; the Bell Tower is more formal.

103 rooms � – ¶¶ € 125/289 – 28 suites

✉ P25 – ☎ 021 421 9000 – www.castlemartyrresort.ie

ⅈ◯ **Bell Tower** – See restaurant listing

CAVAN · AN CABHÁN
Cavan – Regional map n° **20**-C2

at Cloverhill North: 12 km by N3 on N54

ⅈ◯ Olde Post Inn   ⇦ ⇦ ⅋ AC ⅇ ⇧ P

TRADITIONAL CUISINE · RUSTIC ⅩⅩ Start by enjoying a fireside aperitif in the flag-floored bar of this old 1800s post office, then dine either in the atmospheric original building or in the appealing conservatory. The experienced chef-owner uses top local ingredients to create flavoursome dishes that are classic in essence; game is a speciality. Stylish bedrooms complete the picture.

Menu € 49 – Carte € 49/66

☎ 047 55555 – www.theoldepostinn.com – Closed 2-16 January, 1-16 July, Monday, Tuesday, Wednesday - Saturday lunch

CELBRIDGE
Kildare – Regional map n° **21**-D1

❀❀ Aimsir ◎

MODERN CUISINE · ELEGANT XxX Start with a drink in the cocktail lounge overlooking the garden then head past hanging meats and colourful jars of foraged produce into the elegant dining room. Jordan Bailey calmly leads the chefs in the open kitchen, while his wife heads the delightful service team – and their infectious pride radiates through all who work for them.

Originally from Cornwall, Jordan worked at the Elephant and Sat Bains, before heading off to Norway, where he quickly rose through the ranks to become head chef at Three-Starred Maaemo. He brings with him overwhelming passion, a great understanding of flavours, and supreme craftsmanship, resulting in superbly balanced, original dishes with real depth of flavour. The 18+ labour-intensive courses are all very different and make good use of preserved and fermented ingredients sourced from around Ireland.

Specialities: Dublin Bay skate wing, three-cornered leek and chicken skin butter sauce. Achill Mountain mutton shoulder, heather and mutton bone glaze. 'A taste of the forest'.

Menu €115

Cliff at Lyons, Lyons Road ⊠ W23 HXH3 – ℰ 01 630 3500 – www.aimsir.ie –
Closed 22 December-14 January, Sunday, Monday, Tuesday, Wednesday - Saturday lunch

ⓘ○ Canteen Celbridge

MODERN CUISINE · FRIENDLY X A local chef and his endearing French wife have created this relaxed, understated restaurant, where abstract art stands out against grey walls. Well-crafted dishes are boldly flavoured and Irish produce takes centre stage.

Menu €32 – Carte €47/51

4 Main Street ⊠ W23 – ℰ 01 627 4967 – www.canteencelbridge.com –
Closed 1-14 January, 15 August-1 September, Sunday, Monday, Tuesday - Friday lunch

CLONAKILTY · CLOICH NA COILLTE

Cork – Regional map n° **21**-B3

ⓘ○ Gulfstream

MODERN CUISINE · CHIC XX Contemporary New England style restaurant set on the first floor of a vast hotel and offering superb views over the beach. Modern menus highlight produce from West Cork and feature plenty of fresh local seafood.

Carte €45/65

Inchydoney Island Lodge and Spa Hotel ⊠ P85 X258 – ℰ 023 883 3143 –
www.inchydoneyisland.com – Closed Sunday - Saturday lunch

ⓘ○ Deasy's

TRADITIONAL CUISINE · PUB X An appealing pub in a picturesque hamlet, offering lovely views out across the bay. Its gloriously dated interior is decorated with maritime memorabilia. Menus are dictated by the seasons and the latest catch from the local boats.

Menu €34 – Carte €32/47

Ring ⊠ P85 AD80 – ℰ 023 883 5741 – Closed Sunday dinner, Monday, Tuesday

🏨 Inchydoney Island Lodge and Spa

SPA AND WELLNESS · CONTEMPORARY Superbly located on a remote headland and boasting stunning views over the beach and out to sea; all of the contemporary bedrooms have a balcony or terrace. The impressive spa boasts a seawater pool and 27 treatment rooms. Dine in the modern restaurant or nautically styled bistro-bar.

67 rooms ⊇ – 🛏 €169/269 – 3 suites

⊠ P85 X258 – ℰ 023 883 3143 – www.inchydoneyisland.com –
Closed 24-26 December

ⓘ○ **Gulfstream** – See restaurant listing

CLONEGALL • CLUAIN NA NGALL
Carlow – Regional map n° **21**–D2

🐷 Sha-Roe Bistro
MODERN CUISINE · FRIENDLY 𝕏 A welcoming 17C former coaching inn set in a picturesque village; it's a simple place with a relaxed, intimate feel and candlelit tables in the evenings. Menus offer carefully presented, unfussy dishes with clear flavours and a classical base. Sourcing of local and farmers' market ingredients is paramount.

Specialities: Bengali vegetable cakes, Madras sauce and frisée salad. Slow-braised beef cheek with button mushroom and pancetta. Banana custard, pecans, honeycomb, caramelised banana and salted caramel ice cream.

Carte € 34/45

Main Street ⊠ Y21 KH61 – ℰ 053 937 5636 – www.sha-roebistro.ie –
Closed 1 January-6 February, 24 August-3 September, Sunday dinner-Wednesday, Thursday-Saturday lunch

CLONTARF • CLUAIN TARBH – Dublin ➜ See Dublin

CLOVERHILL • DROIM CAISIDE – Cavan ➜ See Cavan

CONG • CONGA
Galway – Regional map n° **20**–A3

⭑⚪ George V   🐬 ≤ 🛒 🆑 🅿
CLASSIC CUISINE · ELEGANT 𝕏𝕏𝕏 A visit to the stunning wine cellars is a must at this grand, sophisticated hotel restaurant, where wood-panelling and Waterford Crystal chandeliers set the tone. Classic French flavours are delivered using subtly modern techniques.

Menu € 95/150

Ashford Castle Hotel, Ashford Castle Hotel ⊠ F31 CA48 – ℰ 094 954 6003 –
www.ashfordcastle.com – Closed Sunday - Saturday lunch

⭑⚪ Cullen's at the Cottage   🛒 🏡 🆑 🅿
TRADITIONAL CUISINE · BISTRO 𝕏𝕏 Set within the grounds of Ashford Castle is this pretty little thatched cottage with an attractive landscaped terrace and lovely views. It has a stylish, subtly rustic look and a relaxed feel. Menus list appealing classics.

Carte € 33/60

Ashford Castle Hotel, Ashford Castle Hotel ⊠ F31 CA48 – ℰ 094 954 5332 –
www.ashfordcastle.com – Closed Sunday dinner

🏰 Ashford Castle   🎏 🐬 ≤ 🛒 🖼 🛎 🏯 💪 🛗 🆑 🧖 🅿
HISTORIC BUILDING · ELEGANT Hugely impressive lochside castle surrounded by extensive grounds; try archery, falconry, clay pigeon shooting or zip-lining; take to the water; or relax with loch views in the spa. Handsome guest areas display plenty of historic splendour and bedrooms are sumptuously appointed. Dine in the stone cellars in Dungeon, casually in Cullen's or formally in elegant George V.

83 rooms ⥄ – 🛏 € 325/1950 – 12 suites

⊠ *F31 CA48 – ℰ 094 954 6003 – www.ashfordcastle.com*

⭑⚪ **Cullen's at the Cottage** • ⭑⚪ **George V** – See restaurant listing

CORK • CORCAIGH
Cork – Regional map n° **21**–B3

⛣ Ichigo Ichie (Takashi Miyazaki)   🆑
JAPANESE · ROMANTIC 𝕏𝕏 Chef-owner Takashi Miyazaki spent three years tempting the taste buds of the diners of Cork with his small Japanese takeaway before eventually opening this smart restaurant in the heart of the city. It's a dark, moody place with something of an industrial feel; a lucky few get seats at the small five-seater counter to watch the deft preparation close up.

The interesting omakase menu changes every 6 weeks and mixes long-standing Japanese traditions with more modern touches. Irish ingredients – including supreme quality fish and shellfish – are cleverly balanced with time-honoured Japanese techniques. Colourfully presented dishes are artfully arranged on handmade crockery and are brought to the table by the chef and his knowledgeable team – they are also paired with sakes chosen by Takashi himself.

Specialities: Duck with white asparagus, soy pulp and cucumber vinegar. Cod with salted rice malt, okura and daikon. Watermelon with berries, kanten, adzuki beans and kuromitsu.

Menu €120/135

5 Fenns Quay, Sheares Street – ☎ 021 427 9997 –
www.ichigoichie.ie – Closed Sunday, Monday, Tuesday, Wednesday - Saturday lunch

‖○ Orchids   ⌲ ⅙ AC P

MODERN CUISINE · ELEGANT XxX Sophisticated formal dining room in a well-appointed country house. Pillars dominate the room, which is laid with crisp white tablecloths. Menus offer refined dishes with some modern twists.

Menu €72

Hayfield Manor Hotel, Perrott Ave, College Road – ☎ 021 4845900 –
www.hayfieldmanor.ie – Closed Sunday lunch, Monday, Tuesday, Wednesday, Thursday - Saturday lunch

‖○ Greenes   AC ⊗

MODERN CUISINE · FRIENDLY XX Head down the alleyway at the side of the Isaacs Hotel, towards the waterfall, to access this formal yet friendly restaurant. The chef is a local and uses his cooking to showcase ingredients from West Cork producers.

Menu €33 (lunch)/49 – Carte €53/62

48 MacCurtain Street – ☎ 021 455 2279 –
www.greenesrestaurant.com – Closed Monday - Wednesday lunch

‖○ Perrotts   ⌲ ⌂ ⅙ AC ⇆ P

MODERN CUISINE · BRASSERIE XX A conservatory restaurant overlooking the gardens of a luxurious country house. It's smart but comfortably furnished, with an adjoining wood-panelled bar. The menu offers a modern take on brasserie classics.

Menu €38 – Carte €40/60

Hayfield Manor Hotel, Perrott Ave, College Road – ☎ 021 484 5900 –
www.hayfieldmanor.ie

‖○ da Mirco ⑩

ITALIAN · SIMPLE X Let owner Mirco transport you to Italy at this authentic osteria in the heart of the city. Light pours over the tightly packed tables, which are skirted by plant-lined walls. Both Irish and imported ingredients feature in the rustic home-style dishes; all of the pastas and sauces are homemade.

Carte €25/40

4 Bridge Street ✉ P47 – ☎ 021 241 9480 –
www.damirco.com – Closed Sunday lunch, Monday, Tuesday, Wednesday - Saturday lunch

‖○ Farmgate Café

REGIONAL CUISINE · BISTRO X Popular, long-standing eatery above a bustling 200 year old market; turn right for self-service or left for the bistro. Daily menus use produce from the stalls below and are supplemented by the latest catch. Dishes are hearty and homemade.

Carte €22/40

English Market, Princes Street (1st Floor) – ☎ 021 427 8134 –
www.farmgate.ie – Closed 25-29 December, Sunday, Monday, Tuesday - Wednesday dinner

🍴○ **Oyster Tavern**

IRISH · SIMPLE X Cork's residents have frequented this charming pub since 1792. Stay on the characterful ground floor for drinks or head upstairs to eat in the smarter restaurant. It sits adjacent to the English Market and this is reflected in the menu. Oysters lead the way, closely followed by unbelievably succulent steaks.

Carte €22/44

54 St Patrick's Street (1st Floor) – ℰ 021 735 5677 – www.oystertavern.ie – Closed Sunday dinner

🏨 **Hayfield Manor**

HISTORIC · CLASSIC Luxurious country house with wood-panelled hall, impressive staircase and antique-furnished drawing rooms; the perfect spot for afternoon tea. Plush bedrooms have plenty of extras, including putting machines. Well-equipped residents' spa.

88 rooms ⌂ – ♥♥ €239/405 – 4 suites

Perrott Ave, College Road ⊠ T12HT97 – ℰ 021 484 5900 – www.hayfieldmanor.ie

🍴○ **Orchids** · 🍴○ **Perrotts** – See restaurant listing

CROSSHAVEN · BUN AN TÁBHAIRNE
Cork – Regional map n° **21**–B3

🍴○ **Cronin's**

SEAFOOD · PUB X A classic Irish pub filled with interesting artefacts. It's been in the family since 1970 and is now run by the 3rd generation. Unfussy seafood dishes feature local produce. The limited opening restaurant offers more ambitious fare.

Carte €25/47

1 Point Road ⊠ P43 – ℰ 021 483 1829 – www.croninspub.com – Closed 25 December

DELGANY · DEILGNE
Wicklow – Regional map n° **21**–D2

🍴○ **Pigeon House**

MODERN BRITISH · BISTRO X You'll find this large restaurant located above a bakery and deli in a former pub. Good value, all-encompassing menus morph from breakfast into coffee, then lunch and dinner. There's a tempting counter filled with homemade cakes and in the evening, rotisserie chicken and pizza from the wood-oven feature.

Carte €25/50

The Delgany Inn ⊠ A63 T285 – ℰ 01 287 7103 – www.pigeonhouse.ie – Closed Monday, Tuesday - Wednesday dinner

DINGLE • AN DAINGEAN
Kerry - Regional map n° **21**-A2

⊛ Chart House   🅰️🄲

REGIONAL CUISINE • RUSTIC ✗ This characterful former boathouse sits in a pleasant quayside spot. The charming open-plan interior features exposed stone and stained glass, and the room has a cosy, intimate feel. Seasonal local ingredients feature in rustic, flavoursome dishes and service is friendly and efficient.

Specialities: Risotto of Dingle Bay prawns with Parmesan tuile. Roast breast of Irish chicken, apricot and sage stuffing, sweet potato mousseline and plum sauce. Espresso tart with crème fraîche and malt syrup.

Menu € 36 – Carte € 36/48

The Mall ⊠ V92 T2R9 – ℰ 066 915 2255 –
www.thecharthousedingle.com – Closed 2 January-12 February, Sunday - Saturday lunch

⊛ Land to Sea 🄽

IRISH • BISTRO ✗ The name sums it up perfectly, as the chef uses produce from the surrounding fields and nearby waters to full advantage. Local meats and wonderfully fresh fish and shellfish are prepared with care and a good understanding of flavours. If the crab salad is on the menu, be sure to choose it.

Specialities: Dingle Bay crab salad with radish and pesto. Pork cheek cooked in Cronin's cider with crackling. Honey and whiskey mousse, honeycomb and sea salt ice cream.

Menu € 20/40 – Carte € 35/50

Main Street ⊠ V92 –
ℰ 066 915 2609 – www.landtoseadingle.com –
Closed 1 November-29 February, Sunday - Saturday lunch

⫯○ Global Village   🅰️🄲 🝙

TRADITIONAL CUISINE • BISTRO ✗✗ This well-run restaurant has a pleasingly homely, laid-back feel. Despite having visited 42 countries, the chef likes to keep things regional, with herbs and salad leaves coming from their kitchen garden and meats and vegetables sourced from the fertile peninsula. The local fish dishes are fantastic.

Menu € 33/37 – Carte € 40/58

Upper Main Street ⊠ V92 – ℰ 066 915 2325 – www.globalvillagedingle.com –
Closed 5 January-7 March, Sunday - Saturday lunch

⫯○ Out of the Blue   🝚 🅰️🄲

SEAFOOD • RUSTIC ✗ Its name is perfectly apt: not only is it painted bright blue, but this simple harbourside restaurant keeps its focus firmly on ingredients that come from the sea. Menus are decided each morning, based on the latest local catch.

Menu € 33 (lunch), € 45/65

Waterside ⊠ V92 T181 –
ℰ 066 915 0811 – www.outoftheblue.ie –
Closed 9 December-29 February, Monday - Saturday lunch

DONEGAL • DÚN NA NGALL
Donegal – Regional map n° **20**-C1

🏨 Solis Lough Eske Castle   🛝 🛎️ 🔟 🆂 🜋 🖨️ 🔽 ♿ 🛁 🅿️

LUXURY • CLASSIC Beautifully restored 17C castle, surrounded by 43 acres of sculpture-filled grounds. There's a fantastic spa and a swimming pool overlooking an enclosed garden. Bedrooms are a mix of contemporary and antique-furnished; go for a Garden Suite.

97 rooms ⊈ – 🛉 € 215/440 – 20 suites

ℰ 074 974 3250 – www.lougheskecastlehotel.com

DONNYBROOK • DOMHNACH BROC – Dublin ➜ See Dublin

DOONBEG • AN DÚN BEAG
Clare – Regional map n° **21**–B2

🏵 Morrissey's   ⬅ ⓧ 🏠 ⅛

SEAFOOD · PUB ⅹ Smartly refurbished pub in a small coastal village; its terrace overlooks the river and the castle ruins. The menu may be simple but cooking is careful and shows respect for ingredients; locally caught fish and shellfish feature heavily and the crabs in particular are worth a try. Bedrooms are modern – two overlook the river – and they have bikes and a kayak for hire.

Specialities: Wild Doonbeg crab claws. Fillet of hake with prosecco velouté. Local berry Eton mess with salted caramel.

Carte € 28/40

✉ V15 – ℰ 065 905 5304 – www.morrisseysdoonbeg.com –
Closed 1 January-7 March, Monday, Tuesday, Wednesday - Saturday lunch

DROGHEDA • DROICHEAD ÁTHA
Louth – Regional map n° **20**–D3

ⅢO The Kitchen   ⅛ 🆎 ⟷

MEDITERRANEAN CUISINE · BISTRO ⅹ By day, this glass-fronted Georgian eatery opposite the river in the town centre is a café serving homemade cakes, pastries, salads and sandwiches. By night, it offers a more interesting Spanish and Eastern Mediterranean menu with influences from North Africa and the Middle East.

Carte € 22/45

2 South Quay – ℰ 041 983 4630 – Closed 25-27 December, Monday, Tuesday

DUBLIN • BAILE ÁTHA CLIATH

Dublin – Regional map n° **21**–D1

Top tips!

Dublin's handsome squares and facades took shape some 250 years ago, designed by the finest architects of the time, but its Georgian properties have now been joined by the more modern architecture of grand hotels, smart restaurants and impressive galleries.

A must-visit is the historic Trinity College, home to the magnificent Old Library and the world's most famous medieval manuscript, the Book of Kells. From here, head for the smart shops of Grafton Street and then on to St Stephen's Green, a stunning 22 acre Victorian park. Further west are the impressive structures of Dublin Castle and Christ Church Cathedral.

Ireland's capital is on a roll when it comes to eating out. It boasts two Two-Starred restaurants – **Patrick Guilbaud** and **The Greenhouse** – and several One Stars, including long-standing **Chapter One** and the stylishly laid-back **Variety Jones**; along with a host of Bib Gourmands.

Z. Steger/age fotostock

Restaurants

✿✿ **Patrick Guilbaud** (Guillaume Lebrun)

MODERN FRENCH · ELEGANT XXX Patrick Guilbaud is one of Ireland's most celebrated chefs and this well-regarded restaurant is high on the list of any serious foodie living in or visiting Dublin. He has run a tight ship here for many years and you cannot deny that he has earned his place in Irish culinary history. The lounge is decorated in bold, eye-catching colours, while the sumptuous restaurant's period features are softened by pastel shades.

The owners are ever-present and they work their way around the room making sure that every diner is warmly welcomed and made to feel special. Accomplished, original cooking is rooted in the traditional French school but introduces some modern techniques. Bold flavours are superbly balanced, the presentation is stunning, and luxurious Irish ingredients are always to the fore. Both the wine cellar and the wine list are works of art.

Specialities: Blue lobster ravioli with coconut scented lobster cream, toasted almonds and curry dressing. Lamb fillet, wet garlic and black olive oil. Opalys chocolate and tropical fruit "Cocoon".

Menu € 52 (lunch), € 135/203 – Carte € 125/151

Town plan G3-e – *21 Upper Merrion Street* ✉ *D2* – *☎ 01 676 4192* – *www.restaurantpatrickguilbaud.ie* – *Closed 25 December-3 January, Sunday, Monday*

✿✿ **Greenhouse** (Mickael Viljanen)

MODERN CUISINE · ELEGANT XXX The Greenhouse is a chic, intimate restaurant that has steadily evolved over the years. The staff are friendly and personable and the atmosphere is refreshingly relaxed, and while the trams may rumble past outside, no-one seems to notice, as the focus here is the food on the plate.

Chef Mickael Viljanen hails from Finland and has been working in kitchens since he was 14. Food is his life and he regularly travels to Paris both to enhance his knowledge and to source some excellent quality produce. Accomplished, sophisticated cooking presents some stimulating flavour combinations and while it's classically based, has creative elements and plenty of personality. This is a chef who really understands how to get the best out of his ingredients and works with great precision to continually refine each dish.

Specialities: Foie gras Royale with apple, smoked eel and walnut. Lozère milk-fed lamb with kombu, lemon and curry. Amedei chocolate with praline, coffee, orange and rosemary.

Menu € 55 (lunch)/110

Town plan G3-r – *Dawson Street* ✉ *D2* – *☎ 01 676 7015* – *www.thegreenhouserestaurant.ie* – *Closed 13-28 January, 20 July-4 August, Sunday, Monday*

DUBLIN

0 — 850 m
0 — 850 yards

MONAGHAM

A

B

Griffith
Tolka Valley Rd
Finglas Rd Old
Tolka Valley Park
Ballyboggan
ROYAL CANAL
National Botanic Gardens
Finglas Rd
GLASNEVIN CEMETERY
Finglas

NAVAN

ASHTOWN
Navan Rd
Blackhorse Av
Raoath Rd
Raoath Rd
CABRA
Faussagh
PHIBSBOROUGH
Neiphin
Navan Rd
Faussagh Rd
Connaught St
Cabra Rd
Quarry Rd
North Circular Rd
Phibsborough

1

Phoenix Monument

Old Cabra Rd
North Circular Rd
Fish Pond
Blackhorse Av
Aughrim St
Manor St
Enusia St
North
Dublin Zoo
Phoenix Park
People's Garden
Wellington Monument
National Museum of Decorative Art & History
f
King St North
King St North
Church St

2

Conyngham Rd
Conyngham Rd
Usher's Island
Arran Quay
Inns Quay
Chapelizod
South Circular Rd
St James' Church
Thomas St
Francis St
Chapelizod Bypass Con
Colbert Rd
Irish Museum of Modern Art
James's St
Du
Kilmainham Gaol
Mount Brown
Guinness Storehouse
Marrowbone Lane
St
Clanbrassil St
New Patrick St
South Circular Rd
Cork
Lower Clanbrassil St

MULLINGAR

GRAND CANAL
Tyrconnell Rd
Davitt
Dolphin Rd
Herberton Rd
South Circular Rd
Naas Rd
Mourne Rd
BRICKFIELDS PARK
Dolphin Rd
Parnell Rd
h
a
GRAND CANAL
Cooley Rd
Crumlin Rd
Grove
DRIMNAGH
Crumlin Rd
Sundrive Rd
HAROLD'S CROSS

LIMERICK

Drimnagh Rd
Kildare Rd
Kildare Rd
Convent Rd
SUNDRIVE PARK
MOUNT JEROME
PEARSE MEMORIAL PARK
Mourne Rd
CRUMLIN
MOUNT ARGUS PARK
Lower Kimmage Cross Rd
t
Leinster

3

KINMAGE
Nynes St
Stannaway Rd
Kimmage Rd
TERENURE
Clareville
Harold's
Rath
Cromwell's Fort Rd

BLESSINGTON

A

B

REPUBLIC OF IRELAND

Griffith Av.

DRUMCONDRA

KILLESTER

Collins Av. East

Casino
Marino

Griffith Av.

MARINO

Howth Rd

1

Clonliffe Rd

Tolka

FAIRVIEW
PARK

Clontarf Av.

CLONTARF

Castle Rd

Circular Rd

**POINT
VILLAGE**

TOLL

M 50

2

Tolka Quay Rd

Parnell St.

O'Connell St.

Gardiner St Lower

Talbot St.

Amiens St.

Sheriff St. Upper

North Wall Quay

3 Arena

Eden Quay

Liffey

City Quay

Townsend St.

York Rd

OLD LIBRARY

PEARSE

Ringsend
Park

Dawson St.

Kildare St.

Fenian St.

Waterways
Visitor Centre

Bridge St.

RINGSEND

Stephen's
Green

Baggot St. Lower

Mount St. Lower

Northumberland Rd

DODDER RIVER

s

Camden

Adelaide Rd

k

Haddington Rd

a

x

Shore Rd

**DUBLIN
BAY**

t

Canal Rd

a

Waterloo Rd

Shelbourne Rd

e

SANDYMOUNT

Sandymount
Claremont Rd

Ranelagh Rd

Clyde Rd

HERBERT
PARK

Serpentine Av.

Merrion Rd

3

Sandymount Av.

Strand Rd

RATHMINES

DONNYBROOK

g

Sandford Rd

Anglesea Rd

Merrion Rd

Park Av.

Milltown Rd

Eglinton Rd

Stillorgan Rd

Ailesbury

Nutley Lane

Merrion Rd

DUBLIN

0 —— 300 m
0 —— 300 yards

Kirwan St

Morning Star Av.

Brunswick St

Blackhall Pl
Blackhall Parade

SMITHFIELD VILLAGE

Constitution Hill

Prebend St

Upper Church St

Coleraine St

North King St

King St North

Anne St North

Beresford St

Halston St

Green St

North King St

Henrietta St

Bolton St

King's Inns St

Western Way

Dominick St Upper

Temple Cottages

Dominick St Lower

King's Inns

Loftus Lane

Parnell St

Parnell Sq

Dominick St Lower

Dublin Writers Museum

Dublin City Gallery The Hugh Lane

Garden Of Remembrance

Gate Theatr

Rotunda Hospital Chapel Rotun

r

a

Jameson Distillery Bow St

Benburb St

Ellis Quay

Usher's Island

Island St

Queen St

Smithfield

Arran Quay

Usher's Quay

Usher's Quay

May Lane

St Michan's

Mary's Lane

Greek St

Chancery St West

Charles St West

Chancery Pl

Four Courts

Inns Quay

Chancery St

Mary's Abbey

Little Strand St

Arran St East

Ormond Quay Upper

Strand St

Great Strand St

Little Britain St

Capel St

Wolfe Tone St

Jervis Lane Upper

Jervis St

Jervis Lane Lower

Abbey St Upper

Liffey St Upper

Millennium Bridge

Wood Quay

Ha'pen Bridg

Nor

s

Benburb St

Bridgefoot St

Oliver Bond St

Thomas St West

Thomas St

Earl St South

Braithwaite St

John St South

Cork St

Chamber St

O'Curry Av.

Susan Terrace

Donore Rd

O'Donovan Rd

O'Curry Rd

Thomas St Rd

St Augustine St

Watling St

John St

Vicar St

Francis St

Meath St

Molyneux Yard

Swift's Alley

Garden Lane

Carman's Hall

Gray St

The Coombe

Weaver's St

Cork St

Ardee St

Mill St

Clarence St

Mangan Rd

Pimlico

Meath Pl

Meath St

The Coombe

New Row South

Newmarket

Fumbally Lane

Blackpitts

Clanbrassil St Lower New

Daniel St

Lombard St West

Cook St

St Audoen's Gate

St Audoen's

High Street

Back Lane

Ross Rd

Bride Rd

John Dillon St

Bride St

Christ Church Cathedral

Dublinia

St Patrick's Cathedral

Peter St

Peter's Row

Marsh's Library

Bishop St

Kevin St Lower

New Bride St

Camden Row

Pleasants St

Heytesbury St

Arnott St

Golden Lane

CHESTER BEATTY LIBRARY

Lord Edward St

Wood Quay

City Hall

Dublin Castle

Castle St

Olympia Theatre

Meeting House Sq

Dame St

Temple Ba

King St

York St

Aungier St

Mercer St Upper

Liberty Lane

Wexford St

Camden St Lower

Cuffe St

Kevin St

Grantham St

Harcourt St

t

h

m

u

x p

n

E

F

596

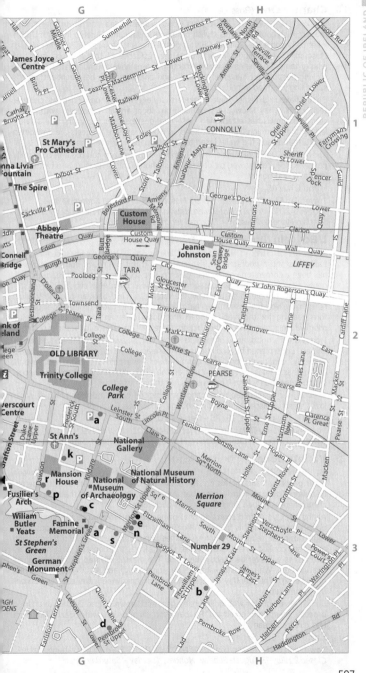

G

H

James Joyce
Centre

Cathal
Brugha St

St Mary's
Pro Cathedral

nna Livia
ountain

The Spire

Sackville Pl

iddle

tts

Connell
Bridge

Abbey
Theatre

Custom
House

Custom
House Quay →

Jeanie
Johnston

Custom
House Quay

North Wall Quay

LIFFEY

CONNOLLY

George's Dock

Mayor St Lower

Sheriff
St Lower

Spencer
Dock

Ferrymans
Crossing

Ossory Rd

Clarion

Burgh Quay

George's Quay

City Quay

Sir John Rogerson's Quay

Poolbeg St

TARA

Gloucester
St South

Westmoreland St

Doller St

Townsend St

Townsend

Hanover

on Quay

et St

nk of
eland

College St

Pearse St

Mark's Lane

Lombard

Pearse

lege
een

OLD LIBRARY

College
St

College

PEARSE

Trinity College

College
Park

Boyne

verscourt
Centre

Leinster
St South

Lincoln Pl

Fenian

Denzille Lane

Hogan Pl

a

Frederick
St South

Clare St

St Ann's

National
Gallery

k

P

Merrion
Sq^tn North

Hollis

Grants Row

Mansion
House

r

National
Museum
of Archaeology

National Museum
of Natural History

Merrion
Square

Grattan St

Fusilier's
Arch

p

c

Merrion Sq^e
Fitzwilliam

Mount St

Stephen's Pl

Verschoyle Pl

Power's
Court

Wiliam
Butler
Yeats

Famine
Memorial

a

e

n

Merrion St Upper

Merrion

South

Mount St Upper

James's
Pl East

James St East

Warrington Pl

St Stephen's
Green

s

Number 29

Baggot St Lower

German
Monument

phen's

Green

Pembroke
Lane

b

Pembroke Row

AGH
RDENS

Eardfort Terrace

Leeson St Lower

Quinn's Lane

d

Pembroke St Upper

Fitzwilliam St Upper

Herbert Lane

Percy Pl

Haddington Rd

Chapter One (Ross Lewis)

MODERN CUISINE · INTIMATE XxX Good old-fashioned hospitality meets with modern Irish cooking in this stylish basement restaurant. Situated in North Dublin – set to become the Cultural Quarter of the city – it's found beneath the Writers Museum, in a building that was once the residence of the Jameson family of whisky fame. The series of interconnecting rooms have an understated elegance, striking bespoke art hangs on the walls and considering its basement setting, it's surprisingly bathed in natural light.

Boldly flavoured dishes have a modern style yet are underpinned by classical techniques. They showcase produce from local artisan producers with whom chef Ross Lewis has established close relationships over the years. The service, led by the charming Danny Desmond, is worthy of note – guests are welcomed as old friends and the well-versed team anticipate their every need.

Specialities: Cured organic salmon, Lambay crab, smoked cod roe and buttermilk pancake. Brill, cauliflower, pickled red dulse, horseradish. Flavours and textures of Irish milk and honey.

Menu € 42/115

Town plan F1-r – *The Dublin Writers Museum, 18-19 Parnell Square* ⊠ *D1* – ℘ *01 873 2266* – *www.chapteronerestaurant.com* – *Closed 24 December-7 January, Sunday, Monday, Tuesday - Thursday lunch, Saturday lunch*

L'Ecrivain (Derry Clarke)

MODERN CUISINE · CHIC XxX Derry Clarke is one of Ireland's finest culinary ambassadors and a godfather of Irish cuisine, and this old coach house conversion has been a cornerstone of the Irish gastronomic scene for nearly 30 years; indeed, many a successful chef has passed through his kitchen. However, this is no stiff and starchy temple to gastronomy: the room has a laid-back air and the friendly team make you feel instantly at ease. Start off in the glitzy ground floor bar before heading for the high-ceilinged first floor restaurant or the private dining room which screens live kitchen action; there's also a terrace for warmer months.

Menus offer a good range of modern dishes which have a hint of the adventurous and are underpinned by a solid classical base and some supreme Irish ingredients. Precisely, confidently prepared combinations have bold yet restrained flavours and he has a knack for only putting on the plate only what is absolutely necessary. His legendary kataifi prawns are not to be missed.

Specialities: Kilkeel crab with mango and pickled beech mushroom. Aged Wicklow Venison, celeriac and Savoy cabbage. Chocolate 'Snickers'.

Menu € 37 (lunch), € 85/115 – Carte € 70/96

Town plan H3-b – *109a Lower Baggot Street* ⊠ *D2* – ℘ *01 661 1919* – *www.lecrivain.com* – *Closed Sunday, Monday - Thursday lunch, Saturday lunch*

Variety Jones (Keelan Higgs)

MODERN CUISINE · FRIENDLY X This tiny restaurant sits sandwiched between other properties and there's no sign above the door, but that all adds to the anticipation. The long, narrow room has a funky, modern style and the cool, relaxed atmosphere is helped along by the laid-back team.

At the back you'll find charming chef-owner Keelan Higgs working calmly in the open kitchen, while his brother Aaron keeps things running smoothly out front. Highly original, refined yet unfussy dishes burst with freshness and flavour, and many are cooked over the open fire; Keelan loves this concept, as it means no two dishes will ever be exactly the same. The menu is divided into the headings Snacks, Cold, Warm, Pasta, Family Style (for sharing) and After (one dessert and one cheese). The monthly changing, mostly organic wine list is equally passionately compiled.

Specialities: Lobster with grilled baby gem and brown butter. Duck with charred broccoli, hearts and confit leg. Rhubarb and almond cake with poached rhubarb and cultured cream.

Carte € 50/60

Town plan E2-t – *78 Thomas Street* ⊠ *D8* – ℘ *01 516 2470* – *www.varietyjones.ie* – *Closed 29 July-13 August, Sunday, Monday, Tuesday - Saturday lunch*

⊕ Pichet

CLASSIC FRENCH · CHIC XX You can't miss the bright red signs and blue and white striped canopies of this buzzy brasserie – and its checkerboard flooring makes it equally striking inside. Have snacks at the bar or classic French dishes in the main room. A good selection of wines are available by the glass or pichet.

Specialities: Roaring Water Bay organic mussels. Cherry Valley duck with figs and confit fennel. Buttermilk panna cotta.

Menu € 24/30 – Carte € 36/51

Town plan F2-g – *14-15 Trinity Street* ⊠ *D2* – ℰ *01 677 1060* – *www.pichet.ie* – *Closed Sunday lunch*

⊕ Clanbrassil House &

MODERN CUISINE · RUSTIC X Bastible's younger sister is a small place seating just 25. The concise menu focuses on the charcoal grill, with everything from homemade sausages to prime cuts. The hash brown chips are a favourite; the early evening menu is a steal; and if you're in a group you can share dishes 'family-style'.

Specialities: Roast leeks, chopped egg and chicken skin. Homemade sausage, potato purée and charred greens. Chocolate mousse with honeycomb and marmalade ice cream.

Menu € 28 – Carte € 35/47

Town plan B3-h – *6 Clanbrassil Street Upper* ⊠ *D8* – ℰ *01 453 9786* – *www.clanbrassilhouse.com* – *Closed Sunday, Monday, Tuesday - Friday lunch*

⊕ Richmond

MODERN CUISINE · NEIGHBOURHOOD X A real gem of a neighbourhood restaurant with a rustic look and a lively feel; sit upstairs for a more sedate experience. The vibrant, gutsy dishes change regularly – apart from the Dexter burger and rib-eye which are mainstays; on Tuesdays they serve a good value tasting menu where they try out new ideas.

Specialities: Roast onion soup, blue cheese and hazelnuts. Slow-cooked lamb neck with glazed sweetbreads, broccoli, swede and anchovy. Richmond date pudding, toffee sauce, salted peanuts and gingerbread ice cream.

Menu € 26/30 – Carte € 35/48

Town plan C3-r – *43 Richmond Street South* ⊠ *D2* – ℰ *01 478 8783* – *www.richmondrestaurant.ie* – *Closed Monday, Tuesday - Friday lunch*

⊕ Uno Mas ⓝ

MEDITERRANEAN CUISINE · NEIGHBOURHOOD X The smell of freshly baked bread lures you into this stripped-back bistro located in a historic building near the city centre. It's run by a very friendly team and offers great value menus of cleanly executed, unfussy Spanish dishes that are packed with flavour. A Spanish wine and sherry list accompanies.

Specialities: Potato and onion tortilla. Whole John Dory with purple sprouting broccoli, mussels and seaweed. Flan de queso.

Menu € 24 (lunch)/28 – Carte € 31/45

Town plan F3-h – *6 Aungier Street* ⊠ *D2* – ℰ *01 4758538* – *www.unomas.ie* – *Closed Sunday, Monday lunch*

⍟○ Glovers Alley

MODERN CUISINE · DESIGN XXX This second floor hotel restaurant looks out over St Stephen's Green and is named in honour of the city's glove-makers who once occupied the neighbouring alleyway. Pinks, greens and floral arrangements give the room a soft touch, while dishes display contrasting bold flavours and textures.

Menu € 45 (lunch)/80

Town plan G3-d – *Fitzwilliam Hotel, 127-128 St. Stephen's Green* ⊠ *D2* – ℰ *01 244 0733* – *www.gloversalley.com* – *Closed 25 December-8 January, Sunday, Monday, Tuesday - Wednesday lunch*

⭑○ **One Pico** AC ⊕ ✿

MODERN CUISINE · ELEGANT XX This discreet, passionately run restaurant tucked away on a side street is a well-regarded place that's a regular haunt for MPs. Sit on comfy banquettes or velour chairs, surrounded by muted colours. The modern Irish cooking has plenty of flavour and dishes are attractively presented.

Menu € 39 (lunch)/50 – Carte € 55/75

Town plan G3-k – *5-6 Molesworth Place* ✉ *D2* – ☏ *01 676 0300* – *www.onepico.com* – *Closed Sunday*

⭑○ **Amuse** AC

MODERN CUISINE · ELEGANT XX Modern, understated décor provides the perfect backdrop for the intricate, innovative cooking. Dishes showcase Asian ingredients – including kombu and yuzu – which are artfully arranged according to their flavours and textures.

Menu € 35 (lunch)/69

Town plan G3-r – *22 Dawson Street* ✉ *D2* – ☏ *01 639 4889* – *www.amuse.ie* – *Closed 24 December-7 January, Sunday, Monday*

⭑○ **Bang** AC ⊕ ✿

MODERN CUISINE · BISTRO XX Stylish restaurant with an intimate powder blue basement, a bright mezzanine level and a small, elegant room above. There are good value pre-theatre menus, a more elaborate à la carte and tasting menus showcasing top Irish produce.

Menu € 35 (lunch)/38 – Carte € 34/62

Town plan G3-a – *11 Merrion Row* ✉ *D2* – ☏ *01 400 4229* – *www.bangrestaurant.com* – *Closed Sunday, Monday lunch*

⭑○ **Dax** AC

FRENCH · BISTRO XX Clubby restaurant in the cellar of a Georgian townhouse near Fitzwilliam Square. Tried-and-tested French dishes use top Irish produce and flavours are clearly defined. The Surprise Menu best showcases the kitchen's talent.

Menu € 35 (lunch)/39 – Carte € 55/70

Town plan G3-d – *23 Upper Pembroke Street* ✉ *D2* – ☏ *01 6761494* – *www.dax.ie* – *Closed 18-22 August, 25 December-5 January, Sunday, Monday, Saturday lunch*

⭑○ **Fade St. Social - Restaurant** 🍸 ⅋ ⅋①⑨ ⊕ ✿

MODERN CUISINE · BRASSERIE XX Have cocktails on the terrace then head for the big, modern brasserie. Dishes use Irish ingredients but have a Mediterranean feel; they specialise in sharing and wood-fired dishes, and use large cuts of meat such as chateaubriand.

Menu € 37 – Carte € 38/70

Town plan F2-u – *4-6 Fade Street* ✉ *D2* – ☏ *01 604 0066* – *www.fadestreetsocial.com* – *Closed Sunday - Wednesday lunch, Saturday lunch*

⭑○ **Mr Fox** 🍴 ⅋⑨

MODERN CUISINE · INTIMATE XX In the basement of a striking Georgian house you'll find this light-hearted restaurant with a lovely tiled floor and a small terrace. The charming team present tasty international dishes, some of which have a playful touch.

Menu € 28 – Carte € 40/51

Town plan F1-a – *38 Parnell Square West* ✉ *D1* – ☏ *01 874 7778* – *www.mrfox.ie* – *Closed 1-8 January, Sunday, Monday*

⭑○ **Pearl Brasserie** AC ⅋⑨

MODERN CUISINE · BRASSERIE XX Formal basement restaurant with a small bar-lounge and two surprisingly airy dining rooms; sit in a stylish booth in one of the old coal bunkers. Intriguing modern dishes have a classical base and Mediterranean and Asian influences.

Menu € 36 (lunch)/39 – Carte € 40/70

Town plan G3-n – *20 Merrion Street Upper* ✉ *D2* – ☏ *01 6613572* – *www.pearl-brasserie.com* – *Closed Sunday*

Peploe's

MEDITERRANEAN CUISINE · COSY XX Atmospheric cellar restaurant – formerly a bank vault – named after the artist. The comfy room has a warm, clubby feel and a large mural depicts the owner. The well-drilled team present Mediterranean dishes and an Old World wine list.

Menu € 38 (lunch) – Carte € 46/70

Town plan G3-p – *16 St Stephen's Green* ✉ *D2* – ✆ *01 676 3144* – *www.peploes.com* – *Closed 25-26 December*

Saddle Room

MEATS AND GRILLS · ELEGANT XX A renowned restaurant with a history as long as that of the grand hotel in which it stands. The warm, inviting room features intimate gold booths and a crustacea counter. Menus offer a mix of grills and classic dishes, with some finished off at the table in front of you.

Menu € 30 (lunch), € 37/50 – Carte € 30/125

Town plan G3-c – *Shelbourne Hotel, 27 St. Stephen's Green* ✉ *D2* – ✆ *01 663 4500* – *www.shelbournedining.ie*

Suesey Street

MODERN CUISINE · INTIMATE XX An intimate restaurant with sumptuous, eye-catching décor, set in the basement of a Georgian townhouse; sit on the superb courtyard terrace. Refined, modern cooking brings out the best in home-grown Irish ingredients.

Menu € 30 – Carte € 38/59

Town plan C3-k – *26 Fitzwilliam Place* ✉ *D2* – ✆ *01 669 4600* – *www.sueseystreet.ie* – *Closed 25-30 December, Sunday, Monday*

Taste at Rustic by Dylan McGrath

ASIAN · RUSTIC XX Dylan McGrath's love of Japanese cuisine inspires dishes which explore the five tastes: sweet, salt, bitter, umami and sour. Ingredients are top-notch and flavours, bold and masculine. Personable staff are happy to recommend dishes.

Menu € 45 – Carte € 40/78

Town plan F2-m – *17 South Great George's Street (2nd Floor)* ✉ *D2* – ✆ *01 526 7701* – *www.tasteatrustic.com* – *Closed 1-8 January, Sunday, Monday, Tuesday, Wednesday - Saturday lunch*

Delahunt

MODERN CUISINE · BISTRO X This old Victorian grocer's shop is mentioned in James Joyce's 'Ulysses' – the clerk's snug is now a glass-enclosed private dining room. Flavoursome dishes take on a modern approach; dinner offers a set price menu, while lunch sees lighter offerings. The speakeasy style bar is a popular spot.

Menu € 39/45 – Carte € 19/45

Town plan F3-p – *39 Camden Street Lower* ✉ *D2* – ✆ *01 598 4880* – *www.delahunt.ie* – *Closed 24 December-2 January, Sunday, Monday, Saturday lunch*

Bastible

MODERN CUISINE · SIMPLE X Its name refers to the cast iron pot which once sat on the hearth of every family home, and they still use it here to make the bread – but this lively neighbourhood spot is far from old-fashioned. Dishes are stripped-back, flavours are bold and servings are generous. Desserts are a highlight.

Menu € 45/55

Town plan B3-a – *111 South Circular Road* ✉ *D8* – ✆ *01 473 7409* – *www.bastible.com* – *Closed 25 December-2 January, Sunday dinner, Monday, Tuesday, Wednesday - Thursday lunch*

REPUBLIC OF IRELAND

Camden Kitchen

CLASSIC CUISINE · BISTRO X A simple, modern, neighbourhood bistro set over two floors; watch the owner cooking in the open kitchen. Tasty dishes use good quality Irish ingredients prepared in classic combinations. Service is relaxed and friendly.

Menu €24 (lunch)/33 – Carte €18/44

Town plan F3-x – *3a Camden Market, Grantham Street* ✉ *D8* – ✆ *01 476 0125* – *www.camdenkitchen.ie* – *Closed 25-28 December, Sunday dinner-Tuesday lunch, Saturday lunch*

Etto

MEDITERRANEAN CUISINE · RUSTIC X The name of this rustic restaurant means 'little' and it is totally apt! Blackboards announce the daily wines and the Worker's Lunch special. Flavoursome dishes rely on good ingredients and have Italian influences; the chef understands natural flavours and follows the 'less is more' approach.

Menu €27 (lunch)/32 – Carte €29/45

Town plan G3-s – *18 Merrion Row* ✉ *D2* – ✆ *01 678 8872* – *www.etto.ie* – *Closed Sunday*

Fade St. Social - Gastro Bar

INTERNATIONAL · CHIC X A buzzy restaurant with an almost frenzied feel. It's all about a diverse range of original, interesting small plates, from burrata with basil purée and cherry tomatoes to Irish sirloin. Eat at the kitchen counter or on leather-cushioned 'saddle' benches.

Carte €25/57

Town plan F2-u – *4-6 Fade Street* ✉ *D2* – ✆ *01 604 0066* – *www.fadestreetsocial.com* – *Closed Monday - Friday lunch*

Fish Shop &

SEAFOOD · RUSTIC X A very informal little restaurant where they serve a daily changing seafood menu which is written up on the tiled wall. Great tasting, supremely fresh, unfussy dishes could be prepared raw or roasted in the wood-fired oven.

Menu €45

Town plan E2-s – *6 Queen Street* ✉ *D7* – ✆ *01 430 8594* – *www.fish-shop.ie* – *Closed Sunday, Monday, Tuesday, Wednesday - Saturday lunch*

Grano

ITALIAN · FRIENDLY X To the northwest of the city you'll find this lovely little osteria specialising in homemade pasta. The owner and his chef hail from Calabria and regularly import produce from their home town. Cooking is fresh and unfussy and the all-Italian wine list features organic and biodynamic wines.

Menu €12 (lunch)/24 – Carte €25/35

Town plan B2-f – *5 Norseman Court, Manor Street, Stoneybatter* ✉ *D7* – ✆ *01 538 2003* – *www.grano.ie* – *Closed Monday, Tuesday lunch*

Locks

MODERN CUISINE · BISTRO X Locals love this restaurant overlooking the canal – downstairs it's buzzy, while upstairs is more intimate, and the personable team add to the feel. Natural flavours are to the fore and dishes are given subtle modern touches; for the best value menus come early in the week or before 7pm.

Menu €30/45 – Carte €30/60

Town plan B3-s – *1 Windsor Terrace* ✉ *D8* – ✆ *01 416 3655* – *www.locksrestaurant.ie* – *Closed Sunday dinner, Monday, Tuesday - Thursday lunch*

Pickle

INDIAN · BISTRO X It might not look much from the outside but inside the place really comes alive. Spices are lined up on the kitchen counter and dishes are fresh and vibrant; the lamb curry with bone marrow is divine. Try a Tiffin Box for lunch.

Menu €24 – Carte €28/57

Town plan F3-n – *43 Lower Camden Street* ✉ *D2* – ✆ *01 555 7755* – *www.picklerestaurant.com* – *Closed Monday*

🍴 Pig's Ear

MODERN CUISINE · BISTRO X Look out for the bright pink door of this three storey Georgian townhouse overlooking Trinity College Gardens. The first and second floors have a homely retro feel while the third floor is a private dining room with its own kitchen and library. Irish produce features in refined yet comforting dishes.

Menu € 23/28 – Carte € 35/49

Town plan G2-a – *4 Nassau Street* ✉ *D2* – ☏ *01 670 3865* – *www.thepigsear.ie* – Closed 1-8 January, Sunday

Hotels

🏨 Shelbourne

GRAND LUXURY · CLASSIC A famed hotel dating from 1824, overlooking St Stephen's Green; this is where the 1922 Irish Constitution was signed. It has classical architecture, elegant guest areas, luxurious bedrooms and even a tiny museum. The lounge and bars are the places to go for afternoon tea and drinks.

265 rooms – 🛉🛉 € 299/850 – 🖵 € 30 – 19 suites

Town plan G3-c – *27 St. Stephen's Green* ✉ *D2* – ☏ *01 663 4500* – *www.theshelbourne.com*

🍴 **Saddle Room** – See restaurant listing

🏨 Merrion

TOWNHOUSE · CLASSIC A Georgian façade conceals a luxury hotel with a compact spa and impressive pool. Opulent drawing rooms are filled with antiques and fine artwork; enjoy 'Art Afternoon Tea' with a view of the parterre garden. Stylish bedrooms have a classic, understated feel and marble bathrooms. Dine from an all-day menu in the brasserie, whose windows fold back to create a terrace.

143 rooms – 🛉🛉 € 250/420 – 🖵 € 33 – 9 suites

Town plan G3-e – *Upper Merrion Street* ✉ *D2* – ☏ *01 603 0600* – *www.merrionhotel.com*

🏨 Fitzwilliam

BUSINESS · CONTEMPORARY This stylish hotel is set around an impressive roof garden. Contemporary bedrooms come in striking colours with good facilities – some overlook the courtyard garden and others St Stephen's Green. Dine on original Mediterranean dishes in the brasserie or boldly flavoured dishes in Glovers Alley.

139 rooms – 🛉🛉 € 229/700 – 🖵 € 25 – 3 suites

Town plan F3-d – *127-128 St. Stephen's Green* ✉ *D2* – ☏ *01 478 7000* – *www.fitzwilliamhoteldublin.com*

🍴 **Glovers Alley** – See restaurant listing

at Ballsbridge – Regional map n° **21**–D1

🍴 Shelbourne Social

CONTEMPORARY · BRASSERIE XX A smart high rise plays host to this large brasserie deluxe with its profusion of glass and modish feel. Choose from a great selection of cocktails in the first floor loft-style bar, then pick from the wide-ranging menu which sees global dishes sitting alongside local steaks. Sharing is encouraged.

Menu € 35 (lunch)/40 – Carte € 27/68

Town plan D3-e – *Number One, Shelbourne Road* ✉ *D4* – ☏ *01 963 9777* – *www.shelbournesocial.com* – Closed Sunday - Monday dinner

🍴 Chop House

MEATS AND GRILLS · PUB X An imposing pub not far from the stadium. For warmer days there's a small terrace; in colder weather head up the steps, through the bar and into the bright conservatory. The relaxed lunchtime menu is followed by more ambitious dishes in the evening, when the kitchen really comes into its own.

Carte € 33/56

Town plan D3-x – *2 Shelbourne Road* ✉ *D4* – ☏ *01 660 2390* – *www.thechophouse.ie* – Closed Saturday lunch

REPUBLIC OF IRELAND

� Old Spot   ⅃ AC �

TRADITIONAL CUISINE · PUB X This grey pub is just a stone's throw from the stadium. The appealing bar has a stencilled maple-wood floor and a great selection of snacks and bottled craft beers. Downstairs, the relaxed, characterful restaurant is filled with vintage posters and serves pub classics with a modern edge.

Menu € 29 – Carte € 31/51

Town plan D2-s – *14 Bath Avenue* ⊠ *D4* – ℰ *01 660 5599* – *www.theoldspot.ie* – *Closed Saturday lunch*

Dylan   🏠 ⅃ AC 🏊

TOWNHOUSE · DESIGN This old Victorian nurses' home conceals a funky, boutique hotel. Tastefully decorated bedrooms offer a host of extras; those in the original building are the biggest. The stylish restaurant serves modern Mediterranean dishes and comes with a walnut-fronted, slate-topped bar and a smartly furnished terrace.

72 rooms – †† € 169/560 – ⊑ € 25

Town plan C3-a – *Eastmoreland Place* ⊠ *D4* – ℰ *01 660 3000* – *www.dylan.ie*

at Blackrock Southeast : 7. 5 km by R 118 – Regional map n° **21**-D1

✿ Liath (Damien Grey)

MODERN CUISINE · FRIENDLY XX A bohemian suburban market plays host to this intimate restaurant, which is named after chef-owner Damien Grey (Liath is Irish for 'Grey'). It's a chic, elegant place, and the open kitchen at one end allows the chefs to interact with their guests.

Lunch sees a concise fixed price menu, where each course relates to one of the five senses, but it's the set multi-course dinner menu that is the highlight; this evolves constantly and changes fully every 2 weeks, depending on the seasonality of ingredients. Intensely flavoured, well-judged dishes draw on natural flavours and are full of contrasting colours, textures and tastes. Preparation is precise and they take maximum care in everything that they do. There's a good range of non-alcoholic drinks, and warm service completes the picture.

Specialities: Langoustine, wild garlic and morels. Angus beef, kelp and sandwort. Chocolate and preserved raspberries.

Menu € 58 (lunch), € 78/96

Off plan – *Blackrock Market, 19a Main Street* ⊠ *A94 V0D8* – ℰ *01 212 3676* – *www.liathrestaurant.com – Closed 2-16 August, 22 December-5 January, Sunday, Monday, Tuesday, Wednesday - Friday lunch*

☐O 3 Leaves 🅝

INDIAN · SIMPLE X This sweet little eatery sits within a bohemian market and is always packed. Simple lunches follow a 'when it's gone, it's gone' approach – go for the great value 'Taster' menu. Three nights a week they offer dinner, which is a more ambitious affair. They're unlicensed, so BYO.

Menu € 31 – Carte € 25/35

Off plan – *Unit 30, Blackrock Market, 19A Main Street* ⊠ *A94 V0D8* – ℰ *087 769 1361 – www.3leaves.ie – Closed 17-30 August, 30 December-19 January, Sunday dinner, Monday, Tuesday, Wednesday dinner, Thursday lunch, Friday dinner*

at Clontarf Northeast: 5. 5 km by R 105 – Regional map n° **21**-D1

🏵 Pigeon House

MODERN CUISINE · NEIGHBOURHOOD X A slickly run neighbourhood bistro set just off the coast road in an up-and-coming area. It has a lovely front terrace, a lively feel and a bar counter laden with freshly baked goodies. Cooking is modern and assured and dishes are full of flavour. It's open all day and for weekend brunch too.

Specialities: Whipped Fivemiletown goat's cheese with salt-baked beetroot and hazelnuts. Roast cod, cauliflower, smoked bacon and white bean cassoulet. Hazelnut cake with orange salsa and mascarpone.

Menu € 26/30 – Carte € 26/49

Off plan – *11b Vernon Avenue* ⊠ *D3* – ℰ *01 805 7567 – www.pigeonhouse.ie – Closed Monday*

ⅼ○ Fishbone

SEAFOOD · NEIGHBOURHOOD Ⅹ A friendly little restaurant opposite the Bull Bridge, with a cocktail bar at its centre and a glass-enclosed kitchen to the rear. Prime seafood from the plancha and charcoal grill is accompanied by tasty house sauces.

Menu € 25 (lunch)/29 – Carte € 25/45

Off plan – *324 Clontarf Road* ✉ *D3 – ☎ 01 536 9066 – www.fishbone.ie – Closed 25-26 December*

at Donnybrook

ⅼ○ Mulberry Garden

MODERN CUISINE · COSY ⅩⅩ Hidden away in the suburbs is this delightful little restaurant, with an interesting L-shaped dining room set around a small courtyard terrace. The biweekly menu offers three dishes per course and the original modern cooking relies on good quality local produce.

Menu € 45 (lunch), € 55/80

Town plan C3-g – *Mulberry Lane* ✉ *D4 – ☎ 01 269 3300 – www.mulberrygarden.ie – Closed 1-7 January, Sunday, Monday, Tuesday, Wednesday - Saturday lunch*

at Dundrum South : 7. 5 km by R 117

ⅼ○ Ananda

INDIAN · EXOTIC DÉCOR ⅩⅩ Its name means 'bliss' and it's a welcome escape from the bustle of the shopping centre. The stylish interior encompasses a smart cocktail bar, attractive fretwork and vibrant art. Accomplished Indian cooking is modern and original.

Menu € 65 – Carte € 42/57

Off plan – *Sandyford Road, Dundrum Town Centre (Cinema Building, 2nd Floor)* ✉ *D16 VK54 – ☎ 01 296 0099 – www.anandarestaurant.ie – Closed Monday - Thursday lunch*

at Foxrock Southeast : 13 km by N 11

ⅼ○ Bistro One

TRADITIONAL CUISINE · NEIGHBOURHOOD ⅩⅩ Long-standing neighbourhood bistro above a parade of shops; run by a father-daughter team and a real hit with the locals. Good value daily menus list a range of Irish and Italian dishes. They produce their own Tuscan olive oil.

Menu € 29 – Carte € 29/52

Off plan – *3 Brighton Road* ✉ *D18 – ☎ 01 289 7711 – www.bistro-one.ie – Closed Sunday dinner, Monday, Tuesday - Thursday lunch*

at Ranelagh

ⅼ○ Forest & Marcy

MODERN CUISINE · CHIC Ⅹ There's a lively buzz to this lovely little wine kitchen with high-level seating. Precisely prepared, original dishes burst with flavour; many are prepared at the counter and the chefs themselves often present and explain what's on the plate. Choose between a 4 or 6 course tasting menu.

Menu € 49/58

Town plan C3-a – *126 Leeson Street Upper* ✉ *D4 – ☎ 01 660 2480 – www.forestandmarcy.ie – Closed 6-14 April, 17 August-2 September, 23 December-7 January, Sunday lunch, Monday, Tuesday, Wednesday - Saturday lunch*

ⅼ○ Forest Avenue

MODERN CUISINE · NEIGHBOURHOOD Ⅹ This rustic neighbourhood restaurant is named after a street in Queens and has a fitting 'NY' vibe. Elaborately presented tasting plates are full of originality and each dish combines many different flavours.

Menu € 35 (lunch)/68

Town plan C3-t – *8 Sussex Terrace* ✉ *D4 – ☎ 01 667 8337 – www.forestavenuerestaurant.ie – Closed 23 December-7 January, Sunday, Monday, Tuesday, Wednesday lunch*

REPUBLIC OF IRELAND

at Sandyford South : 10 km by R 117 off R 825

🍴○ **China Sichuan** 🏠 ⅃ AC

CHINESE · BRASSERIE XX A smart interior is well-matched by creative menus, where Irish produce features in tasty Cantonese classics and some Sichuan specialities. It was established in 1979 and is now run by the third generation of the family.

Menu € 17 (lunch)/31 – Carte € 29/43

Off plan – *The Forum, Ballymoss Road* ⊠ *D18 –* ℘ *01 293 5100 –*
www.china-sichuan.ie – Closed 25-27 December, Monday, Saturday lunch

at Terenure – Regional map n° **21**–D1

⊛ **Circa** Ⓝ 🏮

MODERN CUISINE · FRIENDLY X Four young friends run this modern neighbourhood restaurant with a laid-back vibe. The appealing monthly menu lists around a dozen dishes – half of which are small plates. Irish produce is kept to the fore and cooking is full of flavour. You can sit in the bar, at the counter or at regular tables.

Specialities: Buttermilk-fried rabbit with pea, bacon and lettuce fricassée. Wicklow lamb rump with potato mousseline, asparagus and salsa verde. Chocolate crémeux with peanut praline and salted banana ice cream.

Carte € 33/51

Off plan – *90 Terenure Road North* ⊠ *D6 –* ℘ *01 534 2644 –*
www.restaurantcirca.com – Closed Sunday, Monday, Tuesday, Wednesday - Thursday lunch

🍴○ **Craft** ⅃ ⓥ

MODERN CUISINE · NEIGHBOURHOOD X A busy southern suburb plays host to this friendly neighbourhood bistro. Concise menus evolve with seasonal availability and there's a good value early bird selection. Dishes are modern and creative with vibrant colours and fresh, natural flavours. The dripping roasted potatoes are delicious.

Menu € 25/30 – Carte € 25/55

Town plan B3-t – *208 Harold's Cross Road* ⊠ *D6 –* ℘ *01 497 8632 –*
www.craftrestaurant.ie – Closed Sunday dinner, Monday, Tuesday, Wednesday - Thursday lunch

DUNCANNON • DÚN CANANN
Wexford – Regional map n° **21**–D2

⊛ **Aldridge Lodge** ⇦ 🛏 🅿

COUNTRY COOKING · FRIENDLY XX This attractive house is set in a great rural location and run by cheery owners. The constantly evolving menu offers tasty homemade bread and veg from the kitchen garden. The focus is on good value fish and shellfish (the owner's father is a local fisherman), with some Asian and fusion influences. Homely bedrooms come with hot water bottles and home-baked cookies.

Specialities: Seared scallops with celeriac and chorizo. Dexter beef strip-loin with corned beef cheek croquette and rocket butter. Chocolate tart with popping candy and salted caramel.

Menu € 38/40

⊠ *Y34 W650 –* ℘ *051 389 116 – www.aldridgelodge.com – Closed 1-9 January, 25 May-11 June, Sunday lunch, Monday, Tuesday, Wednesday, Thursday - Saturday lunch*

DUNDRUM • DÚN DROMA – Dún Laoghaire-Rathdown → See Dublin

DUNFANAGHY • DÚN FIONNACHAIDH
Donegal

🏠 Breac House ❶ 🐾 ≼ 🛏 🏠 & 🅿

LUXURY · DESIGN This superb hillside house affords lovely views over the bay, while luxuriously appointed bedrooms with terraces and highly attentive service from the owners add to its allure. Natural materials and local artisan furnishings feature in the Nordic-inspired interior. A sauna in the Nordic hut is a must.

3 rooms – 👫 € 255/295

☎ 074 913 6940 – www.breac.house – Closed 11 November-9 March

DUNGARVAN · DÚN GARBHÁN
Waterford – Regional map n° **21**-C3

🍴 Tannery ⇦ 🅰🅲 🏠 ⇔

MODERN CUISINE · FRIENDLY ✗✗ Characterful 19C stone tannery, close to the harbour; they also run the cookery school here. Have small plates at the counter or head upstairs to the bright restaurant. Attractively presented, classically based dishes use good seasonal ingredients. Stylish bedrooms are in a nearby townhouse.

Menu € 33 (lunch), € 37/59

10 Quay Street ⊠ X35 – ☎ 058 45420 – www.tannery.ie – Closed Sunday dinner, Monday, Tuesday - Thursday lunch, Saturday lunch

DUN LAOGHAIRE · DÚN LAOGHAIRE
Dún Laoghaire-Rathdown – Regional map n° **21**-D1

🍴 Rasam 🏠

INDIAN · EXOTIC DÉCOR ✗✗ The scent of roses greets you as you head up to the surprisingly plush lounge and contemporary restaurant. Fresh, authentic dishes come in original combinations – they dry roast and blend their own spices.

Menu € 24 – Carte € 32/60

18-19 Glasthule Road (1st Floor, above Eagle House Pub) ⊠ A96 H2N1 – ☎ 01 230 0600 – www.rasam.ie – Closed Sunday - Saturday lunch

DURRUS · DÚRAS
Cork – Regional map n° **21**-A3

🍴 Blairscove House ⇦ ≼ 🛏 🅿

MODERN CUISINE · ELEGANT ✗✗ Charming 18C barn and hayloft, just a stone's throw from the sea, with fantastic panoramic views, pretty gardens, a courtyard and a lily pond. Stylish bar and stone-walled, candlelit dining room. Starters and desserts are in buffet format, while the seasonal main courses are cooked on a wood-fired chargrill. Luxurious, modern bedrooms are dotted about the place.

Menu € 65

⊠ P75 FE44 – ☎ 027 61127 – www.blairscove.ie – Closed 3 November-12 March, Sunday, Monday, Tuesday - Saturday lunch

ENNISCORTHY · INIS CÓRTHAIDH
Wexford – Regional map n° **21**-D2

🏨 Monart 🎋 🐾 🛏 🖼 🕉 🏠 🛗 ⬆ & 🅿

SPA AND WELLNESS · CONTEMPORARY Comprehensively equipped destination spa in 100 acres of beautifully landscaped grounds; a haven of peace and tranquility. The Georgian house with its contemporary glass extension houses spacious, stylish bedrooms with a terrace or balcony. The Restaurant serves light, modern dishes; the minimalistic Garden Lounge offers global dishes in a more informal environment.

68 rooms – 👫 € 300/600 – 2 suites

Forgelands, The Still – ☎ 053 923 8999 – www.monart.ie – Closed 13-27 December

FOXROCK · CARRAIG AN TSIONNAIGH – Dún Laoghaire-Rathdown ➔ See
Dublin

GALWAY • GAILLIMH

Galway – Regional map n° **20**–B3

Top tips!

If you're after the craíc, Galway's the place to go. The city has a wonderfully bohemian vibe and, aside from the popular tourist areas and the impressive cathedral, it's fun just to wander the narrow city streets.

It has a burgeoning arts scene, from buskers and traditional Irish music performances to theatre productions and international arts and literature Festivals. The iconic Galway Races sets the city alive as it welcomes over 250,000 visitors a year and the historic Oyster Festival plays host to the World Oyster Opening Championships. The spectacularly beautiful landscape of Connemara supplies produce for the best restaurants in the city, where eating out is an eclectic affair: choose French at **Le Petit Pois**, tapas at **Cava Bodega** or Italian at **Il Vicolo**. For a wonderful neighbourhood vibe head to Bib Gourmand awarded **Kai** or for modern Irish dishes try Michelin-Starred **Anair** or **Loam**.

A G Baxter/Shutterstock.com

Restaurants

Loam (Enda McEvoy)   & 🄰🄲 ⓥ

CREATIVE · MINIMALIST XX The location in a modern building shared with the bus station and the spartan, industrial-style interior dominated by bare concrete hardly conjure up images of the rich, fertile local soils, that is until you look on your plate. Chef-owner Enda McEvoy was one of the first chefs in Ireland to champion natural ingredients and also to build personal relationships with his suppliers to ensure the quality of his produce – and, as such, his menus are fiercely seasonal.

Dishes are original and creative but have a well-judged simplicity to them, letting natural flavours shine while offsetting them with subtle contrasts – often in the form of acidity, which adds great dimension to the dishes. Vegetables are also used to great effect. The fully open kitchen allows diners to see the intense focus from both Enda and his team and their pride is palpable as they deliver the dishes to the table. Service is smooth and professional yet also relaxed.

Specialities: Squid, egg and shiitake. Duck, blood and mustard. Burnt honey with whiskey and raspberry.

Menu € 55/99

Off plan – *Geata na Cathrach, Fairgreen Road* –
℘ *091 569 727* – *www.loamgalway.com* –
Closed 2-13 February, Sunday, Monday, Tuesday - Saturday lunch

Aniar (JP McMahon)   🄰🄲

CREATIVE · NEIGHBOURHOOD X Both the décor and the cooking at this stylish, laid-back restaurant follow a 'back-to-nature' ethos, with wood and stone setting the scene and menus championing ingredients from Ireland's Atlantic Coast. Aniar means 'From the West' and the majority of the ingredients come from the land and shores around Galway. Chef JP McMahon is well-known for his passion for the local larder and the changing seasons, and his multi-course set menus are only confirmed once all of the day's ingredients have arrived.

Cooking cleverly blends traditional and modern techniques, and contrasts in texture, temperature and acidity all play their part in delicate, well-balanced dishes with a Scandic style. Service is confident and detailed, with many of the dishes delivered to the tables by the chefs themselves, and there are some great wine matches for every menu.

Specialities: Oyster with arrow grass. Brill and sea beet. Sorrel and buttermilk.

Menu € 75/105

Town plan A2-a – *53 Lower Dominick Street* ✉ *H91 V4DP* –
℘ *091 535 947* – *www.aniarrestaurant.ie* –
Closed 5-20 January, Sunday, Monday, Tuesday - Saturday lunch

Kai

MEDITERRANEAN CUISINE · NEIGHBOURHOOD X A laid-back eatery with a gloriously cluttered interior and a bohemian feel; the owners run it with real passion. Morning coffee and cakes morph into fresh, simple lunches and are followed by afternoon tea and tasty dinners. Concise menus list fresh, vibrant dishes and produce is organic, free range and traceable.

Specialities: Clare crab with celeriac and pumpkin seeds. Roscommon lamb chops, beetroot picada and green tahini. Dark chocolate and almond pudding, burnt butter ice cream.

Carte € 32/49

Town plan A2-x – *22 Sea Road* –
℘ *091 526 003* – *www.kaicaferestaurant.com* –
Closed 23-31 December

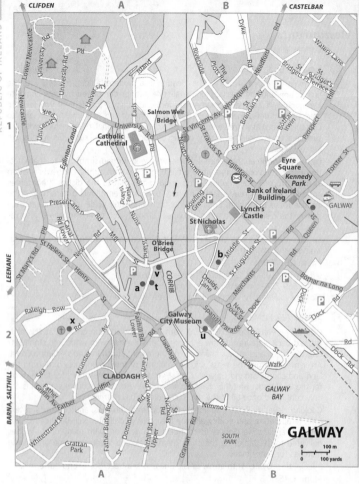

GALWAY

0   100 m
0   100 yards

⊛ **Tartare**   🍴

MODERN BRITISH · SIMPLE ✗ Snug, intimate and endearing, with a rustic feel; this sweet neighbourhood café is a hit with one and all. Sit at multi-level wood-topped tables beneath bright oil paintings and dine on delicious small plates. Simplicity is the key: top seasonal ingredients are well-sourced and carefully prepared.

Specialities: Oysters with sea lettuce and trout roe. Beef tartare, pickled onion and smoked egg. Rhubarb and buttermilk panna cotta, hazelnut crumble.

Carte € 21/42

Town plan A2-t – 56 Lower Dominick Street – ℰ 091 567 803 – www.tartaregalway.ie – Closed Sunday - Wednesday dinner

⊩○ **Ard Bia at Nimmos**   🕅

MEDITERRANEAN CUISINE · COSY ✗ Pleasingly cluttered, atmospheric riverside restaurant, where tables occupy every space; it's open all day but it's at night that it really comes alive. Sourcing is paramount and dishes take their influences from across the Med.

Carte € 39/56

Town plan B2-u – Spanish Arch – ℰ 091 561 114 – www.ardbia.com

⁏○ Cava Bodega   AC 🍽

SPANISH · TAPAS BAR Ⅹ This split-level tapas bar – with its reclaimed wood tables – has a rustic, neighbourhood feel; sit downstairs to watch the chefs in the open kitchen. It's all about sharing: choose around 3 dishes each and a Spanish beer or wine.

Carte € 20/36

Town plan B2-b – *1 Middle Street* – ☏ *091 539 884* – *www.cavarestaurant.ie* – *Closed Monday - Friday lunch*

⁏○ Le Petit Pois

FRENCH · COLOURFUL Ⅹ A friendly husband and wife team run this simple neighbourhood restaurant. The monthly changing menus are French at heart, with the occasional subtle global influence. Produce is proudly Irish and dishes are packed full of flavour.

Carte € 35/53

Town plan B1-c – *Victoria Place* ✉ *H91 TY40* – ☏ *091 330 880* – *www.lepetitpois.ie* – *Closed 23 December-9 January, Sunday, Monday, Tuesday - Saturday lunch*

⁏○ Il Vicolo   🏠 🍽

ITALIAN · BISTRO Ⅹ Start with an aperitif on the riverside terrace before dining in the characterful cellars of this old mill, whose exposed stone walls provide the perfect backdrop for the chef's rustic Italian cooking. Open by sharing some cicchetti, which will be delivered by a bright and breezy team.

Carte € 33/44

Town plan A2-v – *The Bridgemills, O'Brien's Bridge* – ☏ *091 530 515* – *www.ilvicolo.ie* – *Closed Monday - Friday lunch*

Hotels

🏨 G   🍴 ⊕ 🐾 🛁 🔁 ♿ AC 💪 🚗

LUXURY · DESIGN A small retail park plays host to this smart design hotel, whose eye-catching colour schemes were conceived by Galway native Philip Treacy. Take in distant views of the bay and mountains from the striking atrium's oversized window. Bedrooms are spacious and calming and there's an impressive thermal spa.

101 rooms 🛏 – ♟♟ € 140/850 – 2 suites

Off plan – *Wellpark, Dublin Road* – ☏ *091 865 200* – *www.theghotel.ie*

GLASLOUGH · GLASLOCH
Monaghan – Regional map n° **20**-D2

🏨 Castle Leslie Estate   🍴 🐎 ← 🛎 ⊕ 🐾 🔁 ♿ 💪 P

HISTORIC · CONTEMPORARY An impressive castle in 1,000 acres of peaceful parkland: owned by the 4th generation of the Leslie family. Various lounges are filled with heirlooms and antiques and country house bedrooms are fittingly luxurious; for a chic modern room book into the old hunting lodge. Unwind in the Victorian Treatments Rooms or charming bar before dining on modern Mediterranean fare.

70 rooms – ♟♟ € 180/320

☏ *047 88100* – *www.castleleslie.com* – *Closed 20-27 December*

GLASSON – Westmeath ➜ See Athlone

GOREY • GUAIRE
Wexford – Regional map n° **21**–D2

⚪ The Duck
🍷 ⬚ 🏠 ♻ 🅿

INTERNATIONAL · FRIENDLY ❌ The Duck is a smart, rustic bistro which sits within the grounds of a grand country house, next to a superb kitchen garden which informs its menu. Sit on the wonderful terrace with a glass of wine and dine on unfussy, global cuisine.

Menu € 26/33 – Carte € 29/51

Marlfield House Hotel, Courtown Road – ☎ 053 942 1124 –
www.marlfieldhouse.com/dining/the-duck/ – Closed 5-23 January

🏠 Marlfield House
🏡 ⬚ ⛬ 🅿

COUNTRY HOUSE · ELEGANT Well-appointed, period-style bedrooms look out over the large grounds of this attractive Regency house. Various sitting and draw-ing rooms have a homely, classical feel and all are packed with antiques, oil paint-ings and curios. Have afternoon tea in the garden while watching the peacocks wander by, then dine in the conservatory restaurant or the terrace café and bar.

19 rooms ⚏ – ♥♥ € 240/700

Courtown Road – ☎ 053 942 1124 – www.marlfieldhouse.com –
Closed 7 January-1 February

⚪ **The Duck** – See restaurant listing

GREYSTONES • NA CLOCHA LIATHA
Wicklow – Regional map n° **21**–D1

⚪ Chakra by Jaipur
⛬ 🆎 🛅

INDIAN · EXOTIC DÉCOR ❌❌ An elegant, intimate restaurant with bold décor, un-usually set within a shopping centre. Interesting dishes represent the country from north to south. Spicing is delicate, flavours are refined and desserts are a highlight.

Menu € 24 – Carte € 32/55

Meridian Point Centre, Church Road (1st Floor) ✉ A63 HD43 – ☎ 01 201 7222 –
www.chakra.ie – Closed Monday - Wednesday lunch, Friday - Saturday lunch

INISHMAAN • INIS MEÁIN – Galway ➜ See Aran Islands

KENMARE • NEIDÍN
Kerry – Regional map n° **21**–A3

⚪ Park
⮜ ⬚ ⛬ 🅿

CLASSIC CUISINE · ELEGANT ❌❌ Start with canapés in the lounge then move on to the elegant dining room of this luxurious hotel. Silver candelabras, cloches and gueridon trolleys all feature and service is top-notch. Classically based dishes have a modern touch and local ingredients are kept to the fore.

Menu € 80/95

Park Hotel, Shelbourne Street ✉ V93 X3XY – ☎ 064 664 1200 –
www.parkkenmare.com – Closed 4 January-4 February, 10-22 December, Sunday -
Saturday lunch

⚪ Mulcahys
🆎

MODERN CUISINE · INTIMATE ❌❌ Come for cocktails and snacks in the bar or settle in for the evening in the intimate restaurant. Modern dishes utilise Irish in-gredients, including plenty of local beef and fish. Start with two of the delicious homemade brioche and, for dessert, try the tarte Tatin to share.

Carte € 31/52

Main Street ✉ V93 – ☎ 064 664 2383 – www.mulcahyskenmare.ie –
Closed Sunday - Monday lunch, Tuesday, Wednesday - Saturday lunch

⭑○ Boathouse Bistro ≤ 🍴 🏠 🅿

SEAFOOD · **BRASSERIE** ✗ Converted boathouse in the grounds of Dromquinna Manor; set on the waterside, overlooking the peninsula and mountains. It has a nautical, New England style and a laid-back vibe. Simple, appealing menus focus on seafood.

Carte € 32/54

Dromquinna – ☏ 064 664 2889 –
www.dromquinnamanor.com – Closed 1 January-7 February

⭑○ Mews AC

MODERN CUISINE · **BISTRO** ✗ Owners Gary and Maria provide a warm welcome at this cosy, intimate, three-roomed restaurant. Many different ingredients combine to create colourful dishes with rich flavours. There's plenty of choice, including daily specials.

Menu € 34 – Carte € 28/50

Henry Court, Henry Street ⊠ V93 – ☏ 064 664 2829 –
www.themewskenmare.com – Closed 2 January-17 March, Sunday, Monday,
Tuesday - Saturday lunch

⭑○ No. 35 🆕

IRISH · **BISTRO** ✗ This appealing village restaurant comes with a laid-back vibe. The owner is a famous pig breeder and pork is used to great effect in unfussy, rustic dishes which have an Irish heart – daily specials could feature any part of the beasts. Desserts are a highlight, particularly the poire belle Hélène.

Menu € 35 – Carte € 35/45

35 Main Street ⊠ V93 – ☏ 064 664 1559 –
www.no35kenmare.com – Closed 9 January-9 February, Monday-Tuesday lunch,
Wednesday-Friday lunch

🏠 Park 🏕 🦢 ≤ 🍴 🖼 🔲 🧖 🏵 ⅃ℴ 🔁 ⅊ 🅿

GRAND LUXURY · **CLASSIC** One of Ireland's most iconic country houses sits in the town centre and looks out over wonderful gardens to the bay and the hills. It's elegantly furnished, with a charming drawing room, a cosy cocktail lounge and tastefully styled bedrooms. The stylish spa adds a modern touch.

46 rooms ☖ – 👫 € 210/470

Shelbourne Street ⊠ V93 X3XY – ☏ 064 664 1200 –
www.parkkenmare.com – Closed 4 January-4 February, 10-22 December
  ⭑○ **Park** – See restaurant listing

🏠 Sheen Falls Lodge 🏕 🦢 ≤ 🍴 🔲 🧖 🏵 ⅃ℴ 🔁 ⅊ 🏊 🅿

LUXURY · **PERSONALISED** Modern hotel in an idyllic spot, where the waterfalls drop away into the bay. It has a welcoming wood-fired lobby, a lovely indoor swimming pool and well-appointed bedrooms overlooking the falls. Unusually, the restaurant serves a brasserie menu on the upper level and more refined dishes on the lower level.

72 rooms ☖ – 👫 € 200/640 – 14 suites

☏ 064 664 1600 – www.sheenfallslodge.ie – Closed 3-31 January

KILCOLGAN · CILL CHOLGÁIN

Galway – Regional map n° **20**-B3

⭑○ Moran's Oyster Cottage 🏠

SEAFOOD · **PUB** ✗ An attractive thatched pub hidden away in a tiny hamlet – a very popular place come summer. It's all about straightforward cooking and good hospitality. Dishes are largely seafood based and oysters are the speciality.

Carte € 30/70

The Weir – ☏ 091 796 113 –
www.moransoystercottage.com – Closed 23-27 December

KILDARE • CILL DARA
Kildare – Regional map n° **21**-D1

⭕ Harte's
A/C ⇦

CLASSIC CUISINE · PUB ꭓ Sample a home-brewed beer in the snug open-fired bar before heading through to the small restaurant for hearty, well-prepared dishes with a modern twist. All produce is sustainable and traceable. They also have their own deli selling food from local artisan producers, as well as a cookery school and bedrooms.

Menu € 29 – Carte € 30/46

Market Square – 𝒞 045 533 557 – www.harteskildare.ie – Closed Monday

KILKENNY • CILL CHAINNIGH
Kilkenny – Regional map n° **21**-C2

🕸 Campagne (Garrett Byrne)
🕭 A/C ꭲ 🕅

MODERN BRITISH · INTIMATE ꭖꭖ This might not be the smartest part of town, and there's no denying that the setting opposite the railway arches is somewhat incongruous, but all is forgotten once you cross the threshold. The interior is surprisingly sleek, with curved banquettes, spotlights illuminating dark wood tables, and striking local artwork hanging on the walls; and you can watch the experienced chef-owner hard at work in the open kitchen while you wait.

The best Irish produce is used to create refreshingly understated, unfussy dishes which are packed with flavour, and the minute you start eating it becomes apparent that the classically based combinations are much more complex than they first appear. The early bird menu is a steal, the wine list has something to suit every purse, and service by the chef's partner is smooth, relaxed and friendly.

Specialities: Black pudding & pig's trotter with green tomato chutney, foie gras and crispy pig's ear. Roast brill with sprouting broccoli and seaweed butter sauce. Seville orange marmalade soufflé with chocolate ice cream.

Menu € 38/60

5 The Arches, Gashouse Lane – 𝒞 056 777 2858 – www.campagne.ie –
Closed 14 January-1 February, 1-10 July, Sunday dinner, Monday, Tuesday,
Wednesday - Thursday lunch

⭕ Anocht
🕭

MODERN CUISINE · DESIGN ꭖꭖ Set above the Design Centre in an old 1760s grain store is this daytime café, which morphs into an intimate candlelit restaurant at night. Colourful, creative dishes are full of flavour; influences range from the Med to Asia.

Menu € 25 – Carte € 34/46

Kilkenny Design Centre, Castle Yard (1st Floor) – 𝒞 056 772 2118 –
www.anochtrestaurant.ie – Closed Sunday-Wednesday, Thursday-Saturday lunch

⭕ Ristorante Rinuccini
A/C

ITALIAN · CLASSIC DÉCOR ꭖꭖ Set in the basement of a townhouse and named after the 17C papal nuncio, this family-owned restaurant is well-known locally. Classic Italian cuisine with homemade ravioli a speciality. Some tables have views through to the wine cellar.

Menu € 29 – Carte € 29/50

1 The Parade – 𝒞 056 776 1575 – www.rinuccini.com

⭕ Foodworks
🕭 A/C ⇱

TRADITIONAL CUISINE · FRIENDLY ꭓ A former bank in the town centre: its bright, fresh look is a perfect match for the style of cooking. Unfussy dishes use top local produce, including fruit and veg from the experienced chef-owner's farm.

Menu € 26/29 – Carte € 28/42

7 Parliament Street ✉ R95 X577 – 𝒞 056 777 7696 – www.foodworks.ie –
Closed Sunday dinner, Monday, Tuesday

KILLARNEY • CILL AIRNE

Kerry – Regional map n° **21**–A2

⁺○ **Panorama**   ⟨☲ ⌂ & AC P

MODERN CUISINE · ELEGANT XₓX Large, formal restaurant set within a luxurious hotel. Panoramic windows afford superb views across the lough to the mountains. Creative modern menus follow the seasons and use the very best Irish produce.

Carte € 39/68

Europe Hotel, Fossa ⊠ V93 KHN6 – ℰ 064 667 1300 – www.theeurope.com – Closed 8 December-6 February, Sunday, Monday - Saturday lunch

⁺○ **Park**   ⌂ & AC P

TRADITIONAL CUISINE · ELEGANT XₓX Elegant hotel restaurant with chandeliers, ornate cornicing and a pianist in summer. Classically based menus use some modern combinations; Irish meats are a feature and the tasting menu is a highlight.

Carte € 70/82

Killarney Park Hotel ⊠ V93 CF30 – ℰ 064 663 5555 – www.killarneyparkhotel.ie – Closed 16-30 December, Sunday - Saturday lunch

⁺○ **Brasserie**   ⊘⑈ ⟨☲ ⌂ ⌂ & AC P

INTERNATIONAL · BRASSERIE XX Set in a sumptuous lakeside hotel; a modern take on a classical brasserie, with water and mountain views – head for the terrace in warmer weather. The accessible all-day menu ranges from salads to steaks.

Carte € 34/62

Europe Hotel, Fossa ⊠ V93 KHN6 – ℰ 064 667 1300 – www.theeurope.com – Closed 8 December-6 February

🏨🏨 **Europe**   ⟨⌂ ⌂ ⟨☲ ⌂ ⦿ ☆ Ⓢ ⟨ & 🛁 P

GRAND LUXURY · CONTEMPORARY A superbly located resort boasting stunning views over the lough and mountains. It has impressive events facilities and a sublime three-level spa. Bedrooms are lavishly appointed; some overlook the water.

187 rooms ⊊ – ⁑⁑ € 255/550 – 6 suites

Fossa ⊠ V93 KHN6 – ℰ 064 667 1300 – www.theeurope.com – Closed 8 December-6 February

⁺○ **Panorama** • ⁺○ **Brasserie** – See restaurant listing

🏨🏨 **Aghadoe Heights H. and Spa**

⟨⌂ ⌂ ⟨☲ ⌂ ⦿ ☆ ⟨ & AC 🛁 P

LUXURY · DESIGN An unassuming hotel with stunning views over the lakes, mountains and countryside. It boasts an impressive spa and a stylish cocktail bar which comes complete with an evening pianist. Bedrooms are spacious and many have balconies or terraces. The split-level restaurant makes the most of the views.

74 rooms – ⁑⁑ € 200/599

ℰ 064 663 1766 – www.aghadoeheights.com

🏨🏨 **Killarney Park**   ⟨⌂ ⌂ ⦿ ☆ ⟨ & AC 🛁 P

LUXURY · CLASSIC A well-versed team run this smart hotel, with its plush library and lavish drawing room. Bedrooms mix modern furnishings with original features. Lunch and afternoon tea are served in the clubby, wood-panelled bar.

67 rooms ⊊ – ⁑⁑ € 225/485 – 7 suites

⊠ V93 CF30 – ℰ 064 663 5555 – www.killarneyparkhotel.ie – Closed 6-17 January, 23-27 December

⁺○ **Park** – See restaurant listing

KILLORGLIN • CILL ORGLAN
Kerry – Regional map n° **21**–A2

🏠 Giovannelli

ITALIAN · RUSTIC 🍴 A sweet little restaurant, hidden away in the town centre, with a traditional osteria-style interior and an on-view kitchen. The concise, daily changing blackboard menu offers authentic Italian dishes which are unfussy, fresh and full of flavour. The pasta is homemade and herbs are from the owners' garden.

Specialities: Caprese salad. Swiss chard and ricotta ravioli. Tiramisu.

Carte € 29/39

Lower Bridge Street ✉ *V93 RD68 – 𝓒 087 123 1353 –*
www.giovannellirestaurant.com – Closed Sunday dinner, Monday, Tuesday -
Saturday lunch

🍴🄾 Sol y Sombra   🛖 🦽 📱 🔔

SPANISH · TAPAS BAR 🍴 Its name means 'Sun and Shade' and the huge tower of this former church provides the latter! The cavernous interior still has its pews and stained glass windows. Cooking is fresh and vibrant: go for the raciones.

Carte € 27/39

Old Church of Ireland, Lower Bridge Street ✉ *V93 – 𝓒 066 976 2347 –*
www.solysombra.ie – Closed 6-31 January, Sunday lunch, Monday, Tuesday -
Saturday lunch

KINLOUGH • CIONN LOCHA
Leitrim – Regional map n° **20**–C2

🍴🄾 Courthouse   🗲

ITALIAN · TRADITIONAL 🍴🍴 A boldly painted former courthouse with a pretty stained glass entrance, run by a passionate Sardinian chef-owner. Extensive seasonal menus offer honest, authentic Italian dishes, and local seafood and imported produce feature. Service is friendly and the simply styled bedrooms are good value.

Menu € 33 – Carte € 35/50

Main Street ✉ *F91 – 𝓒 071 9842391 – www.thecourthouserest.com –*
Closed 1-7 January, 22 June-2 July, Sunday lunch, Monday, Tuesday, Wednesday -
Saturday lunch

KINSALE • CIONNE TSÁILE
Cork – Regional map n° **21**–B3

🏵 Bastion (Paul McDonald)   🍴🕉

MODERN CUISINE · FRIENDLY 🍴 Set in the very centre of town, Bastion is an intimate wine bar cum bistro run by a keen young couple: Paul cooks, while his wife Helen looks after the service. A large bar splits the room in two and while its dark décor might give it a moody feel, twinkling candles add a welcoming touch.

Chef-owner Paul McDonald might be Scottish born but the cooking here has a strong Irish base, with regional ingredients leading the way – although he's happy to search further afield if the quality of the produce dictates. Natural flavours are kept to the fore and local seafood is a highlight. The skilfully prepared, exacting dishes take on a modern style and often exhibit a playful, innovative element, while at the same time showing depth in their flavours and textures.

Specialities: Pea mousse & soup with lemon, mint and basil. Cannon of lamb with aubergine and wild garlic. Caramelised milk with chocolate & mandarin crumble and milk & honey sorbet.

Menu € 57/77

Market Street ✉ *P17 – 𝓒 021 470 9696 – www.bastionkinsale.com –*
Closed 15 January-15 February, Sunday lunch-Tuesday, Wednesday-Saturday lunch

⫿○ **Finns' Table**

REGIONAL CUISINE · FRIENDLY ✕✕ Behind the bright orange woodwork lie two attractive rooms – one with colourful banquettes, the other in powder blue with wine box panelling. Meat is from the chef's family farm and everything from bread to ice cream is homemade.

Menu € 37 – Carte € 36/55

6 Main Street ✉ P17 DC85 – ✆ 021 470 9636 – www.finnstable.com –
Closed 25 October-5 December, Sunday - Tuesday lunch, Wednesday, Thursday -
Saturday lunch

⫿○ **Max's** 🄰🄲

SEAFOOD · COSY ✕✕ An efficiently run, two-roomed restaurant on a quaint main street, with a simple yet smart rustic style – a spot well-known by the locals! The unfussy, classical seafood menu offers plenty of choice; try the tasty 'Fresh Catches'.

Menu € 27/40 – Carte € 40/55

Main Street ✉ P17 – ✆ 021 477 2443 – www.maxs.ie –
Closed 15 December-20 February, Sunday, Monday - Saturday lunch

⫿○ **Fishy Fishy** 🎪 ♿ 🄰🄲

SEAFOOD · DESIGN ✕ Dine alfresco on the small terrace, amongst 'fishy' memorabilia in the main restaurant or on the quieter first floor; the photos are of the fishermen who supply the catch. Concise, all-day menus feature some interesting specials.

Carte € 28/48

Pier Road ✉ P17 EK27 – ✆ 021 470 0415 – www.fishyfishy.ie – Closed 10-25 January

🏠 **Perryville House** 🅿

TOWNHOUSE · CLASSIC A luxuriously appointed house in the heart of town, named after the family that built it in 1820. It boasts three antique-furnished drawing rooms and a small courtyard garden. Bedrooms are tastefully styled – the top rooms have feature beds, chic bathrooms and views over Kinsale Harbour.

33 rooms ⌑ – 👫 € 200/600

Long Quay ✉ P17 – ✆ 021 477 2731 – www.perryvillehouse.com –
Closed 29 October-10 April

LAHINCH · AN LEACHT
Clare – Regional map n° **21**–B1

🏠 **Moy House** ✿ 🐾 ⩽ 🚲 🅿

COUNTRY HOUSE · ELEGANT An 18C Italianate clifftop villa, overlooking the bay and run by a friendly, attentive team. Homely guest areas include a small library and an open-fired drawing room with an honesty bar; antiques, oil paintings and heavy fabrics feature throughout. Individually designed, classical bedrooms boast good extras and most have views. Formal dining is from a 6 course set menu.

9 rooms – 👫 € 165/395

✆ 065 708 2800 – www.moyhouse.com – Closed 28 October-10 April

LETTERKENNY · LEITIR CEANAINN
Donegal – Regional map n° **20**–C1

⫿○ **Browns on the Green** ⩽ 🄰🄲 🅿

MODERN CUISINE · FRIENDLY ✕✕ Situated on the first floor of a golf club but with views of the mountains rather than the course. A cosy lounge leads into the intimate modern dining room. Refined dishes are modern interpretations of tried-and-tested classics.

Menu € 25 (lunch), € 27/46 – Carte € 23/48

Letterkenny Golf Club, Barnhill ✉ F92 – ✆ 074 912 4771 –
www.brownsonthegreen.com – Closed Monday, Tuesday, Wednesday, Thursday

⅋○ Lemon Tree 📱ⓥ

REGIONAL CUISINE · FAMILY ✕✕ This established family-run restaurant sees brother, sisters and cousins all working together to deliver surprisingly modern dishes which draw from Donegal's natural larder. The early evening set dinner menu is good value.

Menu € 25 (lunch)/30 – Carte € 27/45

32 Courtyard Shopping Centre, Lower Main Street ✉ F92 – ☏ 074 912 5788 – www.thelemontreerestaurant.com – Closed Monday - Saturday lunch

LIMERICK · LUIMNEACH
Limerick – Regional map n° **21**–B2

⅋○ East Room at Plassey House ⓝ 🍽 ♿ ⇆ 🅿

MODERN CUISINE · HISTORIC ✕✕ Start with an aperitif in the drawing room of this whitewashed Palladian-style house, then head through to the grand restaurant with its ornate plasterwork, Corinthian pillars and impressive art collection. Beautifully presented modern dishes have a sophisticated feel, with bold flavours and a deft touch.

Menu € 33 (lunch) – Carte € 40/56

University of Limerick, Castletroy ✉ V94 PX58 – ☏ 061 202 186 – www.eastroom.ie – Closed 21 July-12 August, 24-28 December, Sunday, Monday, Tuesday - Wednesday dinner

⅋○ Sash ♿ 🆎

TRADITIONAL CUISINE · BRASSERIE ✕✕ A relaxed, modern bistro with a feature wall hung with pictures and mirrors. Set on the first floor of a boutique hotel, it's named after the type of window found in houses of this era. Menus have an Irish heart and modern touches; ingredients are sourced from their 40 acre farm and the local market.

Carte € 25/59

No.1 Pery Square Hotel, Pery Square – ☏ 061 402 402 – www.oneperysquare.com – Closed 24-28 December

🏠 No.1 Pery Square 🍽 🕸 🛋 🆎 🅿

TOWNHOUSE · CONTEMPORARY A charming boutique townhouse in the Georgian Quarter, with a superb spa and a spacious drawing room overlooking the gardens. Choose a luxurious 'Period' bedroom or more contemporary 'Club' room.

20 rooms ☲ – ♟ € 165/225 – 1 suite

Pery Square – ☏ 061 402 402 – www.oneperysquare.com – Closed 24-28 December

⅋○ **Sash** – See restaurant listing

LISCANNOR · LIOS CEANNÚIR
Clare – Regional map n° **21**–B1

⅋○ Vaughan's Anchor Inn ⇐ ♿ 🆎 🅿

SEAFOOD · PUB ✕ A characterful family-run pub in a small fishing village. Nautical memorabilia lines the walls and along with the impressive fish tank, gives a clue as to the focus of the menu, where locally sourced seafood underpins the cooking. Bright, stylish bedrooms are hung with photos of local sights.

Menu € 20/30 – Carte € 25/45

Main Street ✉ V95 – ☏ 065 708 1548 – www.vaughans.ie – Closed 25-26 December

LISDOONVARNA · LIOS DÚIN BHEARNA
Clare – Regional map n° **21**–B1

Wild Honey Inn (Aidan McGrath)

CLASSIC CUISINE · PUB This personally run inn set in the heart of The Burren started life as an 1860s hotel serving those visiting the town's spas. For this reason, it doesn't look much like a pub – but once inside all is forgotten, as it's warm, cosy and full of pubby character. Tables are arranged around a central bar, all manner of bric-a-brac hangs on the walls and there's a welcoming open fire for colder nights. There might be a few seats at the bar but you'll find that most people are here to dine.

Aidan McGrath is a mature and experienced chef and his two fixed price menus change weekly – sometimes even daily – in line with which produce is at its best. Dishes have a classical French base and showcase the county's produce in neat, confidently prepared combinations which are beautifully balanced and packed with bold flavours.

Comfy bedrooms have a fittingly traditional feel and the breakfast room overlooks the pretty garden.

Specialities: Smoked eel with fennel, apple, beetroot and chive crème fraîche. Rump and braised neck fillet of lamb, wild garlic pesto, morels and asparagus. Poached pineapple with vanilla cream, hazelnuts and pistachios.

Menu € 50/60

*Kincora Road ⊠ V95 – ℰ 065 707 4300 – www.wildhoneyinn.com –
Closed 31 October-6 March, Sunday, Monday, Tuesday - Saturday lunch*

LISTOWEL · LIOS TUATHAIL
Kerry – Regional map n° **21**–B2

Allo's Bistro

TRADITIONAL CUISINE · COSY Former pub dating back to 1873; now a simple, well-run and characterful restaurant. Series of homely rooms and friendly, efficient service. Wide-ranging menus rely on regional produce, with theme nights on Thursdays and an adventurous gourmet menu Fri and Sat evenings. Individual, antique-furnished bedrooms.

Carte € 27/50

*41-43 Church Street ⊠ V31 – ℰ 068 22880 – www.allosbarbistro-townhouse.com –
Closed Sunday, Monday, Tuesday, Wednesday dinner*

LONGFORD · AN LONGFORT
Longford – Regional map n° **20**–C3

VM

MODERN CUISINE · INTIMATE This smart, rustic hotel dining room sits in the old stables of a Georgian house and comes with stone-faced walls and views over a Japanese garden. Orchard and garden produce features in surprisingly creative, modern dishes which have a sophisticated style.

Menu € 35 (lunch), € 60/65

*Viewmount House Hotel, Dublin Road – ℰ 043 334 1919 –
www.viewmounthouse.com – Closed 26 October-4 November, 24-26 December,
Sunday dinner, Monday, Tuesday, Wednesday - Saturday lunch*

Viewmount House

COUNTRY HOUSE · CLASSIC Set in 4 acres of mature grounds, a welcoming house with 15C origins and a charming period feel. Bedrooms are traditionally styled, furnished with antiques and have good modern facilities; go for a duplex room. Delicious breakfasts are taken under an original ornate vaulted ceiling.

12 rooms ⊊ – †† € 80/90 – 5 suites

*Dublin Road – ℰ 043 334 1919 – www.viewmounthouse.com –
Closed 25 October-4 November, 24-26 December*

VM – See restaurant listing

MALAHIDE • MULLACH ÍDE
Fingal – Regional map n° **21**–D1

⑪○ Jaipur

INDIAN · ELEGANT XX A friendly basement restaurant in a Georgian terrace. The origins of the tasty, contemporary Indian dishes are noted on the menu. The monkfish with lime, ginger, coriander root & fried okra is a speciality.

Menu €24 – Carte €29/54

5 St. James's Terrace ⊠ K36 RD29 – ☏ 01 845 5455 – www.jaipur.ie – Closed Monday - Saturday lunch

⑪○ Bon Appetit

MODERN CUISINE · BRASSERIE X Smart Georgian terraced house near the harbour. The intimate, dimly lit bar offers cocktails and tapas; below is a modern brasserie with a lively atmosphere. Modern dishes have a classical French base; the steaks are a highlight.

Menu €17 – Carte €35/60

9 St. James's Terrace ⊠ K36 – ☏ 01 845 0314 – www.bonappetit.ie – Closed 25 December, Monday - Friday lunch

⑪○ Old Street

MODERN CUISINE · CHIC X A pair of converted cottages house this lively split-level restaurant which boasts designer touches and a stylish cocktail bar with a lovely panelled ceiling. The experienced team carefully craft appealing modern dishes that are made up of numerous different flavours and textures.

Menu €28 – Carte €35/49

Old Street ⊠ K36 – ☏ 01 845 5614 – www.oldstreet.ie – Closed Monday, Tuesday - Thursday lunch

MIDLETON • MAINISTIR NA CORANN
Cork – Regional map n° **21**–C3

⑪○ Farmgate Restaurant & Food Store

REGIONAL CUISINE · SIMPLE X A friendly food store with a bakery, a rustic multi-roomed restaurant and a courtyard terrace. Lunch might mean soup, a sandwich or a tart; dinner features regional fish and meat – the chargrilled steaks are popular. Cakes are served all day and brunch is offered on Friday and Saturday.

Carte €33/54

Broderick Street, Coolbawn ⊠ P25 DT99 – ☏ 021 463 2771 – www.farmgate.ie – Closed 24 December-4 January, Sunday, Monday, Tuesday - Wednesday dinner

⑪○ Sage

REGIONAL CUISINE · BISTRO X A passionately run restaurant with a rustic feel. Hearty, classical cooking is full of flavour – ingredients are sourced from within a 12 mile radius and their homemade black pudding is a must. To accompany, try a biodynamic wine or artisan beer. The next door Greenroom café serves lighter dishes.

Menu €35 – Carte €32/46

The Courtyard, 8 Main Street ⊠ P25 – ☏ 021 463 9682 – www.sagerestaurant.ie – Closed 27 January-8 February, Monday, Tuesday - Friday lunch

MONKSTOWN • BAILE NA MANACH
Dún Laoghaire-Rathdown – Regional map n° **21**–D1

⑪○ Bresson

MODERN CUISINE · BRASSERIE XX Enter via a small courtyard into this smart, characterful neighbourhood brasserie. It's named after a French photographer who pictured subjects in their natural state rather than studio settings – a reflection of their cooking being honest and natural. Rich, hearty dishes use classic French techniques.

Menu €25/30 – Carte €50/72

4A The Crescent ⊠ A94 VK30 – ☏ 01 284 4286 – www.bresson.ie – Closed Monday, Tuesday - Wednesday lunch

NAAS • AN NÁS
Kildare – Regional map n° **21**–D1

⑪○ **Vie de Châteaux** 🛜 ⅙ 𝔸�ℂ 🅿

CLASSIC FRENCH · BISTRO ✗ A smart modern bistro with a great terrace overlooking the old harbour. The keenly priced menu of carefully cooked, fully flavoured Gallic dishes will evoke memories of holidays in France; save room for 'Les Mini Desserts'.

Menu € 28 – Carte € 30/59

The Harbour ⊠ W91 XO21 – ℰ 045 888 478 – www.viedechateaux.ie –
Closed Monday - Tuesday lunch, Saturday lunch

at Two Mile House Southwest: 6. 5 km by R448 on L 2032

⑪○ **Brown Bear** 🛜 ⅙ 𝔸�ℂ 🅿

MODERN BRITISH · BRASSERIE ✗✗ Set in a sleepy village, the Brown Bear comprises a locals' bar and a clubby bistro with tan leather booths and candlelit tables. Ambitious dishes are creatively presented and full of flavour. Service is smooth and assured.

Menu € 27/35 – Carte € 33/54

⊠ W91 – ℰ 045 883 561 – www.thebrownbear.ie – Closed Sunday dinner, Monday,
Tuesday, Wednesday - Saturday lunch

RANELAGH – Dublin → See Dublin

RIVERSTOWN • BAILE IDIR DHÁ ABHAINN
Sligo – Regional map n° **20**–B2

🏠 **Coopershill**   🅿

TRADITIONAL · CLASSIC A magnificent Georgian house set on a 500 acre estate and run by the 7th generation of the same family. Spacious guest areas showcase original furnishings – now antiques – and family portraits adorn the walls. Bedrooms have a warm, country house style. Dining is fittingly formal and takes place amongst polished silverware.

8 rooms ⊇ – 👫 € 101/125

ℰ 071 916 5108 – www.coopershill.com – Closed 1 November-1 April

ROSMUCK
Galway – Regional map n° **20**–A3

🏠 **Screebe House**  🅿

COUNTRY HOUSE · CLASSIC An old Victorian fishing lodge in a stunning spot on Camus Bay; it has the look of a country house and a friendly, laid-back atmosphere. Understated bedrooms feature good quality furnishings and character beds. Enjoy tea by the fire in the sitting room, then dine on classic dishes featuring garden produce.

11 rooms – 👫 € 180/250

⊠ H91 – ℰ 091 574 110 – www.screebe.com – Closed 23 December-14 February

ROSSCARBERY • ROS Ó GCAIRBRE
Cork – Regional map n° **21**–B3

⑪○ **Pilgrim's**

MODERN CUISINE · RUSTIC ✗ It's been a guesthouse and the village bookshop among other things, but this cosy, proudly run restaurant has always kept its name. The concise daily menu lists generously proportioned dishes prepared from a mix of local and Asian ingredients. The sweet, caring service really stands out.

Carte € 30/45

6 South Square ⊠ P85 – ℰ 023 883 1796 – www.pilgrims.ie –
Closed 13 January-13 March, Sunday dinner, Monday, Tuesday, Wednesday -
Saturday lunch

SALLINS · NA SOLLÁIN
Kildare – Regional map n° **21**–D1

⑬ Two Cooks
A/C

IRISH · NEIGHBOURHOOD X This delightful first floor restaurant overlooking the Grand Canal is run by – you've guessed it – two chefs; he cooks, while she keeps things running smoothly out front. Cooking is honest, well-judged and generous. Even the lesser cuts are transformed into dishes which are packed with flavour.

Specialities: Ballotine of chicken with morel duxelle. Brill with asparagus and garlic leaf emulsion. Hazelnut and chocolate mousse.

Menu € 38 – Carte € 36/47

5 Canal View ⊠ W91 C786 – ℰ 045 853 768 – www.twocooks.ie –
Closed 12-28 January, 3-18 August, Sunday, Monday, Tuesday - Saturday lunch

SANDYFORD · ÁTH AN GHAINIMH – Dún Laoghaire-Rathdown ➜ See Dublin

SHANAGARRY · AN SEANGHARRAÍ
Cork – Regional map n° **21**–C3

🏠 Ballymaloe House
☆ ⑤ ⇐ 🛏 🏊 ⚒ ⚘ P

FAMILY · CLASSIC With its pre-18C origins, this is the very essence of a country manor house. Family-run for 3 generations, it boasts numerous traditionally styled guest areas, comfortable, classical bedrooms and a famed cookery school. The daily changing fixed price menu offers local, seasonal produce.

30 rooms – ♥♥ € 295/500

ℰ 021 465 2531 – www.ballymaloe.ie – Closed 6 January-1 February

SKERRIES
Fingal – Regional map n° **21**–D1

⑩ Potager ⓝ

MODERN CUISINE · NEIGHBOURHOOD XX The first solo venture for experienced chef Cathal Leonard is this laid-back neighbourhood restaurant set in the old Munster and Leinster bank – the original bank vault acts as the wine cellar. Good quality produce from the north of Dublin features on a set menu of modern Irish dishes.

Menu € 35 (lunch), € 55/75

7 Church Street ⊠ K34 – ℰ 01 802 9486 – www.potager.ie – Closed 1-14 January, Sunday dinner, Monday, Tuesday, Wednesday - Friday lunch

SLIGO · SLIGEACH
Sligo – Regional map n° **20**–B2

⑩ Montmartre
A/C

CLASSIC FRENCH · BISTRO XX An experienced French chef runs this smart restaurant in the shadow of the cathedral. Walls decorated with subtle Gallic references give a clue as to the cooking: classic French dishes which use ingredients from the surrounding land and sea. The all-French wine list offers some lesser-known choices.

Menu € 24/37 – Carte € 28/52

Market Yard – ℰ 071 916 9901 – www.montmartrerestaurant.ie –
Closed 5-29 January, 11-19 October, Sunday, Monday, Tuesday - Saturday lunch

⑩ Hargadons Bros
🍷 ⑪ 🍴 ☆ A/C

TRADITIONAL CUISINE · PUB X At over 150 years old, this hugely characterful pub delivers everything you might hope, with its sloping floors, narrow passageways, dimly lit anterooms and a lovely "Ladies' Room" complete with a serving hatch. Cooking is heart-warming and satisfying, and offers the likes of Irish stew followed by tasty nursery puddings.

Menu € 10 (lunch) – Carte € 25/43

4-5 O'Connell Street – ℰ 071 915 3709 – www.hargadons.com – Closed Sunday, Monday dinner

STRAFFAN • TEACH SRAFÁIN
Kildare – Regional map n° **21**–D1

🏨 K Club
🏌 🐾 🛏 📷 🗻 📶 🏋 📺 ♿ 🧖 🅿

GRAND LUXURY · CLASSIC A golf resort with two championship courses, an extensive spa and beautiful formal gardens stretching down to the Liffey. The fine 19C house has elegant guestrooms and luxurious bedrooms; those in the wing are newer. Choose from a range of dining options; the clubhouse brasserie offers great views.

122 rooms 🍽 – 👫 € 219/339 – 12 suites
☎ 01 601 7200 – www.kclub.ie

TERENURE – South Dublin → See Dublin

THOMASTOWN • BAILE MHIC ANDÁIN
Kilkenny – Regional map n° **21**–C2

✤ Lady Helen
⪦ 🛏 ♿ 🅿

MODERN CUISINE · ROMANTIC 🆇🆇🆇 This impressive country house sits on a 1,500 acre estate and is one of the best examples of Georgian architecture in Ireland; it still boasts its original stuccowork and hand-carved marble fireplaces, and its well-appointed bedrooms follow the period style.

The luxurious restaurant comprises two high-ceilinged rooms which look out over the estate towards the River Nore – be sure to ask for a seat by the window to take in the view. While the grand room comes with all the comfort and elegance one would expect from such a historic place, refreshingly, the service is smooth, relaxed and free of pomposity. Boldly flavoured, visually impressive dishes are skilfully prepared and ingredients come from the estate, the county and the coast. Playful desserts make a memorable finish to the meal. For the full experience go for the tasting menu.

Specialities: Cromesquis of crubeen with foie gras, Pedro Ximénez and sauce gribiche. Turbot with fennel, preserved lemon and chervil emulsion. Tiramisu.

Menu € 75/115

Manor House Hotel, Mount Juliet Estate –
☎ *056 777 3000 – www.mountjuliet.ie – Closed Sunday, Monday, Tuesday - Saturday lunch*

🍽 The Hound
🍷 🛏 🏠 ♿ 🆎 🅿

MODERN CUISINE · BRASSERIE 🆇🆇 This eye-catching restaurant is named after the Kilkenny Hounds, who were kept on the estate for many years. Irish ingredients feature in refined dishes with robust flavours. Ask for a table in the conservatory overlooking the greens of the golf course; start with a drink in the Saddle Bar.

Carte € 35/49

Hunter's Yard Hotel, Mount Juliet Estate ✉ R95 E096 –
☎ *056 777 3000 – www.mountjuliet.ie*

🏨 Manor House
🏌 🐾 ⪦ 🛏 📷 🗻 📶 🏋 📺 ♿ 🧖 🅿

HISTORIC · CLASSIC Within this Irish Estate's 1,500 acres you can enjoy fishing, falconry, horse riding and golf. The house was built in the 1700s and is a fine example of Georgian architecture, with original stuccowork and hand-carved fireplaces. Well-appointed bedrooms have a period style; ask for a River Nore view.

32 rooms 🍽 – 👫 € 230/620 – 2 suites
Mount Juliet Estate ✉ R95E096 –
☎ *056 777 3000 – www.mountjuliet.ie*
✤ **Lady Helen** – See restaurant listing

🏠 Hunter's Yard

COUNTRY HOUSE · PERSONALISED The former stable block of the Mount Juliet Estate provides a pleasing contrast to the original Manor House, with bright modern bedrooms and up-to-date amenities. Rooms by the walled garden are quieter and more secluded and come with Juliet balconies. Facilities are shared with the Manor House.

93 rooms 🖵 – ♔ €155/425

Mount Juliet Estate – ☏ 056 777 3000 – www.mountjuliet.ie
🍴 **The Hound** – See restaurant listing

TIMOLEAGUE · TIGH MOLAIGE
Cork – Regional map n° **21**–B3

🐝 Dillon's

MODERN CUISINE · BISTRO X A former pub-cum-grocer's named after its first owner. The original bar counter and shelves remain and the room has a homely feel. Flavoursome dishes are eye-catchingly presented and make good use of local ingredients, some of which they grow in the garden – the purple sprouting broccoli is wonderful.

Specialities: Bacon with Jerusalem artichokes and parsnip. Pan-fried cod with asparagus, peas and smoked haddock cream. Caramel chocolate mousse with toasted hazelnut and physalis sorbet.

Carte €34/50

Mill Street ⊠ P72 R288 – ☏ 023 886 9609 – www.dillonsrestaurant.ie –
Closed Sunday-Tuesday lunch, Wednesday, Thursday, Friday-Saturday lunch

TRAMORE
Waterford – Regional map n° **21**–C2

🍴 Copper Hen Ⓝ

TRADITIONAL CUISINE · SIMPLE X A whitewashed building located on a narrow road behind the main promenade houses this Mediterranean-style restaurant; sit in one of three rooms or in the sheltered courtyard. Cooking is wholesome and dishes are keenly priced. Be sure to ask about the catch of the day.

Menu €23/30 – Carte €23/36

20 Queens Street ⊠ X91 TD81 – ☏ 051 330 179 – www.thecopperhen.ie –
Closed 15 September-1 October, Monday, Tuesday, Wednesday - Thursday lunch

TUAM · TUAIM
Galway – Regional map n° **20**–B3

🐝 Brownes

MODERN BRITISH · COSY X A husband and wife own this sweet former pub, which previously belonged to the chef's grandfather. The snug front bar has a welcoming open coal fire and a collection of family photos – and the dining room has a homely feel. The availability of ingredients writes the great value modern daily menu.

Specialities: Castlemine Farm pig's head croquettes, chicory and pear. Braised beef cheek with salt-baked celeriac and charred onions. White chocolate mousse with rhubarb and honeycomb.

Carte €28/39

The Square ⊠ H54 VP96 – ☏ 093 60700 – www.brownestuam.ie –
Closed 1-10 January, Sunday dinner, Monday, Tuesday, Wednesday - Saturday lunch

TULLAMORE · TULACH MHÓR
Offaly – Regional map n° **21**–C1

🍴○ Blue Apron

CLASSIC CUISINE · BISTRO 🅇 Friendly, engaging service sets the tone at this intimate restaurant, which is run by an enthusiastic husband and wife team. All-encompassing menus offer generous, flavoursome dishes that are prepared with care and understanding.

Menu € 30 – Carte € 31/58

Harbour Street ⊠ R35V6X0 – ℰ 057 936 0106 – www.theblueapronrestaurant.ie –
Closed 15-29 January, 12-26 August, Monday, Tuesday, Wednesday - Saturday lunch

TWO MILE HOUSE – Kildare ➜ See Naas

WATERFORD · PORT LÁIRGE
Waterford – Regional map n° **21**–C2

🍴○ La Bohème

FRENCH · INTIMATE 🅇🅇 A characterful candlelit restaurant set in the vaulted cellar of a Georgian house and run by a friendly team. The French chefs offer an array of Gallic dishes and daily market specials, with the simpler dishes often being the best. Seafood is a highlight, particularly the lobster.

Menu € 31/40 – Carte € 44/63

2 George's Street – ℰ 051 875 645 – www.labohemerestaurant.ie –
Closed 6-23 January, Sunday, Monday, Tuesday - Saturday lunch

🍴○ Everett's ❿

MODERN CUISINE · BISTRO 🅇 This unpretentious bistro is set in the heart of the city and dates from the 15C; sit on the ground floor with its barrel-fronted bar or in the intimate vaulted brick cellar. Modern menus showcase the best of the Irish larder and dishes are assured, unfussy and well-balanced. Service is friendly and relaxed.

Menu € 28 (lunch)/42

22 High Street – ℰ 051 325 174 – www.everetts.ie – Closed 1 January, 6-21 January, 25-28 December, Sunday, Monday, Tuesday - Thursday lunch

🏰 Waterford Castle H. and Golf Resort

HISTORIC BUILDING · CLASSIC An attractive part-15C castle set on a charming 310 acre private island in the river. The carved stone and wood-panelled hall displays old tapestries and antiques, and the beautiful dining room boasts a delightful hand-carved fireplace. Elegant bedrooms come with characterful period bathrooms.

19 rooms – 👫 € 158/365 – 5 suites

The Island, Ballinakill – ℰ 051 878 203 – www.waterfordcastleresort.com –
Closed 6-27 January

WESTPORT · CATHAIR NA MART
Mayo – Regional map n° **20**–A2

🍴○ An Port Mór

CLASSIC CUISINE · COSY 🅇 The friendly chef-owner named this restaurant after his home village. It's tucked away down a narrow town centre alleyway and its cosy interior has a simple, shabby-chic style. Local produce is showcased in classically based dishes with an Irish heart. The daily specials are more adventurous.

Menu € 24 – Carte € 26/48

Brewery Place, Bridge Street ⊠ F28 – ℰ 098 26730 – www.anportmor.com –
Closed 24-26 December, Sunday - Saturday lunch

⅋○ Cíans on Bridge Street

MODERN BRITISH · NEIGHBOURHOOD 🕽 A cheery team run this town centre bistro where you'll find white wooden slatted walls, vintage lighting and modern art. The straightforward menu sees modern dishes sitting alongside those of a more traditional bent. Seafood is always a good bet and local scallops, oysters and mussels feature highly.

Menu €30 – Carte €31/47

1 Bridge Street ✉ F28 – ℰ 098 25914 – www.ciansonbridgestreet.com –
Closed 1-21 January, Sunday, Monday, Tuesday - Saturday lunch

⅋○ Cronin's Sheebeen

TRADITIONAL CUISINE · PUB 🕽 Pretty pub with lovely bay and Croagh Patrick views. Hearty, unfussy dishes feature shellfish and lobsters from the bay, and lamb and beef from the fields nearby. Sit outside, in the rustic bar or in the first floor dining room.

Carte €25/45

Rosbeg ✉ F28 – ℰ 098 26528 – www.croninssheebeen.com

WEXFORD · LOCH GARMAN

Wexford – Regional map n° **21**-D2

⅋○ La Côte

MODERN CUISINE · NEIGHBOURHOOD 🕽 On the main promenade of a historic town, you'll find this welcoming, personally run restaurant. It comprises two homely rooms with grey oak flooring and Cape Cod inspired blues. Local seafood is at the heart of the good value menu.

Menu €33 – Carte €42/53

Custom House Quay – ℰ 053 912 2122 – www.lacote.ie – Closed 1-16 January,
Sunday, Monday, Tuesday - Saturday lunch

YOUGHAL · EOCHAILL

Cork – Regional map n° **21**-C3

⅋○ Aherne's

SEAFOOD · FRIENDLY 🕽🕽 A traditional place dating from 1923, keenly run by the 2nd and 3rd generations of the same family. Have lunch in one of the bars or dinner in the restaurant. Seafood is from the local boats and hot buttered lobster is a speciality. Some of the antique-furnished bedrooms have balconies.

Menu €25/35 – Carte €25/60

163 North Main Street ✉ P36 – ℰ 024 92424 – www.ahernes.com

627

Index
of towns

INDEX OF TOWNS

INDEX OF MAPS

Map number in parentheses (6)

Adam Petto/iStock

TOWN PLAN KEY

Sights

Place of interest
Interesting place of worship

● Hotels
● Restaurants

Road

Motorway, dual carriageway
Junctions: complete, limited
Main traffic artery
Unsuitable for traffic; street subject to restrictions
Pedestrian street

Piccadilly [P] Shopping street • Car park
Gateway • Street passing under arch
Tunnel
Station and railway
Funicular
Cable car, cable way

London

BRENT WEMBLEY Borough • Area
Borough boundary
Congestion Zone • Charge applies
Monday-Friday 07.00-18.00
Nearest Underground station to the hotel or restaurant

Various signs

Tourist Information Centre
Place of worship
Tower or mast • Ruins • Windmill
Garden, park, wood • Cemetery
Stadium • Golf course • Racecourse
Outdoor or indoor swimming pool
View • Panorama
Monument • Fountain
Pleasure boat harbour
Lighthouse
Airport
Underground station
Coach station
Tramway
Ferry services:
passengers and cars, passengers only
Main post office with poste restante
Town Hall • University, College

645

Tell us what you think about our products.

Give us your opinion

satisfaction.michelin.com

Michelin Travel Partner

Société par actions simplifiée au capital de 15 044 940 €
27 cours de l'Ile Seguin - 92100 Boulogne - Billancourt (France)
R.C.S. Nanterre 433 677 721

© 2019 **Michelin Travel Partner** – All rights reserved
Legal deposit: September 2019
Printed in Italy - August 2019
Printed on paper from sustainably managed forests

Typesetting: JOUVE, Ormes (France)
Printing - Binding: Lego Print (Lavis)

Town plan : © MICHELIN et © 2006-2018 TomTom. All rights reserved.

United Kingdom: Contains Ordnance Survey data © Crown copyright and database
right 2018.
Code-Point® Open data:
Contains Royal Mail data © Royal Mail copyright and database right 2018.
Contains National Statistics data © Crown copyright and database right 2018.

Northern Ireland: Ordnance Survey of Northern Ireland.

Our editorial team has taken the greatest care in writing this guide and checking the information in
it. However, practical information (prices, addresses, telephone numbers, internet addresses, etc.)
is subject to frequent change and such information should therefore be used for guidance only. It is
possible that some of the information in this guide may not be accurate or exhaustive as at the date
of publication. We therefore accept no liability in regard to such information.